Amalfi Coast

LAURA THAYER

Contents

Welcome to the Amalfi Coast.. 7
  10 Top Experiences 9
  Planning Your Time. 18
  - If You Like 21
  - If You Have 22
  Best of The Amalfi Coast 24
  - Best Souvenirs 27
  Sorrento and Island-Hopping 28
  - Tips for a Day at the Beach 30
  Outdoor Recreation and Seaside
    Relaxation. 32
  - Tasting the Amalfi Coast 34

Amalfi Coast 35
  Itinerary Ideas 44
  Positano 48
  Praiano 66
  Furore 72
  Conca dei Marini 76
  Amalfi 80
  Atrani. 101
  Ravello. 105
  Scala 119
  Tramonti 124
  Minori 126
  Maiori 131
  Cetara 136
  Vietri sul Mare 142
  Salerno 149

Sorrento and the Sorrentine
  Peninsula. 166
  Itinerary Idea. 170
  Sorrento 172
  Sorrentine Peninsula 192

Capri. 196
  Itinerary Idea 200
  Sights 201
  Beaches. 211
  Sports and Recreation. 214
  Festivals and Events 220
  Shopping 221
  Food 224
  Nightlife 227
  Accommodations 228
  Information and Services 230
  Transportation. 230

Ischia and Procida 234
  Itinerary Ideas 240
  Ischia Town 244
  Casamicciola Terme 255
  Lacco Ameno 261
  Forio 268
  Serrara Fontana, Sant'Angelo,
    and Barano d'Ischia. 274
  Procida 281

Naples 290
  Itinerary Ideas 296
  Sights 300
  Sports and Recreation. 322
  Entertainment and Events. 324
  Shopping 326
  Bars and Nightlife 329
  Food 331
  Accommodations 337
  Information and Services 340
  Getting There 340
  Getting Around. 342

Pompeii, Herculaneum, and Vesuvius 346
    Itinerary Ideas 349
    Pompeii....................... 351
    Herculaneum 362
    Vesuvius 368

Background 372
    The Landscape 372
    Plants and Animals 374
    History........................ 376
    Government and Economy........ 384
    People and Culture 385

Essentials 391
    Transportation................. 391
    Visas and Officialdom 396
    Festivals and Events 398
    Recreation..................... 399
    Food 400
    Shopping 403
    Accommodations 403
    Health and Safety 405
    Conduct and Customs 406
    Practical Details................ 407
    Traveler Advice 412

Resources 417
    Glossary....................... 417
    Italian Phrasebook.............. 418
    Suggested Reading.............. 421
    Suggested Films 424
    Internet and Digital Resources 425

Index 427
List of Maps 435

Amalfi

WELCOME TO

The Amalfi Coast

There are few places in the world that capture the heart as quickly as the Amalfi Coast. With pastel-hued homes clinging to the cliffs between mountain and sea, beaches lined with candy-colored umbrellas, and postcard-worthy views in every direction, the Amalfi Coast lives up to its name: the Divina Costiera.

Although one of Italy's most popular destinations, the Amalfi Coast is so much more than a bucket-list destination. It's a place that beckons you to spend time not only seeing its sights but also discovering its spirit. Beyond the popular towns of Amalfi, Positano, and Ravello, there are 10 more villages—each one uniquely charming—to experience along the coastline.

The extraordinary Campania region is a stunning combination of natural beauty, culture, and history. Home to some of the most important archaeological sites in the world, spend time walking among the well-preserved Greek temples of Paestum and the ancient frozen-in-time cities of Pompeii and Herculaneum.

To shop and island-hop, start out in sunny Sorrento and catch the boat to impossibly chic Capri. Or pamper yourself at the thermal spas on the island of Ischia, which are famous for their curative powers. Don't miss tiny Procida, where the sea laps at brightly colored fishing boats in the island's picturesque Marina Corricella harbor.

When you're ready for a burst of energy, head to Naples, a pulsating city set to the soundtrack of buzzing scooters and Neapolitan songs. Naples is as gritty, loud, and chaotic as it is bustling, vibrant, and inspiring. Amid its fascinating tangle of ancient ruins, medieval castles, and baroque architecture, you won't have to go far to find the best pizza of your life.

Get ready to experience a part of Italy that will capture your heart and leave you longing for more.

Positano's Spiaggia Grande

1 Hiking the Pathway of the Gods amid stunning coastal views (page 55).

2 Climbing the grand staircase of the **Duomo di Amalfi** in the charming Piazza Duomo (page 81).

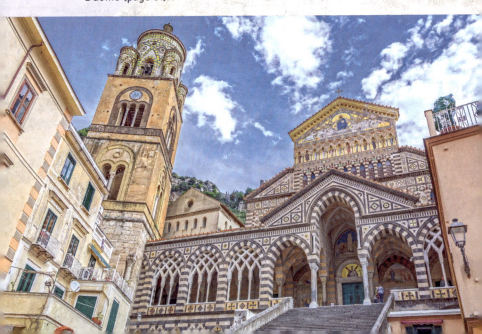

3 Wandering Salerno's atmospheric **centro storico,** with its piazzas, museums, and religious sights (page 152).

4 Taking in the view from atop the medieval **Castello Aragonese** on the tiny islet off Ischia (page 244).

5 Appreciating the incredible archaeological heritage of the Gulf of Naples at the **Museo Archeologico Nazionale** in Naples (page 300).

6 Journeying to the tip of the Sorrentine Peninsula to **Nerano and Marina del Cantone** to hike or kayak (page 192).

7 Finding your own personal paradise at one of the **Amalfi Coast's best beaches** (page 54).

8 Strolling away from Capri's crowds on beautiful walks to **Villa Jovis** (page 206) and to the **Arco Naturale and Belvedere di Tragara** (page 214).

9 Tasting as much traditional **Neapolitan pizza** as you can in Naples, where pizza is the stuff of legends (page 333).

10 Escaping to the vibrant villages on the tiny island of **Procida** (page 281).

Planning Your Time

WHERE TO GO

Amalfi Coast
The first sight of the Amalfi Coast is a travel experience not easily forgotten. Whether you're sailing into Amalfi's harbor or inhaling the sweet scent of wisteria mixed with salty sea air in Positano, you'll be captivated by the **rugged coastline,** rocky **secluded beaches,** and **famous views** that have been luring travelers for centuries.

Positano's cascade of pastel-colored buildings and seemingly unreal beauty makes it one of the most visited spots on the Amalfi Coast—and for good reason. **Amalfi,** the namesake town of the coastline, has a scenic port and a fascinating history as Italy's first maritime republic, dating back to the Middle Ages. Set high in the mountains, the town of **Ravello** is a big draw, with its lovely gardens and romantic views. And there are 10 more towns and tiny villages to discover on this UNESCO World Heritage-protected coast. Just east of the coast lies the city of **Salerno,** with its attractive lungomare (waterfront), a maze of medieval streets in its historic center, and a remarkable cathedral. It's a good home base in this area for travelers who enjoy a city vibe.

Sorrento and the Sorrentine Peninsula
Sorrento is a popular spot for travelers looking to explore all the top destinations in the area thanks to its convenient setting between Naples and the Amalfi Coast. With **panoramic views** across the Gulf of Naples, a **historic center**

view overlooking Amalfi's harbor

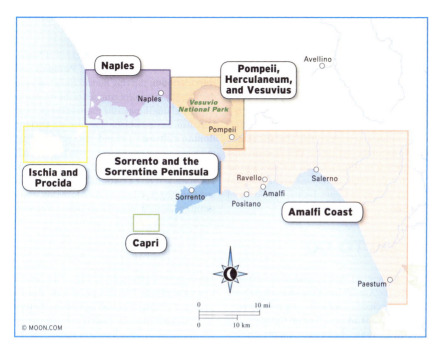

full of shops and restaurants, and picturesque **Marina Grande harbor,** this vacation setting combines beauty, charm, and convenience. Ferry service from Sorrento's harbor offers connections to Naples, Capri, Ischia, and the Amalfi Coast. Along the **Sorrentine coastline,** there are **quaint towns** and **beautiful coves** for swimming that are a bit farther off the beaten path than you'll find on the nearby Amalfi Coast.

Capri

One of Campania's biggest draws, the island of Capri is justifiably famous for its stunning views. Expect crowds, especially during the high season, but don't let that discourage you from experiencing the island's exceptional beauty. Stop in the bustling **Piazzetta,** the heart of Capri town, pick up a souvenir or just browse along the **chic shopping streets,** and don't miss the iconic **Faraglioni rocks.** Yet there's also a quieter side of the island to discover as you **hike** to incredible overlooks, ride a chairlift to **Monte Solaro,** the island's highest point, and get lost exploring narrow pathways past bougainvillea-draped villas. Whether you're planning a day trip from the Amalfi Coast, Sorrento, or Naples or staying longer, there are plenty of ways to enjoy Capri's beauty without becoming part of the crowds.

Ischia and Procida

Head to these two islands in the Gulf of Naples for an abundance of natural beauty and local charm without the day-tripping crowds of Capri. Known as the Green Island, **Ischia** is a lush retreat with little towns, beautiful beaches, and **thermal spas** that have been drawing people here since ancient Roman times. Spend a day dedicated to wellness and relaxation in a thermal spa or discover natural hot springs and steaming sand beaches around the island. Located nearby is the tiny island of **Procida,** famous for its **colorful architecture** and **scenic beaches.**

Naples

Although it has a reputation for being chaotic, Naples buzzes with a vibrant energy and magnetism truly its own. Once you get to know the city, it's easy to succumb to its allure while exploring the many layers of **history** and incredibly **dynamic culture.** How could you not fall for a city with royal palaces, world-class museums, castles, and some of Italy's tastiest **street food?** Around every corner there's something unexpected to discover, and it's also a great base for day trips to famous archaeological sites as well as to Capri, Ischia, Procida, and Sorrento.

Pompeii, Herculaneum, and Vesuvius

Mount Vesuvius looms over the Gulf of Naples and the archaeological sites of **Pompeii** and **Herculaneum,** thriving Roman cities that were destroyed by the violent eruption of the volcano in 79 CE. Walking through the streets of Pompeii and Herculaneum is a unique chance to see **ancient Roman culture** firsthand. Although the last major eruption of this volcano was in 1944, it is still considered active and is monitored continuously. The volcano is now a **national park,** and it's an awe-inspiring experience to climb to the top, where steam occasionally seeps through the rocky crater.

WHEN TO GO

With its plentiful beaches and Mediterranean climate, the Amalfi Coast region is a top choice for travelers looking for a relaxing summer holiday. **High season** runs **Easter-October,** and **July-August** are the busiest months. During this peak period, everything is open and in full activity, and you can expect higher prices for accommodations and even rentals for sun beds and umbrellas at some stabilimenti balneari (beach clubs). For the best beach days, visit during this time, though warm days often extend into September as well.

The **shoulder seasons** are gorgeous on the Amalfi Coast, especially as the wisteria blooms and the temperatures warm up. **April-May** are two of the best months, before things get too warm and busy. The weather usually stays very nice through **October,** when you can hike on the Amalfi Coast and catch a glimpse of autumnal hues across the mountainsides.

Low season runs **November-Easter.** The Amalfi Coast and islands of Capri, Ischia, and Procida are much quieter, but still offer the fine views. Many accommodations and restaurants will close for a period, especially on the Amalfi Coast and islands. Whether you visit the Amalfi Coast and islands off-season depends on the type of travel experience you want: If you're dreaming of a beach holiday, you'll need to visit during the summer. If you'd prefer cooler temperatures for sightseeing and hiking, a shoulder season may be preferable. Though it can be a bit rainy off-season, it usually doesn't last for long and there are many clear, crisp days.

Note that the impact of high and low season will be more noticeable in beach destinations on the Amalfi Coast and islands than in larger cities like Salerno and Naples. On the Amalfi Coast, many hotels and restaurants and some shops close, and ferry service stops during low season. You'll find fewer seasonal closings in the Sorrento area or on the islands of Ischia and Procida, but check in advance as many places do still close for the winter period, including the thermal parks. Accommodations and restaurants in Naples and Salerno are usually open all year, with the Christmas holiday time being very popular for both cities.

If You Like...

PURE RELAXATION

- **Ischia:** Nothing says tranquility like thermal spas where you can soak up the healing properties of the water in serene natural settings.
- **Conca dei Marini** or **Nerano:** These little towns along the Amalfi coastline are secluded, quiet spots full of seaside charm and excellent restaurants.

HISTORY

- **Naples:** Go underground to see the ancient urban plan of the city, and don't miss the stunning baroque churches, royal palaces, and museums big and small.
- **Pompeii** and **Herculaneum:** History enthusiasts shouldn't miss a visit to these ancient cities, which were frozen in time by the eruption of Mount Vesuvius in 79 CE.
- **Paestum:** This ancient city features well-preserved Greek temples that date from the 5th and 6th centuries BCE.

FOOD AND WINE

The Campania region is incredibly rich when it comes to delicious food and locally produced wines.

- **Sorrento:** Discover the flavors of the Sorrentine Peninsula—visiting a historic lemon grove, cooking traditional recipes, or simply enjoying a limoncello spritz with a view of the Gulf of Naples.
- **Tramonti, Furore,** and **Ravello:** The vineyards in and around these towns, a few of which offer tours and tastings, produce the Costa d'Amalfi DOC (controlled designation of origin) wines.
- **Cetara** and **Capri:** Seafood is a gastronomic highlight of the entire region, with standout offerings like the anchovies in Cetara and sea urchin in Capri.
- **Naples:** As the birthplace of pizza, no foodie visit to Campania is complete without a stop in Naples for traditional Neapolitan pizza.

HIKING AND OUTDOOR ADVENTURE

Once only connected by footpaths and trails, the towns of the Amalfi Coast are a dream for hikers.

- **Pathway of the Gods, Positano:** With endless coastal views, this trail (Sentiero degli Dei in Italian) above Positano is one of the most popular hikes in the area.
- **Valle delle Ferriere, Amalfi:** This trail above Amalfi passes by the ruins of the town's once busy paper mills and leads to waterfalls and an almost tropical landscape.

BEFORE YOU GO

Passports and Visas

For travelers visiting Italy from the **United States, Canada, Australia,** and **New Zealand,** the period of visa-free visits to the European Union is coming to an end. Planned to launch in 2025, all visitors will be required to apply for an **ETIAS** (European Travel Information and Authorization System) visa waiver before entering Italy. Check the official ETIAS website (https://travel-europe.europa.eu/etias_en) for the latest information. Apply well in advance to avoid any delays before your travel dates. The ETIAS visa waiver costs €7 and is valid for 3 years or until the end of the validity of your passport. Remember that you're also required to have a passport that is valid at least 3 months after your planned departure date from the European Union. For stays longer than 90 days, you will need to apply for a visa at the Italian embassy in your home country before you travel.

For **EU citizens,** or citizens of the non-EU member states of the EEA or Switzerland, there are no visa requirements for traveling to Italy. You can enter Italy with your passport or National Identity Card. After Brexit, **UK citizens** can enter Italy with a UK passport and an ETIAS visa waiver for visits of fewer than 90 days within any 180-day period. Passports must be less than 10 years old and valid for at least three months beyond the travel dates.

Travelers from **South Africa** will need to procure a Schengen Visa to enter Italy. This currently costs €80 adults, €40 ages 6-12, free under age 6.

You can check for the latest information on visa requirements and other restrictions at Italy's Farnesina website (https://vistoperitalia.esteri.it).

Transportation

By Air

The **Aeroporto Internazionale di Napoli,** also referred to as Capodichino, is the main airport for the region, and it's well connected with flights from across Italy as well as international flights from more than 80 cities. Direct flights from North America, however, are limited and are only available May-October. The airport is only about 3.7 miles (6 km) northeast of Naples city center.

By Train

Naples and Salerno are major stops for trains operated by the Italian national railway company **Trenitalia** (www.trenitalia.com), with Regional, InterCity, and high-speed trains connecting the region to destinations across Italy. The private company **Italotreno** (www.italotreno.it) also offers high-speed trains to both Naples and Salerno from Torino, Milan, Venice, Bologna, Florence, Rome, and many other smaller cities. The **Circumvesuviana** train line (www.eavsrl.it) connects Naples with Pompeii, Herculaneum, and Sorrento. The closest train stations to reach the Amalfi Coast are in **Salerno** and **Sorrento**.

If You Have...

- **Three Days:** Enjoy the highlights of the Amalfi Coast, spending one day each in **Amalfi, Positano,** and **Ravello.**

- **Five Days:** With two extra days, you can add on a day trip to the island of **Capri** and a day in **Cetara,** a lovely seaside village known for its seafood, especially alici (anchovies).

- **One Week:** If you have a full week, add a couple of days in **Sorrento,** and make it your base to explore the city's charming historic center and the ruins of one of the ancient towns near Mount Vesuvius, like **Pompeii,** an easy day trip from Sorrento by train.

- **Two Weeks:** With an additional week, base yourself in **Naples** for 2-3 days, visiting the city's incredible museums and churches and, of course, eating plenty of pizza. Take a day trip to the **Reggia di Caserta,** a lavish 18th-century royal palace, among the largest in Europe. End your trip on the island of **Ischia,** famous for its thermal spas, with the option of hopping over to neighboring **Procida.**

Where you are visiting or staying determines which train station is the best choice. Salerno is generally the most convenient option as it's well connected by ferries to the Amalfi Coast and the port is only a short and easy walk from the station.

By Ferry

Ferries offer an excellent way to move around the Amalfi Coast and Sorrentine Peninsula, and are necessary to reach Capri, Ischia, and Procida. The **Porto di Napoli** (Port of Naples) is one of the largest in Italy, offering ferry service to Capri, Ischia, Procida, and destinations on the Sorrentine Peninsula and Amalfi Coast. Ferry service from Salerno and along the Amalfi Coast runs seasonally Easter-October.

By Bus

Bus companies like **Flixbus** (www.flixbus.com) offer service to Naples and Salerno from cities across Italy. Local buses provide an inexpensive option to get around the Amalfi Coast, islands, and larger cities like Naples and Salerno. Since ferry service along the Amalfi Coast is seasonal, buses are the best way to get around during the off-season (Nov.-Easter).

By Car

Given the famously chaotic traffic of Naples, the narrow and curvy Amalfi Coast Road, and congested island roads, driving is not recommended in this area. With train, bus, and ferry options available, try to stick to public transportation, especially in high season.

What to Pack

When packing for the Amalfi Coast, think relaxed yet elegant resort wear. Formal clothes may be required for fine dining and opera in Naples, but even nice restaurants in the coastal areas and islands are often a more casual affair. For women, a scarf can come in handy for layering, and to use as a shoulder wrap when you visit churches, where modest dress is recommended and tank tops and short skirts or shorts are not considered appropriate attire.

Beachwear and swimsuits are a must if you're traveling during the summer. Cover-ups are a good idea too, as it's not permitted to walk around most towns (even beachside towns) only wearing swimwear. Some towns, including Sorrento and Praiano, even have local ordinances that include fines for walking around town in swimwear or shirtless. Pack sun protection and a hat for beach days.

Whether you're climbing the steps of Positano, visiting the museums of Naples, or walking along the dusty streets of ancient Pompeii, comfortable shoes are a must. If you plan to hike on the Amalfi Coast or islands, bring good footwear with plenty of support. For the rocky beaches, a pair of flip-flops or water shoes will save your feet.

Pack a European **plug adapter** and **converter** for your electronic devices. You'll also want to bring plenty of memory cards or film for photos, as the endless fine views and landscape will inspire you to snap more photos than you expect.

BEST OF
The Amalfi Coast

While the Amalfi Coast's alluring vistas are what first draw travelers to this rugged coastline, with so much to see and do in the area it's well worth spending a week to see the highlights. This seven-day itinerary includes the top spots on the Amalfi Coast along with time to enjoy the charms of Sorrento, discover historic Naples, walk among the ruins of ancient Pompeii, and take in the natural beauty of Capri. This itinerary works best in season (Easter-Oct.) when the ferries are running and everything is open.

Day 1: Amalfi

With its central location on the Amalfi Coast, the town of Amalfi is the ideal home base for sightseeing. Start your first day in the town's **Piazza Duomo** with coffee and a freshly baked sfogliatella. Join the **Amalfi Lemon Experience** tour in the morning to visit a sixth-generation family-run lemon grove. Nearby, visit the **Museo della Carta** to learn more about Amalfi's fascinating history of papermaking. Enjoy shopping along the town's main street and climb the steps to visit the **Duomo di Amalfi,** with its peaceful Cloister of Paradise, excellent small museum, and crypt dedicated to the town's patron Sant'Andrea. Take a leisurely evening stroll along the harbor or savor a sunset aperitivo before enjoying a relaxed dinner overlooking the sea.

Day 2: Positano

Start your second day on the Amalfi Coast by catching a ferry in the morning to Positano, a short, scenic 30-minute cruise along the coastline. You'll arrive right on the **Spiaggia Grande** beach with the **Chiesa di Santa Maria Assunta** in the middle. Climb the steps to visit the church and see its much-loved Byzantine icon. From the Spiaggia Grande, follow the cliff-hugging Via Positanesi d'America pathway over to **Spiaggia**

di Fornillo, a very scenic and quieter spot for a swim. Rent a sun bed and enjoy a fresh lunch at a beachside restaurant. Later in the afternoon, head back to Positano's town center to explore the maze of streets lined with tempting boutiques before catching the last evening ferry back to Amalfi.

Day 3: Ravello

Head into the mountains above the Amalfi Coast by bus or taxi to Ravello. Visit the town's elegant central piazza and stop in the **Duomo** before taking a pleasant walk through the quiet streets of Ravello to reach the **Villa Cimbrone.** Stroll along the wisteria-covered pathway to the Terrace of Infinity, where the blue sea and sky blend into one breathtaking vista. Enjoy shopping for ceramics in Ravello's town center before heading to the **Ristorante Garden** for evening cocktails or dinner on the romantic terrace overlooking the coastline. Catch a late bus or taxi back down to Amalfi.

Day 4: Sorrento

From the Amalfi Coast, move your base over to the north side of the Sorrentine Peninsula to the city of Sorrento. After dropping off your bags at your lodging, head out to explore the **centro storico,** the historic center of Sorrento, which is largely pedestrian-only and lined with shops and restaurants. Enjoy beautiful views over the Gulf of Naples from the **Villa Comunale** gardens and stop for a light lunch in the pretty **Piazza Sant'Antonino.** Head to the **Museobottega della Tarsialignea** to admire the collection of inlaid woodwork, a traditional craft in Sorrento. In the evening, stroll down to the **Marina Grande** harbor. With its old-world fishing village atmosphere, it's a charming spot for dinner by the sea.

Day 5: Capri

Spend a day on the enchanting island of Capri. The ferry from Sorrento's Marina Piccola will

1: arriving in Positano by ferry **2:** Villa Cimbrone in Ravello **3:** fishing boats moored in Sorrento's Marina Grande harbor

Faraglioni rocks off Capri

take you to this beautiful island in only about 30 minutes. From the Marina Grande port, take a boat tour around the island with the option to see the **Grotta Azzurra,** with its shimmering electric-blue water. Back in Marina Grande, take the **funicular train** up to Capri town. Stroll down to the **Giardini di Augusto,** where you'll find a perfect view of the **Faraglioni rocks.** On the way back, shop for beautiful Capri-made perfumes, soaps, and home scents at **Carthusia.** Enjoy an aperitivo in the bustling **Piazzetta,** Capri's place to see and be seen, before hopping on the funicular train back down Marina Grande to catch the ferry back to Sorrento.

Day 6: Naples

Today, move to Naples, reached from Sorrento by ferry (the more scenic option, a 45-minute ride) or Circumvesuviana train. Start in the morning at the **Museo Archeologico Nazionale,** where you can explore one of the world's most important archaeological collections. Then head over to the **Piazza del Gesù Nuovo** and enjoy a walk down **Spaccanapoli,** a straight street that is named for the way it cuts right through the historic center. Take a left on Via San Gregorio Armeno, where you can see artisans creating traditional Nativity scenes. Not far away, stop in the **Duomo di Napoli** to see the city's most important church and the lavishly decorated chapel dedicated to San Gennaro. Next, head over to Piazza del Plebiscito to admire the elegant **Palazzo Reale** and **Basilica di San Francesco da Paola,** with its curved colonnade. Stop for true Neapolitan espresso at the **Gran Caffè Gambrinus** at the edge of the piazza. Cross the Piazza Trieste e Trento and go inside the **Galleria Umberto I** shopping center to admire the soaring glass dome. Watch the sunset from the **Castel dell'Ovo** with fine views of the Gulf of Naples. For dinner, have a traditional **Neapolitan-style pizza.**

Day 7: Day Trip to Pompeii

Set off today for a day trip to the ruins of Pompeii, which you can easily reach on the Circumvesuviana train from Naples. After about a 45-minute ride, get off at the "Pompeii Scavi—Villa dei Misteri" stop and cross the street to the **Porta Marina** entrance. Plan on about 3 hours to explore the museum and archaeological site to see the highlights and really experience what life was like in an ancient Roman town, stopping for a light lunch at the on-site café. Don't miss the experience of standing in the center of Pompeii's ancient **Amphitheater** where gladiators once battled or exploring the **Villa of the Mysteries,** named for its captivating and enigmatic frescoes. After returning to Naples, take time to explore your neighborhood and enjoy some Neapolitan street food, like the classic fried pizza.

Best Souvenirs

The warm colors and brilliant landscape of the Amalfi Coast has long inspired artists, creating a strong local craft tradition and a laid-back yet chic sense of style when it comes to fashion. Shopping on the Amalfi Coast is truly a feast for the eyes. Here are some of the traditional crafts that are sure to tempt you if you want to bring home something special.

CERAMICS

In a landscape so full of color and beauty, the local tradition for equally vibrant ceramics is a natural fit. **Vietri sul Mare** is a shopper's paradise with streets lined with one shop after the other full of handcrafted ceramics (page 146). While Vietri sul Mare is the traditional home of ceramics on the Amalfi Coast, you'll also find lovely shops in Ravello, Amalfi, and Positano as well as on Capri. Most shops can ship internationally, so don't worry about trying to fit all the ceramics you're sure to fall in love with into your suitcase!

INTARSIA

In sunny **Sorrento,** the beauty of the natural landscape and local scenes are captured in fine detail by local woodworkers. The traditional intarsia (inlaid woodwork) started in the 16th century but reached its peak in the 19th century. With a museum completely dedicated to the craft and many shops to explore, you'll want to bring home a music box, frame, or table decorated with the intricate intarsia (page 179).

COASTAL FASHION

The Amalfi Coast exudes a colorful and relaxed style, no place more than Positano. **La Moda Positano** (Positano Fashion) refers to the unique style that you'll see spilling out of the town's many boutiques onto the narrow streets and steep staircases. Find a summer dress in Mediterranean hues that's ideal for a sunset aperitivo on the beach or the perfect linen shirt (page 59). **Handmade sandals** are also a firm fixture on the Amalfi Coast, Capri, and Ischia, where you can have a pair custom made while you wait.

NATIVITIES

While in **Naples,** enjoy a stroll down Via San Gregorio Armeno to see all the presepe (Nativity) workshops (page 309). This is the heart and soul of the Neapolitan Nativity tradition, a local craft that has been going strong for centuries. See artisans at work and choose from Nativities and figurines of all shapes and sizes to take home holiday decorations that will bring back travel memories for years to come.

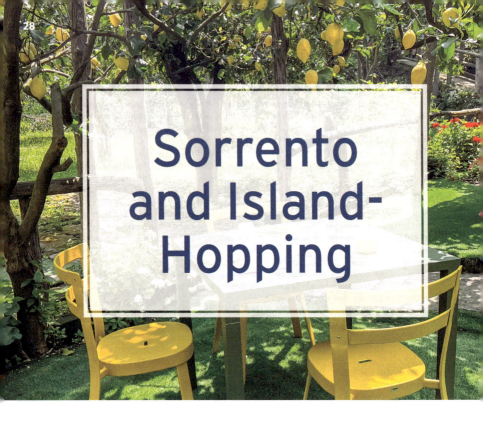

Sorrento and Island-Hopping

If you've seen and done the Amalfi Coast and are looking to explore Sorrento and the beautiful islands of the Gulf of Naples, this itinerary has you covered. Spend a couple of nights in Sorrento before hopping over to Ischia, an oasis of relaxation and beauty.

Day 1: Sorrento

Start off your day in Sorrento's central **Piazza Tasso,** watching the busy square come to life while sipping a cappuccino. Spend the morning exploring the historic center, seeing the **Cattedrale di Sorrento,** and visiting **La Limonaia,** a historic lemon grove, for a tour and tasting of Sorrento's famous citrus. Meander down to the Marina Grande seaside village for lunch by the sea. In the afternoon, discover Sorrento's tradition of inlaid woodwork at the **Museobottega della Tarsialignea.** End a fine day of sightseeing by admiring the sunset view of the Gulf of Naples from the **Villa Comunale** gardens followed by a delicious meal at **L'Antica Trattoria** in the historic center.

Day 2: Day Trip to Capri

Catch the ferry from Sorrento's Marina Piccola port for the quick 30-minute ride over to Capri. After landing in the Marina Grande port, catch a bus or taxi up to **Anacapri.** Stroll down **Via Axel Munthe** for a lovely view overlooking Marina Grande. Hop on the chairlift up to the top of **Monte Solaro,** the highest point on the island, for panoramic views of the island and across the Gulf of Naples to Ischia and Procida. Take a bus or taxi down to Capri town and stroll through the bustling **Piazzetta,** grabbing a relaxed lunch with beautiful views over the island at **Pulalli.** Enjoy a picture-perfect glimpse of the Faraglioni rocks from the **Giardini di Augusto** before heading back to the Piazzetta to catch the funicular train down to Marina Grande and the ferry back to Sorrento.

Days 3-4: Ischia
Take the first morning ferry from Sorrento across the gulf to Ischia, only a 60-minute ferry ride. You'll arrive at the port in Ischia town, a convenient base for exploring the island. Drop your bags at your lodging and set off via taxi or bus to the town of **Lacco Ameno,** on the northwest side of the island, where you can stroll along the waterfront and enjoy a light and fresh lunch. Hop in a taxi for a quick ride up to the **Giardini La Mortella** and soak up the luscious terraced gardens. Catch another taxi outside over to the **Chiesa del Soccorso** in Forio, a small church with a brilliant white facade set atop a panoramic overlook. Walk down through the historic center of Forio before catching a bus or taxi back to Ischia Porto for an evening stroll along the lively **Corso Vittoria Colonna.**

Start off your second day on the island in Ischia Ponte, a great area for shopping near the **Castello Aragonese,** accessible via a pedestrian causeway. Spend the morning exploring the fascinating walled castle with its churches, ruins, and fine views. Next take a taxi from Ischia Ponte up to the **Fonte delle Ninfe Nitrodi** thermal spa, where you can enjoy a one-of-a-kind experience soaking up the healing properties of the hot spring water. Explore the southern side of the island by heading down to the pedestrian-only seaside village of Sant'Angelo for a tranquil dinner by the sea.

Day 5: Day Trip to Procida
From the port at Ischia town, catch a morning ferry over to nearby **Procida,** just a 20-minute ride away. Stop to try the traditional la lingua

Castello Aragonese

pastry at **Bar dal Cavaliere** in the port before meandering through the charming streets of the island up to **Terra Murata,** the medieval fortified town on the island's highest point. Visit the impressive **Abbazia di San Michele Arcangelo** church before walking down to **Marina Corricella,** a charming seaside village with buildings awash in pastel colors. Walk along the harbor lined with fishing boats before making your way back to the port to catch a ferry returning to Ischia and say farewell to the islands.

Marina Corricella

Tips for a Day at the Beach

With a rugged coastline dotted with picturesque swimming spots, the beaches of the Amalfi Coast and around the Gulf of Naples are among the area's most alluring features during the summer months. Keep an eye out for **Blue Flag beaches,** a special ranking that the Foundation for Environment Education gives to beaches with the finest water quality. If you're dreaming of soaking up the Mediterranean atmosphere and diving into the turquoise sea, here's what to expect and how to make the most of your time.

BEACH CLUBS

The coast in this region is quite rocky, and most beaches are pebbly rather than sandy. Bring a pair of **beach flip-flops** or **water shoes** to make walking on the beach easier. Since lounging on the rocks is not always very comfortable, nearly all beaches along the Amalfi Coast and on the islands of Capri, Ischia, and Procida have at least one **stabilimente balneare** (beach club), wooden structures built right on the beach that offer sun beds and umbrella rentals as well as showers (often just an outdoor shower to rinse off), changing rooms, restrooms, and usually a bar for snacks and drinks, or a full restaurant. Although you do have to pay to rent a sun bed and umbrella (usually starting around €15 per person, depending on the location and the season), the rates include all the other services available. A few stabilimenti balneari also offer kayaks for rent, but don't expect to find snorkeling gear or the like available for rent.

FREE AREAS

Although the beach clubs are the most comfortable way to spend a day at the beach, it's not a required expense. Nearly all beaches have a free area (spiaggia libera), where you can just throw down a towel. This is where the locals tend to be, sometimes fully outfitted for the day with their own umbrellas, chairs, and picnics.

WHEN TO GO

The best time to head to the beach depends on when the sun hits it, but mornings are often nicest, when you'll find the beaches less crowded and the water clearer. The sun is hottest in the early hours of the afternoon, so if you're going at that time of day, you might want to opt for an umbrella rental, especially in the peak summer months of July-August. In general, the beach season begins in late spring and stretches through October, and this is when most stabilimenti balneari are open.

BEST BEACHES

- **Amalfi Coast:** Beautiful beach spots are around every corner of the Amalfi Coast, and you'll find everything from rows of multicolored umbrellas and sun beds on Positano's Blue Flag beach **Spiaggia Grande** (page 53) to secluded rocky beaches like **Santa Croce** in Amalfi (page 88).
- **Sorrento and the Sorrentine Peninsula:** With limited space available, Sorrento's beaches stand out from other beaches since they're largely constructed on swimming platforms where you can rent sun beds and umbrellas and dive directly into the sea. However, at **Marina del Cantone,** located near the tip of the Sorrentine Peninsula, you'll find gorgeous beaches and ideal kayaking (page 193).
- **Capri:** Enjoy a day at the beach clubs that dot the rocky seaside at the base of the **Faraglioni** (page 212) or soak up the charm of the island's **Marina Piccola** beach, popular with locals and visitors alike (page 212).
- **Ischia and Procida:** Surrounded by tempting beaches, some with dark sand, hidden coves, and even bubbling hot spring seawater, these islands are a dream for beach lovers (page 248).

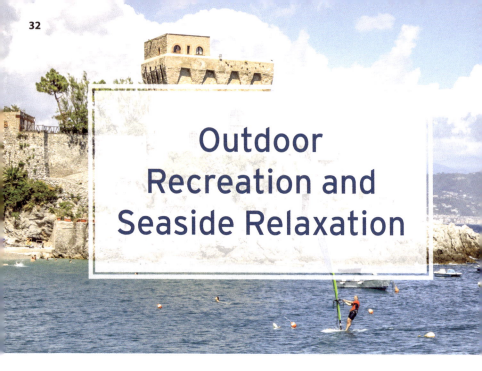

Outdoor Recreation and Seaside Relaxation

From soaring mountains to tiny beach coves, the Amalfi Coast offers such a varied natural landscape to explore and enjoy. This itinerary is based in Amalfi, taking advantage of its central location, and highlights the best outdoor experiences, including a good deal of hiking balanced with time spent discovering the beauty of the coastline and recovering with relaxing beach time.

Day 1

Set off in the morning to explore the beautiful green valley above Amalfi. Follow Amalfi's main street up from Piazza Duomo and continue following signs to the **Valle delle Ferriere.** The hike leads past ruins of old mills and along a peaceful stream with waterfalls and deep into the valley where you'll discover an almost tropical setting. Continue back down the mountain and to the center of Amalfi and stop for a refreshing gelato in **Piazza Duomo,** and then head to the **Marina Grande** beach in Amalfi for a swim to relax. For dinner, stroll over to the neighboring village of Atrani.

Day 2

Start the day with a good breakfast at your lodging before lacing up comfortable walking shoes, packing some water, and catching the bus from Amalfi up to Agerola. Get off in Bomerano to begin the Sentiero degli Dei, or the **Pathway of the Gods,** one of the most impressive and scenic walks on the Amalfi Coast. The walk takes 3-4 hours and ends in **Nocelle,** a frazione (hamlet) above Positano. Continue along the road to **Montepertuso,** another frazione, for a hearty lunch. Catch a local bus down to the center of Positano and head all the way down to the beach to give your legs a rest or go for a swim at the

Spiaggia Grande, with the town's vertical stack of colorful buildings the perfect backdrop. Catch the last ferry back to Amalfi.

Day 3

Give your legs a rest from hiking and take the ferry to **Cetara.** Or, for the more adventurous, rent a scooter in Amalfi and head east down the coastline on the curvy **Amalfi Coast Road** (SS163) through Minori, Maiori, and all the way to Cetara. Park your scooter down by the port and enjoy a walk along the pretty harbor. Stop to savor some of the local seafood specialties—don't miss trying the **alici** (anchovies)! Afterward, head back in the direction of Amalfi and keep an eye out just west of Cetara for the road that leads down to **Erchie.** This secluded seaside village is the perfect spot for a peaceful afternoon swim. Hop back on your scooter and enjoy the evening ride back to Amalfi. If you're traveling by ferry, consider a stop off for a sweet treat from **Sal de Riso** bakery in Minori.

Day 4

Take the bus up into the mountains to the town of **Ravello.** Stop for a coffee in the **Piazza Duomo** and watch the town come to life. Visit **Villa Rufolo,** where you can climb to the top of the 13th-century Torre Museo watchtower to get a bird's-eye view over town and down the coastline. Enjoy the town's best pizza and local specialties at **Mimi' Bar Pizzeria,** and then work off lunch by walking down the **ancient stone steps** connecting Ravello to the seaside town of Minori. The walk takes about an hour and leads through sleepy villages and terraced olive groves. Reward yourself with a leisurely aperitivo and dinner along the lungomare (waterfront) before catching the bus back to Amalfi.

Day 5

For a final day of pure relaxation, catch the boat service to **Santa Croce** beach just west of Amalfi to spend the day lounging in the sun. As the sun begins to fade behind the mountains, head back to Amalfi by boat and enjoy a **limoncello spritz** and people-watching at one of the outdoor cafés in **Piazza Duomo.**

Pathway of the Gods

Tasting the Amalfi Coast

The Amalfi Coast is just as rich with gastronomic experiences as it is with fine views.

LEMONS AND LEMON PRODUCTS

The Amalfi Coast's distinctive lemons grow on terraced groves along the coastline and are ubiquitous in the region's cuisine, from pasta sauces to desserts. In Amalfi, the **Amalfi Lemon Experience** tour and cooking classes (page 89) give you the chance to visit the lemon gardens of the Aceto family, who have been cultivating lemons for six generations. See how they make limoncello, the traditional lemon-infused liqueur, and bring some home with you from their shop, **La Valle dei Mulini** (page 94), located at the entrance to the lemon grove. Lemon groves can also be seen on a scenic walk called the **Pathway of the Lemons** (page 127), connecting the towns of Minori and Maiori.

NEAPOLITAN PIZZA

Nowhere else will you taste pizza quite like the Neapolitan style, which was invented in Naples in 1889. Finding your favorite means stopping in a few of the most iconic pizzerias, like **L'Antica Pizzeria da Michele** (page 332), as well as some of the newer top-ranked spots in the city, such as **Pizzaria La Notizia** (page 336). Outside Naples you'll also find excellent pizza, with both classic and creative options on the menu at **Pizzeria Resilienza** in Salerno (page 158).

SEAFOOD

Seafood is the area's true gastronomic specialty. Some of the most traditional dishes are pasta with vongole (clams) or cozze (mussels), but also freshly caught tuna and other fish, squid, and octopus. **Trattoria Da Lorenzo** in Scala (page 122) on the Amalfi Coast is an excellent spot for seafood, as is **Porta Marina** (page 186) in Sorrento, where the seafood is caught by local fishermen just steps away. A very localized specialty can be found in Cetara on the Amalfi Coast: alici, or anchovies, served fresh and preserved with oil. Colatura di alici is a strong fish oil made from anchovies that adds flavor to many dishes. Cetara's **Ristorante San Pietro** (page 139) is a great spot to try anchovies.

WINE

Wine enthusiasts will want to plan some time exploring the vineyards of the Amalfi Coast, where grapes are grown in steep terraces on the mountainside at **Cantine Marisa Cuomo** (page 74) in Furore, tucked away in a mountain valley at the **Tenuta San Francesco** (page 124) and **Cantine Giuseppe Apicella** (page 124), and overlooking the coastline at **Le Vigne di Raito** in Vietri sul Mare (page 144). On the slopes of Monte Epomeo on Ischia, **Casa D'Ambra** (page 272) is one of the island's leading wine producers and has been growing grapes since 1888. The **Bosco de' Medici Winery** (page 360) grows grapes in their lovely vineyard near the ruins of ancient Pompeii and on the slopes of Mount Vesuvius.

BAKED GOODS

Always save a little room for dessert because the pastry specialties from Naples and the Amalfi Coast are not to be missed. Start your day with a classic Neapolitan **sfogliatella,** a shell-shaped pastry with citrus-infused ricotta filling (page 335). On the Amalfi Coast, try the sfogliatella Santa Rosa, which is named after the birthplace of the sfogliatella at the Monastero Santa Rosa in Conca dei Marini. You'll find tempting local pastries throughout the area, such as the **lingue di bue** (ox tongues) unique to the island of Procida (page 287). Named for their long oval shape, they're puff pastries filled with pastry cream, chocolate, or the most traditional option, a lemon-infused cream.

Above: limoncello

Amalfi Coast

With a beauty that has captivated travelers for ages, the Amalfi Coast, a UNESCO World Heritage Site, has dramatic scenery, charming villages, rocky beaches, and famous views that have made it one of Italy's most popular travel destinations. Positano, known as the Vertical City, is one of the biggest draws, with its pastel-hued buildings scattered down the mountainside to the beach. Amalfi is the namesake town and was the seat of a powerful maritime republic in the Middle Ages. High above Amalfi in the mountains, Ravello stretches out across a promontory with sweeping views of the coast.

While Positano, Amalfi, and Ravello are the most visited, the coastline is home to 10 other towns and tiny villages, each offering unique local culture and intense natural beauty. Linger in Praiano to enjoy

Itinerary Ideas	44
Positano	48
Praiano	66
Furore	72
Conca dei Marini	76
Amalfi	80
Atrani	101
Ravello	105
Scala	119
Tramonti	124
Minori	126
Maiori	131
Cetara	136
Vietri sul Mare	142
Salerno	149

Highlights

Look for ★ to find recommended sights, activities, dining, and lodging.

★ **Finding Your Favorite Beach:** From the colorful umbrellas of Positano's stylish Spiaggia Grande to the quaint wooden fishing boats of Marina di Praia in Praiano, the Amalfi Coast's beaches rank among the best in the world (page 54).

★ **Hiking the Pathway of the Gods:** Enjoy sweeping views of the Amalfi coastline on this beautiful and rugged hike high in the mountains above Praiano and Positano (page 55).

★ **Duomo di Amalfi:** Step back in time to the splendor of Amalfi's medieval past at this impressive cathedral atop a grand staircase in the town's main square (page 81).

★ **Villa Cimbrone, Ravello:** Gaze into endless beauty from the Terrace of Infinity in these finely landscaped gardens, where the sky and sea blend into one tantalizing view (page 110).

★ **Cetara's Anchovies:** With a fishing history dating back to Roman times, Cetara is known for its seafood. Anchovies are a specialty in the local dishes of this small town off the main tourist path, and they're celebrated with a festival every July (page 140).

★ **Centro Storico, Salerno:** Meander through the maze of narrow streets in Salerno's medieval historic center, with its lively atmosphere, excellent shopping options, and important historic landmarks (page 152).

★ **Paestum Greek Temples and Museum:** Marvel at the well-preserved Greek temples, and admire the archaeological treasures uncovered at the museum (page 162).

the best vantage point for sunsets, eat freshly caught seafood in a hidden cove in Conca dei Marini, and wash it down with wine grown in improbably steep vineyards in Furore. Hike to medieval watchtowers and crumbling church ruins in Scala, walk among the lemon groves high above Minori, and try the local anchovies in Cetara. It's well worth the time to wander a bit off the beaten path.

So pack a pair of comfortable shoes and set off to explore the Amalfi Coast with all its magnificent twists and turns, history, and exquisite Mediterranean beauty.

ORIENTATION

The Amalfi Coast is a captivating destination with towns and charming villages sprinkled along the coast between Positano and Vietri Sul Mare. Nearby Salerno and Paestum are centers of history and architecture not to be missed.

TRANSPORTATION
Getting to the Amalfi Coast

Salerno is the closest major train station to the Amalfi Coast. **Trenitalia** (www.trenitalia.com) operates frequent train service between Naples and Salerno daily with travel times ranging 40 minutes to 1 hour 25 minutes, depending on the type of train. From the station you can catch SITA SUD buses to the Amalfi Coast or walk a short distance to the nearby port, where ferries depart for the Amalfi Coast towns and to Capri April-October.

There is also a train station in **Sorrento**. The **Circumvesuviana train line** operated by EAV (www.eavsrl.it) connects Naples with the archaeological sites of Pompeii and Herculaneum as well as Sorrento. The full journey from Naples to Sorrento takes about 1 hour. This regional commuter train runs frequently throughout the day and is an inexpensive way to travel between Naples and Sorrento. To reach the Amalfi Coast from Sorrento, you can catch a SITA SUD bus right outside the Sorrento train station, or if you are headed to Positano, Amalfi, Atrani, Minori, Maiori, Cetara, or Vietri sul Mare April-October, you may also be able to take a ferry.

Getting Around the Amalfi Coast

The landscape of the Amalfi Coast is rugged, with its famously twisty road weaving up and down, connecting towns situated both at sea level and dotted across the mountainsides. While it's certainly not the most straightforward area to explore, with a little preparation you'll be navigating the Amalfi Coast like a pro in no time.

By Car

The **Amalfi Coast Road** (Strada Statale 163, abbreviated as **SS163**) winds its way along the Amalfi Coast from Vietri sul Mare west to Positano. The only road along the coastline, this very narrow and curvy route can become quite packed, especially during peak seasons, around Easter and July-August. Driving the Amalfi Coast Road is not for the faint of heart. If you're up for the challenge, be prepared for the unexpected: tight squeezes, backing up if necessary, and the occasional traffic jam. If you're the driver, don't expect to enjoy those famous views, because it's hard to take your eyes off the road even for a moment. Locals know the route like the backs of their hands, and overtaking is very common. If the traffic behind you wants to move faster than you're comfortable, pull over when possible to let cars pass. Parking can be a challenge, especially during summer, but there are paid parking lots or spaces in every town where you can pay hourly or daily.

By Scooter

For the adventure of driving the Amalfi Coast Road but without the stress of a large vehicle, consider renting a scooter. They make it easier to negotiate tight roads and allow you

Previous: view of Atrani from the sea; ancient Greek temple in Paestum; Amalfi Coast scooter.

Amalfi Coast and Paestum

to zip around (or even through!) traffic jams. This is recommended only if you're already familiar riding a motorcycle or scooter as the Amalfi Coast Road isn't an easy place to learn. You can rent scooters in most of the towns on the Amalfi Coast, especially the larger ones like Positano, Praiano, Amalfi, Ravello, and Maiori. Many companies will even deliver a scooter right to your accommodations for a small fee. Bring an ID if you plan to rent a scooter. While parking can be a bit easier with a scooter, it can still be a challenge July-August. There are paid parking areas for scooters in every town along the coastline.

By Bus
Public Buses

The Amalfi Coast towns are well-connected with buses operated by **SITA SUD** (tel. 089/386-6701; www.sitasudtrasporti.it; from €1.30 per person) that run along the Amalfi Coast Road and to towns located

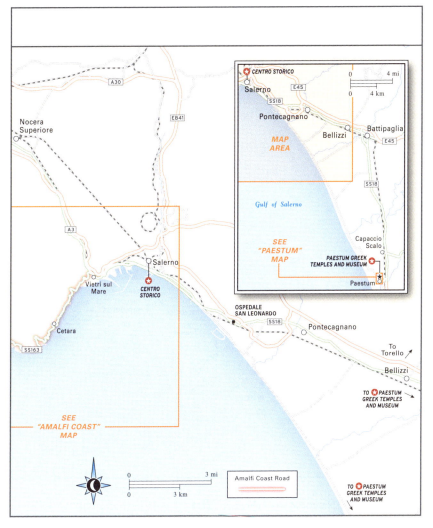

higher in the mountains. Amalfi is a central bus hub along the Amalfi Coast Road, with the main bus lines running from Salerno to Amalfi and from Amalfi to Sorrento. Buses for Ravello and Scala depart from Amalfi. Positano has internal bus lines operated by **Mobility Amalfi Coast** (tel. 089/813-077; info@mobilityamalficoast.com; €1.30-1.80) that circle the internal road though town and to the areas in the mountains above town.

SITA SUD tickets need to be purchased in advance in local tabacchi (tobacco) stores, some bars, or via the Unicocampania app (www.unicocampania.it). Tickets follow the Unicocampania pricing system, where you can pay for individual journeys or daily passes. Ticket prices depend on the length of the journey and start at €1.30. Or opt for a **COSTIERASITA ticket** for €10 that covers all bus rides for 24 hours to and from Agerola, Amalfi, Atrani, Cetara, Conca dei

Amalfi Coast

Marini, Furore, Maiori, Massa Lubrense, Meta di Sorrento, Minori, Positano, Piano di Sorrento, Praiano, Ravello, Salerno, Sant'Agnello, Scala, Sorrento, Tramonti, and Vietri sul Mare. Validate your ticket at the small machine located behind the driver only on the first bus you take, and be sure to write your name and birth date on the ticket where indicated. Ticket inspectors do circulate on the routes and will fine you if you haven't properly validated your ticket.

Tips

Buses are an inexpensive way to get around the Amalfi Coast and avoid the stress of driving on the Amalfi Coast Road. The road, however, remains busy and tricky, which means that bus schedules rarely run precisely on time. If you're planning to travel by bus, be prepared to wait and to deal with crowds in the summer. The public SITA SUD buses are popular with locals and travelers alike and can be absolutely jam-packed during peak season. Lines for getting the bus are chaotic,

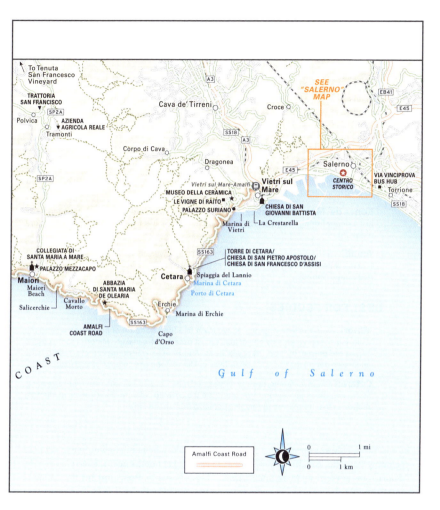

and buses can be so full that they are unable to stop to pick up passengers.

You need to push a button to request your stop; SITA SUD buses don't stop unless requested or there are passengers to pick up. Stops are not numbered or announced in advance in any way, so finding your stop can be a bit of a challenge. Some drivers will announce the biggest stops, for instance in Positano, but it is best not to rely on it. If you have an international data plan for your smartphone, Google Maps can be helpful for tracking your location and helping you know when to get off. Bus stops are marked by a small blue sign saying SITA.

If you are traveling with large luggage, it will need to be stored below the bus before boarding. Be sure to let the driver know you must retrieve luggage before getting off the bus.

By Ferry

Traveling around the Amalfi Coast by ferry is the most comfortable and least stressful way to navigate the coastline, and it offers scenic views from the sea. Ferry service

Which Amalfi Coast Town Is Best for You?

With 13 different towns to choose from and each one more beautiful than the last, it can be hard to decide where to stay during your holiday on the Amalfi Coast. If you're planning a quick visit to the Amalfi Coast of 1-3 days, Amalfi is the most convenient base, with its easy bus and ferry connections to Positano and Ravello. If you're staying for longer or just enjoy being a bit off the beaten path, this will help you find the right spot.

BEST FOR BEACHES

- **Positano:** For a beach-themed holiday, Positano offers a host of different options, from the colorful Spiaggia Grande to the more secluded Spiaggia di Fornillo and tiny beaches reached by boat (page 48).
- **Conca dei Marini:** The seaside Marina di Conca retains an old-world feel from when it was just a sleepy fishing village, and boasts a very scenic beach at the Capo di Conca promontory (page 76).
- **Amalfi:** The namesake town of the Amalfi Coast is a convenient option for beach lovers. You'll find many beaches right in town as well as the beautiful Santa Croce beach only a short boat ride away (page 80).

BEST FOR FOODIES

- **Minori:** From the lemon groves above town to a long tradition of pasta-making and the tempting sweets created by one of Italy's most noted pastry makers, Minori is connected to its past and present by food. Every year in late August or early September these traditions are celebrated during the Gusta Minori (A Taste of Minori) food and cultural festival (page 126).
- **Cetara:** Famous for fishing, fresh anchovies, and tuna, Cetara is home to many fine restaurants where you can enjoy seafood specialties like the coveted colatura di alici, an oil made from anchovies that is similar to the ancient Roman garum (page 136).

connects many towns on the Amalfi Coast, including Positano, Amalfi, Atrani, Minori, Maiori, Cetara, Vietri sul Mare, and Salerno. Amalfi and Positano are the main ferry terminals along the coastline, with the option to transfer to smaller boats to reach Atrani, Minori, Maiori, Cetara, and Vietri sul Mare. Boat service to Salerno and Capri is also available seasonally from the towns of Positano, Amalfi, Minori, Maiori, Cetara, and Vietri sul Mare and to Naples and Sorrento from Amalfi and Positano.

Travelmar (tel. 089/872-950; www.travelmar.it; €3-15 per person) and **Alicost** (tel. 089/871-483 Mon.-Fri., tel. 089/948-3671 Sat.-Sun.; www.alicost.it; €23-28 per person) are the main ferry companies connecting Salerno and the Amalfi Coast with Capri. Tickets can be purchased online in advance or at ticket booths near the ferry terminals. From Positano, **Positano Jet** (tel. 089/811-164; www.lucibello.it; €10-35 per person) offers ferry service connecting Positano, Amalfi, Capri, Sorrento, and Naples. **Grassi Junior** (tel. 089/811-605; www.grassiboat-positano.com; €9-14 per person) runs ferry service connecting Positano to Salerno, Amalfi, Minori, Maiori, and Cetara.

Keep in mind that ferry service is seasonal and only runs from about **Easter** through the beginning of **November.** Naturally, the service is also dependent on the weather and sea conditions. Even though rough seas rarely prohibit service in the summer, during the shoulder seasons of April-May and October, it's a good idea

BEST FOR HIKING

- **Scala:** Hike to a 15th-century watchtower, explore the valley above Amalfi with its paper mill ruins, and wander through sleepy villages that are among the most charming on the Amalfi Coast (page 119).
- **Ravello:** Set on a scenic promontory, Ravello is well situated for hikes to neighboring valley towns like Minori and Atrani (page 105).
- **Nocelle (Positano):** Sitting right by the starting point of the famous Pathway of the Gods (Sentiero degli Dei), Nocelle is a tiny village with immense views (page 52).

BEST FOR ART LOVERS

- **Amalfi:** As the heart of the Republic of Amalfi in the Middle Ages, Amalfi boasted wealth that brought the town many artistic treasures, which can be seen in the Duomo di Amalfi and excellent small museums (page 80).
- **Vietri sul Mare:** The Amalfi Coast's homegrown art form is hand-painted ceramics, and the center of ceramic production in the area is the town of Vietri sul Mare. Visit the scores of ceramic shops and don't miss the town's ceramics museum, Museo della Ceramica (page 142).
- **Salerno:** Salerno has a selection of excellent small museums, including the archaeological treasures at the Museo Archeologico Provinciale and an excellent collection of religious art at the Museo Diocesano (page 149).

ceramic donkey symbol of Vietri sul Mare

to have a backup plan for other transportation options.

By Taxi

Taxis are a comfortable way to get around the Amalfi Coast, but this is the most expensive option. Taxis that transport visitors between towns operate differently from city taxis insofar as the fares aren't usually based on time or distance but on the journey. A ride from one town to the next can cost €40 or more, even if it's a short drive, and this can add up quickly, so be sure to negotiate and agree with the driver on a price before departing.

One time you may want to splurge on a taxi transfer is when you arrive or depart from the Amalfi Coast. Public transportation is not particularly easy to negotiate with luggage, so booking a private transfer to or from the airport or other point of arrival can help alleviate some stress.

PLANNING YOUR TIME

Many travelers see the Amalfi Coast on a day excursion from a cruise ship, or from nearby Naples or Sorrento. Though spending a day is better than not visiting at all, a single day only gives you a small taste of what the towns along the coast have to offer. To explore the area more deeply, plan to spend at least 3 days to visit the three main towns on the coast—Amalfi, Positano, and Ravello—along with a bit of time to relax on the beach. With a week, there is plenty of time for hiking, visiting smaller towns, enjoying water sports along the coastline, and adding day trips to nearby destinations, such as Capri or Sorrento and archaeological sites like Pompeii and Paestum.

Expect bigger crowds—especially **June-August**—in Positano, Amalfi, and Ravello, as they're the most visited towns on the coast. Visit during the shoulder seasons or consider staying in smaller towns like Atrani, Minori, Scala, or Cetara to avoid the crowds.

For shorter visits, Amalfi makes an excellent home base, thanks to its central location and transportation connections. Although Positano is well connected to other towns by ferries, the public buses that pass by at the top of town are often very crowded during peak season.

Itinerary Ideas

ESSENTIAL AMALFI COAST

Make the most of a shorter stay on the Amalfi Coast by hitting the three most popular towns. Amalfi is a great starting point for delving deeper into the region's history, before heading up into the mountains to explore Ravello, famous for its fine views and peaceful gardens. Of course, a visit isn't complete without seeing Positano. After seeing the most popular spots, spend a quieter day exploring the seaside town of Cetara.

Day 1: Amalfi and Ravello

1 Start in the Piazza Duomo, where you'll find a striking view of the Duomo di Amalfi. Visit the historic bakery and coffee shop **Pasticceria Pansa** for the best espresso and cappuccino in town, and for one of their tempting sfogliatelle (shell-shaped pastries).

2 Climb the long staircase to visit the **Duomo di Amalfi,** taking time to savor the peacefulness of the Cloister of Paradise, admire the treasures in the museum, and see the crypt of Sant'Andrea, the town's patron saint.

3 Find out more about Amalfi's important role in the history of papermaking at the **Museo della Carta.** You can even try your hand at making paper!

4 To take home a souvenir of traditional handmade paper, which is still produced at an antique mill in the valley above Amalfi, stop in **Dalla Carta alla Cartolina** near the Museo della Carta for a lovely selection of stationery, journals, and gifts.

5 Hop on a bus or taxi for the short drive up to Ravello. Savor lunch with a panoramic view from the **Ristorante Garden** located right near Ravello's main bus stop.

6 After lunch, stroll through the charming Piazza Duomo and visit the **Duomo di Ravello** to see the 12th-century paneled bronze doors and the mosaic-covered pulpit and ambon.

7 Enjoy a leisurely walk through Ravello to the **Villa Cimbrone** to explore the famous garden and peer out from the Terrace of Infinity across the Gulf of Salerno.

8 Return to Amalfi and watch the sunset accompanied by the sound of the sea with drinks at **Gran Caffè,** which overlooks Marina Grande beach.

9 Enjoy a relaxed dinner overlooking the beach at **Ristorante Marina Grande.**

Day 2: Positano

1 If you're not based in Positano, the best way to arrive during the main tourist season (Easter-October) is by ferry to enjoy the spectacular view of the town from the sea. The ferry docks right at the Spiaggia Grande beach. During off-season (November-Easter), you can reach Positano by public bus. Spend time walking along the beach and climb the steps to visit the **Chiesa di Santa Maria Assunta.** Step inside to see the town's prized Byzantine icon hanging above the altar.

2 Stroll along Via Positanesi d'America over to the Spiaggia di Fornillo beach and pick out a sun bed from **Da Ferdinando** for some relaxation in the sun. When it's time for lunch, enjoy a fresh meal just steps from the beach at their restaurant.

3 Spend the afternoon exploring all the little pathways lined with boutiques. Stroll along Viale Pasitea to find an excellent selection of some of Positano's popular fashion and homeware shops. Stop for a fresh juice from **Casa e Bottega.**

4 Shop for perfume at **Profumi di Positano** to take a little of the sweet scent of Positano home with you.

5 As the sun begins to set, enjoy a spritz at **Franco's Bar** before hopping on the ferry to wave *arrivederci* to Positano.

Day 3: Cetara

1 Spend a peaceful day exploring the picturesque seaside town of Cetara. Arriving by ferry is the most beautiful option from Easter to October, but you can also easily reach Cetara by SITA SUD bus year-round. Follow the main street, Corso Garibaldi, to the short staircase on the right leading up to the **Chiesa di San Pietro Apostolo,** where you can admire the modern bronze doors depicting Saint Peter and Saint Andrew.

2 Next to the church, follow the staircase up to the road and continue right until you reach the **Torre di Cetara.** Visit the tower's museum and stop outside on the balcony of the tower for a beautiful view over Cetara.

3 Return to the main street and stop for lunch at the **Ristorante al Convento** overlooking a pretty piazza. Find a table in the tree-lined outdoor area and enjoy sampling Cetara's famous alici (anchovies) in a variety of ways.

4 Find a spot along the **Marina di Cetara** and soak up the Mediterranean sun and views alongside locals as their kids splash in the sea.

5 Enjoy a leisurely walk back toward the ferry along the beach and stop in **Cetarii** to take home a taste of Cetara, such as their jarred alici, tuna, and other locally made products.

Itinerary Ideas

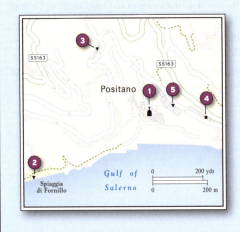

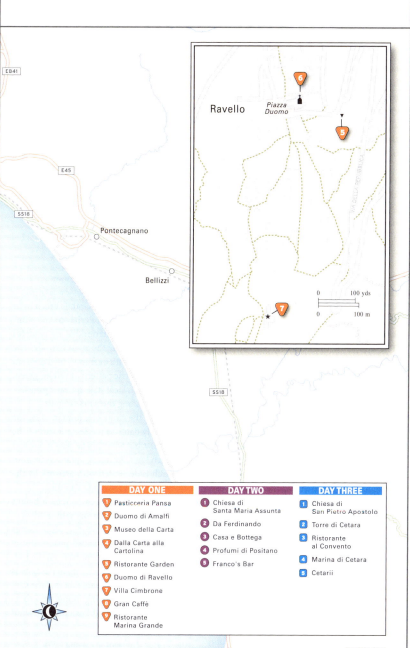

Positano

With its romantic mosaic of pastel-hued buildings clinging to the cliff side, Positano has a seemingly impossible beauty that captures the heart. Set in a steep ravine, the town climbs from the beach to the mountains above. The Amalfi Coast Road winds its way through the top of Positano, leaving much of the town accessible only by a meandering smaller road or the town's famous steps. Whether you arrive by boat at sea level or by car or bus higher up, steps are everywhere in Positano. What did you expect in a town nicknamed the Vertical City? Fortunately, there are plenty of captivating views to stop and enjoy along the way.

With a relaxed yet chic atmosphere, Positano is a place for shopping, soaking up the sun, and perfecting la dolce vita, Amalfi Coast style.

ORIENTATION

The center of town is near the Spiaggia Grande beach; **Via Marina Grande** runs along the beach, lined with restaurants and shops. Overlooking the beach, the **Chiesa di Santa Maria Assunta** sits right in the heart of Positano with the town rising behind it. Ferries arrive and depart from the large cement pier at the westernmost edge of Spiaggia Grande. From near the pier, the Via Positanesi d'America hugs the cliff side and leads to the Spiaggia di Fornillo. Along the way, you can see the Li Galli islands, an archipelago of three small islands located off the coast of Positano.

From the Chiesa di Santa Maria Assunta, Via dei Mulini is a bougainvillea-covered pedestrian-only walkway that leads up to **Piazza dei Mulini.** Local Positano buses also circulate around Viale Pasitea through Positano. By car or bus, the Piazza dei Mulini is the closest spot that you can reach to the Spiaggia Grande, and from there you have to walk. Positano is a town best explored on foot, but expect a lot of steps and steep walkways.

High above Positano in the mountains are two frazioni, or small villages, **Montepertuso** and **Nocelle.** These are peaceful areas noted for their breathtaking views and convenient location for hiking around Positano. To the east of Positano along the coastline are several smaller beaches, the largest and easiest to reach being the **Arienzo beach** and **Laurito beach.** Set into rocky coves, these beaches are accessible by long staircases from the Amalfi Coast Road or by boat service from Positano's Spiaggia Grande.

SIGHTS
Chiesa di Santa Maria Assunta

Via Marina Grande; tel. 089/875-480; www.chiesapositano.it; 8am-1pm and 3pm-8pm daily; free

Situated near the Spiaggia Grande beach right in the heart of the town, Positano's most important church is surrounded by colorful buildings climbing up the mountainside. The church is topped with a ceramic-tiled dome in a striking geometric pattern of yellow, green, blue, and white, a local style appearing on several churches along the Amalfi Coast.

Built over the ruins of a Roman villa, the church likely dates to the second half of the 10th century, but what can be seen today was built much later. An open square in front of the church is decorated with artwork by the noted Italian artist Mimmo Paladino.

Step inside the church to find a bright white neoclassical interior with gold decorative elements. Above the altar hangs the church's most treasured possession, a Byzantine icon of the Madonna from the 13th century. How the icon ended up in Positano is the stuff of legends. It is said that that the icon was aboard a ship sailing along the coastline, but when it reached Positano, the wind

1: the Chiesa di Santa Maria Assunta **2:** Via Positanesi d'America **3:** Li Galli islands

Positano

stopped and the boat was stranded. After trying everything, the sailors heard a voice calling out, "Posa, posa!" ("Put me down, put me down!") The captain took the icon ashore and suddenly the wind began blowing. This is also, according to local legend, how Positano came by its name.

The Museo Archeologico Romano Santa Maria Assunta, or **MAR Positano** (Piazza Flavio Gioia 7; tel. 331/208-5821; www.marpositano.it; 9am-9pm daily Apr.-Oct., 10am-4pm daily Nov.-Mar.; €15, credit card only), offers guided visits of the Roman villa and archaeological area. Groups are limited to a maximum of 10 people and the visit lasts about 30 minutes. To preserve the site, it is kept at a cool temperature, so a jacket or layers are recommended. Tickets can be booked in advance or purchased at the ticket booth next to the bell tower.

Via Positanesi d'America

Via Positanesi d'America from Via Marina Grande to Via Fornillo

This pathway, carved into the mountainside, connects Positano's two main beaches, Spiaggia Grande and Fornillo. Surrounded by the warm scent of pine trees in the sun and

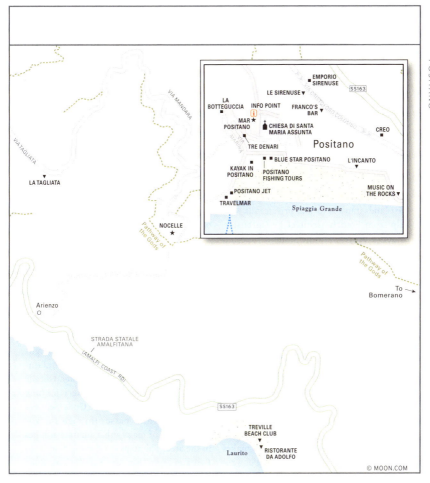

looking over at the stunning turquoise sea below, it's a lovely walk to escape the crowds on Spiaggia Grande.

The pathway begins with a small staircase near the cement ferry pier at the western end of Spiaggia Grande and follows the curve of the mountains past the **Torre Trasita** watchtower. Continue along the pathway and you'll spot a tiny beach called Marinella di Positano, tucked away in a tiny cove below. In the distance, you'll see the **Spiaggia di Fornillo** with its distinctive Torre di Clavel watchtower. The walk over to Fornillo takes about 15 minutes and is mostly an inclined walkway that is a bit steep in parts, with only a few stairs along the way.

Li Galli Islands

Sirenuse Islands, Positano

Just off the coast of Positano lie three small islands that have captivated travelers since ancient times. According to the ancient Greek historian and geographer Strabo, these islands were home to mythical siren creatures with human heads and birdlike bodies. Li Galli (The Roosters) refers to this half-bird characteristic. According to myth, the sirens lured sailors to their death with their beautiful music and songs. You may recall the story in Homer's *Odyssey*: Odysseus filled his sailors' ears with wax and had them bind him to the mast of his ship as they sailed past the sirens, so he could hear their intoxicating song and live to tell the tale. When they failed to enchant Odysseus, the sirens, named Ligea, Leucosia, and Parthenope, died from humiliation, it is said, and were transformed into the three islands we see today.

Eventually, the islands were sold to private owners. In 1924, Russian choreographer and dancer Léonide Massine transformed the islands into a luxurious private villa with help from French architect Le Corbusier. Rudolf Nureyev, another famous Russian dancer, later added lavish decorative touches. Although the property is still privately owned today, you can swim in the beautiful waters around the islands if you rent a boat or go on a private or group boat tour from Positano. Onshore looking west, you'll have a fine view of the islands from Spiaggia Grande or from Via Positanesi d'America.

Montepertuso

Located improbably high in the mountains above Positano, Montepertuso is a quiet little part of town that seems worlds away from the busy beach below. Its quiet and spectacular setting overlooking Positano makes Montepertuso a fine spot for hiking or a relaxed lunch or dinner to savor the views.

Situated at about 1,150 ft (350 m) elevation, this area is best known for the distinctive hole in **Monte Gambera,** which can be seen from far below. This pertuso (the Neapolitan word for hole) gives the village its name. Local legend says that the hole was created during an epic battle between the Madonna and the devil, and as she called on divine strength to defeat evil, a hole was driven straight through the mountain. This dramatic story is reenacted every summer during the town's local festival on July 2 with fireworks set off from the hole and a firelight procession that begins near the hole and travels to the church of Montepertuso, dedicated to Santa Maria delle Grazie.

Hiking through the hole above Montepertuso offers remarkable views over Positano. To reach it, follow the steps that start near the restaurant Il Ritrovo in the center of Montepertuso. The village can be reached by local bus from Positano or by hiking about 1,500 steps from the center of Positano, which start from the Amalfi Coast Road in the upper part of town at the Liparlati bus stop. Follow the steps up Via Liparlati that lead toward the town's cemetery. Not far after the well-marked Villa San Giacomo, the steps split; continue up the steps at the divide as they wind up through olive groves to Montepertuso.

Nocelle

For centuries, Nocelle was reachable only by rugged pathways through the mountains. This area, which sits at about 1,475 ft (450 m) elevation, was likely settled in the 10th century by people fleeing for safety after Saracen pirate attacks. Given the remote setting, it's no surprise that a rural lifestyle still reigns here. Terraced gardens dot the mountainside around the quiet village center. Nocelle is mostly a stopover point for hikers finishing or starting the Pathway of the Gods (Sentiero degli Dei), which passes through the village, or one of many other mountain hikes in the area. The steps connecting Nocelle to Positano begin from the Amalfi Coast Road near Arienzo beach at the Arienzo bus stop just east of the entrance to the Villa Treville hotel. Note that there are over 1,200 steps to reach Nocelle, which makes it much easier to take the local Positano bus up to start in Nocelle and walk down instead of starting in Positano and going up.

BEACHES

Life in Positano has always been intimately connected to the beach, from the Spiaggia Grande in the heart of Positano to tiny beaches set in coves a short boat ride away. Three of the most popular beaches are also designated **Blue Flag beaches,** a special ranking that the Foundation for Environment Education gives to beaches with the finest water quality. Whether you like being in the center of activity or are looking for seclusion and romance, there's a beach for you in Positano.

Spiaggia Grande
Via Marina Grande

This picture postcard of a town wouldn't seem complete without the unique burst of color and buzz of activity found here. Surrounded as it is by the cascade of buildings spilling down the mountainside right to the edge of the beach, it is an absolutely stunning setting. Standing on the beach, you get one of the best views of the vibrant Vertical City.

More than 1,000 ft (300 m) long, this Blue Flag-designated beach is lined with a series of beach clubs. Located in the middle of the beach, **L'Incanto** (Marina Grande 4; tel. 089/811-177; www.lincantopositano.com; daily May-Oct.; from €35 for 1 bed and umbrella) is a good choice with sun beds, umbrellas, beach services, and drinks and snacks available at the Blue Bar right on the beachfront. However, there is also a free section of the beach, where you can simply throw down a towel in any open space you can find. Expect crowds on the Spiaggia Grande, especially during summer, but that's an essential part of the scene. With a lot of boat traffic in summer, a safe but somewhat limited swimming area is marked off by lines of buoys.

Spiaggia di Fornillo
Via Fornillo

Positano's second-largest beach is a wonderful option for a relaxing day by the sea with a little less hustle and bustle. Sitting below the Fornillo neighborhood, this beach is reached on foot by following the scenic Via Positanesi d'America. Pass the Torre Trasita watchtower and continue until the pathway leads through a tunnel and down to the beach level.

There are several beach clubs here to choose from, such as **Da Ferdinando** (from €30 for a sun bed and umbrella). If you walk all the way to the end of the beach, near where it ends at the large rocks, there is a free beach with lovely swimming. The water at this Blue Flag beach is clear and refreshing, particularly in the morning.

During the beach season (Apr.-Oct.), the stabilimenti balneari (beach clubs) at Fornillo also offer boat service from near the corner of Positano's cement pier. The boat service is complimentary for clients, so keep in mind that when you hop off you'll be expected to rent a sun bed or dine at the beachside restaurant.

Arienzo
Via Arienzo

In a ravine east of Positano's Spiaggia Grande, this picturesque little Blue Flag beach is accessible by 269 steps from the Amalfi Coast Road. It's one of the few rocky beaches near Positano that is reasonably accessible from the road. However, the **Bagni d'Arienzo** beach club (Via Arienzo 16; tel. 089/812-002; www.bagnidarienzo.com; 10am-6:15pm daily mid-May-mid-Oct.) offers free boat service from Positano's main pier for clients. With sun beds, umbrellas, showers, changing rooms, and an excellent restaurant and bar, it's a lovely escape from the busy beaches in Positano. Sun bed and restaurant reservations in advance are strongly recommended. With a southwesterly setting, the beach days are longer here than at Positano's other beaches, and it's a fine spot for swimming with very clear water.

Laurito
Via Laurito

Halfway between Positano and Praiano, this rocky beach is set in a cove far below the Amalfi Coast Road. Named after the lauro (laurel) plants growing in the area, it's accessible by a long staircase of about 500 steps through thick Mediterranean vegetation. The most comfortable way to arrive is by boat service from Positano's main cement pier. Look for the small boats from **Ristorante Da Adolfo** (Via Laurito 40; tel. 089/875-5022; www.daadolfo.com; reservations only by

TOP EXPERIENCE

☆ Best of the Beaches

From the buzz of Positano's main beach, with its rows of brilliantly colored beach umbrellas, to hidden-away rocky coves, the Amalfi Coast has many gorgeous beaches to discover. Here's a guide to help you find the right beach scene for your holiday.

BEST BEACHES FOR SWIMMING AND WATER SPORTS

- **Marina di Praia, Praiano:** This is a beautiful small beach for swimming and windsurfing (page 68).

- **Duoglio, Amalfi:** On a rocky beach west of Amalfi, this is a popular local spot for windsurfing and kayaking (page 88).

- **Spiaggia Grande, Minori:** The beach here is lovely for swimming; you can also rent a kayak and paddle over to a waterfall west of town (page 127).

Viceregal Tower seen from Marina di Cetara

BEST BEACHES TO SEE AND BE SEEN

- **Spiaggia Grande, Positano:** A large beach with colorful umbrellas and the iconic view of Positano in the background (page 53).

- **Laurito, Positano:** This beach is home to the Treville Beach Club, one of the chicest beach clubs on the Amalfi Coast (page 53).

BEST BEACHES FOR FAMILIES

- **Spiaggia di Fornillo, Positano:** This is a quieter beach in Positano, away from the hustle and bustle of the Spiaggia Grande (page 53).

- **Marina di Atrani:** This beach's fine, dark sand is more comfortable for kids than the pebbly and rocky beaches along the coast (page 102).

- **Maiori Beach:** The longest beach on the Amalfi Coast is made of small pebbles and sandy areas, with a waterfront area perfect for seaside walks and for kids to run and play (page 132).

HIDDEN GEMS

- **Arienzo, Positano:** In a small cove east of Positano, this beautiful little beach is reached by a long flight of steps or by boat (page 53).

- **Santa Croce, Amalfi:** One of the prettiest and most secluded rocky beaches on the Amalfi Coast, only accessible by boat (page 88).

- **Marina di Cetara:** One of the coast's most picturesque beaches, surrounded by a fishing village and a 14th-century watchtower (page 138).

phone) or the **Treville Beach Club** (Laurito Beach; tel. 089/811-580; www.trevillebeach-club.it; 10am-6pm daily May-Sept.; from €100 per person). As space is limited at this secluded beach, booking in advance is strongly recommended at both establishments to reserve a sun bed or restaurant table. Although it's a small beach, the water is beautiful and it's an excellent spot for swimming and exploring the rocky coastline surrounding the beach.

SPORTS AND RECREATION

With a naturally dramatic landscape stretching from pebbly beaches to soaring mountains, Positano is an ideal location to spend time outdoors exploring the area's natural beauty. Get out on the water on a kayak tour or boat to discover the hidden coves and tiny beaches nearby. The mountain pathways above Positano are excellent for hiking, or for the more adventurous, climbing. No matter what activity you choose, you'll be rewarded with incredible views along the way.

TOP EXPERIENCE

★ Hiking the Pathway of the Gods (Sentiero degli Dei)

Distance: *3.7 mi (6 km)*
Time: *3 hours one-way*
Trailhead: *Piazza Paolo Capasso, Bomerano or Nocelle*
Information and Maps: *www.carteguide.com; English and Italian versions available online; €5 each*

In a landscape famous for beautiful views and hiking, there's one particular trail that is often considered the most breathtaking. The Pathway of the Gods is a rugged mountain trail stretching from Bomerano in Agerola to Nocelle above Positano. Passing along the mountains high above the sea, the trail is dotted with Mediterranean vegetation and offers panoramic views overlooking Praiano, Positano, and Capri in the distance. The pathway can be hiked in both directions, but most people choose to start in Bomerano's Piazza Paolo Capasso and enjoy the hike toward Positano.

While the Pathway of the Gods has become very popular in recent years, it is not considered an easy hike. It is quite remote and rugged along the way. Bring water with you and be prepared for the sun since much of the hike is not shaded.

The pathway is more popular during the hot summer months of June-August. If you're hiking in summer, get an early-morning start and take plenty of water, which can be refilled at public fountains in Bomerano and Nocelle. Spring and autumn are excellent times to hike the Pathway of the Gods. It is important to wear proper footwear for the rocky areas and to pay attention to the trail at all times. With such stunning views, it is easy to become distracted. Stay on clearly marked paths and avoid areas that are indicated as closed. If you have an emergency while hiking, call 118 and look for the nearest ceramic marker to indicate your location.

Getting There

To reach Bomerano by public transportation, you'll need to take the SITA SUD bus on the line from Sorrento to Amalfi, which you can catch at either the Chiesa Nuova stop or the Sponda stop in Positano, and then transfer to the bus from Amalfi to Agerola. Mention to the driver when boarding that you're hiking the Sentiero degli Dei, and they'll usually announce the stop in Bomerano. Look for the signs for the Sentiero degli Dei from the Piazza Paolo Capasso and follow the walkway out of town. Eventually, the road ends and a trail begins, passing by some lonely abandoned houses with sweeping views between mountains and the sea. You'll want to allow for plenty of time to stop and take photos.

The hike from Bomerano to Nocelle takes about 3 hours, depending on how much rest you take. From Nocelle, you can take a local bus or the steps down to Positano.

Hiking
Guided Hikes
A local guide can also add to your enjoyment of the Pathway of the Gods hike and others, helping you to learn about the area's history and vegetation. Guides can also recommend the best hikes tailored your abilities and time available. For a private guided excursion, **Anna Naclerio** (tel. 335/731-5259; annanaclerioguida@gmail.com; 5-6-hour private hiking tour €200) loves sharing her passion for the landscape. **Zia Lucy** (tel. 339/272-0971; www.en.zialucy.com; Mar.-Dec.; small group tours €55-60 per person, minimum 4 people) also offers private and small-group hiking excursions.

Rock Climbing
With rugged Mediterranean landscape and incredible views, the Lattari Mountains are a dream setting for mountain climbers.

Direzione Verticale
tel. 338/727-9878; www.direzioneverticale.it; climbing excursions year-round; from €150

Direzione Verticale, founded by expert climber Francesco Galasso, offers sport climbing excursions with equipment and guide in the Positano area as well as all of the climbing areas of the Amalfi Coast and Capri. They also organize deep water soloing combined with kayak or boat tours.

Associazione La Selva
tel. 347/166-9308; www.associazionelaselva.it

For more than 17 years, Cristiano Bacci from the Associazione La Selva has curated excellent climbs in the Positano area around Montepertuso, Nocelle, and the Pathway of the Gods. Close to the climbing area above Positano, the Associazione La Selva also offers yoga retreats, natural cosmetic products, and room rentals in a gorgeous rustic setting that is dedicated to natural living.

1: Spiaggia di Fornillo 2: hiking the Pathway of the Gods

Water Sports
Kayak in Positano
Spiaggia Grande; tel. 333/614-5247; www.kayakinpositano.it; 8am-8pm daily Apr.-mid-Nov.; tours from €70 pp

With a convenient location right on Spiaggia Grande, Kayak in Positano offers kayak rentals as well as tours along the Amalfi Coast. Start from as little as €15 for 1 hour; half-day and full-day rentals for longer excursions are also available. Want some expert guidance on finding hidden grottoes, caves, and the best beaches? A variety of excursions from Positano to Praiano and along the coastline are available (€45-120 per person).

Positano Fishing Tours
Spiaggia Grande cement pier; tel. 334/980-674; www.positanofishingtours.com; Apr.-Nov.; from €400 per group

Founded by Alberto Russo and his father, two passionate fishermen, this family-run company offers a unique way to experience the Mediterranean Sea. Choose from half-day, full-day, sunset, night, or even giant squid fishing options. It's not often you can learn traditional fishing techniques to catch giant squid from the depths of the Mediterranean. All fishing excursions are private and customized to your interests and schedule.

Boat Tours
Blue Star Positano
Via Del Brigantino 1; tel. 334/235-4122; www.bluestarpositano.it; Easter-early Nov.; small group tours from €85 pp, private tours from €600 per group

Seeing the Amalfi Coast from the sea is a must, and Blue Star offers small-group or private boat excursions along the Amalfi Coast or to Capri. With a team dedicated to customer service, offering excellent assistance in English and many other languages, Blue Star is a popular choice with travelers. Join a small group tour with a maximum of 12 people for a day-trip excursion along the Amalfi Coast, with free time ashore in Amalfi. You can also book a private tour for a fully customized experience. Book in advance online or simply head to the booth right on the Spiaggia Grande.

Cooking Classes
Latteria Cooking Class
Via Pasitea 67; tel. 089/875-081; www.latteriacookingclass.com; 1:30pm Mon.-Sat. Apr.-Oct., advance reservation required; from €150 pp

Set in what was once a dairy for Positano, this small cooking school is a fun spot to learn about the local cuisine while gaining hands-on experience preparing traditional recipes like fresh homemade pasta, gnocchi, meatballs, eggplant parmigiana, and desserts. Small-group classes last 2.5-3 hours and have a maximum of 12 people, with private classes also available. You'll enjoy tasting the recipes you prepare and enjoy beautiful views of Positano during the class.

Wine Tours
Swirl the Glass
Positano; tel. 329/421-9392; www.swirltheglass.com; flexible hours daily Apr.-Oct.; tastings from €70 pp, tours from €190 pp

Discover the wines of Campania and the Amalfi Coast with the guidance of a true wine expert. Tours are led by professional sommelier Cristian Fusco, who was born and raised in Positano. Let him guide you on a wine tour where you'll have a wonderfully authentic experience visiting a local vineyard to learn more about the unique Amalfi Coast winemaking process, from the vine to the bottle. Wine tours include transportation, a vineyard and winery tour, lunch, and wine-tasting. Wine-tastings in Positano are also available.

FESTIVALS AND EVENTS

If you enjoy local experiences and cultural events, time your visit for one of Positano's annual festivals.

Ferragosto
Spiaggia Grande and various locations; Aug. 14-15

Although Ferragosto is a public holiday celebrated in August throughout Italy, it takes on special meaning in Positano. Because Positano's main church is dedicated to the Santa Maria Assunta, or the Assumption of the Virgin, Ferragosto is the town's largest religious celebration of the year. Festivities start on August 14 with a re-creation of the arrival of the icon of the Virgin Mary and continue through August 15, capped off by an incredible fireworks display over the sea. Check with the tourist office for the schedule of events.

Positano Premia la Danza Léonide Massine
Spiaggia Grande and various locations; tel. 089/812-2535; www.positanopremialadanza.it; early Sept.

Positano celebrates its long tradition with the world of dance during this annual festival in early September, named in honor of the great Russian ballet dancer and choreographer Léonide Massine, who was enamored of Positano and once owned the Li Galli islands. Each year, usually in early September, this festival brings dancers from around the world for events, workshops, and performances on a special stage constructed on Spiaggia Grande.

SHOPPING

Shopping in Positano has been all about fashion since the 1960s, when the seaside town became a favorite of stylish vacationers, and there are still shops that create their designs right in Positano. The perfect complement to your summer wardrobe is a pair of custom-made leather sandals, another local tradition still going strong in Positano.

The main shopping area centers on the Chiesa di Santa Maria Assunta and follows **Via dei Mulini** up to where it meets the internal road **Viale Pasitea** that winds through Positano at **Piazza dei Mulini.** Follow Viale Pasitea west to find some of Positano's most traditional fashion and housewares shops. In the other direction, follow **Via Cristoforo Colombo** east uphill toward Sponda, at the intersection with the Amalfi Coast Road, to enjoy a gorgeous view overlooking Positano and a treasure trove of shops to browse along the way.

La Moda Positano

There's one thing you can't miss while shopping in Positano, and that's all the boutiques with colorful displays of clothing spilling out into the narrow streets of the town. Positano is known for fashion, and it has its own unique style called La Moda Positano (Positano Fashion). Perfect for a seaside town, the local style includes flowing linen in Mediterranean hues, lace, and relaxed chic beachwear perfect for a day of lounging in the sun.

You'll be spoiled for choice as you stroll along the streets and climb the famous staircases of Positano. If you're looking for . . .

- **A crisp linen shirt:** Nothing says Positano style quite like **Emporio Sirenuse,** with lines for women and men available (page 59).
- **A beach cover-up: Luisa Positano** has stylish beachwear in vibrant hues and patterns inspired by the Amalfi Coast (page 59).
- **Handmade sandals:** For the finishing touch, have a pair of sandals custom made to fit your feet at **La Botteguccia** (page 59).

Clothing and Shoes
Luisa Positano
Via Pasitea 78; tel. 089/875-549; www.luisapositano.it; 9am-9pm daily

Full of beautifully patterned fabrics, classic linen, and summery styles, this boutique was founded by Luigia Pollio, known as Luisa, who was a model during the glamorous '60s in Positano. Her children have continued the family enterprise, and all of their traditionally Positano designs are handmade in the workshop located right below the boutique. Come here to add a touch of Positano's color and style to your wardrobe.

Emporio Sirenuse
Via Cristoforo Colombo 107; tel. 089/812-2026; www.emporiosirenuse.com; 9:30am-8:30pm daily Apr.-Oct.

Just across the street from the elegant Le Sirenuse hotel, this equally chic boutique features the ready-to-wear resort fashion line and home decor collection custom-curated by Carla Sersale, the wife of Le Sirenuse's owner Antonio Sersale. Featuring collaborations with top artists and designers from around the world, this one-of-a-kind boutique keeps Positano's artistic tradition alive.

Tre Denari
Via del Saracino 8-9; tel. 089/875-062; mcpositano@yahoo.com; 8:30am-9pm daily Mar.-Dec.

Find beautiful sandals and a large selection of both men's and women's shoes at this friendly shop at the foot of the Chiesa di Santa Maria Assunta. Comfortable handmade leather loafers come in every color under the sun to match vibrant Positano fabrics.

La Botteguccia
Via Regina Giovanna 19; tel. 089/811-824; www.labotteguccia positano.it; 9am-10pm daily Mar.-Oct.

This tiny shop has been a Positano fixture since the early 1960s. Inside, you'll find Dino, son of the shop's founder, pounding away at work, creating handmade sandals. Stop by and have your measurements taken, and he'll create a custom pair while you wait.

Ceramics and Home Goods
Da Vincenzo Shop
Via Pasitea 200; tel. 089/875-128; shop@davincenzo.it; 10am-9:30pm daily fall-spring, 10am-10pm daily summer

A tempting and well-curated selection of ceramics, custom linen designs, tableware, and locally sourced products are on display in this inviting shop. A highlight is the La Selva natural soap and skin-care line, all handmade in the mountains above Positano.

Perfume
Profumi di Positano
Via Cristoforo Colombo 175; tel. 089/875-057; www.profumidipositano.it; 10am-10pm daily June-Sept., 11am-1pm and 3pm-7pm Apr.-May and Oct.

Since the 1920s, the Barba family have produced soaps and perfumes right in Positano. Take home the sweet scents of Positano with their locally made products featuring classic Mediterranean scents that are natural to the area, such as lemon, jasmine, wisteria, citrus, and almond blossoms.

Accessories
CREO
Via Cristoforo Colombo 163a; tel. 339/317-4554; www.positanoglasses.com; 10am-10pm daily

Local artisan Crescenzo Parlato creates handmade sunglasses fashioned from more than 50 types of wood, cork, and natural materials. Glasses can also be customized and made to fit during your stay in Positano. A unique reimagining of the woodworking and intarsia tradition in Sorrento, a pair of glasses make a great souvenir or gift from Positano.

FOOD

Positano's diverse landscape, stretching from the sea deep into the mountain forests high above town, is reflected in the local cuisine, which ranges from freshly caught seafood to heartier staples like grilled meat and locally grown vegetables. There's a wide range of high-quality restaurants, whether you're just visiting for the day or making Positano your home base. Reservations are a good idea for much of the season.

Seafood
Da Vincenzo
Via Pasitea 172; tel. 089/875-128; www.davincenzo.it; 12:15pm-2:45pm and 6:15pm-10:45pm daily Mar.-mid-Nov.; €16-30

An excellent spot for traditional Positano cooking in a friendly setting. The indoor dining area spills out onto the sidewalk during nice weather. While you'll find a varied menu, including a very popular Genovese sauce, seafood is a specialty here and is nicely prepared. The pasta is handmade, and when it's paired with fresh seafood like mussels or prawns, it is a sure win. Reservations are a must, especially for dinner.

Ristorante Max
Piazza dei Mulini 22; tel. 089/875-056; www.ristorantemax.it; noon-3pm and 6pm-10pm daily Apr.-Oct.; €20-55

This eatery is located just off Positano's busy pedestrian-only Via dei Mulini. Follow a narrow staircase down to find a peaceful restaurant opening onto a pretty garden patio. With walls lined with wine and an impressive art collection, the setting is one of a kind. The menu is predominantly seafood-based, and the zuppa di pesce (fish soup) is a definite highlight. Cooking classes are offered in the mornings on the terrace (€170 per person, reservation required).

Regional Cuisine
Da Ferdinando
Spiaggia di Fornillo; tel. 089/875-365; daferdinando1953@gmail.com; 8am-8pm daily mid-May-mid-Oct.; €10-25

Whether you're looking for a relaxing day at the beach or a refreshing seaside meal, this stabilimento balneare (beach club) and restaurant is a great choice right on Spiaggia di Fornillo. Sun beds and umbrellas are available (from €30), and when you're ready to eat, just head up to the restaurant area overlooking the beach. The caprese (salad with tomatoes and buffalo mozzarella) tastes even better by the sea, as does parmigiana di melanzane (eggplant parmesan) and their unique caponata, a refreshing take on a panzanella bread and tomato salad, which they prepare with tomatoes, mozzarella, tuna, olives, and bread. There's also a selection of first and second dishes, often based on the fresh seafood catch of the day. Catch their boat service from Positano's main cement pier.

★ Casa e Bottega

Viale Pasitea 100; tel. 089/875-225; casaebottegapositano@gmail.com; 8:30am-3pm Tues.-Sun. Apr.-Oct.; €15-30

When you're ready for a break from pizza and pasta, this is your place. The menu highlights delicious organic fare and features plenty of healthy options like salads, smoothie bowls, and juices. The brunch choices are as beautiful as they are delicious and there's also a tempting selection of seafood dishes with lovely raw and marinated options too. A buffet displaying freshly made sweets is tempting for dessert. The restaurant includes a shop with a well-curated selection of ceramics, linens, and housewares that might just find their way home with you.

La Tagliata

Via Tagliata 32B, Montepertuso; tel. 089/875-872; www.latagliata.com; noon-3pm and 6pm-10:30pm daily mid-Mar.-mid-Nov.; fixed-price menus €40-60 pp

Head high into the mountains to Montepertuso for an entirely different take on local dining in Positano. Here, far from the sea, the menu is based on organic vegetables grown on terraces around the restaurant, handmade pasta, and, above all, grilled meat. The portions are generous and the setting has a rustic charm. The views overlooking Positano and the coastline are as popular as the excellent food. The restaurant is sometimes open off-season November-March, usually for lunch on Sunday, but call in advance to confirm.

NIGHTLIFE

Positano as the sun sets is a magical place to be. Though the town isn't known for its lively nightlife, it is one of the finest spots to enjoy a sunset on the Amalfi Coast. Grab a table at a bar or beachside restaurant and enjoy cocktails as the sun sinks behind the mountains. Compared to the hustle and bustle of Positano during the day, when ferries bring in crowds of day-trippers, the evening delivers a much more relaxed atmosphere.

For a memorable evening, consider dinner with a sea view followed by drinks or dancing at the town's one notable nightclub. Or enjoy a moonlit stroll along the sea and after-dinner drinks by the water's edge.

Music on the Rocks

Località Grotte Dell'incanto 51; tel. 089/875-874; www.musicontherocks.it; 7pm-4am daily Apr.-Oct.

The one vibrant exception to Positano's otherwise sedate nightlife scene is Music on the

shrimp, rice, and fresh organic ingredients at Casa e Bottega

Rocks. This nightclub is literally on the rocks, as it's set in a cave carved out of the mountainside just steps from the sea. For more than 40 years, this has been a hot spot for music and dancing on the Amalfi Coast, and it still attracts national and international DJs and musicians. There is a cover charge, but it varies depending on the events taking place.

Franco's Bar
Via Cristoforo Colombo 30; tel. 089/875-066; www.francosbar.com; 6pm-11:30pm daily May-Oct.

Next door to the stylish Le Sirenuse hotel and named after one of its founders, Franco's Bar is one of the chicest spots in Positano. As the sun sets and Positano turns all rosy-hued, a spritz never looked so good. The warm ambience lingers on well into the night, making this a great choice for after-dinner drinks. Note that there is a minimum spend of €20 required.

ACCOMMODATIONS

Positano is a great place to consider splurging on your accommodations for your Amalfi Coast stay. With hotels that are regularly voted among the best in all of Italy by travelers, Positano knows how to do luxury and service without losing the laid-back style and local family-run feel of the Amalfi Coast. There are also affordable options that are still centrally located and provide the same views for which Positano is so famous.

Whatever your budget, one key to enjoying your stay in Positano is booking well in advance. Positano is one of the most popular destinations on the Amalfi Coast, and accommodations of all sizes fill up very early, despite the large number of options in town. If you have your heart set on a particular hotel or budget range, book as early as possible.

When it comes to your arrival and departure, check with your lodging to see if they offer assistance with luggage. Sometimes available for an extra charge, in Positano this is well worth it, especially if you're staying near the beach or the lower part of Positano and arriving by car or bus. Nothing puts a damper on a holiday faster than hauling a suitcase through the cobblestone walkways and up or down the steps of Positano!

Under €100
Hostel Brikette
Via G. Marconi 358; tel. 334/904-8692; www.hostel-positano.com; Easter-Oct.; from €80 shared room

The Amalfi Coast doesn't boast many hostels, but this one makes up for the shortage, offering gorgeous views at a very good rate. The super-clean rooms are decorated with a cheery design, and all feature air-conditioning, a nice plus during the summer months. Room configurations vary, and you can choose from shared dorms that sleep 4-10 people. All but two rooms offer en suite baths, sea views, and terraces. A private room with double bed and an en suite bath is also available. There are plenty of breakfast options, and the staff are friendly and ready to help with local information and tips. The hostel is located at the top of Positano just 300 ft (100 m) west of the Chiesa Nuova bus stop.

€200-300
★ Villa delle Palme
Viale Pasitea 252; tel. 089/875-162; www.inpositano.com; May-Oct.; €200 d

Family-run since 1959, this charming small hotel near the top of Positano really has a knack for making guests feel at home. The family is always on hand to help with recommendations, getting around, and anything needed for a pleasant stay. With panoramic views over town and decor in classic Amalfi Coast shades of turquoise and blue, all nine rooms include a private terrace or balcony. Breakfast is served on the shared terrace or on your own private terrace, which is a lovely way to start your day in Positano.

Pensione Casa Guadagno
Via Fornillo 34/36; tel. 089/875-042; www.pensionecasaguadagno.it; mid-Mar.-early Nov.; €220 d

Situated above Fornillo beach, this small pensione with seven rooms offers a comfortable stay in a quieter area of Positano. The sea-view rooms are worth the extra splurge and feature private terraces. Fornillo beach is accessible via steps; you can also walk along Viale Pasitea or hop on an internal bus nearby to reach the center of Positano quickly. Rates are much more affordable outside high season.

Over €300
Palazzo Talamo
Via Pasitea 117; tel. 089/875-562; www.palazzotalamo.it; mid-Apr.-Oct.; €320 d

Set in a panoramic spot with great views and excellent restaurants nearby, this small hotel is a little hidden treasure in Positano. The 11 rooms are bright and colorful with balconies or terraces perfect for enjoying breakfast while taking in the sea views. It's a very romantic setting without all the fuss of Positano's better-known addresses.

Le Sirenuse
Via Cristoforo Colombo 30; tel. 089/875-066; www.sirenuse.it; late Mar.-Oct.; €2,200 d

Since 1951, the Sersale family have specialized in personalized luxury and unforgettable stays in a setting that exudes modern elegance while still retaining the air of a family home. Le Sirenuse's 58 rooms and suites embody classic Positano style with traditional ceramic floors, a medley of antique and modern design, and private balconies or terraces with sea views in most rooms. You'll feel like a movie star as you lounge by the outdoor heated pool or enjoy dining at one of the many restaurants, including La Sponda Restaurant, Aldo's Cocktail Bar & Seafood Grill, the Poolside Bar and Restaurant, and Franco's Bar.

INFORMATION AND SERVICES
Tourist Information
Info Point
Via Regina Giovanna; tel. 331/208-5821; 9am-9pm daily Apr.-Oct., 10am-4pm daily Nov.-Mar.

Positano's tourist office operates multiple Info Points around town during the season June-September. You'll find the main office located not far from **Spiaggia Grande** and the ferry terminal along Via Regina Giovanna. Another is located at **Piazza dei Mulini**, and there are QR codes to access more information in various points around Positano as well as Montepertuso and Nocelle. You can also get information at the **MAR Museum ticket booth** near the Chiesa di Santa Maria Assunta. English-speaking staff are on hand to answer your questions about Positano and any special events that might be on during your visit, and they offer a selection of maps and local information.

Postal Services
Post Italiane
Via Guglielmo Marconi 318; tel. 089/875-142; www.poste.it; 8:20am-1:45pm Mon.-Fri., 8:20am-12:45pm Sat.

To mail letters and packages, Positano's post office is located in the upper part of town near the Comune (town hall).

GETTING THERE
By Car and Scooter
Positano is situated toward the western end of the Amalfi Coast, 11 mi (17.7 km) west of **Amalfi** and 27 mi (43 km) west of **Salerno** on the **Amalfi Coast Road (SS163)**. From **Ravello,** which is 15.5 mi (25 km) east of Positano, take the **SS373** road down the mountain to connect with the Amalfi Coast Road (SS163) and continue west on the road to Positano. **Sorrento** is 9 mi (14.5 km) away on the northern side of the Sorrentine Peninsula. You have to follow **SS145** south over the mountains of the Sorrentine Peninsula until it merges with the Amalfi Coast Road (SS163) and head east to reach Positano. **Naples** is 37 mi (60 km) from Positano, and the drive is along the **A3** autostrada south until Castellammare di Stabia, where the SS145 road begins. Follow SS145 west along the coastline to Sorrento and then continue on to reach the Amalfi Coast Road (SS163) for Positano. Although the distances don't seem far, keep in mind that the roads along the Sorrentine Peninsula are very twisty and narrow. Drive time to Positano is usually 50

minutes from Amalfi, a little over 1 hour from Ravello, and about 45 minutes from Sorrento. From Salerno, the drive is about 2 hours, while from Naples plan for 2 hours, and that's without traffic. During the tourist season, Easter-October, expect longer drive times.

Parking in Positano can come with a hefty price tag, €3-5 per hour or €20-30 per day, depending on the season and location. You'll find parking lot options as you drive along Viale Pasitea, especially in the Piazza dei Mulini area. This is a convenient parking area as the Spiaggia Grande and heart of Positano are just a short walk down Via dei Mulini. If you're staying in Positano, check with your lodging in advance for the best parking options.

By Ferry

Ferry service on the Amalfi Coast runs seasonally, from around Easter to the beginning of November. Ferries arrive at, and depart from, the large cement pier on the western end of the Spiaggia Grande beach. Tickets can be purchased at the ticket booths along the pier. Because there is no port and the pier is open to the sea, ferry service to Positano is dependent on good weather and sea conditions. Sometimes even if ferries are running, stops in Positano can be limited or canceled if the sea is rough, a stronger possibility in the shoulder seasons of early spring or October. So if you're traveling by ferry, it's good to have alternative transportation options in mind, just in case.

Ferry service to Positano from Amalfi, Minori, Maiori, Cetara, and Salerno is operated by **Travelmar** (tel. 089/872-950; www.travelmar.it; €9-14 per person). There are ferries throughout the day every 1-2 hours approximately 9:30am-6pm. For some routes, you may need to transfer boats in Amalfi to reach Positano. Travel time to Positano by ferry from Salerno is about 70 minutes, from Cetara about 35 minutes, 40 minutes from Maiori (with a change in Amalfi), 35 minutes from Minori (with a change in Amalfi), and 25 minutes from Amalfi. It's a good idea to purchase your tickets in advance online or via the Travelmar app, especially during the peak season June-September.

Alicost (tel. 089/811-986; www.alicost.it; €15-21.30 per person) is the main ferry service connecting Capri and Sorrento to Positano, with service from Amalfi and Salerno as well. They offer one daily trip from Capri (more available June-Sept.) and two daily trips from Sorrento. The ferry ride from Capri to Positano takes about 45 minutes, while from Sorrento it's about 50 minutes. Tickets can be purchased online in advance. Another option to Positano from Capri is **Positano Jet** (tel. 089/811-164; www.lucibello.it; €9-21 per person). Operated by the Lucibello boat company, this ferry service runs three trips each day, and the journey is about 40 minutes. They also operate 2-3 ferries a day from Amalfi to Positano, and the journey is about 25 minutes. **Grassi Junior** (tel. 089/811-605; www.grassiboatpositano.com; €9-14 per person) also runs more limited ferry service connecting Salerno, Amalfi, Minori, Maiori, and Cetara to Positano.

By Bus

The public bus line connecting Positano to Sorrento, the rest of the Amalfi Coast, and Salerno is operated by **SITA SUD** (tel. 089/386-6701; www.sitasudtrasporti.it; from €1.50). Buses stop in Positano at Chiesa Nuova and Sponda. If you're staying in the upper part of Positano, the **Chiesa Nuova stop** is likely more convenient; the **Sponda bus stop** is the best choice if you're staying in the center of Positano near the beach. To reach Positano from Ravello or towns east of Amalfi to Salerno, you will first need to take the bus to Amalfi and then transfer to the Amalfi-Sorrento line. The bus ride from Sorrento to Positano takes about 1 hour, and from Amalfi the journey takes less than 1 hour.

By Taxi

To get to Positano by taxi, it's best to book in advance. **Positano Drivers** (tel. 338/888-6572 and 339/886-9182; www.positanodrivers.

com; from €100) offers transfers from Naples, Sorrento, and other destinations along the Amalfi Coast.

GETTING AROUND
By Car and Scooter
There's a one-way internal road through Positano that starts on the western edge of town near the Chiesa Nuova. To access the lower part of Positano, follow Viale Pasitea, which winds through Positano down to Piazza dei Mulini and then changes its name to Via Cristoforo Colombo as it climbs out of town to rejoin the Amalfi Coast Road at Sponda, the intersection with the Amalfi Coast Road. To reach Montepertuso and Nocelle, follow the Amalfi Coast Road west from the center of Positano, and soon you'll find a large turnoff with a sign pointing toward Montepertuso and Nocelle. This is Via Corvo, and it becomes Via Monsignor Saverio Cinque, which leads first to Montepertuso and continues along to Nocelle. The drive to Montepertuso takes about 10 minutes, and it's about 15 minutes to Nocelle.

With the narrow roads of the Amalfi Coast, a small rental car is a good idea. **Positano Car Service** (Via Cristoforo Colombo 2; tel. 089/875-541; www.positanocarservice.com; from €110 per day) offers pint-size Smart cars. If you want to rent a scooter, **Positano Rent a Scooter** (Via Pasitea 99; tel. 331/748-1311; www.positanorentascooter.it; from €90 per day) offers a variety of options, including the classic Italian brand Vespa.

By Bus
Mobility Amalfi Coast (tel. 089/813-077; info@mobilityamalficoast.com; €1.30-1.80) provides bus service along Positano's internal road and to Nocelle, Montepertuso, and Praiano. Buses pass about every half hour for the internal route 9am-midnight daily. The service to Nocelle, Montepertuso, and Praiano is more limited and runs more or less hourly. Tickets can be purchased in tabacchi or on board.

By Taxi
Taxis in Positano are independently owned high-quality vehicles, and they charge flat fees based on destination rather than calculating according to distance or drive time. As a result, prices are higher than you might expect compared to taxis in most cities. April-October you can generally find a taxi at Piazza dei Mulini, but budget for more than €40 just to move around Positano; a ride from Positano to Nocelle and Montepertuso can cost €40-50. Before departing, tell the driver where you need to go and agree on a price.

On Foot
Positano isn't called the Vertical City for nothing. Getting around town means navigating a lot of steps and inclines. From Piazza dei Mulini down to the beach, you'll walk on a cobblestone path mixed with steps, a bit of an expedition if you have a lot of luggage. If you're staying near the beach, it's worth asking in advance if your lodging offers a luggage service; there may be an additional fee, but it will be well worth it. Comfortable shoes and sandals are a good idea for getting around Positano. Forgo those elegant heels and opt for a nice pair of flats for evenings out.

Praiano

Despite its mountainside setting, Praiano has always had a strong connection with the sea. Its ancient name, Antica Plagianum, likely derives from the Latin for "open sea." The town has long been known for fishing, including the production of nets, and later coral fishing. Evidence of this tradition can be seen at the Marina di Praia beach, often covered with small wooden boats and heaps of fishing cages and nets.

For some time, Praiano has been a hidden oasis for those who enjoy going off the beaten path. With its dreamy setting suspended between the mountains and sea, Praiano offers a quiet charm that is closely connected to nature. Though this town is certainly no longer off the radar, it is by no means as busy as its next-door neighbor Positano. It's an excellent home base if you're looking for a quieter and more local experience than you'd find in larger towns along the coast.

ORIENTATION

Between Positano and Furore, the Amalfi coastline juts out into the sea and Praiano spills down two sides of a mountain ridge that ends in a gently curved cape, **Capo Sottile**. The eastern side is called Praiano, while **Vettica Maggiore** is the name of the western side of town. One thing is guaranteed: The views are gorgeous on both sides.

In Vettica Maggiore on the western side of Capo Sottile, you'll find the beautiful **Chiesa di San Gennaro** with a large terrace in front, offering spectacular views of Positano. At sea level far below is the rocky **La Gavitella** beach. Just east of the Chiesa di San Gennaro, a narrow road leads up into higher parts of Praiano and meanders through the town until meeting back down at the Amalfi Coast Road on the eastern side of Capo Sottile. Continue on the Amalfi Coast Road east to find the charming **Marina di Praia** beach set in a tiny cove.

SIGHTS
Chiesa di San Gennaro
Piazza San Gennaro, Vettica Maggiore; tel. 089/874-799; piobozza@virgilio.it; 9am-noon and 4pm-8pm daily fall-spring, 4pm-10pm daily summer

Driving through Vettica Maggiore on the Amalfi Coast Road, you'll see the colorful ceramic-tiled dome and bell tower of the Chiesa di San Gennaro sitting just below the road. This large church dates to 1589 and was constructed on the site of an older church, which was also dedicated to San Gennaro (Saint Januarius), an important bishop, martyr, and patron saint of Naples. The baroque interior is richly decorated with an equally ornate ceramic floor. The large piazza in front of the church is a lovely spot to admire the view of Positano in the distance and gaze all the way down the coastline to the island of Capri. Here is where the dramatic Luminaria di San Domenico celebrations take place at the beginning of August. If you're in Praiano on September 19, December 16, or the first Sunday in May, you'll likely catch the local celebrations with special masses and processions honoring San Gennaro.

Chiesa di San Luca Evangelista
Piazza San Luca; tel. 089/874-247; donluigiamendola@gmail.com; 3pm-7pm Mon.-Fri., 8:30am-noon and 3pm-7pm Sat.-Sun. fall-spring, 3pm-10pm Mon.-Fri., 8:30am-noon and 3pm-10pm Sat.-Sun. summer

Although not as striking as the Chiesa di San Gennaro with its majolica dome, the Chiesa di San Luca Evangelista holds a special place in Praiano, as it is dedicated to the town's patron saint. The pretty piazza in front of the church is reason enough to visit, and inside this 16th-century church are lovely baroque ornaments, including a hand-painted

1: Chiesa di San Gennaro **2:** traditional boat near Marina di Praia **3:** La Gavitella beach

majolica floor from 1789, depicting San Luca surrounded by a decorative pattern of flowers and birds. Praiano celebrates its patron saint with a festival, including special masses and processions, on October 18, the first Sunday of July, and Easter Monday.

Praiano NaturArte
various locations; free

Walking is the best way to discover the charms of the Amalfi Coast's towns. Praiano offers extra incentive with a unique artistic experience: The town has created more than 150 permanent art installations around town and strung them together into eight suggested walks, each one leading to a collection of ceramic or stone artworks created by eight different artists. The works blend harmoniously with the landscape to create an outdoor museum, and pieces by local artists showcase the town's traditions, myths, and history. Walks vary in length and difficulty; itinerary no. 5 is an excellent choice, with artwork created by Lucio Liguori, a ceramic artist from Vietri sul Mare. Inspired by the sea, the pathway is dotted with brightly colored ceramic sea creatures like anchovies, squid, and tuna, as well as ceramic panels showing scenes from the traditional fishing life in Praiano. To enjoy this walk, follow Via Breve down from the Amalfi Coast Road to Via Massa, which leads to the Chiesa di San Gennaro and continues on as Via Rezzola. Plan for about 40 minutes for this walk. Visit the **Ufficio Informazioni Turistiche di Praiano** for a map of the NaturArte walks.

BEACHES

Given the town's setting above the sea, Praiano is a little more limited when it comes to beach access than some of the other towns on the Amalfi Coast.

La Gavitella
Cala della Gavitella, Vettica Maggiore

Situated below Vettica Maggiore, this small and very rocky beach is a bit of a hike from the center of Praiano, but it's lovely with great views down the coast toward Positano. Be prepared for the climb back up, which is just over 400 steps. The beach is served by a stabilimento balneare (beach club), but there is also space where you can sunbathe and swim for free. Head to the rockier end of the beach if you're looking for a more secluded spot; the water is lovely here for swimming and access to the sea is via a ladder.

Marina di Praia
Via Marina di Praia

An important access point to the sea since ancient times, Marina di Praia is one of the most captivating beaches on the entire coast. Set in a deep ravine with little houses and a tiny whitewashed church, this beach still has the atmosphere of a fishing village. Sunbathers vie for space with brightly painted wooden fishing boats, nets, and cages pulled up on the beach. Besides the incredibly clear and clean water, one of the most appealing features of Marina di Praia is the **walkway** cut into the cliff side that leads about 1,300 ft (400 m) from the beach along the rugged coastline. Follow the scenic pathway past the medieval **Torre a Mare** watchtower all the way to the entrance of the iconic Africana Famous Club.

One of the best aspects of Marina di Praia is its easy access. A small road leads from the Amalfi Coast Road to a gentle slope of steps down to the beach. Like much of the coastline, the beach is pebbly. Sun beds are available for rental, or find a spot in the crowded free area among the fishing boats. There are also some cement platforms along the walkway where locals sunbathe and where rock jumping is popular.

With steep cliffs on both sides, the sun hits Marina di Praia only during the middle hours of the day, but the location is just as enchanting in the evening or after dark, thanks to the beautiful walk along the sea and excellent restaurants.

SPORTS AND RECREATION

Praiano's rocky stretch of coastline is ideal for water sports. Just head down to Marina di Praia, where you'll find options for kayaking, boat trips, and even diving excursions.

Windsurf & Kayak Praiano

Marina di Praia; tel. 377/474-7089; www.windsurfpraiano.com; 10am-5pm daily May-Oct.; kayak rental from €15 per hour

Set off from the beach and explore the coastline kayaking or stand-up paddleboarding around Praiano. It's the best way to enjoy the area's natural beauty while getting a bit of exercise. In addition to kayak and paddleboard rentals, they offer kayak excursions (€80 per person) along the coastline.

La Boa Charter & Diving

Marina di Praia; tel. 340/654-9621; www.laboa.com; 8am-9pm daily May-Oct.; from €90 pp

Discover the underwater beauty of the Amalfi Coast on a diving excursion from Praiano. La Boa Charter & Diving has two diving centers on the Sorrentine Peninsula, where the company offers immersions and boat excursions. The one in Marina di Praia is the starting point for dives along the Amalfi Coast. All immersions include an instructor and equipment. There are many types of dives possible, ranging in experience level from easy immersions below Vettica Maggiore to challenging dives around the Li Galli islands for very advanced divers. Also available are both small group excursions (from €90 per person) and private boat excursions with a captain (from €600 per group) along the Amalfi Coast and to Capri without diving experiences.

ENTERTAINMENT AND EVENTS

Praiano is a tranquil town known mostly for its moving religious and cultural celebrations throughout the year.

Classical Music
I Suoni degli Dei (The Sounds of the Gods)

Sentiero degli Dei; tel. 089/874-557; www.isuonideglidei.com; generally Sat. in Apr.-May and Sept.-Oct.; free

There are few more impressive settings for an open-air concert than the Sentiero degli Dei pathway high above Praiano. This incredible concert series of classical and contemporary music is not only set against the backdrop of the Amalfi Coast, but also immersed in nature in various settings, including among the ruins of the Santa Maria a Castro church that sit at 1,194 ft (364 m) above the sea. Accessing the concerts means hiking the **Pathway of the Gods;** the hike is strenuous but extremely rewarding. Bring plenty of water and dress accordingly with hiking or good walking shoes. For more details on reaching the concert locations from where you're staying, contact the organization or tourist office for tips or to arrange a guide.

Praiano Chambre and Jazz Music

various locations; tel. 333/965-7612; www.praianochambreandjazzmusic.com; concerts May-Sept.

Dedicated to bringing classical and jazz music to the historic settings and beautiful piazzas in Praiano, this series of concerts is curated by Carmine Laino, the first double bass of the Teatro San Carlo in Naples. Concerts take place at various locations around Praiano, including in the piazzas in front of the churches of San Gennaro and San Luca Evangelista.

Festivals and Events
Luminaria di San Domenico

Piazza San Gennaro, Piazza San Luca, and various locations; www.luminariadisandomenico.it; Aug. 1-4; free

Every summer, the Luminaria di San Domenico—a stunning festival imbued with cultural and religious significance—takes over Praiano. Celebrated for more than 400 years, this event starts from the Convento di

Santa Maria a Castro above Praiano, where there was once a strong devotion to San Domenico. The festival re-creates the legend of San Domenico's mother, who had a dream before he was born of a dog with a torch in his mouth setting the world on fire; this was believed to signify that the newborn would carry the word of God to the world. Today the journey of the fire is represented with thousands of candles around town and religious celebrations. The events culminate with about 3,000 candles decorating the Piazza San Gennaro, where performing fire dancers re-create the story of San Domenico.

FOOD
Seafood
Trattoria da Armandino
Via Praia 1; tel. 089/874-087; www.daarmandino. it; 1pm-3:30pm and 7pm-11pm daily mid-Mar.-Oct.; €18-34

Right at the edge of the sea in picturesque Marina di Praia, this restaurant has a way of making you feel right at home. Owners Armando and Carmela have been running this restaurant since 1986, and it's a popular spot with locals. Seafood is the specialty, with a home-cooked touch. Try the pasta with totani (squid), the delicious risotto with lemon and shrimp, or fried fresh seafood. The restaurant is also open as a bar for coffee and drinks 9am-11pm daily.

Il Pirata
Via Terramare; tel. 089/874-377; www. ilpiratamalficoast.com; noon-4pm and 7pm-10pm daily Easter-Oct.; €22-60

From the beach in Marina di Praia, follow the Via Terramare walkway carved into the mountain, and before long you'll happen across this restaurant with outdoor seating on terraces overlooking the sea. Naturally, this is the place to enjoy seafood, including excellent crudo di pesce (raw fish), totani e patate (squid and potatoes), or pasta with freshly caught fish, yellow tomatoes, and basil. Il Pirata is also open 9am-6pm daily as a solarium for visitors to enjoy the sun, and the bar, carved into the mountain, is usually open late.

Cafés
Café Mirante
Via Masa 55; tel. 366/171-8593; cafemirante.praiano@ gmail.com; 10am-10pm daily May-Oct.; €5-18

For a drink with a picture-perfect view of the coastline all the way to Capri, stop in this café for a refreshing fruit shake or creative cocktails made with ingredients that capture the flavors and scents of the Amalfi Coast, mostly collected direct from the property's garden. This is the place to truly savor those famous Praiano sunset views.

ACCOMMODATIONS
€100-200
Locanda Costa Diva
Via Roma 12; tel. 089/813-076; www.hotelspraiano. com; Mar.-Oct.; €180 d

Enjoy lovely views of the coastline dotted with watchtowers from this hotel nestled between terraces of lemon and olive trees and lush gardens. All of the rooms and suites feature special touches like vaulted ceilings and frescoed walls, ceramics from Vietri sul Mare, and colorful decor. The hotel's restaurant, with an outdoor dining terrace surrounded by lemon trees, is a dreamy dining spot.

Over €300
Hotel Margherita
Via Umberto I 70; tel. 089/874-628; www. hotelmargherita.info; mid-Mar.-Oct.; €434 d

With a bright and classic Amalfi Coast decor and extremely friendly service, Hotel Margherita offers a peaceful escape thanks to its lovely pool overlooking the sea, excellent on-site restaurant, cooking class experiences (from €80 per person), and handy services like a shuttle van to the beach and to Positano. If you want a sea-view room (and you do), make sure to request one of the 24 rooms (out of 28) that include private terraces.

INFORMATION AND SERVICES
Ufficio Informazioni Turistiche di Praiano
Via Gennaro Capriglione 116b, Vettica Maggiore; tel. 089/874-557; www.praiano.org; 9am-1pm and 5pm-9pm daily June-Sept., 9am-1pm and 4:30pm-8:30pm daily Oct.-May

Praiano's tourist office is located just across the street from the easy-to-spot Chiesa di San Gennaro with its multicolored dome. Stop in here for friendly help in English; you'll find all the information you need to explore the town and the entire Amalfi Coast during your stay.

GETTING THERE AND AROUND

Praiano is located only about 3.7 mi (6 km) east of **Positano,** but getting here will require a bit more work. There is no port in Praiano, so unless you are driving, the only connection between Praiano and other towns is via taxi or bus.

By Car and Scooter

The **Amalfi Coast Road (SS163)** runs right through Praiano, making it easy to reach from nearby **Positano,** which is only about a 20-minute drive. The next nearest town to the east on the Amalfi Coast Road is **Conca dei Marini,** which is also about a 20-minute drive. The main sights in Praiano are located along or very near the Amalfi Coast Road. An internal road passes through the upper area of Praiano above the Amalfi Coast Road, intersecting the Amalfi Coast Road east of Chiesa di San Gennaro where the road is called Via Giuglielmo Marconi. Eventually, it splits into Via Costantinopoli to the left, a scenic drive through the upper part of town, and Via Umberto I, which meanders through a pretty area of town with restaurants and hotels, and eventually meets up with the Amalfi Coast Road on the eastern side of Capo Sottile in Praiano.

Driving east from Praiano right on the edge of town, look for the sharp turnoff to the right onto a narrow road, Via Marina di Praia, that leads down to the beach cove. **Parking** is available in Praiano and Marina di Praia in paid areas along the side of the road, or in paid parking lots that usually charge from €3 per hour.

Located right beside the Chiesa di San Gennaro, **Mr Rent a Scooter** (Via Gennaro Capriglione 99, Vettica Maggiore; tel. 089/813-071; www.mrentascooter.it; 9am-6pm daily May-Oct. and by reservation; from €65 per day) has a selection of scooters you can rent daily or for longer periods. This is a fun and often less stressful way to get around the Amalfi Coast compared to a car.

By Taxi

Taxis can usually be found at the beginning of Via Giuglielmo Marconi, just off the Amalfi Coast Road east of the Chiesa di San Gennaro in Vettica Maggiore, and at the crossroads of the Amalfi Coast Road and Via Umberto I in Praiano. Look for the orange Taxi sign for more information. Taxis are independently owned, but the town of Praiano has set taxi fares to most locations on the Amalfi Coast, available for 1-4 people and 5-8 people, starting from €20 within Praiano town limits. It's €40 to Positano, €60 to Amalfi, €100 to Ravello or Sorrento, and €130 to Salerno. Be sure to notify the driver if you want a fixed rate before departure. All other journeys are metered and start at €6. The tourist office in Praiano can offer the latest rates and help with any questions about taxis. It is a good idea to book a taxi in advance, especially for arrival and departure, or if you need to be somewhere at a specific time, as buses can be delayed.

By Bus

Public buses operated by **SITA SUD** (tel. 089/386-6701; www.sitasudtrasporti.it; from €1.50) pass through Praiano on the Amalfi Coast Road, but they can be very crowded, so it's best to be patient. Buses can be so full before arriving in Praiano that they are unable to stop to pick up passengers. Stops are located throughout Praiano and Vettica Maggiore, including near the Chiesa di San Gennaro, intersections with Praiano's internal road, and above Marina di Praia.

To reach Praiano by bus from Positano, catch the bus heading to Amalfi from one of the two stops in Positano (Chiesa Nuova or Sponda); the journey is about 25 minutes. From Amalfi, take the bus heading to Sorrento; the journey is about 25 minutes. To travel to Praiano from Ravello and Salerno, you must first take a bus to Amalfi and then transfer to the bus to Sorrento.

You can also get to Praiano from Positano and get around Praiano by a local bus service, **Mobility Amalfi Coast** (tel. 089/813-077; info@mobilityamalficoast.com; €1.30-1.80). These smaller buses stop throughout Praiano, including at the Chiesa di San Gennaro and Marina di Praia, roughly every hour. Tickets are available in local tabacchi and some shops, or on board for a slightly higher fare.

Furore

Following the Amalfi Coast Road along the coast, it's easy to understand Furore's nickname, "Il paese che non c'è" (The Town that Doesn't Exist). Clinging to the cliff side high above, the only part of Furore you'll see from the road is a brief glimpse of the impressive Fiordo di Furore, a dramatic fjord with a tiny beach. You'll have to meander off the Amalfi Coast Road and head up into the mountains to find this village, which does actually exist. You'll find it spread out along the mountainside with houses set between terraced gardens. As you follow the hairpin curves that zigzag up the mountain, you'll discover Furore's name for itself, "Il Paese Dipinto" (The Painted City), a much more fitting title. The town is full of beautiful murals, sculptures, and artistic embellishments.

Though Furore doesn't have a cohesive town center, its evocative location, peaceful atmosphere, and stunning views make it a fine town to explore if you want to be surrounded by nature and don't mind if you're not close to the beach. With excellent hiking options nearby, Furore is an ideal base for mountain lovers.

SIGHTS
Fiordo di Furore
SS163 (Amalfi Coast Rd.) at Fiordo di Furore

The sliver of Furore's fjord with its tiny beach and old fishing village is one of the Amalfi Coast's most iconic images. However, you can only catch a quick view of it while driving along the Amalfi Coast Road. The best way to enjoy the view and visit the beach is to arrive by bus, because there is no parking nearby. Ask the driver to stop at the Fiordo di Furore stop, and after gazing down at the view, take the staircase starting at the western side of the bridge that clings to the cliff, and follow it down to reach the beach. The little cluster of houses carved into the mountainside and some wooden boats are all that's left of a fishing village that has always been Furore's only access point to the sea. It was in this romantic spot that Italian film director Roberto Rossellini and actress Anna Magnani had a passionate affair during the filming of his 1948 movie *L'Amore*.

This nearly hidden beach still has a mesmerizing atmosphere of bygone days. During the summer season, especially around midday when the sun arrives on the beach, you'll find beachgoers along with boats arriving below the bridge to show travelers the scenic beach, and kayakers pulling up for a rest on the shore. The small beach doesn't offer a lot as far as amenities, but it makes up for it with fine views. For the more adventurous, the rocks along the walk down to the beach are popular for cliff-jumping.

1: Fiordo di Furore beach **2:** Furore village

SPORTS AND RECREATION
Adventure Sports
Zipline Italia Furore—Conca
Via Aldo Moro 1; tel. 089/202-7209; www.ziplineitalia.it; 9am-7pm Tues.-Sun. Apr.-Sept.; from €40

Offering a fantastic bird's-eye view of the Fiordo di Furore, the Zipline Furore—Conca is a thrilling experience. The zip line starts in Furore and runs 0.4 mi (650 m) down the mountainside to Conca dei Marini. Rides can be single or in pairs and take a little over a minute from start to finish.

VINEYARDS
Cantine Marisa Cuomo
Via Giambattista Lama 16/18; tel. 089/830-348; www.marisacuomo.com; wine-tasting and tours Mar.-Oct., tours only Nov.-Feb., reservations required; tour and tasting €75 pp

Set in an improbable location along the steep slopes of Furore, this is one of Campania's most celebrated vineyards. A labor of love of husband-and-wife team Andrea Ferraioli and Marisa Cuomo, Cantine Marisa Cuomo produces highly esteemed wines from grapes grown on nearly 25 acres (10 ha) of steeply sloped and terraced vineyards. After grapes are harvested, the wine is produced in the winemakers' cantine, situated in a cave carved out of the mountain. The winery is noted for both white and red wines, making this an excellent vineyard to try some of the Amalfi Coast's unique grape varietals. Falanghina and biancolella grapes create the lovely Furore Bianco wine, with delicate fruit and Mediterranean scents, while aglianico and piedirosso, also called per'e palummo, are used to make the classic Furore Rosso, a ruby-red-colored wine with a hint of cherry and spices. Wine-tastings and vineyard tours include a tour of the cantine and vineyard, and lunch or dinner accompanied by a selection of wines. Menus can vary, with gluten-free and vegetarian options available. Tours are also offered during the winter months. Booking in advance is required.

FOOD AND ACCOMMODATIONS
Hostaria di Bacco
Via Giambattista Lama 9; tel. 089/830-360; www.baccofurore.it; restaurant 12:30pm-3:30pm and 7:30pm-10pm daily June-Aug., 12:30pm-3:30pm and 7:30pm-10pm Wed.-Mon. Sept.-May; €15-28; hotel Mar.-Jan. 7; €250 d

With a long tradition of welcoming guests since 1930, this friendly restaurant and hotel will make you feel right at home. Restaurant specialties blend seafood and traditional mountain dishes in just the way Furore sits between land and sea. Try the pasta with beans and mussels or the squid stuffed with seafood and locally grown vegetables. "Slow Food" and vegan tasting menus are available. The hotel offers beautifully decorated rooms in its central building, which has been designated the first "albergo dipinto" (painted hotel) of the Amalfi Coast. Each of these rooms feature murals inspired by the natural beauty and history of the area by local artists. There are also additional guest rooms in a separate location nearby. In both locations, the rooms are bright and lovely with balconies or terraces and views of the sea, grapevines, or lemon groves.

Agriturismo Sant'Alfonso
Via San Alfonso 6; tel. 089/830-515; www.agriturismosantalfonso.it; mid.-Mar.-mid.-Jan.; €130 d

This 17th-century farmhouse nestled along the slopes of Furore offers a comfortable spot to get away from it all while surrounded by beautiful views in a rustic setting. The nine rooms are cozy, and the agriturismo offers a generous breakfast with freshly baked sweets included in the rates. For lunch or dinner you can also dine out on the terrace overlooking the sea during good weather. There's a small chapel on-site dedicated to Sant'Alfonso Maria de' Liguori that was once part of a monastery (now the farmhouse). An air of tranquility reigns in this splendidly natural spot.

The Vineyards of the Amalfi Coast

terraces of vineyards on the steep slopes of Furore

The idea of Italian vineyards usually conjures up images of gently rolling hills in Tuscany lined with evenly spaced rows of vines. To see the vineyards of the Amalfi Coast is quite a different experience, and one that often starts with looking up. The steep slopes and rocky terrain of the Amalfi Coast certainly doesn't seem like the place to grow grapes, but with a hefty dose of hard work, some incredible wines are produced in the coastline's vertical vineyards.

Grapes have been grown here for generations on terraces carved out of the mountainside using a clever system of pergolas. In this incredibly challenging landscape, the wines that are produced are infused with the salty scent of sea breeze and the unique Mediterranean microclimate. The wines of the region are of the Costa d'Amalfi DOC, or denominazione di origine controllata, the Italian system to indicate quality and geographically protected wine-production areas. The slopes of Furore, Ravello, and higher into the Lattari Mountains in Tramonti are noted for their wine production. In Tramonti you can sample wines created with grapes handpicked from vines that are more than a century old. Tramonti's remote location allowed it to escape a mid-19th-century blight caused by an aphid species from the United States that destroyed many of the vines in France and Italy.

Along the Amalfi Coast you'll find wine varieties that might be new to your palate but have long been cultivated in the region of Campania. For white wines, look for the very traditional falanghina, fiano, greco di tufo, or biancolella grape varieties. The most common varieties of red wine grapes in the area are aglianico, piedirosso, and tintore. A few visits to the vineyards will show you how the landscape and mix of varieties creates strikingly different wines from one town to the next.

WINE-TASTING

- **Furore:** Visit the **Cantine Marisa Cuomo** (page 74) to try the Costa d'Amalfi DOC wines made from the grapes grown along the slopes of Furore and the Amalfi Coast.

- **Tramonti:** Along with Tramonti's rare vines, you'll find the classic local red varietals like aglianico, piedirosso, and tintore. If you prefer white, you'll find lovely blends with falanghina, ginestra, pepella, and biancolella grapes. Local producers like **Tenuta San Francesco** (page 124) and **Cantine Giuseppe Apicella** (page 124) offer vineyard tours and tastings, and you'll see their wines at many local restaurants.

- **Vietri sul Mare:** Travel down the coast to Raito, a small village above Vietri sul Mare, to visit **Le Vigne di Raito** (page 144), a newer vineyard that is continuing the local traditions of winemaking on the Amalfi Coast.

GETTING THERE

Furore is located between Praiano and Conca dei Marini, with the center of the town on the mountainside above the **Amalfi Coast Road (SS163).** To reach Furore, you'll need to drive up the **SS366** road, which intersects the Amalfi Coast Road (SS163) about 1.2 mi (2 km) west of Amalfi. Look for a well-marked intersection with signs indicating Furore. Continue on SS366 as it climbs into the mountains and passes through the upper part of Conca dei Marini. Stay on SS366, and after about 3.7 mi (6 km) more you'll arrive in Furore. The drive to Furore is about 40 minutes from Praiano, 25 minutes from Amalfi, 15 minutes from Conca dei Marini, and 40 minutes from Ravello.

The **SITA SUD** (tel. 089/386-6701; www.sitasudtrasporti.it; from €1.40) bus line connecting Amalfi to Agerola provides access to the upper part of the town. The Fiordo di Furore is located on the Amalfi Coast Road and is accessible via the SITA SUD bus line connecting Amalfi and Sorrento. It takes about 25 minutes to reach the center of Furore from Amalfi by bus. The Fiordo di Furore is a 20-minute bus ride from Amalfi and a 50-minute bus ride from Positano. From Ravello and Salerno, you first have to take the bus to Amalfi (about 25 minutes from Ravello to Amalfi, and 1 hour 15 minutes from Salerno to Amalfi) and then transfer to the Amalfi to Agerola bus line. To reach the town by ferry, the closest port is Amalfi, where you can then transfer to the SITA SUD bus to reach Furore.

Conca dei Marini

The town is most noted for the picturesque harbor of Marina di Conca, a small cluster of houses built around the beach that were once home to the town's fishermen. Here you'll find one of the Amalfi Coast's most charming beaches and gorgeous water. This sleepy fishing village was put on the map in the 1960s when the jet-set crowd, including Jacqueline Kennedy, favored the quiet setting of Conca dei Marini for summer holidays. The town still has a secluded charm that makes it a popular spot for travelers looking for a relaxed escape.

ORIENTATION

Conca dei Marini climbs vertically from the sea, more than 1,300 ft (400 m) straight up the mountainside. Access to the lower part of town is via the Amalfi Coast Road and the upper part of town via the SS366 road leading up into the mountains toward Furore and Agerola. In Conca dei Marini, you can go from swimming in the sea up to the top of town for sweeping views of the coastline and back down to the distinctive **Capo di Conca** promontory with its 16th-century stone watchtower. In the small bay by the watchtower is the entrance to the **Grotta dello Smeraldo** (Emerald Grotto) with its mesmerizing green waters.

SIGHTS
Grotta dello Smeraldo (Emerald Grotto)

Via Smeraldo; tel. 089/831-535; 9am-4pm daily Apr.-Oct., 9am-3pm daily Nov.-Mar.; €10

While Capri has its famous Blue Grotto, the Amalfi Coast has a cave of its own that is just as notable for its beautiful colors. The Grotta dello Smeraldo (Emerald Grotto) is named after the intense green water inside. Situated in the pretty bay at Capo di Conca, the large grotto was discovered in 1932 by a local fisherman. Unlike the Blue Grotto, however, the Emerald Grotto has an easily accessible entrance. After walking into the grotto, you climb aboard small boats to be rowed around to see the underwater sights, including the impressive stalactites and stalagmites, and, of course, the emerald water. The boat tour lasts about 15 minutes. Access to the grotto is from the Amalfi Coast Road via elevator (the steps are not in service) or by boat from Amalfi, offered by the **Gruppo Battellieri Costa d'Amalfi** (Via Largo Duchi Piccolomini 4, Amalfi; tel. 089/873-446; www.gruppobattellieriamalfi.com; Mar.-Nov.; €15 boat fare plus €10 entrance) with frequent departures 9:40am-4:20pm daily.

Chiesa di San Pancrazio
Via Don Gaetano Amodio 22; hours vary; free

Follow the narrow road that leads from the Amalfi Coast Road up into the heart of Conca dei Marini, and after a few steep twists and turns you'll find this church surrounded by olive trees. There's a beautiful open space in the front lined with trees and oleander. Inside you'll find a baroque altar with marble inlays, above which is a 16th-century triptych showing the Madonna and Child with San Pancrazio and San Leonardo. Across from the church, follow the walkway leading out to the Punta Vreca overlook, which is marked by a large cross. Here, the view stretches down the coastline all the way to the Faraglioni rocks off Capri.

BEACHES
Marina di Conca
Via Marina di Conca

Unless you know where to peek over the edge, you could easily drive right by one of Conca dei Marini's most appealing spots. Set far below the Amalfi Coast Road, the town's tiny beach and seaside village is often called the Borgo Marinaro, because it is where fishermen once lived. Though their homes near the beach have been transformed into restaurants, the local connection to the sea is still strong, and dining on fresh fish here is a must. The incredibly clear turquoise water and charming atmosphere make this one of the best beaches on the Amalfi Coast, well worth the walk down the 300 steps from the Amalfi Coast Road. You'll enjoy panoramic views looking toward Amalfi in the distance. The beach has small pebbles and an easy slope into the sea, where the water is clear and the swimming terrific.

Just before reaching the beach, you'll pass the **Cappella della Madonna delle Neve,** a small chapel with important religious ties for the community and the site of a celebration that includes a boat procession every August 5.

In the 1950s and 1960s, visitors like Jacqueline Kennedy and Britain's Princess Margaret brought a touch of glamour to Conca dei Marini's beach. Here or on the nearby Marinella di Conca and La Vite beaches, there's still a chance of spotting a movie star or two.

Capo di Conca
Via Capo di Conca; tel. 089/831-512; www.capodiconca.it; mid-May-Sept.; from €20

Along the Capo di Conca promontory, just below the 16th-century watchtower, this is less a beach and more a rocky outcropping and series of terraces that is home to one stabilimento balneare (beach club). With a restaurant, bar, sun beds, and umbrellas, there's everything you need for a day by the sea—and to stretch that day into the evening with dinner by the water's edge. Climb the steep staircase near the tower for a stunning view along the coastline in both directions.

SPORTS AND RECREATION
Boat Tours
Exclusive Cruises
Via Smeraldo 14; tel. 331/441-4506; www.exclusivecruisescapri.com; Mar.-Dec.; from €250 self-drive, from €500 with a captain

Experience the natural beauty of the Amalfi Coast up close on a relaxing private boat excursion with an expert local captain at the helm. Discover hidden grottoes and the best swimming spots, and admire the coastline from the sea, away from traffic and crowds. Exclusive Cruises offers a variety of boat options, from classic Sorrentine-style wooden boats to Itama luxury speedboats and larger yachts that are ideal for groups of family or

friends. Smaller boats are also available for self-drive rentals without the need of a license. Boat excursions and transfers are available not only from Conca dei Marini, but also from all the towns along the Amalfi Coast, Sorrento, Capri, Salerno, and Naples.

SHOPPING
Ceramiche Piccadilly
Via SS163 at the Grotta dello Smeraldo; tel. 089/831-630; www.mcpiccadilly.com; 8:30am-7pm daily Mar.-Oct., 8:30am-6pm daily Nov.-Jan. 9 and Feb., closed Jan. 10-31

Located just across from the entrance to the Grotta dello Smeraldo on one of the prettiest curves of the Amalfi Coast Road, this family-run store is a treasure trove of ceramics. You'll find an excellent collection lining the walls of the shop, which has been carved into the mountainside. Choose from a selection of patterns for dinnerware, vases, gifts, and beautiful ceramic tables made with lava stone. Go upstairs for even more choices and to see the tables and vases displayed on the garden terrace with a gorgeous view.

FOOD AND ACCOMMODATIONS
Le Bontà del Capo
Via I Maggio 14; tel. 089/831-515; www.lebontadelcapo.it; 9am-11pm daily Apr.-Oct.; €10-22

Located in the upper part of Conca dei Marini with a view overlooking the Capo di Conca and its watchtower far below, this restaurant is open all day, with lunch served 12:30pm-2:30pm and dinner 6:30pm-11pm. It's also perfect if you're looking for a relaxing spot for drinks or a sweet place to try out local desserts. Specialties include seafood as well as other delightful options like the ravioli with ricotta and lemon. The chef also offers limoncello and **cooking classes** (from €50 per person).

Monastero Santa Rosa
Via Roma 2; tel. 089/832-1199; www.monasterosantarosa.com; mid-Apr.-Oct.; €900 d

Right at the edge of a cliff, a picturesque spot with impossibly beautiful views, Monastero Santa Rosa is one of the finest hotels on the coastline. Located in a convent that dates to the 17th century, this hotel has an air of complete tranquility and lovely rooms that have preserved the space's unique architectural heritage. All 20 rooms have been individually decorated and boast spectacular sea views. The lush gardens dotted with lounge chairs and beautiful landscaping are spread out over four terraces and lead down to the heated infinity pool with views you simply have to see to believe. The on-site spa offers luxurious treatments, and the hotel's Michelin-starred restaurant, **Il Refettorio,** offers fine dining in an enchanting setting. It's ideal for a secluded escape surrounded by the beauty of the Amalfi Coast.

GETTING THERE AND AROUND
By Car
Conca dei Marini is situated between the **Amalfi Coast Road (SS163)** and the **SS366** road that makes its way up into the mountains through the upper part of town before continuing on to Furore and Agerola. There's a narrow and steep road that winds through the town, connecting the two roads with the center of the town. From the Amalfi Coast Road, look for a very large ceramic sign for Conca dei Marini; the road begins there as **Via Don Gaetano Amodio** and leads very steeply up. The name changes to **Via Miramare** as the road continues up and then again changes to **Via Roma** before meeting the SS366 road immediately next to the Monastero Santa Rosa hotel.

From **Amalfi,** the drive to Conca dei Marini takes about 15 minutes. To reach the Marina di Conca, Grotta dello Smeraldo, and the lower part of town, take the Amalfi Coast Road (SS163) west. For the upper part of Conca dei Marini, take the Amalfi Coast

---

1: Peer down over the edge of the Amalfi Coast Road to see Marina di Conca. **2:** octopus and potato antipasto **3:** Capo di Conca watchtower and beach

Road (SS163) west about 1.2 mi (2 km), and at the well-marked intersection with SS366, bear right and continue for about 2.5 mi (4 km). From **Ravello,** take the **SS373** road down the mountain to connect with the Amalfi Coast Road (SS163) and continue west, following the directions from Amalfi. The drive from Ravello to Conca dei Marini takes about 30 minutes. From **Furore,** follow SS366 down the mountain about 10 minutes to reach the upper part of Conca dei Marini.

By Bus

For the lower part of town, the Marina di Conca, and Grotta dello Smeraldo, take the **SITA SUD** (tel. 089/386-6701; www.sita-sudtrasporti.it; from €1.40) bus line from Amalfi to Sorrento; it runs roughly every hour 6:30am-7pm daily. The journey to Conca dei Marini is about 15 minutes from Amalfi and about 35 minutes from Positano. To reach the upper part of town, take the Amalfi to Agerola line, which runs every 1-2 hours 7:10am-9pm daily and takes about 15 minutes. To reach Conca dei Marini by bus from Ravello, you first have to get to Amalfi (about 25 minutes from Ravello) and then transfer to one of these two bus lines.

Amalfi

It only takes one glimpse of Amalfi to understand why the Amalfi Coast's namesake town is one of the most popular spots along the coastline. The town is nestled in a valley with pastel-hued buildings climbing up both sides of the mountain and interspersed with terraces of lemon groves. The bell tower of the town's impressive cathedral marks the center of Amalfi, the beautiful Piazza Duomo. A powerful sea republic in the Middle Ages, Amalfi has a fascinating history populated by dukes and duchesses, wars and wealth, innovation, and undaunted curiosity for exploration that can still be seen in the town today.

With a seeming maze of streets and staircases, Amalfi is a town best explored on foot. While Piazza Duomo and the main street are home to most of the town's activity, shops, and restaurants, do spend some time wandering and exploring the quieter side streets, where you'll find arched passageways, hidden gardens overflowing with lemons, and tiny piazzas. Amalfi is about these quiet spots just as much as it is about the buzz.

Amalfi has one of the most picturesque harbors along the coastline. A scenic passeggiata (stroll) leads from the Marina Grande beach along the sea all the way to the end of the Molo Foraneo, the largest pier in Amalfi, with its red port marker. From the walkway along the pier, enjoy a stunning view across the harbor, captivating during the day but especially after dark with the lights of Amalfi stretching out across the water and the salty sea breeze filling the air.

ORIENTATION

Amalfi's harbor is defined by three piers, the largest being the **Molo Foraneo** on the western side of the town. The central pier is referred to locally as the **Molo Pennello** and serves as the ferry terminal. The pier to the east nearest Marina Grande beach is called the **Molo Darsena.** Near the Molo Darsena is a large traffic circle around **Piazza Flavio Gioia,** the main transport hub for buses and taxis. The Amalfi Coast Road (SS163) runs through Amalfi along the waterfront and through Piazza Flavio Gioia. Two small roads lead from Piazza Flavio Gioia to the **Piazza Duomo,** the heart of Amalfi, where you'll find the **Duomo di Amalfi.**

Follow the covered passageway opposite the Duomo to find a small traffic-free square called **Piazza dei Dogi.** It's surrounded by cafés, restaurants, and shops. On the opposite side of town is the quiet **Piazza Municipio** where the Comune (town hall) is located. Amalfi has one main street called **Via Lorenzo d'Amalfi** (changing names to Via Pietro Capuano, Via Cardinal Marino del Giudice, and Via delle Cartiere) starting from Piazza Duomo and leading far into the valley above town. This main street and Piazza Duomo are the best shopping areas, lined with boutiques, restaurants, and cafés.

Many of Amalfi's beaches are located right in town; **Marina Grande** is the largest. Walking along the waterfront by the port, you'll find the **La Marinella** beach, the **Spiaggia del Porto,** and at the westernmost side of town beyond the Molo Foraneo, the **Le Sirene** beach. The **Duoglio** and **Santa Croce** beaches are located in rocky coves west of Amalfi, most easily reached by boat.

The waterfront, Piazza Duomo, and main street of Amalfi leading into the valley are all relatively flat by Amalfi Coast standards (except for the stairs up to the Duomo). On quieter side streets, you can expect to find plenty of steps.

SIGHTS

Amalfi's highly photogenic **Piazza Duomo** is the place to start exploring town. Before climbing the steps of the Duomo, take a moment to admire the **Fontana di Sant'Andrea** in the Piazza Duomo. This fountain has an 18th-century central marble statue of Sant'Andrea in front of the X-shaped cross (one of the saint's symbols), surrounded by angels, a siren, and mythical creatures. The other top sights are all located within a short walk of the cathedral.

TOP EXPERIENCE

★ Duomo di Amalfi

Piazza Duomo; tel. 089/871-324; www.museodiocesanoamalfi.it; 9am-6pm daily Mar.-June, 9am-7:30pm daily July-Aug., 9:30am-6:30pm daily Sept.-Oct., 10am-3:30pm daily Nov.-Dec., closed Dec. 25 and Jan. 7-Feb.; €4

Sitting atop a grand staircase and overlooking Piazza Duomo, Amalfi's cathedral is dedicated to the town's beloved patron Sant'Andrea Apostolo (Saint Andrew the Apostle). Most often simply referred to as the Duomo, meaning the most important church, it is a monumental complex of incredible beauty and interest. The connection to Sant'Andrea dates to the arrival of the saint's relics in 1208.

While climbing the 57 steps to visit the cathedral, stop along the way to gaze up at the bell tower, which was built between 1180 and 1276. It is topped with a central round tower surrounded by small towers, all featuring interlacing arches and geometric patterns created with yellow and green ceramic tiles. Looking up to the facade of the church, you'll see black and white striped details, mosaics glimmering in the sun, and prominent arches with white tracery opening to the entrance portico. Despite being full of medieval architectural elements, the facade was not completed until 1891, based on a design by Neapolitan architects Errico Alvino and Guglielmo Raimondi after the earlier baroque facade collapsed during an earthquake in 1861. The current design, inspired by details of the 13th-century original, was implemented in a distinctly colorful 19th-century revival fashion.

At the top of the steps in the entry portico, you'll find a set of large bronze doors that date from 1065. On the left side of the portico is the entrance to the **Complesso Monumentale di Sant'Andrea,** which includes the **Cloister of Paradise, Museo Diocesano, Crypt of Sant'Andrea,** and the **Duomo.** The aptly named Cloister of Paradise is a peaceful garden cloister surrounded by 120 columns and intertwined arches. Built between 1266 and 1268, it was once the cemetery for Amalfi's nobility.

From the cloister, you'll enter the **Basilica of the Crucifix,** which dates to the 6th century, the oldest part of the cathedral complex. It now houses the **Museo Diocesano,** which displays the most impressive treasures of the Duomo di Amalfi, including reliquaries, chalices, religious paintings and sculptures, and a precious 13th-century miter made of gold,

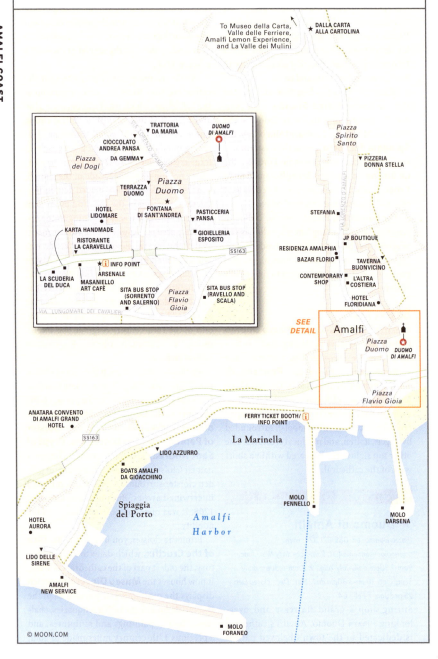

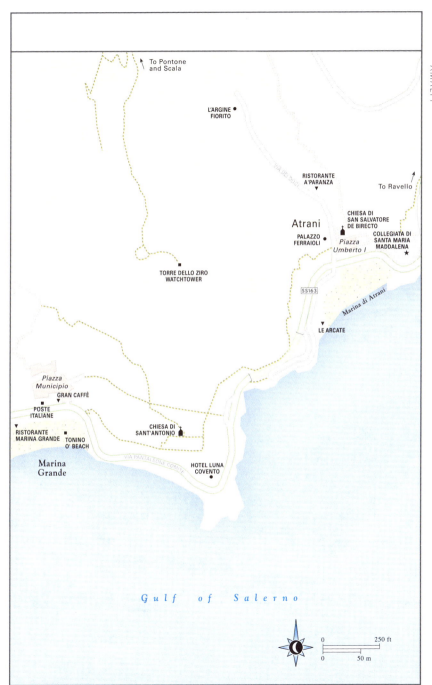

silver, and gems and covered in tiny pearls. Follow the steps down to the **Crypt** where the relics of Sant'Andrea are held below the altar, topped with a large bronze statue of the saint. The final stop on the visit to the complex is the grand **nave** of the cathedral, decorated in a baroque style dating from the early 18th century. The elegant gold-paneled ceiling has four large inset paintings depicting scenes of the life of Sant'Andrea. The columns are covered with richly detailed marble polychrome work and lead to an altar that features an 18th-century painting of the saint's crucifixion.

If you visit when the Complesso Monumentale di Sant'Andrea is closed in January-February, you can still enter the Duomo, as it is open and free to the public 7:30am-11:30am and 4pm-6:30pm daily.

Arsenale

Largo Cesareo Console 3; tel. 089/873-6222; www.arsenalediamalfi.it; 10am-9pm daily Apr.-May, 10am-10pm daily June-Sept., 10:30am-1:30pm and 4pm-7pm Tues.-Sun. Oct.-Dec.; €3

Dating from the 11th century, the Arsenale, where Amalfi's naval fleet and trading ships were constructed, is the only medieval shipyard in Italy to have remained nearly intact. Just off Piazza Flavio Gioia, all that is left are two long naves with cross vaults and pointed arches. Today the Arsenale is home to the **Museo della Bussola e del Ducato Marinaro di Amalfi** (Museum of the Compass and Duchy of Amalfi). The museum's collection of archaeological finds, historic prints, coins, compasses, and photos tells the story of Amalfi's naval heritage and medieval splendor, and its important role in the development of the compass and early maritime codes.

Chiesa di Sant'Antonio

Via Pantaleone Comite; tel. 089/871-485; hours vary

Just below the Hotel Luna Convento and before Amalfi's watchtower, a long zigzag staircase leads from the Amalfi Coast Road and seems to disappear. At the top of the staircase, you'll find the entrance to the Chiesa di Sant'Antonio, one of Amalfi's larger churches after the Duomo. Once dedicated to San Francesco (Saint Francis), it's next to the cloister of San Francesco that is now part of the Hotel Luna Convento. The church was founded in 1220 on the site of an even older church. The original Gothic structure was later covered in the baroque style you see today. Just behind the altar are beautiful baroque wooden chorus stalls dating from 1593. Below in the crypt is an altar with a series of paintings depicting scenes from the life of San Francesco. The church is usually only open during mass, and the tourist office can provide more details on the schedule.

Dalla Carta alla Cartolina

Via Cardinale Marino del Giudice 82; tel. 089/872-976; www.ricordidiamalfi.it; 10am-6pm Mon.-Sat. Mar.-Nov.; free

Situated in a historic paper mill that was built over the ruins of a 13th-century church, Dalla Carta alla Cartolina (From Paper to Postcard) is a special space in Amalfi, part museum dedicated to Amalfi's papermaking history and part shop and gallery space. The multimedia museum is inspired by the countless travelers who have been moved by Amalfi's beauty over the centuries, using a series of postcards to tell their stories. Inside, you'll find a darkened room decorated with objects from Amalfi's papermaking tradition. Take a postcard and drop it in a mailbox, and you'll be taken back in time by the narration of travelers' stories (Italian and English versions are available) brought to life with videos showing historical images of Amalfi. After listening to the stories, spend some time browsing the fine selection of paper products, journals, prints, art, and even vintage postcards—the perfect memento for your own Amalfi experience!

1: Duomo di Amalfi **2:** cliff-side buildings in Amalfi **3:** a captivating view of Amalfi from the sea

Museo della Carta

Via delle Cartiere 23; tel. 089/830-4561; www.amalfipapermuseum.com; 10am-7pm daily Mar.-Oct., 10am-5pm Tues.-Sun. Nov.-Jan.; from €4.50

Discover Amalfi's long tradition of papermaking in the town's paper museum, which is located in a 13th-century mill near the top of town. The working mill offers a rare look at how paper was made in Amalfi before industrialization. Even older papermaking equipment is on display inside the mill, and during the guided tour included in the admission cost, you'll learn about ancient and more modern methods of papermaking and get a chance to try your hand at making traditional Amalfi paper.

BEACHES

Amalfi's harbor has several beaches, ranging from the popular Marina Grande beach with its rows of candy-colored umbrellas to beaches tucked away in nearly hidden spots. There are even more options for a more secluded beach day if you head west, down the coastline to the small beaches located in rocky coves a short boat ride away.

Marina Grande

Via Marina Grande

Historic photos show fishing boats lined up along Amalfi's largest beach, located just east of Piazza Flavio Gioia and the Molo Darsena. Today the scene is a little different, with the beach's buzz of energy and colorful umbrellas and sun beds. Much of the beach is lined with restaurants that also offer sun bed and umbrella rental, along with shower and changing room facilities. For a small fee, you can pick out a sun bed and an umbrella in your favorite color and enjoy a comfortable day at the beach. **Tonino O' Beach** (Via Marina Grande; tel. 089/873-364; www.toninobeach.com; Apr.-Oct.; from €35 for two sun beds and an umbrella) is located on the eastern side of the beach in the best swimming area, and offers sun bed and umbrella rentals, changing rooms, showers, restrooms, and boat rentals. However, the beach also has two free areas, located at either end of the beach. The eastern end is most popular with locals; look for the arches supporting the Amalfi Coast Road as it winds its way out of town and head that way. Though the free beach is quite busy during the summer (that's just part of the scene), the water is gorgeous on this rocky side, especially if you swim out a bit. The water is nicest in the morning, so if you're an early riser, head straight to this beach.

La Marinella

Via Lungomare dei Cavalieri

Stroll along the harbor and just beyond Molo Pennello you'll spot this minuscule beach with transparent water. Part of the **La Marinella** restaurant, this beach is only accessible via the stabilimento balneare (beach club) (tel. 089/871-043; www.lamarinella.net; June-Oct.; €4 entrance only, €20 per person sun bed). Though the beach area is limited, a platform for sunbathing is constructed during the summer months. There are steps down from the platform to the sea, and it's a good spot for families with young children because the beach has small pebbles and easy access to calm water.

Spiaggia del Porto

Via Lungomare dei Cavalieri

Often just called the porto (port), this beach is along the waterfront of the harbor, with floating docks and boats moored nearby. Because there aren't any beach club services here (although there is a shower to rinse off), it's truly a local beach. The view of the harbor with boats puttering to-and-fro is a relaxing sight while sunbathing. The swimming area is somewhat limited, but it's refreshing for a dip in the sea.

Le Sirene

Piazzale dei Protontini 4

Located on the western edge of Amalfi just outside the port, this is a beautiful rocky beach

1: Marina Grande beach **2:** Santa Croce beach **3:** Lido delle Sirene **4:** hiking to the Valle delle Ferriere

with clear water for swimming and nice light well into the afternoon. The beach is private and accessible only via the **Lido delle Sirene** restaurant and beach club (tel. 089/871-756; daily Apr.-Oct.; €6 entrance only, from €22 beach entrance, sun bed, and umbrella), where you can rent sun beds and umbrellas and use the shower and changing facilities. Given its setting only a short stroll from the busy center of Amalfi, this is a good option for a quieter day at the beach.

Duoglio
Spiaggia Duoglio

Along the rocky coastline west of Amalfi is this small beach with restaurants and stabilimenti balneari (beach clubs) that are set up during the summer season, leaving two small areas on either end of the beach for free swimming. The beach is accessible via 400 steps down from the Amalfi Coast Road, starting from a small stone gate just east of the intersection for SS363. The gate is usually open 8am-7pm during the summer season, but not always. However, the best way to reach the beach is by boat service.

For a small fee, the Duoglio beach service boat run by **Gruppo Battellieri Costa d'Amalfi** (www.gruppobattellieriamalfi.com; about every 30 minutes 9:30am-4pm daily June-Sept.; €4 per person round-trip) departs from the Molo Pennello in Amalfi. Or, if you're planning to visit one of the restaurants that offers sun bed and umbrella rental (the best option at this rocky beach), you can take a free boat shuttle service from Molo Darsena. **Lido degli Artisti** (tel. 331/996-5635; www.lidodegliartisti.it; May-Oct.) runs a boat service if you're heading to their restaurant or beach club.

Santa Croce
Spiaggia di Santa Croce

Not far west of Duoglio is one of the Amalfi Coast's most beautiful beaches. Beneath a sheer cliff and surrounded by large rocks, this secluded beach has stunning water and lots of beautiful natural spots to explore. Because a storm damaged the steps leading to the beach in 2011, the only way to access this beach is by boat. There are two restaurants that offer stabilimento balneare (beach club) services and free boat service from Amalfi for clients from the Molo Darsena. Look for the small boats marked **Da Teresa** (www.ristorantedateresa.eu; May-Oct.) or **Santa Croce** (www.ristorantesantacroce.it; Apr.-Oct.). If you're a good swimmer, you can swim along the coastline a short distance to the arco naturale, a natural arch that is also called the Lover's Arch.

SPORTS AND RECREATION
Hiking
Valle delle Ferriere

Distance: *3 mi (5 km)*
Time: *2.5 hours round-trip*
Trailhead: *Via Paradiso (follow to the top of the valley)*
Information and Maps: *Cart&guide maps and www.lavalledelleferriere.com*

To immerse yourself in the natural beauty of the Amalfi Coast, hike into the valley above Amalfi, where you'll find ruins of old mills covered in natural growth, a cool mountain stream, and a surprisingly tropical landscape with waterfalls, wild orchids and cyclamens, and even a rare prehistoric fern called *Woodwardia radicans*. This area is sometimes called Valle delle Ferriere and sometimes Valle dei Mulini, names referring to the ironwork factories and paper mills that once lined the valley, powered by the Canneto stream. At the top of Amalfi, beyond the Museo della Carta, look for the signs for Valle delle Ferriere and continue along Via Paradiso past terraces of lemons until it turns into a dirt path. The walk follows the Canneto and passes by the town's former industrial area. Near the top you'll find some impressive waterfalls. Stop and dip your toes in the water, which is cold even in the peak of summer. The uppermost part of the Valle delle Ferriere is a nature reserve (tel. 338/560-5550; www.lavalledelleferriere.com; €5) and requires advance booking and a small fee to enter.

There are nice areas to stop for a picnic alongside the mountain stream. Or take a break at **Agricola Fore Porta** (Via Paradiso 22; tel. 339/243-6450; www.agriturismoamalfi.it; 10am-6pm daily Easter-Nov., sometimes closed Tues. or Thurs., advance booking recommended), an agriturismo nestled into the valley along the hiking pathway about 25 minutes from Amalfi. Set in a rustic farm building, they offer freshly made drinks and traditional dishes made with organic ingredients from their gardens.

Amalfi Outdoor Experience

various locations, Amalfi; tel. 331/315-9177; www.amalfioutdoorexperience.com; Apr.-Oct.; from €75 pp

For a more in-depth experience hiking the Valle delle Ferriere, join a small group tour led by a local guide that takes you deep into the valley to discover its history and natural beauty. Other excellent guided hiking experiences are available in the Amalfi area as well as the Sentiero dei Limoni (Pathway of the Lemons) in Minori.

Boat and Kayak Tours
Amalfi Kayak

Spiaggia Duoglio, Via Mauro Comite 41; tel. 338/362-9520; www.amalfikayak.com; Apr.-Oct.; from €49 pp

For active travelers, a kayak tour is one of the best ways to experience the natural beauty of the Amalfi Coast. Amalfi Kayak offers multiple half-day and full-day excursions, where expert local guides show you the best spots along the coast. The most popular is the half-day tour from Amalfi to the Runghetiello Grotto: Glide by the villa where Sophia Loren once lived in Conca dei Marini, and see one of the Amalfi Coast's rugged grottoes up close. Longer full-day tours are available to Cetara and Positano, and Capri kayaking experiences are also available.

During the summer months (June-Sept.), excursions depart from the Spiaggia Duoglio beach, and during the shoulder season (Apr.-May and Oct.), excursions depart from the Le Sirene beach in Amalfi. Only guided tours are available, and all equipment is included in the price.

Boats Amalfi da Gioacchino

Via Lungomare dei Cavalieri 286; tel. 338/264-0895; www.boatsamalfi.it; Apr.-Oct.; from €250

Started by Amalfi local Giacchino Esposito, who left his career as a chef to be closer to the sea, this friendly family-run operation offers boat rentals and excursions with or without a captain. For independent travelers, rent a traditional wooden boat or small motorboat without the need for a nautical license and spend a day exploring the coastline. Larger boats and yachts with captain are also available for private tours along the Amalfi Coast or to Capri. Though the main season is April-October, Gioacchino usually has boats in the water year-round. You never know when a beautiful winter day might call you out for a day on the sea.

Amalfi WaterSport

various locations, Amalfi; tel. 338/362-9520; www.amalfiwatersport.com; Apr.-Oct.; from €59 pp

The same expert and adventurous team from Amalfi Kayak also offers a variety of water sports from Amalfi, including parasailing, wakeboarding, waterskiing, and water tubing experiences along with sea scooter and snorkel rental. Contact them as well for help planning custom snorkeling experiences along the Amalfi Coast.

Local Tours
Amalfi Lemon Experience

Via delle Cartiere; tel. 089/873-211; www.amalfilemonexperience.it; 10am Mon.-Sat. Mar.-Oct.; from €30 pp

The lemon and Amalfi have been inextricably connected for centuries. There's no better way to experience this firsthand than to walk among Amalfi's historic lemon groves as you learn about the cultivation of this very special product. Since 1825, six generations of the Aceto family have been growing lemons on the steep slopes of the Amalfi Coast. The family is passionate about maintaining traditional techniques, from the dry stone wall construction that creates the garden terraces to the details of running an organic farm. A daily group tour offers the chance to meander through the Aceto family's lemon gardens, enjoy a taste of their lemon products, and visit the family's **Museum of Rural Life Arts and Crafts,** a fascinating collection of historic pieces from Amalfi's past. The final touch is a visit to the production lab, where the Acetos transform their lemons into limoncello and other traditional products. Book your spot for the lemon tour in advance; private tours and experiences can also be arranged, such as a sweet Honey Lemon Experience and Tour that showcases the honey made in the lemon grove. There are also wine-tastings, botanic tours, ceramic painting experiences, and cooking classes that, of course, highlight the lemon.

FESTIVALS AND EVENTS

Amalfi's scenic setting and the beautiful Piazza Duomo make for a stellar backdrop for concerts, fashion shows, and festivals. Events take place throughout the year but are often not promoted very extensively or far in advance, so stop in the tourist office in Amalfi to find out about upcoming programs.

You can count on Amalfi coming to life during several annual religious festivals, when the town becomes the setting for elaborate processions and spectacular fireworks displays. Capodanno (New Year's Eve) is capped off by the biggest fireworks show of the year, which makes Amalfi the most popular location on the coast to celebrate.

Easter in Amalfi
Piazza Duomo and various locations; Holy Week and Easter Sun.
Easter is one of the biggest holidays in Italy, with events taking place throughout the week leading up to Easter Sunday. Many towns along the coastline have Good Friday and Via Crucis (Stations of the Cross) processions, and Amalfi's are some of the most impressive. The Via Crucis often takes place on Holy Thursday and meanders through the streets, retelling the story of Christ's crucifixion. The procession on Good Friday, representing Christ's funeral and burial, is one of the most moving on the Amalfi Coast. After dark, the lights are turned off in Piazza Duomo, and a candlelit procession starting from the Duomo moves down the steps and through the town. Accompanied by haunting choral music, masked figures carry the statue of Christ after being taken down from the cross, followed by a statue of the Madonna Addolorata (Virgin Mary in mourning).

Easter Sunday is a joyous day in Amalfi and is followed by Pasquetta (little Easter), which is a day traditionally spent outdoors and with family and friends. The Easter holiday is the unofficial start of the tourist season on the Amalfi Coast, and it's often very busy with traffic and visitors. Book your accommodations well in advance.

Festival of Sant'Antonio
Chiesa di Sant'Antonio and various locations; June 13
The summer season gets off to a festive start thanks to the procession and celebrations in honor of Sant'Antonio (Saint Anthony) on June 13. Both Amalfi and Atrani honor this saint because the Chiesa di Sant'Antonio is located not far from the tunnel that leads to Atrani. The procession is one of the most unique on the Amalfi Coast and takes place on both land and sea. It starts from the Chiesa di Sant'Antonio and follows the Amalfi Coast Road to Atrani, where it descends through town to the beach. From the beach, the statue of Sant'Antonio is carefully loaded onto a small boat. Then, every member of the procession—marching band included—boards small boats that continue in a water procession to Amalfi, where they all disembark and continue on land to the Duomo di Amalfi. There's a festive atmosphere, including a fireworks display over the harbor after dark.

Festival of Sant'Andrea
Piazza Duomo and various locations; June 27 and Nov. 30

Twice a year Amalfi honors its patron Sant'Andrea (Saint Andrew) with a grand religious festival that is one of the biggest and most popular of the year on the Amalfi Coast. Celebrations take place June 27 to remember the time Sant'Andrea is said to have heeded the prayers of the town's faithful in 1544 and protected Amalfi from a pirate attack by bringing on a sea storm so intense that it destroyed the invading ships. The November 30 celebration marks the traditional festival day honoring Sant'Andrea.

The festivals center on the Duomo di Amalfi. It does get very crowded, so arrive early in Piazza Duomo to get a good view. After a special mass, a large 18th-century silver-and-gold statue of Sant'Andrea is taken down the long staircase of the Duomo and carried throughout Amalfi. The statue is even carried down to the beach, where boats gather in the harbor for a blessing. The grand finale has to be seen to be believed: The large group of men carrying the statue pause at the bottom of the Duomo's 57 steps before running the statue back to the top. Once they reach the top, the piazza packed full of people bursts into applause as Sant'Andrea returns safely home.

The festive atmosphere continues with music in Piazza Duomo and a spectacular fireworks display over the harbor after dark. The two events honoring Sant'Andrea are similar, though the summer festival usually comes with excellent weather. In June, the procession begins after evening mass, and in November it starts after a midmorning mass. This centuries-old festival offers a wonderful glimpse into the religious traditions of Amalfi. Since these are the biggest celebrations of the year in Amalfi, book your accommodations well in advance, especially for the June 27 festival.

Byzantine New Year
Piazza Duomo and various locations; Aug. 31-Sept. 1

During the Middle Ages, September 1 was the start of the legal and fiscal new year, according to the calendar of the Byzantine Empire. Given Amalfi's strong ties to that part of the world, that date was used to appoint the town's elected officials with an elaborate ceremony. This cultural event is celebrated today with a historical procession including more than 100 people dressed in costumes of the former Republic of Amalfi. The event includes selecting a local Amalfitan or important figure to represent the Magister di Civiltà Amalfitana in a ceremony at the Chiesa di San Salvatore de Birecto in Atrani, followed by a procession to the Duomo in Amalfi. It's a fascinating event, even more elaborate than the historical parade during the Regatta of the Ancient Maritime Republics.

SHOPPING

Amalfi has a wonderful array of shops, mostly arrayed around Piazza Duomo and the main street leading from the piazza up into the valley and through the center of town. You'll find plenty of opportunities to discover the Amalfi Coast's traditional crafts and products, such as handmade paper, limoncello and lemon-themed items, ceramics, and clothing. Shops in Amalfi rarely close for lunch from Easter-October, but during the winter, especially January-February, some shops close midday for a break, on certain days during the week, or for an extended holiday. Most of the shops below are open year-round, with exceptions noted.

Clothing
JP Boutique
Via Pietro Capuano 12; tel. 329/371-8648; www.jp-amalfi.com; 9am-9pm daily May-Oct., 10:30am-6pm daily Nov.-Apr., winter hours may vary

This friendly shop has a unique and refreshing selection of clothing, canvas and jute bags, and gifts. Many items are decorated with the hand-drawn designs by the young owner Gianpiero (JP for short) that include fun sayings in Italian, Amalfi-inspired patterns with anchors, and a simple yet classic pattern with fish. Just around the corner, don't miss the JP

Regatta of the Ancient Maritime Republics

Regatta of the Ancient Maritime Republics

Amalfi celebrates its rich heritage and the medieval splendor of the Duchy of Amalfi each year at the Regatta of the Ancient Maritime Republics (Regata delle Antiche Repubbliche Marinare). This festival brings together the four powerful maritime republics of Italy from the Middle Ages—Amalfi, Pisa, Genoa, and Venice—in a rowing contest and historical parade. Conceived in the 1940s, the first event was held in 1955, and has been held annually since. Each city takes turns holding the regatta, which arrives in Amalfi every 4 years, usually taking place on the first Sunday in June. If your visit happens to coincide with the regatta in Amalfi, you are in for a very special experience.

PARADE

The Regatta of the Ancient Maritime Republics begins with a historical parade that starts from Atrani and follows the Amalfi Coast Road into Amalfi. The procession arrives in Piazza Duomo and then climbs the steps to the Duomo, a grand sight to see. Each of the four cities is represented in the parade with figures from their history; for Amalfi, the period highlighted is the apex of the Duchy of Amalfi around the 10th century with rich costumes made of silk, brocade, damask, and linen. Locals from Amalfi dress as all types of historical figures for the parade, from sailors and rowers to knights, magistrates, judges, and the Duke of Amalfi. The theme for Amalfi's parade is the celebration of the marriage of the Duke's son to a noblewoman. Each town is accompanied by a band and some include flag throwers.

REGATTA

After the parade, all eyes turn to the sea for the regatta. Each city has a team of eight rowers and a helmsman who compete in wooden galleys styled after 12th-century boat designs. It's easy to spot Amalfi's team with its boat painted the traditional blue color of the Republic of Amalfi. Pisa's boat is red, Genoa's is white, and Venice's is green. The course of the regatta is 1.2 mi (2,000 m) long and begins near Cape Vettica west of Amalfi with the finish in front of the Marina Grande beach in the center of town.

BEST VIEW

Anywhere in the center of town with a view of the sea is a good spot to watch the race, but Gran Caffè (Corso delle Repubbliche Marinare 37/38) is great for enjoying an aperitivo with a view of the race finish line.

Market (Supportico Rua 5) shop with locally made ceramics, art, and design.

Contemporary Shop
Via Pietro Capuano 2; tel. 335/121-9319; www. officinezephiro.it; 9am-9:30pm daily
A beautifully curated and tempting selection of clothing, jewelry, accessories, and ceramics are on display in this tiny shop tucked away in an arched passageway just off Amalfi's main street. There's also a nice selection of books on the area, as well as detailed maps for the hiking paths along the Amalfi Coast.

Accessories
Gioielleria Esposito
Via Duca Mansone I 10; tel. 089/871-088; avvesp@tiscali.it; 10am-9pm daily Apr.-Oct., 10am-1pm and 5pm-8pm Sat. and Mon.-Thurs., 10am-1pm Sun. Nov.-Mar.
Just off Piazza Duomo you'll find this beautiful jewelry store that has been family-run for four generations. They have a large selection of silver and gold jewelry along with traditional coral and cameo pieces, charms, crosses, and men's jewelry. The pieces inspired by the Tarì, the currency of the Republic of Amalfi during the Middle Ages, make unique souvenirs or gifts. Necklaces, bracelets, and charms are available with the Tarì design in gold and silver.

Bazar Florio
Via Pietro Capuano 5-7; tel. 089/871-980; www.amalfibazar.com; 8:30am-10pm daily
This is the place to find a large selection of beautiful Italian leather bags and accessories of all shapes, sizes, and colors. The owners stock their own production line of bags as well as notable brands from around Italy. Need a purse to match those sandals you had custom-made in Positano or Capri? Stop in here and you'll find something tempting to bring home.

Stefania
Via Pietro Capuano 29; tel. 089/871-541; amalfibystefania@gmail.com; 10am-10pm daily mid-Mar.-Oct.

Stop in this shop for a colorful selection of Italian leather loafers, shoes, and handmade sandals. There's no need to go to Capri for handmade sandals as this shop has a woman sandal-maker at work creating custom designs. Choose from a wide selection of designs and shades of leather straps and have a pair of sandals fitted and made while you wait.

Paper
La Scuderia del Duca
Largo Cesareo Console 9; tel. 089/872-976; www.carta-amalfi.com; 10am-7pm daily Apr.-Oct., 10am-6pm Mon.-Sat. Nov.-Mar.
Situated near the ancient arsenals where Amalfi's ships were built in the Middle Ages, this treasure trove of a shop offers an incredible selection of paper products, stationery, and prints, all created with paper handmade in Amalfi. They also have an intriguing selection of artwork, ceramics, and antiques. Look for two additional locations in Amalfi's main square (Piazza Duomo 31 and 41) as well as at **Dalla Carta alla Cartolina** (Via Cardinale Marino del Giudice 82), located in a historic paper mill.

Karta Handmade
Largo Cesareo Console 9; tel. 089/871-685; paoladelucakarta@gmail.com; 10am-7pm Mon.-Sat.
A unique and artistic spot in Amalfi, here you'll find a lovely selection of handmade journals and artwork along with books and ceramics. The journals especially are one-of-a-kind souvenirs. Each one is handcrafted and stitched using Amalfi-made paper and featuring artistic covers created by shop owner and artist Paola De Luca. The collage of designs on the covers tell a story, and the joy is finding one that speaks to you where you can capture your own stories.

Ceramics
L'Altra Costiera
Via Lorenzo d'Amalfi 34; tel. 089/830-4536; www.shopaltracostiera.com; 9am-10pm daily Apr.-Oct., 9:30am-1:30pm and 3:30pm-8pm daily Nov.-Dec. and Feb.-Mar.

A love for the Amalfi Coast's ceramic traditions shines through in the handpicked collections on display in this colorful ceramic shop. Here you'll find pieces by renowned local ceramic artists like Paolo Sandulli, Rosalinda, Mirkò, and the next generation of the Solimene family artisans. This is a unique opportunity to support artists who are keeping alive the important ceramic-making tradition on the Amalfi Coast.

Specialty Foods
Cioccolato Andrea Pansa
Via Lorenzo d'Amalfi 9; tel. 089/873-282; www.andreapansa.it; 8am-midnight daily mid-Apr.-mid-June and mid-Sept.-mid-Oct., 8am-1am daily mid-June-mid-Sept., 8am-11pm daily mid-Oct.-mid-Apr.

If you love chocolate or have chocolate enthusiasts on your shopping list, this is the place for you. All the products are handmade in the Pansa chocolate workshop in Piazza Municipio, using local or high-quality sourced ingredients. Try the chocolate with lemon or the candied lemon and orange rinds dipped in chocolate. The citrus is grown on the Pansa family property called Villa Paradiso, located in the valley above Amalfi.

La Valle dei Mulini
Via delle Cartiere 57; tel. 089/873-211; www.amalfilemon.it; 9:30am-1:30pm and 3:30pm-6:30pm Mon.-Fri., 9:30am-1:30pm Sat., winter hours may vary

Stepping into this shop feels like you've arrived in lemon heaven. All of the limoncello and liqueurs are made in Amalfi in the adjacent laboratory at this shop located at the top of the town in the Valle dei Mulini. The lemons are grown on the family's organic farm on the terraces just above the shop, so it doesn't get more local than this. Their lemon honey is especially lovely.

FOOD

Dining along the waterfront in Amalfi, with its beautiful harbor setting, is a memorable experience. However, don't forget to explore the side streets and little piazzas in the heart of town for other unique dining choices. You'll find plenty of eateries around Piazza Duomo for a quick break or aperitivo with a view. Reservations are recommended, especially at the seaside restaurants.

Seafood
Lido Azzurro
Via Lungomare dei Cavalieri 5; tel. 089/871-384; www.ristorantelidoazzurro.it; 12:30pm-3pm and 7pm-10:30pm Tues.-Sun. Mar.-Jan. 9; €19-38

With a beautiful little terrace right on the harbor of Amalfi, this restaurant is a picturesque spot for lunch or dinner. The menu is focused on local ingredients, and given the setting, seafood is naturally a specialty. Yet there's something for all tastes, with especially tempting risotto and pasta dishes. Reservations are recommended, especially for one of the coveted tables right around the edge of the terrace by the sea.

Terrazza Duomo
Largo Duchi Piccolomini 1; tel. 089/872-608; www.terrazzaduomo.com; 12:30pm-2:30pm and 7pm-10:30pm daily Apr.-Nov.; €25-45

One of Amalfi's most picturesque dining spots, this restaurant has a rooftop terrace directly opposite the town's cathedral. Specializing in seafood and with an exceptional crudo menu, there are also a variety of tasting menus (from €80 per person). The spaghetti with local lobster and cherry tomatoes is superb, as is the grilled tuna steak with soy sauce. Reserve in advance for one of the tables right at the edge of the terrace overlooking Piazza Duomo.

Regional Cuisine
Trattoria Da Maria
Via Lorenzo D'Amalfi 14; tel. 089/871-880; www.amalfitrattoriadamaria.com; noon-3pm and 6:30pm-10pm Tues.-Sun.; €12-22

For authentic home cooking and excellent wood-fired-oven pizzas, head to this friendly trattoria and pizzeria just off Piazza Duomo. You truly can't go wrong here, whether you choose pizza or the seasonal pasta options like spaghetti with zucchini or fresh clams and mussels in the summer. The fried alici (anchovies) are a local specialty that should be experienced in Amalfi. Ask for whatever verdure is in season to experience the local ways of cooking fresh veggies. The comfortable air-conditioned dining room is great for hot summer days.

Taverna Buonvicino
Largo Santa Maria Maggiore 1; tel. 089/873-6385; www.tavernabuonvicino.it; noon-2:30pm and 6:30pm-10:30pm daily Apr.-Oct.; €12-23

Set on a tiny piazza under the bell tower of the Santa Maria Maggiore church, this taverna is a great restaurant choice for excellent home cooking and delicious pizza in a tranquil setting. Try the pappardelle con crostacei e sfusato amalfitano (thick pasta noodles with shellfish and local Amalfi lemon), a house specialty that highlights the fresh flavors of Amalfi. Save room for the house-made artisanal desserts. Afterward, stroll through the side streets and catch a glimpse of the quieter side of Amalfi.

★ Ristorante Marina Grande
Viale della Regione 4; tel. 089/871-129; www.ristorantemarinagrande.com; noon-2:45pm and 6:30pm-9:45pm Thurs.-Tues. mid-Mar.-mid-Nov.; €18-40

Enjoy the view overlooking Amalfi's main beach while dining at Marina Grande. The menu changes seasonally throughout the year and highlights regional specialties served with a creative flair, and is well balanced with seafood and meat choices. Locally sourced ingredients take pride of place, including freshly caught seafood and Gentile pasta produced in Gragnano in the hills above Sorrento. This casually elegant restaurant also offers beach service with comfortable lounge chairs just steps from the sea.

Ristorante La Caravella
Via Matteo Camera 12; tel. 089/871-029; www.ristorantelacaravella.it; noon-2pm and 7pm-10pm Wed.-Mon., Feb. 11-mid-Nov. and Dec. 26-Jan. 9; lunch tasting menu €80 pp, minimum 2 people, dinner tasting menu from €130 pp

This gem of a restaurant was the first in southern Italy to earn a Michelin star. Amalfi born and raised, chef Antonio Dipino is a proud custodian of tradition. The restaurant is in a building dating to the 1100s that once belonged to the Piccolomini Family, early Dukes of Amalfi. Only one of 10 restaurants in Italy to be classified as a Ristorante-Museo, the restaurant and nearby art gallery house the finest collection of local ceramics on the Amalfi Coast. Tasting menus change seasonally, but the Tubettoni di Gragnano con ragù di pesce (Gragnano pasta with fish ragout) is an exceptional first course followed by locally caught pezzogna fish stewed with greco di tufo wine, fennel, sun-dried tomatoes, and fresh mint. Il Sole nel Piatto (The Sun in the Dish), the restaurant's lemon soufflé, deserves special mention. For wine enthusiasts, the enoteca offers a remarkable selection. Reservations are strongly advised.

Pizzeria
Pizzeria Donna Stella
Via Salita d'Ancora 4; tel. 338/358-8483; donna.stella@alice.it; noon-3:30pm and 6pm-10:30pm Wed.-Mon. Apr.-Oct., 6pm-10:30pm Wed.-Mon. Nov.-Mar.; €12-20

If eating delicious pizza under a lemon tree pergola sounds just right, then you'll enjoy this pizzeria. A small indoor dining area is available during inclement weather. There are plenty of options for different pizzas, with lots of fresh toppings to try. The specialty is Pizza Annabella, prepared with mozzarella and ricotta di bufala, black olives, and arugula. Appetizers, seasonable vegetables, and a selection of pasta and main course dishes are also available.

Bakeries and Cafés
★ Pasticceria Pansa
Piazza Duomo 40; tel. 089/871-065; www.pasticceriapansa.it; 7:30am-midnight daily mid-Apr.-mid-June and mid-Sept.-mid-Oct., 7:30am-1am daily mid-June-mid-Sept., 7:30am-11pm daily mid-Oct.-mid-Apr.; pastries €2-3.50

Since 1830 this bakery has been a fixture of

Amalfi's Piazza Duomo. The fifth generation of the Pansa family proudly runs the family bakery and have made it one of the most popular in the area for pastries, traditional Christmas and Easter desserts, and chocolates. The candied lemon and citrus peels start in the family's property above Amalfi and are transformed into delicious sweets. Try the sfogliatelle (shell-shaped pastry), delizia al limone (lemon cake), or any of the sweets on display. You truly can't go wrong!

Gran Caffè
Corso delle Repubbliche Marinare 37/38; tel. 089/871-047; www.bargrancaffeamalfi.it; 7:30am-1am Tues.-Sun. Mar.-Jan.; €5-10

Open all day with an outdoor dining area overlooking Marina Grande beach, this is a popular spot with locals and travelers for everything from a morning espresso or cappuccino to a light lunch or an aperitivo as the sun sets. During the summer months the lively atmosphere continues until late. The bruschetta and salads are particularly good and fresh, but they also offer pizzas and daily specials for those who want something more substantial. There's an extensive drink menu, but you can't go wrong with a classic spritz or their unique version with limoncello.

NIGHTLIFE
Masaniello Art Café
Largo Cesareo Console 7; tel. 339/471-0752; www.masanielloartcafe.it; 11am-2am daily Mar.-Oct., 6pm-2am Nov.-Feb.; €8-12

If you're looking for nightlife in Amalfi, this is the place. Popular during the day for drinks and for the best hamburger (yes, you read that right) in town, the Masaniello Art Café really comes to life after dark. The cocktails are on point; if you're a gin fan, don't miss their house-made version. Locally produced beers are also on the menu. Live music and events are scheduled throughout the year. This is the go-to spot for the younger crowd in Amalfi, and in a town that can feel somewhat touristy, it's refreshingly local.

ACCOMMODATIONS
Amalfi offers a large range of accommodations, from small B&Bs to extraordinary five-star hotels with that family-run touch that is an inviting characteristic of luxury on the Amalfi Coast. If you're looking for a unique experience, consider a stay in one of Amalfi's two former monasteries that have been transformed into lovely hotels with incredible views overlooking the harbor.

€100-200
Hotel Lidomare
Largo Piccolomini 9; tel. 089/871-332; www.lidomare.it; €180 d

This family-run hotel is situated in a historic palazzo dating to the 1400s that was once the home of the wealthy Piccolomini family. On a quiet piazza near Piazza Duomo, the palazzo offers 18 large rooms, 9 of which include balconies with sea views, decorated with colorful ceramic tiles and antique touches. Also interesting is the well-preserved kitchen with its antique wood-burning stove and ceramic tiles from Vietri sul Mare. The hotel is open year-round, so it's a great option for off-season stays.

Hotel Floridiana
Salita Brancia 1; tel. 089/873-6373; www.hotelfloridiana.it; Apr.-Oct.; €190 d

Situated in the center of Amalfi, this hotel is a wonderful choice for easy access and beautiful rooms. The 12th-century palazzo includes beautiful features like a salon from the 1700s with a sumptuously frescoed ceiling. The 13 guest rooms vary in style from standard to junior suites with jetted tubs. Parking is available at no extra charge.

1: lemons growing around Amalfi **2:** Anantara Convento di Amalfi Grand Hotel **3:** outdoor seating at the Gran Caffè

€200-300
Residenza Amalphia
Via Pietro Capuano 1; tel. 349/353-4999; www. amalphia.it; Apr.-Nov.; €250 d

This boutique B&B has four beautiful rooms in an incredibly central location on Amalfi's main street near Piazza Duomo. With soaring frescoed ceilings, locally made ceramic tiled floors, and well-soundproofed windows and doors, this is a stylish and comfortable stay. An abundant breakfast is served in the lovely central dining room. Family-owned and run by brother-and-sister team Gerardo and Giovanna Del Pizzo, you'll feel right at home during your stay.

Hotel Aurora
Piazzale dei Protontini 7; tel. 089/871-209; www. aurora-hotel.it; Apr.-Oct.; €260 d

Well situated in a quiet spot overlooking a rocky beach and Amalfi's harbor, this family-run hotel has 28 spacious rooms with sea views, some with large terraces that are perfect for sunbathing. You can also take advantage of the hotel's private beach access nearby. Service is very friendly, and breakfast is served on a bougainvillea-covered terrace with fine views. Three fully equipped apartment rentals (3-night minimum, from €180) are also available in the center of Amalfi.

Over €300
Hotel Luna Convento
Via Pantaleone Comite 33; tel. 089/871-002; www. lunahotel.it; Mar.-Dec.; €420 d

One of Amalfi's most romantic spots, the Hotel Luna Convento is situated in a former monastery that dates to the 1200s near the seaside watchtower at the eastern edge of town. Inside, a peaceful cloister transports you back in time. All of the rooms have sea views, each with its own unique style thanks to the historic nature of the building. The hotel also owns the **Torre Saracena** restaurant across the street, offering the chance to dine with incredible views. Below the watchtower, down a meandering staircase of about 80 steps, you'll find a saltwater pool and sunbathing terrace with access to the sea and splendid views of Atrani.

Anantara Convento di Amalfi Grand Hotel
Via Annunziatella 46; tel. 089/873-6711; www.anantara. com; Apr.-early Jan.; €700 d

A remarkable 13th-century Capuchin monastery has been completely transformed into this five-star hotel that retains the peaceful atmosphere and incredible architectural details of the original building, including the stunning cloister and church of San Francesco. Set more than 260 ft (80 m) above the sea, with an elevator from the Amalfi Coast Road for easy access, this property offers spectacular views, beautifully framed by the terraced lemon gardens and the Monks' Walk with bougainvillea-covered columns. Part of the exclusive Anantara collection, the hotel's 52 rooms and suites have sea views and a refined style. Enjoy fine dining at the Dei Cappuccini restaurant or a true taste of Neapolitan-style pizza at La Locanda della Canonica Pizzeria by Gino Sorbillo, both with stunning views over Amalfi. An infinity pool overlooks Amalfi and is the place to be in the summer.

INFORMATION AND SERVICES
Tourist Information
Info Point
Arsenale, Largo Cesareo Console 3; www.visitamalfi. info; 10am-9pm daily Apr.-May, 10am-10pm daily June-Sept., 10:30am-1:30pm and 4pm-7pm Tues.-Sun. Oct.-Dec.

Local information can be found at the info point located inside the Arsenale year-round or seasonally April-October at the info point at the ferry ticket booths (9:30am-6:30pm daily). Maps and helpful information are available in English on local sights, getting around, and more.

Medical and Emergency Services
Ospedale Costa d'Amalfi
Via Civita 12; www.aslsalerno.it

The only hospital along the Amalfi Coast is in Castiglione, a frazione of Ravello, a little more than 1 mi (1.7 km) east of Amalfi. Follow the Amalfi Coast Road east to the crossroads of SS373 road to Ravello. After a tight hairpin curve, the hospital is located on the left. There is a 24-hour pronto soccorso (emergency room). For **emergency services,** dial 118.

Postal Services
Poste Italiane
Corso delle Repubbliche Marinare 31; tel. 089/830-4831; www.poste.it; 8:20am-1:35pm Mon.-Fri., 8:20am-12:35pm Sat.

Amalfi's post office is opposite the Marina Grande beach and is the main spot in town that offers shipping services for mailing letters and packages.

GETTING THERE

With its larger harbor and convenient central location, Amalfi is a transportation hub along the coastline for buses and ferries. This makes it a popular base for exploring the area by public transportation.

By Car and Scooter

Amalfi is centrally located along the Amalfi Coast, about 15.5 mi (25 km) west of **Salerno** and 10 mi (16 km) east of **Positano.** The **Amalfi Coast Road (SS163)** runs right through Amalfi at sea level. The drive from Salerno to Amalfi takes about 1 hour, while the drive from Positano to Amalfi is about 45 minutes to 1 hour or more, depending on the time of year. From **Ravello,** follow **SS373** down to where it intersects the Amalfi Coast Road at Castiglione and take a right to continue to Amalfi. The drive from Ravello takes about 20 minutes. From **Naples,** there are multiple options for driving to Amalfi: There are two passes over the mountains, the Valico di Chiunzi above Tramonti and the pass through Agerola. Since the tract of road between Tramonti and Ravello is technically closed (although traffic does pass through), many travelers choose to take the pass via Agerola. Follow the **A3** highway south out of Naples, exit at Castellammare di Stabia, and follow **SS145** to the intersection with **SS366** that leads up the mountains, through Agerola, and down to the Amalfi Coast on the other side. It ends at the Amalfi Coast Road (SS163), where you'll bear left and shortly arrive in Amalfi. This drive from Naples to Amalfi takes about 1 hour 30 minutes. You can also stay on the A3 highway until Vietri sul Mare and then take the Amalfi Coast Road west to Amalfi to see more of the coastline. This option takes about 1 hour 45 minutes.

Amalfi has several paid **parking lots,** including limited parking right along the waterfront near Piazza Flavio Gioia, behind the Molo Foraneo, and the **Luna Rossa** parking garage (www.amalfimobilita.com) carved entirely out of the mountain. Prices range €4-5 per hour, depending on the time of year, with the highest rates April-September. During peak periods it is not unusual for all parking to be full. If you're arriving by car, contact your lodging in advance to reserve a spot, as many offer parking at an additional cost.

By Ferry

Right in the center of Amalfi's harbor is the **Molo Pennello pier,** where the ferries arrive and depart. Along the western side of the pier, you'll find the smaller boats that travel to and from nearby beaches. The end of the pier is where the larger ferries from Salerno, Positano, Capri, and Sorrento dock. Tickets can be purchased at the booths at the beginning of the pier, or in advance from many operators, a good idea during the busiest time of year, June-September.

The most frequent ferry service to Amalfi is operated by **Travelmar** (tel. 089/872-950; www.travelmar.it; €3-10 per person). During the ferry season, April-early November, there are 6-11 regular arrivals, depending on the departure point, throughout the day from Atrani, Positano, Minori, Maiori, Cetara, Vietri sul Mare, and Salerno. From Positano the ferry ride is about 25 minutes, from Minori about 10 minutes, from Maiori 15 minutes, from Cetara 40 minutes, and from Salerno about 35 minutes. Tickets can be purchased online in advance, or via the Travelmar app.

Alicost (tel. 089/811-986; www.alicost.it; €20.80-23.30 per person) offers daily ferry service to Amalfi from Capri, Positano, Minori, Maiori, Cetara, Vietri sul Mare, and Salerno. There are usually 1-4 departures from Capri to Amalfi, more during the peak summer period June-September. Exact times can vary seasonally, so check the schedule in advance. The ferry from Capri to Amalfi takes about 1 hour 20 minutes. To reach Amalfi from Sorrento, there are 1-2 ferries daily, and the journey time is about 1 hour. Many of the ferries from Capri and Sorrento also stop in Positano.

By Bus

Amalfi is the central hub along the coastline for the public **SITA SUD** buses (tel. 089/386-6701; www.sitasudtrasporti.it; from €1.30), with service from all the most popular spots in the area. Two main bus lines run along the Amalfi Coast Road and arrive in Amalfi. From Salerno, buses pass through Vietri sul Mare, Cetara, Maiori, Minori, and Atrani before arriving in Amalfi. The other main line departs from Sorrento and passes through Positano, Praiano, and Conca dei Marini before arriving in Amalfi. From Salerno, the bus ride to Amalfi is about 1 hour 15 minutes. From Sorrento, expect the ride to be about 1 hour 40 minutes. From Positano, the bus journey takes about 50 minutes. There is also a bus line that circulates between Ravello and Scala to Amalfi, with a travel time of about 25 minutes to Amalfi from either Ravello or Scala.

Buses for Salerno and Sorrento arrive and depart from **Via Lungomare dei Cavalieri** at the western edge of Piazza Flavio Gioia. The signage for each route is not very clear, but the final destination is listed on the top front of each bus. Buses to Ravello and Scala arrive and depart from the eastern side of **Piazza Flavio Gioia** near the beach, where there's a sun-blocking awning marked for Ravello and Scala.

Pintour (tel. 081/879-2645; www.pintourbus.com; €20 adults, €10 under age 13) offers a convenient and affordable bus service to Amalfi from the Naples airport (Aeroporto Internazionale di Napoli at Capodichino). The service is available seasonally April-early November. Buses depart from the bus terminal located outside the arrivals hall at the airport. The bus stops at Pompeii and every town along the Amalfi Coast from Vietri sul Mare to Amalfi, where it stops right in Piazza Flavio Gioia. Tickets can be booked in advance online (a good idea). There are usually about five departures from the airport for Amalfi daily, but check exact times in advance, as they can change from season to season. The journey takes about 2 hours.

By Taxi

Amalfi Turcoop (tel. 081/873-1522; www.amalfiturcoop.it; from €110) offers private transfers from any point of arrival in the area to Amalfi. Booking a transfer in advance is the most convenient and easiest way to arrive in Amalfi.

GETTING AROUND
By Bus

Amalfi does have a small minibus service, **Amalfi Mobilita** (tel. 089/873-518; www.amalfimobilita.com; €1), that runs from the western end of the port near the Piazzale dei Protontini to near the top of the town at the Valle dei Mulini stop, passing through Piazza Flavio Gioia and Piazza Duomo along the way. Service runs about every half hour 8am-8pm daily. Tickets cost €1 and can be purchased on board. However, Amalfi is very walkable from end to end.

By Car and Scooter

Looking to explore the coastline by car or zip around like a local on a scooter? **Amalfi New Service** (Piazzale dei Protontini; tel. 089/871-087; www.amalfinewservice.it; 8:30am-7pm daily) offers scooters and a variety of car rentals, including new and vintage options. Car rental rates start at €120 per day, while scooters are €70 per day. Scooters are available to rent March-November, and car rentals are available year-round.

By Taxi

Taxis are easy to find year-round in Amalfi. The taxi stand is located on the eastern side of Piazza Flavio Gioia. The city has set taxi fares, clearly marked on the sign near the taxi stand or on the Comune di Amalfi website (https://comune.amalfi.sa.it/taxi-tariffe). Set fares depend on the number of passengers and the distance covered. To ride around Amalfi to hotels in the area (convenient if you have luggage), fares begin at €20 for 1-4 people and €25 for 5-8 people. There are also set fares from Amalfi to Ravello (€55-60), from Amalfi to Positano (€90-100), and most of the towns on the Amalfi Coast. All other journeys are based on the taxi meter, starting at €6. If you want the fixed rate, you must let the driver know before you depart.

Atrani

If you haven't heard of Atrani, that might be because it is the smallest town in all of Italy by surface size, with a footprint of only 0.05 sq mi (0.12 sq km). Located just east of Amalfi, this pint-size town packs quite a punch when it comes to charm. The town is settled into the Valle del Dragone, with its pastel-hued buildings seemingly stacked one on top of the other. The Amalfi Coast Road curves around the Collegiata di Santa Maria Maddalena, with its colorful dome, and cuts right across the front of town with an arched bridge.

Atrani's beautiful jumble of buildings and maze of streets have inspired many artists and writers over the centuries, perhaps most notably M. C. Escher, who was captivated by the labyrinthine setting. Around town you'll see ceramics by notable local ceramic artists, including Lucio Liguori from Vietri sul Mare, with many pieces inspired by M. C. Escher. Travelers feel like they've stumbled across a hidden gem in little Atrani, which has all the conveniences of Amalfi just a short walk away. If you're looking for a central stay with an out-of-the-way feel, consider making Atrani your base on the Amalfi Coast.

SIGHTS
Piazza Umberto I

This is one of the Amalfi Coast's most charming squares: When you step into Piazza Umberto I, it's like you've taken a big step back in time. Surrounded as it is by buildings with arches, balconies, and the staircase leading up to the **Chiesa di San Salvatore de Birecto,** it feels like time has stood still in this little piazza. In fact, it's a popular location for films and commercials looking for an old-world feel. Find a seat at a café, order an aperitivo, and take some time to soak up the peaceful atmosphere.

Collegiata di Santa Maria Maddalena

Largo Maddalena; hours vary, usually from 5pm daily for mass

In a dramatic location, jutting out above Atrani's beach, the Collegiata di Santa Maria Maddalena was built in 1274 in honor of Saint Mary Magdalene, to whom the town is strongly devoted. Built and remodeled over the centuries, the church has a fascinating patchwork of architectural styles and designs, including its striking yellow and green majolica-tiled domes, its stark white and stone 16th-century bell tower, and its gleaming white facade, the only example of rococo architecture on the Amalfi Coast. Inside, the church's baroque decor is well preserved, including 17th- and 18th-century paintings and a 16th-century portrait of Santa Maria Maddalena with Sant'Andrea and San Sebastiano above the altar by Giovanni Angelo d'Amato, a painter from Maiori active on the Amalfi Coast and in Naples from the late 16th to early 17th centuries.

Chiesa di San Salvatore de Birecto

Piazza Umberto I; hours vary

This small church is among the most interesting on the Amalfi Coast, and thanks to a local association, it is occasionally open for a small fee. Climb the staircase from Piazza Umberto I; beyond the iron gate is the entrance to the church, founded in the 10th century. The interior has been restored to reveal layers of history that are well worth uncovering. It was here that the dukes of the Republic of Amalfi were crowned in the Middle Ages. In addition to the beautiful interlaced arches inside, there are bronze doors from 1087, architectural elements uncovered during the restoration, and marble sculptures, including a unique piece with peacocks as well as religious sculptures and paintings.

BEACHES
Marina di Atrani

With a quaint town setting and the Collegiata di Santa Maria Maddalena rising above, this beach is one of the most photographed on the Amalfi Coast. During the summer months, it's lined with umbrellas and sun beds. Yet even on the busiest days it tends to be less crowded than the Marina Grande beach in Amalfi nearby. The water is extremely clear, and the beach even has some dark sandy areas that are a welcome relief from the pebbles and large stones of most of the beaches along the coast. Several stabilimenti balneari (beach clubs) offer everything needed for a relaxing day by the sea.

Spiaggia di Castiglione

SS163 (Amalfi Coast Rd.) at Castiglione

Although it's located just around the corner from Atrani, this beach technically belongs to the city of Ravello and is named after the Castiglione area of Ravello that is just above the beach. It is only accessible by a long staircase of a little more than 180 steps from the Amalfi Coast Road, just east of Atrani, or by swimming over from the Marina di Atrani, which is only about 460 ft (140 m) away. During beach season, there's a stabilimento balneare (beach club) that offers sun bed and umbrella rentals as well as food. With its beautiful water and small soccer field, this beach is very popular with local teenagers during the summer.

FESTIVALS AND EVENTS
Festival of La Maddalena

Collegiata di Santa Maria Maddalena, Piazza Umberto I, and various locations; July 22

Atrani celebrates its patron Santa Maria Maddalena, or La Maddalena, with a grand summer festival every year on July 22. Colorful lights are lit all over town, and a stage is erected in Piazza Umberto I for concerts. The procession begins at the Collegiata di Santa Maria Maddalena and follows the road down to the beach and through the village, with several stops for blessings along the way. After dark, a fabulous fireworks show is set off from barges just off the coastline. The spectacular show offers a unique glimpse into Atrani's deep devotion to La Maddalena and a fun way to spend a warm summer evening on the Amalfi Coast.

FOOD
Le Arcate

Largo Orlando Buonocore; tel. 089/871-367; www.learcateatrani.it; noon-3pm and 7pm-11pm Tues.-Sun. early-Mar.-mid-Nov.; €8-26

It doesn't get much more romantic than the outdoor dining area situated under a series of arches (arcate) that give this place its name. The indoor dining area is carved into the mountain like a little sea cave, but when the weather is warm, a table right by the sea is the place to be. Seafood here is excellent, starting with the classic Antipasto Le Arcate, a mix of seafood served in different styles.

1: L'Argine Fiorito hotel **2:** colorful ceramics in Atrani **3:** Marina di Atrani

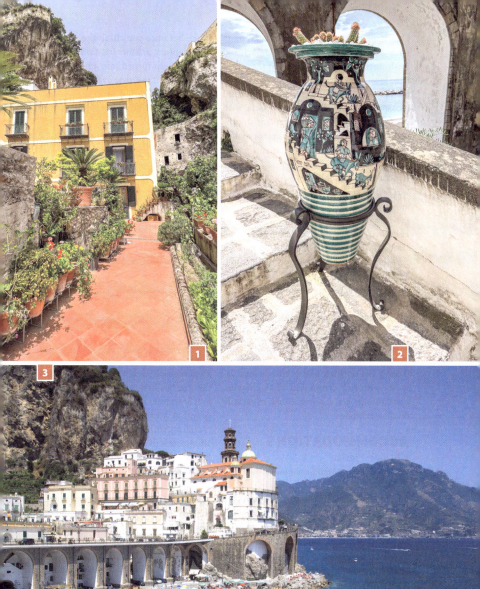

Or try the Spaghettoni alla Scogliera, pasta with clams, mussels, shrimp, calamari, and fresh cherry tomatoes, followed by the mix of fried locally caught seafood. There are plenty of non-seafood options as well, like zucchini blossoms stuffed with ricotta, pasta with smoked provola cheese and eggplant, or provola grilled on lemon leaves. The pizza cooked in a wood-fired oven is also excellent.

Ristorante A'Paranza
Via Comunale Traversa Dragone 1; tel. 089/871-840; www.ristoranteparanza.com; 12:30pm-2:30pm and 7pm-10pm Wed.-Mon.; €15-35

Follow Atrani's main street from the Piazza Umberto I, and after a short distance you'll find this restaurant tucked away on the right. You'll feel as if you've stumbled across a hidden gem. The setting is elegant and the menu is dedicated to local traditions. Seafood is the specialty, such as the pacchero di gragnano (large pasta tubes made on the Sorrento Peninsula) or the zuppa di pesce (fish soup) made with the fish of the day. Save room for dessert and try their pasticciotto, a local favorite with rich cream and black cherries. Reservations are recommended, especially on the weekend.

ACCOMMODATIONS

L'Argine Fiorito
Via dei Dogi 45; tel. 089/873-6309; www.larginefiorito.it; Apr.-Oct.; €150

Located in a peaceful spot near the top of Atrani, this lovely small hotel is set alongside the mountain stream in what was once a pasta factory in the 1700s. The six guest rooms are classically decorated and the entire residence has the feeling of home. The setting is especially lovely if you enjoy the sound of running water. The setting is remarkably central while still giving you the sense of being surrounded by nature.

Palazzo Ferraioli
Via Campo 16; tel. 089/872-652; www.palazzoferraioli.it; mid-Apr.-Oct. 31; €220

It's a little tricky to find the entrance to this hotel, but once you climb the steps to this 19th-century aristocratic family residence that has been turned into a boutique hotel, you'll see that the view over Atrani with the sea beyond is worth every step. Inside you'll be surrounded by modern design, with an elegant dining room, spa, and roof terrace offering sun beds and a fabulous view. The 25 rooms vary in style and size, but all have a clean modern design, with some guest rooms inspired by iconic actresses.

GETTING THERE AND AROUND

Getting to and around Atrani is quite easy. The **Amalfi Coast Road (SS163)** winds right around the tiny town, over the beach and main piazza on a bridge supported by arches. There's a bus stop in the middle of the bridge for **SITA SUD** buses (tel. 089/386-6701; www.sitasudtrasporti.it; from €1.30) from Amalfi, Salerno, Scala, and Ravello. The bus journey from **Salerno** to Atrani is about 1 hour 15 minutes; from **Ravello** and **Scala** it is about 25 minutes. To reach Atrani from Positano, take the bus first to Amalfi and continue on foot or transfer to the bus line to Salerno and get off at Atrani (only worthwhile if you're traveling with luggage). **Amalfi** is just a 10-minute walk along the Amalfi Coast Road. Be aware that this is the often busy main road and there is no sidewalk or pedestrian walkway. Be careful at all times, especially with young children. Once you're through the tunnel along the Amalfi Coast Road on the west side of Atrani, look on the right for a well-marked pedestrian tunnel entrance for a more direct and traffic-free (but less scenic) walk directly to Piazza Municipio in Amalfi. Hourly **parking** for cars and scooters is available in a small lot near the beach or at the **Luna Rossa** parking garage (www.amalfimobilita.com) between Atrani and Amalfi.

Travelmar (tel. 089/872-950; www.travelmar.it; €3-13 per person) now offers limited ferry service to and from Atrani's small pier located near the Le Arcate restaurant. While you can reach Amalfi, Positano, Minori,

Maiori, Cetara, Vietri sul Mare, and Salerno by ferry, note that you will need to change ferries in Amalfi to reach all other towns.

The **Pintour** (tel. 081/879-2645; www.pintourbus.com; €20 adults, €10 under age 13) bus service connecting the Naples airport to the Amalfi Coast stops at Atrani. Service is available seasonally April-early November. Catch the bus outside the arrivals hall at the airport. The bus stops at Pompeii and along the Amalfi Coast. It's a good idea to book tickets in advance via the Pintour website. The bus ride from Naples airport to Atrani takes about 1 hour 45 minutes.

Ravello

Along with Positano and Amalfi, Ravello is one of the most visited towns on the Amalfi Coast, and for very good reason. The city sits 1,200 ft (365 m) above sea level and stretches across a long, flat promontory that juts out of the mountains between two deep valleys. Eye-catching from every angle, Ravello offers a completely different experience from the seaside towns, as well as a unique vantage point and sweeping views down the coastline in both directions.

Ravello's history is tied closely to Amalfi, as Ravello was a part of the Republic of Amalfi in the Middle Ages. Its grand villas and palazzos, many now home to luxury hotels, were once the residences of wealthy merchants who built the remarkable churches that dot the town. Today the grounds of two of the largest estates, Villa Rufolo and Villa Cimbrone, offer visitors the chance to explore their beautifully landscaped gardens and take in their famous views.

A place of inspired beauty, Ravello has been a haven for artists for centuries. Known as the City of Music, the town produces a rich and varied calendar of performances throughout the year, including the annual summer Ravello Festival.

While Ravello is popular with travelers, the town remains tranquil even during the busy summer months. Charming pedestrian-only areas, including Piazza Duomo, feel far away from traffic. Summer evenings are especially enchanting when the day-trippers have moved on and music is in the air during the Ravello Festival. If you can't get enough of the famous Amalfi Coast views, be sure to plan time to explore Ravello's beautiful gardens and enjoy one of the most relaxing towns on the coast.

ORIENTATION

The center of Ravello sits high above sea level, and the **Amalfi Coast Road (SS163)** passes through **Castiglione,** a frazione (hamlet) of Ravello. From the Amalfi Coast Road in Castiglione, the **SS373** road leads up into the mountains to the town center. This road is even narrower than the Amalfi Coast Road, and a traffic light controls the flow of cars, alternating directions in high season (roughly Easter-Oct.) and during winter holidays. Along the drive from Castiglione up to Ravello, you will pass through **Civita,** another frazione of Ravello, as well as two crossroads, the first leading to Pontone and the second to Scala. Keep following the road straight past the well-marked turnoff on the left to Pontone, and at the Scala crossroad, bear right to reach Ravello's town center.

Approaching Ravello from the SS373 leads to one of the town's two tunnels. Before the tunnel to the right, **Via della Marra** leads to the Chiesa di Santa Maria a Gradillo and beyond to Ravello's largest paid parking area. Continuing through the tunnel from SS373 leads to the other side of Ravello. After exiting the tunnel, take a right and follow **Via Giovanni Boccaccio;** it ends at a small piazza in front of the town's second tunnel, which leads directly into the Piazza Duomo. Traffic is restricted through this tunnel.

The heart of Ravello is **Piazza Duomo,**

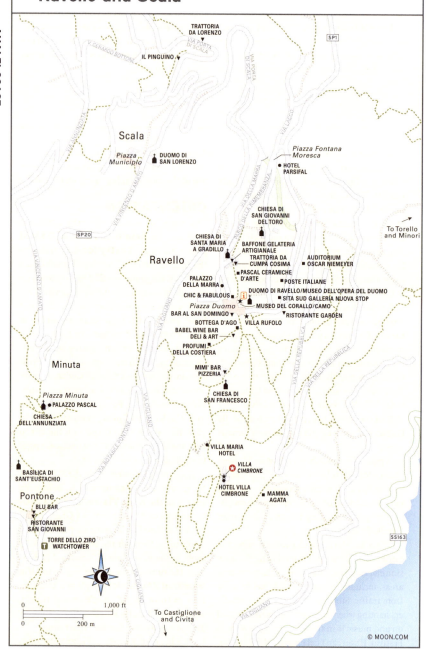

in the center of town, where you'll find the town's largest church, great shopping and dining options, and the entrance to Villa Rufolo, one of the two noted gardens in town. The Villa Cimbrone is located at the tip of the promontory and is well worth the 15-minute walk to reach it, not only to see the splendid views and gardens but also to pass through a quietly beautiful part of town. To reach Villa Cimbrone, head down **Via dei Rufolo** from Piazza Duomo and follow signs that lead up a series of staircases and meandering pedestrian-only walkways to the entrance of the gardens.

SIGHTS
Duomo di Ravello
Piazza Duomo; tel. 089/858-029; 9am-11am and 5pm-7pm daily Apr.-Oct., hours vary Nov.-Mar.; free

Founded in the 11th century, Ravello's most important church has gone through many renovations, but the latest refurbishments restored many of the medieval features and preserved later baroque additions. At the top of a small flight of steps, the entrance to the church is marked by a pair of bronze doors that were created in 1179 by Barisano da Trani.

The nave of the church seems stark in comparison to the richly decorated raised transept with its baroque design. The columns that line the nave are topped with antique capitals taken from ancient sites in the area. Along the nave are two remarkable works of religious art. On the left side is a 12th-century ambon with mosaics depicting the story of Jonah and the whale. The winged monster devouring Jonah is a pistrice, a mythical sea creature with a long, snakelike tail and wings. Just opposite, a pulpit from the 13th century fills a large section of the aisle. Covered with intricate mosaics, the pulpit features six spiral columns supported by lions. It was created for Nicola and Sigilgaida, two members of the wealthy Rufolo family who were the founders of this church.

To the left of the altar is an ornate chapel that is dedicated to San Pantaleone (Saint Pantaleon), the town's patron saint. Behind the 17th-century chapel altar is a reliquary containing the blood of the saint. It is said that every year on July 27, the saint's festival day, the blood liquefies in the reliquary: a religious miracle that just can't be explained!

Museo dell'Opera del Duomo
Piazza Duomo 7; tel. 089/858-029; www.museoduomoravello.com; 11am-5pm daily May-Oct., by advance reservation Nov.-Mar.; €3

Historical treasures are on display in the crypt of the Duomo di Ravello, which houses the Museo dell'Opera del Duomo. Among the pieces on display are reliquaries, paintings, and architectural pieces like the remains of an impressive tabernacle from 1279 that was donated by Matteo Rufolo and was above the main altar until the 18th century. When the church doors are closed, you can still visit the church by paying a small fee to visit the museum.

Villa Rufolo
Piazza Duomo; tel. 089/857-621; www.villarufolo.com; 9am-8pm daily; €8

Take a walk back in time in the gardens of the Villa Rufolo. This sprawling estate belonged to the wealthy Rufolo family during the Middle Ages. The property was largely saved from ruin thanks to Scottish industrialist Francis Nevile Reid in the 19th century. Climb to the top of **Torre Museo,** a 13th-century tower that has been transformed into a museum, to learn the fascinating history of the villa through historic photos, videos, and archaeological finds. As a bonus, you get an incredible bird's-eye view over Ravello from the top. While exploring the villa, you'll spot traces of the unique architectural style of the Amalfi Coast, blending Arabic, Sicilian, and Norman influences. Don't miss the cloister with its delicate twin columns supporting intricate interlocking foliate arches.

There's an air of enchantment in the terraced gardens, which inspired the scenography for Richard Wagner's opera *Parsifal* after a memorable visit he made in 1880. Today the musical tradition continues as the Villa Rufolo hosts the celebrated **Ravello Festival** every year June-August. While the gardens are at their best from early spring through fall, the views and Torre Museo make a visit to Villa Rufolo worthwhile throughout the year.

Museo del Corallo

Piazza Duomo 9; tel. 339/775-6298; www. museodelcorallo.com; free with advance appointment

Just to the left of the stairs leading up to the Duomo, look for the entrance to this lovely shop created by master coral carver Giorgio Filocamo and now run with love by his family. Though the shop looks small from the outside, waiting within is a treasure trove of coral masterpieces. Enter the small museum area at the back of the shop to see the impressive collection that represents the family's heritage and long tradition in coral carving. There's everything from beautiful jewelry and decorative pieces to religious art. To visit the museum, it's best to make an appointment in advance. After visiting the collection, stop in for a look at the fine jewelry and carved pieces for sale in the shop **CAMO.**

Chiesa di San Giovanni del Toro

Via San Giovanni del Toro 3; hours vary

Located atop the highest spot of Ravello, this church sits in what was once the walled-off noble quarter of town. With architectural elements reflecting Byzantine and Sicilian-Arab influences, the church reveals the wide influences the town's merchants brought back with them during the Middle Ages. The church was founded in 975 and the original portico has been lost to time, although a small flight of stairs remains to reach the church. Major restorations over the course of the 20th century have preserved many of the original elements of the church's medieval design. Along the nave is a splendid mosaic-covered pulpit that most likely dates to the 13th-14th centuries. There are still traces of the frescoes that once covered the walls along the apse as well as some 14th-century frescoes in the crypt.

Chiesa di Santa Maria a Gradillo

Via Gradillo; hours vary

Founded around the 11th century, this church has three apses and architectural elements (like its interlacing arches) that bear a resemblance to the nearby Chiesa di San Giovanni del Toro. Nobles of Ravello met here to discuss public affairs. An intense restoration 1958-1963 removed the baroque elements that were added in the 18th century and restored many of the original medieval features, which reveal Ravello's unique blend of Byzantine and Sicilian-Arab architectural influences. Small glass panels in the floor reveal the original mosaic floor below. Unlike other churches in Ravello, this one is often open throughout the day.

Piazza Fontana Moresca

This pretty piazza has an 18th-century fountain with statues of a lion and an ox that are replicas of the originals that once stood in the Duomo (the originals were stolen in 1975). Near the fountain, what remains of the **Chiesa di Sant'Agostino** was transformed into a memorial in 1968 with a plaque on the right of the portico listing the names of Ravello citizens who perished in World War I and World War II. Just beyond the fountain to the right is a terrace where you can enjoy a nice view of the coastline. This piazza is a 10-minute walk north from Piazza Duomo.

Chiesa di San Francesco

Via San Francesco 13; tel. 089/857-146; www. ravellofrancescana.it; hours vary; free

The Chiesa di San Francesco is located through a large portico along the walkway to Villa Cimbrone. The church dates from the 13th century and is said to have been founded when Saint Francis of Assisi passed through on the way to Amalfi in 1222. The original Gothic-style interior was later covered during a late-baroque renovation. Below the altar is a memorial for the beatified Bonaventura

1: Piazza Duomo **2:** the entrance to Villa Rufolo

1

2

da Potenza, a Franciscan monk who died in Ravello in 1711. To the right of the church entrance is a doorway leading to the cloister of San Francesco, which is often used to display artwork. It's a peaceful spot to stop and rest on the way to Villa Cimbrone.

★ Villa Cimbrone

Via Santa Chiara 26; tel. 089/857-459; www. hotelvillacimbrone.com; 9am-sunset daily; €10

At the tip of the promontory where Ravello sits is this lush green estate, now a five-star hotel with beautiful gardens that are open to the public. A 15-minute walk with some hills and steps to navigate from the center of Ravello, the peaceful gardens and stunning views make this one of the highlights of the entire Amalfi Coast. The estate has been in this coveted location in Ravello since ancient Roman times, when it was called Cimbronium. Villa Cimbrone was home to noble Ravello families during the Middle Ages, but by the end of the 19th century, it was largely abandoned. It was rediscovered by Ernest William Beckett, Lord Grimthorpe, an English banker and politician, who fell in love with and purchased it in 1904. He revived the gardens with the help of local as well as notable English garden designers and architects like Gertrude Jekyll, Vita Sackville-West, and Edwin Lutyens. The result blended original Renaissance features like a long central avenue with English elements, such as the temples, grottoes, a tearoom, and a lovely rose garden.

As you enter the gardens, visit the serene **Gothic cloister** with its pointed arches and spiral columns, blending Arab, Sicilian, and Norman architectural details. Continue down the aptly named **Avenue of Immensity,** the main artery through the garden, leading from the entrance to the Terrace of Infinity. From the Avenue of Immensity, wander off and explore the beautifully landscaped gardens. You'll see the **Rose Terrace,** with its geometric flower beds of roses that bloom May-October. Nearby the open pavilion tearoom is decorated with columns in the style of the cloister at **Villa Rufolo** and green and yellow ceramic tiles. It was here that Lord Grimthorpe often gathered with members of the Bloomsbury Group, an association of English writers, philosophers, and artists that included Virginia Woolf.

At the end of the Avenue of Immensity, the pathway leads through a pavilion with a statue of Ceres before opening to the **Terrace of Infinity.** Here, at the very tip of Ravello, the sweeping view blends sky and sea into a panorama that seemingly never ends. Looking down the sheer cliff is not for the faint of heart. Follow the pathway back to the entrance that leads through terraced gardens dotted with sculptures, grottoes, and little overlooks; don't miss the pathway leading under oak, alder, and chestnut trees to Eve's Grotto, where you'll find a marble statue of Eve by Bolognese artist Adamo Tadolini (1788-1868).

SPORTS AND RECREATION

Although Ravello doesn't have beaches near the center of town like other vacation spots in this region, there are interesting hikes to nearby villages. Or spend the day delving into local culinary traditions at a cooking class, complete with a picture-perfect view.

Hiking

With its setting on a promontory between two mountain valleys, Ravello is a great starting point for hiking in the area. Plan to take your time, because there are a lot of steps and panoramic views along the way. The local hiking maps produced by **Cart&guide** (www.officinezephiro.it; English and Italian versions available; €5 each) make excellent companions for exploring on foot. Maps are also available at **Bric a' Brac** (Piazza Duomo 4; tel. 089/858-6228), a shop located in Piazza Duomo.

Ravello to Minori

Distance: 1.5 mi (2.5 km)
Time: 1 hour one-way
Trailhead: Piazza Duomo, Ravello
Information and Maps: Tourist office or Cart&guide maps

Set in the valley below Ravello, the town of **Minori** is your destination on a beautiful hike down an ancient stone pathway that was the only connection between the two towns before roads were built in the 19th century. There are several different pathways leading down the mountain from Ravello to Minori, but the most enjoyable starts at the center of Ravello and passes through the tiny village of **Torello** before meandering through terraces of lemon trees and olive groves. The walk descends from about 1,200 ft (365 m) elevation down to sea level, so be prepared for a lot of steps. There aren't places to stop for refreshments, so bring water.

Start in Piazza Duomo in Ravello and follow the pathway just to the left of the entrance tower to Villa Rufolo. Ceramic signs point the way to Minori as the steps lead past several tiny churches. Stop in Torello to admire the **Chiesa di San Michele Arcangelo.** While usually only open during mass, this small church has a charming piazza and portico. After Torello the steps are steeper but the views are spectacular as you zigzag down, with the sea seemingly just beyond. Follow the steps down all the way to the lungomare (waterfront) in Minori, which has some nice benches: a welcome sight after all those steps. If you walk at a leisurely pace, the hike takes about 1 hour. To return to Ravello from Minori, you first have to get to Amalfi, since there are no direct buses from Minori to Ravello. Catch the ferry from the pier in Minori to Amalfi and then take the SITA SUD bus back up to Ravello. Or on Via Roma along the waterfront in Minori, you can catch the SITA SUD bus to Amalfi and then transfer to the bus to Ravello.

Ravello to Atrani

Distance: 2 mi (3 km)
Time: 1.5 hours one-way
Trailhead: Via della Repubblica, Ravello
Information and Maps: Tourist office or Cart&guide maps

Hiking down the valley on the western side of Ravello will take you to **Atrani,** and Amalfi is located just a short stroll beyond on the Amalfi Coast Road. Just like the hike to Minori, there are various routes. One option is to follow the steps near Santa Maria a Gradillo down the valley and follow the signs to Atrani. You'll walk along a pathway with stone steps that follows the river valley down to the top of Atrani and then passes through the tiny village to the sea.

Another scenic option is to follow Via della Repubblica past the Auditorium Oscar Niemeyer down to the **Chiesa di San Cosma.** Follow Via San Cosma, a footpath that alternates between flat walkways and steps beyond the church, hugging the mountainside below Villa Cimbrone. Very steep steps lead down toward the sea through the Civita area of Ravello, just above Castiglione. Look for Via San Nicola near Civita, a gorgeous walk high above the Castiglione beach, that takes you directly down into Atrani.

It's good to have a map because some options can lead to long stretches of walking along SS373, the narrow road connecting Ravello and Scala with the Amalfi Coast Road, an unpleasant walk compared to the other options described here. Hiking from Ravello to Atrani will take 1 hour or a little longer, depending on the route you choose. The landscape is quite secluded and you won't find many options for refreshments during the walk, so carry your own water. From Atrani, along the bridge over the center of town or from Piazza Flavio Gioia in Amalfi, you can catch the SITA SUD bus back up to Ravello.

Hiking on the Amalfi Coast

With spectacular views and rich natural beauty, the mountainous landscape of the Amalfi Coast is truly ideal for hiking. The towns and tiny villages dotted along the coastline are interconnected by pathways that were the only way to get around before the Amalfi Coast Road was built in the 19th century. Most of the original footpaths have been preserved and are relatively well maintained. What this means for hikers today is that getting from town to town on foot is actually quite easy, as long as you plan for a lot of steps!

TIPS

Here are a few suggestions for enjoying walks and hikes on the Amalfi Coast.

- **Footwear:** Unless you need added support, you'll be fine with a pair of comfortable sneakers or walking shoes.
- **Maps:** Popular hikes and pathways connecting the towns along the Amalfi Coast are fairly well marked. However, **Cart&guide** (www.officinezephiro.it; English versions available; €5 each) makes detailed maps that can be purchased in bookstores and shops in the area.
- **Steps:** Expect a lot of steps wherever you are hiking on the Amalfi Coast. The ancient stone steps and pathways can be very irregular and steep, and going down can be hard on the knees. If this is an issue, consider walking from the lowest starting point to the highest, and plan a more relaxed activity after a long hike.
- **Essentials:** Bring plenty of water as well as sun protection and a hat in the summer months. Fountains along the way all have potable water to refill bottles.

HIKES

Trail	Starting Point	Hiking Time	Description
Pathway of the Gods (page 55)	Bomerano (in Agerola) or Nocelle (near Positano)	3 hours	Mountain trail with panoramic views of Praiano, Positano, and Capri.

Cooking Class
Mamma Agata

Piazza San Cosma 9; tel. 089/857-845; www.mammaagata.com; classes Mon.-Tues. and Thurs.-Fri. Apr.-Aug. 10 and Aug. 29-Oct.; from €300 pp

Located in a tranquil spot in Ravello, Mamma Agata is a little culinary haven where cooking is a passion and truly a family affair. Mamma Agata, who began cooking on the Amalfi Coast at a very early age, was the inspiration for this cooking school created by her daughter Chiara Lima. In cooking classes, Mamma Agata and Chiara share their traditional family recipes, home-cooking style, locally produced and organic products, and a wealth of cooking secrets. After the cooking class, an exquisite lunch is served on the terrace with panoramic views over their gardens and the Amalfi Coast.

ENTERTAINMENT AND EVENTS

Known as the City of Music, Ravello offers no shortage of concerts and musical events throughout the year. Though the town is rather quiet at night when it comes to nightclubs, you'll find an assortment of bars with outdoor seating surrounding the Piazza Duomo. During the Ravello Festival, these are lively places for pre- or post-concert drinks.

Trail	Starting Point	Hiking Time	Description
Valle delle Ferriere (page 88)	Amalfi	2.5 hours	Hike in the valley above Amalfi, passing old paper mills and waterfalls.
Ravello to Minori (page 111)	Ravello	1 hour	Ancient stone steps lead down through lemon and olive trees to Minori.
Ravello to Atrani (page 111)	Ravello	1.5 hours	Follow stone pathways down the valley to Atrani and farther to Amalfi.
Torre dello Ziro Watchtower (page 121)	Pontone (near Scala)	2 hours	Visit this 15th-century watchtower via a mountainside trail with views of Atrani from above.
Scala to Amalfi (page 122)	Scala	45 minutes	Stairway hike through villages with a quick detour to the ruins of an old basilica. Can be combined with Valle delle Ferriere hike.
Pathway of the Lemons (page 127)	Minori	1 hour	Walk through lemon groves on this mountain trail that was once the only way to get between Maiori and Minori.

Performing Arts
Auditorium Oscar Niemeyer
Via della Repubblica 12; tel. 089/858-360; www.fondazioneravello.com

Since 1997, the Amalfi Coast has been a UNESCO World Heritage Site, which tells you there has been very little new construction in the area. One distinctive exception is the Auditorium Oscar Niemeyer, which takes its name from its designer, Brazilian architect Oscar Niemeyer. With Ravello's music and art tradition, a state-of-the-art concert hall for year-round performances was needed, and this venue was inaugurated in 2010. The sweeping curved roofline of the bright white building is a striking addition to Ravello's cityscape. A variety of shows are staged here throughout the year, from concerts during the Ravello Festival to movies during the winter months. The large terrace in front of the auditorium is often used for art installations during the Ravello Festival.

Festivals and Events
Ravello Festival
Villa Rufolo and various locations; tel. 089/858-422; www.ravellofestival.info; July-Sept.; €35-60

Inspired by 1880 Ravello visitor Richard Wagner, the Ravello Festival began in the 1930s and became a yearly event in the 1950s. While exploring the Villa Rufolo gardens, Wagner was inspired to create the scenography for the magical garden of Klingsor in his opera *Parsifal*. The town transformed that musical moment into a tradition of performances and events. At first, the festival was dedicated primarily to Wagner's music, but over time it has become more varied, with classical, opera, jazz, and contemporary performances as well as ballet, dance, theater, and cultural events and exhibitions. The majority of the performances take place on a specially constructed stage in the Villa Rufolo gardens, the scene of Wagner's inspiration, with the Amalfi Coast serving as a one-of-a-kind backdrop. Other events are held in the Auditorium Oscar Niemeyer and at various locations in Ravello. Concerts take place throughout the week during the festival, and the schedule is usually announced around May each year, with tickets available online shortly thereafter. Tickets frequently sell out for concerts, so book as soon as tickets go on sale.

Festival of San Pantaleone

Duomo di Ravello and various locations; July 27; contact tourist office for program of events

Ravello celebrates its patron San Pantaleone (Saint Pantaleon) with a religious festival that starts in the Duomo and takes over the entire town. The festivities take place on July 27, the date San Pantaleone was martyred in 305 CE, and the date that it's said the blood of the saint miraculously liquifies each year. After a special mass, a procession following a statue of the saint meanders through the narrow streets, accompanied by the town's faithful. Concerts take place in the piazza, and after dark a huge fireworks display is set off above Ravello. The sight is just as magnificent overhead as it is from across the valley in Scala, where you can enjoy a full view overlooking Ravello.

SHOPPING

With a fine selection of boutiques, ceramic stores, and local products, Ravello is a nice spot for shopping. You'll find most of the shops around Piazza Duomo and the two streets that branch off from the square: **Via San Francesco** heading toward Villa Cimbrone, and **Via Roma** in the opposite direction.

Camo

Piazza Duomo 9; tel. 339/775-6298; www.museodelcorallo.com; 9:30am-8pm daily May-Oct., 9:30am-3pm Tues.-Sat. Nov.-Apr.

Master cameo and coral carver Giorgio Filocamo created one of Ravello's most remarkable shops, located right below the Duomo. While the shop looks tiny from the outside, step inside to find a treasure-house of jewelry. His family now continue to share Filocamo's passion and have preserved his prized collection of coral carving masterpieces in the museum at the back of the shop.

Bottega d'Ago

Via Trinità 7; tel. 347/097-7207; www.bottegadago.it; 10am-1pm and 2pm-8pm daily

In this small, intimate family-run boutique, custom-designed women's clothing and accessories are handmade on-site. Every piece is created by designer Laura D'Agostino, and the boutique is a collaboration with her husband, Anthony Cantarella. There's always a tempting selection, from handprinted fabrics to stylish crocheted bags and elegant pieces you'll want to add to your wardrobe.

Pascal Ceramiche d'Arte

Via Roma 22; tel. 089/858-576; www.ceramichedarte.com; 9am-9pm daily Mar.-Oct., 9am-5pm daily Nov.-Feb.

A fine selection of ceramics is on display at this large shop in the center of Ravello. The pieces are curated by Pasquale Sorrentino, who is passionate about handpicking and creating beautiful designs. You'll find a tempting choice of dishes as well as garden furniture, tables, and vases in the courtyard and in an additional shop located just around the corner.

1: the Ravello Festival **2:** Pascal Ceramiche d'Arte

Profumi della Costiera

Via Trinità 37; tel. 089/858-167; www. profumidellacostiera.it; 9am-6pm daily May-Oct., 9am-5pm daily Nov.-Apr.

Stop in to find a large selection of locally made liqueurs, including the iconic limoncello (lemon liqueur) made with Amalfi Coast lemons. For something a little different, don't miss the liqueur with finocchietto selvatico (wild fennel) or other popular varieties made with melon, strawberries, or licorice.

FOOD

With a setting suspended between land and sea, Ravello offers traditional cuisine that reflects both the mountains and the ocean. Expect to find options ranging from freshly caught seafood to hearty meat dishes or crespolini, a local dish of rich and creamy stuffed crepes baked in the oven. If you're just visiting for the day, you'll want to pick a restaurant where you can enjoy the view. Longer stays will present you with the chance to try some of the excellent local pizzerias and trattorias too.

Regional Cuisine
Ristorante Garden

Via Boccaccio 4; tel. 089/857-226; www.gardenravello. com; noon-3pm and 7pm-9:30pm Thurs.-Tues. Easter-mid-Nov.; €20-26

With a large terrace and sweeping views, this is a great choice for dining with those iconic Ravello views as the backdrop. The menu is varied and offers excellent choices, even if you aren't into seafood. However, if you are, it is very delicately prepared here, including spaghetti con le vongole (with clams) that is top-notch.

Trattoria da Cumpà Cosima

Via Roma 44; tel. 089/857-156; noon-3pm and 6:30pm-10pm daily Mar.-Nov., noon-3pm and 6:30pm-9pm Tues.-Sun. Dec.-Feb.; €15-40

Tucked away on a small street near the Chiesa di Santa Maria a Gradillo, this trattoria is the real deal. Netta Bottone, with her apron neatly tied around her waist, serves up hearty local specialties. Can't choose just one pasta from the menu? Try the sample platter that combines some of the restaurant's daily choices, or go for the crespolini—Netta's take on this local dish of baked stuffed crepes is out of this world. The meat is also a great choice; it's especially fresh because the family runs the butcher shop next door.

Pizzeria
Mimi' Bar Pizzeria

Via San Francesco 12; tel. 089/857-134; www. mimiravello.com; 12:30pm-3pm and 7pm-10pm Thurs.-Tues. May-Sept., contact for hours Oct.-Apr.; €15-25, pizzas €8-16

With indoor seating and a pretty outdoor garden terrace, as well as outdoor seating along the charming street near the Chiesa di San Francesco, this restaurant specializes in pizza and does it exceptionally well. Top-quality ingredients and a tempting selection of pizzas makes this a tasty spot for lunch or dinner. The menu also features an excellent selection of first and second courses, and their spaghetti with Cetara anchovies, yellow cherry tomatoes, and crumbled garlic bread is a house specialty.

Wine Bar
Babel Wine Bar Deli & Art

Via Santissima Trinità 13; tel. 089/858-6215; www. babelravello.com; 11:30am-3pm and 7pm-9:30pm Mon.-Sat. late Mar.-early Nov., €12-22

For a light lunch, dinner, or drinks, head to this wine bar, just a short jaunt from Piazza Duomo. Try one of the excellent salads for a refreshingly healthy option with a local twist, like the fabulous buffalo bresaola (air-dried salted meat) and fig salad with white truffle honey. There are also lovely pizzas and creative bruschette topped with lovely combinations like goat cheese and caramelized onion, or creamy burrata cheese with pesto and tomato confit. Choose from local beer and wines in an artistic setting. Plenty of vegetarian and gluten-free options are also available.

Gelato and Cafés
Baffone Gelateria Artigianale
Via Roma 48; 11am-8pm daily Apr.-Oct.; €3-5

When you're ready for something sweet and refreshing, stop by this small gelato shop that makes both classic and creative flavors. Try the lemon sorbetto or richer lemon crumble gelato, or try out their unique mojito and Aperol spritz varieties.

Bar Al San Domingo
Piazza Duomo 2; tel. 089/857-142; www.alsandomingo.it; 8am-midnight Wed.-Mon. May-Oct., 8am-8pm Wed.-Mon. Nov.-Apr.; €8-15

On a corner of Piazza Duomo, this friendly local coffee shop, bar, and pasticceria (pastry shop) has great indoor and outdoor seating. The outdoor area has a lovely view of the Duomo and is a great spot to enjoy drinks after dark and soak up the atmosphere. The pastries made on-site are a special treat if you're looking for something sweet to go with your cappuccino in the morning or for dessert after dinner. They also offer light meals and snack options.

ACCOMMODATIONS

Ravello is noted for its five-star hotels, but there are also cute B&Bs set in historic buildings and seaside villas. It's a good idea to book well in advance, especially because it's a popular location for destination weddings. If relaxing by the sea or pool is key for your holiday, keep in mind that there aren't any beaches in Ravello near the center of the town. You can compensate by picking a hotel with a lovely pool.

Under €100
Palazzo della Marra
Via della Marra 3; tel. 089/858-302; www.palazzodellamarra.it; Feb.-Dec.; €80 d

Just a few steps from Piazza Duomo, this simple B&B is set in a historic palazzo once belonging to the Della Marra family, who were important nobles in 13th-century Ravello. The four guest rooms have views over the Piazza Duomo or across the valley to Scala. The family also offers an apartment rental right in the center of Ravello. This B&B offers a central location and friendly service.

€100-200
Hotel Parsifal
Viale Gioacchino d'Anna 5; tel. 089/857-144; www.hotelparsifal.it; €185 d

Taking its name from Wagner's opera inspired by Ravello, this hotel certainly has an enchanting setting. Sitting high atop Ravello, it was founded as a convent in 1288 and was converted into a hotel in 1948. There's a tranquil atmosphere in the hotel's lovely terraces, central cloister, and 17 rooms. This charming boutique hotel has a family feel and offers the kind of gorgeous Amalfi Coast views that you'd find at the five-star hotels nearby, yet at a much more affordable price point. It's also open year round, which means you can enjoy Ravello's charms off-season too.

€200-300
Villa Maria Hotel
Via Santa Chiara; tel. 089/857-255; www.villamaria.it; Apr.-Oct.; €230 d

Near the entrance to the Villa Cimbrone gardens you'll find this hotel through a small garden courtyard, beautifully decorated and with the air of a noble residence. The spacious rooms are full of light from the large windows, and there are terraces with excellent views of the tranquil valley and the sea. With hand-painted majolica tiled floors and antique furnishings, the rooms boast historic elements as well as all the modern comforts. The hotel restaurant is set below a wisteria-covered pergola in the courtyard and is a top choice in Ravello.

Over €300
Hotel Villa Cimbrone
Via Santa Chiara 26; tel. 089/857-459; www.hotelvillacimbrone.com; Apr.-Oct.; €850 d

Nestled in beautiful gardens, Villa Cimbrone is a stunning property, offering the rare chance to enjoy a luxurious stay on a 12th-century estate. The hotel and its rooms are full of historic charm and remarkable details like frescoed ceilings, marble fireplaces, and hand-painted ceramic floors. The pool and private garden area for guests are perfectly manicured. The hotel isn't accessible by car, but it's a pleasant 10-minute walk from Piazza Duomo.

INFORMATION AND SERVICES
Tourist Information
Agenzia Regionale Campania Turismo
Viale Richard Wagner 4; tel. 089/857-096; www.agenziacampaniaturismo.it; 9am-1:30pm and 3pm-7pm daily June-Sept., 9am-3pm daily Oct.-May, hours can vary

Ravello's tourist office is located in the pretty Giardini del Vescovo located behind the Duomo. Stop in if you have questions or need local information, and the English-speaking staff will be happy to help.

Medical and Emergency Services
Ospedale Costa d'Amalfi
Via Civita 12; tel. 089/935-8180; www.aslsalerno.it

The Amalfi Coast's only hospital is located in Ravello, but not in the center of town. It is on the SS373 road that connects Ravello with the Amalfi Coast Road (SS163). The hospital is located in Castiglione, a frazione of Ravello, just before the intersection with the Amalfi Coast Road. It is a little more than 3 mi (5 km) and a 15-minute drive (without traffic) from the center of Ravello. The hospital has a 24-hour pronto soccorso (emergency room). To receive **emergency services** in Italy, dial 118.

Postal Services
Poste Italiane
Via Giovanni Boccaccio 21; tel. 089/858-6611; www.poste.it; 8:20am-1:35pm Mon.-Fri., 8:20am-12:35pm Sat.

To find Ravello's post office from the central Piazza Duomo, walk through the large tunnel to the left of the Villa Rufolo entrance, take a left, and walk along Via Giovanni Boccaccio only a short distance to find the post office on the left. This is where you go to mail letters or packages.

GETTING THERE
By Car and Scooter
Ravello, at 1,200 ft (365 m) above sea level along the Amalfi Coast, is about 4 mi (6.7 km) from Amalfi. It is not located along the Amalfi Coast Road (SS163), but can be reached by following **SS373** from the crossroads at Castiglione. The road to Ravello is among the trickiest on the coast, as one section is very narrow. During the tourist season, Easter-October, there is a traffic light limiting traffic to one-way during the day. If you're driving this road, go slowly and be prepared to back up if needed. The drive from **Amalfi** to Ravello takes about 20 minutes, depending on traffic. From **Positano,** the drive is about 1 hour along the Amalfi Coast Road east to SS373 and then up to Ravello. To reach Ravello from **Salerno,** the drive is about 1 hour along the Amalfi Coast Road west to SS373, and then up to the center of town.

By Bus
Given the tricky roads and limited parking, one of the best ways to arrive is by bus. The local public bus company **SITA SUD** (tel. 089/386-6701; www.sitasudtrasporti.it; from €1.40) has a bus line connecting Ravello with Scala and Amalfi. Buses arrive every 30-60 minutes throughout the day, depending on the time of year, at the **Galleria Nuova stop** located on Via Giovanni Boccaccio near the entrance to the tunnel that leads to Piazza Duomo. The bus ride from Amalfi to Ravello takes about 25 minutes. To reach Ravello by bus from Salerno, Positano, and other locations on the Amalfi Coast, you first have to arrive in Amalfi and then transfer to the SITA SUD bus line to Ravello. Travelers with an affinity for walking can take the bus up to Ravello and then walk down to the coastal towns, such as Atrani (1-1.5 hours) or Minori (1 hour), following scenic stairs and pathways.

GETTING AROUND

Ravello is a small town and is best explored on foot once you've arrived by bus or parked your car or scooter. A well-marked paid **parking lot** below Piazza Duomo is accessed by following Via della Marra below the Chiesa di Santa Maria a Gradillo. A small parking lot is available below the Auditorium Oscar Niemeyer, and paid parking is also available along the side of the roads surrounding Ravello. Expect to pay about €3 per hour for parking. Scooter parking is available near the Chiesa di Santa Maria a Gradillo and on Via della Repubblica leading down to the Auditorium Oscar Niemeyer. Scooter parking costs €1.50 per hour or €8 for the day.

If you'd like to rent a scooter in Ravello, stop by **Chic & Fabulous** (Via della Marra 4; tel. 333/380-8288; www.amalficoastrentalcf.com; Mar.-Oct.; from €70) just off Piazza Duomo for a variety of rental options.

Scala

Considered the oldest settlement on the Amalfi Coast, Scala is believed to have been founded in the 5th century by shipwrecked Romans who fled to the rugged mountains for protection. Over time, the town's prosperity grew in connection with the Republic of Amalfi, which led to a period of great affluence and the construction of Scala's impressive churches.

Scala's serene atmosphere feels worlds away from modern-day life and makes it the ideal base, surrounded by nature. You'll enjoy hiking and savoring the beauty of the Amalfi Coast just a short distance from two of the coastline's major destinations.

ORIENTATION

Located just across the valley from Ravello in the mountains above Amalfi and Atrani, Scala is one of the Amalfi Coast's hidden gems. It stretches across the mountainside and is composed of six different frazioni, or villages: **Minuta, Campidoglio, Santa Caterina, San Pietro,** and **Pontone.** The center of Scala is at Piazza Municipio, where the Duomo di San Lorenzo is located as well as the main bus stop and shopping area in town. Via Torricella heads south out of Piazza Municipio and makes a large circuit around town, connecting Minuta, Campidoglio, Santa Caterina, and San Pietro. The peaceful village of Pontone is reached by taking Via Valle delle Ferriere from the SS373 road; Pontone lies in a more secluded area between Scala and Amalfi.

SIGHTS

Scala's setting, stretching out across the valley, is one of its most attractive sights. While exploring the town's frazioni, stop to visit the churches, as they offer a glimpse into Scala's important history as a part of the Republic of Amalfi. Wealthy families built large estates in the area and founded the churches you can still visit today.

Piazza Municipio

Piazza Municipio between Via Vescovado and Via Torcella

This square is the heart of Scala. It is where you'll find the Duomo di San Lorenzo as well as all the town's shops and city hall. The piazza is dominated by the facade of the Duomo, but just to the right you'll find a stone fountain, and beyond that a terrace with great views of Ravello across the valley. In the piazza opposite the Duomo, a plaque honors Gerardo Sasso, a monk from Scala who, during the 12th century, was the founder of the Order of the Knights of Malta (Cavalieri dell'Ordine dell'Ospedale di San Giovanni di Gerusalemme). At that time, Scala was a part of the Republic of Amalfi, which is why you'll spot the familiar symbol of Amalfi, the eight-pointed Maltese cross, on the plaque.

Duomo di San Lorenzo
Piazza Municipio; hours vary; free

Dedicated to San Lorenzo, the Duomo of Scala is an impressive church for what is now a small, peaceful town. Step inside and you'll see a massive space with large white columns, crowned with three large paintings on the ceiling depicting the life of San Lorenzo, the town's patron saint. In the center of the aisle on the floor, there's a large majolica ceramic scene from 1853 of a shield with a lion climbing a ladder, which refers to the town's name (*scala* means steps). The shield is surrounded by cherubs holding an ornate garland of flowers. Follow the steps on the right aisle down to the church's crypt, the Gothic-style Cripta del Paradiso, with delicate pink and white detailing, home to the striking tomb of Marinella Rufolo, a 14th-century Ravello noblewoman.

Chiesa dell'Annunziata
Piazza Minuta; open only during mass, generally 6pm Sun.; free

Set in the frazione of Minuta, one of the prettiest spots in Scala, this church is among the oldest on the Amalfi Coast. Founded in the 11th century, it features a portico with a 15th-century fresco of the Madonna above the central door. Be sure to visit the crypt to see the extraordinary 12th-century frescoes with a variety of scenes including the Miracle of San Nicola of Bari. From the piazza outside the church there's a panoramic view down the valley and just a glimpse of Amalfi in the distance.

Basilica di Sant'Eustachio
Via Sant'Eustachio; www.discoverscala.com; hours vary; free

Located between Minuta and Pontone, the ruins of the 12th-century Basilica di Sant'Eustachio are a romantic sight sitting atop a small promontory. This was once a lavish church built by the noble d'Afflitto family of Scala, but what remains today are just traces of its former glory. Walk through the ruins and enjoy the marvelous panoramic views across the valley to the Villa Cimbrone in Ravello and down the valley to Atrani, Pontone, and Amalfi.

Pontone
Via Valle delle Ferriere, Pontone, Scala

This tranquil frazione of Scala sits halfway between Scala and Amalfi, and is often a peaceful respite for hikers exploring the area. Its pretty little piazza is full of trees, and **Blu Bar** (Piazza San Giovanni 2; tel. 089/872-639; 8am-11pm daily Mar.-Oct., 8am-1pm and 5pm-8pm Mon.-Sat. Nov.-Feb.) is a great spot to relax. Also on the piazza, you'll find the bell tower and **Chiesa di San Giovanni Battista,** which was founded in the 12th century. If the church is open, step inside to find a baroque interior and an 18th-century organ with Venetian rococo decorations.

Pontone is reachable by steps from Minuta or Amalfi, and more easily by a small road that branches off the SS373 between Castiglione on the Amalfi Coast Road and Ravello. There's a handful of public SITA buses on the Amalfi, Scala, and Ravello line that also stop in Pontone.

HIKING
Torre dello Ziro Watchtower
Distance: *1.6 mi (2.5 km) round-trip*
Time: *2 hours round-trip*
Trailhead: *Via Valle delle Ferriere, Pontone*
Information and Maps: *Cart&guide maps (www.officinezephiro.it)*

Sitting atop the mountain between Amalfi and Atrani is the 15th-century Torre dello Ziro watchtower, built on top of an earlier defensive tower from the 12th century. Though it is much more visible from Amalfi and Atrani, the only way to reach the watchtower is by hiking from Scala. Start in Pontone where Via Pisacane branches off the Via Valle delle Ferriere and follow the signs to the Torre dello Ziro. The rugged pathway hugs the mountainside as it climbs toward the tower. The

---

1: ruins of the Basilica di Sant'Eustachio **2:** view of Amalfi while walking down the steps from Scala **3:** Pontone's little piazza

pathway follows roughly the same elevation from Pontone to the tower, and along the way there's a spectacular view looking down on Atrani. You can explore the area around the tower and walls before climbing to a higher viewpoint for a bird's-eye view of Amalfi. Plan for about 2 hours round-trip to hike to the tower and back.

Scala to Amalfi

Distance: *0.6 mi (1.5 km) one-way*
Time: *45 minutes one-way*
Trailhead: *Piazza Minuta, Minuta*
Information and Maps: *Cart&guide maps (www.officinezephiro.it)*

This gorgeous hike leads from Scala down through the mountain valley to Amalfi and passes through the villages of Minuta and Pontone along the way. Start by following the steps from Via Torricella down to Minuta to the Chiesa dell'Annunziata. From the piazza in front of the church, take the staircase behind the fountain down and follow signs to Amalfi. When you reach the top of Pontone, the pathway divides with two options for passing through Pontone. Take the pathway on the right to visit the ruins of the **Basilica di Sant'Eustachio** before descending a steep staircase. Stop for a rest in the piazza before continuing down toward Amalfi.

The staircase zigzags through terraces of lemon groves and hugs the mountainside before it reaches the first houses at the top of Amalfi. The pathway leads down to Amalfi's main street and eventually the Piazza Duomo.

Another option once you arrive in Pontone is to hike into the Valle delle Ferriere to explore the waterfalls and ruins of ancient mills before descending back into Amalfi. From Piazza San Giovanni in Pontone, follow signs for the Valle delle Ferriere leading deep into the valley. From the Valle delle Ferriere, follow signs pointing back down to Amalfi. The hike from Scala to Amalfi takes 45 minutes, but plan to spend at least twice as long if you're going to explore the **Valle delle Ferriere.**

ENTERTAINMENT AND EVENTS

While Scala's peacefulness is one of its best features, the town also knows how to put on a good festival. Whether it's feting the town's patron saint or one of the best food festivals along the Amalfi Coast, Scala's annual events are worth marking your calendar.

Festival of San Lorenzo

Piazza Municipio; Aug. 10

Scala's patron saint is celebrated with a big summer festival on August 10, the traditional day the saint is honored. Events center on the Duomo di Scala—which is dedicated to San Lorenzo—and include a religious procession with a statue of the saint, music in the piazza, stalls selling food, and a fireworks display over the town after dark.

Festa Della Castagna (Chestnut Festival)

Piazza Municipio; www.discoverscala.com; Oct., dates vary

Chestnut trees fill the valley around Scala, and in autumn the annual harvest is celebrated with a big sagra (food festival) completely dedicated to chestnuts. The entire center of town is transformed into a rustic setting with various stalls selling local specialties like gnocchi and pasta made with chestnuts or chestnut flour and a variety of tempting chestnut cream-filled desserts as well as roasted chestnuts. Traditional games take place in Piazza Municipio, including tug of war and a donkey race with each of the frazioni of Scala vying to win. A stage is set up in the piazza for concerts by local bands. The festival usually takes place over two weekends in October, with the dates varying depending on the harvest.

FOOD

Trattoria Da Lorenzo

Via Frà Gerardo Sasso 10; tel. 089/858-290; www. trattoriadalorenzo.com; 12:30pm-2pm and 7:30pm-9:30pm Sat.-Sun., 7:30pm-9:30pm Tues.-Fri. Apr.-mid-Oct.; €16-45

The entrance to this gem of a restaurant is

through a pretty garden with olive trees, where you can sample creative cocktails for a relaxed aperitivo. Inside there's a small seating area and, just beyond, a beautiful terrace for alfresco dining with a glimpse of Ravello in the distance. You'll want to try their array of antipasti, a selection of fish and local vegetable dishes. Seafood is the highlight here, and the pasta and fresh local fish like scorfano (red scorpionfish) or rana pescatrice (angler) are exceptionally good. Save room for the creative desserts if you can!

Il Pinguino

Via Frà Gerardo Sasso 7; tel. 089/857-304; bbpinguino@hotmail.com; 7pm-10:30pm Wed.-Mon. Mar.-Dec.; €15-35

This family-run restaurant and B&B is a local favorite with its excellent home cooking, wood-fired-oven pizza, and warm hospitality. The eggplant parmesan is a great place to start, followed by spaghetti with beans and mussels, a regional specialty you won't find on many menus. The pizza is also top-notch. The rooms (€150 d) are clean and bright, and the breakfast options are delicious.

Ristorante San Giovanni

Via Santa Maria, Pontone; tel. 089/872-582; www.ristorantesangiovanni.com; noon-3pm and 6pm-midnight daily Mar.-Nov.; €10-20

Located next to the Chiesa di San Giovanni Battista in Pontone, this is a great spot to stop for lunch while hiking in the Scala area. There's both an indoor dining area and a lovely outdoor covered terrace with views across the valley to Ravello. You'll enjoy excellent pizza, hearty pasta dishes, and an especially good grilled meat platter.

ACCOMMODATIONS

Palazzo Pascal

Piazza Minuta 1; tel. 089/858-312; www.palazzopascal.it; Mar.-Oct.; €400

Ideally situated in Minuta with panoramic views of Ravello and the sea, this five-star hotel offers the comfort and style of a luxury stay, a secluded setting, and top-notch service. The entire property has been impeccably remodeled, and the seven suites all feature colorful ceramic tiles and balconies or terraces. The pool is the perfect spot to soak up the sun in complete peace. The excellent restaurant **Gli Ulivi** (noon-3pm and 7:30pm-10:30pm daily Apr.-Oct.; €18-25) is open to non-guests with a menu highlighting traditional recipes and fresh ingredients. Try the spaghetti with yellow tomatoes, anchovies, and bread crumbs or seared sea bass with a fresh sauce made from sfusato amalfitano lemons. Vegetarian, vegan, and gluten-free menus are also available.

GETTING THERE AND AROUND

Scala is located across the Valle del Dragone from Ravello and is easily reached by car or bus. From Ravello, you can even walk to Scala in about 30 minutes. To reach Scala from the **Amalfi Coast Road,** follow the **SS373** road at Castiglione up toward Ravello. Before reaching Ravello, look for the large ceramic sign for Scala and turn left. From there the road leads to the center of town, and if you continue to follow it, it makes a large loop around the different parts of town. The drive to Scala is about 5 minutes from **Ravello,** 20 minutes from **Amalfi,** and a little over 1 hour from either **Positano** or **Salerno.**

The local bus company **SITA SUD** (tel. 089/386-6701; www.sitasudtrasporti.it; from €1.40 per person) has a bus line that connects Scala to Ravello and Amalfi, with service every 30-60 minutes throughout the day, with more frequent service April-October. All buses to Scala stop in the **Piazza Municipio** in the center of town, while only a handful each day stop in the frazioni of Scala, including Pontone and Minuta. The bus ride from Ravello to Scala is about 5 minutes; from Amalfi it's about 25 minutes. To reach Scala by bus from Positano or Salerno, first take the bus to Amalfi where you can transfer to the bus line serving Scala and Ravello.

Tramonti

Deep in the Lattari Mountains above Ravello and Maiori, Tramonti is the green heart of the Amalfi Coast. The town once played an important role in defending the Republic of Amalfi along the pass through the mountains, while the river Reginna, which runs down the valley to Maiori, was used to power the local ironworks and paper mills.

The town's name means "among the mountains," which perfectly describes its setting nestled in a lush valley and spread out into 13 different areas that are connected by a narrow road that winds through sleepy villages, terraced gardens, olive groves, and pergolas of grapevines so close to the road that it seems you could reach out and touch them while driving by. It's those grapevines that bring most visitors to quiet Tramonti because wine from this region is a real treasure of the Amalfi Coast. Vines have been growing here for more than a thousand years. If you enjoy a rural and natural landscape or good wine, plan to stop in Tramonti.

VINEYARDS

Tramonti's rolling mountain setting is best appreciated while exploring the different villages spread out around the valley. Along the way, you can stop to visit some of the top vineyards on the Amalfi Coast.

Tenuta San Francesco Vineyard

Via Solficiano 18, Corsano; tel. 089/876-434; www.vinitenutasanfrancesco.com; reservation required; from €40 pp

Since 2004, Tenuta San Francesco has been at the forefront of producing highly respected wines from the Amalfi Coast. They've brought modern production into a cantina dating to the 1700s, and with a little more than 22 acres (9 ha), this is one of the largest vineyards in Tramonti. Vineyard tours and a variety of tasting options are available, including a lovely wine tour and lunch tasting (from €80 per person). Reservations are required.

Cantine Giuseppe Apicella

Via Castello S. Maria 1, Capitignano; tel. 089/876-075; www.giuseppeapicella.it; reservation required; tour and tasting from €50

For generations the Apicella family has produced wine in the Tramonti valley. In 1977 the first wines were bottled by Giuseppe Apicella, and today the vineyard is run by his son Prisco Apicella. The new generation of the Apicella family is passionate about continuing the important wine-producing tradition and tending the vines, the oldest dating to the early 20th century. Wine-tastings and tours through the vineyards and the cantina are available.

FOOD AND ACCOMMODATIONS

Tramonti's local specialties are inspired by the land and include hearty meat dishes, locally produced cheese, chestnuts, and pizza.

Trattoria San Francisco

Piazza Polvica 17, Polvica; tel. 339/440-1041; s.francisco2000@libero.it; 7pm-11pm daily; €8-18

Head to this welcoming restaurant and pizzeria to try Tramonti's unique style of pizza, a little different and a bit thicker than the traditional Neapolitan style. Pizza maker Francesco Maiorano and his wife, Pamela Viggiano, are the masterminds behind this restaurant, which is dedicated to Tramonti's traditional home cooking based on high-quality ingredients. Try the pasta with locally grown beans or sauces prepared with the variety of tomato called re fiascone, cultivated in Tramonti.

Azienda Agricola Reale

Via Cardamone 75A, Gete; tel. 089/856-144; www.aziendaagricolareale.it; 12:30pm-3pm and 7:30pm-10pm Thurs.-Tues. May-Nov., 12:30pm-3pm and 7:30pm-10pm Sat.-Sun. Dec.-Apr.; €10-22

This lovely farm is the place to experience Tramonti's gastronomic diversity at the on-site Osteria Reale. The menu highlights locally sourced meat and farm-fresh vegetables as well as seafood options and great pizza. Enjoy views of the surrounding vineyards, which are over 100 years old. Sample their excellent wines while dining or opt for a tour through the vineyards, which includes a wine-tasting of their four locally produced wines along with a full lunch or dinner (€110 per person). Extend your stay in this tranquil spot in Tramonti at one of the two on-site B&B rooms (€95 d).

GETTING THERE AND AROUND

Given Tramonti's rural setting, with 13 different areas sprawling across a valley in the Monte Lattari, the best way to get to and explore the town is by car or scooter. Two main roads pass through Tramonti, connecting it with Ravello and Maiori on the Amalfi Coast. The **SP1** (Strada Provinciale 1) road begins in Ravello and runs through the western side of Tramonti, while the **SP2a** starts in Maiori and passes along the eastern side of Tramonti. Both SP1 and SP2a meet at the Valley of Chiunzi (Valico di Chiunzi), the pass over the Lattari Mountains from the southern side of the Sorrentine Peninsula to the northern side. From there, **SP2b** continues down the northern side of the mountains, where it meets the highway to Naples and Salerno. A narrow internal road connects the small rural areas of Tramonti. From SP2a on the eastern side of Tramonti, take a left at a well-marked intersection onto **SP141** and follow the road as it meanders through the terraced vineyards and tiny hamlets to the other side of Tramonti, connecting to SP1 on the western side of the town.

To reach Tramonti from **Maiori,** follow the SP2a road up into the valley, and you'll reach the town after a 15-minute drive. From **Amalfi** and **Positano,** follow the **Amalfi Coast Road (SS163)** east to Maiori and then take SP2a to Tramonti. From **Salerno,** take the Amalfi Coast Road west to Maiori and continue along SP2a. The drive to Tramonti from Amalfi takes about 35 minutes, from Positano about 1 hour 15 minutes, and from Salerno a little over 1 hour. From **Naples,** follow the **A3** highway south, exit at Angri Sud, and follow signs for Valico di Chiunzi. Continue along SP2a to the pass, where you can continue along either SP1 or SP2a to Tramonti. From Naples, plan for about a 1-hour drive to Tramonti.

Minori

Minori sits at the base of a beautiful valley surrounded by terraced gardens. Called Rheginna Minor in the Middle Ages, this town has a vibrant cultural and gastronomic heritage. Minori's mountain stream, called Regginolo, once powered papermaking mills and pasta factories. Yet it was the town's agricultural tradition of lemon farming that left a lasting mark on Minori.

Minori is home to an archaeological treasure in the form of an expansive Roman villa dating from about the 1st century BCE. The excavated parts of the villa are located right in the center of town. Not far away is the grand Basilica di Santa Trofimena, dedicated to Minori's very special patron saint. The small, well-manicured waterfront stretches along the beach and is the popular spot for locals to enjoy a passeggiata (stroll) throughout the day. Across from the lungomare in Piazza Umberto I, spot the Fontana Moresca, a fountain with two carved stone lions and, in the middle, a column that was most likely taken from an ancient site.

Though it is not far from Amalfi and Ravello, Minori has a more laid-back feel because it is just that little bit off the beaten path. It's an excellent base to enjoy a holiday surrounded by the Amalfi Coast's charms.

SIGHTS

Most of Minori's sights are located along the waterfront or right in the center of the town. Though its main sights can be visited in a half day, plan to linger because there are some great walks in the area and a picturesque beach to soak up the sun.

Basilica di Santa Trofimena

Piazza Cantilena; tel. 089/854-1503; www.santatrofimena.it; 9am-1pm and 5pm-7:30pm daily

The religious heart of Minori, the Basilica di Santa Trofimena sits in a small piazza not far from the beach. The first church to stand on this spot dates to the 7th century, but when Santa Trofimena's relics miraculously arrived on the beach in 640 after she was martyred in Sicily, a new and much grander church was constructed to honor this miracle. The church is one of the most lavish and largest on the Amalfi Coast, and from 987 to 1818 it was even the seat of a bishop and therefore held the position of a cathedral.

The church you see today dates from the baroque period, though it underwent significant 19th-century restorations. The elegant stucco architectural details in gray and white blend baroque and neoclassical into one unique style. Its interior has a Latin cross floor plan with a nave, two side aisles, and a dome. The oldest part of the church is the crypt holding the relics of Santa Trofimena.

Villa Romana

Via Capo di Piazza 28; tel. 089/852-893; 9am-7pm Tues.-Sat., 9am-1:30pm Sun., closed May 1, Dec. 25, and Jan. 1; free

Enjoying the natural landscape of Minori has been a pastime since the Romans sailed along the coast and spotted this scenic beach and lush valley setting. We know this thanks to a large Roman villa dating from about the 1st century BCE that has been excavated right in the center of town. Of all the ruins uncovered along the Amalfi Coast, the Villa Romana is the largest. Sprawling out over 2,500 sq ft (232 sq m), the villa offers a rare glimpse into the Roman lifestyle along the Amalfi Coast.

The multilevel villa includes a large dining area and nymphaeum, with beautiful mosaics, frescoes, and the remains of what was once a waterfall. Though much of the villa is closed to visitors, you can envision how grand the villa was if you walk around the portico surrounding the courtyard. The pool was once in the center of the villa, meaning the garden area was much larger than we can see today. Near the entrance is a small museum of archaeological items uncovered in Minori and the surrounding areas.

Campanile dell'Annunziata
Via Torre Annunziata

On the eastern mountain slope above Minori, you can spot a striking bell tower, which is all that remains from the Chiesa dell'Annunziata, a church from the 12th century. While there are only ruins of the church that the bell tower was once connected to, from the outside on the steps next to the tower you can see the Byzantine-Arab architectural influences in the intricate geometric diamond and cross patterns and style of the bell tower. To reach the tower, follow the steps from the center of Minori for the Campanile dell'Annunziata. A narrow staircase leads through a residential area with little terraced gardens to the top of town and the bell tower. If you would like to continue your walk, the Sentiero dei Limoni begins nearby.

BEACHES
Spiaggia Grande
Via Roma

Minori's pretty beach stretches out in front of the town and offers a lovely view of the surrounding valley. The beach has several stabilimenti balneari (beach clubs) like **Chalet de Mar** (Lungomare; tel. 089/851-721; www.chaletdemaramalficoast.it; May-Oct.; from €15 for two sun beds and umbrella), offering sun bed and umbrella rentals as well as showers, changing rooms, and beachside snack bars or restaurants. On both ends of the beach are open areas where you can throw down a towel and enjoy the beach for free. The beach is popular with families because it faces south for sunshine most of the day and is a pleasant spot for swimming. **Boat Service** (tel. 375/528-4587; www.boatservice.org; May-Oct.; kayak rental from €15 per hour) offers kayak, clear kayak, and pedal boat rentals right on the beach in Minori.

HIKING
Pathway of the Lemons
(Sentiero dei Limoni)
Distance: 2 mi (3 km)
Time: 1 hour one-way
Trailhead: Campanile dell'Annunziata
Information and Maps: Pro Loco

Before the Amalfi Coast Road was built in the first half of the 19th century, the only connection between Maiori and Minori on land was a rugged pathway over the mountain. This scenic walk is now called the Sentiero dei Limoni (Pathway of the Lemons) because it passes through the terraces of lemon groves above Minori and Maiori. This was once the largest area for growing the local sfusato amalfitano lemons, which were harvested and carried down the mountain to Minori and Maiori and then exported around the world. The lemon groves are still lovingly maintained and the walk offers beautiful views along the way.

Starting from the **Campanile dell'Annunziata** in Minori, follow Via Torre, which hugs the mountainside with terraced lemon gardens above and below. Stop at the **Belvedere Mortella,** a little overlook off the walkway that offers great views of the town, the Basilica di Santa Trofimena, and the beach below. The pathway passes through a little area called Torre with a small church dedicated to San Michele Arcangelo before continuing around to Maiori. It takes about 1 hour to walk from Minori to Maiori.

Enhance your walk along the Pathway of the Lemons with a visit to **Agriturismo Villa Maria** (Via Pioppi; tel. 089/877-197; www.agriturismovillamaria.it; tastings from €35 per person, reservations preferred) in Minori to visit a working lemon grove up close and enjoy a limoncello tasting.

FESTIVALS AND EVENTS

During the summer months, Minori often hosts concerts and cultural events along the waterfront or in the Villa Romana, so keep an eye out for event postings around town. In

addition to the festivals for the town's patron saint throughout the year, Minori also celebrates Easter with moving religious processions from the Basilica di Santa Trofimena.

Festival of Santa Trofimena

Basilica di Santa Trofimena; July 13, Nov. 5, and Nov. 26-27

Minori's faithful have a deep connection to their patron saint, Santa Trofimena. The early Christian martyr is celebrated with three religious festivals throughout the year. November 5 marks the traditional saint day for Santa Trofimena, while the November 26-27 events celebrate the relics being found again after they were lost in the church, a fascinating story: In the 9th century, the highly prized relics were stolen by the powerful prince of Benevento. Eventually, they were brought back to Minori, and the festival each year on July 13 marks the return of the relics. After this momentous occasion, the relics were well hidden in the church for safekeeping. Unfortunately, they were hidden a little too well and their exact location was lost over the centuries. When they were rediscovered, it was a grand event for the town. The festivals for Santa Trofimena include special masses in the Basilica, religious processions with a treasured statue of the saint, and fireworks displays over the sea.

Gusta Minori
(A Taste of Minori)

various locations; tel. 089/854-1609; www.gustaminori.it; Sept.

Once an important center for pasta making and still strongly connected with the Amalfi Coast's traditional lemon cultivation, Minori is proud of its gastronomic heritage. This culinary tradition is feted during the last week of August with a multiday festival called Gusta Minori, which celebrates local products and blends food, art, and cultural events into a fun summer event.

1: Spiaggia Grande **2:** the Festival of Santa Trofimena in Minori **3:** looking down to the ancient Villa Romana **4:** Minori's Basilica di Santa Trofimena

SHOPPING
Liquorificio Carlo Mansi

Via Vescovado 1; tel. 089/853-717; www.carlomansi.com; 9am-1:30pm and 3:30pm-7:30pm Mon.-Sat.

Head toward the bell tower of the Basilica di Santa Trofimena and just behind it you'll find one of the Amalfi Coast's top producers of liqueurs. You'll find the classic limoncello along with some other unique blends like Cicerenella, made with orange and anise, or Concerto, a liqueur unique to Minori, made with their secret blend of herbs, barley, and coffee.

FOOD AND ACCOMMODATIONS
Sal de Riso

Via Roma 80; tel. 089/877-941; www.salderiso.it; café 7am-1am daily; Gourmet 12:30pm-3pm and 7:30pm-10:30pm daily, reservations required; individual pastries €7-8, entrées and pizzas €8-16, Gourmet €16-28

Saving room for dessert is a must thanks to Minori's famous pastry chef Salvatore de Riso, who has created a heavenly spot not only for sweets but also for excellent dining in his hometown. The beautiful café features indoor and outdoor seating and serves gourmet pizza, salads, sandwiches, and even a great hamburger. Next door, the Gourmet restaurant maintains the same focus on the highest-quality local ingredients with a fine dining experience often accompanied by live music and entertainment. Whichever location you choose, you really do want to save room for dessert: You'll find an incredible selection of pastries, gelato, and cakes, all beautifully presented. You really can't go wrong, but the delizia al limone, a lemon cream infused cake, and ricotta pera e cioccolato, a lovely cake made with ricotta, pears, and chocolate, are both divine.

Giardiniello

Corso Vittorio Emanuele 17; tel. 089/877-050; www.ristorantegiardiniello.it; 12:15pm-3pm and 6:30pm-11pm daily; €16-32

Along the main street that cuts through the center of Minori, you'll find this restaurant with a beautiful pergola-covered garden where you can dine outside when the weather is fine. The menu highlights seafood, and it's done remarkably well. However, you could also go for the local ndunderi, a traditional Minori pasta dish of small dumplings made with flour and ricotta served with a meat ragù sauce. The menu also includes plenty of excellent non-seafood options, including pizza.

Agriturismo Villa Maria

Via Pioppi; tel. 089/877-197; www. agriturismovillamaria.it; €110 d

Enjoy a stay surrounded by lemon groves at this family-run agriturismo located above Minori. Each of the 6 guest rooms has a view overlooking Minori to the sea, and there's a lovely patio. Enjoy local flavors in a garden setting at the on-site restaurant. Cooking classes (from €180 per person) and limoncello tastings (from €35 per person) can also be arranged.

INFORMATION AND SERVICES

Pro Loco

Via Roma 32; tel. 089/877-087; www.prolocominori.it; 9am-1pm and 4pm-8pm daily

Located right along the waterfront, Minori's tourist office is friendly and well-stocked with information about the town and surrounding area. The English-speaking staff are happy to share information and answer any questions.

GETTING THERE AND AROUND

Minori is located 2.5 mi (4 km) east of **Amalfi** and about 13 mi (21 km) west of **Salerno** on the **Amalfi Coast Road (SS163).** There is a small public **parking lot** near the beach on the western edge of town where you can park hourly for a small fee. Parking is relatively limited, so arriving by bus or ferry is recommended. Minori is very small and easy to get around on foot.

By Ferry

Minori is well connected to other towns along the Amalfi Coast via ferry service by **Travelmar** (tel. 089/872-950; www.travelmar.it; €3-15 per person). Boats arrive at Minori's small pier from Amalfi, Atrani, Maiori, Cetara, Vietri sul Mare, Salerno, and Positano. Tickets are available online in advance, or via the Travelmar app. Ferries operate seasonally April-early November, with boats departing hourly 8:30am-7pm daily; times vary depending on the departure point. From Salerno the trip to Minori is about 40 minutes, from Positano about 25 minutes, and then after a transfer in Amalfi, only about 10 minutes. **Alicost** (Salerno; tel. 089/227-979; www.alicost.it; €25.50) runs a daily ferry April-October connecting Capri and Minori, with usually only one daily departure in the evening from Capri to Minori and one in the morning from Minori to Capri. The trip takes about 1 hour 30 minutes from Capri to Minori.

By Bus

Minori is served by the public **SITA SUD** (tel. 089/386-6701; www.sitasudtrasporti.it; from €1.40) buses on the Amalfi-Salerno line. Buses arrive every hour or so throughout the day, depending on the time of year. The main stop is along the **Via Roma** (the waterfront) opposite the small road leading to the Basilica di Santa Trofimena. From Amalfi the journey to Minori is about 15 minutes, and from Salerno about 1 hour. From Positano, you have to take the bus to Amalfi and then transfer to the bus to Salerno.

To reach Minori by bus from the Naples airport, **Pintour** (tel. 081/879-2645; www.pintourbus.com; €20 adults, €10 under age 13) runs a seasonal bus service April-early November. Catch the bus at the bus terminal located outside the arrivals hall at the airport. The bus stops at Pompeii and along the Amalfi Coast, including at Minori along the waterfront on Via Roma and at Via Gatto 59. Book your tickets in advance via the company website. The journey from the airport to Minori takes about 1 hour 35 minutes.

Maiori

Maiori sits at the base of a wide valley with a long beach that is one of the town's key attractions, especially during the summer. With the longest beach on the coast, Maiori was the trading center of the Republic of Amalfi in the Middle Ages and home to the largest arsenals for shipbuilding. Where its beaches were once lined with sailing ships, fishing boats, and nets, today there are rows of brightly colored beach umbrellas and sun beds. The beach itself has been the setting for significant moments in the town's history, starting with the recovery of a statue of Santa Maria a Mare (Madonna of the Sea) in 1204, a focal point for the town's faithful that is now on display in the Collegiata di Santa Maria a Mare.

Maiori's beach was the setting for another historical event on September 8, 1943, when it was the location for part of Operation Avalanche, or the landing of Salerno, during World War II. Allied troops landed on the beach and then followed the pass over Chiunzi on their way to Naples. On October 25, 1954, a massive storm destroyed much of the central part of the town. Many of Maiori's more modern buildings along the seafront and main street, Corso Reginna, date from the period after the flood. Yet the charming and wide lungomare (waterfront) walkway is a beautiful place to enjoy a passeggiata (stroll), a popular local pastime.

ORIENTATION

The **Amalfi Coast Road (SS163)** runs through Maiori at sea level alongside the **lungomare** walkway. In the center of town, the main street of Maiori, **Corso Reginna,** runs perpendicular to the lungomare up into the valley. This pedestrian-only street is lined with shops, cafés, and restaurants. After walking a short distance up Corso Reginna, the small **Piazza Raffaele D'Amato** opens on the left with a narrow yet steep staircase that leads up to the **Collegiata di Santa Maria a Mare.** Continuing on Corso Reginna leads to **Palazzo Mezzacapo** on the left, and more shops and dining options.

Following the Amalfi Coast Road east out of town leads past the **Abbey of Santa Maria de Olearia** (Abbazia di Santa Maria de Olearia). To reach the seaside village of **Erchie,** which is technically part of Maiori, continue east on the Amalfi Coast Road until a small road splits off sharply to the right, the **Via Provinciale,** which meanders down to Erchie, set well below the Amalfi Coast Road.

SIGHTS

One of the most pleasurable things to do in Maiori is to stroll along the lungomare or relax on the beach. **Corso Reginna** is where you'll find the majority of the town's sights, restaurants, and shops.

Collegiata di Santa Maria a Mare

Piazzale Mons. Nicola Milo; tel. 089/877-090; parrocchia.maiori1204@gmail.com; 8:30am-noon and 5pm-8pm daily

Maiori's largest church sits on the western side with a scenic position overlooking the town. Founded as a small church carved into the rocks, it was later expanded in the 13th century after an important sculpture of the Madonna was discovered in Maiori. As the story goes, in 1204 a ship sailing back from the East had aboard a beautiful statue of the Madonna and Child from Constantinople. However, during a terrible storm it was lost overboard, only to be found by fishermen from Maiori. The church was then dedicated to Santa Maria a Mare, and the statue still stands above the high altar of the church. The statue is carved from cedarwood from Lebanon and depicts the Madonna holding the baby Jesus, wearing gold crowns and rich robes in red, blue, and gold.

The church has a simple yet refined pale

yellow baroque-style facade from the 1700s, a 14th-century bell tower, and a dome covered with green and yellow ceramic tiles in a geometric diamond pattern. Inside, the church has three naves and is decorated in a baroque style with the same sense of elegance. The town celebrates its patron saint on August 15 with a grand religious festival that coincides with the national Italian holiday **Ferragosto,** which celebrates the feast of the assumption of Mary.

Palazzo Mezzacapo

Corso Reginna 71; tel. 089/814-204; www.comune. maiori.sa.it; gardens 8:30am-11pm daily; free

Once the home of the marquis Mezzacapo, an influential noble family of Maiori, this beautiful palazzo is now home to the town's Comune (city hall), library, and archive; the palazzo occasionally hosts art exhibitions and events. Elements from the 18th-century structure are still visible, such as the ornate frescoed ceilings, which can be seen in the spaces used for exhibits. The lovely garden to the left of the palazzo is planned in the shape of the Maltese cross, the eight-pointed cross that is the symbol of Amalfi; it is designed to reflect the members of the Mezzacapo family, who had ties with the Order of the Knights of Malta. The garden features fountains, roses, and other seasonal flowers and offers a fine view up to the Collegiata di Santa Maria a Mare.

BEACHES

If you enjoy the buzz of a busy beach scene, head to the main beach in town. Otherwise, enjoy exploring some of the smaller beaches nearby or head down the coast to Erchie, a small seaside village that is technically part of Maiori.

Maiori Beach

Amalfi Coast Rd. (SS163)

Stretching from the port to a historic watchtower on the eastern side, Maiori has the longest beach on the Amalfi Coast at over 0.5 mi (almost 1 km) long. The beach is split nearly in two by the river that runs down the valley. It's lined with a host of beach clubs to choose from, and many hotels have private beach areas for their guests. There are also small free areas along the beach, including the westernmost side near the port. By Amalfi Coast standards, the beach is quite sandy rather than pebbly, and the water is clear and lovely for swimming. The services available and pleasant conditions make this beach a good choice for families.

Salicerchie

SS163, 0.75 mi (1.2 km) east of Maiori

Just beyond Maiori's distinctive watchtower is a tiny beach tucked away in a semicircular bay that gave the beach its name. It can be reached by following a staircase of about 160 steps leading down from the Amalfi Coast Road, which is right above the western side of the beach. There are some small grottoes near the beach for good swimmers and explorers to discover. Because parking is not available near the steps to the beach, it's best to arrive by SITA SUD bus (catch the bus bound for Salerno); the closest stop is at the Torre Normanna watchtower. Continue on foot about 500 ft (150 m) east to find the steps down to the beach. From the center of Maiori, the walk is about 0.6 mi (1 km) and 20 minutes east along the Amalfi Coast Road.

Cavallo Morto

SS163, 1.75 mi (2.8 km) east of Maiori

This incredibly scenic beach is set in a little bay with clear turquoise water. A sheer rock cliff soars from the beach up to the Amalfi Coast Road high above. This pretty spot is accessible only by sea, and it's a popular spot for boats to drop anchor. If you rent a boat or hire a private boat excursion along the Amalfi Coast, stop here to dive into the stunning water and explore the beach.

Marina di Erchie

Erchie

Overlooked by most travelers, the seaside village of Erchie (err-KEY-eh) has a beautiful beach with all the services needed for a relaxing day by the sea. It's a scenic setting with the 16th-century watchtower **Torre Cerniola** set on a rocky peninsula nearby. Though it's well off the beaten path for day-trippers, Marina di Erchie is a popular beach in the summer, thanks to the gorgeous clear water and convenient parking lots. From Maiori, the best way to reach Erchie is via the public SITA SUD bus. Catch the bus in the direction of Salerno along the lungomare in Maiori and ask to get off in Erchie. The stop for Erchie is along the Amalfi Coast Road, and from there you follow the narrow Via Provinciale road about 0.4 mi (700 m) downhill to reach the beach. The center of the beach is occupied by a handful of beach clubs (stabilimenti balneari), and the extreme ends of the beach offer small free beach areas. For a comfortable day at the beach with sun beds, umbrellas, a changing room, and beach services, head to **Lido Edelvina** (Via Capo Tomolo, Erchie; 8am-6:30pm daily May-Sept.; from €20 for two sun beds and one umbrella).

SPORTS AND RECREATION
Boat Rentals
Capone Servizi Marittimi
Lungomare Amendola; tel. 089/853-895; www.caponeservizimarittimi.it; Apr.-Oct.; group tours from €40, half-day (4-hour) self-drive rental €130

The coastline between Maiori and Erchie is one of the most beautiful untouched stretches of the Amalfi Coast. With tiny beaches and grottoes to discover, it's ideal for exploring with a self-drive boat or on a guided boat excursion. Capone Servizi Marittimi offers small boats that can be rented without a license by the hour, as well as small-group and private boat tours along the Amalfi Coast and to Capri. The Minicrociera (mini cruise) is a pleasant 4-hour small-group tour along the coastline with an optional stop to visit the Grotta dello Smeraldo (Emerald Grotto) in Conca dei Marini.

Amalfi Outdoor Experience
meeting point: Via Giovanni Amendola, Maiori; tel. 331/315-9177; www.amalfioutdoorexperience.com; Apr.-Oct.; from €69 pp

For a fun day on the water, join a kayak tour to experience the beauty of the Amalfi Coast from the sea. This small group tour (maximum 12 people) starts in Maiori and passes Minori, historic watchtowers, a natural waterfall in Marmorata, and Atrani before reaching Amalfi and then returning to Maiori. Snorkeling experiences can also be combined with kayaking.

FESTIVALS AND EVENTS
Carnival
Maiori port and lungomare; Sun. and Tues. before Ash Wed.

Maiori comes to life after the winter season with a massive citywide celebration for Carnevale (Carnival), which takes place the Sunday and Tuesday before Ash Wednesday. Groups in Maiori build massive handmade floats, with colorful designs often inspired by historic or mythical characters or contemporary figures, that are paraded down the waterfront along with costumed bands and locals. There are also games, mini amusement park-type rides for kids, and stalls selling candy and toys along the waterfront.

Festival of Santa Maria a Mare
Collegiata di Santa Maria a Mare and various other locations; Aug. 15

The biggest event of the year in Maiori centers on the Collegiata di Santa Maria a Mare and the celebration of the town's patron saint. This is the peak of summer in Italy, as it is also **Ferragosto** (Feast of the Assumption of Mary), a public holiday celebrated throughout the country. All this means busy beaches, big crowds, and religious events. In Maiori you'll find special masses around the holiday, as well a procession through town followed by a huge fireworks display set off from a barge on the sea after dark.

FOOD AND ACCOMMODATIONS

Maiori has plenty of dining options. Along the waterfront and the main street, Corso Reginna, there are bars and bakeries; eateries for a light lunch, pizza, or seafood; and places that buzz after dark and are ideal for an aperitivo or drinks.

Ristorante Pizzeria Nettuno

Via Gaetano Capone 1; tel. 089/877-594; nettunoristorante@live.it; 12:45pm-3:30pm and 7:45pm-11pm daily June-Sept., 12:45pm-3:30pm and 7:45pm-11pm Thurs.-Tues. Oct.-May; €10-25

With a great setting right on the sea at the eastern edge of the beach, this restaurant and pizzeria is an excellent choice for local specialties and pizza. The pasta dishes are generous, and the pizza—with a slightly thicker crust than is common in the area—can also be made larger than the standard personal size, which is great for families or sharing.

Torre Normanna

Via D. Tajani 4; tel. 089/877-100; www.ristorantetorrenormanna.com; 12:30pm-2:30pm and 7pm-10:30pm daily May-Sept., 12:30pm-2:30pm and 7pm-10:30pm Tues.-Sun. Feb.-Apr. and Oct.; €18-32

If you like the idea of dining in a 13th-century watchtower as the waves crash below, you'll enjoy the setting of this restaurant, with its sweeping views of the coastline toward Amalfi. Run by the four Proto brothers, Torre Normanna showcases their passion for local ingredients and love of tradition as well as experimenting with new flavors. Reservations are recommended.

Hotel Botanico San Lazzaro

Via Lazzaro 25; tel. 089/877-750; www.hbsl.com; mid-Apr.-Oct.; €395 d

If you enjoy truly unique hotels, the Hotel Botanico San Lazzaro—set above Maiori and immersed in a garden setting—is the place for you. Set in a 19th-century home belonging to the Cimini family (who are still the owners today), this five-star boutique hotel is one of a kind: It's surrounded by gardens full of everything from lemon trees to exotic plants. The 20 rooms and suites are thoroughly modern while maintaining an old-world feel, and all offer beautiful panoramic views. The two-level Garden Suite immersed in a beautiful garden is especially lovely. With a spa, pool, two gourmet restaurants, and a bar all on-site, this hotel has everything you need. Set above Maiori, the hotel is reached by a panoramic elevator.

INFORMATION AND SERVICES

Info Point

Lungomare near Corso Reginna; 8am-1pm and 3pm-8pm daily Apr.-Oct.

This little kiosk is a handy spot to stop for local information and assistance in English as well as bus tickets and details on special events. It's located along the lungomare, across the street from the sea, not far from Corso Reginna.

GETTING THERE

By Car

Maiori is located at the base of a wide river valley, 3.5 mi (5.7 km) east of Amalfi and about 12.4 mi (20 km) west of Salerno on the **Amalfi Coast Road (SS163).** To reach Maiori by car along the Amalfi Coast Road, the drive is about 40 minutes from **Salerno,** 20 minutes from **Amalfi,** and 1 hour from **Positano.** From **Ravello,** follow **SS373** down to where it meets the Amalfi Coast Road at Castiglione and take a left to continue along the Amalfi Coast Road to Maiori. From **Naples,** take the **A3** highway south, exit at Angri Sud, and follow signs for Valico di Chiunzi. Continue along the **SP2a** road through Tramonti and down the valley to Maiori. The drive from Naples to Maiori takes about 1 hour 20 minutes.

By Ferry

Travelmar (tel. 089/872-950; www.travelmar.it; €3-15 per person) operates ferry services to Maiori from Amalfi, Atrani, Minori, Cetara, Vietri sul Mare, Salerno, and Positano seasonally April-early November. Times and schedules vary by departure point, but ferries generally run about every hour 8:30am-7pm daily. The ferry ride from Salerno to Maiori takes 30 minutes, while from Positano it is 25 minutes to Amalfi, where you'll change ferries, and then 15 minutes to Maiori. From Amalfi and Cetara it's about 15 minutes, and it's only 5 minutes from Minori to Maiori. Tickets are available online in advance, or via the Travelmar app.

To reach Maiori from Capri or Sorrento, **Alicost** (Salerno; tel. 089/227-979; www.alicost.it; €25.50 per person) is the ferry service you want. There's usually only one trip per day, so check the schedule in advance. Plan for the journey from Capri to Maiori to take about 1 hour 40 minutes.

By Bus

Maiori is on the public **SITA SUD** (tel. 089/386-6701; www.sitasudtrasporti.it; from €1.40 per person) bus line from Amalfi to Salerno as well as a line that connects Maiori to Tramonti, Nocera, and Cava de' Tirreni. Buses stop in Maiori at several points along the waterfront. To reach Maiori by bus, the journey is about 20 minutes from Amalfi, 55 minutes from Salerno, and 20-40 minutes from Tramonti, depending on where you depart. From Ravello and Positano, you first have to arrive in Amalfi by bus, then transfer to the Amalfi-Salerno line.

If you're traveling from the Naples airport to Maiori, **Pintour** (tel. 081/879-2645; www.pintourbus.com; €20 adults, €10 under age 13) offers an affordable bus service seasonally April-early November. Catch the bus at the terminal located outside the arrivals hall at the airport. The bus stops at Pompeii and along the Amalfi Coast, including three stops for Maiori, at Erchie, at the crossroads of the SP2a road, and near the port at Via Giovanni Amendola 41. It's a good idea to book your tickets in advance on Pintour's website. The trip from the airport to Maiori takes about 1 hour 30 minutes.

GETTING AROUND

Maiori is a comfortable town for walking and exploring because it is largely flat. The Amalfi Coast Road runs through town, and between the road and the beach is a wide and tree-lined sidewalk called the lungomare (waterfront), which is a popular place to stroll along the sea. Midway along the waterfront, the **Corso Reginna** begins at the Amalfi Coast Road and runs perpendicular to the Amalfi Coast Road up through the town. Corso Reginna is Maiori's main shopping street; it is also pedestrian-only and a great place for walking. To the east of Corso Reginna is the intersection where the SP2a road to Tramonti meets the Amalfi Coast Road.

Although it's part of Maiori, the frazione of **Erchie** is about 5.5 mi (8.6 km) east along the Amalfi Coast Road. To get here by public transport, take the SITA SUD bus in the direction of Salerno and get off in Erchie after about 10 minutes.

You'll find a small paid public **parking lot** by the beach in Maiori at the intersection of Corso Reginna. There's also paid parking along the north side of the Amalfi Coast Road as it runs through Maiori.

Cetara

A town of unexpected charm and deep traditions, Cetara is a wonderful example of just how much there is to discover on the Amalfi Coast. In a relatively isolated valley along the coastline between Vietri sul Mare and Maiori, the town is beautifully preserved with historic buildings along the seafront, a beach scattered with colorful fishing boats, and a maze of streets opening onto piazzas where locals chat and children play.

Here the sea is everything and never seems far away. Cetara has the best-equipped fishing fleet on the Amalfi Coast that is still active in the Mediterranean, with the specialty being tuna. The town is also known far and wide for anchovies, and even if you think you don't care for them, you've got to at least try one: It's a culinary experience not to be missed! Generations of Cetara's fishermen have brought in hauls of these tasty tiny fish that have been a delicacy since ancient Roman times.

For a base on the Amalfi Coast full of charm and off the well-worn path, consider a stay in Cetara, which is also connected to the rest of the coastline by ferry service.

ORIENTATION

Many travelers catch only a glimpse of this beautiful town and its brightly colored church dome from the Amalfi Coast Road (SS163) as they're driving through, which is a real shame. If your time is limited, stop for a stroll along the town's main road, **Corso Garibaldi,** which leads from the **Piazza San Francesco** down to the port and beach; it's one of the prettiest stretches along the coastline. **Via Marina** runs along the town's main beach over to the base of the **Torre di Cetara** watchtower. However, to visit the tower, you'll need to follow the Amalfi Coast Road to the eastern edge of town, as the only entrance is directly from the road. From Piazza San Francesco, Corso Garibaldi goes under the bridge of the Amalfi Coast Road and continues up into town and the **Piazza Martiri Ungheresi,** where more shops and accommodations are located.

SIGHTS
Torre di Cetara
Corso Umberto I 4; tel. 089/262-911; www.torredicetara.it; hours vary; free

Rising above the eastern edge of the beach, the town's historic watchtower dates to the 14th century. A close look reveals multiple layers built one on top of the other over the centuries. The original cylindrical part of the watchtower is closest to the sea, with a larger square-shaped section added later. The top two levels were added at the end of the 1800s. Today, the tower houses a museum that highlights local artists and the town's history and provides a venue for temporary exhibitions. During exhibitions the tower is sometimes open extended hours. Visitors get a rare chance to see the interior of one of the Amalfi Coast's historic watchtowers, while enjoying a fine view overlooking the town.

Chiesa di San Pietro Apostolo
Via San Giacomo; hours vary; free

Dedicated to Cetara's beloved patron, San Pietro Apostolo (Saint Peter), this beautiful church boasts an eye-catching green and yellow majolica tiled dome that is reminiscent of the Chiesa di Santa Maria Assunta in Positano. Though the church dates to 988, it has been remodeled and restored multiple times over the centuries. Today the neoclassical facade has a set of bronze doors, created in 2005 by Italian sculptor and painter Battista Marello. The doors depict Saint Peter and Saint Andrew, both fishermen, surrounded by a swirling net full of tiny fish, a nod to the longstanding fishing tradition that is part of

1: arriving in Cetara by ferry **2:** Marina di Cetara

local life. The interior, a single-nave floor plan with side chapels, boasts a late baroque design with rich decor. Tucked away on the side of the church is a bell tower dating to the 1300s. The church is usually only open during mass.

Chiesa di San Francesco d'Assisi

Piazza San Francesco; open only on special occasions; free

Sitting on a small piazza just below the point where the Amalfi Coast Road winds through the center of town, this convent dates to the end of the 14th century. Once a sprawling structure, a church is all that remains, while the cloister is now a lovely restaurant and other parts of the convent have become the town hall. The church itself dates from 1585, and though the facade is quite simple, inside the single-nave church are beautiful frescoes on the ceiling, from the 1600s. Although located right in the center of town, this small church is open only occasionally. Stop in the **Pro Loco,** the town's tourist information center, just across the street below Piazza San Francesco for more details on when it might be open.

BEACHES

Cetara is set along a particularly scenic and sparsely inhabited stretch of the coastline that is dotted with numerous tiny beaches stretching west toward Erchie and east toward Vietri sul Mare. Though these little beaches are certainly beautiful, the majority are only accessible by sea. The following beaches are right in Cetara or are accessible on foot.

Marina di Cetara

Via Marina

Cetara's main beach stretches out in front of the town's characteristic houses, from the parking lot beside the port to the rocky base of the Torre di Cetara. You'll find beach clubs with sun beds you can rent for the day and, closer to the parking area, a small spiaggia libera (free beach). With its beautiful clear water, colorful houses, and historic watchtower, Cetara's beach is one of the most picturesque of the entire coastline and is a great spot for swimming.

Porto di Cetara

Via Galea

This small beach is located on the western edge of Cetara, just outside the port. Walk all the way down to the end of the parking area at the port, and outside the pier is an angular beach that was created in the mid-1980s during construction after a massive earthquake. Over time, it has become a lovely beach that is often a little less crowded than the main beach, but it is a popular spot with locals for swimming. The beach is mostly accessible via a beach club but there is a small and rocky free area.

Spiaggia del Lannio

Via Lannio

A small walkway starts very near the Amalfi Coast Road-level entrance to the Torre di Cetara; follow it down to reach this secluded beach. Although it might be a little out of the way, that doesn't mean it's not popular. The sandy beach and clear water make this a hot spot in the summer. Find an open space on the free beach, the sandy side of the beach on the right, which gets sun longer into the afternoon, or head to the beach club for all the comforts, including sun bed rentals and dining options.

FESTIVALS AND EVENTS

Festival of San Pietro

Chiesa di San Pietro and various locations; June 29

The biggest event of the year in Cetara is the summer celebration for the town's patron San Pietro. After a special mass, a religious procession leads up to the top of town and then back down to the beach where boats are waiting for the traditional blessing. The procession then returns to the church, where the statue of the saint is run up the flight of steps leading to the church. A unique feature of the procession is that the statue of the saint is carried through town on a platform shaped like a boat, representing San Pietro's role as patron of fishermen. As the statue is taken through town, the bearers lilt back and forth to give the impression that the saint is navigating the sea. Afterward, the town is bustling with people—especially along the beach—waiting for the huge fireworks display.

Notte delle Lampare
Largo Marina and various locations; tel. 089/262-911; www.nottedellelampare.it; July; tasting menu €10

This food festival not only celebrates the town's famous anchovies but also re-creates a traditional fishing technique using large lights attached to a boat. This attracts the fish to the surface, where they are caught in a massive net. It's quite a piece of choreography to pull off, and it's possible to go out on boats and watch the fishing from up close. Boats depart from Cetara at 8pm and cost €10 per person (tickets available at the **Travelmar** ferry ticket booth in the port). The fishermen bring their catch to shore where it is served fresh on the beach. Buy a €15 ticket for the tasting menu and enjoy fish that's as fresh as can be. The celebrations and music continue well into the night. Dates vary depending on the lunar calendar, which plays an important role in anchovy fishing.

SHOPPING
Cetarii
Via Largo Marina 48/50; tel. 089/261-863; www.cetarii.it; 9am-1am Tues.-Sun. June-Aug., 9am-1:30pm and 3:30pm-9pm Tues.-Sun. Sept.-May

Just steps away from the beach, follow a small ramp up to reach this shop, where there's an excellent variety of local products on display. Naturally, the focus is on tuna and anchovies, and this is the spot to find jars of the tonno rosso (red tuna) caught in the Mediterranean, as well as anchovies preserved in oil and salt and the famous colatura di alici. Not sure what to buy, or just curious to try out some of the delicacies? Cetarii also offers product tastings, gourmet sandwiches, and an excellent aperitivo accompanied by locally made Amalfi Coast wines at outdoor tables just steps from the beach.

FOOD AND ACCOMMODATIONS

Gourmands will be glad to have Cetara on their radar. With such a strong fishing tradition, it's no surprise that the local restaurants specialize in fresh seafood, but the lemon trees and vegetables grown in the verdant valley above town play a prominent role in the town's cuisine as well. Here, the flavors of land and sea blend into unique dishes that you'll find only in Cetara.

Casa Torrente-Ristorante al Convento
Piazza San Francesco 16; tel. 089/261-039; www.alconvento.net; noon-3:30pm and 7pm-11pm Thurs.-Tues.; €12-30

As the name suggests, this restaurant is set inside a former convent right next to the Chiesa di San Francesco. It overlooks a pretty square along the town's main street. The space has been transformed into a comfortable dining area with a chic and welcoming feel that's enhanced by the friendly service. There's an outdoor dining area beneath the trees, overlooking the piazza. Chef Gaetano Torrente is the third generation bringing new flavors to the local traditions. The fresh tuna tartare is excellent, and you can't go wrong with the grilled seafood dishes, which highlight local tuna and anchovies. Try the genovese di tonno, a twist on the classic Neapolitan pasta sauce made with tuna instead of beef.

Ristorante San Pietro
Piazza San Francesco 2; tel. 089/261-091; www.sanpietroristorante.it; 12:30pm-3pm and 7:30pm-11pm Wed.-Mon.; €10-25

Cetara's gastronomic traditions are well-preserved in this popular restaurant. Here you can sample locally grown products in fresh seafood in dishes like the risotto with their own house-made tuna bottarga. The zuppa antica pompei is a local specialty made with farro (spelt wheat), fish, and colatura di alici.

⭐ Little Fish with Big Flavor: Cetara's Anchovies

Cetara's fishing tradition is embedded in the town's name, which is thought to come from a host of different Latin or even ancient Greek words all having to do with fishing. Whatever the exact origin, it's clear that fishing has been an important part of the economy for most of the town's history. Cetara's fishing fleet is still very active, and you'll spot both larger fishing boats and the colorful little wooden rowboats bobbing in the port. The specialties are tuna caught in the deeper waters of the Mediterranean and the popular alici (anchovies). Rich in omega-3, iron, and other nutrients, anchovies have long been a key part of the local diet.

Even if you think you're not keen on anchovies, give them a chance in Cetara. The tiny fish are filleted and prepared in a number of different ways, including marinated in vinegar or lemon, breaded and fried, used in a variety of pasta dishes, baked in the oven, and used as a pizza topping. You'll find alici prepared in many traditional ways on the menus in all of Cetara's restaurants.

colatura di alici made in Cetara

COLATURA DI ALICI

The most prized production is colatura di alici, a deep amber-colored oil made from pressing anchovies. This intensely flavored oil is thought to be the descendent of the ancient Roman garum, a creamy fish sauce created by salting and preserving fish, which was produced in Pompeii.

The process to create colatura di alici is passed down through generations of fishermen in Cetara, and many families have their own secret recipes. It starts with freshly caught anchovies placed in wooden barrels, called terzigni, and covered with salt. The fish are usually caught March-July so that the heat of the summer can help advance the maturation process. The barrels are weighted down and the anchovies are slowly pressed inside. Months later, a small hole is punctured in the bottom of the barrel to release the precious liquid, which has a super-concentrated fish and salt flavor.

The colatura di alici is traditionally ready at the beginning of December, when the **Festa della Colatura di Alici** takes place in town. The oil is then used to flavor the pasta and fish dishes customarily made on Christmas Eve. However, colatura di alici is used year-round to add extra flavor to everything from antipasti to pasta dishes and fresh vegetables.

WHERE TO TRY

In addition to the food shops and restaurants in Cetara, not to mention the annual festivals, there are a number of places to try the famous anchovies and anchovy oil. Here are a few that stand out:

- **Trattoria Da Maria, Amalfi:** Fried anchovies are a specialty here (page 94).
- **Pizzeria Resilienza, Salerno:** Try the signature Resilienza pizza with a parsley pesto, anchovies from Cetara, and fior di latte mozzarella cheese (page 158).
- **Il Principe e la Civetta, Vietri sul Mare:** The spaghetti al pesto vietrese combines anchovies with capers, sun-dried tomatoes, pine nuts, and another Amalfi specialty, lemon (page 147).

Vegan and vegetarian menus are available. Reservations are recommended.

Cetara Albergo Diffuso
Piazza Martiri Ungheresi 14/16; tel. 089/262-014; www.cetaraalbergodiffuso.com; €110 d

This hotel is diffuso: spread out in a variety of charming locations around Cetara's main piazza. However, with a central reception and breakfast room, as well as attentive service, it offers all the conveniences of a traditional hotel. There are seven guest rooms and three additional lodgings with mini kitchens available.

Hotel Cetus
Corso Umberto 1; tel. 089/261-388; www.hotelcetus.com; year-round; €349 d

Impressively built into the cliff side below the Amalfi Coast Road, this hotel offers a unique Amalfi Coast stay. Its 37 rooms all have beautiful sea views, and each includes a private balcony or terrace. Located a short 10-minute walk from the center of Cetara, the hotel has an on-site restaurant, bar, and access to the hotel's private beach, Tuoro Vecchio. The beach club offers sun beds, umbrellas, and a bar.

INFORMATION AND SERVICES

Pro Loco
Corso Garibaldi 15; tel. 089/261-593; www.prolococetara.it; hours vary

Located below Piazza San Francesco on Cetara's main road leading down to the beach, the town's friendly tourist office is a great spot to stop in for local information, specific details about openings of the smaller churches, and more. Information and assistance are available in English.

GETTING THERE AND AROUND

Located about 6 mi (10 km) west of Salerno, Cetara offers a more secluded feel while still well connected via ferry and bus to Salerno and other towns along the Amalfi Coast. Cetara is very small and enjoyable to explore on foot.

By Car

The **Amalfi Coast Road** winds through Cetara just above the center of town, passing over the town's main street, **Corso Garibaldi,** with a small bridge. Just east of the bridge, a narrow road called Via Francesco Prudente (marked with a sign for the Centro) splits off the Amalfi Coast Road and leads down to Corso Garibaldi to the left, and Corso Federici leading to Piazza Martiri Ungheresi to the right. To reach Cetara from **Salerno,** it's a 25-minute drive west on the Amalfi Coast Road. From **Positano** and **Amalfi,** follow the Amalfi Coast Road east to Cetara with a drive time of about 1 hour 25 minutes from Positano or 40 minutes from Amalfi. From **Ravello,** the drive takes about 50 minutes; first follow the **SS373** road down to the Amalfi Coast Road at Castiglione and then continue east to Cetara. Once you're in Cetara, hourly paid **parking** is available in a large lot next to the port.

By Ferry

Travelmar (tel. 089/872-950; www.travelmar.it; €4-15 per person) operates ferry services from Salerno, Vietri sul Mare, Maiori, Minori, Amalfi, Atrani, and Positano to Cetara. Ferry service is available seasonally April-early November, with departures roughly hourly 9am-6pm for Cetara; times vary depending on the departure point. A ferry ride from Salerno or Maiori to Cetara takes about 15 minutes, from Minori about 25 minutes, from Amalfi about 40 minutes, and from Positano about 65 minutes. For Positano and Atrani, you'll need to change ferries in Amalfi. Tickets are available online in advance, or via the Travelmar app.

It's possible to reach Cetara from Capri by the **Alicost** (Salerno ticket office tel. 089/227-979; www.alicost.it; €25.50) ferry service, which offers one departure for Cetara in the evening and one return to Capri in the morning. The ferry ride from Capri to Cetara takes a little less than 2 hours.

By Bus

Cetara is located along the public **SITA SUD** (tel. 089/386-6701; www.sitasudtrasporti.it; from €1.30) bus line from Amalfi to Salerno, and buses arrive about every hour, depending on the time of year. The main stop in town is right in the center, where Corso Garibaldi meets the Amalfi Coast Road. The bus journey from Salerno takes about 30 minutes and from Amalfi about 45 minutes. From Positano and Ravello, you first have to travel to Amalfi by bus and then continue on the Amalfi-Salerno line to Cetara.

To reach Cetara from the Naples airport, **Pintour** (tel. 081/879-2645; www.pintourbus.com; €20 adults, €10 under age 13) runs a convenient bus service seasonally April-early November. Catch the bus at the terminal located outside the arrivals hall at the airport. The bus stops at Pompeii and along the Amalfi Coast, including a stop right in the center of Cetara. Book your tickets in advance via Pintour's website. The trip from the airport to Cetara takes just over 1 hour.

Vietri sul Mare

From the pastel-hued buildings of Positano to the bright lemons and the brilliant shades of blue in the sea, the Amalfi Coast bursts with color. The most colorful spot of all just might be Vietri sul Mare, famous for its longstanding tradition of ceramics. As the easternmost town on the coastline, Vietri sul Mare is also known as the gateway to the Amalfi Coast. With its colorful ceramics shops spilling out onto the street, artistic heritage, and lovely views down the coast, it makes a thoroughly fetching impression.

While ceramics are the appeal for daytrippers passing through town, Vietri sul Mare has a refreshingly traditional and less touristy feel than many of the more famous towns along the Amalfi Coast. This lesser-known town is an excellent place to discover a different side to the Amalfi Coast.

ORIENTATION

Vietri sul Mare is divided into two areas, with the center of town at the top and Marina di Vietri at sea level, where you'll find a large beach or boats to reach smaller and more secluded beaches nearby. The multihued dome of the town's main church, the **Chiesa di San Giovanni Battista,** marks the center of town and is surrounded by a maze of little streets, including the main **Corso Umberto I.** That's where you'll find one ceramic shop after another, each more tempting than the last. Spend time trying to find your favorite and then head up into the mountains to **Raito,** a frazione of Vietri sul Mare, to visit the town's interesting ceramic museum to learn more about the history of ceramic production in the area.

SIGHTS

The ceramic shops in town are among Vietri sul Mare's main attractions. The town is practically a ceramic museum, with all the colorful murals and designs decorating the walls, houses, and shops.

Chiesa di San Giovanni Battista

Via San Giovanni 18; tel. 089/210-219; s.giovannidivietri@diocesiamalficava.it; 8:30am-12:30pm and 4:30pm-9pm daily

Vietri sul Mare's religious and artistic traditions blend beautifully at this church right in the center of town, with its bold blue, yellow, and green ceramic-tiled dome. Situated on a

1: Marina di Vietri beach **2:** Vietri sul Mare **3:** Le Vigne di Raito

tiny yet charming little piazza surrounded by houses, the entrance of the Chiesa di San Giovanni Battista features a round ceramic mural above the entrance showing San Giovanni Battista (Saint John the Baptist) against a backdrop of Vietri sul Mare. The mural dates from 1946 and replaced a rose window that was damaged during World War II. The church was originally founded toward the end of the 10th century, but the structure we see today dates to the last major restoration in 1732, in the baroque style. The single-nave church is decorated in a pale pink with ornate white stuccowork and lovely light that comes in from the large windows around the base of the dome.

Museo della Ceramica

Villa Guariglia, Via Nuova Raito, Raito; tel. 089/211-835; 9am-3pm Tues.-Sun., call in advance to confirm; free

If you love the ceramics on the Amalfi Coast and are curious to find out more about the history and traditions, head to Vietri sul Mare's Provincial Museum of Ceramics, located in Raito. The museum is situated in the Torretta Belvedere, an old tower on the grounds of the Villa Guariglia, a large estate now owned by the Province of Salerno. Opened in 1981, the museum tells the story of ceramic production in the Vietri sul Mare area with beautiful pieces of religious art and household items. There is also an excellent collection of pieces from Vietri sul Mare's 20th-century German Period; these are noted for their modern style and for the introduction of decorative themes inspired by the local landscape and traditions. A detailed brochure with information in English is available.

Le Vigne di Raito

Via San Vito 9, Raito; tel. 328/865-1452; www.levignediraito.com; reservation required; wine-tasting and tour from €55

Situated along a mountain slope in Raito, this vineyard is a labor of love for owner Patrizia Malanga. She fell in love with the area in 2001 when she began the intense work of recovering and restoring a 5-acre (2-ha) plot of terraced land. She set to work planting a new vineyard and creating wine that would be infused with the scents of the beautiful landscape. Since 2007, Malanga has been producing Ragis Rosso, a deep and rich red wine made with aglianico and piedirosso grapes. Later came Vitamenia, a dry rosato with notes of citrus. Since 2011, Le Vigne di Raito has been certified organic. Patrizia's hospitality makes you feel right at home during a visit to the vineyard. Stop by for a wine-tasting and tour that lasts about 2.5 hours, or stay longer for lunch or dinner after the wine-tasting and tour (4 hours, from €125 per person). You can also take a cooking class that highlights traditional local dishes like eggplant parmesan, homemade pasta, and local desserts (6-7 hours; €280 per person).

BEACHES

Marina di Vietri

Via Cristoforo Colombo

Vietri sul Mare's seaside frazione, called Marina di Vietri, has one of the most expansive beaches on the Amalfi Coast. While the beach was created naturally, its size is the result of a 1954 flood that washed massive amounts of mud down the valley from the mountains high above town. The beach is divided into two sections by the river Bonea, and both sides offer a large selection of stabilimenti balneari (beach clubs) as well as free areas. From the eastern side, you can get an especially good view of the **I Due Fratelli** rock formation, with two large rocks jutting out of the sea off the coastline; it is one of the symbols of Vietri sul Mare. The beach is popular in summer as it's the first large beach on the coast near Salerno. The water is great for swimming.

La Crestarella

Via Cristoforo Colombo 27

Surrounded by rocky cliffs, this small beach stretches out below the 16th-century Torre Crestarella watchtower just east of I Due Fratelli. During the summer, the beach is reached via a private entrance from Via Cristoforo Colombo to the beach club **La Crestarella** (Via Cristoforo Colombo 27; tel. 327/576-6591; www.torrecrestarella.eu; 9am-6:30pm daily May-Sept.; €30 for 2 adults, umbrella, and two sun beds). La Crestarella offers parking, sun bed and umbrella rentals, and a restaurant.

FESTIVALS AND EVENTS

With its large beach area, Marina di Vietri is a popular spot for concerts during the summer. Most events are seasonal and dates are posted locally. Check with the tourist office for any scheduled events during your visit.

Festival of San Giovanni Battista

Chiesa di San Giovanni Battista and various locations; June 24

On June 24 the town of Vietri sul Mare honors its patron, San Giovanni Battista (Saint John the Baptist), with a town-wide celebration. After mass in the evening, the statue of the saint is carried through town on a long procession accompanied by a marching band and the town's faithful. Find a spot in the small piazza in front of the Chiesa di San Giovanni Battista for a good view of the procession.

CERAMICS SHOPPING

Ceramics are naturally the focus for shopping in Vietri sul Mare, and the joy comes in the sheer abundance of choices. Though ceramic shops seem to be tucked away in every nook and cranny, you'll find the majority of shops along **Corso Umberto I** in the heart of town. Spend time exploring, visiting shops, and talking to the locals, and find the style that catches your eye. All the shops can help you arrange shipping services so you don't have to overload your luggage.

Ceramica Artistica Solimene

Viadotto Madonna degli Angeli 7; tel. 089/210-243; www.ceramicasolimene.it; 9am-2pm and 4pm-8pm daily May-Sept., 9am-6pm daily Oct.-Apr.

A visit to this ceramic factory is a must for ceramic or architecture enthusiasts, as it is one of Vietri sul Mare's—and perhaps the entire Amalfi Coast's—most distinctive buildings. The factory is literally covered in small circular orange and green tiles in a unique design that was created in the 1950s by Italian architect Paolo Soleri, who had studied with Frank Lloyd Wright in the United States. Inside you'll find a large selection of ceramics ranging from iconic designs featuring various animals to more abstract artistic pieces. You can also catch a glimpse inside the ceramic factory where artists are at work producing the famous Solimene ceramics.

Ceramica Pinto

Corso Umberto I 31; tel. 089/210-271; www.ceramicapinto.it; 10:30am-1:30pm and 3:30pm-7pm Mon.-Sat.

One of Vietri sul Mare's important ceramic-making families, the Pinto family have produced beautiful ceramics in the factory located along Corso Umberto I in the center of town since Vincenzo Pinto purchased the entire building in 1910. Today his granddaughter, Rosaura Pinto, continues the family tradition and runs the ceramic factory, which you can spot easily by the large ceramic murals decorating the walls. Stop in the showroom to see a display of their tableware, vases, lamps, tiles, and more.

Artemika

Corso Umberto I 63; tel. 340/428-7478; www.ceramicaartemika.it; 9am-1:30pm and 4pm-8pm daily

This small and colorful shop is full of tempting ceramics that are all created and produced by owner Enza d'Arienzo and her family. The designs are bright and modern with a touch of whimsy, and are hand-painted on everything from vases to candleholders, lamps, platters, decorative objects, and dishes. In the back of the shop, you'll likely see the ceramic production in process.

Zuma Ceramiche

Corso Umberto I 69; tel. 339/831-4991; www.zumaceramiche.it; 10am-1pm and 4pm-8pm daily

Ceramics in Vietri sul Mare

The Salerno area has a long tradition of ceramic production dating to the 5th century BCE thanks to natural clay caves. Archaeological excavations have revealed that vessels were produced to transport wine, oil, and other products even before Romans settled the area. But ceramic production began on a larger scale at the end of the 15th century when the local ceramic factories began working in a more industrial manner.

GERMAN PERIOD

Production ebbed and flowed over the centuries, with slower periods interspersed with moments when creativity flourished and brought new life to the ceramic factories. One of the most notable peaks is known as the German Period, which started in the early 20th century with the arrival of German artists and other Europeans, who brought with them new styles and influences, such as the Expressionism movement. The peak of this design period took place from the 1920s to the start of World War II.

ceramics in Vietri sul Mare

THEMES AND MOTIFS

Artists like Richard Dölker, Irene Kowaliska, Lisel Oppel, and Barbara Margarethe "Bab" Thewalt Hannasch, to mention just a few, developed a distinctive style as they experimented with new colors and found inspiration in the local people and the warm Mediterranean landscape. Everyday scenes like fishermen and women carrying water urns on their heads, local architecture, and elements of daily life served as colorful artistic inspiration. Even the humble and hardworking donkey was memorialized in clay, and has ever since been one of the ceramic symbols of Vietri sul Mare. The local ceramic style in Vietri sul Mare varies by artist but often involves bright Mediterranean colors like turquoise, yellow, and blue.

WHERE TO SEE AND BUY CERAMICS

Ceramic production continues today with a handful of ceramic factories, smaller shops, and individual artists who carry on this creative tradition on the Amalfi Coast. Simply stroll through Vietri sul Mare and you'll find one tempting shop after another.

- Both **Ceramica Pinto** and **Ceramica Artistica Solimene** (page 145) have long played an important role in the town's ceramic production and offer a large selection.
- Take time to visit smaller shops as well, such as **Zuma Ceramiche** (page 145), where local artist Lucia Carpentieri brings a modern and distinctive touch to traditional designs.

Inside this beautiful shop you'll find the work of ceramic artist and painter Lucia Carpentieri, who learned the craft starting at a young age from her father and talented painter Michele Carpentieri. With a style ranging from traditional landscapes and iconic Vietri sul Mare images to delicate floral designs and strikingly bold geometric patterns, there's something for every taste on display.

FOOD AND ACCOMMODATIONS
Il Principe e la Civetta
Via Giuseppe Mazzini 137; tel. 089/763-2201; www.ilprincipeelacivetta.it; noon-3pm and 7pm-11pm daily Apr.-Oct., noon-3pm and 7pm-11pm Mon.-Tues. and Thurs.-Sat., noon-3pm Sun. Nov.-Mar.; €15-25

Located in the center of Vietri sul Mare, this restaurant is tucked away in the former display galleries of the historic Ceramica Pinto factory. Beautiful ceramics and a spacious dining area are the setting for an excellent gastronomic experience. Choose from plenty of seafood options: The spaghetti al pesto vietrese is a house specialty made with fresh anchovies, capers, sun-dried tomatoes, pine nuts, herbs, and a touch of lemon. You'll also find meat and vegetarian options on the menu.

Ristorante 34 Da Lucia
Via Scialli 48; tel. 089/761-822; www.risto34dalucia.altervista.org; noon-3pm and 6pm-midnight Mon. and Wed.-Sat., noon-3pm Sun.; €14-30

Find this welcoming restaurant in a pretty little piazza tucked away in the center of town. During nice weather the outdoor tables are the place to enjoy excellent home-cooked dishes in a quiet setting. Seafood is prepared exceptionally well; try the spaghetti with fresh anchovies and cherry tomatoes.

Bed-and-Breakfast Palazzo Pinto
Via Giuseppe Mazzini 137; tel. 340/101-2255; www.palazzopinto.it; Mar.-mid-Jan.; €100 d

Surround yourself with the beauty of Vietri sul Mare's ceramics at this small B&B. The four double rooms feel like you're staying in a ceramic museum as they are designed with ceramics from the Pinto family ceramic factory, including decorative floors, fully tiled en suite baths, and gorgeous tables and lamps everywhere you look. The B&B is connected to the factory and is located in the center of Vietri sul Mare, off of Corso Umberto I.

Palazzo Suriano
Via Madonna Dell'Arco 30; tel. 089/234-450; www.palazzosuriano.it; €300 d

Situated in a beautiful palazzo from the 1700s and surrounded by terraced gardens, this property is a remarkable find. On the western side of Vietri sul Mare in a scenic spot below the Amalfi Coast Road, the beach at Marina di Vietri is accessible on foot by following a small road and about 40 steps. Six rooms, some with balconies and sea views, are decorated in a warm style that blends beautifully with the historic wood-beamed ceilings and frescoed walls. The public spaces, including a library with sea views, are all curated with antiques and historical and artistic touches. Enhance your stay with the hotel's exclusive cooking classes where you can learn how to prepare local dishes, the iconic limoncello liqueur, or pizza.

INFORMATION AND SERVICES
Pro Loco
Via Orazio Costabile 4; tel. 089/211-285; www.prolocovietrisulmare.it; 9am-12:30pm Tues.-Sun. May-Sept., 10:30am-12:30pm Fri.-Sun. Oct.-Apr.

Vietri sul Mare's tourist info point is located just above Piazza Matteotti and can easily be reached following Via XXV Luglio up to the small triangular piazza where the Pro Loco is set in a small well-marked building. The friendly English-speaking staff can offer information on Vietri sul Mare and getting around, and can help answer any Amalfi Coast travel questions.

GETTING THERE
By Ferry
Vietri sul Mare's ferry terminal in Marina di Vietri is small yet characteristically decorated with colorful ceramics. It is well connected to other towns along the Amalfi Coast by ferry service operated by **Travelmar** (tel. 089/872-950; www.travelmar.it; €4-15 per person) seasonally April-early November. Catch the ferry to Vietri sul Mare from Salerno, Cetara, Maiori, Minori, Amalfi, Atrani, and Positano with departures roughly hourly 9am-6pm; times and frequency vary depending on the departure point. A ferry ride from Salerno or

Cetara to Vietri sul Mare takes about 5 minutes, from Maiori about 25 minutes, from Amalfi about 45 minutes. From Positano or Atrani, you have to change ferries in Amalfi. Tickets are available online in advance, or via the Travelmar app.

Ferry service to Vietri sul Mare from Capri is operated by the **Alicost** (Salerno ticket office tel. 089/227-979; www.alicost.it; €28), with one departure for Cetara in the evening and one return to Capri in the morning. The ferry ride from Capri to Vietri sul Mare takes about 2 hours.

Keep in mind that the ferry terminal is not on the same level as the center of town. Plan on about a 15-minute walk between the terminal in Marina di Vietri and the center of town with the ceramic shops and sights. Or catch one of the local buses to reach the center of town instead of the uphill walk.

By Car

Vietri sul Mare is the eastern gateway to the Amalfi Coast. The town begins just west of the Port of Salerno and marks the starting point for the **Amalfi Coast Road (SS163).** From the lungomare and center of Salerno, follow **Via Roma (SS18)** west from the historic center. The road climbs above the port and in about 10 minutes leads directly to Vietri sul Mare. From **Positano** and **Amalfi,** follow the Amalfi Coast Road east to Vietri sul Mare. From **Ravello,** first drive down **SS373** to reach the Amalfi Coast Road at Castiglione before continuing east. The drive to Vietri sul Mare from Positano takes about 1 hour 45 minutes; it's about 50 minutes from Amalfi, and 1 hour from Ravello. If you're coming from **Naples,** take the **A3** highway south to the Vietri sul Mare exit, and expect a drive time of about 50 minutes.

By Bus

Vietri sul Mare is located along the **SITA SUD** (tel. 089/386-6701; www.sitasudtrasporti.it; from €1.30 per person) bus line connecting Amalfi to Salerno. Buses run roughly every hour 5:15am-9pm daily from Amalfi in the direction of Salerno, and 5:55am-9:30pm daily from Salerno toward Amalfi. The bus ride from Amalfi to Vietri sul Mare takes about 1 hour, while from Salerno it's about 15 minutes. To reach Vietri sul Mare from Positano and Ravello, first take the bus to Amalfi and transfer to the Amalfi-Salerno line. Buses stop at the western side of town at the start of the Amalfi Coast Road (SS163) across from Piazza Matteotti, and at the eastern side of town near the Ceramica Artistica Solimene building.

You can also take **Busitalia Campania** (www.fsbusitaliacampania.it; from €1.20 per person) lines 1 or 4 to get from Salerno to Vietri sul Mare. Bus line 1 runs every 30-60 minutes 7am-10pm daily. Bus line 4 runs about every hour 6:45am-11pm daily. The ride to Vietri sul Mare takes about 10 minutes.

To arrive in Vietri sul Mare from the Naples airport, **Pintour** (tel. 081/879-2645; www.pintourbus.com; €20 adults, €10 under age 13) offers a convenient bus service seasonally April-early November. Catch the bus at the terminal located outside the arrivals hall at the airport. The bus stops at Pompeii and along the Amalfi Coast including two stops in Vietri sul Mare: one near Piazza Matteotti at the start of the Amalfi Coast Road, and one at the crossroads leading up to Raito and Albori. It's a good idea to book your tickets in advance via the Pintour website. The trip from the airport to Vietri sul Mare takes about 50 minutes.

By Train

Vietri sul Mare is the only town on the Amalfi Coast with a train station. The **Vietri sul Mare-Amalfi station** is situated above the center of town and is serviced by local **Trenitalia** (www.trenitalia.com) trains from Salerno and Naples. Trains from Salerno depart every 30-60 minutes about 5am-9pm daily. The journey is about 8 minutes and costs €1.30. From Naples, trains depart every 30-60 minutes about 7am-10pm daily. The journey takes about 50-80 minutes and fares start at €5.10. There's an elevator near the station that goes down to Piazza Matteotti, or it's a 10-minute downhill walk following a winding cobblestone street to the center of town from the train station.

GETTING AROUND

The center of Vietri sul Mare, where all the shops are located, is relatively flat and walkable. To reach the Marina di Vietri, follow Via Orazio Costabile from Piazza Matteotti down through town to sea level. Along the way, don't miss the "Case Colorate" (colorful house) along Via Giuseppe Pellegrino in Marina di Vietri. This narrow street is lined with houses painted in bright shades of blue and decorated with ceramics.

By Car

The center of Vietri sul Mare is easy to navigate on foot, so if you have a car, you may want to leave it parked while you're here. Limited paid **parking** is available in Piazza Matteotti or in parking areas along the beach in Marina di Vietri. The six frazioni (hamlets) of Vietri sul Mare are scattered along the mountainside west of the center of town. To reach **Raito,** follow the Amalfi Coast Road west, and shortly you'll see a sign marking Raito and a turnoff to the right. This road, the **SP75,** winds up the mountain to Raito and takes about 10 minutes. Parking is available along the side of the street in Raito.

By Bus

The **Busitalia Campania** (www.fsbusitaliacampania.it; from €1.20 per person) bus lines connect Vietri sul Mare with Cava de' Tirreni and provide local bus service to the frazioni of Vietri sul Mare, and between the town center and Marina di Vietri. Look for line 68 to reach Marina di Vietri and Raito from the center of Vietri sul Mare. Buses run every 60-90 minutes 6:30am-8:30pm daily; the journey from the town center to Marina di Vietri takes 6-8 minutes, and to Raito takes about 8 minutes. Early June-early September, the line 63 bus runs between Marina di Vietri and the center of town every 30 minutes 7am-6:30pm daily; it is a comfortable way to reach the beach in Vietri sul Mare without the walk.

Salerno

Just beyond Vietri sul Mare, where the Lattari Mountains drop down to a flat plain, the city of Salerno stretches out along a large gulf. Set between two of the most beautiful coastlines in Italy—the Amalfi Coast to the west and the Cilento Coast to the south—Salerno is a vibrant and traditional southern Italian city. Despite its scenic setting and proximity to the Amalfi Coast, Salerno has an off-the-beaten-path atmosphere that appeals to many travelers. You can explore the medieval historic center, catch a show at the elegant Teatro Giuseppe Verdi, stroll along the waterfront, or visit the Castello di Arechi for a bird's-eye view over Salerno.

Salerno has a rich heritage dating to the early Middle Ages, when it was a flourishing Lombard principality that was noted for its culture and learning. This town was the birthplace of the Schola Medica Salernitana, the first medical school in the West. The history of Salerno can be seen in the city's impressive Romanesque cathedral dedicated to Saint Matthew, and in the Museo Archeologico Provinciale. Not far from Salerno you can uncover even more of the area's ancient origins while visiting the ruins of Paestum, where you'll find some of the best-preserved Greek temples in the world.

For travelers who enjoy a city vibe, a stay in Salerno is a great alternative to Naples. With a train station and port right in the center of the city, you'll have easy access to day trips to the Amalfi Coast, Paestum, Capri, and also to Pompeii and Naples. There's a wealth of history to uncover, and all the top spots in the area are just a train or ferry ride away.

ORIENTATION

Though Salerno is a large city, the top sights are primarily located in the historic center or along the waterfront (lungomare). An important shipping center, Salerno's large **port** on the western side of the city is where cruise ships dock, and ferry service for the Amalfi Coast and Capri departs from the Molo Manfredi at the **Stazione Marittima di Salerno.** From the port, the lungomare is a pleasant place to stroll along the sea and stretches to **Piazza della Concordia,** where you'll find another touristic port called the **Masuccio Salernitano.** This port offers more frequent ferry service to the Amalfi Coast.

Salerno's **train station** is about two blocks north of Piazza della Concordia. Roughly parallel to the lungomare, the **Corso Vittorio Emanuele** starts at the train station and continues west through the city to the **Piazza Sedile di Portanova.** From there, Via Mercanti leads into the medieval **centro storico** (historic center) of Salerno. The city's museums, most intriguing churches, and excellent shopping are all located along Corso Vittorio Emanuele and the historic center.

At the western end of the lungomare is a lovely park called the Villa Comunale, and next to it is the Teatro Giuseppe Verdi. The best way to get around Salerno is on foot, because as you visit the sights you can explore the maze of streets in the medieval city center, one of the most characteristic and charming spots in the city.

SIGHTS
Centro Storico

between Piazza Sedile di Portanova and Piazza Matteo Luciani, and between Via Roma and Via Torquato Tasso

The centro storico (historic center) of Salerno has origins dating to Roman times, around 197 BCE, when the city was founded as Salernum. A few remains of the ancient city can be seen at the Tempio di Pomona, ruins of a Roman temple, next to the Duomo, which is often the setting for art exhibits throughout the year. The centro storico as it appears today is largely the same as the medieval layout, with the main artery, the **Via Mercanti** (Merchant's Street), running from Piazza Sedile di Portanova past Via Duomo, leading up to the cathedral and past the Chiesa di San Pietro a Corte to where it disperses into a seeming labyrinth of even narrower streets. With its cobblestone streets and historic buildings, the centro storico is a lovely area to walk and explore, as many of the streets are lined with shops, cafés, and little restaurants.

Cattedrale di Salerno

Piazza Alfano I; tel. 089/231-287; www.salernosacra.it; 9:30am-6:30pm daily; €7

One of the architectural gems of Campania, the Cattedrale di Salerno, also called the Cathedral of San Matteo or the Duomo, was consecrated in 1085; it houses the relics of San Matteo (Saint Matthew). Behind the neoclassical facade lies a masterpiece of Norman architecture. Climb the steps and enter through the Porta dei Leone, a Romanesque portal flanked by two lions that leads into a grand atrium. Look up on the right to see the 12th-century bell tower, an impressive sight with its sturdy square levels and rounded top decorated with interlacing arches. Around the atrium runs a portico with a loggia above supported by antique columns. The impressive doors to the main portal to the church were made in Constantinople in 1099 and feature 42 decorative panels.

Step inside to find a soaring nave with baroque decor and two ambons from the 12th century covered in intricate mosaics. While many of the original decorations have been lost over time, in the transept the three apses have beautiful 13th-century Byzantine mosaics. The apse to the right of the altar is the **Cappella dei Crociati** (Chapel of the Crusaders), where crusaders would receive

Salerno

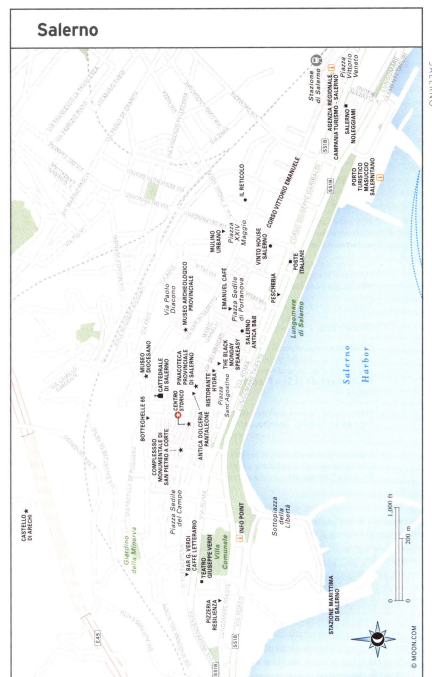

TOP EXPERIENCE

⭐ Walking Tour of Salerno's Centro Storico

At first glance Salerno can feel like a larger city, especially compared to the towns along the Amalfi Coast, but the centro storico is easily walkable, and its narrow streets, lined with shops and restaurants, have a pleasant, historical atmosphere. This walk covers about 1 mi (1.6 km) through the historic center, and depending on how long you stop at sights, is easily done in a couple of hours.

- Begin in **Piazza Sedile di Portanova,** a broad square that opens to the Corso Vittorio Emanuele to the east, and to the west the much narrower entrance to Via Mercanti.

- Follow **Via Mercanti** into the heart of Salerno's old town and what was historically the center of commerce. The street is still lined with elegant buildings and small shops to explore, with many fine jewelry and clothing stores.

- After a few blocks you will find the **Pinacoteca Provinciale di Salerno** on the left side of the street in the 17th-century Palazzo Pinto. Stop in to visit the collection of religious paintings and artwork inspired by the local landscape.

- Just beyond the Pinacoteca Provinciale di Salerno, take a right on Via Duomo and follow it about two blocks to reach the **Cattedrale di Salerno.** Climb the steps and enter to see the courtyard and visit the cathedral.

- If you're interested in more religious art, take a right outside the cathedral at Via Nicola Monterisi and walk until it ends at Largo Plebiscito, where you'll find the entrance to the **Museo Diocescano,** with a large collection of religious art and exquisitely carved medieval ivories.

- Return down Via Duomo and take a right on Via Mercanti until you reach an arched passageway. Continue straight under the arch on Via Dogana Vecchia. Take a right at Via dei Canali, and shortly after, on your right, you'll find Larghetto S. Pietro a Corte. Visit the **Complesso Monumentale di San Pietro a Corte** for a fascinating glimpse of centuries of Salerno's history.

- Return along Via dei Canali and take a right at Via Giovanni da Procida and follow to reach **Piazza Sedile del Campo,** a small piazza surrounded by historic palazzi. Elements of the fountain date to the 1600s; two metal sculptures of dolphins were added later.

- From here you can continue to explore the many small streets that crisscross the centro storico. Or continue along Via Portacatena until it reaches Piazza Matteo Luciani. Cross the street to visit the **Villa Comunale** gardens and relax on a bench for a peaceful break.

---

a blessing before sailing for the Holy Land. This is also the final resting place for Pope Gregorio VII, who died in exile in Salerno in 1085. In the apse to the left of the altar is the grand 15th-century monument to Margherita di Durazzo, Queen of Naples and Hungary. Follow the steps on the left down to the crypt, which is resplendent with its baroque decor, complete with polychromatic marble designs and shimmering golden elements. Here is where the relics of Saint Matthew are held, below the two central bronze statues of the saint by Michelangelo Naccherino from 1622. The ticket price gives you access to the Museo Diocesano, located around the corner from the Duomo.

Museo Diocesano

Largo Plebiscito 12; tel. 089/239-126; www.salernosacra.it; 9:30am-6:30pm daily; museum €5, combined entrance with Cattedrale di Salerno €7

Housed in the former seminary of the Cattedrale di Salerno, this museum contains an important collection of religious art spanning medieval times to the 20th century. The impressive collection is beautifully displayed on one level of the seminary and is well illustrated, with information in English available throughout the galleries. You'll see the fine collection of medieval ivory carvings and notable reliquaries and crosses, including one said to have belonged to Roberto il Guiscardo, ruler of Salerno in the 11th century. There's also a rich collection of paintings, antique coins, and illuminated manuscripts and scrolls.

Museo Archeologico Provinciale
Via San Benedetto 28; tel. 089/231-135; www. museoarcheologicosalerno.it; 9am-7pm Tues.-Sun.; free
Salerno's Archaeological Museum has a fine collection of finds that were uncovered in sites across the province of Salerno. Housed in the former abbey of San Benedetto, dating from the 11th century, the museum offers an evocative setting for visitors to admire the collection, including ceramics, bronze vases, jewelry, and objects from daily life that date from prehistoric to Roman times. A large part of the collection documents the Etruscan-Campano settlement of Fratte in the northern part of modern-day Salerno, where a large part of the museum's collection was uncovered. A special room is dedicated to the museum's important bronze statue of the Head of Apollo dating from the 1st century BCE. A detailed map and information are available in English.

Pinacoteca Provinciale di Salerno
Via Mercanti 63; tel. 089/258-3073; museibiblioteche@ provincia.salerno.it; 9am-7:45pm Tues.-Sun.; free
Set in the historic center along Via Mercanti, this museum is located in the 17th-century Palazzo Pinto. The collection is based on the original collection belonging to the Pinto family, predominantly paintings and other works from the 15th-18th centuries that were donated or saved from churches or other locations throughout the province. The collection comprises mainly religious works but also includes landscapes and portraits. Important works include 17th-century paintings by Giovanni Battista Caracciolo and 18th-century works by Francesco Solimena, two important Neapolitan artists. An interesting section is dedicated to foreign artists who were inspired to visit the area by earlier travelers on the Grand Tour, and features paintings and drawings of scenes from the Amalfi Coast. The museum also hosts special exhibits throughout the year. Information is available in English throughout the museum.

Complesso Monumentale di San Pietro a Corte
Larghetto San Pietro a Corte; tel. 347/688-9701; www. ambientesa.beniculturali.it; 10am-6:30pm Tues.-Sun.; free
This interesting church offers a glimpse into the many layers of Salerno's history and is well worth a visit while in the historic center. Located in a peaceful courtyard, the church was founded in the 8th century and constructed over what used to be Roman baths. A stone bell tower from the early 10th century marks the entrance to the archaeological site. Inside you'll find only the bare bones of the single-nave church as you follow a specially constructed platform that offers a view down through different moments of history. You'll see ruins of the baths from the 3rd century, remains of the early Christian church, and frescoes from the 12th century.

Villa Comunale
Via Roma and Via Lungomare Trieste; 8am-midnight Apr.-Oct., 8am-8pm Nov.-Mar.; free
Just next to the Teatro Giuseppe Verdi, along the waterfront, you'll find this public garden, constructed in 1874 as a quiet retreat around an 18th-century fountain called the Fontana del Tullio. Statues of political and military figures are dotted throughout the garden. During the Luci d'Artista Christmas light festival (Nov.-Jan.), the Villa Comunale is transformed into a magical garden with light installations, tunnels, and plenty of whimsy. For Luci d'Artista, the Villa Comunale may

be closed during the day and stays open until midnight.

Giardino della Minerva
Vicolo Ferrante Sanseverino 1; tel. 089/252-423; www.giardinodellaminerva.it; 9:30am-8pm Tues.-Sun. June-Aug., may close earlier Sept.-May; €3

In the early 1300s this garden was used as the botanical garden for the Schola Medica Salernitana medical school, which makes it one of the oldest in the world. Tucked away in a residential area, the gardens are spread out along the slope in the upper part of Salerno below the Castello di Arechi. After an in-depth restoration in 2001, the gardens were revitalized and replanted with many of the species mentioned in medieval medical texts. The gardens now have more than 380 species of plants and are as educational as they are beautiful, offering a peaceful spot with some lovely panoramic views overlooking Salerno and the sea.

Castello di Arechi
Via Croce; tel. 089/227-237; www.ilcastellodiarechi.it; 9am-5pm Tues.-Sat., 9am-3:30pm Sun.; €4

Situated in the mountains about 980 ft (300 m) above Salerno, this castle, dating to the 8th century, is named after the Lombard duke Arechi II, who transferred his kingdom from Benevento to Salerno. The castle was part of the Lombard defensive system and was added to over the centuries with each new invasion and change of power in Salerno. The on-site **Museo Medievale** (Medieval Museum) houses historical finds uncovered during various restoration projects on the castle, including collections of ceramics, glass vessels, iron and bronze objects from daily life, and weapons. Besides the fine views overlooking the city and Gulf of Salerno, the castle's rugged walls are an evocative setting to delve deeper into Salerno's history.

The castle can be reached from the center of Salerno on the **Busitalia Campania** (www.fsbusitaliacampania.it; from €1.10) line 19 that departs from the Via Vinciprova bus hub (about 15 minutes' walk east of the train station) and runs through the center of Salerno along Corso Giuseppe Garibaldi. Take the bus to the end of the line at Croce, which is at the entrance to the Castello di Arechi.

SPORTS AND RECREATION

Lungomare di Salerno
Lungomare Trieste

Stretching out nearly 1 mi (1.5 km), the lungomare (waterfront) of Salerno is a pedestrian-only garden lined with trees overlooking the Gulf of Salerno and Amalfi Coast. It leads from near the Villa Comunale gardens to Piazza della Concordia and is a popular spot to enjoy a passeggiata (stroll) with a lovely view with the ports of Salerno nearby and the beginning of the Amalfi coastline to the west.

ENTERTAINMENT AND EVENTS

Salerno has a lively entertainment scene. Even in winter, when the Amalfi Coast is sleepy, Salerno's **Luci d'Artista** Christmas light festival attracts large numbers of visitors during the holiday season.

Performing Arts
Teatro Giuseppe Verdi
Piazza Matteo Luciani; tel. 089/662-141; www.teatroverdisalerno.it; Sept.-May; concerts €10-25, operas and ballets €10-50

Inaugurated in 1872, Salerno's Teatro Giuseppe Verdi is an impressive venue for a concert or show. Inspired by the grand Teatro San Carlo in Naples, the architects created a smaller version that was then decorated by celebrated Neapolitan artists. The stunning interior of the theater, one of the few remaining original wooden 19th-century theaters in Italy, has been beautifully restored with its brilliant red seats, four tiers of boxes, shimmering gold details, and a ceiling mural depicting Gioachino Rossini surrounded by muses. The lyric, concert, and ballet season

---

1: approaching Castello di Arechi **2:** Villa Comunale gardens

runs September-May with a pause in the summer months, but there are often concerts and performances throughout the year.

Festivals and Events
Festival of San Matteo
Cattedrale di Salerno and various locations; Sept. 21

On the traditional day honoring San Matteo, September 21, Salerno celebrates its patron saint with a religious festival that is fittingly grand for an apostle and evangelist. The evening procession leads through the streets of the centro storico with statues of San Matteo, San Giuseppe, San Gregorio VII, and the saints Gaio, Ante, and Fortunato, accompanied by marching bands. As the procession makes its way through the narrow streets, balconies are packed with onlookers and the streets are lined with people leaving just enough room for the procession to squeeze through. For a moment, city activity pauses and time seems to stand still during this annual event that has taken place for centuries. After the procession a mass is given in the crypt of the Duomo, followed by concerts in Piazza Alfano I, Piazza Cavour, and Piazza Amendola. The finishing touch is a huge fireworks display after dark.

Luci d'Artista
Villa Comunale and the historic center; www.lucidartistasalerno.com; early Nov.-mid-Jan.

There are holiday lights, and then there's the Luci d'Artista, which takes Christmas lights to a whole new level. Starting in November, the entire city is decorated with elaborate light displays that transform an evening stroll through the city into a dreamlike experience. Every little street and piazza is covered with lights, each with its own theme. A soaring Christmas tree graces Piazza Sedile di Portanova, and the Villa Comunale is always decked out with an abundance of light displays, often shaped like animals and whimsical floral designs, to create an enchanted garden setting.

SHOPPING

Salerno's centro storico is a fun destination for shopping for a variety of larger Italian brands as well as locally owned shops. The best spots are along two main streets and the area around them. Keep in mind that Salerno keeps to traditional shop hours: Most will close for lunch around 1:30pm-4:30pm, and many are also closed Monday morning, especially in winter.

Luci d'Artista Christmas lights

Shopping Districts
Corso Vittorio Emanuele
Corso Vittorio Emanuele between Piazza Vittorio Veneto and Piazza Sedile di Portanova

Corso Vittorio Emanuele is the main shopping street in Salerno and runs from the train station at **Piazza Vittorio Veneto** to **Piazza Sedile di Portanova.** Lined with shops, cafés, and restaurants, this tree-lined street has limited traffic and makes a pleasant place to stroll. Along the way, you'll find larger department stores as well as Italian and international brand clothing, jewelry, and shoe shops.

Centro Storico
Via Mercanti starting from Piazza Sedile di Portanova and turning into Via Dogana Vecchia and Via Portacatena, plus cross streets like Via Duomo and many more

Cross Piazza Sedile di Portanova and look for the narrow entrance to Via Mercanti, the original merchant area of medieval Salerno. This is the entrance into the oldest part of the city, where you'll find smaller artisanal shops mostly selling clothing and jewelry. The maze of little streets that cross Via Mercanti are also fun to explore.

Clothing and Accessories
La Botteguccia al Duomo
Via Duomo 43; tel. 089/222-687; vm@viamercanti.sa.it; 9:30am-1:30pm and 4pm-8:30pm Tues.-Sat., 10am-1:30pm Sun., 4pm-8:30pm Mon.

La Botteguccia al Duomo is located across from the Cattedrale di Salerno and is a lovely artisanal leather workshop where you'll find handmade bags, shoes, and accessories.

Sciglio
Via Duomo 46; tel. 089/296-1785; www.scigliovintage.com; 10am-1pm and 5pm-8:30pm Tues.-Sun., 5pm-8:30pm Mon.

Stop in Sciglio for a beautifully curated selection of vintage clothing as well as illustrations, ceramics, jewelry, accessories, and artwork all created by a group of young and talented local artists.

Ceramics
DecoBirds Ceramiche
Via Portacatena 21/23; tel. 347/480-5208; 10am-1pm and 5pm-8pm Mon.-Sat.

Keep following Via Mercanti west as it changes into Via Dogana Vecchia and Via Portacatena, and don't miss exploring all the little cross streets, like Via Duomo, in the historic area. At the western end of the centro storico, look for DecoBirds Ceramiche, where owner Donatello Ciao is often at work hand-painting the cheerful ceramics on display; many pieces feature birds, which is his unique personal touch.

FOOD
Much larger than the towns along the Amalfi Coast, Salerno has a thriving restaurant scene with an abundance of options. You'll find excellent pizza with influences from nearby Naples, as well as trattorias to enjoy local specialties, and even a variety of international options. You don't have to walk far in the centro storico to find a host of restaurant options; there are also plenty of choices along the lungomare and near the Villa Comunale.

Seafood
Pescheria
Corso Giuseppe Garibaldi 227; tel. 089/995-5823; www.pescheriasalerno.it; 1pm-3pm and 8pm-11pm daily; €20-30

Head to this restaurant for fresh seafood served in a simple yet delicious way with a focus on the highest-quality ingredients. There's an excellent selection of raw fish. While the specialties vary depending on what's fresh, this is a great spot to try spaghetti with riccio (sea urchin) if available.

Regional Cuisine
Botteghelle 65
Via Botteghelle 65; tel. 089/232-992; www.botteghelle65.it; noon-3pm and 8pm-11pm Mon.-Sat.; €6-12

One of the tastiest spots in Salerno, this little salumeria is the oldest in the city. Owner Pino Adinolfi, a certified wine, cheese, and olive oil specialist, is passionate about sharing the best flavors of Campania. Local wines and products are available to buy, or grab a seat and let Pino guide your dining experience. Try a Tagliere Degustazione to sample local cured meats and cheeses or try some of their daily specials, which are also available for takeaway.

Ristorante Hydra
Via Antonio Mazza 30; tel. 089/995-8437; www.ristorantehydra.com; lunch noon-3pm Fri.-Sun., dinner 7pm-11:30pm daily; €20-75

Just off of Via Mercanti, this is a fine spot for lunch or dinner. With a beautiful minimalist decor, the restaurant offers the opportunity to dine inside or outside in their garden setting, right in the historic center. The menu is creative and highlights both seafood and meat; their grilled menu is a highlight, as is the wine list with over 500 labels.

Mulino Urbano
Piazza XXIV Maggio 12; tel. 089/214-6836; www.mulinourbano.it; 7am-midnight Mon.-Fri., 7am-1am Sat., 8am-midnight Sun.; €6-18

Much more than a bakery, although you can pick up excellent fresh bread and pastries, the menu at Mulino Urbano highlights regional fare and also includes pizza. With a lovely outdoor seating area, it's a great place for a tasty break, light lunch, or even just drinks while exploring the historic center.

Pizzeria
Pizzeria Resilienza
Via Santa Teresa 1; tel. 347/607-3735; www.resilienza.pizza; 12:30pm-3pm and 7:30pm-midnight Mon.-Sat., 7:30pm-midnight Sun.; €5-10

Located near the Villa Comunale gardens and with a pleasant outdoor dining area, this pizzeria was created in 2013 by Gennaro Coppeta with a focus on locally sourced and organic ingredients. Very popular with locals, you'll find a delicious selection of pizzas to choose from as well as traditional dishes on the menu. The classic pizza Margherita with organic tomatoes is perfection, or try their namesake pizza, Resilienza, with a parsley pesto,

anchovies from Cetara, and fior di latte mozzarella cheese.

Bakery
Antica Dolceria Pantaleone
Via Dei Mercanti 75; tel. 089/227-825; www.dolceriapantaleone.it; 8:30am-1:45pm and 4:30pm-8pm Mon. and Wed.-Sat., 8:30am-1:45pm Sun.; €2-4

Right in the historic center, this bakery was founded in 1868 and is still the spot to try classic Campania desserts as well as Salerno specialties. You'll catch the sweet scent even before you arrive at the entrance to what was once a church. For something very local, try the scazzetta, a brilliant red-hued cake with chantilly cream, wild strawberries, and a strawberry glaze. Or try the dolce della strega (witch's dessert) flavored with Strega liqueur made in Benevento, a city inland in Campania.

NIGHTLIFE

Salerno's nightlife scene keeps the centro storico and lungomare buzzing well after dark. On Via Roma from Via Antica Corte to the Villa Comunale, you'll find about every type of bar and restaurant.

Bar G. Verdi Caffè Letterario
Piazza Matteo Luciani 28; tel. 320/897-2096; barverdi1910@yahoo.it; 6:30am-2pm and 4:30pm-12:30am daily Sept.-July, 6:30am-2pm and 4:30pm-12:30am Mon.-Sat. Aug.; €3-6

Located across the street from the Teatro Giuseppe Verdi, this café has been a hub of creativity since it opened in 1910. Inside, you'll find photos of the artists who have visited, which is a tradition that continues today during the theater season. The eclectic decor and quirky style are the perfect setting for a literary café that also hosts weekly events that range from music and theater to book presentations and children's programs. There's even a small independent bookstore inside. They roast their own beans, so this is the place for coffee lovers. You'll also find organic teas, fresh juices, and homemade desserts as well as wine and cocktails.

The Black Monday Speakeasy
Via Mazza 26; tel. 348/263-7594; 9:30pm-3am daily; €10-20

This unique speakeasy offers incredibly creative and sophisticated cocktails and drinks, a vintage vibe, a friendly local setting, and frequent live music performances. While open year-round, this is a cozy spot to warm up with a drink after seeing the holiday Luci d'Artista lights. Look for the black door with the lion-head knocker for the entrance.

Emanuel Café
Corso Vittorio Emanuele 234; tel. 089/221-112; midnight-2am daily; €6-15

Set on one of Salerno's most vibrant and busy pedestrian-only streets, this café is a popular spot for an aperitivo or after-dinner drink thanks to its fine selection of cocktails and drinks. You'll also be tempted by a menu that changes monthly with a choice of sandwiches and salads for a light lunch or first and second courses for something more substantial.

ACCOMMODATIONS
Il Reticolo
Via Giovan Angelo Papio 14; tel. 089/995-8585; www.ilreticolobebsalerno.it; €75 d

In the historic center about a 10-minute walk from the train station, this B&B offers four bright rooms, each named after a town in the area that is featured in a panoramic photo in the room. The building has an elevator and two wheelchair-accessible rooms. Private parking is also available for a daily fee.

Vinto House Salerno
Via Adolfo Cilento 13; tel. 393/907-5795; www.vintohouse.com; €80 d

For a stay in Salerno with a creative touch, this boutique hotel is beautifully designed in every detail with the atmosphere of an art gallery—fitting since the owner's photography is on display, with changing exhibits throughout the hotel. Each of the four rooms has a distinct vibe and is exquisitely designed and decorated. Located just around the corner from Corso Vittorio Emanuele and just a short walk from the port and train station, it's an ideal central setting in the heart of Salerno.

Salerno Antica Bed-and-Breakfast
Via Masuccio Salernitano 8; tel. 328/331-1881; www.salernoantica.com; €90 d

With an ideal location just off of Piazza Sedile di Portanova, this lovely B&B is set in a historic palazzo dating to the 1400s. The building has been remodeled and has an elevator. The three large rooms are all beautifully appointed, and owner Daniele Abbondanza is on hand to help with information and suggestions. This is a wonderful find right in the heart of Salerno's historic center.

INFORMATION AND SERVICES
Tourist Information
Agenzia Regionale Campania Turismo-Salerno
Piazza Vittorio Veneto; tel. 089/209-5340; www.agenziacampaniaturismo.it; 9am-6pm Mon.-Sat., 9am-2pm Sun.

With a kiosk conveniently located outside the Salerno train station, this info point is a great spot to get information on the entire area, including the city of Salerno and the Amalfi Coast. The English-speaking staff can help with detailed info, events, and transportation in the area. There is also a tourist info point across the street from the southeast corner of the Villa Comunale (Via Lungomare Trieste 13; tel. 089/231-432; 9am-2pm Mon.-Sat.).

Medical and Emergency Services
Ospedale San Leonardo
Via San Leonardo; tel. 089/671-111; www.sangiovannieruggi.it

Salerno's hospital is located about 5 mi (8 km) southeast of the historic center in the San Leonardo area of the city. The fastest way to reach it from the center of Salerno is to take the Tangenziale di Salerno highway just east of the train station south to the exit for Ospedale-San Leonardo; the hospital is directly at the exit. The drive is about

15 minutes, depending on traffic. It is a large hospital with a 24-hour pronto soccorso (emergency room). If you need **emergency services** to come to you, dial 118.

Postal Services
Poste Italiane
Corso Giuseppe Garibaldi 203; tel. 089/275-9749; www.poste.it; 8:20am-7:05pm Mon.-Fri., 8:20am-12:35pm Sat.

For letter- and package-mailing services, you'll find Salerno's main post office along the Corso Giuseppe Garibaldi in the city center. There's also a smaller post office near the train station (Piazza Vittorio Veneto 7; tel. 089/229-998; 8:20am-1:35pm Mon.-Fri.).

GETTING THERE
By Car
Salerno is east of the Amalfi Coast and is quite easy to reach from all towns along the coastline. From **Positano** and **Amalfi,** head east on the **Amalfi Coast Road (SS163);** Salerno is located just beyond Vietri sul Mare. The drive from Positano takes 1 hour 45 minutes, while from Amalfi it's about 1 hour's drive. From **Ravello,** first follow **SS373** down to where it intersects the Amalfi Coast Road and take a left to continue east until you reach Salerno. The drive time from Ravello is about 1 hour 15 minutes. From **Naples,** follow the **A3** highway south to the Salerno exit. From Naples to Salerno, plan for about a 1-hour drive.

By Train
Salerno's train station, the **Stazione di Salerno** (Piazza Vittorio Veneto), is conveniently located in the center of the city and is served by Italy's national train line, **Trenitalia** (www.trenitalia.com), as well as **Italo** (www.italotreno.it). There are local, regional, and high-speed trains to Salerno from cities across Italy, with trains arriving direct to Salerno or by transferring in large cities like Naples and Rome. From Naples, trains depart every 15-30 minutes or more frequently, depending on the time of day, about 5:30am-11:30pm daily. The length of the journey ranges 40-90 minutes, depending on the type of train, and fares start at €5.10.

From Rome, trains also run frequently (every 10-30 minutes) about 5am-11pm daily. The journey time varies greatly, depending on the type of train and the number of transfers. The fastest and most convenient trains are the Frecciarossa high-speed trains that travel from Rome to Salerno in about 2 hours. Fares vary, depending on the train type, number of changes, and season, but a direct Intercity train can start around €30 and takes about 3 hours. The piazza in front of the station is also a bus hub, and it's a short walk to reach the Porto Turistico near Piazza della Concordia for ferries.

By Bus
To reach Salerno by bus from the Amalfi Coast, **SITA SUD** (tel. 089/386-6701; www.sitasudtrasporti.it; from €1.30) runs a bus line from Amalfi to Salerno. Buses run roughly every hour 5:15am-9pm daily, and the journey takes about 1 hour 15 minutes. The bus passes through Atrani, Castiglione (Ravello), Minori, Maiori, Cetara, and Vietri sul Mare before arriving in Salerno. To reach Salerno from points west of Amalfi, such as Positano, first take the bus to Amalfi and then transfer to the Amalfi-Salerno line. From Ravello, take the bus to Amalfi and transfer to the Amalfi-Salerno line. Buses from the Amalfi Coast pass along the waterfront in Salerno, where you can get off at multiple stops as well as Piazza della Concordia before the bus arrives at the **Via Vinciprova bus hub,** about 15 minutes' walk east of the train station. For the center of Salerno, you'll want to get off along the waterfront or **Piazza della Concordia.**

From Naples, buses for Salerno depart from near the Piazza Immacolatella along the port about every 30 minutes 6am-9pm daily, and the journey takes about 1 hour 15 minutes. Note that the bus arrives at the bus hub at Via Vinciprova.

FlixBus (www.flixbus.it; from €6) offers 136 routes to Salerno from destinations all across Italy. The most central of the four stops in Salerno is the stop at **Piazza della Concordia**.

By Boat

Salerno's large port is divided into several areas. On the western side is the city's commercial port, where large cruise ships often dock. On the eastern side, not far from the train station, is the Porto Turistico, where ferries arrive from the Amalfi Coast. In the center is the Stazione Marittima di Salerno (Maritime Station), or Molo Manfredi, where ferries arrive from the Amalfi Coast, Capri, and the surrounding area.

Porto Turistico Masuccio Salernitano

Piazza della Concordia

Salerno's main port for ferries is the Porto Turistico, also called the Marina Masuccio Salernitano, located at Piazza Concordia. **Travelmar** (tel. 089/872-950; www.travelmar.it; €5-15) ferries arrive at the end of the pier from Vietri sul Mare, Cetara, Minori, Maiori, Atrani, Amalfi, and Positano. Ferry service is seasonal and runs April-early November. Departures are every 1-2 hours 9am-7pm daily, depending on the departure location, and the ferry ride from Positano to Salerno takes about 70 minutes. From Amalfi, it takes about 35 minutes, from Minori about 40 minutes, from Maiori about 30 minutes, and from Cetara about 15 minutes. Note that some Travelmar ferries arrive at Molo Manfredi instead of Piazza della Concordia. Tickets are available online in advance, or via the Travelmar app.

Stazione Marittima di Salerno

Molo Manfredi; tel. 800/115-110; www.salernostazionemarittima.it

Salerno's maritime station at Molo Manfredi is located on the western side of the port. Architect Zaha Hadid designed the Stazione Marittima di Salerno, with its sleek lines and sweeping roofline. **Alicost** (tel. 089/871-483; www.alicost.it; from €28 per person) ferries from Capri and Ischia arrive at this port, often stopping at Positano, Amalfi, Minori, Maiori, Cetara, and Vietri sul Mare along the way. Ferry service is available seasonally April-October, but exact start and end dates vary each year. From Capri there are usually one or two ferry services in the evening, and the journey is a little over 2 hours. Ferries only run from Ischia to Salerno during the peak summer months, mid-June-August or September, and the journey takes about 3 hours.

GETTING AROUND

Salerno's historic center is not that large, and the best way to get around is on foot. The majority of the city's main sights are very walkable. However, there are local buses that run along the town's main thoroughfares to speed up crossing the city.

By Car and Scooter

If you want to rent a car or scooter, many of the internationally known names like Hertz and Avis have offices near the Stazione di Salerno train station. Though traffic in Salerno is tame compared to nearby Naples, keep in mind that it is still a good-size city and you should be cautious, especially when navigating traffic on a scooter. Located just across the street from the train station, **Salerno Noleggiami** (Corso Giuseppe Garibaldi 63; tel. 089/252-579; www.salernonoleggiami.it; scooter from €45 per day, cars from €39 per day) offers daily and longer rentals of scooters and cars.

By Bus

Salerno's local buses are run by **Busitalia Campania** (www.fsbusitaliacampania.it; from €1.20). A large number of urban lines crisscross the city, along with lines to nearby towns like Vietri sul Mare. Many bus lines run along the waterfront of Salerno, from west to east on Lungomare Trieste and from east to west on Corso Giuseppe Garibaldi. Main stops along the waterfront and the centro storico are near the Villa Comunale. There are also several stops along Lungomare Trieste and Corso Giuseppe Garibaldi, along with Piazza della Concordia near the tourist port. Bus lines 4, 5, and 6 run frequently throughout the day, but if you're just moving around the center of Salerno to see the sights, nearly every bus that runs along the Lungomare Trieste and Corso Giuseppe Garibaldi will get you from one side of the centro storico to the other. Buses run frequently about 6am-11pm daily. Tickets need to be purchased before boarding and can be found in most tabacchi (tobacco shops), as well as some coffee shops and bars. Don't forget to validate your ticket after boarding using the machine usually located near the driver.

To reach the Amalfi Coast by bus, take the **SITA SUD** (tel. 089/386-6701; www.sitasudtrasporti.it; from €1.30) bus line from Salerno to Amalfi. From Amalfi, you can transfer to other bus lines to reach Ravello, Positano, and Sorrento. Buses depart from Via Vinciprova, with a stop in **Piazza Vittorio Veneto** in front of the train station as well as on Via Roma on the western edge of town, across from the Teatro Giuseppe Verdi. Bus tickets can be purchased in local tabacchi shops or via the Unicocampania app (www.unicocampania.it).

★ DAY TRIP FROM SALERNO: GREEK TEMPLES AT ANCIENT PAESTUM

Not far south of Salerno is one of Italy's most remarkable archaeological treasures, the ruins of the city of Paestum, with its incredibly well-preserved Greek temples. The site makes an excellent day trip from Salerno and the Amalfi Coast.

Parco Archeologico di Paestum

Via Magna Grecia 919; tel. 082/811-023; https://museopaestum.cultura.gov.it; site 8:30am-7:30pm daily, museum 8:30am-7:30pm Tues.-Sun., closed Jan. 1 and Dec. 25; archaeological site and museum €12 Mar.-Nov., €6 Dec.-Feb., family rates available

The ancient city of Paestum was founded by Greek colonists around 600 BCE as Poseidonia, a defensive outpost of Magna Graecia. Once surrounded by an impressive wall over 23 ft (7 m) tall with towers and four entry gates, parts of the original wall still exist, although not at the original height. Named after Poseidon, the Greek god of the sea, the colony was later conquered by the Lucanians, an Italic tribe on Italy's mainland, at the end of the 5th century BCE. Excavations

ancient ruins of Paestum

Paestum

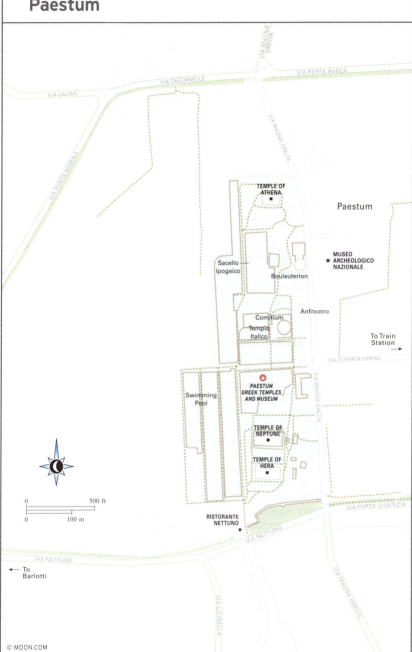

on the site have revealed how the Greek and Italic cultures blended and then continued to transform until, in 273 BCE, the city became a Roman colony called Paestum.

While visiting the archaeological site, you'll see both Greek and Roman ruins, and it is all worth exploring in detail. A modern-day road called **Via Magna Grecia** cuts through the center of the ancient city with the archaeological area on the west side and a museum on the east side. Enter through one of the two gates along the pedestrian-only section of Via Magna Grecia and the ancient city spreads out in front of you. What captures the most attention, however, are the three incredible temples, and for very good reason, as they are remarkable examples of Greek architecture.

Temples

The oldest on the site is the **Temple of Hera,** also referred to as the Basilica, located near the southern side of the city. Dating from around 560 BCE, it's the finest and best-preserved example anywhere of early Greek temple architecture. Just to the north is the **Temple of Neptune,** the largest in Paestum, which was built in the mid-5th century BCE. It's an essential example of a Doric-style temple, and although its name refers to Neptune, the later Roman name of the god of the sea, archaeological evidence has revealed it was likely dedicated to Hera or perhaps even Zeus. On the northern side of the site is the **Temple of Athena,** dating from around 500 BCE; this is the only temple in Paestum where excavations have revealed with certainty that the temple was originally dedicated to Athena. Along with the temples, you can see the ruins of the agora—later transformed into the Roman forum, which was the heart of the city—as well as part of an amphitheater, baths, and more.

Museo Archeologico Nazionale

Opposite the archaeological area across Via Magna Grecia, the Museo Archeologico Nazionale is a must during your visit to Paestum. The museum houses artifacts uncovered at Paestum, and rarely is it possible to see such a detailed portrait of an ancient city and how it changed over the centuries. Inside you'll find areas dedicated to the prehistory and protohistory of Paestum, a large area dedicated to the Greek and Lucanian city, and a section on the Roman period.

Don't miss the extensive collection of ancient vases produced in local workshops, the room dedicated to the carved stone metopes from temples in the area, and the many incredible tombs. The most famous is the Tomb of the Diver, the only known example of a Greek burial tomb with painted figures. Captivating in their simplicity and elegance, the painted scenes date from 470 BCE and show figures taking part in a symposium as well as the namesake scene depicting a man diving.

Note that the museum is closed Monday. During winter, December-February, admission for the archaeological site and museum is reduced to €6. The archaeological area is open until 7:30pm (last tickets at 6:30pm) year-round and is illuminated after dark. Seeing the temples lit at night is a special experience, but keep in mind that you'll need to stick to the illuminated trail only if you visit after sunset.

Food
Ristorante Nettuno

Via Nettuno 2; tel. 082/881-1028; www. ristorantenettuno.com; noon-3pm and 7pm-11pm Thurs.-Sat., noon-3pm Sun. mid-Mar.-Oct.; €12-20

Located right at the southern Porta Giustizia entrance to Paestum, this is a lovely restaurant to stop for lunch or dinner during your visit. Not only are you steps from Paestum, but there are views of the temples and archaeological site from the indoor and outdoor dining areas. The menu is broad and offers both seafood and meat-based specialties. In an area famous for buffalo mozzarella, this is an excellent spot to sample locally made cheese.

Barlotti

Via Torre di Paestum 1; tel. 082/881-1146; www.barlotti.it; café and shop 8am-8pm daily, restaurant noon-3pm daily; tours from €40, reservation required; €12-23

A visit to Paestum isn't complete without sampling the famous locally made mozzarella di bufala. Barlotti is one of the most noted producers in the area and they're conveniently located very near the archaeological park. Tours are available in English with advance booking and last about 30 minutes. Since the cheese is produced during the night, the tour shows the buffalo and explains the process with photos. You can also see the buffalo without a tour as they're located right next to the shop, café, and restaurant. Enjoy a tasting at the restaurant of their fresh and seasoned cheeses and buffalo milk products as well as unique menu items featuring buffalo meat. Or simply stop in for a coffee, yogurt, or gelato made with buffalo milk at the café.

Getting There

From Salerno, the easiest way to reach Paestum is to catch a local train operated by **Trenitalia** (www.trenitalia.com; 30 minutes; departures every 30-60 minutes 6am-9pm daily; from €3.10) and get off at the Paestum stop. Just across the street from the station is the Porta Sirena entrance to the archaeological area. It's a 15-minute walk through the park to reach Via Magna Grecia with the museum to the right and the archaeological area directly ahead. By car, the **SP175** road runs south from Salerno and along the coastline and leads to the site after a 50-minute drive.

Sorrento and the Sorrentine Peninsula

Itinerary Idea 170
Sorrento 172
Sorrentine Peninsula . . . 192

A picturesque setting atop a rocky terrace

along the rugged coastline, a well-preserved historic center, and a warm Mediterranean atmosphere are just a few of the elements that make Sorrento such a popular holiday destination. Add to that panoramic views of the Gulf of Naples and a convenient central location on the Sorrentine Peninsula, and you'll really understand Sorrento's appeal. Yet it's not until you're walking along the water's edge watching the colorful fishing boats bob in the harbor of Marina Grande, or examining the detailed inlaid woodwork on a music box that plays "Torna a Surriento" ("Return to Sorrento") that it begins to sink in. This is a city that draws you in with its colorful streets, refreshing limoncello liqueur, and those stellar views.

Highlights

Look for ★ to find recommended sights, activities, dining, and lodging.

★ **Food Experiences in Sorrento:** With citrus groves, local wines, and traditional recipes as well as the best wine bar with a view, enjoy delicious food experiences while in Sorrento (page 173).

★ **Cattedrale di Sorrento:** Visit Sorrento's cathedral, with its ornate baroque interior and exquisite examples of intarsia, the local tradition of inlaid woodwork (page 173).

★ **Centro Storico, Sorrento:** The historic center of Sorrento, with an urban footprint dating to ancient Greek and Roman settlements, is full of shops and dining spots (page 176).

★ **Museobottega della Tarsialignea:** This excellent museum is dedicated to Sorrento's long history of inlaid woodwork. You'll learn about every step of the process while exploring the extraordinarily rich collection (page 176).

★ **Marina Grande:** Incongruously named, the smaller of Sorrento's two ports is charming, with its traditional fishing boats lining the harbor and restaurants perfect for relaxed dining by the sea (page 180).

★ **Marina del Cantone:** Swim or sunbathe at this small, secluded beach near the tip of the Sorrentine Peninsula (page 193).

Sorrento and the Sorrentine Peninsula

Though Sorrento is the main draw for most visitors to the area, there are many scenic spots to explore. Discover panoramic vistas and secluded seaside villages where time seems to have stood still in Marina del Cantone, one of the most charming and lesser-known spots on the peninsula. Take some time to explore a bit off the beaten path, and you'll be rewarded with kayak trips into hidden coves, hikes among rugged terrain overlooking the sea with a mesmerizing view of Capri, and time to soak up the untouched natural beauty of the Sorrentine Peninsula.

ORIENTATION

The Sorrentine Peninsula juts out from the coastline south of Naples, separating the Gulf of Naples from the Gulf of Salerno to the south. Named after **Sorrento,** its largest and most populous city, the peninsula begins west of Castellammare di Stabia and stretches to the very tip of the peninsula, called **Punta**

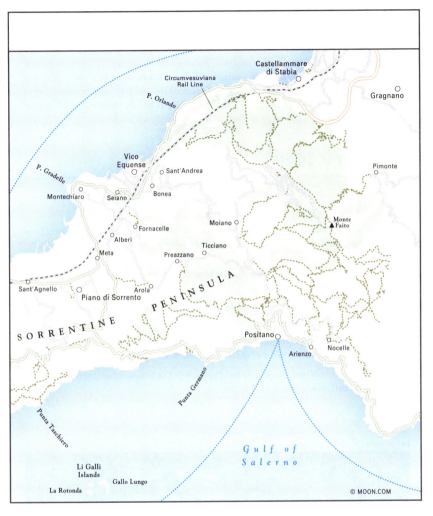

Campanella. This beautiful area is surrounded by the Area Marina Protetta di Punta Campanella (Punta Campanella Protected Marina Area). Along the southern coastline of the peninsula near the tip, you'll find the quiet mountain town of **Nerano** and its charming seaside village **Marina del Cantone.** To the east, a rugged and largely undeveloped mountainous landscape stretches out until you reach Positano, which is where the Amalfi Coast begins.

PLANNING YOUR TIME

Though many travelers spend only a day in Sorrento, there's much to enjoy with a longer stay in the city and the time to explore other highlights of the Sorrentine Peninsula. Two or three days is enough time to enjoy

Previous: Sorrento lemon garden; wine-tasting at Vrasa; Marina Grande.

Sorrento's fine small museums and historic center, but stay longer to enjoy local flavors as well as the beautiful natural surroundings. Sorrento is also well situated, with a central location and excellent transportation connections, to serve as your home base for a longer stay to explore the entire area. From Sorrento, you can hop on a ferry to Capri or Ischia to explore the islands. During the season (May-Oct.) there are also ferries connecting Sorrento with Amalfi and Positano on the Amalfi Coast; year-round, buses connect these areas as well. With the Circumvesuviana train line, it's also easy to reach Naples and the archaeological cities of Pompeii and Herculaneum.

Itinerary Idea

ONE DAY IN SORRENTO

Sorrento's historic center is quite compact and it's easy to explore the top sights on foot. Even if you only have a day to visit Sorrento, the city's relaxed Mediterranean charm makes it a favorite with many travelers.

1 Start your day in the charming **Piazza Sant'Antonino,** with a cappuccino or tea and some people-watching at D'Anton.

2 Visit **La Limonaia** to stroll through the citrus grove on a guided tour while learning about Sorrento's famous lemons.

3 Enjoy shopping and strolling through the historic center and the **Villa Comunale** gardens. Walk all the way to the edge for a sweeping panoramic view of the Gulf of Naples.

4 Stop for a lunch break to sample local specialties like lemon-infused seafood pasta at **L'Antica Trattoria** in the historic center.

La Limonaia

Itinerary Idea

ONE DAY IN SORRENTO
1. Piazza Sant'Antonino
2. La Limonaia
3. Villa Comunale
4. L'Antica Trattoria
5. Museobottega della Tarsialignea
6. Cattedrale di Sorrento
7. Stinga Tarsia
8. Marina Grande

5 Follow Via Accademia/Via San Nicola to the **Museobottega della Tarsialignea** to learn more about Sorrento's long tradition of inlaid woodwork artistry.

6 Head to the **Cattedrale di Sorrento** for a look at the intricate intarsia work around the entrance.

7 Pick up some beautiful woodwork of your own as a souvenir at **Stinga Tarsia.**

8 Stroll down to **Marina Grande** for a seafood dinner at Porta Marina, overlooking the tiny harbor of the quaint old fishing village.

Sorrento

Sorrento, the land long associated with the mythical sirens, has been captivating travelers for centuries. On a long, flat terrace of craggy coastline, where the cliffs drop straight to the sea, the Greeks and later Romans built a fortified town protected by its inaccessible setting and thick stone walls, parts of which are still visible around the city today. Although much of the historic center's urban plan dates back to the ancient Roman city of Surrentum, the Sorrento we see today is a refined modern holiday destination.

This friendly place, noted for its hospitality and Mediterranean charm, became a popular spot in the 18th century during the Grand Tour. Weary after a long journey through Italy, travelers found in Sorrento a true respite where the sweet scent of citrus blossoms mingled with the salty breeze. Elegant hotels like the Hotel Bellevue Syrene are the bastions of Sorrento's old-world style and elegance, with large terraces, gardens, and captivating views, still savored today by travelers from around the world. Visiting the city's small yet fascinating museums reveals centuries of artwork inspired by Sorrento, including the city's important artisanal craft of intarsia (inlaid woodwork). Tradition and hospitality combine beautifully in Sorrento; come discover for yourself the city's eternal allure.

ORIENTATION

Sorrento is a small city where all of the top sights and the charming historic center are easily explored on foot. Indeed, walking is a pleasure in Sorrento compared to much of the Amalfi Coast area because it is quite flat. However, the town's two harbors, **Marina Piccola** and **Marina Grande,** are both located below the city center, which sits on a cliff. **Piazza Tasso** is the heart of Sorrento, with the city's main thoroughfare, **Corso Italia,** running through it roughly east-west and parallel to the sea. Following Corso Italia east of Piazza Tasso leads to the train station at **Piazza Giovanni Battista de Curtis.** From Piazza Tasso heading west, Corso Italia is pedestrian-only for a long stretch until Via degli Aranci. Lined with shops, restaurants, pubs, and cafés, Corso Italia is a lively spot for shopping and dining during the day and especially for the evening passeggiata (stroll).

The **historic center** of Sorrento is north of Corso Italia, up to the steep cliff side overlooking the Gulf of Naples. It's a relatively small and highly walkable area stretching from Piazza Tasso on the east to Via Sopra le Mura on the west. An ancient urban plan dating back to the Romans, the historic center is a grid, with Via San Cesareo and Via Accademia/Via San Nicola running parallel to Corso Italia and intersected by many small cross streets, where you'll find excellent shopping and dining options. From Piazza Tasso, Via Luigi di Maio leads to **Piazza Sant'Antonino;** from there you can follow Via San Francesco to the Villa Comunale garden.

The names are pretty misleading: Marina Piccola (Small Harbor) is the largest port in town, where ferries arrive and depart for destinations in the Gulf of Naples, including Naples, Capri, Ischia, and the Amalfi Coast. Marina Grande (Large Harbor) is a small port west of the historic center with a charming atmosphere that's perfect for a quiet swim or dining by the sea.

SIGHTS
Piazza Tasso

Piazza Tasso, the bustling heart of Sorrento, was only developed in the mid-1800s, yet you'll find plenty of history here, starting with the **Santuario della Madonna del Carmine** (Piazza Tasso 158; tel. 081/878-1416; 7am-noon and 4:30pm-7:30pm daily), a cheery, yellow, 16th-century baroque church with elaborate white ornamental features on

★ Food Experiences in Sorrento

Not only is Sorrento a beautiful and convenient base for exploring the area, it's also a great spot for enjoying the traditional food and wine that makes Campania such a favorite foodie destination. From citrus groves to locally made wines and cocktails with a panoramic view of the Gulf of Naples, here are some of the best gastronomic experiences in Sorrento.

Nonna Flora cooking school

- **La Limonaia:** Right in the historic center of Sorrento, don't miss visiting this citrus grove to learn more about Sorrento's famous lemons. The tour includes a delicious tasting of lemon-based and other local products (page 182).

- **Nonna Flora Sorrento Family Kitchen:** Enjoy cooking traditional recipes in a fun and family setting at this cooking school created by local chef Anna Maione. Choose from Sorrentine classics, handmade pasta, or pizza classes available for small groups or privately (page 182).

- **L'Antica Trattoria:** Enjoy seafood pasta and an expansive wine list beneath a bougainvillea-covered pergola terrace in this family-run restaurant (page 188).

- **That's Panaro:** This small and friendly restaurant highlights local specialties made with carefully sourced ingredients from small producers on the Sorrentine Peninsula, the Cilento, and throughout Campania (page 188).

- **La Colonna Sunset Bar:** One of the best spots for drinks with a view in Sorrento—especially at sunset looking at the perfect view of Mount Vesuvius across the Gulf of Naples. With a "kilometer zero" philosophy, local ingredients inspire the drinks and menu items as much as the setting right at the edge of the cliff that drops straight down to the sea (page 189).

---

the eastern side of the piazza. Walk up **Viale Enrico Caruso** about a block and peer down at the **Vallone dei Mulini,** a deep valley that at one point extended all the way down to Marina Piccola, where you can spot the ruins of an old abandoned mill.

Piazza Tasso is named after poet Torquato Tasso (1544-1595), who was born in Sorrento. A statue of him stands in a little park in the piazza's southwestern corner, while in the center of the square is a statue of Sant'Antonino Abate, Sorrento's patron saint. The piazza has a buzzing vibe all day long. In the evening, grab a table at one of the bars surrounding the square and people-watch. Corso Italia, the city's main east-west road, runs right through the piazza; this means there's usually a lot of traffic here and along Viale Enrico Caruso to the south. The western side of Piazza Tasso, where the pedestrian-only part of Corso Italia begins, is less chaotic.

★ Cattedrale di Sorrento

Via Santa Maria della Pietà 44; tel. 081/878-2248; www.cattedralesorrento.it; 8am-8pm daily Apr.-Sept., 8am-noon and 4pm-7pm daily Oct.-Mar.; free

Along Corso Italia not far from Piazza Tasso, Sorrento's Cathedral is dedicated to San Filippo and San Giacomo (Saints Philip and James). The first cathedral in Sorrento was founded as early as the 10th century, but it was completely rebuilt in the 16th century after being damaged during the Turkish invasions in 1558. The beautifully preserved baroque

Sorrento

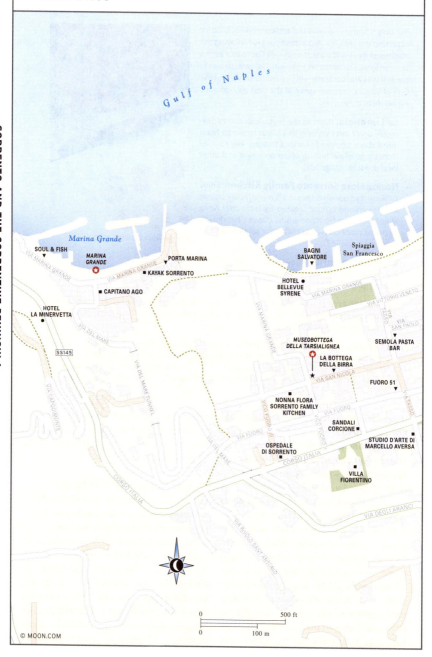

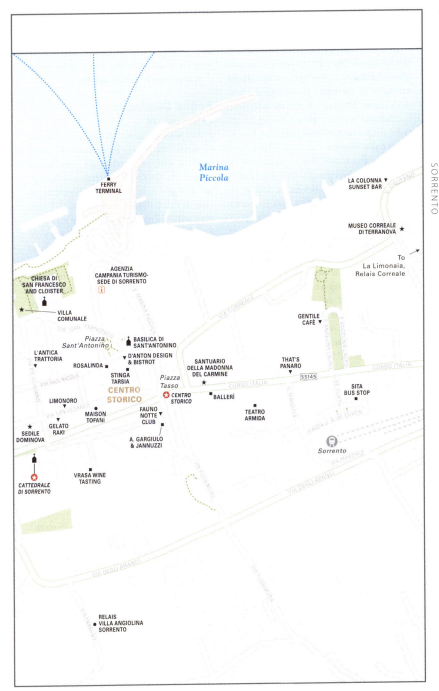

decorations inside the church date from an 18th-century restoration.

In fact, beyond the cathedral's simple neo-Gothic facade from 1924 there's a treasure trove of architectural design and remarkable examples of Sorrento's famed inlaid woodwork inside. The warm feel of the woodwork is enhanced by ornate golden ceiling decorations, deep-orange marble panels on the columns down the nave, and terra-cotta-colored detail on the arches that complement the wood accents throughout the church. Look for the detailed intarsia work inside around the wooden entrance, depicting stories from the church's history, as well as the Stations of the Cross along the two side aisles and the incredible choir stalls behind the altar. In the central nave near the altar stand two interesting elements: On the left is the Cattedra, the Bishop's throne, which dates from 1573 and incorporates columns and pieces from ancient Roman temples. Opposite is a marble pulpit, also from the 16th century, with a bas-relief sculpture depicting the baptism of Christ. Back outside, you'll spot the bell tower, constructed around the 11th century in the Romanesque style, located not far from the church.

★ Centro Storico

Via San Cesareo north to Villa Comunale and Via Marina Grande between Via Luigi de Maio and Via Sopra le Mura

Sorrento sits on a foundation dating to an ancient Greek settlement that later became an important urban center for the Romans, who called the town Surrentum. Their footprint is still evident in the grid of streets that make up the centro storico (historic center). Until the late 1800s, when Corso Italia was built, the main street of the historic center was Via San Cesareo, which corresponds to the ancient Greek decumano maggiore (most important street). Walking down the cobblestoned streets today, look for grand stone entrance portals where the noble families and wealthy merchants of Sorrento built stately homes. Meander through the small historic center, which is now home to a host of shopping and dining spots, as well as churches and historic sights. Largely pedestrian-only, this area is ideal for popping in and out of shops or stopping for lunch or dinner at one of the many restaurants with outdoor seating.

Sedile Dominova

Via San Cesareo 68

While walking down the historic Via San Cesareo, you'll pass by a dark-gray stone building with large arches. It's worth a stop to peer over the stone balustrade and through the wrought-iron fence at the beautiful arcade of this building. Built in the 15th century with a distinct Renaissance style, the building was originally a gathering place for the town's noblemen. The ornate frescoes with their elaborate architectural details date from the 18th century. Since 1877, the Sedile Dominova has been the home of the Società Operaia di Mutuo Soccorso (Workers Mutual Aid Society), a place for workers of Sorrento to gather and assist one another. Given the private nature of this building, it is most respectful for travelers to admire the frescoes and architecture from outside.

★ Museobottega della Tarsialignea

Via San Nicola 28; tel. 081/877-1942; www.museomuta.it; 10am-6:30pm daily Apr.-Oct., 10am-5pm daily Nov.-Mar.; €8, €5 over age 65 and under age 19

Dedicated to Sorrento's history of intarsia (inlaid woodwork or marquetry), this museum brings to life the traditional craft and houses a large collection of pieces by master crafters. It's set in the remarkable Palazzo Pomarici Santomasi, a five-floor building from the 1700s that was once surrounded by intarsia workshops. The building itself is a work of art and maintains many original features, including 18th-century hand-painted wallpaper, wooden vaults, frescoed ceilings, and unique architectural details like the spiral

---

1: Piazza Tasso **2:** Vallone dei Mulini near Piazza Tasso **3:** Basilica di Sant'Antonino **4:** Chiesa di San Francesco and Cloister

stone staircase that was uncovered during restoration.

The museum's collection is displayed in three sections that span five floors. The first is dedicated to showing Sorrento in the 1800s with paintings, prints, and photographs of the town. The next section highlights intarsia in Italy from the 1400s to the 1800s, while the third area is the largest and highlights the intarsia work of Sorrento artisans in the especially rich period of the 19th century. Along with the remarkable pieces of art and furniture with inlaid designs, the museum does an excellent job demonstrating the process with displays of work tools and materials, discussions of technique, and explanations about design and innovation. Exhibits include pieces by Sorrentine artists and artists from around the world. The museum has detailed information available in English, and pullout trays below many displays contain samples of wood and additional didactics that add to an excellent visitor experience.

Basilica di Sant'Antonino

Piazza Sant'Antonino 2; tel. 081/878-1437; 9am-7pm daily Apr.-Oct., 9am-noon daily Nov.-Mar., closed during mass 9am Mon.-Sat., 10am and 11:30am Sun. and holidays; free

Set on a small piazza, this church holds a special place in the hearts of Sorrento's faithful because it is dedicated to the town's patron saint, Sant'Antonino. Dating from the 11th century, the original church design included many elements found in ancient Roman temples and villas along the coastline. In the 17th century, the church was updated in a baroque style with gilded accents while the highly decorative friezes and stuccowork were added later in the 18th century. The crypt is set below the main altar area; it is accessed via two marble staircases and is supported by four marble columns from ancient temples. Even if the church is closed when you pass through Piazza Sant'Antonino, stop to peer through the gates to the right of the entrance and you'll spot a large whale bone. According to legend, this belongs to a whale that swallowed a baby who was then miraculously saved by Sant'Antonino.

Chiesa di San Francesco and Cloister

Via San Francesco 12; tel. 081/878-1269; 8am-noon and 3:30pm-8pm daily Apr.-Oct., 9am-noon and 4pm-7pm daily Nov.-Mar.; free

Founded in the 8th century as a Benedictine convent, this complex was later transformed into a Franciscan monastery, and today the church and adjacent cloister are still dedicated to San Francesco (Saint Francis). While the church was redecorated many times over the centuries, the current baroque design dates from 1690-1727 and seems infused with a touch of Sorrento sunshine with its warm yellow tone. Be sure to visit the peaceful cloister dating to the 13th century. It is a unique amalgam of architectural styles, with two sides featuring pointed interlaced arches and the other two with rounded arches, along with octagonal columns and pieces from ancient sites incorporated into the design. Generally open 8am-9pm daily, this romantic setting is a popular spot for weddings, concerts, and other events.

Villa Comunale

Via San Francesco; 7:30am-8:30pm daily Nov.-Jan., 7:30am-11pm daily Apr. and Oct., 7:30am-midnight daily May, 7:30am-1am daily June-Sept.; free

Just beyond the Chiesa di San Francesco, this small square is a popular spot, primarily for the panoramic view it offers across the Gulf of Naples. With shady spots to sit beneath the trees, you can relax a moment and savor the view across to Naples and Vesuvius. Walk right to the edge of the park and peer down the sheer cliff to Sorrento's beach area below. You can get down to the beach via a zigzag staircase, or pay a small fee to take the elevator (Sorrento Lift, Villa Comunale; tel. 081/807-2543; www.sorrentolift.it; same hours as Villa Comunale; one-way €1.10, round-trip €2).

The Intarsia of Sorrento

Sorrento's tradition of intarsia (wood inlay or marquetry) dates back centuries and is kept alive today by the town's artisans. The craft has been associated with Sorrento since at least the 16th century and flourished in the 19th century; an intarsia school was even founded here in the 1880s. The labor-intensive process involves creating mosaic-type designs by inlaying thin slivers of wood into a base. Different types of wood provide different colors, and the tiny pieces are hand cut to create elaborate designs, from landscapes to ornate floral and geometric patterns. Today you can find intarsia on music boxes, decorative boxes and trays, frames, and tables. Classic motifs include lemons and images of Sorrento and its surrounding landscape. These pieces make lovely keepsakes from your visit. You'll find fine examples of intarsia throughout Sorrento, but here's a guide to the highlights around town.

WHERE TO SEE AND BUY INTARSIA

- **Cattedrale di Sorrento:** Look at the panels surrounding the portal on the inside of Sorrento's Cathedral, as well as the early-20th-century choir stalls and the Stations of the Cross (page 173).

- **Museobottega della Tarsialignea:** This museum is entirely devoted to intarsia and the contribution Sorrento's artisans have made over the centuries. You can learn about the process and explore an impressive collection spread across five levels (page 176).

- **Museo Correale di Terranova:** While not exclusively focused on intarsia like the Museobottega della Tarsialignea, this museum has many inlaid woodwork pieces, including especially fine examples of tables and other furniture (page 179).

- **Stinga Tarsia:** Brothers Franco and Roberto Stinga are third-generation woodworkers whose music boxes, frames, and furniture feature inlaid designs that range from delicate floral motifs to modern geometric patterns (page 185).

- **A. Gargiulo & Jannuzzi:** Located just off Piazza Tasso, this family-run store has offered fine crafts, including intarsia, for six generations. Sometimes you can even see artisans at work creating inlaid woodwork designs (page 185).

Museo Correale di Terranova

Via Correale 50; tel. 081/878-1846; www.museocorreale.it; 9am-6pm Tues.-Sat., 9am-1pm Sun.; €15

Set in the historic residence of the noble Terranova family, this museum opened in 1924 thanks to the donation of the estate by Alfredo and Pompeo Correale, counts of Terranova. Their incredible gift offers a glimpse into Sorrento's history through an extensive collection of paintings from the 15th-19th centuries, extraordinary porcelain, furniture, and ceramics. The museum occupies four floors; on the ground level is a gallery dedicated to the Correale family with beautiful inlaid woodwork pieces and fascinating archaeological finds, including Greek and Roman statues and two sculptures from Egypt that were uncovered near the Sedile Dominova, which arrived in Sorrento during Roman times.

On the upper floors, paintings are displayed among fine examples of furniture, ceramics from China and Japan, and historic clocks, many of which are ticking away and periodically fill the galleries with their chimes. The Room of Mirrors is resplendent with its late-18th-century gold-embellished mirrors and consoles. The upper level is entirely dedicated to ceramics and porcelain created by the most significant European producers.

The museum's estate includes a citrus grove first planted in the 17th century that can now be visited in part at **La Limonaia** (Via Bernardino Rota 4; tel. 081/807-3265; www.lalimonaiasorrento.it; Apr.-Oct.; group tours from €30). Before leaving the museum, follow the uneven pathway that leads through a rough garden to the Terrazza Belvedere for a stunning and peaceful view across the Gulf of Naples.

BEACHES
Spiaggia San Francesco
Located just west of Marina Piccola and directly below the Villa Comunale, Sorrento's main beach area is not like most beaches in that there is a distinct lack of beach. While there is a small sandy area nearest the port and shoreline, most sunbathing space consists of specially built stabilimenti balneari (beach clubs) that are constructed on a series of jetties. The platforms have sun beds, umbrellas, facilities like changing rooms and showers, and access to the sea via steps. Located on the western side of the beach area, **Bagni Salvatore** (tel. 081/878-1214; www.bagnisalvatore.com; Apr. 25-mid-Oct.; sun beds €13, umbrellas €6) offers friendly service, tranquil water for swimming, and a unique glimpse of Roman ruins as a backdrop. Marina Piccola can be reached via the port area directly, or from the Villa Comunale if you follow the zig-zag staircase or take the elevator down.

★ Marina Grande
Via Marina Grande

Only a short walk from the center of Sorrento, the Marina Grande harbor feels worlds away from the hustle and bustle of the city center. You can stroll along the water's edge, enjoy a peaceful swim, or dine by the sea at a number of restaurants. Fishing is still an important local activity as well, as the piles of nets, colorful fishing boats, and fisherfolk at work would attest. For swimmers, there's a small sandy beach area in the middle of the harbor, or sunbathing platforms built out into the harbor. For a relaxing beach experience, head to the small beach at **Soul & Fish** (Via Marina Grande; tel. 081/878-2170; www.soulandfish.com; May-Oct.; sun bed and umbrella from €22), which offers sun beds, umbrellas, hot showers, and changing rooms in a spot that feels pleasantly hidden away. With direct sea access, you can swim with stunning views of the Gulf of Naples—and excellent food at the ready thanks to their casual terrace dining and beach service. You can reach the Marina Grande by car or bus along Via del Mare. However, if you opt to go on foot, a pleasant walk leads you down Via Marina Grande near Piazza della Vittoria. As you near the sea, you'll pass through a stone arch that dates to the 3rd century BCE and the Greek origins of the city.

WATER SPORTS
Capitano Ago
Via Marina Grande 92; tel. 081/188-62797; www.capitanoago.com; Mar. 15-Oct.; group tours from €85 pp, private tours from €900 for up to 12 people

See the Sorrento coastline up close, or enjoy Capri or the Amalfi Coast by boat from Sorrento, with Capitano Ago's small-group and private boat excursions. Small-group excursions have room for a maximum of 12 people and include options like a Capri tour, an Ischia and Procida tour, an Amalfi Coast tour with stops ashore at Positano and Amalfi, and sunset or fishing excursions. Private tours are available to the Amalfi Coast, Capri, Ischia, and Procida. SUP tours are available (€50 per person) or, for an adventurous experience, try parasailing on the Gulf of Naples (€65 per person).

Kayak Sorrento
Via Marina Grande 90; tel. 328/702-1422; www.kayaksorrento.com; Mar.-Nov.; group tours from €50 pp, private tours from €50 per hour

Spend time immersed in the natural beauty of the Sorrento coastline with a kayak excursion starting from Marina Grande. Guided 2-3-hour excursions are available following the coastline west toward the Bagni della Regina

1: Sorrento's Marina Grande harbor **2:** swimming platforms at Spiaggia San Francesco

Giovanna past caves, beautiful coves, and historic sites. Learn about the landscape with its legends and history while gliding along the sea. Group tours are available daily, usually departing early afternoon, or you can take a sunrise or sunset tour starting 2 hours before sunrise or sunset. Group tours can accommodate up to 35 people, or you can opt for a private guided excursion.

COOKING CLASSES AND TASTINGS

La Limonaia

Via Bernardino Rota 4; tel. 081/807-3265; www.lalimonaiasorrento.it; Apr.-Oct.; group tours from €30 pp

Visit this beautiful citrus grove in the heart of Sorrento for a closer look at the town's prized lemons. Many of the trees are over 100 years old, and you can see the special variety of lemons only grown in the Sorrento area, distinct from the varieties grown on the nearby Amalfi Coast. While the setting is peaceful, it's also fascinating to learn how lemons are grafted onto local wild orange trees, and about the unique growing and harvesting traditions. At the end of the guided tour, enjoy a tasting under a pretty lemon grove. The tour and tasting can be combined with lunch or dinner from the home-style restaurant. Cooking classes are also available (from €130 per person).

Nonna Flora Sorrento Family Kitchen

Via San Nicola 42; tel. 331/414-8009; www.nonnaflora.it; year-round, advance booking required; classes from €125 pp

Learn how to prepare traditional Sorrento dishes in a home setting with chef Anna Maione at her small cooking school named after her grandmother Nonna Flora. Passionate about sharing good food and recipes, Anna has created a setting that's cheerful and relaxed, with several classes to choose from, including the classics like gnocchi Sorrento-style or handmade pasta or pizza classes, and a food tour and cooking class. Lunch and dinner courses are available as well as private classes and events or family classes that are perfect for kids who love to cook. The cooking school is conveniently located in the historic center near the Museobottega della Tarsialignea.

Vrasa Wine Tasting

Via Santa Maria della Pietà 30; tel. 340/427-3961; www.vrasa.it; Wed.-Mon., advance booking required; wine-tastings from €95

Set in a peaceful garden just around the corner from Piazza Tasso, this is the spot to enjoy a wine-tasting accompanied by cheeses, cured meats, and other local products while learning about Campania wines from an expert sommelier. The relaxed setting, fine quality, and deft guidance make this an ideal experience for wine novices and enthusiasts alike.

HIKING

Sorrento Hiking

tel. 339/649-6418; www.sorrentohiking.com; group tours from €60 pp, private tours from €220 per group

Immerse yourself in the natural beauty of the Sorrentine Peninsula on a hiking tour to the coastline's most scenic spots. Sorrento Hiking is a group of guides offering tours throughout the region, but especially concentrated in the Sorrento and Nerano areas. Hikers won't want to miss exploring the rugged and untouched Punta Campanella area at the very tip of the peninsula. The views along the way are gorgeous enough, but at the end you'll be rewarded with a captivating view across to Capri. Or explore the lesser-known and very beautiful Ieranto Bay near Nerano for panoramic views and brilliant turquoise swimming coves. Many more options are available on the Sorrento coastline as well as the Amalfi Coast, possible as private tours or in small groups, with a variety of lengths to suit your hiking level and time. If time is limited, the sunset tour to Punta Campanella is especially enchanting.

1: La Limonaia **2:** Vrasa Wine Tasting **3:** Nonna Flora Sorrento Family Kitchen

ENTERTAINMENT AND EVENTS

Performing Arts

Sorrento Musical Show
Teatro Armida, Corso Italia 219; tel. 081/377-1850; www.cinemateatroarmida.it; May-Nov.; from €25 pp

Be swept away to the Sorrento of bygone days with a vibrant and entertaining Sorrento Musical Show that brings to life moments of Sorrento's history and tradition. Classic songs like "O Sole Mio" ("My Sunshine") and "Torna a Surriento" ("Return to Sorrento") are highlights. Check in advance for show schedules. Performances are staged at the Teatro Armida near Piazza Tasso.

Villa Fiorentino
Corso Italia 53; tel. 081/878-2284; www.fondazionesorrento.com; 10am-1pm and 4pm-7pm Mon.-Fri., 10am-1pm and 4pm-8pm Sat.-Sun.; exhibits from €5

Set back from Corso Italia, the Villa Fiorentino was constructed at the beginning of the 1930s for Antonino Fiorentino and his wife Lucia Cuomo, who had a successful business producing and selling fine embroidered fabrics. Surrounded by gardens with many varieties of roses and camellias, the villa is now home to the Fondazione Sorrento, a center for exhibits, concerts, and cultural events throughout the year. While special exhibits generally require a ticket, entrance to the villa's gardens is free, and it's a lovely spot to rest on a sunny day.

Festivals and Events

Festival of Sant'Antonino
Basilica di Sant'Antonino and various locations; Feb. 14

Sorrento's patron saint is celebrated every year on February 14 with a festival commemorating the day of his death in 625 CE. Special masses and a procession are held, where a silver statue of the saint is borne through the historic center. The procession, which usually takes place about 9am, not only is an important event for the town's faithful but also is seen as a harbinger of spring weather and a good year to come. Festival lights, stalls selling food and toys, and crowds of people coming to honor the saint create a lively atmosphere in Piazza Sant'Antonino and the historic center of Sorrento.

Easter Holy Week
historic center; Holy Week and Easter Sun.

Easter is one of the most important religious holidays of the year in Italy, and in most towns, it is celebrated with processions, especially during Holy Week (the week leading up to Easter Sunday). Sorrento has a series of processions that are among the largest and most moving in the region. The procession that takes place on Good Friday starts with the Processione Bianca (White Procession), which begins before dawn: Hundreds of people dressed in hooded white costumes carry the statue of the Madonna Addolorata (Our Lady of Sorrows) and other elements that commemorate the Passion of Christ. The torchlit procession moves through the streets of the historic center and finishes around dawn. That same night is Processione Nera (Black Procession), a tradition dating to the 1300s. It takes place after dark and represents the final moments of the Passion of Christ, with statues of Christ—after being taken down from the cross—and the Madonna Addolorata carried through the streets of Sorrento by people dressed all in black. With the torches flickering, sorrowful music, and thousands of faithful, the processions are incredibly poignant to witness.

Festival of Santi Anna e Gioacchino
Marina Grande; July 26-30

Taking place right at the peak of summer, the Festival for Sant'Anna and San Gioacchino in Marina Grande is an eagerly anticipated summer festival for the town's faithful and a fun event to experience for visitors. Centering on the Chiesa di Sant'Anna along the waterfront in Marina Grande, the religious and traditional events happen over several days, including a procession on July 26, musical concerts by the sea, games, and a fireworks display over the harbor on July 30.

SHOPPING
Woodwork and Artisan Crafts
Stinga Tarsia
Via Luigi de Maio 16; tel. 081/878-1165; www.stingatarsia.com; 9:30am-10pm daily Apr.-Oct., 9:30am-1:30pm and 4pm-8:30pm Nov.-Mar.

As third-generation woodworkers, brothers Franco and Roberto Stinga are passionate about continuing the family tradition of creating handcrafted furniture, decorative items, and their particularly fine music boxes. Along with the intricate carved patterns in a style dating to the 19th century, a selection of contemporary inlaid pieces with creative geometric designs bring a new look to Sorrento's traditional artisanal craft. You can also find a selection of beautifully restored antique pieces with intarsia.

A. Gargiulo & Jannuzzi
Viale Enrico Caruso 1; tel. 081/878-1041; www.gargiulojannuzzi.it; 9am-8pm daily

For six generations this store has been a source of artisanal crafts right on Piazza Tasso in the heart of Sorrento. There's a fine and large selection of inlaid woodwork, including enchanting music boxes, gorgeous furniture, and even chess sets. You'll also find other local crafts, such as ceramics, hand-embroidered linens, and laces. Occupying three floors, this shop invites you to take time to browse, and you might just see artisans at work. Check the open hours in advance, as the store may close later in the summer and slightly earlier in the winter.

Studio d'Arte di Marcello Aversa
Via Sersale 3; tel. 081/877 1535; www.marcelloaversa.it; 9:30am-1:30pm and 5:30pm-9:30pm daily Apr.-Oct., 9:30am-1:30pm and 4:30pm-8:30pm daily Nov.-Dec. and Feb.-Mar.

Tucked away on a small street behind the Cattedrale di Sorrento is the workshop and showroom of artist Marcello Aversa. Born in nearby Sant'Agnello, Marcello started in his family's business, which has made bricks for wood-fired ovens since the 16th century. However, at a young age he discovered his passion for sculpting with terra-cotta, especially in the Neapolitan presepe (Nativity) tradition. From impossibly tiny figurines to entire large grottoes filled with sculptures, he creates captivating landscapes full of movement and intricate detail that suggest hours upon hours of passionate work. Stop by and you'll often find Marcello at his workbench, focused on his next creation.

Shoes
Ballerì
Corso Italia 187; tel. 081/224-8970; www.ballerisorrento.com; 10am-10pm daily June-Sept., 10am-1:30pm and 4:30pm-9pm daily Oct.-May

Just a few steps from Piazza Tasso you'll find this cheerful shop with a collection of shoes designed by Gaia de Lizza and inspired by Neapolitan musical traditions, fine craftsmanship, and Gaia's family's heritage. Ballerì is a family affair, created by Gaia and her siblings Sergio and Solange. The classic ballerina flats are finely made, and the designs inspired by Sorrento with hand-embroidered lemons will add a sunny bounce to your step as you're reminded of beautiful moments in Sorrento.

Sandali Corcione
Corso Italia 28; tel. 338/349-3632; www.sandalicorcione.com; 9am-11pm daily Apr.-Oct., 9am-1pm and 4pm-8pm daily Nov.-Mar.

This lovely boutique is located along the pedestrian-only part of Corso Italia near the Villa Fiorentino and has specialized in handmade sandals and shoes since 1925. Quality Italian leather is used, and everything from classic designs to Swarovski crystal-decorated sandals are on display. The sandals and shoes can all be custom made.

Specialty Foods
Limonoro
Via San Cesareo 49; tel. 081/878-5348; www.ninoandfriends.it; 9am-10pm daily May-Sept., 9am-9pm daily Oct., 9am-8pm daily Nov.-Apr.

If you're strolling down the Via San Cesareo through the historic center, you'll notice that this bright shop seems to be permeated with lemons. Stop in to sample their locally made limoncello (lemon-infused liqueur) and a variety of other tempting products. The limoncello comes in many different bottle shapes and sizes, and there are lemon-filled candies and cookies, candied lemon and citrus peel dipped in chocolate, and so much more. For even more chocolate temptations, continue down the street to the **Nino & Friends Chocolate Store** (Via San Cesareo 67c; tel. 081/877-1693; 9am-10pm daily May-Sept., 9am-9pm daily Oct., 9am-8pm daily Nov.-Apr.).

Ceramics
Rosalinda
Piazza Sant'Antonino 9; tel. 081/877-1831; www.rosalindacampora.com; 9am-1pm and 4pm-8pm daily Apr.-Oct., hours vary Nov.-Mar.

Rosalinda Acampora is the creator of vibrant ceramics that decorate some of Sorrento's most stylish homes, restaurants, and hotels. From the iconic ceramic dishes with blue and red geometric designs to sculptures and home decor, here you'll find a selection of her work to bring home the colors of Sorrento.

FOOD
Seafood
Porta Marina
Via Marina Grande 25; tel. 349/975-4761; anna1984esposito@gmail.com; noon-3:30pm and 6pm-10:30pm daily Apr.-Oct.; €15-25

Set right along the water's edge in Marina Grande, this small and casual seafood restaurant is run by six brothers who are a fourth-generation fishing family dedicated to bringing in the best daily catch. The menu is determined by what they've caught and is written up on a board. You might find fried calamari or grilled octopus, spaghetti with clams, or grilled fresh local fish. With a glass of crisp white Campania wine and the view of Marina Grande harbor, it just can't be beat.

Soul & Fish
Via Marina Grande; tel. 081/878-2170; www.soulandfish.com; noon-3pm and 7pm-11pm daily; €18-30

For elegant yet relaxed seaside dining in Marina Grande, reserve a table at this restaurant that—as the name suggests—specializes in seafood. Start with the tuna with crunchy almond breading or the raw seafood appetizer and then follow with the daily catch or baccalà prepared with unexpected flavor combinations. There's an extensive wine menu and light and fresh desserts that you'll want to save room for at the end of the meal.

Regional Cuisine
Semola Pasta Bar
Via Torquato Tasso 53/55; tel. 081/1900-4857; www.semolapastabar.com; noon-2:30pm and 6pm-10pm Tues.-Sun. Mar.-Jan.; €13-23

While pasta is a fixture on nearly every menu in Italy, Semola Pasta Bar focuses on handmade pasta served in a variety of traditional and creative dishes. This is an excellent place to try the classic gnocchi alla sorrentina (potato and flour dumplings served with a tomato sauce enriched with mozzarella and basil), and there's a large selection of tasty vegetarian and gluten-free choices. The restaurant is located on a quiet street in the historic center with nice outdoor seating. Takeaway service is also available.

D'Anton Design & Bistrot
Piazza Sant'Antonino 3; tel. 081/807-5839; www.dantonsorrento.com; 10am-midnight daily Apr.-Oct. and Dec.; €6-20

A family interior design boutique transformed into a cocktail bar and bistro, D'Anton reflects one family's passion for good fresh fare and design. Stop in for coffee and you'll likely leave with the coffee cup or something else tempting. Enjoy brunch, a light lunch or dinner, or simply stop by for drinks. The limoncello

1: Villa Fiorentino **2:** seared tuna on arugula at Soul & Fish **3:** cocktails and aperitivo snacks at La Colonna Sunset Bar **4:** focaccia at That's Panaro

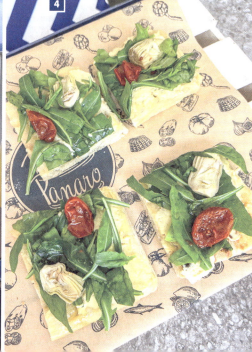

cocktail is a signature, made with a touch of Sorrento's famous lemon liqueur.

L'Antica Trattoria
Via Padre Reginaldo Giuliani 33; tel. 081/807-1082; www.lanticatrattoria.com; noon-11:30pm daily Mar. 20-Jan. 6; €30-42

With beautiful seating areas, including a bougainvillea-covered pergola terrace, this is a welcoming spot with a familial atmosphere for excellent dining in Sorrento. The menu has many tempting choices, but a favorite is the Tagliolini Antica Trattoria, a pasta dish served with a lemon cream sauce, red prawns, and lumpfish on creamed spinach. The large wine cellar, stocked with more than 30,000 bottles, is the work of owner Aldo D'Oria and his son Luca, both of whom are passionate about wine and fine dining.

That's Panaro
Corso Italia 206/A; tel. 340/291-0731; www.thatspanaro.com; 10:30am-11:30pm daily June-Oct., noon-6pm Mon.-Thurs., noon-11:30pm Fri.-Sun. Nov.-May; €4-12

A delicious food experience is waiting at this unique restaurant dedicated to serving local products in a fast and convenient way. All ingredients are sourced from small producers in the Sorrento area as well as other parts of Campania, with special attention to the Cilento. Fabulous vegetarian, vegan, and gluten-free options are on the menu. Located right on Corso Italia, there's a cute dining area outside, or pick up your order for takeaway. A panaro is a traditional wicker basket used for harvesting in Campania, and you can also order fully stocked baskets for boating and hiking experiences.

Vrasa
Via Santa Maria della Pietà 30; tel. 340/427-3961; www.vrasa.it; 7pm-11pm Wed.-Mon., noon-3pm and 7pm-11pm Sat.-Sun.; €16-70

Named for the traditional antique woodfire heaters once used to warm homes in the Naples area, this restaurant is a unique dining experience focused on fresh ingredients all grilled to perfection. The gastronomic experience can be paired with wine from the extensive list carefully curated by expert sommelier Francesco Gargiulo. Wine-tastings are also available in the beautiful garden surrounding the restaurant.

Gelato
Gelato Raki
Corso Italia 96 and Via San Cesareo 48; tel. 081/1896-3351; www.rakisorrento.com; 11am-1am daily; €2.50-7

Raki stands out as the top choice for gelato in the historic center thanks to the owners' focus on top-quality fresh and all-natural ingredients. The artisanal gelato is made on-site, and the mouthwatering selection often includes a refreshing limone gelato made with Sorrento's lemons. Try the soft-serve gelato too!

Cafés
Gentile Cafè
Piazza Angelina Lauro 20; tel. 081/314-2438; www.pastificiogentile.com; 7am-10:30pm daily; €2-8

Set in a covered arcade, this lovely coffee shop has a great selection of pastries and desserts as well as a savory breakfast items like avocado toast and omelets. Sandwiches as well as lunch and dinner options are also available. Created by the Pastificio Gentile pasta making company from Gragnano, near Sorrento, stop in to pick up locally made pasta and products to take home.

BARS AND NIGHTLIFE
Bars
Fuoro51
Via Fuoro 51; tel. 081/878-3691; www.fuoro51.it; 11am-midnight daily Apr.-Oct., 11am-midnight Tues.-Sun. Nov.-Dec. and Feb.-Mar.

For a relaxed setting and a selection of more than 800 wines, head to this enoteca (wine bar) in the historic center. There's an excellent choice of wines with a special focus on Italian producers, especially those of Campania. If you're interested in wine, this is a great place to try many Campanian wines that are challenging to find outside the area. A selection of cured meats, salami, and cheese trays as well as a full menu specializing in grilled meat and seafood are available to enjoy along with your wine.

La Colonna Sunset Bar
Via Aniello Califano 4; tel. 081/1902-2620; www.loreleisorrento.com; 11am-11:30pm daily Apr.-Oct.; €15-20

With one of the most scenic locations in Sorrento, this bar is beautiful any moment of the day but becomes enchanting as the sun sets across the Gulf of Naples. Relax with a creative cocktail and a stellar view or stay longer to sample from the menu, which includes a raw seafood platter, light snacks, and main course options.

La Bottega della Birra
Via San Nicola 13; tel. 340/591-6271; www.labottegadellabirra.it; 6pm-1am daily

Beer enthusiasts will enjoy this welcoming spot in the historic center, where Nunzio Manna cultivates his passion for discovering the best beers. La Bottega della Birra offers a vast selection of artisanal beers from across Italy, as well as beers from Belgium, England, America, and more. A variety of local dishes, cheese and meat plates, and bruschette designed to pair well with beer are also available.

Clubs
Fauno Notte Club
Piazza Torquato Tasso 13; tel. 081/878-1021; www.faunonotte.it; 11pm-4am daily Apr.-Oct.

For the nightclub scene in Sorrento, head to Fauno Notte Club right in Piazza Tasso. There's always something going on here after dark, as the club hosts visiting DJs, live music, and themed dance nights. During the week entrance is free and you pay only for drinks, which cost about €10. On Saturday and for special events the cover charge is €15-25.

ACCOMMODATIONS
€100-200
★ Maison Tofani
Via San Cesareo 34; tel. 081/878-4020; www.maisontofani.com; Feb. 13-Jan. 7; €189 d

Right in the historic center, not far from Piazza Tasso, this gorgeous hotel in an 18th-century building is full of historical charm. Each of the 10 rooms is different, with some featuring unique touches like exposed wood beams. Traditional terra-cotta floors with majolica tiles add a warm touch that's perfectly complemented by contemporary furnishings and colorful accents. Some rooms have balconies overlooking the town center. Breakfast is served in a beautiful room full of historical accents, with ornate doors and a frescoed ceiling.

€200-300
Relais Villa Angiolina Sorrento
Via Parsano 12; tel. 081/878-4523; www.villangiolina.com; Apr.-Dec.; €209 d

In a nice residential area south of Piazza Tasso, this B&B is set in a historic farmhouse with citrus trees and a pretty property. Although the surrounding landscape has changed, the owners' respect for tradition is evident in the 12 large double rooms decorated in natural tones. Hand-painted ceramics add a touch of color to the baths. Some rooms have steps to access the bath, so inquire when booking if this is a concern. Apartments and suites are also available in the center of Sorrento.

Relais Correale
Via Bernardino Rota 4; tel. 081/807-3265; www.relaiscorreale.it; Mar.-Oct.; €250 d

Located right in the La Limonaia citrus grove, this small hotel has 6 rooms decorated with bold Mediterranean colors and ceramic tiled floors. Many rooms have an outdoor patio area and an independent entrance. Start your day with a wonderful selection of homemade pastries and breakfast options served in the lemon garden. A full restaurant and cooking classes are also available on-site from La Limonaia.

Over €300
★ Hotel La Minervetta
Via Capo 25; tel. 081/877-4455; www.laminervetta.com; closed most of Jan.; €735 d

While located a bit outside of Sorrento's historic center, the position of this extraordinary boutique hotel affords enviable views of Marina Grande and all of Sorrento. Stepping inside is like seeing the pages of a design magazine come to life. Every angle and detail is beautifully curated with crisp modern design in a palette of predominantly blue, red, and white. There are large windows with panoramic views, and contemporary ceramics and art on display. The 12 rooms all have sea views, and each one is wonderfully unique. Follow the steps down to find a pool clinging to the cliff side and continue down the zigzag steps to reach Marina Grande. Stop by Bazar (Via Capo 17), the hotel's nearby boutique, for a curated selection of stylish home decor, ceramics, and design.

Hotel Bellevue Syrene
Piazza della Vittoria 5; tel. 081/878-1024; www. bellevue.it; mid-Mar.-Jan. 3; €820 d

Situated along the cliff side of Sorrento where there was a Roman villa in the 2nd century BCE, this hotel is set in an 18th-century villa that was transformed into a hotel in 1820. The historical character has been finely preserved, while at the same time the property has been updated to offer a thoroughly luxurious stay. Sea-view rooms come in a variety of sizes and are worth the splurge. If you're looking for a truly special stay, check out their extraordinary suites. The hotel has excellent dining options as well as its own private bathing platform, which is reached by elevator or via a long staircase carved into the rocks that passes by Roman ruins.

INFORMATION AND SERVICES
Tourist Information
Agenzia Campania Turismo- Sede di Sorrento
Via Luigi de Maio 35; tel. 081/807-4033; www. agenziacampaniaturismo.it; 9am-2pm daily Apr.-Oct.

In addition to its office on Via Luigi de Maio, the Sorrento tourist office has a main information point conveniently located in the center of town at Piazza Tasso (10am-1pm and 4pm-7pm daily Mar.-June and Oct.-Feb., 10am-1pm and 5pm-8pm July-Sept.). Piazza Tasso is large and busy, so look for the building on the western edge with the large clock; the info point is located nearby.

Medical Services
For emergency services in Italy, dial 118 for ambulance and urgent care. The hospital, **Ospedale di Sorrento** (Corso Italia 1; tel. 081/872-9111), is located at the western end of Corso Italia and has a pronto soccorso (emergency room) open 24-7. You'll find several **pharmacies** along Corso Italia and right in Piazza Tasso for nonemergency assistance.

GETTING THERE
By Car and Scooter
From **Naples,** follow the **A3** highway out of the city south to Castellammare di Stabia, where you'll continue on the **Strada Statale della Penisola Sorrentina (SS145)** road along the coastline all the way to the center of Sorrento. Drive time from Naples to Sorrento is about 1 hour 30 minutes, but expect a slightly longer drive when there's traffic during the summer months.

From the Amalfi Coast, follow **SS163** (the Amalfi Coast Road) until it meets **SS145,** at which point you can continue straight along SS145 into Sorrento from the east. Or take a left on SS145 and follow a route about 5 mi (8 km) longer via Sant'Agata sui Due Golfi to arrive in Sorrento from the west. Either way, the drive from **Amalfi** to Sorrento takes about 1 hour 30 minutes with no traffic, and about 45 minutes from **Positano** to Sorrento.

There are many paid **parking lots,** including at Marina Piccola harbor, near Piazza Tasso on Via Fuorimura, on Via Correale not far from the Museo Correale di Terranova, and on Via del Mare near Corso Italia. Expect to pay €2-3 an hour or more.

By Bus
From the **Aeroporto Internazionale di Napoli** (also called Capodichino Airport),

Curreri Service (tel. 081/801-5420; www.curreriviaggi.it) offers bus service from the airport to Sorrento with various stops along the way, including Pompei and Vico Equense, before arriving at the **Sorrento train station.** The bus departs from Capodichino every 1-1.5 hours 9am-7:30pm daily, and tickets cost €10. At the airport, tickets are available from an automatic vending machine just outside the arrivals area, and buses depart from the bus terminal outside the arrivals area near the bus parking area. Advance booking and payment can be made on the website.

To reach Sorrento from the Amalfi Coast, **SITA SUD** (tel. 089/386-6701; www.sitasudtrasporti.it; from €2.20) has a bus line connecting Amalfi to Sorrento with stops along the coast, including Positano. Buses depart roughly every hour 6:20am-10:30pm daily from Amalfi, with fewer buses Sunday, holidays, and during the winter. Travel time from Amalfi to Sorrento is about 1 hour 40 minutes; it's about 1 hour from Positano to Sorrento. Buses arrive in Sorrento at the Piazza Giovanni Battista de Curtis in front of the train station. Tickets can be purchased at local tabacchi (tobacco) stores or sometimes right at the bus departure point in Sorrento from a small booth.

By Train

From Naples, you can take the **Circumvesuviana** train line operated by **EAV** (www.eavsrl.it) from Piazza Garibaldi at the Napoli Centrale train station to **Sorrento's train station.** There are departures about every 30 minutes daily, and the trip takes about 60 minutes from Naples to Sorrento. Tickets cost €4.20 and can be purchased at the station. Keep in mind that the Circumvesuviana trains are primarily commuter- or metro-style trains, so there are many stops in between Naples and Sorrento, including Vico Equense and Castellammare di Stabia on the Sorrentine Peninsula, as well as Pompeii and Herculaneum. The train can get quite crowded, so don't be surprised if you have to stand for part of the journey during peak hours in the morning and evening.

By Ferry

Ferries arrive at Sorrento's **Marina Piccola** from destinations around the Gulf of Naples. There are many companies to choose from, from high-speed jet boats to aliscafo (hydrofoil) and slower traghetti (ferries) that transport passengers and vehicles.

Alilauro (tel. 081/878-1430; www.alilaurogruson.it; from €18.20 per person) offers routes connecting Sorrento to Naples, Capri, Ischia, Procida, and the Amalfi Coast seasonally April-October. From Capri, **Gescab** (tel. 081/428-5259; www.gescab.it; from €17.50) offers many daily trips for each destination. **Laser Capri** (tel. 081/837-5208; www.lasercapri.com; from €20) also offers several departures a day. **Caremar** (tel. 081/189-66690; www.caremar.it; from €16.40 passengers, €32.30 vehicles) also offers passenger and car ferries from Capri. **NLG** (tel. 081/807-1812; www.nlg.it; from €13.10 per person) operates jet routes from Capri and Naples to Sorrento, with the trip taking about 30 minutes from Capri and 40 minutes from Naples. **SNAV** (tel. 081/428-5555; www.snav.it; from €20) operates a Capri-to-Sorrento line as well, with a journey of about 30 minutes. Easter-October, **Alicost** (tel. 089/871-483; www.alicost.it; from €18.50 per person) offers ferry service from Salerno, Vietri sul Mare, Maiori, Amalfi, and Positano to Sorrento. The ferry ride from Positano to Sorrento takes about 50 minutes, and from Amalfi about 1 hour 15 minutes. Gescab, Caremar, NLG, and SNAV all offer year-round service to Sorrento, but with a more limited schedule off-season (Nov.-Mar.).

GETTING AROUND

Sorrento's historic center and main sights are quite easy to explore on foot. Local buses run through town and provide a good way to ride between the center of town and Marina Piccola or Marina Grande because they are located beneath the rest of Sorrento.

By Bus

EAV (www.eavsrl.it; departures every 20-30 minutes; from €1.30) offers four lines that cover the town with buses every 20 minutes. Bus schedules are not available online from EAV; the tourist office and info points are the best places to find the latest schedules and information. Linea A (Line A) runs from Sorrento to Capo di Sorrento. Linea B and Linea C run from Marina Piccola to Piazza Tasso and the train station. Linea D and Linea E circulate around town with various stops that include Marina Grande, Piazza Tasso, and the train station. Tickets must be purchased before boarding at tabacchi (tobacco) shops and news agents.

Sorrentine Peninsula

While Sorrento draws the most visitors, there are many beautiful spots and interesting towns to discover along the northern coastline of the Sorrentine Peninsula. Located along the Gulf of Naples, and given its proximity to Naples, the Sorrento coastline is definitely on the radar of Italian travelers, especially during the summer months. However, the charming town of Nerano and its picturesque Marina del Cantone seaside village are less known by international travelers, which gives them a charm well worth discovering. Add a laid-back element to your holiday by spending a day hiking or kayaking, swimming in little coves, and experiencing all the natural beauty the Sorrentine Peninsula offers.

BAGNI DELLA REGINA GIOVANNA

Traversa Punta Capo

West of Sorrento, you'll see verdant mountain slopes running down the rugged coastline all the way to Capo di Sorrento, the cape that juts out west of the city. Near the Punta del Capo, tucked into a little cove in a particularly scenic spot, is the Bagni della Regina Giovanna, a tiny lagoon with an arched entrance opening to the sea. The beautiful natural pool is named after Giovanna II, Queen of Naples in the 15th century, who legend says loved to swim here. Entrance to the sea is rocky, but the water is splendid. Note that there are no beach facilities here. The beach can be reached by taking the Line A bus from Sorrento to Capo di Sorrento and following signs to Ruderi della Villa Romana di Pollio (Ruins of the Pollio Roman Villa) for about 15 minutes down to the lagoon. Not far beyond the Bagni della Regina Giovanna, a rugged pathway continues toward Punta del Capo, where you'll find the ruins of an ancient Roman villa. You can walk around the ruins and imagine how scenic and grand this ancient Roman seaside villa would have been in its heyday. Beyond the ruins is a sloping rocky area that is popular with locals for sunbathing. Entering the sea is for the adventurous, but it's also just a beautiful spot for a walk or for photos of the Gulf of Naples.

TOP EXPERIENCE

NERANO AND MARINA DEL CANTONE

Very near the tip of the Sorrentine Peninsula along the southern coastline, the small town of Nerano and its seaside village of Marina del Cantone seem worlds away from the busy streets of Sorrento and the popular Amalfi Coast. A narrow and winding road zigzags down the mountain through the sleepy town of Nerano, where you can catch a glimpse of the turquoise sea as the road makes its way down to Marina del Cantone. Here you can enjoy a true escape surrounded by nature while relaxing on the beach, kayaking to isolated coves, or savoring a fine meal by the sea as little boats putter back and forth to the seaside restaurants.

The scenic road that connects Sorrento to Nerano and Marina del Cantone is one of the loveliest on the Sorrentine Peninsula. Less busy than the Amalfi Coast Road, the drive along Via Capo winds along the rugged coastline, through quiet villages, and around twists and turns that open to splendid views of Capri. The narrow two-lane road splits from SS145 west of Sorrento and passes above picturesque Marina di Puolo before becoming Via Nastro d'Oro and continuing through Massa Lubrense and Termini, where it zigzags through olive groves dotted with secluded villas. Just when you think it couldn't get any tighter, an even narrower road leads down the mountainside to Nerano and Marina del Cantone. While only a little over 10.5 mi (17 km) from Sorrento to Nerano, plan about 40 minutes just for the drive. You'll want longer to enjoy the view, stopping off at scenic spots or exploring villages along the way.

Beaches

★ Marina del Cantone

Set in a beautiful bay, Marina del Cantone has a secluded atmosphere at once natural and exclusive. The beach is lined with hotels and restaurants that are among the most popular spots in the area for VIP and celebrity travelers. The long and pebbly beach gently slopes down into the sea, which is clear and calm here, so it's a particularly good beach for swimming. The beach is one of the few Blue Flag-designated beaches along the southern coastline of the Sorrentine Peninsula. You'll find free areas as well as sun bed rentals and beach services offered by beach clubs like **Bar Bagni Mimì** (Via Marina del Cantone 8; tel. 081/808-1174; www.bagnimimi.it; Apr.-Oct.; from €15 per person), noted for its delicious and refreshing granita.

Water Sports and Hiking
Chasing Syrens

Marina del Cantone; tel. 333/277-2987; www. chasingsyrens.com; tours year-round; group tours from €70 pp, private tours from €350 for up to 4 people

The best way to experience the natural landscape and beautiful coastline surrounding Marina del Cantone is by kayak. This friendly company offers kayak rentals and tours as well as stand-up paddleboard (SUP) rentals. For a unique experience on these scenic waters, enjoy a paddle along the coastline with one of their clear kayaks. Hourly rentals are available, but consider joining one of their small-group tours to explore the area with a local guide. The 4-hour Ieranto Tour includes stops at caves, small coves, and the Ieranto Bay, as well as breaks for swimming, snorkeling,

Marina del Cantone beach

or relaxing. For a shorter jaunt, join the 90-minute Easy Tour that covers about 1 mi (1.5 km) around Marina del Cantone. Groups start with a minimum of 1 person and top out at 11 people. SUP tours are also available and can be combined with a boat tour to enjoy an SUP experience in Ieranto Bay, the Li Galli islands, and Capri. Hiking excursions to the beautiful Ieranto Bay and other scenic spots around Nerano are great when you're ready to explore on land.

Cooperativa S. Antonio

Piazza delle Sirene 2, Marina del Cantone; tel. 331/857-2856; www.coopsantonio.com; mid-Mar.-mid-Nov.; shared tours from €50 pp

Although Marina del Cantone has a secluded section, this boat company makes it easy and affordable to see the Amalfi Coast and Capri by sea thanks to their shared boat tours. Both are 8 hours, and the Amalfi Coast tour includes free time on shore in both Amalfi and Positano, while the Capri tour includes 6 hours of free time on the island. Small boats are available for rental without a skipper, or you can hire a boat with skipper for a private boat excursion.

Food and Accommodations
Ristorante Lo Scoglio

Piazza delle Sirene 15, Marina del Cantone; tel. 081/808-1026; www.hotelloscoglio.com; 12:30pm-4:30pm daily Apr.-Nov. 5, 12:30pm-5:30pm daily June-Aug., 12:30pm-4:30pm Sat.-Sun. Nov. 6-Mar.; restaurant €20-80, rooms from €250 d

Much loved by travelers from around the world who come to enjoy the incredibly simple yet fresh fare overlooking the sea in Marina del Cantone, the De Simone family's restaurant is a gastronomic haven. Whether you're enjoying fresh vegetables from the family garden prepared in traditional styles, or the popular local Nerano dish of spaghetti with zucchini, or ravioli with yellow tomatoes, the light, fresh flavors are divine. Seafood is exquisite here; try the linguine with sea urchin, grilled lobster, or locally caught pezzogna, a flaky whitefish. If you're like most visitors to Lo Scoglio who arrive and never want to leave this enchanting spot, there are also 14 simple yet stylish double or triple rooms with sea views (hotel open Apr.-Nov. 5).

Conca del Sogno

Via Amerigo Vespucci 25, Nerano; tel. 081/808-1036; www.concadelsogno.it; 12:30pm-4:30pm and 8pm-9:30pm daily Easter-mid-Oct.; restaurant €25-100, rooms from €250 d

Along the rocky cove overlooking the beautiful Baia di Recommone with its Blue Flag beach, Conca del Sogno offers beach club services as well as a top-notch restaurant and a small hotel with five charming rooms. With its seaside location, naturally the seafood is excellent here; the lobster pasta and salt-crusted freshly caught fish are fine choices. You could also opt for the classic Nerano dish of spaghetti with zucchini. The hotel rooms are bright and fresh, with private terraces overlooking the sea.

★ Regional Ristorante Don Alfonso 1890

Corso Sant'Agata 11/13; tel. 081/878-0026; www.donalfonso.com; 7:30pm-10:30pm Wed.-Sun. Nov.-Mar., 7:30pm-10:30pm Wed.-Fri., 12:30pm-2:30pm and 7:30pm-10:30pm Sat.-Sun. Apr.-Oct.; restaurant €46-65, tasting menu from €195 pp, rooms from €520 d

In a historic building right in the center of Sant'Agata sui Due Golfi is one of the finest restaurants on the Sorrentine Peninsula. In this rural setting at the tip of the peninsula, the Iaccarino family creates exquisite dishes that use local traditions as a firm foundation for innovation. The menu changes seasonally based on the fresh produce grown at the family's nearby terraced organic farm. The tasting menus let you sample the finest of the season and are the best option. With two Michelin stars, at Ristorante Don Alfonso 1890 you'll experience fine dining that is well worth the splurge.

A true gastronomic gem on the Sorrentine Peninsula, the restaurant is located roughly halfway between Sorrento and Nerano. Sant'Agata sui Due Golfi is located just off the **SS145** road that connects Sorrento with the Amalfi Coast Road (SS163). The town is in the mountains about 6.2 mi (10 km) from Sorrento and 10.5 mi (17 km) from Positano. Plan for a drive of about 25 minutes from **Sorrento,** 15 minutes from **Nerano,** and 30 minutes from **Positano.** There are limited SITA SUD bus connections, but arriving by car is the better option. For a peaceful experience, Don Alfonso 1890 also has eight lovely rooms and suites available in its **boutique hotel.** The decor blends historic furnishings from the 1700s-1800s with modern design and all the conveniences of a luxury hotel.

Getting There and Around
By Car
Nerano and Marina del Cantone are quite secluded areas along the Sorrentine Peninsula and are most easily reached by car or scooter. From **Sorrento** it's about a 40-minute drive following the **SS145** west out of Sorrento and continuing to reach Sant'Agata dui Due Golfi. From there, follow **Via dei Campi** southwest out of town; that road becomes Via Santa Maria della Neve, then Via Leucosia, and Via Capo D'Arco. Follow signs for Nerano and stay on **Via Capo D'Arco** as it winds down through Nerano and then to Marina del Cantone. If you're starting in **Sant'Agata dui Due Golfi,** plan on a 15-minute drive to Nerano and about 20 minutes to Marina del Cantone. **Parking** is available in parking lots and along the road in Marina del Cantone.

By Bus
If you're traveling by public transportation, the closest train station is in Sorrento, where you can continue by **SITA SUD** (tel. 089/386-6701; www.sitasudtrasporti.it; from €1.80) bus. Catch the bus heading to Nerano in the piazza in front of the train station; the bus stops at both Nerano and Marina del Cantone. The ride will take about 1 hour. The bus first passes through Massa Lubrense and Sant'Agata sui Due Golfi before reaching Nerano.

Capri

Itinerary Idea	200
Sights	201
Beaches	211
Sports and Recreation	214
Festivals and Events	220
Shopping	221
Food	224
Nightlife	227
Accommodations	228
Information and Services	230
Transportation	230

With a natural beauty that's famous around the world, the island of Capri is one of Italy's most popular travel destinations. What this small island lacks in size it easily makes up for with its mesmerizing blue sea, soaring cliffs, and Mediterranean charm. In this place of stunning scenery, there is so much to discover beyond the breathtaking views—but you won't want to miss those views!

Split between two towns called Capri and Anacapri, the island's sights spread from rocky beaches to mountain peaks, with historic sites and, of course, shopping to enjoy along the way. Visit La Piazzetta, a bustling square at the heart of Capri; enjoy iconic views of the famous Faraglioni rock formations that jut straight out of the water off the coastline, and stroll along the chic shopping streets. Then get away from it all by

Highlights

Look for ★ to find recommended sights, activities, dining, and lodging.

★ **Giardini di Augusto:** Visit these beautifully curated gardens to enjoy some of the best views over the Capri coastline, including the stunning I Faraglioni rock formation (page 203).

★ **Villa Jovis:** Hike to the top of Monte Tiberio to explore the ruins of the once palatial villa of Roman Emperor Tiberius. More stunning views are an added bonus (page 206).

★ **Villa San Michele:** Vistas and gardens blend beautifully at this museum located in what was once the home of Swedish doctor and writer Axel Munthe (page 209).

★ **Monte Solaro:** Ride the chairlift to Capri's highest point to see across the island to the Gulf of Naples (page 210).

★ **Marina Piccola:** Capri's smaller harbor is a picturesque spot to swim on the rocky beach or dine overlooking the turquoise sea (page 212).

★ **Arco Naturale to Belvedere di Tragara Walk:** A pleasant walk through Capri town leads to a large natural arch, immersed in a quiet spot of immense beauty, and continues to the Belvedere di Tragara, a beautiful overlook above the Faraglioni (page 214).

★ **Capri's Grottoes:** Enjoy a private or group boat tour or kayak around the island to see Capri's natural grottoes, including the Grotta Azzurra (Blue Grotto), up close (page 218).

Capri

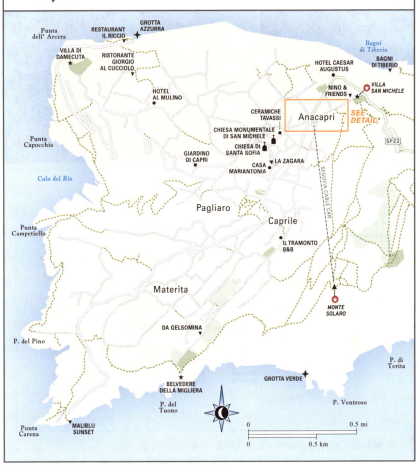

exploring the island's quieter side. Hike to incredible overlooks, ride a chairlift to the top of Monte Solaro, and meander down pedestrian-only pathways past bougainvillea-draped villas. Once you've enjoyed the top sights on land, get out on the water to take in the landscape from the sea, explore the island's grottoes, and find tiny coves where you can dive into the sea for a swim.

While its popularity means plenty of crowds during the busy season, Capri should still be on every traveler's list. Whether you're planning a day trip or staying longer, there are plenty of ways to enjoy Capri, from popular spots to tranquil corners of the island immersed in nature. Find those quiet moments, and Capri will surely capture your heart just as it has so many travelers for ages.

Previous: view of the Faraglioni rocks from the Giardini di Augusto; Giardini di Augusto; Arco Naturale.

ORIENTATION

Located just off the tip of the Sorrentine Peninsula, Capri is the best-known island in the Gulf of Naples. Measuring only about 4 sq mi (10.4 sq km), it packs an intense amount of beauty into its small area. Capri is mountainous, dominated by **Monte Solaro** soaring to 1,932 ft (589 m) on the western side of the island, and **Monte Tiberio** rising to 1,095 ft (334 m) on the northeastern side. The island's largest town, also called **Capri,** is situated along the dip between the two mountains just east of the middle of the island, while **Anacapri** spreads out around the base of Monte Solaro on the higher western side.

Capri has two harbors, with the main ferry harbor and tourist port of **Marina Grande** on the northern side of the island. This is where ferries arrive and depart, and is the main transportation hub of the island. On the southern side of the island, **Marina Piccola** is a beautiful little area with lovely, albeit rocky, swimming spots and plenty of excellent beach clubs for swimming and dining by the sea.

With the island's incredibly narrow and twisty roads and extremely limited parking, the best way to get around Capri is via public transportation or taxi. Small local buses connect Capri town, Anacapri, and the two harbors, while taxis are a quicker yet more expensive option. Marina Grande and Capri town are connected with a funicular train line that runs up and down the mountainside. During peak summer season, allow extra time to get around the island, especially if you have a ferry to catch.

PLANNING YOUR TIME

Even on a day trip, you can see many of the highlights of the island (the following Essential Capri itinerary is an excellent place to start). However, staying longer gives you the chance to see Capri's beauty at a slower pace, go hiking, and enjoy the quieter atmosphere in the evening after the last ferry departs. However, for the best experience and to support more sustainable tourism on the island, plan at least 3-4 days on Capri.

Capri's main sights are clustered around the island's two towns, Capri and Anacapri. Plan to divide your time between them. If you're staying longer, after seeing the main sights in the center of Capri and Anacapri, such as the **Piazzetta, Giardini di Augusto, Certosa di San Giacomo,** and the **Villa San Michele,** consider walking farther afield. For history lovers, the **Villa Jovis** offers the chance to meander through the ruins of the grand palace of Roman Emperor Tiberius. Or marvel at the **Arco Naturale,** a massive natural arch, on a pleasant walk from the center of Capri town.

Capri's rocky cliffs, famous grottoes, and tempting turquoise sea can be enjoyed in a variety of ways depending on the amount of time available. You'll find everything from hour-long group boat tours around the island that depart regularly from Marina Grande to private boat excursions and self-drive boat rentals. Even if your time is limited on the island, get out on the water to take in Capri's impressive beauty from a different vantage point.

Itinerary Idea

ESSENTIAL CAPRI

Thanks to its small size, Capri and its most famous sights can be seen in a whirlwind of a day.

1 If seeing the **Grotta Azzurra** (Blue Grotto) is on your bucket list, begin your day with an early visit before all the crowds arrive. There are a number of group and private tour options readily available from Marina Grande, where your ferry to Capri docks.

2 After seeing the grotto, take a local bus or taxi up to Piazza Vittoria in Anacapri and hop on the chairlift to the top of **Monte Solaro** to enjoy the view from the island's highest point.

3 Ride the chairlift back down and stroll through Anacapri to the **Chiesa Monumentale di San Michele** to see the remarkable 18th-century hand-painted ceramic floor.

4 Head to Capri by taxi or bus and enjoy a leisurely lunch of freshly caught seafood dishes, like pasta with fresh prawns, at **Il Geranio,** in a garden setting with unforgettable sea views.

5 Nearby, visit the **Giardini di Augusto** for a remarkable view, overlooking the Faraglioni rocks jutting out from the water and the zigzagging Via Krupp, carved into the mountainside.

Itinerary Idea

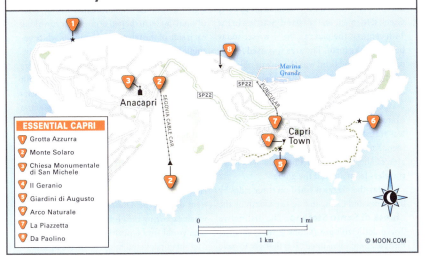

6 Take a walk out to the dramatic **Arco Naturale** rock formation and back to get even more of a sense of the landscape; it's just over 2 mi (3.5 km) to the arch and back.

7 Back in Capri town, head to **La Piazzetta** for a coffee and some window-shopping before heading back on the ferry if you're on a day trip.

8 If you're staying on the island, dine on Caprese (Capri-style) specialties in a charming and rustic setting under lemon trees at **Da Paolino.**

Sights

CAPRI TOWN

Capri's iconic Torre dell'Orologio clock tower is the first sight when arriving in Capri town by bus, taxi, or funicular train. Here you'll find the buzzing Piazzetta, the heart of Capri and the crossroads of town. Stop at a local café to watch the vibrant scene play out. Capri's international allure has created a welcoming atmosphere where daily life for the locals blends seamlessly with visitors from around the world, and there's no place better to take it all in than the Piazzetta. While there, visit the Chiesa di Santo Stefano, one of the island's most important churches, and the Centro Caprense Ignazio Cerio, which offers a sweeping view over the Piazzetta and Marina Grande harbor. Just off the Piazzetta, meander through a maze of little streets lined with shops or follow the elegant Via Vittorio Emanuele, which turns into the Via Federico Serena, on a slightly downhill stroll past Via Camerelle, the island's most exclusive shopping address, to reach the beautiful Giardini di Augusto for the best views of the Faraglioni rocks and the nearby Certosa di San Giacomo.

La Piazzetta
Piazza Umberto I
Its official name is Piazza Umberto I, but this busy little piazza is more commonly known as

La Piazzetta. It has had a long history as the nucleus of the community since Roman times, and probably even dating back as far as early Greek settlement on the island. Starting in the 16th century, the piazza's shape we see today began to take form. The area was used for occasional markets and was the hub of religious celebrations until the 1930s, when the first café opened on the square. This is when the Piazzetta as a center of socializing truly began. Many more cafés followed, and the Piazzetta was transformed into the place to see and be seen. Known as the "salotto del mondo" (theater of the world), the Piazzetta welcomes travelers from around the globe.

Today the piazza is lined on three sides by buildings and cafés, and on the fourth by the **Chiesa di Santo Stefano.** The distinctive Torre dell'Orologio (Clock Tower) has the form today of a bell tower. It is thought to have been a part of the defensive walls of the medieval city, or maybe the only remaining piece of a large church and monastery that once occupied the site where Santo Stefano stands today. Whatever its origins, locals think of the tower, with its colorful majolica tile design dating from the 1800s, as the symbol of Capri.

Beyond the Piazzetta and through the arch to **Via Longono** and **Via le Botteghe** is the **medieval quarter** of the city, with its maze of little streets and courtyards. This is an intriguing area to explore, home to lovely little boutiques and restaurants.

With Capri's transportation hub—buses, taxis, and the funicular to Marina Grande—nearby, all life seems to pass through the Piazzetta. Stop for a coffee or aperitivo during the day to watch the world go by, or find a table after dark to watch the Piazzetta truly come to life.

Chiesa di Santo Stefano

Piazza Umberto I; tel. 081/837-0072; 8am-1pm and 4pm-8pm daily Apr.-Oct., 8am-1pm and 4pm-7pm daily Nov.-Mar.; free

Located at the top of a small flight of steps from the Piazzetta, the facade of Capri's largest church feels squeezed into an impossibly narrow passageway. You'll need to look from a few different angles to take in the baroque design and spot the even more interesting series of small lantern-shaped domes that run along each side of the nave. The luminous white baroque interior is filled with light from the windows and domes along the nave and the large dome over the crossing. The church was built in the late 17th century on the site of an earlier church and is dedicated to Santo Stefano (Saint Stephen). However, there's also a special reverence here for San Costanzo (Saint Constantius), Capri's patron saint. The church holds an important silver bust reliquary statue of the saint from 1715, and that statue is carried during the procession for the saint's festival on May 14. Don't forget to look down when exploring the church: In the main altar area you'll find a multicolored marble floor that was uncovered at the Villa Jovis, and in the side chapel to the left of the altar there's another Roman-era marble floor, likely from ruins near Punta di Tragara.

Centro Caprense Ignazio Cerio

Piazzetta Cerio 5; tel. 081/837-6681; www.centrocaprense.org; 11am-4pm Tues.-Wed., 11am-3pm Thurs.-Sat. May-Oct., hours vary Nov.-Apr.; €3

Situated opposite the Chiesa di Santo Stefano, the Palazzo Cerio—also known as the Palazzo Arcucci—is one of the most historic buildings around the Piazzetta. It was built in the 14th century for Giacomo Arcucci, the founder of the Certosa di San Giacomo. Today it houses the Centro Caprense Ignazio Cerio, a cultural center dedicated to Capri history with a library and museum displaying archaeological, paleontological, and naturalistic finds. The center was founded in 1947 by Edwin Cerio, a noted writer and engineer, in honor of his father, Ignazio Cerio, a doctor and naturalist. The museum's collection and role in preserving Capri's history in many forms makes this a fascinating spot to explore. Don't leave without heading up to the rooftop terrace for a bird's-eye view overlooking the Piazzetta. The center also organizes cultural events, meetings, and concerts throughout the year.

Capri Town

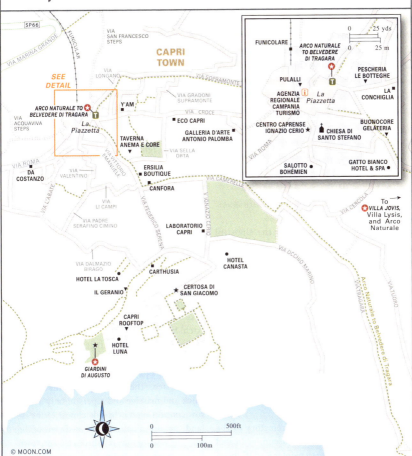

★ Giardini di Augusto

Via Matteotti 2; tel. 353/452 3908; www.capriculturaeturismo.it; 9am-8pm daily Apr.-Oct., 9am-5pm Nov.-Mar.; €1.50

The beautiful Giardini di Augusto (Gardens of Augustus) were created on land purchased at the end of the 1800s from the nearby Certosa di San Giacomo Carthusian monastery by German industrialist Friedrich Alfred Krupp. While there is a strong connection between Capri and ancient Rome, the gardens didn't receive their name in honor of Augustus until after World War I. Spread across several terraces, the lush gardens are full of seasonal flowers as well as plant and flower species that are typical of Capri, like ginestra (broom), bougainvillea, cacti, and bird of paradise. The terraced garden offers shaded spots with ceramic-tiled benches, giving you a relaxing spot to sit and rest. However, the main draw here is the sweeping view from the edge of the garden of the Faraglioni rocks and the Certosa di San Giacomo in one direction, and the bay of Marina Piccola in the other.

Look down from the highest terrace of the garden to see the famous **Via Krupp,** a zigzagging pathway down the mountain connecting Capri with Marina Piccola below. Excavated out of the mountainside, this remarkable pathway was created at Krupp's expense by the engineer Emilio Mayer. A particularly scenic way to walk between Capri town and Marina Piccola, it has recently reopened after many years of work to secure the area for falling rocks. Even if you're not tempted by the vertiginous walk, the view looking down on Via Krupp with the bright turquoise sea just beyond is not to be missed.

Certosa di San Giacomo

Via Certosa 1; tel. 081/837-6218; www.musei.campania. beniculturali.it; 10am-4pm Tues.-Sun.; €6

Easy to spot on the way to the Giardini di Augusto, the Certosa di San Giacomo was built starting in 1371 by the nobleman Giacomo Arcucci as a Carthusian monastery. The complex included a series of buildings and gardens organized around two cloisters, a large one and a small one, much of which can be visited today. The church off the small cloister has an impressive vaulted ceiling that reveals its Gothic origins amid the remains of the late-17th-century decor. Walking around the cloisters offers a chance to enjoy a shady and peaceful moment, an especially appealing break from the summer sun.

Since 1974, the former refectory of the monastery has housed a museum dedicated to the works of German painter Karl Wilhelm Diefenbach, who arrived on Capri in 1900 and remained until his death in 1913. The collection contains 31 of his paintings—many of them impressively large, dramatic, and dark—along with five plaster sculptures and one portrait. For more detailed information during your visit, an audio guide is available in English and is included in the ticket price.

I Faraglioni

Punta di Tragara

Perhaps Capri's most iconic symbol, the Faraglioni are three large rocks located just off the Punta di Tragara. With sheer cliffs and only a scattering of vegetation along the top, the three Faraglioni are majestic to behold. The rock closest to the land is connected to the island and rises to 358 ft (109 m), while the center rock with the hole in the middle rises to 266 ft (81 m), and the farthest one out is 341 ft (104 m) high. On the outer rock and the nearby rock formation called Monacone lives a rare type of lizard called the lucertola azzurra (blue lizard), which has an incredible blue tint, the color of the deep sea surrounding the Faraglioni. The rocks can be admired from many vantage points around the island, including the Giardini di Augusto and Belvedere di Tragara, and from high above in Anacapri from the top of Monte Solaro. You can also see the Faraglioni close-up from the sea; small boats can cruise right through the opening in the center rock.

Arco Naturale

Via Arco Naturale

To immerse yourself in Capri's natural beauty, take a walk to the Arco Naturale (Natural Arch) from the Piazzetta. Set about 656 ft (200 m) above sea level, the craggy natural arch is about 66 ft (20 m) tall and 39 ft (12 m) wide. Located in a peaceful landscape surrounded by pine trees, the outside part of the arch is thick and massive and tapers to only a narrow connection on the side closest to the island, creating a naturally framed view of the sea. The walk to the arch through Capri town becomes quieter and more secluded as you go, and leads to a set of steps down to a series of small overlooks where you can admire the arch from a variety of different viewpoints. In the distance, you'll spot the **Sorrentine Peninsula** and beyond to the right the **Li Galli islands** off Positano. The setting is nearly untouched nature, where you can listen to the wind blowing through the pine trees and catch the scent of the sea far below as boats pass by. You can also spot the Arco

---

1: La Piazzetta **2:** Chiesa di Santo Stefano **3:** Certosa di San Giacomo **4:** Arco Naturale

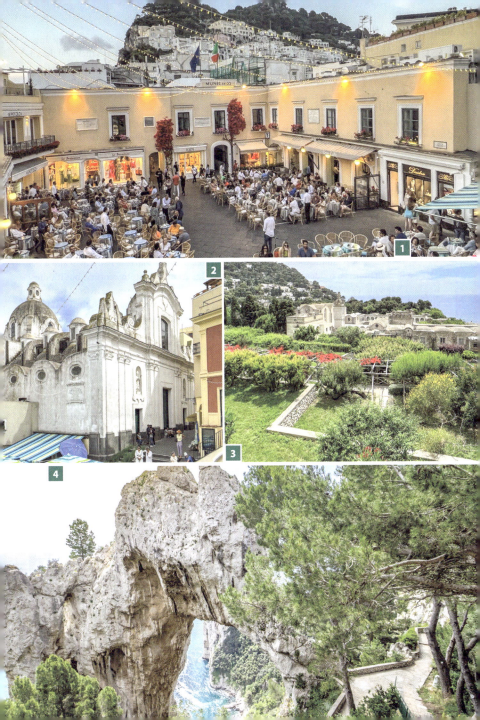

Naturale from the sea on a boat tour around the island.

TOP EXPERIENCE

★ Villa Jovis

Via Tiberio; tel. 081/837-6218; www.musei.campania. beniculturali.it; 10am-6pm Thurs.-Sun. Apr.-Oct., check for hours Nov.-Mar.; €6

Sitting atop the highest point of Monte Tiberio on the northeastern point of Capri are the ruins of a lavish villa built for Emperor Tiberius. From this perch, Tiberius ruled the Roman Empire from 27 to 37 CE. The largest of Tiberius's villas on the island, Villa Jovis was a massive estate that functioned as a fortress yet included all the modern comforts of a Roman imperial residence.

Though it's hard to imagine the original design from the state of the ruins, the Villa Jovis was once a splendid example of Roman architecture, and visiting offers a chance to imagine the ancient Roman lifestyle on Capri. Given the limited surface area near the top of Monte Tiberio, the villa occupied many levels rather than following the more traditional sprawling layout of Roman imperial villas. Exploring the site's multiple levels, you can see parts of the imperial residence as well as the servant's quarters, baths, and the ingenious series of large cisterns that held the villa's water supply, fundamental because Capri has no natural water sources. Although there is not a lot of historical information offered throughout the site, it's still a moving experience to walk through the ruins.

The villa's setting is dramatic, overlooking a sheer cliff that drops straight to the sea; this is sometimes called Tiberius's Leap, where it's said people the emperor wasn't pleased with were shown the exit. Take your time admiring the sweeping views across the Gulf of Naples and the Sorrentine Peninsula. Adjacent to the ruins you'll find a small **church** with a plain gray facade and arched entrance. It is dedicated to Santa Maria del Soccorso and dates from around the 16th century, but it's most popular for the large terrace in front with panoramic views over the ruins, the island, the Gulf of Naples, and the Gulf of Salerno.

Getting There

Located at the extreme northeastern tip of the island at the highest point of Monte Tiberio, the walk to Villa Jovis is about 1.25 mi (2 km) and takes around 45 minutes. The walk is almost entirely uphill from the center of Capri and includes sections with uneven stone

Villa Jovis

steps, especially as you approach the site. Starting from La Piazzetta, look for the signs to Villa Jovis and follow Via Longono, Via Sopramonte, and Via Tiberio. Comfortable shoes are recommended, and during the summer months don't forget to bring water as there are limited opportunities to purchase refreshments as you near Monte Tiberio. Walking is the only way to reach Villa Jovis.

Villa Lysis

Via Lo Capo 12; tel. 377/359-0709; www. capriculturaeturismo.it; 10am-6pm daily Mar.-Apr. and mid Sept.-Oct., 10am-7pm daily May-mid Sept., check for hours Nov.-Feb.; €1.50

Along the pathway leading through the rugged mountainous landscape up to the summit of Monte Tiberio lies one of Capri's most curious villas. Set in an extraordinarily scenic spot at the edge of the cliff overlooking the Gulf of Naples and Marina Grande below, the secluded and inaccessible location was exactly what the villa's owner, the French writer Jacques d'Adelswärd-Fersen, was looking for when he built the villa starting in 1904. After being arrested in Paris the previous year for scandalous behavior, he fled to Capri, a place he had visited at a young age, where he built a refuge from the world. And quite a refuge it was: Villa Lysis defies any one architectural style, rather blending inspiration from his travels around the world, from Louis XVI to art nouveau and Asian influences. The Villa Lysis became a meeting point for d'Adelswärd-Fersen, his companion Nino Cesarini, and the many artists and writers who visited Capri at the beginning of the 20th century.

After d'Adelswärd-Fersen's death, the villa fell into disrepair and has gone through subsequent restorations. While much has been lost, the romantic and decadent atmosphere is still captivating. The villa and gardens are open to explore. Though the rooms are not decorated in the lavish style they once were, there is an air of the original elegance and flair, especially in the large salon with its columns decorated with gold mosaic details. The gardens are the highlight, with many terraces and picturesque spots to enjoy the fine views over Marina Grande below. Don't miss the view from the rooftop terrace looking toward the Sorrentine Peninsula in the distance. During the summer the villa often hosts concerts, theatrical performances, and exhibitions.

Getting There

To reach Villa Lysis, follow the same directions for Villa Jovis. The walk takes approximately 45 minutes from the Piazzetta and is mostly uphill. Especially if you enjoy architecture, it's a pleasant stop on the way to or from visiting Villa Jovis.

ANACAPRI

Spread out around the base of Monte Solaro, the island's highest peak, the town of Anacapri is quieter than Capri town. Piazza Vittoria is the main transport hub and also the location of the chairlift to reach the top of Monte Solaro. Following Via Capodimonte from Piazza Vittoria leads to the Villa San Michele, the former home of Swedish writer and doctor Axel Munthe. Or follow Via Giuseppe Orlandi through a charming shopping area, past the colorful Casa Rossa, a small museum full of art inspired by Capri's beauty, to reach the Chiesa Monumentale di San Michele, with a hand-painted 18th-century tile floor that's too beautiful to walk on.

Anacapri's most famous sight, the Grotta Azzurra, is located in the ruggedly beautiful northwestern area of the island. While it is more popular to arrive by boat from Marina Grande, it is also possible to reach the grotto from land. While in the area, stop to visit the Roman ruins of the Villa di Damecuta.

Grotta Azzurra

Grotta Azzurra; tel. 081/837-5646; www.musei. campania.beniculturali.it; 9am-6pm daily Apr.-Oct., 9am-2pm daily Nov.-Mar., weather permitting; €15

Synonymous with Capri around the world, the Grotta Azzurra (Blue Grotto) is one of the island's most popular sights. This natural cavern is about 197 ft (60 m) long and 82 ft (25 m) wide, but the entrance to the grotto is

Best Views on Capri

view from Villa Jovis

If there's one thing Capri has in abundance, it's beautiful views—the kind you never forget. The island's small size seems only to enhance the captivating views of the soaring mountains, sheer cliffs, and impossibly blue sea that changes from brilliant turquoise to electric blue. Here are the top spots on the island to savor Capri's views.

BEST VIEWS ON LAND

- **Giardini di Augusto:** Only a short stroll from the central Piazzetta, these gardens are easy

very small and can only be accessed by rowboats that hold up to four people. You must lie nearly flat as your skipper carefully pulls the boat into the grotto to row you around. Inside, you'll see deep electric-blue water that shimmers with a silvery glow thanks to the refraction of light from an opening below sea level. This magical space led to a Roman nymphaeum, or shrine dedicated to nymphs, where statues have been uncovered. For ages it was largely forgotten and mostly feared by local fisherfolk until it was rediscovered by German travelers August Kopisch and Ernst Fries in 1826.

Given its popularity and limited access, the Grotta Azzurra can be a bit challenging to visit, especially during the busy summer season. Before you can enter, be prepared for a lengthy wait, which for some travelers can seem disproportionate to the limited amount of time you actually get to stay inside (about 10 minutes). However, if seeing the Grotta Azzurra is on your bucket list, it is quite a unique experience, and the colors certainly don't disappoint.

Getting There

The entrance to the Grotta Azzurra can be reached by land or sea, but you can only enter the grotto by boat. Several boat companies, including **Motoscafisti Capri** (Marina Grande; tel. 081/837-5646; www.motoscafisti-capri.com; from €21 per person) and **Laser Capri** (Via Cristoforo Colombo 69; Marina

to reach to enjoy a view of the Faraglioni rocks. The beautiful garden setting is an extra perk (page 203).

- **Villa Jovis:** If you have time for a longer walk, visit the ruins of Villa Jovis, set atop the island's second highest point, with spectacular views over the island as well as toward the Sorrentine Peninsula and Gulf of Naples. The villa is especially interesting to history lovers (page 206).
- **Monte Solaro:** Hands down, the finest view on Capri is from the island's highest point atop Monte Solaro. Hop on the chairlift for a scenic ride to the top to enjoy the 360-degree views over the island (page 210).

BEST SEA VIEWS

- **Marina Piccola:** Of Capri's beaches, one of the most enjoyable and beautiful is the island's Marina Piccola with its turquoise water and view of the Faraglioni in the distance (page 212).
- **Boat Tour around the Island:** Capri is perhaps even more breathtaking when seen from the sea. Choose a tour, or rent a boat and cruise around on your own. Any way you go, you'll see grottoes up close and enjoy spotting Capri's wild goats along the cliffs (page 217).

A TABLE WITH A VIEW

- **Il Geranio, Capri:** Tucked away in a peaceful spot above the Giardini di Augusto, this is a lovely restaurant with a view over the Faraglioni (page 226).
- **Capri Rooftop, Capri:** Perfect for a relaxed drink anytime of day, this bar situated next to the Giardini di Augusto in Capri town has picture-perfect views of the Faraglioni (page 227).
- **Maliblu Sunset, Anacapri:** Located on Punta Carena at the westernmost tip of the island, this beach club offers a stunning setting, surrounded by the natural beauty of Capri, to enjoy drinks and live music during their summer sunset parties (page 228).

Grande; tel. 081/837-5208; www.lasercapri.com; from €21 per person) offer group boat service from Marina Grande to the Grotta Azzurra, with the option to add on a boat tour around the island for an additional fee. Note that the fee for the boat transfer is separate from the €15 entrance fee, which is paid to access the grotto. By land, you can reach the grotto by taxi or via the local Capri bus to the Grotta Azzurra, but you have to walk down some steps to the spot near the entrance where you can board the rowboats to enter.

If you're on a day trip, it's a good idea to visit the grotto in the morning, as occasionally wind or weather changes can require the grotto to close in the afternoons. A visit is not guaranteed, as even on days when the weather seems nice, the sea conditions near the grotto might make it unsafe to enter. Though the Grotta Azzurra is often closed during the winter, November-March, it may occasionally be open if the weather and sea conditions are appropriate. Throughout the year, if the Motoscafisti Capri ticket booths are open in Marina Grande, that means the grotto is open.

★ Villa San Michele

Viale Axel Munthe 34; tel. 081/837-1401; www.villasanmichele.eu; 9am-4:30pm daily Mar., 9am-5pm daily Apr. and Oct., 9am-6pm daily May-Sept., 9am-3:30pm daily Nov.-Feb.; €10

Immersed in nature, Villa San Michele was the home of noted Swedish doctor and writer Axel Munthe (1857-1949). In his will, he bequeathed the estate to the Swedish government to welcome and promote ties between Sweden and Italy and to inspire Italian artists, writers, and researchers. Munthe is largely known today for his autobiographical work *The Story of San Michele,* first published in 1929. Admission includes a visit to his home, which has been transformed into a museum, and the chance to explore the gorgeous garden dotted with statues. Stroll along the pergola-covered walkway to the very end to find a loggia with an Egyptian sphinx and you will enjoy an extraordinary view overlooking Marina Grande below and the Gulf of Naples. Nearby is a little chapel dedicated to San Michele. Above the villa rises Monte Barbarossa, where birds rest during spring and autumn migrations. In 1904, Munthe bought the entire mountain to protect the birds from local hunters. Atop the Villa San Michele is Café Casa Oliv (9:30am-6pm Tues.-Sun.), a lovely spot with a serene outdoor terrace. The café can be accessed without visiting the museum via a side entrance. The Villa San Michele also hosts concerts and cultural events during the summer season.

★ Monte Solaro

chairlift: Via Caposcuro 10; tel. 081/837-1438; www.capriseggiovia.it; 9:30am-4pm daily Mar.-Apr., 9:30am-5pm daily May-Oct., 9:30am-3:30pm daily Nov.-Feb.; €14

At 1,932 ft (589 m), Monte Solaro is Capri's highest point and offers a splendid bird's-eye view overlooking the island. From here you'll also enjoy an excellent vantage point to take in the entire area from the Sorrentine Peninsula to Ischia, Procida, and Mount Vesuvius, all located across the Gulf of Naples. Standing at the edge of the cliff, the yachts below seem so far away, yet the turquoise sea so temptingly close. With the sound of the wind blowing through ragged pine trees, the sun-baked Mediterranean vegetation, and the call of seagulls in the air, this is one of Capri's most majestic spots and simply must be experienced.

Getting to the top of Monte Solaro is an experience in itself, thanks to the **Seggiovia Monte Solaro,** a chairlift that runs from Piazza Vittoria to the summit. Simply hop on one of the 156 single seats that run continuously and enjoy the 13-minute ride to the top. The chairlift seats are individual and are not designed to accommodate large bags. You will be assisted on and off, but you'll need to hop off as the chairlift moves continuously. Along the way, you'll pass over a quiet residential area of Anacapri before everything drops away and you're surrounded by nature. On the way down, there's an excellent view from the chairlift across the gulf, especially on a clear day. Purchase a one-way ticket (€11) if you would like to hike up or down, which takes about an hour.

Chiesa Monumentale di San Michele

Piazza San Nicola; tel. 081/837-2396; www.chiesa-san-michele.com; 10am-2pm daily Mar., 9am-7pm daily Apr.-Oct., closed Nov.-Feb.; €2

One of Anacapri's gems, this baroque church dedicated to San Michele Arcangelo was constructed from 1698 to 1719 and features a central floor plan with an octagonal shape and a large dome. The entire floor of the church is covered with marvelous hand-painted majolica tiles depicting Adam and Eve in the Garden of Eden. Created by master majolica artist Leonardo Chiaiese in 1761, the floor is a remarkable work of art and visitors are not allowed to walk on it. From a narrow platform along the edge, you can examine the garden scene with its 18th-century images of exotic animals and the serpent wrapped around the tree of life. Climb the spiral staircase to the upper level near the organ for an even better view of the scene.

Casa Rossa

Via Giuseppe Orlandi 78; tel. 081/838-7260; www.museocasarossa.it; 10:30am-1:30pm and 4:30pm-8pm Tues.-Sun. June-Sept., 10am-4pm Tues.-Sun. Oct.-May; €3.50

It's impossible to miss this eccentric house, with its distinctive red color, located on

Via Giuseppe Orlandi not far from Piazza Vittoria. It's not only the red color that grabs attention but also its eclectic architectural style. Built between 1876 and 1899 for American colonel John Clay MacKowen, the house is a treasure trove of architectural elements and is home to a museum featuring paintings of Capri from the 1800s to 1900s. MacKowen was keenly interested in archaeology; he was the first to recover Roman statues from the Grotta Azzurra, and four of these sculptures are featured in a multimedia display that brings their history vibrantly to life. Climb to the top level for a view overlooking Anacapri. Guided visits in English are offered throughout the day.

Villa di Damecuta

Via Antonio Maiuri; tel. 081/370-0381; www.musei. campania.beniculturali.it; 10am-noon and 4pm-7pm Tues.-Sun. Apr.-mid-Oct., 10am-1pm and 2:30pm-4:30pm Tues.-Sun. mid-Oct.-Mar.; free

Set in a secluded area on the western edge of the island, the Villa di Damecuta is something of a mystery. All we know is that it was once a grand imperial Roman villa used by Augustus or Tiberius, or perhaps by both emperors. Only a few remnants of the buildings remain, as the site was poorly preserved over the centuries. It even served as a military training ground at the beginning of the 19th century as the French and English battled over control of the island. Little is left of the ruins other than a general idea of the footprint of the imperial palace, outlined by the walls that are barely visible above ground level. You can make out a long path leading to a semicircular terrace situated to make the most of the views across the Gulf of Naples to Ischia and Procida in the distance.

Beaches

With gorgeous colors ranging from deep cobalt blue to shockingly bright turquoise, the sea around Capri just beckons for a swim. However, be prepared for higher prices compared to other towns in the area. For private beach clubs, there's usually a set price per person that includes a chair and access to a shower and changing rooms; there's often an additional cost to rent umbrellas. Given that the beaches are very rocky, it is generally worth the splurge for a comfortable beach experience.

Marina Grande
Capri

Just steps beyond the Marina Grande port to the west is a long, narrow stretch of beach that's a good spot if you only have time for a quick swim. **Le Ondine Beach Club** (Via Marina Grande; tel. 081/277-9056; www.dagemma.com; 9:30am-7pm daily mid-Apr.-mid-Oct.; beach chair €25, sun bed €25, umbrella €10) offers sun bed and umbrella rentals along with changing rooms and showers. Or head to the westernmost side of the beach for a free area where you can just throw down a towel. The water is clear and pleasant for swimming, with the western side offering finer pebbles and gentler slope into the sea. It's a popular and busy beach with tourists, but you'll find the western side has a more local scene.

Small boats depart from the eastern side of the beach for the nearby **Bagni di Tiberio** (Via Palazzo a Mare 41; tel. 081/837-0703; www.bagnitiberio.com; May-Sept.; entrance €15 per person plus €15 for sun beds, €8 for umbrellas), a beach club located west of Marina Grande. With incredible water and set in an area rich with Roman history, Bagni di Tiberio offers a more secluded beach experience. The beach can also be reached on foot after a 25-minute walk from Marina Grande; follow Via Marina Grande to Via Palazzo a Mare and continue along to reach the beach.

Faraglioni

Punta di Tragara, Capri

One of Capri's most dramatic and exclusive beach experiences is right at the foot of the Faraglioni rocks. Two notable beach clubs are located on the rocky stretch connecting the island with the first Faraglioni. The beach clubs are nestled right into the rocks with platforms and ladders for sea access. **Da Luigi ai Faraglioni** (Via Faraglioni 5; tel. 081/837-0591; www.luigiaifaraglioni.com; late Apr.-Sept.; €100 per person for entrance and deck chair, which includes €55 for the on-site restaurant or bar) is located right at the base of the Faraglioni, while just to the west with a spectacular view is **La Fontelina** (Località Faraglioni; tel. 081/837-0845; www.fontelina-capri.com; late Apr.-mid-Oct.; from €40 per person for entrance and seating), a popular spot with VIP travelers. Both beach clubs have excellent restaurants where you can dine steps from the sea. Note that restaurant reservations are required for beach access at both Da Luigi ai Faraglioni and La Fontelina. Advance booking at La Fontelina requires a 3-day minimum. The setting is rocky, so expect to access the sea by ladders and steps. Yet once you're in the water it's exquisite swimming.

To reach the Faraglioni beach clubs, follow the pathway from the **Belvedere di Tragara** that leads down steeply about 985 ft (300 m) to sea level. The beach clubs also offer a pickup or drop-off boat shuttle service from Marina Piccola; the service is €7 per person for Da Luigi ai Faraglioni clients and starts at €30 for up to four La Fontelina clients.

★ Marina Piccola

On Capri's southern side between the Faraglioni to the east and the rugged coastline below Anacapri is the island's very charming Marina Piccola. It's a buzzing seaside spot during the summer months thanks to the beautiful, albeit rocky, beaches and restaurants that are popular with locals and tourists alike. While it can seem a maze of zigzag staircases, the marina is split in two by the Scoglio delle Sirene, a small, rocky promontory that juts out into the bright turquoise sea, with swimming areas, beach clubs, and small free beaches on both sides.

Given the rugged setting, a sun bed is a good idea here, and you'll find plenty of options to rent one from the restaurants and stabilimenti balneari (beach clubs) along the little marina. Try **Bagni Internazionali** (Via Marina Piccola 95; tel. 081/837-0264; www.bagninternazionali.com; daily May-Oct.; from €25 for entrance and deck chair, €35 for sun bed) for a sunny spot. Or head to **La Canzone del Mare** (Via Marina Piccola 93; tel. 081/837-0104; www.lacanzonedelmare.com; late Apr.-Sept.; €90 per person for entrance, sun bed, and pool access, includes €45 credit for the bar or restaurant) for elegant dining in the iconic hotel founded by English actress and singer Gracie Fields.

Beyond Marina Piccola in a tiny cove, the water at **Spiaggia Torre Saracena** is an impossibly bright shade of turquoise. It's a secluded spot with beach access available via the **Torre Saracena Beach Club** (Via Marina Piccola; tel. 081/837-0646; www.torresaracenacapri.com; daily May-Oct.; from €35 for entrance and sun bed). You can reach this tiny beach by taking Via Krupp off of Via Marina Piccola and following the signs to Spiaggia Torre Saracena. Once you reach the entrance, there are over 150 steps down to the beach, where you'll be well rewarded for the effort by the beautiful sea.

Marina Piccola can be reached by bus or taxi from all the main points on the island. You can also enjoy a pleasant walk down from Capri town by following Via Roma from the Piazzetta to the rotary intersection where the road splits to go up to Anacapri or down to Marina Grande. Continue along Via Mulo, which leads through the quiet residential area of Marina Piccola. It's a more direct and enjoyable walk compared to following the zigzagging road connecting Marina Piccola

1: Le Ondine Beach Club in Marina Grande **2:** beach clubs at Marina Piccola

1

2

and Capri town. The walk takes about 25 minutes from the Piazzetta and is largely downhill once you start along Via Mulo, so a bus is a good option for the return. Buses run regularly from Marina Piccola to Capri and less frequently direct to Anacapri. If you need to reach Anacapri in the periods when there aren't direct buses, take a bus to Capri town, where you can find frequent service to Anacapri.

Punta Carena
Str. Faro di Carena, Anacapri

The pink and white striped lighthouse that sits on the Punta Carena is one of the prettiest sights on Capri. This spot marks the southwesternmost point of the island and is surrounded by impressive craggy mountains. Easily spotted from the sea on a boat trip around the island, the **Lido del Faro** (Str. Faro di Carena; tel. 081/837-1798; www.lidofaro.com; 10am-sunset daily June-Sept.; €100 per person for entrance, sun bed, and sea and pool access, includes €50 credit for the bar or restaurant) beach makes this a popular area for swimming in the summer months. This area is about as rugged as swimming gets on Capri, so be prepared for rocky entrances to the sea and a higher price tag in the peak of summer due to the isolated and exclusive setting. From Anacapri, local buses on the Anacapri-Faro route run back and forth about every 30 minutes and provide a convenient way to reach the beach.

Sports and Recreation

With its remarkably varied landscape, from rugged mountains to sea grottoes, Capri is a fun destination for active travelers.

WALKS

Exploring Capri on foot is one of the best ways not only to enjoy the island's natural beauty but also to get away from the crowds. You won't have to wander very far off the well-beaten path to find quiet spots, residential streets lined with beautiful villas, and incredible views.

Capri Town

TOP EXPERIENCE

★ Arco Naturale to Belvedere di Tragara Walk

Distance: 2.2 mi (3.6 km) round-trip
Time: 2.5 hours round-trip
Trailhead: *Piazzetta, Capri*
Information and Maps: *Local tourist offices or the Cart&guide Island of Capri map (www.carteguide.com; English version available; €5)*

Explore Capri's quieter side on this enjoyable walk that leads from the busy Piazzetta through peaceful side streets to a large natural arch and scenic overlook above the Faraglioni rocks. This walk is a loop that starts in the center of town and returns to the Via Camerelle. Much of the walk doesn't involve too many steps, but there is a stretch that requires a good number. If stairs are an issue, consider either doing the first part leading to the Arco Naturale and then turning back, or starting on the Via Camerelle, walking to the Belvedere di Tragara, and returning without doing the entire loop. To walk the entire loop takes about 2 hours, depending on the number of times you stop to take photos, of course.

Start off in the Piazzetta opposite the **Chiesa di Santo Stefano** and look for an arched walkway and signs pointing to the Arco Naturale. The walk is well-marked as it leads through the narrow streets and begins to head east out of the center of town along Via Matermania; keep following signs along Via Arco Naturale. As you approach the natural arch, there's a series of terraces and steps you can follow down to enjoy various viewpoints of the arch and the turquoise sea.

Walk back up the steps from the Arco Naturale and look for the signs nearby for the **Grotta di Matermania.** From there a steep staircase called Via del Pizzolungo leads down the forested mountainside past the Grotta di Matermania, a large cavern that the Romans once used as a luxurious nymphaeum (a monument dedicated to nymphs). Continue along Via del Pizzolungo, which becomes a more level and well-maintained walkway hugging the cliff side. Along the way you'll pass above the **Villa Malaparte,** a striking red villa that stands out against the natural setting. This private home was created by Italian writer Curzio Malaparte and is an intriguing example of Italian modern architecture. With its intense red hue and clean lines, the building stands out vividly atop Punta Massullo, with its steep cliffs dropping straight to the sea. The villa was donated to the Giorgio Ronchi Foundation in 1972 and is not open to the public.

Not far beyond the Villa Malaparte, the captivating Faraglioni rocks come into view. The landscape along this section of the Via del Pizzolungo is rugged cliffs and untouched nature; the only sounds are birds singing and boats puttering by in the sea below. When you reach the **Belvedere di Tragara,** you'll find a shady spot with an incredible view overlooking the Faraglioni rocks. From here, continue along Via Tragara, which leads to Via Camerelle and takes you right back into the heart of Capri town.

Anacapri
Belvedere della Migliera Walk
Distance: 1.4 mi (2.2 km) one-way
Time: 30 minutes one-way
Trailhead: Piazza Vittoria, Anacapri
Information and Maps: Local tourist offices or the Cart&guide Island of Capri map (www.carteguide.com; English version available; €5)

One of Capri's most peaceful and easy walks leads to a remarkable view at the **Belvedere della Migliera** (Via Migliera, Anacapri), where you can see all the way from the Faraglioni to the tip of the Punta Carena with its pink and white lighthouse. Starting in Piazza Vittoria, look for the chairlift to Monte Solaro. To the left of the chairlift, follow **Via Caposcuro** until it bends to the left and becomes **Via Migliera.** Continue along this road to the viewpoint at the very end. The relatively level walkway leads you through a rural landscape with terraces of grapevines, gardens, and a view in the distance across the Gulf of Naples to Ischia.

HIKING

Capri is excellent for hiking: The island's small size and public transportation routes make hikes relatively accessible. If you're looking to explore the natural landscape of Capri away from the crowds, there are plenty of options that feel very much off the tourist path along rugged dirt trails and beautiful cliffs, and they offer spectacular views. There will be plenty of steps and elevation changes during hikes, so sturdy, comfortable walking shoes are recommended. Because much of the landscape is exposed to the strong Mediterranean sunshine, a hat, sunscreen, and plenty of water are also strongly recommended. Trails are generally well marked with signs throughout the island, with the more rugged and rural hikes located in Anacapri.

Capri Trails
tel. 347/368-1699; www.capritrails.com; year-round; 3-hour private hike from €160

Experience Capri's most beautiful hikes with Luigi Esposito, a local Capri hiking guide who is passionate about sharing the island's natural treasures and scenic spots. Luigi can organize private guided hikes around Capri based on your experience and schedule, from shorter 3-hour hikes to full-day (6-8 hours) hikes. Contact him in advance to find out which of Capri's hikes is the best one for your time on the island.

Anacapri
Hiking to Monte Solaro
Distance: 1.4 mi (2.2 km) one-way
Time: 1.5 hours one-way

Trailhead: *Piazza Vittoria, Anacapri*
Information and Maps: *Island of Capri map by Cart&guide (www.carteguide.com; English version available; €5)*

While the chairlift to the top of Monte Solaro is a fun and easy way to reach Capri's highest point, the hike up the mountain to reach the summit is an equally beautiful experience. From Anacapri's central Piazza Vittoria, head down Via Capodimonte, and after a few minutes' walk, look for signs indicating Monte Solaro and a staircase leading up on the right. Follow Via Monte Solaro as it climbs up the mountainside; you'll traverse stone steps as well as concrete and dirt pathways. It's a steep walk that takes about 1 hour. At the top of the climb, you'll be rewarded with spectacular 360-degree views over the island. Enjoy a well-deserved rest before returning back down, or hop on the chairlift for the ride back to Piazza Vittoria.

BOAT TOURS AND RENTALS

Seeing Capri from the water is one of the best ways to enjoy the island's natural beauty up close. There are a number of different options readily available, from group boat tours that depart regularly from Marina Grande to private boat excursions. Marina Grande offers the most options for last-minute booking of group tours, which can be purchased right before boarding. But if you're traveling during the summer season, especially in July-August, it's a good idea to book a private boat excursion in advance.

Marina Grande
Laser Capri

Via Cristoforo Colombo 69; tel. 081/837-5208; www.lasercapri.com; 9am-4:30pm daily; from €21 pp

For an easy and affordable way to see Capri by sea and visit the Grotta Azzurra, check out the offerings from Laser Capri, right in Marina Grande. This provider offers a variety of group boat tour options. The classic boat tour highlights the most popular grottoes and cruises through the Faraglioni rocks. If you would like to visit the Grotta Azzurra, take an island tour that includes a visit (admission to Blue Grotto paid separately). The boats are medium-size and can be spotted easily, marked "Grotta Azzurra." Tours depart about every 30 minutes 9am-4pm daily from Pier 23 in Marina Grande, with the ticket office just opposite the pier.

Motoscafisti Capri

Private pier at dock no. 0; tel. 081/837-5646; www.motoscafisticapri.com; 9am-5pm daily; from €21 pp

Also located right in Marina Grande, this local company offers group boat tours to the Blue Grotto and around the island with an option to visit the Blue Grotto (admission to Blue Grotto paid separately). Tours depart 9:30am-2pm daily from the pier nearest where ferries arrive, located opposite the funicular train entrance. The tour to the Blue Grotto takes about 1 hour, while the tour around the island plus a stop at the Blue Grotto takes about 2 hours. Book your tickets online in advance to save time at the ticket office.

Capri Excursions

Marina Grande; tel. 366/317-0573; www.capriexcursions.com; Apr.-Oct.; from €250

Local captain Vittorio De Martino offers a variety of private boat excursions around the island aboard a comfortable Sorrento-style wooden boat. Tour guests meet in Marina Grande, and excursions can be customized or themed to include activities such as snorkeling, fishing, or photography experiences.

Marina Piccola
Capri Blue Boats

Via Mulo 72; tel. 339/619-2151; www.caprieblueboats.com; Apr.-Oct.; from €100

Located right on the beach in Marina Piccola, which is more tranquil than busy Marina Grande, Capri Blue Boats offers smaller self-drive boats that can be rented

---

1: Boat tours to the Grotta Azzurra depart from Marina Grande. **2:** path atop Monte Solaro **3:** chairlift to Monte Solaro

★ Cruising Around Capri's Sea Grottoes

Grotta Azzurra

Though the Grotta Azzurra, the Blue Grotto, gets most of the attention, Capri has many beautiful, colorful grottoes, and the best way to see them is on a boat tour around the island. Pack a picnic for the day, and remember to bring your swimsuit and plenty of sunscreen! While there are many small grottoes, the following self-guided tour takes in the largest and most impressive ones to visit around the island. There are tons of options for boat tours or rentals from Marina Grande. If you decide to rent your own boat, small boats can be rented without a boat license. Plan for at least 2 hours just to cruise around, but a half day is the better option to give you time to stop and swim.

without a license, as well as private boat excursions with captains. For both options, Capri Blue Boats uses wooden boats that are very traditional in the area. Self-drive rentals can be 2-7 hours, and excursions with a captain range from a 2.5-hour tour of the island all the way up to full-day excursions or sunset cruises.

Capri Hydro
Spiaggia di Marina Piccola; tel. 350/046-9234; www.caprihydro.com; Apr.-Oct.; from €40 pp

Experience the natural beauty of Capri up close with a kayaking or stand-up paddleboard (SUP) tour or with the more adventurous Fliteboard eFoil or SEABOB rentals or private lessons. Join experienced guides for either a group or private kayak and SUP tour to explore Capri's famous caves and beaches. Group kayak tours are for a maximum of 30 people, with a dedicated guide for every 10 kayakers, while for SUP group tours the maximum is 10 people.

COOKING CLASSES
Giardino di Capri
Traversa Monticello 3 and Via Vecchia Grotta Azzurra, Anacapri; tel. 347/334-6696; www.giardinodicapri.com; cooking classes and experiences vary by season; from €125 pp for a group, €150 private; advance booking required

With over a decade of sharing traditional Caprese dishes at their popular restaurant and cooking school Michel'angelo, husband-and-wife team Gianluca D'Esposito and Holly Star have started a new chapter that has taken

- Head out from Marina Piccola west toward the **Grotta Verde** (Green Grotto), noted for its intensely green water. It's a popular spot to stop and swim through little caves and a natural arch in the water.

- Continue along the coastline to the westernmost tip of the island, **Punta Carena,** which is marked by a pink and white lighthouse.

- Cruise along the rugged western coastline of the island past old **watchtowers** and **forts** perched at the edge of the cliffs.

- On the northwestern side of the island you'll find the famous **Grotta Azzurra** (Blue Grotto). Stop for a visit inside to see the light shimmering across the electric blue water. Here, you'll have to pay an entrance fee and transfer aboard a rowboat to be taken inside the grotto.

- Enjoy the views of Marina Grande while continuing east past the port. Look up high to catch a glimpse of the **Villa Lysis,** and around the northeast corner of the island the setting of the ruins of **Villa Jovis.**

- Cruising along the eastern coastline, stop to see the **Grotta Bianca** (White Grotto), a large cave that gets its name from the white hue of the calcareous material on the cliff side. Most impressive when seen from the sea, peering deeper inside reveals the **Grotta Meravigliosa** (Marvelous Grotto) high above.

- Not far from the White Grotto, keep gazing up to the mountain to look for the **Arco Naturale,** a large natural arch located high above the sea. This is a beautiful area to drop anchor for a swim, with soaring cliffs of unspoiled natural beauty and incredible turquoise water.

- Soon you'll see the striking red **Villa Malaparte,** a modern villa nestled right on top of the Punta Massullo promontory.

- End the day with a spectacular cruise right through the hole in the middle **Faraglioni** rock before returning to Marina Piccola.

their passion for Capri's traditional cooking and the finest locally sourced ingredients directly to the source in Anacapri at their peaceful garden home and nearby multi-terraced garden that cascades down the mountainside to the sea.

For an experience that celebrates the rural and agricultural traditions of Capri, don't miss the chance to enjoy a cooking class or tasting with Gianluca. Learn how to cook authentic Caprese dishes with seasonal menus inspired by what's fresh in the garden, sample delicious flavors with a cheese, wine, or EVOO tasting, or join a fun gelato or sorbet workshop. Cooking classes are held at their garden villa in Anacapri, while other experiences, such as olive harvests, yoga, meditation, and art classes, are held in the seaside garden terraces surrounded by nature with the sound of the sea as your backdrop. Discover one of the most peaceful spots on the island, with a spectacular view overlooking the Gulf of Naples with the islands of Ischia and Procida and the slopes of Mount Vesuvius in the distance. Contact them in advance for seasonal offerings and experiences available during your stay. Advance booking is required.

DRIVING TOURS

If hiking and water sports aren't for you, see the island in style and take home photos of the unique experience on a fun driving tour to Capri's most beautiful locations.

500 in Capri
Various locations; tel. 340/358-3818; www.500incapri.it; Mar.-Oct.; from €280; advance booking required

Capture beautiful holiday memories on Capri with a vintage car tour and private photo shoot in scenic spots around the island. Hop in an iconic lemon-yellow Fiat 500 from 1969 or a light blue Bianchina from 1962 and relax as your driver shows you a local side of the island. You'll stop in picture-perfect locations for photos with the classic cars and Capri as your backdrop.

Festivals and Events

Capri has a vibrant cultural scene with festivals and concerts throughout the summer season. Watching a religious procession weaving through the narrow streets of the island, you'll find that Capri's beauty is a stunning backdrop to some of the island's most memorable moments. In addition, the Villa San Michele in Anacapri and the Centro Caprense Ignazio Cerio and Villa Lysis in Capri host concert programs and events throughout the season.

CAPRI
Rolex Capri Sailing Week
info@rolexcaprisailingweek.com; www.rolexcaprisailingweek.com; early-mid-May

For a week every year in May, Capri is a top sailing hub of the Mediterranean. The Rolex Capri Sailing Week includes a variety of races and the celebrated sailing Regata dei Tre Golfi that starts dramatically at midnight in Naples and ends in Capri. Activity centers on Marina Grande, but a good viewpoint from high on the island is the panoramic terrace below the bell tower in the Piazzetta, with views over the Gulf of Naples.

Festa di San Costanzo
Piazzetta and Marina Grande; May 14

Celebrations for Capri's patron San Costanzo take place May 14 and include a grand procession that starts from the Chiesa di Santo Stefano in the Piazzetta and leads down to the Chiesa di San Costanzo along the road to Marina Grande. The heart of the procession is a large and very precious silver reliquary of the saint dating from 1715. Carried on a flower-covered platform and accompanied by music and the town's faithful, the statue is kept in the Chiesa di San Costanzo for a week before being returned to the Chiesa di Santo Stefano with another procession.

ANACAPRI
Festa di Sant'Antonio
Chiesa di Santa Sofia; June 13

Anacapri honors Sant'Antonio every year on June 13 with a colorful summer festival. Every neighborhood along the procession route is adorned with elaborate altars and designs created with flower petals on the ground. Balconies are draped with flowers and brightly colored blankets, and onlookers shower the statue of the saint with flowers as the procession passes. The procession begins at the Chiesa di Santa Sofia in Anacapri and leads through the streets of town before returning to the church.

Settembrata Anacaprese
www.comunedianacapri.it; starts last week of Aug.

Beginning the last week of August and lasting several days, this festival celebrates the annual grape harvest as well as Anacapri's culture and cuisine, with parades, music, local crafts, and, of course, good food. Each year the festival has a special theme, and the different areas of Anacapri compete to make the best floats and costumes for the parade.

Shopping

Famous around the world for fashion, Capri truly is a dream for shoppers, whether you're picking out a perfume made with flowers on the island, enjoying the iconic Capri experience of having sandals custom made, or splurging at a big-name designer boutique. Even if you're not big on shopping, it's still quite fun to browse the shop windows while strolling through Capri town or Anacapri.

CAPRI

Capri town is known for fine shopping, and you'll see why as soon as you arrive. The main shopping spots include the areas immediately surrounding the Piazzetta, **Via Vittorio Emanuele** and elegant **Via Camerelle**. This is where you'll find boutiques from top Italian and worldwide fashion designers, including Dolce & Gabbana, Salvatore Ferragamo, Valentino, Dior, Chanel, and more. Because those powerhouse brands speak for themselves, the selection of shopping spots listed here are more unique stores that represent Capri's artistic heritage, traditions, and style. Many are also smaller spots you might miss if you don't know where to look.

Perfume
Carthusia

factory: Viale Matteotti 2d; tel. 081/837-5393; www.carthusia.it; 9am-8pm daily May-Sept., 9am-4:30pm daily Oct.-Apr.

The air in Capri seems extra sweet, especially when you walk by one of the many Carthusia shops on the island. Legend has it that the first Carthusia perfume dates to 1380, when the prior of the Carthusian monastery, Certosa di San Giacomo, noticed that the water from a special floral bouquet he made for a visit by Queen Joanna I of Anjou had been infused with a captivating scent. The origin of the scent was traced back to a variety of wild carnation that grew on the island and became the first perfume of Capri.

Carthusia produces perfumes, soaps, lotions, and home products inspired by the flowers of Capri, and here you'll find distinctive souvenirs that reflect the island's history and capture its natural scents so you can take them home. Craftsmanship is this provider's top priority, and every step of the production is done by hand and with great care. Each scent is inspired by the island's native plants, featuring the sweet fragrances of geranium and lily of the valley, the woody scent of cedarwood, and the fresh smell of citrus blossoms. You can watch fragrances being produced in Carthusia's factory and main store.

You'll also find stores in **Marina Grande** (Via Marina Grande), **Anacapri** (Viale Axel Munthe 26), and **Capri** (Via Camerelle 10, Via F. Serena 26, Via Fuorlovado 2, Piazzetta Umberto I). Stores are also located in **Sorrento** (Corso Italia 117), **Naples** (Capodichino airport, Piazza San Domenico Maggiore 16), and **Positano** (Via della Tartana).

Sandals
Canfora

Via Camerelle 3; tel. 081/837-0487; www.canfora.com; 9:30am-11pm daily Apr.-Oct., 10:30am-5pm daily Nov.-Mar.

One of Capri's historic sandal boutiques, Canfora helped make handmade sandals synonymous with the jet-set life on Capri. In 1946, Amedeo Canfora decided to open a sandal shop across from the elegant Grand Hotel Quisisana. It was a small storefront with soles of shoes and decorative strips of leather lining the walls, and a workbench to create the shoes. The measurements of regular clients were kept in special books. Before long, word spread about the exquisite sandals created by Amedeo Canfora, and famous clients, including Britain's Princess Margaret, Grace Kelly, Maria Callas, and Jacqueline Kennedy, came to have custom-fitted sandals made.

The Canfora boutique has always been a cornerstone for tradition, quality, and creativity. Whether you're looking for something classic or glam, you'll find it here. Amedeo Canfora passed his skills down to his children, and then to his grandsons Fabrizio and Costanzo, who now can be found making sandals and running the shop in Capri. For a unique piece of Capri history you can wear and enjoy, have a pair of sandals custom made to fit while you wait.

Da Costanzo
Via Roma 49; tel. 081/837-8077; caprimania@ supereva.it; 10am-8:30pm daily Apr.-Oct.

A classic spot for handmade sandals since 1963, this little boutique is not far from the Piazzetta. Inside is a huge selection of beautiful sandals in a tiny space, where you can choose just the style you want and enjoy watching them being made right before your eyes.

Clothing and Accessories
Eco Capri
Via Fuorlovado 14; tel. 081/837-4510; www.ecocapri.com; 10am-8pm daily Apr.-Oct.

Tucked away on one of Capri's most charming shopping streets in the historic medieval center, this remarkable boutique captures the style and beauty of Capri with custom clothing, accessories, and home decor inspired by the incredibly creative Cerio family. Federico Alvarez de Toledo, the grandson of artist Letizia Cerio, has created a shop that is imbued with the spirit of Capri. Look for the stunning scarves, clothing, and decorative objects made with authentic prints and designs from the 1940s and 1950s reimagined in a modern resort style for today.

Y'am
Via Madonna delle Grazie 7; tel. 081/837-5510; www.yamcapri.it; 10:30am-8:30pm daily Apr. and Sept.-Oct., 10:30am-10pm daily May-Aug.

Capri-born designer Valeria De Gregorio launched this label in 2016 and created a clothing line inspired by Capri's fashion history and local style. The dresses and caftans are uniquely Capri with their colors and simple elegance, and the T-shirts with fun Neapolitan sayings make great souvenirs.

Ersilia Boutique
Via Vittorio Emanuele 53; tel. 081/837-7127; www.ersiliacapri.com; 10am-10pm daily mid-Mar.-Oct.

This is the spot to head for iconic Capri linen in a tempting array of Mediterranean blues and classic crisp white. There are plenty of styles to choose from, from tailored shirts to light, summery dresses. The quality is top-notch and the linen wears beautifully.

Laboratorio Capri
Via Ignazio Cerio 6; tel. 081/837-6296; www.laboratoriocapri.it; 10am-9pm daily Apr.-Oct.

Stroll down this quiet street a bit off the beaten path to find this treasure trove of Capri fashion and design. From classic to whimsical, you'll find an appealing selection of locally made clothing, bags, and accessories that recall the elegance of Capri in the 1950s and 1960s.

Books and Art
La Conchiglia
Via Le Botteghe 12; tel. 081/837-6577; www.edizionilaconchiglia.it; 9am-9pm daily Apr.-Sept., 9:30am-1pm and 3:30pm-7:30pm Mon.-Sat. Oct.-Mar.

Brimming with books and art, this bookstore will catch the eye of any book lover. Inside you'll find an excellent selection of books on local Capri history, culture, and landscape. Many of the works are published by their own publishing house, Edizioni La Conchiglia, with versions of popular titles available in English. You'll also find a bookshop in **Anacapri** (Via Giuseppe Orlandi 205; 9:30am-1pm and 3:30pm-7:30pm Mon.-Sat.).

Galleria d'Arte Antonio Palomba
Via Padre Reginaldo Giuliani 6/A; tel. 081/837-6751; antoniopalomba10@libero.it; 10am-8pm daily Mar. 19-Nov. 15

Tucked away in a blissfully quiet spot just off stylish Via Fuorlovado is the charming art gallery of artist Antonio Palomba. A third-generation painter from Capri, Antonio's artwork captures the color and magical light of the island in oil, watercolor, and other mediums. For a special souvenir from Capri, check out his paintings created directly on historic doors and window shutters—a unique architectural and creative piece of history.

ANACAPRI

Though you won't find as many high-fashion designer names in Anacapri as in Capri town, Anacapri is a lovely area for shopping with many wonderful small boutiques, local artisans, and a quieter pace. The best shopping area is around the busy **Piazza Vittoria, Via Giuseppe Orlandi,** and **Via Capodimonte.** You'll find shops selling ceramics, linen clothing, sandals, and jewelry. These streets are also home to the top sights in town, which means you can enjoy a bit of shopping while strolling to the Chiesa Monumentale di San Michele or Villa San Michele.

Ceramiche Tavassi

Via Giuseppe Orlandi 129; tel. 081/838-2067; ceramichetavassi@virgilio.it; www.tavassicapri.com; 9am-9pm daily Apr.-Dec.

This shop is as bright and beautiful as the ceramics on display, featuring traditional design elements like decorative tiles, coral, lemons, and fish, with a creative touch. Walk to the back of the shop to see new designs being hand-painted in the little studio.

Mik Mak

Via Giuseppe Orlandi 62; tel. 081/838-2210; d.farace@alice.it; 9:30am-11pm daily June-Aug., 9:30am-10pm daily Apr.-May and Sept.-Oct.

For fine-quality linen clothing and accessories for men and women, stop in this colorful shop in Anacapri. Unlike many shops, here you'll find beautiful pieces that are custom designed on Capri, made in Italy, and unique to this Anacapri shop.

Nino & Friends

Via Axel Munthe 16; tel. 081/837-3967; www.ninoandfriends.it; 9am-6pm daily Apr.-Oct.

The delicious scent from this large shop will lure you in as you walk along the tree-lined Via Axel Munthe. Selling chocolates, limoncello, coffee, and candies, the owners share a firm belief that you must sample their products to savor the flavors—this truly is a sweet stop. You'll find Capri-inspired perfumes and elegant sandals as well. They also have a location in **Capri** (Piazza Ignazio Cerio 4) just off the Piazzetta near the Chiesa di Santo Stefano.

Salvatore Federico

Via Capodimonte 58; tel. 081/837-3061; fabio@capri.it; 10am-6pm daily Apr.-Oct.

An Anacapri native with a grand passion for painting and music, Salvatore Federico has been capturing the ever-changing beauty of the island in his paintings and drawings since he was 7 years old. Along the walkway to Villa San Michele, you'll find his gallery full of captivating pieces, from large oil paintings down to delicate watercolors and charcoal sketches. Whatever your budget or space allows, you'll find a unique view of Capri by Salvatore to help you remember your visit.

Food

MARINA GRANDE
Seafood
Ristorante Da Gemma

Via Cristoforo Colombo, Capri; tel. 081/277-9056; www.dagemma.com; 9:30am-6:30pm daily (lunch 11am-6:30pm) mid-Apr.-mid-Oct.; €15-30

Just beyond the harbor at Marina Grande, this restaurant has a seafront terrace along with a lounge bar and **Le Ondine Beach Club.** Family-run for more than 80 years, this iconic Capri restaurant moved to its current location in 2017. With its setting overlooking the sea, the natural choice here is seafood. Each dish is as beautiful as it is delicious, focusing on freshness and tradition, from a tempting raw fish menu to creative appetizers and dishes combining seafood with other traditional Campania flavors to tempt your palate.

Regional Cuisine
Da Paolino

Via Palazzo a Mare 11, Capri; tel. 081/837-6102; www.paolinocapri.com; 12:30pm-2:15pm and 7pm-11:30pm daily late Apr.-May, 7pm-11:30pm daily June-late Oct.; €30-80

One of Capri's most romantic spots, this restaurant has an enchanting dining terrace nestled into a lemon grove. The menu is varied but very traditional, and includes beautiful pasta dishes as well as meat and fish main courses. The fresh pasta or ravioli with lemon sauce is a classic choice while dining under the lemon trees. Sautéed mussels and clams are divine, and the catch of the day is grilled to perfection. Booking in advance is necessary to secure a table.

Cafés
Bar Il Gabbiano

Via Cristoforo Colombo 76, Capri; tel. 081/837-6531; www.gabbianocapri.it; 7am-8pm daily Mar.-Nov.; €3-10

Whether you need a strong espresso after getting off the ferry or a spritz and a rest at the end of a day of sightseeing before leaving Capri, this friendly family-run bar along the harbor is a good choice. Just steps from where the ferries arrive and depart, choose from a great selection of cocktails, local wine, and freshly made juices. Next door, their tavola calda has an excellent menu with sandwiches, salads, bowls, and traditional dishes that can be enjoyed on-site or prepared for takeaway—especially handy if you're planning a boat trip around the island.

CAPRI
Seafood
Pescheria Le Botteghe

Via le Botteghe 19; tel. 081/837-6942; www.pescherialebotteghe.it; 12:30pm-3pm and 7pm-11pm Tues.-Sun. Apr.-Oct.; €10-30

Tucked away on a narrow street very near the Piazzetta, this local fish shop transforms into an excellent seafood diner for lunch and dinner with casual bar-style seating. You'll enjoy only the freshest fish, oysters, crudo di pesce (raw seafood), and outstanding fried calamari and alici (anchovies).

Regional Cuisine
Pulalli

Piazza Umberto I 4; tel. 081/837-4108; pulallicapri@gmail.com; noon-3pm and 7pm-midnight Wed.-Mon. Apr.-mid Nov.; €20-30

Dine right in the Piazzetta but above the crowds at this charming restaurant and wine bar next to Capri's famous bell tower. You'll enjoy great views in all directions from its panoramic terrace overlooking the piazza and Chiesa di Santo Stefano in one direction and toward the sea in the other. The menu has a young and refreshing approach that highlights fresh ingredients with a nice balance of seafood and meat as well as vegetarian options. The "Ricci e Capri . . . cci" pasta with

---

1: Carthusia perfume shop **2:** Taverna Anema e Core **3:** pizza at Lo Sfizio

sea urchin, roasted Piemonte hazelnuts, and orange-infused buffalo butter cream is exceptional. Wine enthusiasts will enjoy the extensive list of over 250 wines.

★ Il Geranio
Viale Giacomo Matteotti 8; tel. 081/837-0616; www.geraniocapri.com; noon-3pm and 7pm-11pm daily Apr.-Oct.; €20-35

Situated above the Giardini di Augusto, with the same gorgeous view overlooking the Faraglioni, this is one of Capri's most romantic dining spots. Whether you're looking for lunch with a view or a peaceful candlelit dinner under the pine trees, this is a great choice. Try the pappardelle (thick noodles) with fresh prawns followed by the grilled seafood platter. There's an excellent wine selection, and great desserts to finish off a delicious meal in an unforgettable setting.

Pizzeria
Lo Sfizio
Via Tiberio 7/e; tel. 081/837-4128; www.losfiziocapri.com; noon-3pm and 7pm-midnight Wed.-Mon. Apr.-mid-June, noon-3pm and 7pm-midnight daily mid-June-mid-Sept., noon-3pm and 7pm-midnight Wed.-Mon. mid-Sept.-Nov.; pizzas €7-18, pasta €10-24

This casual and friendly dining spot is located halfway between the Piazzetta and Villa Jovis. With both indoor and outdoor dining options, this pizzeria offers fresh pasta and meat and fish options as well as delicious pizza from the wood-fired oven. Try the Caprese Doc pizza inspired by the island favorite with mozzarella di bufala, fresh tomatoes, and basil. Popular with locals, this is a great affordable option away from the crowds, as long as you don't mind the 15-minute walk from the town center.

Gelato
Buonocore Gelateria
Via Vittorio Emanuele 35; tel. 081/837-7826; buonocore.capri@libero.it; 8am-10pm daily Apr.-May, 8am-midnight daily June-Oct.; €3.50-6

Stroll down Via Vittorio Emanuele from the Piazzetta to Via Camerelle and the divine scent of handmade cones from this gelateria and bakery will stop you in your tracks. It's a popular spot offering excellent quality. There's a selection of gelato you can buy at the window right off the street, but go inside to find baked goods like their caprilù (lemon and almond cookies) as well as savory dishes you can eat at one of the small bars inside.

ANACAPRI
Seafood
Restaurant Il Riccio
Via Gradola 4; tel. 081/837-1380; www.capripalace.com; 12:30pm-3:30pm Mon.-Wed., 12:30pm-3:30pm and 7:30pm-10:30pm Thurs.-Sun. June-mid Sept.; €46-80

Capri's most exclusive seaside dining address is on the rugged northwest tip of the island near the famed Blue Grotto. Boasting a Michelin star, this is the spot for seafood dining overlooking the sea. Start with their divine plateau royal with assorted raw fish, and then try the spaghetti with sea urchins, a local specialty. Just save room for dessert and a visit to the Temptation Room full of traditional Neapolitan and Caprese desserts. This is a Capri experience worth the splurge, but do make reservations in advance.

Regional Cuisine

★ Da Gelsomina
Via Migliara 72; tel. 081/837-1499; www.dagelsomina.com; noon-3:30pm and 7pm-11pm daily mid-Apr.-mid-Oct.; €12-26

Escape from the crowds near the beautiful Belvedere Migliera overlook, a pleasant walk from the center of Anacapri. Da Gelsomina also offers a complimentary shuttle service from the center of town if you call ahead. This family-run restaurant has a welcoming atmosphere and serves local favorites like ravioli filled with caciotta cheese as well as traditional chicken and rabbit dishes. If you're looking for a quiet escape, Da Gelsomina also has a small B&B (from €225) and a large pool nearby.

Ristorante Giorgio al Cucciolo

Via La Fabbrica 52; tel. 081/837-2675; www. giorgioalcucciolo.com; noon-3pm and 7pm-11pm Thurs.-Sun. mid-Oct.-mid-Apr., noon-3pm and 7pm-11pm Thurs.-Sun., 7pm-11pm Mon.-Wed. mid-Apr.-mid-Oct.; €15-30

Traditional Caprese dishes are the heart of this family-run restaurant with a remarkable view overlooking the Gulf of Naples. Located along the road to the Grotta Azzurra and surrounded by a peaceful natural setting, this eatery celebrates local fare that exudes simplicity and freshness. There's excellent seafood as well as other options if you're looking for a break from fish. With a reservation, shuttle service is available from the center of Anacapri.

La Zagara

Via Giuseppe Orlandi 180; tel. 081/837-2923; www. casamariantonia.com; noon-3pm and 7pm-11pm daily Apr.-Oct.; €18-58

Located at the serene Casa Mariantonia, right in the center of Anacapri, this lovely restaurant is set among the villa's lemon grove, where citrus scents blend perfectly with the Mediterranean flavors. The menu options are well balanced between seafood specialties like spaghetti with lobster or fresh sea bass and the excellent veal fillet or savory duck. Reservations are required, especially for dinner. For an aperitivo or light bistro-style meal, the Vinoteca della Zagara wine bar next to the restaurant's garden is a great spot.

Nightlife

If you enjoy a night out, stay in Capri town, the center of the island's chic nightlife scene. Capri town offers a variety of lively spots to sip cocktails, relax with a prosecco at a rooftop bar, or dance until the early hours of the morning in one of the island's hottest nightclubs.

CAPRI

Salotto Bohémien

Via Padre Serafino Cimmino 4; tel. 328/127-4890; www.salottobohemiencapri.it; 5:30pm-1am daily Feb.-Dec.; €8-27

With a panoramic terrace and a delightfully hidden-away vibe, this is the Capri spot you'll love so much that you'll want to keep it a secret. Salotto means "living room," and this wine bar has a relaxed atmosphere that's perfect for watching the sunset. Located right next to the Piazzetta, grab a spot at the long bar overlooking the view or at one of the small tables. A great drinks menu can be paired with even more tempting cheese and salami trays, sandwiches, and creative daily specials.

Taverna Anema e Core

Via Sella Orta 1; tel. 081/837-6461; www.anemaecore. com; 11pm-4am daily Apr.-Sept.; admission from €50 pp

A Capri nightlife institution in the best possible way, Gianluigi Lembo continues the tradition of his father, Guido Lembo, who created a nightlife spot that's truly full of heart and soul. A lively and fun atmosphere and performance style brings the audience into the experience in a way that has made this nightclub one of the most famous in the world. You might catch sight of international movie stars, musicians, athletes, and VIP visitors in a truly unique hot spot that stands apart from other clubs. Admission is €50 per person, and for a table, prices start at €100. Reservations for tables are strongly recommended July-August.

Capri Rooftop

Via Matteotti 7; tel. 081/837-8147; www.caprirooftop. com; 10am-2am daily mid-May-mid-Sept., 9am-midnight daily mid-Apr.-mid-May and mid-Sept.-Nov.; from €20

If your idea of evening entertainment is a cocktail and a gorgeous view, head to Capri Rooftop. Set above the Hotel Luna next to the Giardini di Augusto, this rooftop bar affords spectacular views of the Faraglioni in the distance. Choose from a tempting selection of classic cocktails and signature creations like the Luna Caprese, made with limoncello, vodka, citrus, and soda.

ANACAPRI
Maliblu Sunset
Faro Punta Carena; tel. 081/837-2560; www.maliblusunset.com; noon-9:30pm daily Apr.-Oct.; €10-12

With a gorgeous setting on Punta Carena at the southwest tip of Capri, this beach club is popular with sunbathers during the day, and the fun kicks up a notch as the sun begins to set. Summer events include sunset parties with DJs and live music.

Accommodations

Although not a very large island, Capri has an abundance of accommodations. Because it's one of the most popular destinations in the Campania region, it's not unusual for hotels to be fully booked for much of the season. It's always a good idea to book in advance for Capri, especially if you have a certain hotel or experience in mind. Capri isn't cheap when it comes to accommodations, which gives you even more reason to book an affordable room well in advance.

CAPRI

Capri town is the hub of activity on the island and a good place to base your stay, especially if you enjoy the shopping scene, nightlife, and easy access to the beach at Marina Piccola.

€100-200
★ Hotel La Tosca
Via Dalmazio Birago 5; tel. 081/837-0989; www.latoscahotel.com; late Mar.-early Nov.; €180 d

Set in one of the loveliest areas of Capri, yet at a price point that's easy on the wallet, this small hotel has been created in a traditional home with a setting surrounded by gardens with views of the Certosa di San Giacomo monastery and the Faraglioni beyond. The 11 large rooms are peaceful and some even have little terraces with sea or garden views. Breakfast is served on the terrace with a view of the sea, or in your room for no extra charge. This is a top affordable option in the heart of Capri town.

€200-300
★ Hotel Canasta
Via Campo di Teste 6; tel. 081/837-0561; www.hotelcanastacapri.it; Apr.-Oct.; €200 d

Set in a tranquil spot not far from the Certosa di San Giacomo monastery, this boutique hotel is a little Capri gem. Inside you'll find only 15 rooms, but all are nicely appointed and very welcoming. Standard rooms have a patio with internal view, while medium rooms offer a terrace with garden view. For a sea view, try to score one of the two superior double rooms with a terrace. There's also a top-notch restaurant, **Villa Margherita** (tel. 081/837-7532; www.ristorantevillamargheritacapri.com; noon-2pm and 7pm-11pm daily Apr.-Oct.; €26-45), which serves a lovely raw seafood starter and their specialty Fettuccine Villa Margherita, lemon fettuccine with shrimp infused with lemon peels. With a swimming pool and lovely outdoor lounge area, this is a place you will love to call home on Capri.

Gatto Bianco Hotel & Spa
Via Vittorio Emanuele 32, Capri; tel. 081/837-0203; www.gattobianco-capri.com; Apr.-Oct.; €300 d

For three generations, this family-run hotel right in the center of Capri has welcomed guests as well as artists and writers from around the world. With an incredibly private yet central location, the atmosphere still has the essence of the 1950s La Dolce Vita spirit of Capri with its mix of antique decor, paintings, and beautiful ceramic-tiled floors. The

44 rooms and 4 suites are colorfully decorated and welcoming, while the indoor and outdoor garden sitting areas are perfect for conversation. The hotel's name comes from the resident white cat—the latest incarnation called Mirò.

Over €300
★ Hotel Luna

Viale Giacomo Matteotti 3; tel. 081/837-0343; www.lunahotel.com; May-Oct.; €400 d

With a dream location tucked away between the Giardini di Augusto and the Certosa di San Giacomo, this hotel boasts stellar views of the Faraglioni as well as a large pool, a gym with a sea view, a small spa, and beautifully landscaped grounds. All the rooms are recently renovated and furnished with Mediterranean accents and Caprese style. Rooms range from Standard to Imperial, but here you'll want to go for one of the 18 Camera Deluxe, 2 Imperial, or 4 Suites to have a private terrace with a view of the sea and Faraglioni. Dining well is right at your fingertips with two restaurants and two bars on-site, including the **Capri Rooftop** bar (Via Matteotti 7; tel. 081/837-8147; www.caprirooftop.com; 10am-9:30pm daily Apr.-Nov.).

ANACAPRI

Anacapri's setting, higher on the island than Capri town, lends it a sense of calm that makes it a quieter spot for a holiday stay. You'll find secluded B&Bs, luxury five-star hotels, and everything in between.

€100-200
Il Tramonto Bed-and-Breakfast

Via Migliera 30/b; tel. 366/426-3757; www.iltramonto.it; €140 d

Immersed in the natural landscape of Anacapri along the walk to Belvedere della Migliera, this welcoming B&B is aptly named with the Italian word for sunset because the views are extraordinary from the garden. The four lovely rooms all open to the sun terrace, which is well equipped with chairs, umbrellas, and comfortable places to lounge.

Hotel Al Mulino

Via La Fabbrica 11; tel. 081/838-2084; www.mulino-capri.com; Easter-Oct.; €180 d

Located in a former farmhouse, this small rural-chic hotel, run by the grandchildren and family of the original owners, has a beautiful setting surrounded by fruit trees, olive trees, and charming gardens. The eight rooms are bright and cheerfully decorated. All open onto private terraces surrounded by nature. The pool is perfect for a refreshing dip while relaxing on the sun terrace.

Over €300
★ Casa Mariantonia

Via Giuseppe Orlandi 180; tel. 081/837-2923; www.casamariantonia.com; late Mar.-early Nov.; €340 d

One of the prettiest spots on the island, this boutique hotel is set in a lemon grove and offers a peaceful escape right in the center of Anacapri. Named after the grandmother of the current hosts, the hotel has a welcoming family feel and the service is as warm and inviting as the nine rooms and relaxing pool. Dine under lemon trees at the hotel's restaurant **La Zagara** or enjoy an evening aperitivo at the well-stocked wine bar Vinoteca della Zagara.

Hotel Caesar Augustus

Via Giuseppe Orlandi 4; tel. 081/837-3395; www.caesar-augustus.com; mid-Apr.-Oct; €790 d

Perched on the edge of a cliff boasting a breathtaking view of Mount Vesuvius, Ischia, and the entire sweep of the Gulf of Naples, this remarkable property began as a private home two centuries ago. It later became an exclusive retreat for artists and intellectuals from around the world, and today it's a popular spot for travelers looking for a luxurious and calm oasis on Capri. The double infinity pool is a place of dreams, and just beyond is a 2-acre (0.8-ha) garden where the majority of produce used in the on-site restaurant is grown. There are 49 finely appointed rooms and six exclusive suites, each one more beautiful than the last. This is where you definitely want to splurge on a sea-view cliff-side room.

Information and Services

If you need to store your bags for the day on Capri, you'll find a staffed **luggage storage office** near the arrival area in the Marina Grande port, to the left of the Bar Grotta Azzurra. Most hotels work with porters to help transfer your luggage upon arrival and for departure, and the service is well worth the cost. If you're staying in a vacation rental or smaller B&B that doesn't arrange the service, you can contact the porters at **Cooperativa Portuali Capresi** (Via Prov. Marina Grande 270, tel. 081/837-0896, www.coopportualicapresi-capri.it, from €10 per bag to Capri, €15 per bag for Anacapri).

TOURIST INFORMATION
**Agenzia Regionale
Campania Turismo**
Piazza Umberto I, Capri; tel. 081/837-0686; www.capritourism.com; 8:30am-8pm daily June-Sept., 8:30am-4:15pm Mon.-Fri. Nov.-May

Capri's tourist office has information points in the three main areas of the island. Upon arrival at Marina Grande, you'll find an info point at the Molo "0" pier (tel. 081/837-0634; 8:30am-1:30pm and 2pm-6pm Mon.-Sat.). In Capri town, the info point is in an easy-to-spot location in the Piazzetta directly below the bell tower (tel. 081/837-0686). In Anacapri, the info point is at Piazza Vittoria 5 and is open the same hours as the Piazzetta info point.

HEALTH SERVICES
Should medical services be needed or an emergency arise, Capri's hospital, **Ospedale Capilupi** (Piazzale Anacapri 3, Capri; tel. 081/838-1206), is located at the rotary intersection of the road to reach Capri town's center and the road up to Anacapri. In an emergency, head to the emergency room (pronto soccorso) or dial 118.

Transportation

Capri is reachable by boat year-round from Naples and Sorrento, and seasonally from other locations in the Gulf of Naples and Amalfi Coast. Capri is a small island with two towns that are easy to reach from the Marina Grande harbor, where all boats arrive. Transportation options are readily available near where ferries dock, including taxis, buses, and the funicular train to Capri town.

GETTING THERE
All ferries to Capri arrive at **Marina Grande,** also the island's **Porto Turistico** (www.portoturisticodicapri.com). Cruise ships drop anchor off of Marina Grande and shuttle passengers to the port. In the Gulf of Naples, there's a variety of ferry companies offering year-round regular connections to Capri from Naples and Sorrento, and seasonal service from the Amalfi Coast, Salerno, Ischia, and Procida. Prices and speed vary depending on the type of ferry, with options ranging from fast jet boats and hydrofoils to slower ferries that also transport cars. The faster the boat, the higher the price, but they all arrive in Marina Grande on Capri. All are comfortable options, and the departure port and time usually determine which company to use, as nearly all providers offer a variety of boats. Tickets from most companies can be purchased online in advance or at ticket booths at the departure port. For peak summer travel, buying tickets in advance is a good idea to ensure you get a seat. Check when booking

online if you need to pick up the tickets at the ticket booth before departure, as some companies may require it. If so, plan extra time in case of queues at the ticket booths.

From Naples

To reach Capri from Naples, head to the Molo Beverello in the Naples port, where the majority of the passenger ferries depart and arrive. If you're looking for speed, opt for a jet or aliscafo (hydrofoil) from **NLG** (tel. 081/552-0763; www.nlg.it; from €23.50), **Gescab** (tel. 081/704-1911; www.gescab.it; from €24), or **SNAV** (tel. 081/428-5555; www.snav.it; from €25.50). If you're transporting a car, you'll need to book on a traghetto or motonave (ferries) operated by **Caremar** (tel. 081/189-66690; www.caremar.it; passengers €15.40-21.20, vehicles €39.10). Crossing to Capri takes about 1 hour from Naples, but can vary slightly depending on the type of ferry.

From Sorrento

Ferries for Capri depart from Sorrento's Marina Piccola harbor and offer regular connections throughout the year with more departures during the busy season April-October. The companies **NLG** (tel. 081/807-1812; www.nlg.it; from €21.10), **Alilauro** (tel. 081/878-1430; www.alilaurogruson.it; from €21.60), and **Gescab** (tel. 081/428-5259; www.gescab.it; from €21.60) offer frequent service from Sorrento to Capri. **Caremar** (tel. 081/189-66690; www.caremar.it; passengers from €17.60, vehicles €29.90) also offers passenger and car ferries from Sorrento to Capri. **Laser Capri** (tel. 081/837-5208; www.lasercapri.com; from €20) also offers several departures a day. It is a quick 30-minute ferry ride from Sorrento to Capri.

From the Amalfi Coast

While ferry service to Capri runs year-round from Naples and Sorrento, ferries from the Amalfi Coast only run from about Easter-early November. **Alicost** (tel. 089/871-483; www.alicost.it; from €23.50) offers regular ferry service from Salerno, Vietri, Cetara, Maiori, Minori, Amalfi, and Positano on the Amalfi Coast. From Salerno there are usually 1-3 ferry services in the morning, and the journey is a little over 2 hours. From Cetara and Vietri, there is one ferry departure in the morning and it takes just under 2 hours to reach Capri. From Maiori and Minori there's usually only one departure in the morning for Capri, and it takes about 1 hour 40 minutes from Maiori, and 1 hour 30 minutes from Minori. From Amalfi and Positano, there are 1-4 departures daily for Capri and the journey takes about 1 hour 20 minutes from Amalfi and 45 minutes from Positano. From Amalfi and Positano, **Lucibello** (tel. 089/875-032; www.lucibello.it; from €23.50) also offers a ferry service to Capri with Positano Jet; it runs three times a day and takes 40 minutes from Positano and 1 hour from Amalfi.

Car Restrictions

Due to its small size and narrow roads, the island of Capri limits the number of cars on the island during the busiest times of the year. Early April-early November and December 18-January 7, nonresidents are not permitted to bring a car to Capri. So if you're traveling around Italy by car, you'll need to leave it in a garage on the mainland before continuing on to Capri via ferry. If you're visiting outside those dates, you will be able to bring your car on one of the larger ferries, usually called a traghetto. However, even off-season, navigating Capri by car isn't recommended, as parking is extremely limited and the island is quite small and fairly easy to navigate by public transportation.

GETTING AROUND

With plenty of transportation options and the island's small size, Capri is easy to navigate—in theory. The challenge comes when the island gets crowded, especially during peak summer season. Be prepared for lines, and allow extra time to get around on public transportation. The good news is that, although it can be busy, Capri is full of inexpensive ways to get around. Note that large pieces of luggage are not allowed on the small Capri buses or the funicular train. You can travel with a small bag, maximum size 9 by 12 by 20 in (23 by 30 by 50 cm) and not more than 22 lbs (10 kg), which is about the size of a carry-on, but be sure to purchase a supplementary ticket of €2.20. For large luggage, you'll need to take a taxi or arrange porter service to transfer your luggage to your accommodation.

By Bus

Capri's public buses are pint-size to match the island and connect all the main points on Capri, including Marina Grande, Capri town, Anacapri, Marina Piccola, Punta Carena, and the Grotta Azzurra. Buses are operated by **A.T.C.** (tel. 081/837-0420) and the cost is €2.20 per ride if you purchase tickets before boarding at the bus terminals, or €2.70 if you buy them on board. Tap your ticket on the machine near the driver to validate it when you board. Buses run every 15-30 minutes about 6am-midnight daily on most routes, but the buses are small and can be very crowded in summer. The bus lines on Capri run between Marina Grande and Capri town, Marina Grande and Anacapri, Capri town and Anacapri, and Capri town and Marina Piccola, as well as from Anacapri to Punta Carena and Anacapri to the Grotta Azzurra. The bus from Marina Grande to Capri town and from Capri town to Anacapri takes about 15 minutes, while from Marina Grande to Anacapri takes about 20 minutes.

In Marina Grande, the bus terminal is located on the western side of the port next to the ticket booths. In Capri town, the main bus terminal is on Via Roma very near the Piazzetta. In Anacapri, buses pick up in Piazza Vittoria and the nearby terminal at Viale T. De Tommaso 22. Given the high demand, there are usually points indicating where to wait for each bus line.

By Funicular

Capri's **Funicolare** (Servizio Funicolare S.I.P.P.I.C.; Piazza Umberto I, Capri; tel. 081/837-0420; www.funicolaredicapri.it; €2.20 each way) is a train line connecting Marina Grande with Capri town at the Piazzetta. The cable car train runs diagonally up the side of the mountain and offers an inexpensive and relatively quick way to travel between the port and Capri town. Tickets can be purchased before boarding in the office at the entrance in the Piazzetta or across the street from the large entrance marked Funicolare in Marina Grande, near the ferry ticket booths. During the busy season, there can be long lines at Marina Grande in the morning to go up to Capri town as well as to return to the port later in the day. Plan accordingly to avoid stress or rushing, especially if you are going down to Marina Grande to catch a ferry. The funicular runs about every 15 minutes 6:30am-8:30pm or 9pm daily.

By Taxi

Certainly the most comfortable way to get around Capri is by taxi, especially one of the classic open-top ones. You'll find taxis in Marina Grande near where the ferries arrive and depart, in Capri town at Piazza Martiri d'Ungheria near the Piazzetta, and in Piazza Vittoria in Anacapri. Keep in mind that fares are higher than in some other locations, with a minimum fare of €9 and set fare starting at €17 for the short jaunt between Marina Grande and Capri town, and up to €40 for a trip from Marina Grande to the Grotta Azzurra. There are predetermined rates, but it's still essential to agree on the rate with the driver before departing. One reliable company is the **Cooperative Taxi Capri** (tel. 081/837-6464; www.capritaxi.it), which offers round-the-clock service.

By Scooter

If you'd like more freedom to move around the island and have a sense of adventure, renting a scooter on Capri could be a good choice. Keep in mind that the roads are very narrow and twisty, and busy with traffic during the season, early spring-October. Parking is difficult to find too, which can make things a little tricky. However, a scooter does offer the chance to explore the entire island relatively quickly and at your own pace. There are multiple options to rent one on the island, but **Oasi Motor** (Via Cristoforo Colombo 47; tel. 081/837-7138; www.oasimotorcapri.it; 9am-7pm daily Mar.-Oct., 9am-1:30pm and 3pm-7pm Mon.-Sat. Nov.-Feb.; from €30) is conveniently located right in Marina Grande.

Ischia and Procida

Itinerary Ideas 240	
Ischia Town 244	
Casamicciola Terme 255	
Lacco Ameno 261	
Forio 268	
Serrara Fontana, Sant'Angelo, and Barano d'Ischia 274	
Procida 281	

An island with volcanic origins, Ischia offers an exquisite blend of verdant mountain slopes, turquoise sea, thermal spas, and fishing villages. Around every corner there's a varied landscape to discover, from bubbling hot thermal springs to steeply sloped vineyards and historic castles. Although this island is not on every day-tripper's radar, Ischia is an oasis that is ideal for a relaxing holiday surrounded by nature.

Called the Isola Verde (Green Island), Ischia centers on Monte Epomeo, which soars to 2,589 ft (789 m) and is largely covered by thick vegetation and forests. Although its volcanic history has made the island incredibly lush, its name is thought to refer to the unusual

Highlights

Look for ★ to find recommended sights, activities, dining, and lodging.

★ **Castello Aragonese, Ischia:** Enjoy panoramic views while exploring the medieval castle, churches, and ruins perched atop a rocky islet (page 244).

★ **Ischia's Thermal Spas:** Spend time relaxing in one of the island's many thermal spas, which have been famous since ancient times for the healing properties of their waters (page 258).

★ **Giardini La Mortella, Ischia:** Visit the sprawling gardens of English composer Sir William Walton and his wife (page 268).

★ **Chiesa del Soccorso, Ischia:** With its simple white facade, this small church is set on a picturesque promontory overlooking the sea (page 269).

★ **Sant'Angelo, Ischia:** This quaint fishing village on Ischia's southern coast is one of the island's chicest spots (page 275).

★ **Hiking Monte Epomeo, Ischia:** Hike up to the island's highest point on the mountain that forms the green heart of Ischia (page 277).

★ **Marina Corricella, Procida:** Dine seaside in this colorful and much photographed village on Procida (page 281).

★ **Terra Murata, Procida:** Explore the narrow streets and historic churches of Procida's medieval town and take in the views from the island's highest point (page 282).

Ischia and Procida

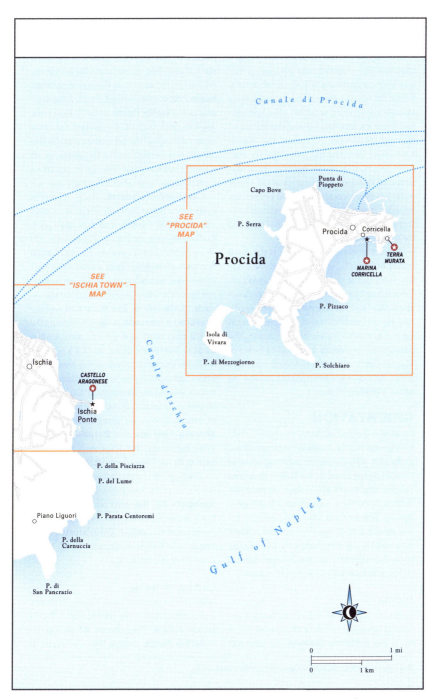

green-hued tufa stone that is found on Ischia, especially on the southern side of the island.

Spilling down the slopes to the rugged coastline, the island's towns have a rich history to discover, dating to early Greek settlers. While the island's natural beauty and quaint villages are alluring, what has attracted visitors since ancient times is the abundance of thermal springs dotted around the island. Known for their healing properties for over 2,000 years, nearly 100 hydrothermal basins and fumarole fields offer a variety of water temperatures and chemical properties. Whether you're looking for pure relaxation or therapeutic treatments, Ischia's spas are good for the body and soul.

A short ferry ride from Ischia is the small island of Procida, easily explored on a day trip from Ischia or Naples. But Procida's relaxed allure begs a longer visit if your travels allow. Stay and meander through the medieval Terra Murata village at the island's highest point, enjoy leisurely lunches among the pastel-hued buildings and fishing boats of Marina Corricella, and experience your own *Il Postino* movie moments biking around the island's residential streets.

ORIENTATION

Located in the Gulf of Naples about 20.5 mi (33 km) west of Naples, Ischia is the largest island in the gulf, with the tiny neighboring island of Procida sitting closer to the Italian mainland not far off the tip of Capo Miseno, the point that defines the northern edge of the Gulf of Naples. Procida sits only about 5 mi (8 km) east of Ischia and about 8.1 mi (13 km) west of Capo Miseno. It's a small island measuring only 1.4 sq mi (3.7 sq km), compared to the much larger island of Ischia, which covers 18.1 sq mi (47 sq km).

Ischia

Ischia is a large island and is home to six towns located along the coastline and spread out on the slopes of **Monte Epomeo,** the mountain that rises up from the center of the island. Ischia's largest port, where the majority of ferries arrive and depart, is located in the town also called Ischia, which covers the northeastern part of the island from the port area, called **Ischia Porto,** down to the Castello Aragonese area called **Ischia Ponte.** Near Ischia's port, you can catch the SP270, the main road that weaves through all the towns and circles back to Ischia town. Getting around the island, which is larger than many travelers expect, can take a bit of patience, especially during high season.

Casamicciola Terme, about 2.5 mi (4 km) west of Ischia Porto on SP270, is another important ferry arrival and departure port. Continuing west about 1.2 mi (2 km) on SP270 along Ischia's north coastline leads to **Lacco Ameno,** stretching from a charming port to the west to a hilly area at the northwestern tip of the island where you'll find the secluded **Spiaggia di San Montano** and the **Giardini La Mortella** gardens. Following the SP270 road southwest out of Lacco Ameno leads to **Forio,** about 2.4 mi (3.8 km) away on Ischia's western coastline; the town's port offers limited ferry service. Continuing the circuit around the island on SP270, the road climbs away from the coastline to the slopes of Monte Epomeo, through the towns of **Serrara Fontana** and **Barano d'Ischia.** From Barano d'Ischia, it's about 4.3 mi (7 km) back to Ischia Porto along SP270.

The popular seaside spots of **Sant'Angelo** (about 4 mi/6 km from Forio) and the **Spiaggia dei Maronti** (about 2 mi/3 km from Barano d'Ischia), on Ischia's southern coast, are not located on SP270; to reach them, you have to follow roads splitting off to the coast from the main road.

Getting to Ischia

With ferries arriving from Naples, Sorrento, and other islands in the Gulf of Naples, Ischia is easy to reach. The majority of ferries arrive in **Ischia Porto,** though they also arrive at

---

Previous: Sant'Angelo; Marina Corricella; Castello Aragonese.

Casamicciola Terme and **Forio**. The main ferry companies serving Ischia are **Caremar** (www.caremar.it), **SNAV** (www.snav.it), **Medmar** (www.medmargroup.it), **Alilauro** (www.alilaurogruson.it), and **Alicost** (www.alicost.it). Though there are restrictions on bringing a car to Ischia, they're only for residents of Campania April-September and don't apply to rental cars. You will want to check in advance with your car rental agency to ensure there won't be any issues taking your car on a ferry. However, getting around the island by car is often an added hassle given the traffic on the narrow roads and parking challenges during the summer. It's often easier to hop around the island by taxi or on the many public buses that circle Ischia.

Buses Around Ischia

Getting around the island is relatively easy thanks to a series of bus lines. Regular bus service is operated by **EAV** (www.eavsrl.it) and is an inexpensive option for exploring the island. The main lines circulating the island are the CS (Circolare Sinistra) and the CD (Circolare Destra). The CS runs from Ischia Porto west to Casamicciola Terme, Lacco Ameno, Forio, Panza, Sant'Angelo, Serrara Fontana, Barano d'Ischia, and back to Ischia Porto. The CD runs the same route in the opposite direction. Bus line 1 connects Ischia Porto, Casamicciola Terme, Lacco Ameno, Forio, and Sant'Angelo, while line 2 follows the same route but goes only as far as Forio. Within Ischia town, line 7 runs between Ischia Porto and Ischia Ponte.

Buses run about 4:30am-2:30am daily, although sometimes service ends around midnight, with buses every 15-30 minutes for the CD and CS lines and most other main lines around the island. Tickets start at €1.60 for a single ride, and there are 1-day passes available for €4.80, 3-day passes for €11, and 7-day passes for €14.50. Tickets need to be validated at the machine near the driver when you board; passes are validated on the first ride only. Tickets can be purchased in local tabacchi (tobacco shops) or in Ischia Porto at the bus terminal in Piazza Trieste near the ferry terminal.

Hiring a Taxi

Taxis in Ischia are all privately owned. The best way to catch one is to head to a taxi stand in any of the towns on the island, usually located in the town center or along the waterfront and marked with an orange Taxi sign. You'll find taxi stands right by the ports in Ischia Porto, Casamicciola Terme, or Forio. Taxi sizes vary from sedans to minivans to very characteristic micro taxis, 4-wheeled or sometimes even 3-wheeled vehicles that can zip around the narrow streets of the island with ease. Some are even open on the sides or top for a breezy ride on a summer day. Set fares vary between towns on the island, but expect to find fares are higher during peak periods. Be sure to ask for the fare to your destination and agree on a price before leaving.

Procida

All ferries to Procida arrive in the island's **Marina Grande** port on the northeast side of the island. From there it's a pleasant walk to reach **Marina Corricella,** a small seaside village with pastel-hued buildings, and **Terra Murata,** the oldest settlement and the highest point on Procida. On the southwest side of the island is the **Marina Chiaiolella,** a small harbor, and beyond the islet of **Vivara,** which is now a nature reserve.

PLANNING YOUR TIME

Given its size and variety of experiences, **Ischia** warrants more than just a day trip. It's an ideal setting for relaxation, with a wealth of thermal spas, water parks, and beaches. If you're looking for a relaxed holiday that will take full advantage of Ischia's charms, plan to spend at least 3 days on Ischia to take in the main sights like the **Castello Aragonese,** beautiful **Giardini La Mortella,** and picturesque **Sant'Angelo.** You'll also want to enjoy some time at the beaches, experiencing a **thermal spa** or two, and hiking along the rugged slopes of **Monte Epomeo.** Using Ischia as a base, **Procida** makes an ideal day trip thanks to its proximity and small size.

Itinerary Ideas

2 DAYS ON ISCHIA

With beautiful vistas, tempting beaches, and soothing thermal spas, Ischia beckons for a leisurely stay. However, if your time is limited, you can still spend a fun couple of days exploring a few of the highlights and getting in a little time at a thermal spa. The fastest and easiest way to get around the island is to hire a taxi to hop from town to town, but the towns on the island are also well connected by the local buses.

Day 1

1 Begin the day in Ischia Porto where the majority of ferries arrive. Head along the northern coastline of the island to the town of **Lacco Ameno.** Stroll along the waterfront of the lovely harbor with a view of the Il Fungo rock.

2 Visit the **Giardini La Mortella,** remarkable terraced gardens between Lacco Ameno and Forio.

3 Head south on the island to Forio to see the **Chiesa del Soccorso** with its stark white facade and sweeping view overlooking the town.

4 Stop for a fresh lunch of local seafood and traditional Ischia specialties at **Saturnino,** overlooking the harbor in Forio.

5 Head back to the charming Ischia Ponte area (plan about 40 minutes by taxi or longer by bus) and admire the view out to the **Castello Aragonese.** Take the elevator to the top of the castle to explore the fascinating medieval site.

6 Take an evening stroll along the lively shop-lined **Corso Vittoria Colonna** in Ischia Porto for great local atmosphere. Enjoy a bit of shopping or perhaps have a pair of sandals made to fit at Mariarosaria Ferrara Sandals.

7 Enjoy a delicious dinner of local seafood at **Cap' e' Fierr,** right on the beach in Ischia town.

Day 2

1 Start the morning by heading up into the mountains southwest of Ischia Ponte to the **Fonte delle Ninfe Nitrodi** thermal spa for some relaxation time. Enjoy lunch at their on-site restaurant, which serves healthy dishes inspired by the natural setting.

2 Take a taxi (about 25 minutes) from the spa to **Sant'Angelo,** where you can meander through the pedestrian-only area and enjoy a stroll along the water's edge in this picturesque fishing village.

3 Elena Ferrante fans can spend a relaxing afternoon by the sea at the **Spiaggia dei Maronti** near Sant'Angelo, featured in her novels. Water taxis are available between the beach and Sant'Angelo's small harbor.

4 For an adventurous thermal experience, hop on a water taxi from Sant'Angelo to the nearby **Baia di Sorgeto,** where you can soak in the hot bubbling water from the thermal springs just below the sea.

5 Return by water taxi to Sant'Angelo and enjoy romantic views overlooking the village while dining on fresh seafood at **Deus Neptunus.**

ESSENTIAL PROCIDA

Procida's small size makes it easy to explore on a day trip. This itinerary is easy to cover on foot, but taxis are also readily available on the island if walking distances or uphill isn't possible.

1 Stroll along the harbor in **Marina Grande** on Via Roma. Stop for coffee and try lingue di bue, a traditional Procida cream-filled pastry, at Bar dal Cavaliere.

2 Head to explore **Terra Murata,** the medieval fortified old town on Procida's highest point.

3 Visit the 16th-century **Abbazia di San Michele Arcangelo** for views of the Gulf of Naples.

4 Follow the steep steps and narrow passageways down to Marina Corricella. Stop for lunch at **La Lampara** just steps from the colorful fishing boats lining the harbor.

5 After lunch, take a leisurely walk around the pastel-hued **Marina Corricella** and stop for a gelato at Chiaro Di Luna.

6 For time at the beach, head to the nearby **Spiaggia della Chiaia.** Rent a sun bed from La Conchiglia and spend the afternoon relaxing.

Deus Neptunus

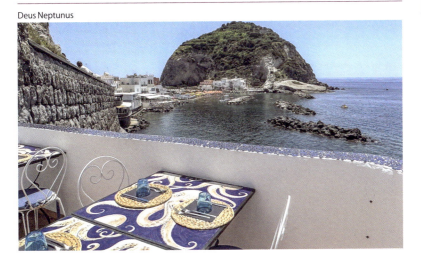

Itinerary Ideas

Ischia Town

Ischia's largest town is also the first point of arrival for many visitors who arrive by ferry at the island's main port. The harbor itself is quite distinctive; its circular shape—which was once a lake—was most likely formed by a crater after a volcanic eruption. In the 1850s, at the behest of King Ferdinand II of Naples, the lake was opened to the sea and laboriously dredged to create a port that officially opened in 1854. Today the town of Ischia spreads out around the port and is the biggest town on the island.

The port area is a bustling place during the high season, with buses and taxis at the ready to take travelers to their destinations on the island. With its convenient setting, beautiful beaches, and lively evening atmosphere, Ischia town makes a great base on the island. You'll find the best shopping in the Ischia Porto area as well as near Castello Aragonese in the charming surrounding area called Ischia Ponte. Whether you're exploring the castle, soaking up the sun on the beach, or dining by the sea after dark, you'll find that the relaxed resort vibe of Ischia town is one of the most enjoyable on the island.

ORIENTATION

Ischia town is split into two areas: **Ischia Porto,** the area surrounding the port and stretching down the northeastern side of the island, and **Ischia Ponte,** where the Castello Aragonese is located. From **Piazza Antica Reggia** near the port, **Via Alfredo De Luca** is the route for buses and traffic, but the best way to explore Ischia town is on foot, following **Via Roma,** which becomes **Corso Vittoria Colonna.** This long street is lined with boutiques as well as restaurants and cafés with outdoor seating. An evening passeggiata (stroll) is a traditional local experience. After dark, the eastern side of the port, locally called the **Riva Destra (Right Bank),** is a popular location for dinner and drinks.

Ischia Ponte spreads out around the **Piazzale Aragonese,** with the causeway leading out to the **Castello Aragonese. Via Luigi Mazzella** and the tiny maze of surrounding streets are fun to explore. Visit the Castello Aragonese to see ruins of ancient churches and panoramic views over Ischia Ponte, Procida, and the Gulf of Naples.

SIGHTS
Ischia Ponte

TOP EXPERIENCE

★ Castello Aragonese

Castello Aragonese; tel. 081/992-834; www.castelloaragoneseischia.com; 9am-sunset daily; €12

Ischia's most iconic image is the view of Castello Aragonese, a medieval castle atop a largely inaccessible rocky islet off the shore of Ischia Ponte. Rising to 371 ft (113 m), the islet has been connected to the island since 1441, and today the causeway called Ponte Aragonese provides an excellent view as you approach the castle on foot. The first fortification on the small island, which dates to 474 BCE, was later inhabited by Romans. However, it was during the 14th century that more in-depth construction began on the island after the eruption of Monte Epomeo in 1301 caused many Ischians to flee to the islet for safety. Often closely connected to Naples, King Alfonso I d'Aragona rebuilt the Angevin castle in the 15th century and began a prosperous period that peaked at the end of the 16th century, when there were 1,892 families residing on the islet, along with 13 churches and a convent of the Monache Clarisse (Poor Clares). During the 18th century, Ischians began to move ashore to more comfortable dwellings, and in 1809 the castle was significantly damaged during the battles between the Bourbon rulers of Naples, with the help of the English navy fighting against the brief

Ischia Town

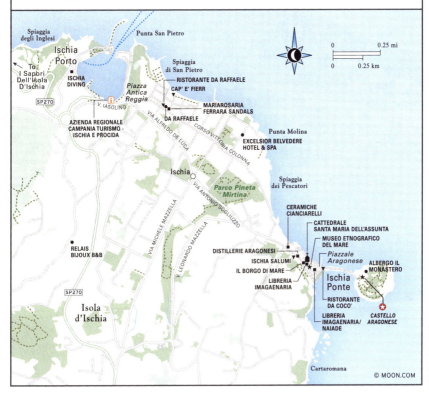

French control of Naples and the surrounding area in the early 19th century. By 1823, King Ferdinand I of Naples expelled the last 30 residents of the island and transformed the castle into a prison, which remained in use until 1860. Since 1911, the island has been privately owned, but it is possible to visit and explore by paying an entrance fee.

When you visit Castello Aragonese, an elevator tunneled out of the rock makes reaching the top quick and easy. A well-marked pathway leads around Castello Aragonese through all the top spots to visit along with panoramic viewpoints. Highlights include the views over Ischia Ponte from the **Terrace of the Immacolata** next to the 18th-century **Chiesa dell'Immacolata,** where art exhibitions are often held under the soaring dome in its beautiful bright-white baroque interior. Nearby is the **Convento di Santa Maria della Consolazione,** which was the convent of the cloistered nuns of the Poor Clares, along with the cemetery below the church. Here you can imagine (or try not to) the macabre scene in the dark crypt where the corpses of the nuns were placed on draining seats to decompose. Moving on, the pathway leads past ruins of churches and terraces now planted with gardens, olive trees, and grapevines, where the houses of the island's many residents once stood. Don't miss the incredible ruins of the Cattedrale dell'Assunta, where you can still get an idea of its former baroque splendor before it collapsed under bombardment in 1809.

To take in highlights of the entire Castello

Aragonese, which is highly recommended, allow at least 2 hours for a leisurely visit. The pathway around the castle has quite a few steps, so comfortable shoes are recommended. On-site there are two tempting restaurants and bars, as well as a lovely gift shop with artisanal crafts and books.

Cattedrale Santa Maria dell'Assunta
Via Luigi Mazzella 72; www.chiesaischia.it; 8:30am-12:30pm daily; free

Follow Via Luigi Mazzella from the small piazza near Ponte Aragonese into the heart of Ischia Ponte, and in a narrow stretch you'll have to crane your neck up a bit to take in the impressive yellow and white baroque facade of the Cattedrale Santa Maria dell'Assunta. Set behind a tall iron gate, the entrance of Ischia's cathedral is at the top of a small flight of steps. The church dates from the 18th century, but the treasures it holds inside go back much farther. Highlights include a baptismal font supported by three caryatids from the late Renaissance and a treasured wooden cross from the 13th century. Opposite the cathedral stands the **Palazzo dell'Oroglogio** (Clock Palace), an 18th-century building that takes its name from the clock at the top.

Museo Etnografico del Mare
Via Giovanni da Procida 3; tel. 338/282-5247; museodelmareischia@libero.it; 10:30am-12:30pm and 6:30pm-9:30pm Tues.-Sat., 11am-1pm Sun.; €5

Around the corner is the small yet fascinating Museo del Mare (Museum of the Sea), dedicated to the island's rich nautical history. Spread across three floors, the collection covers navigation and fishing equipment, archaeological finds, ship models, traditional fishing clothes, and photographs. Many descriptions are in Italian, but it's an enjoyable collection to explore, especially for anyone interested in nautical history.

1: Ischia Porto harbor **2:** Castello Aragonese

BEACHES
Ischia Porto
Spiaggia di San Pietro
between Punta San Pietro and Punta Molino

Just a short stroll from the port, this long and sandy beach stretches along the northeastern edge of the island from the Punta San Pietro, near the entrance to the port, down to Punta Molino. The beach is the largest near Punta San Pietro, and it progressively narrows to a sliver before turning into a series of rocky coves. There are a large number of stabilimenti balneari (beach clubs) alternating with several free areas. The largest spiaggia libera (free beach) can be found at the end of Via Francesco Buonocore off the Via Roma, Ischia Porto's main shopping street. For sun bed and umbrella rental as well as fine dining, head to **Cap' e' Fierr** (Via Venanzio Marone 9; tel. 340/009-7505; www.capefierr.it; 8:30am-7pm daily late Apr.-Oct.; two sun beds and umbrella from €15).

Spiaggia degli Inglesi
Spiaggia degli Inglesi

This small beach is only accessible via a pathway that starts near Ischia's port. To find it, follow Via Iasolino to the western side of the port to where it ends at Via Svincolo Porto. Across the street, follow the pedestrian pathway marked Via S. Alessandro. Continue along for about 15 minutes as it leads uphill and then down a steep staircase. While small, the beach has a secluded feel and lovely clear water. Much of the fine sand here has eroded, but there is still a small public beach area with a mix of sand and pebbles and a sunbathing platform that is part of a small beach club and restaurant. With its secluded setting and position, this beach doesn't get as much sun as some others, but it's a good choice if you enjoy hiking and a bit of an adventure.

Ischia Ponte
Spiaggia dei Pescatori
Via Spiaggia dei Pescatori

Located on the eastern side of the island between Ischia Porto and Ischia Ponte and

Best Beaches on Ischia and Procida

Spiaggia dei Maronti near Sant'Angelo

The islands of Ischia and Procida are a haven for sunbathing and swimming. The sea is temptingly clear, and most beaches are sandier than you'll find on Capri and the Amalfi Coast. With so many beaches to choose from, here's a head start to finding your favorite spot on Ischia and Procida.

BEST BEACHES FOR SWIMMING AND WATER SPORTS

- **Spiaggia di Citara, Forio (Ischia):** Located on the western coastline of Ischia, this is a beautiful spot for long summer-day swims. The fine sandy beach, clear water, and beautiful setting make it one of the best beaches for swimming (page 271).

- **Spiaggia di Sant'Angelo (Ischia):** Not only is this one of the prettiest towns on Ischia, but Sant'Angelo is also a fine area for swimming as well as snorkeling and kayaking (page 276).

BEST BEACHES FOR VIEWS

- **Spiaggia dei Pescatori, Ischia Ponte (Ischia):** From this long, sandy beach you can

slightly closer to Ischia Ponte, the Spiaggia dei Pescatori is a popular sandy beach with a view of Procida in the distance. The beach is named after the small houses that line the beach and once belonged to pescatori (fishermen). Both free areas and stabilimenti balneari (beach clubs) are available. **Bagno Francesca Lido & Snack Bar** (Via Spiaggia dei Pescatori 7; tel. 347/077-4897; 8am-7:30pm daily Apr.-Oct.; from €30 for 2 sun beds and an umbrella) is a friendly spot to spend a day at the beach.

Cartaromana
Via Cartaromana

This secluded beach has a picturesque view of a small bay with the Scogli di Sant'Anna, a cluster of rocks just off the coastline, and the Castello Aragonese in the distance. Just offshore in the bay are the ruins of a Roman town called Aenaria, founded in the 1st century BCE. The beach can be reached by a pathway and about 100 steps down from Via Cartaromana, or in a taxi boat from Ischia Ponte run by **Cassano Barche** (Scivolo

enjoy a picture-perfect view of the Castello Aragonese as well as the island of Procida in the distance (page 247).

- **Spiaggia della Chiaia (Procida):** Spend a peaceful day on this stretch of beach with a view to the pastel-colored buildings of Marina Corricella in the distance (page 285).

BEST BEACHES FOR FAMILIES

- **Spiaggia dei Maronti, Barano d'Ischia (Ischia):** The longest beach on Ischia, this spot offers fine sand, clear turquoise water, and a host of beach services from the beach clubs, making it one of the most popular beaches on the island (page 276).
- **Spiaggia di San Francesco, Forio (Ischia):** This sandy beach is a great choice for families with its easy grade into the sea, calm water, and array of beach clubs (page 271).

MOST ROMANTIC BEACHES

- **Spiaggia di San Montano, Lacco Ameno (Ischia):** This gorgeous beach set in a horseshoe-shaped bay is one of the most romantic on Ischia, as it's truly immersed in the island's natural beauty (page 263).
- **Spiaggia del Pozzo Vecchio (Procida):** Also called the Spiaggia del Postino for the 1994 movie Il Postino that was filmed here, it's an appealing spot for a romantic day at the beach (page 285).

HIDDEN GEMS

- **Cartaromana, Ischia Ponte (Ischia):** This is a tiny beach tucked away south of the Castello Aragonese. Just hop on a boat near the Piazzale Aragonese, close to the causeway leading out to the castle, to reach this secluded beach (page 248).
- **Baia di Sorgeto (Ischia):** This rocky beach set in a small, remote bay on the southwest coast of Ischia is famous for its hot springs that bubble up below the water's surface, creating natural hot pools (page 276).

Piazzale delle Alghe; tel. 338/823-0064; www.cassanobarche.com; €7.50 per person).

SPORTS AND RECREATION
Boat Trips and Water Sports
Il Borgo di Mare
Via Luigi Mazzella 68; tel. 081/230-4911; www.ilborgodimare.com; 9am-1pm and 4pm-8pm Apr.-Oct.; tours from €30 pp

An interesting stop while exploring Ischia Ponte, this cultural center offers a variety of ways to tour and discover Ischia from the sea. Private and small group boat excursions are available as well as diving and snorkeling. The glass-bottom boat tour is a fascinating way to see the underwater ancient Roman ruins off of the Cartaromana beach. Private boat rentals with or without a skipper are also available for tours around the island.

Ischia Diving

Via Iasolino 106; tel. 081/981-852; www.ischiadiving. net; Easter-Oct.; dives from €40 pp plus equipment rental

With an underwater landscape just as remarkably varied as what you'll find on land, Ischia is an excellent spot for scuba diving. Ischia Diving is located very near Ischia's port and offers guided dives for travelers with an international diving certification in the best spots around Ischia and Procida. Equipment rental is also available.

FESTIVALS AND EVENTS
Ischia Film Festival

Castello Aragonese; tel. 081/181-66810; www. ischiafilmfestival.it; last Sat. in June-first Sat. in July; daily tickets €10

Held in the evocative setting of Castello Aragonese, the Ischia Film Festival attracts the top players in Italy's film industry and from around the world. Michelangelo Messina is the creator and artistic director of the festival, which is also called the International Film Location Festival since it celebrates international films that create a captivating sense of place. Film screenings take place throughout the week along with panels and presentations. Ticket prices are reduced if purchasing more than one ticket or for the entire festival.

Festa a Mare agli Scogli di Sant'Anna

Ischia Ponte; tel. 081/333-3206; www.festadisantanna. it; July 26

Since 1932, this popular local festival has combined history, tradition, and folklore. Every year on July 26, Ischia Ponte is transformed into a festival setting surrounding the Castello Aragonese to the Baia di Cartaromana with its Scogli di Sant'Anna rock formations. Centered on the day honoring Sant'Anna (Saint Anne) and the small Chiesa di Sant'Anna overlooking the bay, the festival includes a boat procession, floats decorated in different themes, and a spectacular fireworks display over the Castello Aragonese and Scogli di Sant'Anna. The festival often includes concerts, processions, and other events.

Festa di San Giovan Giuseppe della Croce

Chiesa Collegiata dello Spirito Santo, Via Luigi Mazzella 70; tel. 081/333-4556; www.lafontanadelvillaggio.it; Sept. 3

Celebrating Ischia's patron San Giovan Giuseppe della Croce (Saint John Joseph of the Cross), this multiday festival is centered on the Chiesa dello Spirito Santo near the cathedral in Ischia Ponte. The peak of celebrations takes place September 3 with a sea procession from Ischia Ponte to Ischia Porto and back, along with a food festival, concerts, and fireworks near the Castello Aragonese.

SHOPPING
Spa and Beauty Products
Naiade

Via Mazzella Luigi 32; tel. 328/318-3244; gabriella. naiade@libero.it; 10am-1pm and 5pm-11pm daily June-Sept., 10am-1pm and 4pm-10pm daily Oct.-May

Not far from Castello Aragonese in Ischia Ponte, this sliver of a shop sells beauty products created on Ischia with a special focus on the Ischia Spaeh line of products made with the thermal hot spring water from the Fonte delle Ninfe Nitrodi. The water has been noted for its healing properties since ancient times, and the products are designed to replenish and refresh the skin.

Clothing
Mariaosaria Ferrara Sandals

Via Venanzio Marone 2; tel. 081/985-418; www. mariaosariaferrara.com; 9:30am-1pm and 4:30pm-11pm daily Mar.-Oct., 10am-1pm and 4pm-8pm Mon.-Sat. Nov.-Feb.

Tucked away just off Via Roma not far from Ischia's port, this little boutique is home to Mariaosaria Ferrara and her gorgeous handmade sandals. Born and raised in Ischia, Mariaosaria came back home after studying fashion, and she has mastered the art of sandal-making. Stop in for a friendly chat and beautiful custom-fitted sandals while you wait.

Ceramics
Ceramiche Cianciarelli
Via Luigi Mazzella 113; tel. 081/984-674; www. ceramichecianciarelli.it; 9am-1:30pm and 5pm-11:30pm daily June-Sept., 9am-1pm and 4pm-10pm Mon.-Sat. Oct-May, closed Jan. 6-Mar. 3

A colorful display of ceramics around the entrance tempts you inside this family-owned shop. Inside you'll find a lovely selection of ceramics, including dishes with bright patterns of flowers and lemons as well as lamps, tables, decor, and a series of ceramic tiles hand painted right in the shop or in their laboratory in Barano d'Ischia, with scenes of Ischia that make lovely souvenirs and gifts.

Books
Libreria Imagaenaria
Palazzo dell'Orologio, Via Luigi Mazzella 46/50; tel. 081/985-632; www.imagaenaria.com; 9am-2pm and 4pm-9pm daily

Although perhaps unexpected just a few steps from the sea in Ischia Ponte, this independent bookshop and publishing house is a dream for book lovers. Books in multiple languages are available, as well as an extensive and fine collection of antique prints.

Specialty Foods
Distillerie Aragonesi
Via Luigi Mazzella 77; tel. 081/975-8441; www. distilleriearagonesi.com; 10am-1pm and 4pm-9pm daily May and Sept., 10am-1pm and 5pm-10pm daily June, 10am-1pm and 5pm-11pm daily July-Aug., 10am-1pm and 4pm-8pm daily Apr. and Oct.; tours and tastings from €25 pp

While this is the first distillery on Ischia, owners Anna and Alessandro are preserving ancient methods and traditions on the island with their locally crafted line of liquors as well as brandy, amaro, and orange wine. Learn more about the process and see the distillery on a tour (from €25 per person). Try the Figaro fig liquor, made from dried figs, which grow abundantly on Ischia. Additional tours and tasting experiences can be arranged that include a visit to the Castello Aragonese or a boat tour around the island.

FOOD
Seafood
Cap' E' Fierr
Via Venanzio Marone 9; tel. 340/009-7505; www. capefierr.it; 12:30pm-4:30pm and 7pm-10:30pm daily late Apr.-Oct.; €10-20

Situated along the Spiaggia di San Pietro, this restaurant and beach club is an excellent spot to dine near the popular Via Roma shopping street. Seafood is the specialty here, but there are also tempting vegetarian and meat choices on the menu. The atmosphere is relaxed at lunch and romantic for dinner, with an evening menu of gourmet options that changes daily based on what is caught fresh in the local waters. Make a day of it by renting a sun bed and soaking up the sun.

Ristorante da Coco
Piazzale Aragonese 1; tel. 081/981-823; www. ristorantecocoischia.it; lunch 12:30pm-3pm Thurs.-Tues., dinner 7:30pm-11pm daily Mar.-Oct.; €12-25

With a picture-perfect seaside location right at the Ponte Aragonese walkway leading out to the Castello Aragonese, this restaurant is a great choice for trying traditional Ischia seafood dishes. Ask for the menu of the day featuring the daily local catch. Specialties include spaghetti ai frutti di mare (a variety of seafood), fried calamari, fresh-caught fish grilled to perfection, or their classic impepata di cozze (peppered mussels).

Regional Cuisine
Ischia Salumi
Via Luigi Mazzella 100; tel. 081/992-411; info@ ischiasalumi.it; 9am-midnight daily Mar.-Jan.; sandwiches from €6, platters from €20

This popular spot is the place for locally made salami and other cured meats and cheeses. You can enjoy meat and cheese platters or delicious sandwiches. Try the unique

rabbit salami, reflecting the island's long tradition of rabbit dishes. A small seating area outside is a great spot to sit and enjoy local specialties accompanied by local beer and drinks, just a short stroll from Castello Aragonese.

Ristorante Da Raffaele

Via Roma 29; tel. 081/991-203; www.daraffaele.it; noon-3pm and 6pm-midnight daily Apr.-Oct.; €8-24

Stop in this family-run restaurant on Ischia's main shopping street for a great choice of local specialties as well as delicious Neapolitan-style pizza. Though there are plenty of options, you can't go wrong with the grilled fish or meat, and the local Ischia-style rabbit stewed in wine, tomatoes, and herbs is also a popular choice.

ACCOMMODATIONS
Under €100
Da Raffaele

Via Roma 29; tel. 081/991-203; www.daraffaele.it; Apr.-Oct.; €75 d

Set along Ischia's bustling shopping street, this cheery hotel has large, very clean rooms and friendly service. The location is conveniently close to the port as well as Spiaggia di San Pietro, making it a great base to get around the island and to enjoy leisurely beach time. The hotel has an on-site restaurant and pizzeria, so excellent dining is only steps away. This is the best deal on Ischia for a comfortable room at great rates.

€100-200
Relais Bijoux Bed-and-Breakfast

Via Pendio di Lapillo 1b; tel. 081/333-1034; www.relaisbijouxischia.it; Apr.-Oct.; €180 d

Situated in the hills above Ischia town, this gorgeous B&B is a gem with its stylish rooms, landscaped gardens, and sweeping views over Ischia to Castello Aragonese, Procida, and the Gulf of Naples. Indoor and outdoor spaces flow together, and both are equally well curated. Your day starts with an extensive breakfast, and the pool invites sunbathing. This property is ideal for a relaxed escape surrounded by nature.

Albergo Il Monastero

Castello Aragonese; tel. 081/992-435; www.ilmonasterocastelloaragoneseischia.com; Apr.-Oct.; €190 d

This extraordinary hotel offers the chance to stay at the Castello Aragonese in the historic monastery, which has been transformed into an exclusive and truly one-of-a-kind lodging. Dating to the 16th century, the property offers a tranquil atmosphere and architectural details that remain very much intact, while the hotel has been created to offer every modern comfort. The rooms are fittingly austere in a way that captures the hotel's heritage, and with a setting like the Castello Aragonese, this is the spot to splurge for a sea-view room. This hotel is not recommended for children.

Over €300
Excelsior Belvedere Hotel & Spa

Via E. Gianturco 19; tel. 081/991-522; www.excelsiorischia.it; mid-Apr.-mid-Oct.; €450 d

Nestled in a lush park right by the sea, this property is set in an aristocratic mansion that was beautifully transformed into a hotel with a friendly atmosphere to make you feel right at home. The hotel's 78 rooms are elegant and full of light. The larger deluxe rooms are an excellent choice, or choose one of the 11 suites for impeccably refined style and stunning balcony views to the sea. Although just around the corner from Ischia's best shopping street, the setting is tranquil thanks to the surrounding gardens that lead to a private beach. Soak up the sun at the large outdoor pool or relax at the hot thermal water indoor pool. There's even a "secret pool" in a lovely hidden spot in the gardens. The on-site spa offers a selection of specialized treatments touting the healing properties of the thermal water.

1: owner and designer Maria Rosaria Ferrara creating handcrafted sandals **2:** Ischia Salumi

INFORMATION AND SERVICES
Tourist Information
Azienda Regionale Campania Turismo–Ischia e Procida

Via Iasolino 7; tel. 081/507-4231; areturischiaeprocida@gmail.com; 9am-7pm Mon.-Sat., 9am-2pm Sun. Apr.-Oct., 9am-2pm Mon.-Sat. Nov.-Mar.

This is the main tourist office serving all of Ischia and Procida and is conveniently located right at the port where ferries arrive. Stop in for friendly help in English and assistance with any questions you may have about the islands, getting around, and tours or excursions, as well as the latest information on upcoming special events.

GETTING THERE
By Boat

Frequent ferry service from Naples to Ischia is operated by several different companies offering both high-speed hydrofoils and slower ferries for passengers and vehicles. **Caremar** (tel. 081/189-66690; www.caremar.it; 13-14 departures daily; hydrofoil from €20.40, ferry €14 passengers, from €42.20 vehicles) is the most frequent, with hydrofoils leaving from Molo Beverello and slower ferries departing from the Calata Porta di Massa ferry terminal. Also from Calata Porta di Massa, **Medmar** (tel. 081/333-4411; www.medmargroup.it; 3-6 departures daily; from €14.10 passengers, €45 vehicles) operates passenger and vehicle ferries; **Alilauro** (tel. 081/497-2238; www.alilauro.it; 10-13 departures daily; from €22 per person) also runs frequent hydrofoil service from Molo Beverello. The ferry ride from Naples to Ischia takes about 1 hour by hydrofoil and 1.5 hours by ferry.

Ferry service is operated from Sorrento to Ischia by **Alilauro Gruson** (tel. 081/551-3236; www.alilaurogruson.it; 2-3 departures daily; from €24 per person) seasonally April-September. The ferry ride from Sorrento to Ischia takes about 1 hour.

From Salerno, Amalfi, Positano, and Capri, seasonal ferry service is run by **Alicost** (tel. 089/871-483 Mon.-Fri.; tel. 089/948-3671 Sat.-Sun.; www.alicost.it; 1 departure daily; from €21.50 per person) from June or July to September. The ferry to Ischia takes nearly 3 hours from Salerno, 2.5 hours from Amalfi, 2 hours from Positano, and 1.5 hours from Capri. **Alilauro Gruson** (tel. 081/551-3236; www.alilaurogruson.it; 1 departure daily; from €20 per person) also runs seasonal ferry service from Capri April-September.

By Bus

Local buses operated by **EAV** (www.eavsrl.it; every 15-30 minutes 6:30am-midnight daily; from €1.60) run from Casamicciola Terme (10 minutes on the CD or lines 1, 2, or 3). From Lacco Ameno (15 minutes) and Forio (25-30 minutes), catch the CD or line 1 or 2 buses. From Sant'Angelo (45-55 minutes), catch the line 1 bus or either the CD or CS bus to reach Ischia Porto. From Serrara Fontana (40 minutes) and Barano d'Ischia (20 minutes), catch the CS bus.

By Car

To reach Ischia town by car from **Casamicciola Terme** and **Lacco Ameno,** follow the **SP270** road (the main road that runs around Ischia) along the waterfront east to reach Ischia Porto. It's about a 10-minute drive from Casamicciola Terme to Ischia and about 15 minutes from Lacco Ameno. From **Forio,** take SP270 heading northeast from near the port and continue along through Lacco Ameno and Casamicciola Terme to reach Ischia Porto, a 30-minute drive. From the **Serrara Fontana** and **Barano d'Ischia** areas on the southern side of the island, you also want SP270 heading east, but the road leads through the mountains on the southeastern side of the island and up to Ischia Porto. From Serrara Fontana the drive is about 30 minutes, and from Barano d'Ischia it's 15-20 minutes.

GETTING AROUND

Ischia town is highly walkable. To get between the port area and Ischia Ponte, the most pleasant walk is along largely pedestrianized Corso

Vittoria Colonna. It takes 40-45 minutes to walk from the port to Ischia Ponte. You can also catch the line 7 local bus operated by **EAV** (www.eavsrl.it; 10-minute ride; departures every 15-30 minutes 6:30am-midnight daily; from €1.60) that connects the Ischia Porto bus terminal to Ischia Ponte near the Castello Aragonese.

Taxis also provide a convenient way to get around Ischia town, with stands on Via Iasolino right at the ferry terminal, in Piazza degli Eroi in Ischia town, and Piazzale Aragonese in Ischia Ponte. The set fare for a ride within Ischia is €10, or you could go for the metered rate starting at €3 and with a set minimum of €10.

Casamicciola Terme

Only a short jaunt from Ischia town, Casamicciola Terme cascades down the mountainside to the sea with an area of unique thermal sources on the island's northern edge. In the hills over the town's harbor is an area of underground activity that has created many thermal hot springs. Home to some of Ischia's most historic thermal spas, this has been a popular destination for wellness since the 1600s. However, that same underground activity has brought its share of tragedy to the town. In 1883, Casamicciola Terme was at the epicenter of a massive earthquake that nearly destroyed the entire town and caused a significant number of deaths. In 2017, the town had a reminder that Ischia is indeed a volcanic island when another earthquake struck the area. In 2022, a terrible landslide caused by heavy rain left another deadly mark on the town.

If you're looking for the quintessential Ischia spa experience, support the town of Casamicciola Terme in recovering by spending some time in their historic spas, especially in the peaceful hilly area around Piazza Bagni, or at the Parco Castiglione Resort & Spa along the sea between Casamicciola Terme and Ischia Porto. The Casamicciola port is one of the larger ones on the island after Ischia Porto, which makes it convenient to reach Procida, Naples, and other destinations directly by ferry. With cute shops, cafés, and restaurants, the waterfront by the harbor is a pleasant place to stroll along the tree-lined pedestrian area and the shady Piazza Marina.

SIGHTS
Piazza Marina

Just opposite the harbor, this piazza sits between the busy SP270 road and the pedestrian Corso Luigi Manzi. It's a popular spot for locals to relax and kids to run around the large central fountain. Take a closer look at the series of colorful ceramic tiles around the edge of the fountain. Created in 2016, the panels depict a variety of the town's historic spots, seasonal activities, scenes of daily life, important visitors, and local festivals and traditions. You'll see Henrik Ibsen, who spent time in Casamicciola Terme in 1867 while writing his iconic work *Peer Gynt*. Among historical scenes of the town's piazzas and churches, Giuseppe Garibaldi, the great Italian general who contributed to the unification of Italy in the 19th century, also appears in honor of his visit to the area's thermal spas in 1864. Nearby a panel depicts the Osservatorio Geofisico (Geophysical Observatory) with a portrait of Giulio Grablovitz (1846-1928), an important Italian scientist, seismologist, and volcanologist who founded the observatory above town after the 1883 earthquake.

Chiesa di Buon Consiglio

Piazza Marina; hours vary; free

This little church just off Piazza Marina is dedicated to the Madonna di Buon Consiglio (Our Lady of Good Counsel) and was founded in 1821 by a group of local fishermen. As a result, it is also sometimes referred to as the Chiesa dei Marinai (Church of the

Fishermen). The pale pink and white facade is topped with a distinctive design with two bells flanked by a clock on the left and an anchor on the right. Inside, the altar is the main focal point, decorated with colorful marble and a painting of the patron saint.

SPAS AND BATHS
Parco Castiglione Resort & Spa
Via Castiglione 62; tel. 081/982-551; www. termecastiglione.it; 10am-6pm daily mid-Apr.-mid-Oct.; from €34

Located along the rugged coastline between Casamicciola Terme and Ischia Porto, this thermal spa is a green oasis cascading down to the sea. Enjoy 10 thermal swimming pools along with a natural sauna set inside a grotto, a Turkish bath, plenty of outdoor space for relaxing, dining options, private sea access, and an abundance of beauty and wellness treatments. Admission includes access to the sea and thermal pools, changing rooms, sauna, whirlpool, and sun beds. There's also a hotel on-site for a complete spa escape.

Antiche Terme Belliazzi
Piazza Bagni 122; tel. 081/994-4580; www. termebelliazzi.it; 8am-1pm Mon.-Sat.; spa treatments from €12

This spa is one of Ischia's most historic and is the only spa in Cassamicciola Terme to use water from the Gurgitello Springs, one of the most important hot springs on the island, purported to have healing and regenerative properties since antiquity. The hyperthermal water in the spa and the thermal mud treatments and massages are a specialty.

BEACHES
Spiaggia della Marina
Via Salvatore Girardi

Even with its harbor and long waterfront, there aren't a lot of large beach areas right in Casamicciola Terme. However, there are a few spots to swim while you're visiting the town. There's a little beach to the west of the port and tiny stabilimenti balneari (beach clubs) along the rocky coastline east and west of town. However, your best swimming option is the Spiaggia della Marina, located just east of the port. This small beach area is protected by a jetty and has direct access to the sea from the beach or via a platform built over the jetty.

SHOPPING

While strolling along the waterfront, and especially **Corso Luigi Manzi** to Piazza Marina, you'll pass by the town's main shopping area, which also has plenty of café and restaurant options.

Fischi d'Ischia
Corso Luigi Manzi 11; tel. 081/994-141; www. fischidischia.it; 9am-1pm and 4pm-11pm daily Apr.-Oct., 10am-1pm and 4pm-8pm Mon.-Sat. Nov.-Mar.

This colorful ceramic shop is an Ischia classic thanks to the unique whistles handmade by owner Luigi Mennella. Why whistles? There's an old rhyming expression in Italian: Ad Ischia si mangia, si beve e si fischia ("On Ischia, you eat, you drink, and you whistle"). Here the whistles have a variety of different shapes and purposes. The horn-shaped whistles are inspired by a Neapolitan legend that they ward off evil spirits; different colored whistles are supposed to combat a variety of issues, from solving problems with bad neighbors to finding true love.

I Sapori dell'Isola d'Ischia
Via Duchessa di Genova 2; tel. 081/996-524; www. saporischitani.it; 8:30am-noon daily Apr.-Oct., 9am-1pm and 4pm-8pm Mon.-Sat. Nov.-Mar.

Stop in for a nice selection of Ischia's traditional products, including liqueurs, spices, marmalades, and sweets. This is a good spot to try the local liqueur made with rucola (arugula), which has a spicy and strong kick. There's also a location in Ischia Ponte (Via Luigi Mazzella 150; tel. 081/991-1229).

1: Chiesa di Buon Consiglio **2:** Fischi d'Ischia **3:** Spiaggia della Marina

⭐ Ischia's Thermal Spas

Giardini Poseidon Terme

Visiting a thermal spa in Ischia is a relaxed experience, with a variety of options available, from soaking in heated pools to skin and beauty treatments, massages, and highly specialized healing treatments. All spas are mixed-gender with men and women using the same thermal pools and zones.

WHAT TO BRING

You'll need comfortable beachwear, a bathing suit, flip-flops, and sun protection for an outdoor spa. No particular type of bathing suit is required, but you can expect to see most women in bikinis and men in Speedo-style swimwear. A bathing cap is required for swimming in most pools at thermal spas; caps are usually available to purchase if you don't have one. Though it's not required, a beach coverup is nice to have.

RULES AND ETIQUETTE

Individual spas will detail the rules before entering, but do note that it is common practice to shower before entering thermal pools. Thermal spas are places of relaxation and rest, so music played without headphones is not permitted, and in certain areas of some spas—such as **Regina Isabella** in Lacco Ameno—cell phones and electronic devices are not permitted.

FOOD
Regional Cuisine
Cantinando

Via Monte della Misericordia 81; tel. 081/994-379; https://cantinando.business.site; 7pm-10:30pm daily Easter-Oct.; €12-22

In the upper part of Casamicciola Terme not far from Piazza Bagni, this restaurant's welcoming rustic atmosphere pairs well with its traditional dishes and wine selection. It's an excellent spot to try coniglio all'Ischitana (Ischia-style rabbit) as well as fish specialties.

Taverna Jantò

Via Grande Sentinella 32; tel. 081/994-661; www.villajanto.com; 12:30pm-2:30pm and 5pm-11pm daily Apr.-Oct.; €10-20

With a rooftop setting overlooking Casamicciola Terme, this beautiful spot is excellent for drinks and a fresh take on

SPAS WITH CHILDREN

Children are welcome in most thermal spas on Ischia, but often with some age restrictions in certain areas, depending on the temperature of the water. Many spas offer a discounted or free entry for children and infants. Check with the spa in advance for specific restrictions or guidelines. Certain spas are better suited for families than others: For example, **Negombo**, in Lacco Ameno, has no restrictions on children accompanied by parents, and children will enjoy the two saltwater pools and the beach facilities. Likewise, the **Giardini Poseidon Terme,** in Forio, has three saltwater pools and beach areas that children under age 13 can use.

BEST SPAS ON ISCHIA

With so many thermal spas to choose from on Ischia, it can be hard to know where to start. The good news is that the standards of service and quality are very high, so you truly can't go wrong. If your time is limited or you're searching for the perfect fit, here's a good starting place to find the right spa for your holiday on Ischia.

- **Best for a Day Trip:** If you have limited time, head to **Parco Castiglione Resort & Spa,** the closest thermal park to the ferry terminals in Ischia Porto and Casamicciola Terme, so you'll have more time to relax in the 10 thermal pools, the sauna, or the sea (page 256).
- **Best Bang for Your Buck:** Ischia's largest thermal park, the **Giardini Poseidon Terme,** offers the most options, with 20 thermal spring and saltwater pools, private beach access, and beautiful gardens (page 271).
- **Most Luxurious:** Head to the **Regina Isabella** in Lacco Ameno, part of a luxury five-star hotel. It specializes in treatments using the hyperthermal spring water right from the source (page 263).
- **Best for Healing:** For more than 2,000 years, the water at the **Fonte delle Ninfe Nitrodi** spa on the southern side of the island has been appreciated for its healing properties, especially for skin (page 275).
- **Best for Beauty Treatments:** Set in the natural oasis of the Baia di San Montano, **Negombo** offers a wide selection of beauty treatments, relaxing or therapeutic massages, skin and body-care treatments, and an extensive selection of Ayurvedic treatments (page 263).
- **Most Unique:** A truly natural spa experience, in the **Baia di Sorgeto** thermal water bubbles up from below the sea along the rocky shoreline, and you can soak in natural hot pools (page 276).

traditional Ischia dishes prepared with ingredients grown in their own garden. Lovely vegetarian and vegan options are available. Check for live music and special events throughout the season.

Bakeries and Cafés
Di Massa Pasticceria
Corso Luigi Manzi 61; tel. 081/900-835; www. dimassapasticceria.it; 7am-11pm Tues.-Sun.; €2-6

Stop in this refreshing spot for a delicious gelato or one (or many more!) of their specialty: mignon freddi. These little chocolate-covered gelato desserts come in a variety of flavors and are a real treat. There's seating at the bar or at outdoor tables nearby.

La Bottega Del Pane
Corso Luigi Manzi 33; tel. 081/996-777; www. bottegapane.it; 7am-8pm daily; €3-8

This popular little bakery is the place for freshly baked cornetti (croissants), a variety of breads, sandwiches, snacks, and pizza and food takeaway. Their products are made with lievito madre (natural yeast), making them light and incredibly fresh.

ACCOMMODATIONS

Paradise Relais Villa Jantò

Via Grande Sentinella 32; tel. 081/994-661; www. villajanto.com; €250

This charming family-run B&B makes for a friendly stay with a stupendous view. All the rooms have lovely views, and many have a private balcony or a direct sea view. With both an outdoor and indoor pool and an excellent on-site restaurant and rooftop bar, it's a beautiful spot for a relaxed vacation.

Hotel Casa di Meglio

Corso Vittorio Emanuele 46; tel. 081/994-940; www. casadimeglio.it; mid-Apr.-late Oct.; €140 d

This hotel was founded in 1960 by Antonio Di Meglio, who has a passion for creating welcoming accommodations with a home-like atmosphere. Still family-run by Antonio and his children, the hotel offers 35 comfortable rooms, and guests can also enjoy the outdoor thermal pool, beauty and wellness center, on-site restaurant and rooftop bar, and excursions organized by the owners.

INFORMATION AND SERVICES

For local information, stop at the **Info Point** (Comune di Casamicciola Terme; tel. 081/507-2501; ufficio@procasamicciola.it; 9am-1pm and 4pm-8pm Mon.-Sat., 9am-1pm Sun. summer, 9am-1pm and 3pm-7pm Mon.-Sat. winter) in **Piazza Marina** near the large fountain.

GETTING THERE

By Ferry

Casamicciola Terme has the second-largest port on the island, and ferries arrive here from Naples and Procida. **SNAV** (tel. 081/428-5555; www.snav.it; 4-8 departures daily; from €24.80) offers fast hydrofoil service from both Procida and the Molo Beverello in Naples to Casamicciola. The ferry ride from Naples to Casamicciola Terme is approximately 1.5 hours, and from Procida it's 20-30 minutes, depending on the type of hydrofoil or ferry.

By Bus

Ischia's local bus service operated by **EAV** (www.eavsrl.it; departures every 15-30 minutes 6:30am-midnight daily; from €1.60) is an excellent way to reach Casamicciola Terme. From Ischia Porto (10 minutes), catch the line 1, line 2, or CS bus. From Lacco Ameno (5 minutes) and Forio (15 minutes), you'll want the CD, line 1, or line 2 bus. To reach Casamicciola Terme from Sant'Angelo (35 minutes), the line 1 or CD bus is the best option. From the Serrara Fontana and Barano d'Ischia areas on the southern part of the island, you'll want to catch the CD bus; the ride takes about 1 hour.

By Car

Located on the northern side of the island, Casamicciola Terme is only a little over 3 mi (5 km) from **Ischia Porto,** a 10-minute drive west on **SP270,** and even closer to **Lacco Ameno,** a little more than 1 mi (2 km) to the west, a 5-minute drive. From **Forio,** follow SP270 east for 20 minutes. From **Sant'Angelo,** get to SP270 and head west through Forio and Lacco Ameno before arriving in Casamicciola Terme in 35-40 minutes. From **Serrara Fontana, Barano d'Ischia,** and points on the southeastern side of the island, you can follow SP270 east and take a left onto **Via Duca Abruzzi,** which meanders over the mountain slopes, becoming **Via Vicinale Cretaio** and leading to Casamicciola Terme after a 40-minute drive.

GETTING AROUND

The main circle road around Ischia **(SP270)** runs right along the waterfront and harbor of Casamicciola Terme, while the hilly upper part of town is reached by **Via Monte della Misericordia** from near the port or by a series of other winding roads along the mountain slopes. The town is small and easily walkable, but you have to take a bus or taxi to get between the thermal area around Piazza Bagni and the waterfront. The **EAV** bus line 3 runs from **Piazza Marina** on the waterfront to **Piazza Bagni. Taxis** can be found at the stand right by the ferry terminal. **Parking** is available in a small paid parking lot on the waterfront by the eastern side of the port.

Lacco Ameno

Situated at the northwestern tip of the island, Lacco Ameno has a picturesque setting with its harbor nestled between the slopes of Monte Epomeo and the hill of Monte Vico. Just beyond the harbor and tucked away below Monte Vico is the Baia di San Montano, a semicircular bay surrounded by lush greenery and cliffs. A chic resort since the 1950s, the town has a relaxed yet elegant atmosphere and is one of the island's loveliest spots for a holiday. With a beach right in town and the Negombo hydrothermal water park and Regina Isabella and its unique thermal water, there's a great combination of wellness and relaxation right at hand.

While Lacco Ameno is a picture of resort charm today, the town has a long and somewhat unexpected history. It was here on the hill of Monte Vico that Greek settlers arrived and founded the first colony of Magna Graecia in what is now modern-day Italy. That first settlement was established around 775 BCE, when the island of Ischia was called Pithecusa, and it quickly became an important merchant community thanks to its strategic location in the Gulf of Naples. Ischia's ancient history can be explored at Lacco Ameno's Complesso Museale di Villa Arbusto.

The heart of Lacco Ameno is the waterfront area stretching from the beginning of the harbor in the east to Piazza Santa Restituta near the base of the steep Monte Vico hill. In the center of the harbor is the distinctive mushroom-shaped rock called Il Fungo.

SIGHTS
Chiesa di Santa Restituta
Piazza Santa Restituta; tel. 081/994-774; www.parrocchialacco.it; generally 9:30am-1pm and 5pm-8:30pm daily

Just off Piazza Santa Restituta, this church dedicated to Santa Restituta dates from 1886 after the earlier baroque church was destroyed during the 1883 earthquake. The neoclassical-style facade in pink and white features four pilasters and a small bell tower on the right. Inside, the church has a striking design with ornate wooden details and an impressive coffered ceiling.

Santa Restituta has a strong connection with the community of Lacco Ameno. Legend says that the body of this African martyr arrived by boat from Carthage and landed on the Spiaggia di San Montano. A church has stood on this site since 1036, and excavations below the church have found that it was built on the site of an early Christian basilica. The complex also houses a museum with a collection of important Greek and Roman archaeological finds. However, at press time the museum and archaeological site below Santa Restituta were closed, awaiting renovation work with no definite reopening date.

Museo Archeologico di Pithecusae
Villa Arbusto, Corso Angelo Rizzoli 210; tel. 081/996-103; www.pithecusae.it; check website for hours and admission

Located on the hill above town, Villa Arbusto is a sprawling 18th-century villa that was once

Lacco Ameno and Forio

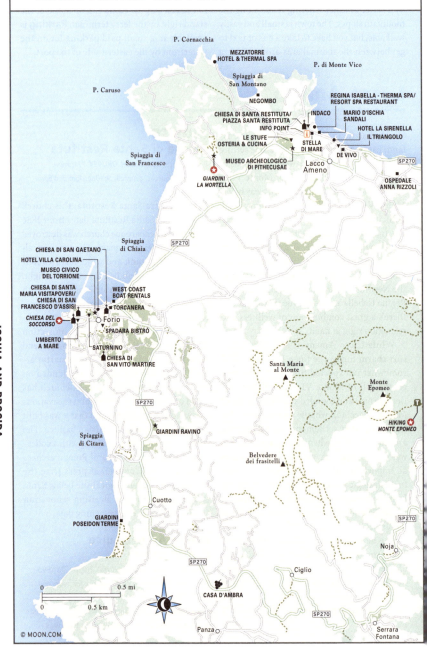

the home of Angelo Rizzoli (1889-1970), the noted Italian film producer and editor. In the 1950s, thanks to his film connections, Rizzoli put Lacco Ameno on the map, drawing chic visitors to his villa and thermal spas in town. The villa was eventually sold to the town of Lacco Ameno, and in 1999 the main buildings were opened as the **Archaeological Museum of Pithecusae.** Dedicated to the island's fascinating heritage, the museum's collection covers prehistory through Greek and later Roman settlements. There's a particularly good collection of rare objects from Ischia's first Greek settlement from the 8th century BCE. Don't miss the Coppa di Nestore (Nestor's Cup), a ceramic cup from circa 725 BCE that has a Greek inscription referencing Homer's *Iliad*; the cup is the oldest object to have been found in the western Mediterranean and is one of the indications that ancient Pithecusae was the earliest Greek settlement of Magna Graecia. In 2023 the museum was temporarily closed for remodeling. Check online for the latest information, hours, and ticket prices.

Also in Villa Arbusto is the **Museo Angelo Rizzoli** (www.museoangelorizzoli.it), a small museum highlighting Rizzoli's life, work, and contributions to Lacco Ameno. Rizzoli's story is told through historic newspaper clippings, photos, and documents. It's a fine testament to the man who did so much to benefit Lacco Ameno. Stroll through the villa's gardens, dotted with citrus trees and tropical plants, and enjoy the view from the pergola; it's easy to see why Rizzoli was so drawn to this picturesque spot on Ischia.

SPAS AND BATHS
Negombo
Via San Montano; tel. 081/986-152; www.negombo.it; 8:30am-7pm daily Apr. 20-Oct. 4; from €55 pp

Set on the beautiful Spiaggia di San Montano, Negombo is a natural oasis offering thermal and saltwater pools, lush gardens, grottoes, and tranquility. The park's 11 pools have a variety of water sources and temperatures, each one with different benefits to the body for rejuvenation and relaxation. The price of admission also includes access to the Turkish bath and the Spiaggia di San Montano beach with sun beds and umbrellas, showers, and changing rooms. The spa offers a wonderful selection of skin-care and body treatments, including massages, facials, and Ayurvedic treatments. There's a variety of on-site options for refreshments as well, with bars offering snacks on the beach, a trattoria tucked away in the gardens, and elegant yet relaxed dining.

Regina Isabella-Thermal Spa
Piazza Santa Restituta 1; tel. 081/994-322; www.reginaisabella.com; 8am-8pm daily Apr.-Oct.; from €55

Part of the luxurious Regina Isabella, these thermal baths and spa are open to the public to visit and experience the healing properties of the waters from the thermal source. The water here is noted for its rare combination of minerals, and it's considered hyperthermal because it flows from the source at a temperature of 171°F (77°C). The properties of this water have been studied since the Middle Ages and even attracted the attention of Marie Curie when she visited in the early 20th century. The spa offers a variety of treatments, including special ones using mud soaked in the thermal water for 6 months.

BEACHES

Lacco Ameno has a series of small beach areas dotted along the waterfront on either side of the harbor area. They're popular places in the summer where you can try to find a spot in the free area or head to one of the many stabilimenti balneari (beach clubs) to rent a sun bed and umbrella for the day. Sit back and watch boats come and go, and enjoy the view of **Il Fungo,** the town's mushroom-shaped rock right in the middle of the harbor.

Spiaggia di San Montano
Via San Montano

For a more secluded beach experience, head to nearby Spiaggia di San Montano, a horseshoe-shaped bay with stunning water and fine white sand. Surrounded by steep cliffs and verdant mountainsides, it's one of Ischia's most beautiful beaches. Sun beds and umbrellas are available to rent, or there's a free area where you can just throw down a towel and enjoy a day at the beach. The Negombo thermal park has a large beach area with sun bed and umbrella rentals, which means you can make a day out of swimming in the sea and experiencing thermal spa treatments.

FESTIVALS AND EVENTS
Festa di Santa Restituta
Chiesa di Santa Restituta and various locations; May 16-18

Lacco Ameno's largest religious festival of the year honors the town's special devotion to Santa Restituta. Starting on May 16, the miraculous arrival of the saint's relics is re-created in the Baia di San Montano. According to legend it was that very day that her body arrived on a boat in the bay after she had been martyred. On the 17th, a statue of the saint is taken by boat in a water procession from Lacco Ameno to Casamicciola Terme, where the statue is welcomed by the faithful and blessed by the bishop. The following day sees the statue of the saint carried on a procession through the streets of Lacco Ameno. The event is capped off with a grand fireworks display at night.

SHOPPING
Lacco Ameno's main shopping area includes the **Corso Angelo Rizzoli,** which runs along the waterfront, as well as the small streets nearby and **Piazza Santa Restituta.**

Stella di Mare
Corso Angelo Rizzoli 148; tel. 081/994-396; stelladimarelacco@gmail.com; 9:30am-1pm and 5:30pm-11pm daily Easter-Oct.

With the most beautiful selection of women's clothing and accessories on the island, stop in here for something lovely to wear on holiday and enjoy at home. Owned by sisters Marilena and Deana Grazioso, their keen eye for fashion means you'll be tempted to take something home from this small and charming shop.

De Vivo
Via Roma 34-36; tel. 081/900-086; www.devivotessilericami.com; 9:30am-1pm and 4:30pm-10pm Mon.-Fri., 9:30am-1pm and 5pm-11pm Sat.-Sun. Apr.-Oct., 9:30am-1pm and 4:30pm-8:30pm daily Nov.-Mar.

An Ischia essential, De Vivo has been producing fine fabric clothing and household linens for more than 50 years. Salvatore De Vivo and his sons are passionate about selecting the finest cotton, linen, and hemp fabrics. Along Via Roma you will find three of the family's shops. Stop in **Tessile Ricami** for beautiful sheets, towels, and fabric. **Veste la tua Notte** specializes in pajamas and lingerie, while the little **Casa De Vivo** has cute gifts and decor items. Don't miss their beach-perfect clothing line at **De Vivi d'amare** (Corso Angelo Rizzoli 48).

Mario D'Ischia Sandali
Corso Angelo Rizzoli 57; tel. 081/900-153; www.mariodischia.com; 10am-1pm and 5pm-10pm daily Apr.-Sept., 9:30am-1pm and 4pm-7pm Mon.-Sat. Nov.-Mar.

Stop in here for fine handmade sandals custom-fit to your feet. Since 1958, this has been the go-to address in Lacco Ameno for high-quality and stylish all-Italian-leather sandals made by hand. Choose from a variety of styles, from simple and classic to elegant sandals glittering with embellishments. There's also a nice selection of dresses and accessories.

FOOD
Il Triangolo
Corso Angelo Rizzoli 2; tel. 081/994-364; www.triangolopasticceria.it; 7am-1am daily; €7-30

This restaurant, pizzeria, and bakery is a popular spot along the waterfront of Lacco Ameno, with its large covered outdoor and indoor dining areas. There's a full range

---

1: Il Fungo in Lacco Ameno bay **2:** Spiaggia di San Montano

1

2

of options, from coffee and pastries in the morning to a broad menu of lunch and dinner options, including classic Neapolitan-style pizzas. Their cute seaside tables at Katerina a Mare (tel. 335/153-6593; 6pm-1am Tues.-Sun.) across the street are a great spot if you're in the mood for seafood.

Le Stufe Osteria & Cucina
Corso Angelo Rizzoli 210; tel. 328/625-0584; lestufeosteriaecucina@gmail.com; 7pm-11:30pm Thurs.-Tues.; €16-42

Set in a secluded area not far from the Museo Archeologico di Pithecusae, this restaurant feels like a hidden gem once you arrive. The setting and service are both welcoming, and the view overlooking Lacco Ameno is especially fine from the outdoor seating area. Ingredients are fresh and seasonal, which means the specialties change throughout the year. However, if available, don't miss the pasta made with cicale di mare, a type of locally caught crustacean.

Indaco
Piazza Santa Restituta; tel. 081/994-322; www.reginaisabella.com; 8pm-10:30pm Wed.-Mon. late Apr.-late Oct.; tasting menu from €170

The Michelin-starred restaurant of the Regina Isabella resort is the place for a romantic or special dinner on Ischia. Headed by chef Pasquale Palamaro, the highlights are seafood and locally sourced ingredients from the island. The dining room and outdoor seating area afford a charming view overlooking Lacco Ameno. Two masterfully created tasting menus are available. Reservations are required because dining space is limited.

ACCOMMODATIONS
Hotel La Sirenella
Corso Angelo Rizzoli 45; tel. 081/994-743; www.lasirenella.net; Apr.-Oct.; €190 d

It doesn't get more central or more friendly than this seaside hotel and restaurant in the heart of town. The decor of the 14 rooms is cheerful and bright, with hand-painted ceramic tiles and balconies overlooking the sea. The restaurant (noon-3:30pm and 6:30pm-midnight daily; €15-30) is also an excellent spot for seafood, and the private beach club (two sunbeds with umbrella €15-35) is a nice perk.

Regina Isabella-Resort Spa Restaurant
Piazza Santa Restituta; tel. 081/994-322; www.reginaisabella.com; Apr.-early Nov.; €637 d

Hotel La Sirenella

One of Ischia's most elegant addresses since it opened in the 1950s, this remarkable five-star property was built by the Italian editor and film producer Angelo Rizzoli. Rizzoli was enamored of Lacco Ameno and had this hotel built to enhance the region. The luxurious rooms are warmly decorated with elegant touches, all of them with striking majolica tiles. Located in three separate buildings set directly on the sea, guest rooms vary from singles to superior doubles, with garden and sea views available. The suites are impeccable in every detail. The hotel's Michelin-starred **Ristorante Indaco** offers a top Ischia dining experience, and two more restaurants and several bars add to an unforgettable dining experience during your stay.

Mezzatorre Hotel & Thermal Spa
Via Mezzatorre 23; tel. 081/986-111; www.mezzatorre.com; Apr.-Oct.; €688 d

Overlooking the Baia di San Montano from a rocky promontory, this remarkable resort is set in a secluded spot surrounded by a lush forest and the tempting blue sea. The hotel is part of the exclusive Pellicano Hotel Group portfolio and includes private sea access, four pools, and an excellent thermal spa situated in the 16th-century tower. The setting is ideal for complete relaxation and seclusion. For gourmet dining, visit the hotel's La Torre Restaurant or enjoy a more relaxed setting at the Restaurant La Baia, overlooking the pool. The 51 rooms and suites are all beautifully decorated and offer a variety of sea or garden views. There's even a state-of-the-art gym located in a cottage immersed in nature and with stunning sea views.

INFORMATION AND SERVICES

Tourist and local information is available at the **Info Point** (Comune di Lacco Ameno; tel. 081/333-0898; 9:30am-12:30pm Mon.-Sat.) in **Piazza Santa Restituta** in the 16th-century tower to the right of the Chiesa di Santa Restituta.

Medical and Emergency Services
Ospedale Anna Rizzoli
Via Fundera 2; tel. 081/507-9111; www.aslnapoli2nord.it; 24 hours daily

The only hospital on Ischia is in Lacco Ameno and offers a 24-hour pronto soccorso (emergency room). For **emergency services** anywhere on the island, the number to dial in Italy is 118 for ambulance and urgent care.

GETTING THERE

Lacco Ameno is located on the northwest corner of Ischia about 1 mi (2 km) west of Casamicciola Terme and 2.5 mi (4 km) from the historic center of Forio on the western side of the island. Although Lacco Ameno has a picturesque port, there is no ferry service directly to the town. The nearest ports are in Casamicciola Terme or Forio.

By Bus

Local buses operated by **EAV** (www.eavsrl.it; departures every 15-30 minutes 6:30am-midnight daily; from €1.60) connect Lacco Ameno with all parts of the islands and drop off in town along the waterfront by the harbor. To reach Lacco Ameno from Ischia Porto and Casamicciola Terme, take the line 1, line 2, or CS bus. It's only a 15-minute ride from Ischia Porto and 5 minutes from Casamicciola Terme. From Forio, you'll want the CD, line 1, or line 2 bus, and the ride is about 10 minutes. From Sant'Angelo, catch the line 1 or CD bus, and the ride takes about 30 minutes. From the Serrara Fontana and Barano d'Ischia areas, the best option is the CD bus, and the trip is about 50 minutes.

By Car

To reach Lacco Ameno by car from **Ischia Porto** and **Casamicciola Terme,** follow the **SP270** road west. It's about a 15-minute drive from Ischia Porto and only about 5 minutes from Casamicciola Terme nearby. From **Forio,** follow SP270 east and it's a 15-minute drive. From **Sant'Angelo,** first reach SP270 and follow it west as it passes through Forio and reaches Lacco Ameno in about 30 minutes. To reach Lacco Ameno from **Serrara Fontana** and **Barano d'Ischia** on the southeastern side of the island, follow SP270 west through Forio to Lacco Ameno and plan on a drive of about 40 minutes.

GETTING AROUND

Lacco Ameno's waterfront and town center are small and enjoyable to walk along. You may, however, want to catch a **taxi** to reach the Spiaggia di San Montano. The taxi stand in town is located near the harbor at the beginning of Corso Angelo Rizzoli, where the SP270 ring road turns inland and passes through the upper part of Lacco Ameno on the way to Forio. There's **parking** in a small paid lot located along the harbor, just east of the intersection of SP270 with Corso Angelo Rizzoli.

Forio

Covering the entire western side of Ischia, Forio is the second-largest town on Ischia and is one of the island's most popular tourist destinations. The town spreads out along the island's western coastline up into the slopes of Monte Epomeo. About midway down the western coastline, the Punta del Soccorso promontory juts out where the stark white Chiesa del Soccorso church sits in a picturesque spot. To the north lies Forio's historic center, the port, and the popular and long stretch of sandy beaches from the Spiaggia di Chiaia to the Spiaggia di San Francesco. Farther south, where the coastline becomes more rugged and rural, is the Spiaggia di Citara, where the popular Giardini Poseidon Terme thermal park is located.

With such an expansive footprint, Forio offers the chance to experience the best that Ischia has to offer, from lush green spaces and a historic town center to thermal spas and sunny beaches. Forio's setting along the west coast of Ischia makes it an exceptional spot to enjoy the sunset, and the waterfront and historic center of Forio hum with people out and about for the traditional passeggiata (stroll) or a relaxed aperitivo (happy-hour drink).

SIGHTS
★ Giardini La Mortella

Via Francesco Calise 45; tel. 081/986-220; www.lamortella.org; 9am-7pm Tues., Thurs., and Sat.-Sun. Apr.-Oct.; €12

On a lush green promontory above Spiaggia di San Francesco, these incredible landscaped gardens were once the private oasis of English composer Sir William Walton (1902-1983) and his Argentinian-born wife, Susana Walton (1926-2010). Spreading over about 5 acres (2 ha), the gardens were lovingly created starting in 1958 by Susana. She worked with passion to expand and develop the gardens for the next 50 years. The garden is divided into two parts that flow together. The plan for the valley garden was originally laid out by British garden designer Russell Page (1906-1985), while the sunnier hill gardens were developed over time.

A well-marked pathway leads through the Mediterranean and subtropical gardens, which feature ponds, little waterfalls, unique buildings, pavilions, and greenhouses. Stop to admire the large fountain with giant Victoria amazonica water lilies. Nearby a small greenhouse is home to more giant lilies and a wall fountain with a large mask inspired by Sir William Walton's piece *Facade*. Exploring the gardens is like a treasure hunt with hidden surprises to discover. There's a cascade with sculpted crocodiles, a Thai-inspired garden with bamboo and lotus flowers, a Greek-style theater where concerts take place in the summer, a stone memorial to William Walton where his ashes are preserved, and many more treasured spots. One of the most artistic is the Tempio del Sole (Temple of the Sun), a small building dedicated to Apollo and decorated with plants, fountains, and phrases from William Walton's compositions. A small museum and recital hall shows a film about Sir William Walton and La Mortella. Stop for a pleasant respite at the lovely tearoom that also serves light lunches.

Allow at least an hour or two to explore the gardens at a leisurely pace, leaving time to stop and rest on one of the many benches dotted throughout the gardens and to take in the views overlooking Forio. The gardens are accessible for disabled visitors. Free parking is available at the upper entrance off Via Zaro. As the gardens are located between Forio and Lacco Ameno, it's a quick taxi ride from either town. Or take the CD or CS bus lines and get off at the Mortella stop and follow signs about 5 minutes' walk to the entrance.

★ Chiesa del Soccorso

Via del Soccorso; generally 9:30am-1pm and 3:30pm-8:30pm daily; free

One of Ischia's most iconic landmarks, the Chiesa del Soccorso sits at the tip of the **Punta del Soccorso** promontory surrounded by a large piazza. Although small, its bright white facade stands out brilliantly against the blue of the sky and the sea beyond. It's a scene evocative of Greece, and its unusual style is part of what makes this such an architectural gem. The church has always been connected with the sea, and its setting and stark color are a point of reference for sailors and fishermen. A church has stood on this site since 1350, but the structure was later remodeled and expanded in the 18th century. The church is accessed via a small flight of stairs with five crosses on the right and ceramic tiles from the 1700s decorating the double-staircase entrance to the church. Inside, the single nave church is moving in its simplicity with its cross-vaulted ceiling and chapels lining both sides. One of the most distinctive features of the church is a collection of ship models that were ex-votos from fishermen in thanks for being saved from shipwrecks.

Chiesa di Santa Maria Visitapoveri and Chiesa di San Francesco d'Assisi

Piazza Municipio; hours vary; free

Near the Chiesa del Soccorso on Piazza Municipio are two more interesting churches side by side. On the right, the unusual double-facade entrance leads to the Chiesa di Santa Maria Visitapoveri, which was founded in the early 1600s. Inside, the single-nave church is lined on each side with large wooden stalls with a series of grand oval paintings just above on both sides of the nave. The rich decoration and small size create a unique closeness rarely felt in baroque architecture. Next door to the left, the Chiesa di San Francesco d'Assisi dates from 1646 and once included a convent and cloister. The plain white facade is in stark contrast to the rich baroque yellow and white decor and elegant marble altar inside the church.

Museo Civico del Torrione

Via del Torrione 32; tel. 333/392-1839; www.iltorrioneforio.it; check website for hours and admission

Set in a round stone watchtower dating from around 1480, this civic museum is set on two levels and offers an interesting look inside a historic watchtower. The museum hosts temporary art exhibits, and on the upper level you can see paintings and sculptures by the local artist Giovanni Maltese (1852-1913), who transformed the tower into his studio and home for nearly 30 years. At press time the museum was undergoing renovations without a set open date. Check the website for updates on visiting.

Chiesa di San Gaetano

Piazza San Gaetano; hours vary; free

Along with the tower of the nearby Museo Civico del Torrione, the other easy-to-spot sight in Forio is the pale orange and white dome of the Chiesa di San Gaetano. Built in 1655 for the town's fishermen, the church was completely redone in 1857, maintaining the structural lines of the exterior and preserving the rich baroque-style interior from the 18th

century, with its pale blue color and elaborate white stucco accents and artistic touches. Look for the sundial on the side of the dome that tells time accurately.

Giardini Ravino

Via Provinciale Panza 140b; tel. 081/997-783; www. ravino.it; 10am-7pm Fri.-Mon. and Wed. Mar. 20-Nov.; €10

In the hills above Forio lies a fascinating tropical Mediterranean park that is home to the largest and most varied collection of cacti and succulents in Europe. Founded by Giuseppe D'Ambra, who has collected plants from around the world, the gardens are beautifully landscaped and dotted with creations by local artists. After exploring the gardens, stop for a rest at the **Cactus Lounge Café,** which serves drinks and light lunch options.

SPAS AND BATHS
Giardini Poseidon Terme

Via Giovanni Mazzella 338; tel. 081/908-7111; www. giardiniposeidonterme.com; 9am-7pm daily mid-Apr.-Oct.; from €40 pp

Set at the tranquil southern end of the Spiaggia di Citara and completely immersed in nature, Giardini Poseidon Terme is the island's largest thermal park. Spreading over nearly 15 acres (6 ha), the park's 20 pools are thermal spring-fed or saltwater and vary in temperature. Following the suggested route through the park emphasizes the therapeutic effects of the thermal and hyperthermal volcanic spring water. The gardens also include private beach access with sun beds and umbrellas, a wellness center for specialized spa treatments, and three dining areas. Everything you need for a relaxing day absorbing Ischia's natural healing properties of sun, thermal waters, and tranquil beaches is right at your fingertips.

BEACHES
Spiaggia di San Francesco

Via Tommaso Cigliano

Stretching out below the mountain slopes of Punta Caruso, the Spiaggia di San Francesco is a long and sandy beach in the northern part of Forio. As it's not in the town center and is surrounded by a primarily residential area, it's a quiet spot that's also popular with families with young children. The beach is lined with free areas and a selection of stabilimenti balneari (beach clubs) where you can rent sun beds and umbrellas, use the shower and changing room facilities, and dine by the sea.

Spiaggia di Chiaia

Via Spinesante

Just north of the port and running along the historic center of Forio, this beach is a popular and often quite crowded spot in the summer. Yet the fine sand and stabilimenti balneari, such as **Lido Mattera** (Via Spinesante 90; tel. 081/218-9685; www.lidomattera.it; daily May-Oct.; from €20 per day for two sun beds and umbrella), lining the beach make this an appealing spot for a swim if you're staying in the historic center. There are free areas where you can just throw down your towel and enjoy a swim toward the northern and southern edges of the beach.

Spiaggia di Citara

Via Giovanni Mazzella

Along the southwestern coastline of Ischia, the Spiaggia di Citara is a beautiful fine sandy beach that stretches south to the verdant Punta Imperatore. It's a lovely natural setting that is also home to the Giardini Poseidon Terme, the largest thermal park on the island. There are free beach areas as well as stabilimenti balneari (beach clubs) to choose from, such as **Bagno Teresa** (Via Giovanni Mazzella 87; tel. 351/866-2203; daily Apr.-Oct.; from €20 per day for two sun beds and umbrella).

1: Chiesa del Soccorso **2:** cacti in the Giardini Ravino **3:** private bay at Mezzatorre Hotel & Thermal Spa **4:** Giardini La Mortella

BOAT RENTALS
West Coast Boat Rentals
Via Cristoforo Colombo; tel. 339/613-7491; www.westcoastischia.it; Apr. 10-Nov. 15; self-drive boats from €130, boat with a captain €280

Located right in Forio's port, this friendly company offers small boat rentals without a skipper (no license required) or excursions with a skipper on a variety of different motorboats and traditional wooden Sorrentine-style boats. Excursions are available to survey the most beautiful spots around the island, or to visit Procida.

VINEYARDS
Casa D'Ambra
Via Mario D'Ambra 30; tel. 081/907-246; www.dambravini.com; May-Oct., reservation required; from €35 pp

Founded in 1888 by Francesco D'Ambra, Casa D'Ambra is Ischia's leading wine producer and offers visitors the chance to visit the family's museum, cantina, and vineyards, and to sample their excellent wines. Situated on the slopes of Monte Epomeo high above Forio, this winery has a truly spectacular natural setting. The master enologist behind Casa D'Ambra's award-winning wines is Andrea D'Ambra, the great-grandson of the vineyard's founder. A wine tour experience is available with advance booking and includes a visit to the vineyard and winery as well as wine-tasting in the cellar tasting room.

FESTIVALS AND EVENTS
Festa di San Vito
Chiesa di San Vito Martire, Piazza Municipio, and various locations; June 14-17

Every summer the town of Forio celebrates its patron and protector San Vito (Saint Vitus) with a 4-day festival. Religious celebrations are centered on the beautiful **Chiesa di San Vito Martire** (Via San Vito 62), located above the center of Forio. Festival events include concerts and performances in Piazza Municipio and in front of the Chiesa di Santa Maria Visitapoveri, processions through town and on the sea, and a big fireworks display over the water.

SHOPPING
Forio's main shopping area starts near the **Via del Soccorso** in the historic center. The long street **Via Avvocato Francesco Regine** turns into **Corso Matteo,** and along this street you'll find the best shopping area, as

Spiaggia di Citara

well as the cross street **Via Erasmo di Lustro** leading to Piazza San Gaetano near the Chiesa di San Gaetano.

Torcanera
Via Erasmo Di Lustro 5; tel. 081/997-262; www.torcanera.it; 9am-7pm daily

Stop in this well-stocked shop close to Piazza San Gaetano to find tempting options lining the shelves and spilling out into displays along the street. Try something new from the variety of amaro (bitter) herbal liqueurs, such as the amaro torcanera alla portulaca, made with purslane, a plant native to Ischia, mixed with aromatic herbs. Other unique Ischia liqueurs include those made with thyme and arugula. The selection of local sweets, wines, and food products is large and varied.

FOOD
Seafood
Saturnino
Via Soprascaro 17; tel. 081/998-296; www.ristorantesaturnino.it; 12:30pm-2:30pm and 7:30pm-11pm daily Apr.-Oct.; €18-28

This restaurant offers a rare gastronomic experience for travelers who enjoy discovering the authentic and creative. Chef Ciro Mattera and his wife, Stefania Coletta, have combined their passions for traditional cooking and friendly service in this restaurant, just a few steps from Forio's port. Choose the fish or traditional menu options and let Stefania guide you through the meal as Ciro prepares dishes based on the freshest ingredients available. If you're not keen on seafood, the rabbit-themed menu is an excellent way to try another side of Ischia's local cuisine.

Umberto a Mare
Via del Soccorso 8; tel. 081/997-171; www.umbertoamare.it; 12:30pm-2:30pm and 6:30pm-10.30pm daily Mar.-Oct.; €18-30

With a gorgeous setting below the Chiesa del Soccorso, this is an iconic spot for dining by the sea in Ischia. Seafood is prepared exceptionally well here. Wine enthusiasts will enjoy the large wine selection. Although the indoor dining rooms offer beautiful views, book in advance to dine at one of the 10 exclusive tables outside by the sea.

Regional Cuisine
Spadara Bistrò
Piazza Giacomo Matteotti 11; tel. 333/132-2249; spadarabistro@gmail.com; 6pm-2am daily; €15-22

Located in a charming piazza in the historic center, this bistro infuses every dish with high-quality ingredients, many grown on the Villa Spadara farm on Ischia, whether it's delicious bruschette or salads for a light lunch, an aperitivo, gourmet burgers, or traditional pasta dishes and main course dishes that highlight fresh seafood. Try their version of the popular Ischia la zingara sandwich made with prosciutto crudo, mozzarella, tomatoes, lettuce, and mayonnaise. The outdoor seating area in the piazza is great for people-watching and atmosphere.

ACCOMMODATIONS
Hotel Villa Carolina
Via Marina 50/55; tel. 081/997-119; www.hotelvillacarolinaischia.com; Apr.-Oct.; €160 d

Located just steps from the port, this hotel is a convenient and friendly place to stay right in the historic center. The rooms are simple yet nicely decorated, and the rooftop pool and solarium have lovely views overlooking the port. The two-level deluxe rooms and junior suites offer extra space and sea views.

GETTING THERE
By Ferry
Located on the western side of the island, Forio's port offers limited ferry service from Naples operated by **Alilauro** (tel. 081/497-2238; www.alilauro.it; about 6 departures daily; from €23.60 per person). The hydrofoil service from Molo Beverello in Naples to Forio takes about 1 hour.

By Bus
The local buses in Ischia are operated by **EAV** (www.eavsrl.it; departures every 15-30 minutes 6:30am-midnight daily; from €1.60)

and provide service from all towns on the island to Forio. To reach Forio from Ischia Porto, Casamicciola Terme, or Lacco Ameno, catch the line 1, line 2, or CS bus. The ride from Ischia Porto is about 25 minutes, from Casamicciola Terme about 15 minutes, and from Lacco Ameno about 10 minutes. From Sant'Angelo, you'll want the CD or line 1 bus, and it's a 10-15 minute ride. From Serrara Fontana and Barano d'Ischia, take the CD bus and the trip is about 40 minutes.

By Car

To get to Forio by car from **Ischia Porto, Casamicciola Terme,** and **Lacco Ameno,** follow the **SP270** road west. Expect a 30-minute drive from Ischia Porto, 15-20 minutes' drive from Casamicciola Terme, and about 10 minutes from Lacco Ameno. From **Sant'Angelo,** take SP270 west and the drive is 10-15 minutes. To reach Forio from **Serrara Fontana** and **Barano d'Ischia** on the southeastern side of the island, follow SP270 west for 20-30 minutes.

GETTING AROUND

The historic center of Forio is easily explored on foot, but the town's footprint is large and covers the western side of the island. You'll want to catch a **bus** or **taxi** to reach areas outside of the town center. A taxi stand is located right at the port where SP270 passes through Forio, and all buses can be caught in this area as well.

Serrara Fontana, Sant'Angelo, and Barano d'Ischia

Ischia's rugged southern coastline is not nearly as developed as the northern side of the island, especially in the southeast where mountains drop straight down to the sea. Along the southern slopes of Monte Epomeo are the towns of Serrara Fontana and Barano d'Ischia, two of Ischia's six official towns. Yet, because the towns are spread out along the mountainside, each comprises many smaller frazioni (hamlets). Though Serrara Fontana and Barano d'Ischia are both set in Ischia's famous green landscape and have a rustic charm, each one has a connection to the sea that is a major lure for travelers.

The least populated of Ischia's six towns, **Serrara Fontana** comprises seven frazioni and is named after the two largest. It is unique on the island because of the way it is scattered across the slopes of the mountain, from the seaside in Sant'Angelo all the way up to Fontana, which sits at 1,181 ft (360 m) above sea level. The area has a strong agricultural heritage that is still important today.

One of Serrara Fontana's frazioni is **Sant'Angelo,** one of the most secluded and picturesque seaside villages on Ischia and the most popular attraction in the area. Here you can relax in a tranquil setting by the sea or take a boat west to the nearby Baia di Sorgeto, where hot thermal water bubbles up in rock pools along the beach. In the other direction you'll find the famous Spiaggia dei Maronti, which is a part of Barano d'Ischia.

Spreading over the hills in the southeastern part of the island, the town of **Barano d'Ischia** sits between Ischia town and Serrara Fontana. Home to some of the oldest thermal springs on Ischia as well as the island's most popular beach, this town encompasses not only the agricultural traditions of the island but also the spas and beaches that Ischia is known for. The entrance to the town from the east is marked by a 16th-century Roman-style aqueduct called Pilastri that was used to carry water from the hills down to Ischia Ponte. However, what has put Barano d'Ischia on the map since the 1960s is the popularity of the Spiaggia dei Maronti. This long, sandy beach is popular not only for its beautiful setting and view of Sant'Angelo in the distance but also for the Cavascura thermal springs nearby.

In the frazione of Buonopane, above the town center of Barano d'Ischia, the Fonte delle Ninfe Nitrodi is this island's most historic thermal spa.

Whether you enjoy hiking to the top of Monte Epomeo or relaxing in the waters of the island's oldest spa, a visit to Ischia isn't complete without time exploring the captivating southern coastline.

SIGHTS
Serrara Fontana Belvedere
Piazza Pietro Paolo Iacono, Serrara Fontana

A stop in the center of Serrara offers a beautiful view of Sant'Angelo below from the belvedere in Piazza Pietro Paolo Iacono. This scenic overlook on the side of the road through Serrara Fontana has benches where you can sit and take in the view of Sant'Angelo, and on a clear day you can see across the Gulf of Naples to the island of Capri and the Sorrentine Peninsula.

★ Sant'Angelo

Jutting out into the Gulf of Naples at Ischia's southernmost post, Sant'Angelo is a seaside village famous for its colorful jumble of houses that used to belong to the town's fishermen. The little village is now a chic holiday setting with a secluded atmosphere, thanks in large part to the fact that the town is pedestrian-only. From the nearest road, a narrow walkway leads down to the Piazzetta Sant'Angelo by the sea, where a small isthmus leads out to the **Torre di Sant'Angelo.** This massive tufa rock is a distinctive symbol of the town, though it is largely inaccessible today. You can walk out to it along the isthmus, which has stabilimenti balneari (beach clubs) for swimming on both sides next to the small harbor where boats depart to reach the Spiaggia dei Maronti and Baia di Sorgeto springs nearby. Above the beach, the seaside village and its multihued buildings are all connected by steps and narrow pathways where you'll find little wine bars, restaurants overlooking the sea, and lovely boutiques as you explore. With its tranquil and exclusive setting, Sant'Angelo is one of the finest spots on the island for a relaxing holiday.

Piazza San Rocco
Barano d'Ischia

The center of Barano d'Ischia is Piazza San Rocco, which is home to the Chiesa di San Sebastiano Martire, from the 17th century. Next to the church, an overlook offers a panoramic view of the coastline, including Sant'Angelo.

SPAS AND BATHS
Fonte delle Ninfe Nitrodi
Via Pendio Nitrodi, Buonopane; tel. 081/990-528; www.fonteninfenitrodi.com; 9am-7pm daily June-Sept., 10am-6pm daily May and Oct., 10:30am-5:30pm daily Apr. and Nov., reservations required; from €28 pp

With more than 2,000 years of history, this unique thermal spa in the mountains northeast of Sant'Angelo is known as one of the oldest in the world, thanks to some very special archaeological finds. A series of carved Roman tablets depicting Apollo and nymphs indicates that even the earliest Roman settlers on the island had discovered the healing power of the waters from the Nitrodi thermal spring. The water's properties are especially beneficial to the skin, and the natural setting is equally soothing for the soul.

The spa is organized on multiple levels, from a solarium to a garden level and the more private Oasi area. You'll find a series of showers where you let the hypothermal water run over your skin and then relax, as the effect is stronger if you dry naturally in the sun. You'll definitely want to book a chair in the Oasi, which is ensconced in beautiful gardens full of herbal plants that create a natural aromatherapy effect. Enjoy herbal infusions to cleanse the body, or opt for treatments from the wellness center. The finishing touch to the experience is to relax in the sun while taking in the sweeping views over the island. The outdoor

Bio Bar serves a tempting menu of fresh and light sandwiches, salads, and drink options for a refreshing break. The spa's specially developed line of skin-care products is produced with water from the thermal spring.

Terme di Cavascura
Via Cavascura; Serrara Fontana; tel. 081/905-564; www.cavascuraterme.it; 9am-5pm daily Apr. 20-Nov. 7; from €12 pp

Carved into a gorge above the Spiaggia dei Maronti, these unique thermal baths have been noted for healing properties since the earliest Greek settlers arrived on Ischia. The thermal spring waters and vapors can be experienced in a natural setting because the spa's outdoor rooms are caverns dug out of the stone. Take a hot shower in a waterfall coming down from the mountain and spend time relaxing in the sauna carved out of the mountainside. Mud treatments are a popular option here. The spa is accessible from the Spiaggia dei Maronti if you walk about 5 minutes uphill into the gorge. A taxi boat is also available from Sant'Angelo by the **Cooperativa San Michele** (Sant'Angelo; tel. 350/585-2653; www.sanmicheleboatservice.com; €4 per person).

BEACHES
Spiaggia di Sant'Angelo
Via Nazario Sauro, Sant'Angelo

Located on the western side of the walkway opposite the small port, this beautiful beach right in the center of Sant'Angelo offers lovely views and spots to swim and sunbathe. The area closest to town is a small free beach, while the rest is lined with very small stabilimenti balneari (beach clubs) offering sun bed and umbrella rentals. **Lido del Sole** (Spiaggia Sant'Angelo; tel. 338/826-0856; from €20 sun bed, €5 umbrella) is a good choice for a comfortable day at the beach.

Spiaggia dei Maronti
Barano d'Ischia

East of Sant'Angelo, the Spiaggia dei Maronti stretches out nearly 2 mi (about 3 km) and is the longest beach on the island. It's also one of the most beautiful, thanks to its protected natural setting, view of Sant'Angelo in the distance, and clear turquoise sea. The sandy golden beach is lined with rows of colorful sun beds and umbrellas. Many restaurants and stabilimenti balneari are interspersed with free swimming areas along the beach. A great spot to stop is **Bar Ristorante Ida** (tel. 081/990-163; www.ristoranteida.it; Easter-Oct.; €30 for covered cabana with 2 sun beds), which is equipped with everything you'll need for a comfortable day at the beach. Fans of **Elena Ferrante's Neapolitan Novels** will enjoy a stroll down **Maronti,** where so many key scenes took place in the second novel, *The Story of a New Name*. The beach is accessible by car or bus, and parking is available in various lots near the beach. A comfortable and easy option is to arrive from Sant'Angelo on a water taxi operated by **Cooperativa San Michele** (Sant'Angelo; tel. 350/585-2653; www.sanmicheleboatservice.com; €5 per person). The sand on this beach can become scorching on hot summer days so be sure to bring flip-flops or beach shoes.

Baia di Sorgeto
Via Sorgeto, Panza, Forio

West of Sant'Angelo, this gorgeous bay is home to one of Ischia's most unusual thermal water experiences. Below the sheer cliffs, this rocky beach has thermal springs underneath the surface of the water near the shoreline that bubble up with hot water. A swim in the hot rock pools offers the rare chance to enjoy a thermal spring experience surrounded by immense natural beauty. Even better? It's free. That is, if you're willing to dare the steep 234 steps from Via Sorgeto down to the beach. Arriving by boat is definitely recommended. Although this bay is technically in Forio, it's only a short boat ride from Sant'Angelo, and regular taxi boat service is operated by **Cooperativa San Michele** (Sant'Angelo; tel. 350/585-2653; www.sanmicheleboatservice.com; €6 per person) during the summer months. A small beach club right on the rocks offers sun bed rentals as well as dining options.

Spiaggia delle Fumarole
Sant'Angelo

Just a short walk between Sant'Angelo and Spiaggia dei Maronti, this small beach is notable for its fumaroles. Hot vapor caused by volcanic activity has created a naturally hot sand beach. As an added bonus, the sea here is beautifully clear for a swim.

HIKING
★ Hiking Monte Epomeo
Distance: *3.1 mi (5 km) round-trip*
Time: *2.5 hours round-trip*
Trailhead: *Via Epomeo, Frazione di Fontana*
Information and Maps: *The island's tourist office in Ischia near the port*

Rising up in the center of Ischia, Monte Epomeo is the island's highest point, reaching 2,589 ft (789 m). From the craggy top of the mountain, there's a truly breathtaking 360-degree view of the entire island. Though there are pathways from various spots on the island, one of the easiest and best marked routes starts in the frazione of Fontana in the mountains above Sant'Angelo. You can reach the village by catching the CD or CS bus, as both pass through Fontana. A sign pointing toward Monte Epomeo is marked on SP270 at Via Epomeo. From here, follow an uphill paved road that winds up the mountains surrounded by forest on both sides and occasional secluded houses, which become even more sparse as you get higher and higher. Continue uphill as the road becomes Via Militare. Follow it up until you reach an intersection where signs point off to the left to a pathway. Here, the hike becomes especially beautiful, as vistas begin to open up over the island. The last part of the hike is steep and rocky but well worth the climb for the views at the top. There are some spots near the top to stop for refreshments, such as **La Grotta da Fiore** (Via Epomeo 21; tel. 339/165-4739; www.epomeolagrotta.com; 9am-6pm daily Feb.-Nov.).

Ischia Hiking
tel. 339/277-8119; ischiahiking@gmail.com; tours year-round; half-day private tour from €175

Ischia-based hiking guide Marianna Polverino offers private and small group tours to Monte Epomeo and many other locations across Ischia. With her expertise and love of the island, you'll discover Ischia's natural landscape in all its many varieties, from the peaks of mountains, through vineyards, and even down to the sea. Tours can combine scenic hikes that include visits to secluded beaches, boat excursions, or—her most popular hike—a wine-tasting. For a unique experience, join Marianna for a hike by night to see Ischia under the stars.

BOAT TRIPS AND WATER SPORTS
Cooperativa San Michele
Sant'Angelo; tel. 350/585-2653; www.sanmicheleboatservice.com; mid-Apr.-Oct.; from €3 pp

Located right in Sant'Angelo, this local cooperative offers boat taxi service to many beaches and thermal springs in the area, including Sorgeto, Fumarole, Cavascura, and Spiaggia dei Maronti, for a small fee (€3-10 per person). For up to 6 people (starting around €120), this provider offers taxi boat service to other destinations around the island like Forio, Lacco Ameno, and Castello Aragonese. Boat excursions around the island are also available.

Nemo
Via Sant'Angelo 85, Sant'Angelo; tel. 366/127-0197; www.nemoischia.it; 9am-6:30pm daily July-Sept. 15; from €30 pp

Explore Ischia's remarkable seascape snorkeling or kayaking with the team at Nemo in Sant'Angelo. Dedicated to sharing and respecting the sea, a passionate team is on hand to help you discover the marine treasures of Ischia firsthand during your stay. All experiences are tailored to your ability and time available, but must be booked in advance. Snorkeling experiences can start right from the beach in Sant'Angelo or by boat around

the island. Hiking excursions around the island and to Monte Epomeo with environmental guides are also available (minimum 8 people; from €20 per person).

FESTIVALS AND EVENTS

'Ndrezzata
Buonopane, Barano d'Ischia; www.gruppofolkndrezzata.com; Easter Mon. and June 24

In the mountains of Barano d'Ischia, the frazione of Buonopane is home to one of the island's most interesting folklore traditions. The 'Ndrezzata is a local dance performed by a group of men in the small piazza near the **Chiesa di San Giovanni Battista.** The folk dance may have ancient origins, although the exact lineage is unknown. It features 18 men dressed in traditional fishermen's costumes from the 17th century, each carrying wooden sticks. The dance is accompanied by a song and rhythmic beating of the wooden sticks and swords, and as the story unfolds the pace becomes more energetic. The tradition is passed down from one generation to the next and is a unique local experience to witness. The dance traditionally takes place for the festival of San Giovanni Battista on June 24 and on the Monday following Easter.

Festa San Michele Arcangelo
Sant'Angelo; Sept. 29-30

The fishing village of Sant'Angelo takes its name from patron San Michele Arcangelo (Saint Michael the Archangel), celebrated every year at the end of September with a festival centered on the little **Chiesa di San Michele.** On the first day after a celebratory mass, a statue of the saint is carried through the maze of streets in town. On the second day, another procession carries the statue to the town's small piazza by the sea, where it is displayed until the evening procession on the sea heads first toward the Baia di Sorgeto and then returns to the Spiaggia dei Maronti.

The evening is capped off with concerts and a spectacular fireworks display over the sea.

SHOPPING

Villa Margherita Boutique
Piazza Sant'Angelo 5, Sant'Angelo; tel. 335/725-5878; www.villamargheritaboutique.com; 10am-11pm daily early Apr.-Oct.

This gorgeous boutique is infused with an air of chic island elegance, and it's a pleasure to explore the diverse collection of clothing, gifts, and homeware on display. The setting is warm and inviting. This is a concept store that captures the true essence of Ischia in the colors and traditional items on display.

Rose Garden Biocosmesi
Via Chiaia di Rose 10, Sant'Angelo; tel. 081/904-367; rosegardenischia@gmail.com; 10am-1pm and 4pm-11pm Mon.-Sat. July-Aug., 10am-1pm and 3pm-10pm Mon.-Sat. Apr.-June and Sept.-Oct.

This cute shop has an excellent selection of natural and organic skin-care lines, including products from the Nitrodi thermal spa. A charming selection of all-natural eco-sustainable gifts, perfume, home scents, and jewelry is also on display.

FOOD
Seafood
Deus Neptunus
Via Chiaia delle Rose, Sant'Angelo; tel. 081/999-135; www.deusneptunus.it; 12:30pm-3pm and 7:30pm-10pm daily June-Aug., 12:30pm-3pm and 7:30pm-10pm Wed.-Mon. Apr.-May and Sept.-Oct.; €15-60

Set in a scenic spot overlooking Sant'Angelo, this restaurant is a dream combination of fine views and excellent dining. Seafood is the specialty here, with fresh ingredients and the local catch at the top of the menu. The pasta sautéed with shrimp and zucchini is excellent, but you can't go wrong with any of the options. The family-run atmosphere as well as the fine views from the dining terrace create the perfect setting.

1: hiking Monte Epomeo **2:** Dolce è La Vita
3: Sant'Angelo

Regional Cuisine
Dolce è la Vita
Via Nazario Sauro 10, Sant'Angelo; tel. 081/999-120; dolcelavitasantangelo@libero.it; noon-3pm and 7:30pm-10:30pm daily July-Aug., noon-3pm and 7:30pm-10:30pm Fri.-Wed. Apr.-June and Sept.-Oct.; €18-25

Just steps from Sant'Angelo's seaside piazza and with a picture-perfect dining terrace overlooking the sea, this is a delicious spot to truly enjoy la dolce vita. The menu features creative options for seafood and meat dishes as well as refreshing salads and sandwiches for something light.

Pizzeria
Pizzeria Da Pasquale
Via Sant' Angelo 79, Sant'Angelo; tel. 081/904-208; www.dapasquale.it; 12:30pm-3pm and 7pm-midnight Wed.-Mon. Apr.-Nov.; €5-15

A family-run pizzeria full of local charm, this is the place to enjoy Neapolitan-style pizza cooked in a traditional wood-fired oven. Seasonal ingredients are key to the fresh flavors. Try their pizza with zucchini flowers or cherry tomatoes and mozzarella di bufala.

ACCOMMODATIONS
Hotel Villa Bina
Via Succhivo 55, Sant'Angelo; tel. 081/278-8311; www.villabinaischia.com; Mar.-Oct.; €150 d

This lovely little hotel has a panoramic view of Sant'Angelo and is only a very short stroll down to the beach and pedestrian-only area of town. The 12 rooms and suites are bright, and all include balconies with either sea or garden views. Relax and take in the fine setting from the rooftop terrace, which features a lounge bar and solarium. All the suites and some of the double rooms have sea views, but it's worth extra for the sea view because this is one you will want to savor.

Miramare Sea Resort & Spa
Via Comandante Maddalena 55, Sant'Angelo; tel. 081/999-219; www.miramarsearesort.it; late Apr.-Oct.; €490 d

Just steps from Sant'Angelo's pretty seaside piazza, this elegant hotel offers a complete Ischia experience with its 55 modern and well-designed rooms, great sea views, private beach access, and a connection to the nearby Apollon Club hotel with its **Aphrodite Apollon Thermal Park and Spa.** The hotel's fine restaurant has a dining area with an unbelievably romantic outdoor terrace.

GETTING THERE
By Bus
The Serrara Fontana, Sant'Angelo, and Barano d'Ischia areas are served by buses operated by **EAV** (www.eavsrl.it; departures every 15-30 minutes 6:30am-midnight daily; from €1.60). The CS and CD buses circulate around the island in both directions and pass through all three areas. From Ischia Porto, take the CD bus and it's about 20 minutes to Barano d'Ischia, 40 minutes to Serrara Fontana, and about 60 minutes to **Cavo Grado,** the stop for Sant'Angelo. If Sant'Angelo is your destination, you can also take the CS from Ischia Porto and the ride is a little shorter, about 45 minutes. From Casamicciola Terme, Lacco Ameno, and Forio, hop on the CS or the line 1 bus to reach Sant'Angelo, or take the CS to reach Serrara Fontana or Barano d'Ischia. The ride from Casamicciola to Sant'Angelo is about 35 minutes, from Lacco Ameno about 30 minutes, and from Forio about 20 minutes.

By Car
The **SP270** road that circles Ischia passes through both Serrara Fontana and Barano d'Ischia, making it easy to reach both areas by car. From **Ischia Porto,** head southwest on SP270 and plan for a 20-minute drive to Barano d'Ischia and 30 minutes to Serrara Fontana. From **Casamicciola Terme,** on the north side of the island, you can take SP270 in either direction to reach the south side of the island. Either head east and pass through Ischia Porto before reaching Barano d'Ischia and Serrara Fontana, or head west and pass through Lacco Ameno and Forio before reaching first Serrara

Fontana and then Barano d'Ischia. Either way it's a 30- or 40-minute drive. From **Lacco Ameno,** follow SP270 and it's a 30-40-minute drive, while from **Forio** you'll follow the same road and the drive is 20-30 minutes.

To reach Sant'Angelo by car, from SP270 southwest of Serrara Fontana, look for signs for Sant'Angelo and follow **Via Provinciale Panza-Succhivo,** which leads down to the Cavo Grado area above Sant'Angelo after about a 10-minute drive. There is a paid **parking** lot near the pedestrian-only pathway down into the village.

GETTING AROUND

The seaside village of Sant'Angelo is a pedestrian-only zone and easily walkable, but the towns of Serrara Fontana and Barano d'Ischia are quite spread out along the mountain slopes on the southern side of the island. To get around these areas you'll need to take a **bus** or **taxi.** The CD or CS buses all pass through Serrara Fontana, Barano d'Ischia, and the **Cavo Grado** bus stop, which is the closest to Sant'Angelo. From there, follow the walkway that leads down to the village, about 10 minutes on foot. There's also a taxi stand located at Cavo Grado.

Procida

TOP EXPERIENCE

In a region full of beautiful colors, such as the pastel-hued cascade of buildings in Positano or the many shades of turquoise and blue sea of Capri, there's one place that is easily the most colorful: the island of Procida. This small island is located between Ischia and Capo Miseno west of Naples. With an area of only 1.4 sq mi (3.7 sq km) and about 10 mi (16 km) of rugged coastline, Procida is the perfect size for exploring. Although you can see all the sights in a day trip, it's a dreamy spot to make your base for a relaxed holiday by the sea.

Ferry service frequently connects Procida with Ischia and Naples throughout the year, with ferries arriving in the island's Marina Grande harbor. Lined with brightly colored buildings and boats, Via Roma, which runs along the waterfront, is a pleasant place to stroll and shop. The rest of Procida's top sights are located above the Marina Grande area to the south, where you'll find the pastel-colored harbor of Marina Corricella, and above that the Terra Murata, the oldest settled area on the highest spot of the island. From Via Roma in Marina Grande, follow Via Vittorio Emanuele uphill and take a left on Via Principe Umberto to reach Piazza dei Martiri, where you can continue down to Marina Corricella or up to Terra Murata; each is about a 20-minute walk from Marina Grande.

To reach the southern points on the island, like the Marina Chiaiolella, beautiful beaches, and the small island nature reserve of Vivara, you have to take a bus or taxi. Or travel like many locals and the lead character in the 1994 movie *Il Postino,* filmed on Procida: Go by bike. Just be prepared to fall in love with Procida, as it truly is an enchanting place that captures the heart.

SIGHTS
★ Marina Corricella
Via Marina di Corricella

With its jumble of pastel houses and colorful wooden fishing boats lining the harbor, Marina Corricella is perhaps the prettiest spot in all of Campania. The oldest harbor on Procida, it was a fishing village, and the piles of nets and boats in the harbor are signs that the tradition is still going strong. Via Marina di Corricella is a small and sometimes narrow walkway along the harbor that, like all of Marina Corricella, is pedestrian-only. To reach it you must walk down sloped steps from Via San Rocco, not far from Piazza

Procida

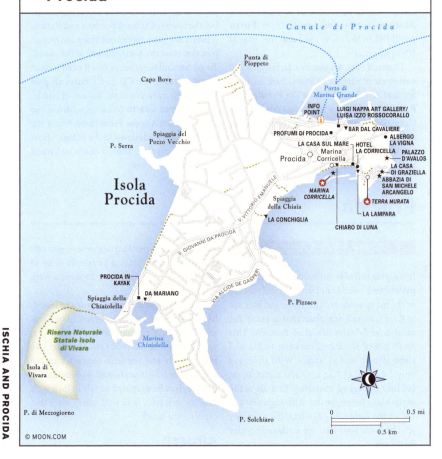

dei Martiri, or a zigzag staircase from Via Marcello Scotti that leads down to the western end of the harbor.

Now lined with restaurants and cafés, Marina Corricella is a romantic spot to dine by the sea or enjoy a leisurely stroll. If you've watched the movie *Il Postino,* you'll have fun picking out some of the locations where it was filmed. Although it's a popular spot, especially in the summer, there's an air of tranquility in this beautiful setting with the pastel colors of the buildings reflected in the harbor and the salty scent of the sea filling the air.

★ Terra Murata

Salita Castello to Via Borgo

Set atop the highest point of Procida, Terra Murata is one of the oldest settled areas of the island and also one of its most intriguing. This fortified area is built right into the rocky cliffs, and its name, Terra Murata, meaning "walled land," reflects the fortified setting, which was created when the island's residents fled here in the 9th century for safety from barbarian and pirate attacks. The oval-shaped walled village is home to the impressive **Abbazia di San Michele Arcangelo** and a small museum called **La Casa di Graziella** where you can learn more about Procida's history.

En route to or from the Terra Murata, stop at the overlook near the Chiesa di Santa Margherita Nuova, which has excellent views over Marina Corricella.

Abbazia di San Michele Arcangelo

Terra Murata; tel. 081/896-7612; www. abbaziasanmicheleprocida.it; 10am-12:45pm and 4pm-6pm Tues.-Sat., 10:30am-12:45pm Sun.-Mon. Easter-Nov., hours vary in winter; free guided visits available

Dedicated to San Michele Arcangelo (Saint Michael the Archangel), the patron saint of Procida, this remarkable abbey holds a rich history that reflects the island's strong religious traditions. Situated at the edge of the Terra Murata with a sheer drop to the sea 299 ft (91 m) below, the abbey dates to the 15th century and has many layers of architectural styles that parallel its past. For example, it has two facades, one being the traditional entrance leading into the nave of the church and the other on the back of the church, which is the main entrance used today that leads into the nave just to the right of the main altar.

The church has a Latin cross shape with 3 naves and 17 altars. The main altar, dating to the 18th century, is richly decorated in marble and paintings. Above the altar are works by the Neapolitan painter Nicola Russo from 1690, one showing San Michele protecting the island of Procida. Above the central nave is a richly decorated 17th-century coffered wood ceiling with carved rosettes all gilded in pure gold. In the center of the ceiling is a fine painting by Roman artist Luigi Garzi from 1699, showing San Michele defeating Satan. The Millennium Cultural Association offers free guided tours as well as information in English for visitors. Just stop and ask at the information desk located right inside the entrance of the abbey.

La Casa di Graziella

Palazzo della Cultura, Terra Murata; tel. 334/115-9502; www.lacasadigraziella.com; 10am-1pm Tues.-Sun. Jan.-Mar. and Nov.-Dec., 10am-1pm and 3pm-6pm Tues.-Sat., 10am-1pm Sun. Apr.-June and Sept.-Oct., 10am-6pm Mon.-Sat., 10am-1pm Sun. July-Aug.; €5

This small museum re-creates a typical 19th-century house in Procida, set high atop Terra Murata in one of the oldest buildings, dating to before the 16th century. In 1656, the palazzo was turned into an orphanage. The name of the museum, which means The House of Graziella, refers to the book *Graziella* by the French writer Alphonse de Lamartine, about his personal experience visiting the island in 1812 and falling in love with a young orphan woman named Graziella. Although the house is a reconstruction and nothing belongs to Graziella of the popular romantic tale, it is a fascinating small museum well worth a visit. The collection is spread across several rooms of the house, each rich with historical objects from daily life, from the kitchen walls covered in pots, pans, and cooking utensils to traditional furniture, clothing, and decor in the sitting room and bedroom. There's also a panoramic rooftop terrace with incredible views from the island's highest point. The small entrance fee includes a guided visit, also in English, that offers excellent context for the items on display.

Palazzo D'Avalos

Via Terra Murata 33; tel. 333/351-0701; asspalazzodavalos@gmail.com; 10am-1pm and 4pm-8pm daily summer, hours vary in winter; entrance €5, with a guided visit €10

Located just outside the fortified walls of the Terra Murata, also atop the highest area of the island, is the Palazzo D'Avalos. Built in the 16th century as a defensive castle and stately home, it later became a royal residence for the Bourbon kings of Naples in the 18th century before being transformed into a prison in 1830. The prison was closed in 1988, but the buildings are once again open and tell the story of a darker side of the island's past. Cross a moat to enter, where you can tour the ground and first floors of the former prison. Information panels, videos, and holograms depict the life of prisoners and how they worked to produce linens.

BEACHES
Spiaggia della Chiaia
Via dei Bagni

Located west of Marina Corricella, this beautiful, long, and narrow beach has fine dark sand and very clear water for swimming. The beach is reached only on foot with access from Via Vittorio Emanuele by following the steps down along Via dei Bagni to the eastern side of the beach. Another pathway called Via Pizzaco starts from Piazza Olmo and leads down about 180 steps to the western side of the beach, where the restaurant **La Conchiglia** (Via Pizzaco 10; tel. 081/896-7602; www.laconchigliaristorante.com; daily Apr.-mid-Nov.; sun beds from €15) offers sun bed and umbrella rentals along with a boat service from Marina Corricella. Much of the beach is a spiaggia libera (free beach), and it's popular with locals and visitors alike for its natural setting surrounded by rocky cliffs and fine views.

Spiaggia del Pozzo Vecchio
Via Cesare Battisti

Also referred to as the Spiaggia del Postino in honor of the 1994 movie *Il Postino,* which was filmed here, this beautiful horseshoe-shaped beach is located along the northwestern side of the island. Sheer cliffs around the beach provide a secluded setting, which has fine dark sand. To reach this beach, follow Via Cesare Battisti, and to the right of the entrance to the island's cemetery is a narrow and inclined walkway, marked with signs saying Spiaggia, that leads down to the beach. Given the setting facing the northwest, this beach gets the best sun in the afternoon and evening in summer.

Spiaggia della Chiaiolella
Lungomare Cristoforo Colombo

On the southwestern tip of the island, this long beach has free areas interspersed with stabilimenti balneari (beach clubs) for sun bed and umbrella rentals. **Lido Vivara** (Lungomare Cristoforo Colombo 4; tel. 081/896-0594; www.lidovivara.com; daily May-Oct.) is a great option for sun beds, umbrella rental, beach services, and seaside dining. Here the sand is also fine and dark, and the water is calm and clear for swimming. The beach is also close to the charming **Marina Chiaiolella,** a small harbor lined with boats, and the bridge leading out to the Vivara island nature reserve. The beach has sun all day, but the sunsets are particularly gorgeous from this beach.

SPORTS AND RECREATION
Water Sports
Procida in Kayak
Via Marina Chiaiolella 30; tel. 348/348-7880; www.procidainkayak.it; excursions daily July-Sept., Sun. Jan.-June; from €35 pp

Set out from the Marina Chiaiolella on a guided kayak excursion led by locals familiar with all the beauty and history of the island. Excursions range from a 1.5-hour trip to the Spiaggia del Pozzo Vecchio to a 3-hour tour focusing on Marina Corricella, or a 4-hour *Il Postino*-themed excursion highlighting movie locations, and a complete tour around the island that also takes about 4 hours.

Parks
Riserva Naturale Statale Isola di Vivara
Ponte di Vivara; tel. 081/283-388; www.vivarariservanaturalestatale.it; guided visits Tues.-Sun., advance booking required; €10

Located off the southwest coast of Procida is a small and lush green island called Vivara that is connected to Procida by a small footbridge built in 1956. Covering 79 acres (32 ha), with 1.9 mi (3 km) of coastline, this reserve is of considerable interest from a geological, historical, and archaeological point of view as well as for its flora and fauna. Since 1974 this has been a protected area, and in 2002 it became a Riserva Naturale Statale (State Nature Preserve), and visits to the island became limited to guided tours. It is a remarkably

---
1: views from Terra Murata **2:** overlooking Marina Corricella from Terra Murata

unspoiled place of natural beauty in the Gulf of Naples and is home to hundreds of species of flora and fauna, as well as resident and migratory birds.

To visit the nature reserve and discover its many natural features, you must book a tour in advance on the website. Guided tours are usually at 9am Tuesday-Sunday. Led by authorized nature guides, the tours last about 3 hours. Arrive about 20 minutes before the scheduled time. Closed-toe shoes are required (no sandals or flip-flops) for the walk. Tours accommodate up to 25 people, and at least 8 people are needed for a tour to take place. Note that there are no restroom facilities and no potable water on the island, so visitors should bring water. Glass bottles and food are not allowed on the island.

FESTIVALS AND EVENTS

Festa di San Michele Arcangelo
Abbazia di San Michele Arcangelo, various other locations; May 8 and Sept. 29

Twice a year Procida celebrates its patron saint, San Michele Arcangelo, with a religious festival centered on the Abbazia di San Michele Arcangelo in Terra Murata. The festival is held in memory of an apparition of the saint that is said to have appeared above the island in 1535. Both festival days include special masses and processions carrying a precious silver and gold statue of San Michele Arcangelo from 1727. On May 8 the statue is carried through the streets of Procida, and during the September 29 celebration it is carried to a small overlook near the Chiesa di Santa Margherita Nuova. From there a benediction is given to protect the island and the mariners who fill the harbor below with boats of all shapes and sizes.

Settimana Santa
Various locations; Easter week

In Italy, Easter is celebrated in most towns with religious processions during the week before Easter, called Settimana Santa (Holy Week). Easter processions in Procida are spiritual, intense, and extremely moving. Among the most impressive religious events of the week are the Processione degli Apostoli on Holy Thursday (the Thursday before Easter Sunday) and the Venerdì Santo (Holy Friday) processions. On the evening of Holy Thursday, a procession takes place where members of various confraternities, completely shrouded in white robes and carrying wooden crosses, walk slowly through the dark streets of Procida, only illuminated by candles. On Holy Friday, an elaborate morning procession departs from the Abbazia di San Michele Arcangelo and follows the streets of Procida down to Marina Grande. Carried in the procession is a statue from 1728 depicting the body of Christ after being taken down from the cross as well as a statue of the Madonna Addolorata (Our Lady of Sorrows). Both processions offer a meaningful way to experience the Easter holiday in Italy.

SHOPPING

Procida is a lovely place to shop, with many locally owned small stores lining the most frequented streets from Marina Grande to Marina Corricella. There's no need to go out of your way to find the best shops because you'll stroll right by them while visiting the top sights on the island.

Luigi Nappa Art Gallery
Via Roma 50; tel. 081/896-0561; www.luiginappa.com; 9:30am-noon and 4pm-10:30pm daily May-Oct., hours may vary

The colorful artwork on display at the Luigi Nappa Art Gallery is created by Procida-born artist Luigi Nappa and captures the joy and explosion of colors of a summer's day on the island. You'll find prints and paintings along with scarves, blankets, and ceramics.

Luisa Izzo RossoCorallo
Via Vittorio Emanuele 6; tel. 081/377-5374; www.luisaizzorossocorallo.com; 10am-1pm and 4pm-11pm daily June-Sept., 10am-1pm and 5pm-7pm Tues.-Sun. Oct.-May

Located just at the start of Via Vittorio

Emanuele near Via Roma on the left, Luisa Izzo RossoCorallo sells handmade coral jewelry.

Profumi di Procida
Via Vittorio Emanuele 55; tel. 081/896-0233; www.profumidiprocida.it; 9am-10pm daily Mar.-Oct.

Stop in for locally made perfumes and home fragrances inspired by the natural scents of Procida. Scents are named for iconic locations around the island, including Vivara, with natural notes of sage, rosemary, mint, and fig, or the Procida scent, inspired by the local citrus groves, with a touch of magnolia.

FOOD
Seafood
La Lampara
Via Marina di Corricella 88; tel. 081/896-0609; www.hotelcorricella.it; noon-2:30pm and 7:30pm-9:30pm daily Apr.-Oct.; €10-24

With one of the most scenic spots in Procida, this restaurant overlooks the harbor and has a full view of Marina Corricella from its dining terrace. Seafood is naturally the specialty here, and it is incredibly fresh, often straight from the local catch. The menu highlights classic flavors of Procida and the Gulf of Naples with a refreshing touch, such as the delicious tortelli, a type of stuffed pasta filled with shellfish with a lime and cream-of-zucchini sauce and served with a seafood ragù.

La Conchiglia
Via Pizzaco 10; tel. 081/896-7602; www.laconchigliaristorante.com; noon-3:30pm and 7pm-10:30pm daily Apr.-mid-Nov.; €15-20

Situated right on Spiaggia della Chiaia, this restaurant is a top choice for relaxed dining and excellent seafood. Try the fresh pasta served with mussels and zucchini or mussels and broccoli. Enjoy a view across the bay to Marina Corricella, where the restaurant offers boat pickup during the season. Make a relaxing day of it by renting a sun bed and umbrella from the restaurant and enjoying the beach just steps from the restaurant. Call in advance to find out the schedule or to arrange a pickup with the boat service from Marina Corricella.

Da Mariano
Via Marina Chiaiolella 32; tel. 081/896-7350; marianolanzuise@libero.it; 5pm-midnight Mon.-Fri., 1pm-4pm and 5pm-midnight Sat.-Sun. Easter-Nov.; €12-20

Seafood enthusiasts will love this restaurant right on the Marina Chiaiolella harbor, a tranquil location away from the hustle and bustle of the Marina Grande. The setting, with an outdoor covered dining terrace just steps from the sea, is the ideal place to enjoy freshly prepared traditional Procida seafood dishes, such as pasta with fresh anchovies, tomatoes, and pecorino cheese; excellent fried calamari and shrimp; or baked fresh fish with the flavor of lemons grown on Procida.

Bakeries and Gelato
Bar dal Cavaliere
Via Roma 42; tel. 081/810-1074; bardalcavaliere@gmail.com; 6:30am-3am daily June-Aug., 6:30am-1am Tues.-Sun. Sept.-May; €2.50-5

Stop in this bakery and coffee shop overlooking the harbor in Marina Grande to try the island's local dessert, called lingue di bue (ox tongues), a name that mercifully refers to the pastry's long oval shape. Traditionally served warm, it is made with puff pastry with a lemon cream filling, or sometimes with pastry cream or chocolate. With its pleasant outdoor dining terrace and late hours, it's also a popular spot for aperitivo or cocktails at night.

Chiaro di Luna
Via Marina di Corricella 87; tel. 333/770-0776; chiarodilunabargelateria@gmail.com; 10am-8pm daily Mar. 15-Apr., 10am-11pm daily May-June and Sept., 9am-2am daily July-Aug.; €2.50-4 takeaway, €4-8 table by the sea

Set right along Marina Corricella with seating beside the sea, this gelato bar creates only handmade artisan gelato and sorbet using fresh ingredients, many homegrown in the family's garden. A great spot to stop for gelato, a light lunch or dinner, or cocktails to enjoy the atmosphere of Marina Corricella.

ACCOMMODATIONS
Hotel La Corricella
Via Marina di Corricella 88; tel. 081/896-7575; www.hotelcorricella.it; Apr.-Oct.; €180 d

Set right in Marina Corricella at the eastern end of the seafront walkway Via Marina di Corricella, this is the perfect place to soak up the atmosphere of Procida's most iconic spot. Guest rooms are decorated with terracotta floor tiles and warm decor in soft Mediterranean colors that blend with the pastel hues of Marina Corricella. All rooms open to a terrace with a view of Marina Corricella, but note that the eight standard rooms share a common terrace while the one superior room has a private terrace. Whatever room you choose, you'll fall in love with the views.

La Casa sul Mare
Via Salita Castello 13; tel. 081/896-8799; www.lacasasulmare.it; Mar.-early Nov.; €220 d

Ideally situated near Piazza dei Martiri and only a short walk from Marina Corricella and Terra Murata, this hotel, in a lovely 18th-century palazzo with 10 rooms, boasts incredible views over the bay of Marina Corricella. Guest rooms are simply yet elegantly decorated with ceramic tile floors, Mediterranean colors, and private balconies where you can soak up the sun and the fine views.

Albergo La Vigna
Via Principessa Margherita 46; tel. 081/896-0469; www.albergolavigna.it; mid-Feb.-early Nov.; €195 d

Set in a vineyard and peaceful residential area near the northeastern tip of the island, this hotel is a great option for a peaceful stay in Procida, surrounded by nature and beautiful design. Although the setting is secluded, it is not remote, and you'll find Piazza dei Martiri only a short stroll away with Marina Corricella and Terra Murata just beyond. Accommodations vary from standard rooms, some featuring sea views, to spacious superior rooms with loft sleeping areas, a dreamy suite with sea views, and a special standard room decorated with works by Procida artist Luigi Nappa. The hotel features an on-site spa with a jetted tub, a Turkish bath, massage, and beauty treatments.

TOURIST INFORMATION
For information on Procida, you'll find an **Info Point** (Via Roma; tel. 081/896-9048; prolocodiprocida@gmail.com; 9am-7pm Mon.-Sat., 9am-2pm Sun., 9am-2pm daily winter) at the ferry terminal on Via Roma at the western end of the port in Marina Grande, next to where ferry tickets are sold. The staff can provide information in English about getting around the island and available guided tours.

GETTING THERE
By Boat
Procida is well connected by ferries from Ischia and Naples that arrive in the island's **Marina Grande harbor.** To reach Procida from Ischia Porto, there are many ferry options each day. **Caremar** (tel. 081/189-66690; www.caremar.it; about 12 departures daily; passengers from €8.90, vehicles €29.90) offers passenger hydrofoil service as well as ferry service for passengers and vehicles. **Medmar** (tel. 081/333-4411; www.medmargroup.it; 1-2 departures daily; passengers from €12.40) runs service from Ischia Porto to Procida, which takes about 20 minutes by hydrofoil and 30 minutes by ferry.

From the port at Casamicciola Terme on Ischia, you can also take the ferry direct to Procida with service provided by **SNAV** (tel. 081/428-5555; www.snav.it; 4 departures daily; from €14.40). The ferry ride from Casamicciola Terme to Procida takes 20-30 minutes, depending on the type of hydrofoil or ferry.

From Naples, ferries depart from the port at **Molo Beverello** and at **Calata Porta di Massa.** During the summer season, especially July-August, it's a good idea to book your ticket in advance on the website. The faster hydrofoils depart from Molo Beverello and take about 45 minutes to cross over to

Procida. Both Caremar (tel. 081/189-66690; www.caremar.it; 12 departures daily; from €16.40) and SNAV (tel. 081/428-5555; www.snav.it; 6 departures daily; from €22.90) offer frequent ferry service throughout the year. The slower ferries for passengers and vehicles depart from Calata Porta di Massa and take about 1 hour to reach Procida. Caremar (tel. 081/189-66690; www.caremar.it; about 7 departures daily; passengers from €12, vehicles €33.40) is the company to use if you're traveling with a vehicle to Procida.

Car Restrictions

Check in advance regarding the regulations about bringing a car onto the island of Procida. Nonresidents are generally not allowed to arrive with a car April-October. You'll need to leave your car rental in Naples or Sorrento before arriving. The island's small size, very narrow streets, and limited parking make a car truly unnecessary and not recommended for Procida.

GETTING AROUND

Procida is small and best explored on foot or via bike, scooter, or taxi. There are some uphill and downhill slopes and some steps to reach Marina Corricella. Don't expect sidewalks along the narrow streets, and do be aware of scooters and bikes zipping up and down. Streets are generally cobblestoned, so if you're arriving with luggage, you may want to opt for a taxi transfer.

Electric bikes, scooters, and even small cars can be rented from **General Rental** (Via Roma 112; tel. 081/810-1132; www.generalrental.it; 8:30am-8pm daily; from €20). Electric bikes are popular because they're not affected by traffic restrictions and make it easier to navigate the hills around the island. Many streets around Procida are one-way and have traffic restrictions during the summer. To avoid the hassle, consider taking a taxi or microtaxi (small three-wheel vehicles), available at the taxi stand near the ferry terminal on Via Roma. Call **Taxi Marina Grande** (tel. 081/896-8785) for a taxi in the Marina Grande area.

Four bus lines operated by **EAV** (www.eavsrl.it; from €1.60) circulate around the island. Line C1 runs from the Marina Grande port to the Spiaggia del Pozzo Vecchio. Line C2 conveniently connects the port at Marina Grande to Terra Murata, with stops near Marina Corricella and the Spiaggia della Chiaia. Buses on both lines run every 30-40 minutes 6:30am-10pm daily September-June, 6:30am-1am daily July-August. Lines L1 and L2 connect the Marina Grande port with Marina Chiaiolella, with buses every 10-40 minutes, more frequently in summer, about 6am-11pm daily September-June, 6am-2am daily July-August. Buy your tickets in advance at local tabacchi (tobacco shops). For one ride, tickets are €1.60, or buy a daily pass for €4.80 for unlimited rides. If you're staying for longer than a day on Procida, there are also 3-day tickets for €11 and 7-day tickets for €14.50. Be sure to validate your ticket after boarding; the machine is near the driver. You'll only need to do this for the first ride if you're using a daily or multiple-day pass.

Naples

Itinerary Ideas	296
Sights	300
Sports and Recreation	322
Entertainment and Events	324
Shopping	326
Bars and Nightlife	329
Food	331
Accommodations	337
Information and Services	340
Getting There	340
Getting Around	342

Often described as tumultuous and gritty,

Naples is a fascinating city teeming with vibrant energy and, yes, a touch of chaos. Travelers who get to know this city's dynamic culture and layers of history often find it captures their heart when they least expect it. From royal palaces to castles, world-class museums, and some of Italy's best street food, Naples is unexpected in the best possible ways.

Naples is a city to be seen from all its many angles. Climb to the top of the Castel Sant'Elmo in the Vomero for a bird's-eye view and then stroll along the waterfront to the Castel dell'Ovo, guarding an unusual legend as well as a picturesque fishing village, perfect for seaside dining. Meander through the narrow streets of the Quartieri Spagnoli

Highlights

Look for ★ to find recommended sights, activities, dining, and lodging.

★ **Museo Archeologico Nazionale:** This museum is a must, as it houses one of the finest archaeological collections in the world, including treasures uncovered at the ancient Roman cities of Pompeii and Herculaneum (page 300).

★ **Spaccanapoli:** Walk down this characteristic and vibrant street in the centro storico. Its name means "Split Naples" after the way it cuts a straight line through the historic center (page 304).

★ **Complesso Monumentale di Santa Chiara:** This Gothic church was built by the Angevin rulers of Naples. Don't miss the excellent museum, ancient Roman archaeological site, and famous cloister featuring 18th-century majolica tiles (page 304).

★ **Duomo di Napoli:** The Cathedral of Naples includes the earliest baptistery in the Western world and the Chapel of San Gennaro, the patron saint of Naples (page 307).

★ **Castel dell'Ovo:** The oldest castle in Naples is set right on the waterfront on an islet near the picturesque little harbor of Borgo Marinari (page 317).

★ **Reggia di Caserta:** Explore the grandiose 18th-century royal palace and gardens of the Bourbon kings of Naples (page 322).

★ **True Neapolitan Pizza:** Naples is famous as the birthplace of pizza. Enjoy a true Neapolitan experience with a classic pizza Margherita cooked to perfection (page 333).

Greater Naples

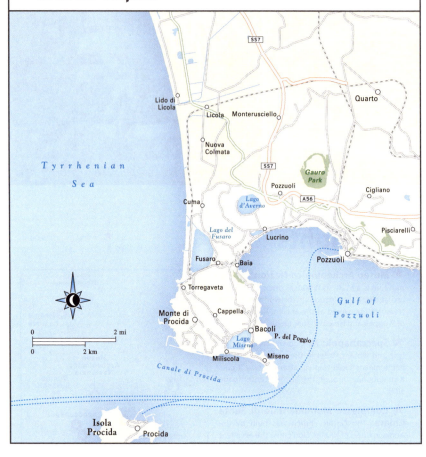

(Spanish Quarter) and centro storico (historic center), discovering remarkable small museums and stumbling across artistic treasures in the city's hundreds of churches. Travel in time through the history of Naples, from Greek walls and Roman streets underground to the lavish Palazzo Reale (Royal Palace) built for the Bourbon kings, and all the way to the modern metro stations brought to life with vibrant contemporary art and design.

Naples is a city of too many contrasts to describe. One moment you're gazing up at the impressive glass dome of the Galleria Umberto I or admiring Roman statues in the Museo Archeologico Nazionale, and the next scooters are zipping past you down impossibly narrow alleyways as you discover artisans continuing centuries-old craft traditions. What's that delicious scent? There's no need to worry about going hungry in Naples, because no matter where you turn, you won't be far from a pizzeria or the sweet scent of sfogliatelle (shell-shaped pastry filled with citrus-infused ricotta) or strong Neapolitan coffee.

While Naples has enough captivating sights and experiences to fill a vacation, it's also a

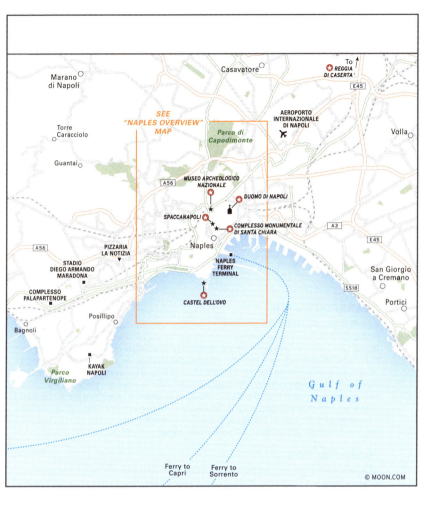

great jumping-off point to explore other popular destinations around the Gulf of Naples such as Capri, Sorrento, and the islands of Ischia and Procida. For a regal day trip, head north to visit the Reggia di Caserta, one of the largest royal palaces in Europe.

ORIENTATION

Set on the Gulf of Naples, the city of Naples stretches out from the waterfront and flat centro storico (historic center) up into the surrounding hilly landscape. Farther afield, about 19 mi (30.5 km) north of Naples lies the **Reggia di Caserta,** the impressive 18th-century royal palace built for the Bourbon kings of Naples.

Centro Storico

Via Toledo cuts a long, straight line through the heart of the centro storico of Naples, from

Previous: view of the city of Naples with famous Mount Vesuvius in the background; pizza in Naples; Reggia di Caserta.

Naples and the Amalfi Coast

Castel Nuovo

TRANSPORTATION

If you're looking to explore the Amalfi Coast from Naples, you can take the ferry from Naples to Positano or Amalfi or take the train to Salerno or Sorrento and continue on by ferry or bus. Ferry service from Naples to the Amalfi Coast is limited and only available during peak tourist season (June-Sept.). If you're visiting outside this season or prefer to take the train, staying in the centro storico puts you close to the Napoli Centrale station, where you can catch a train to Salerno and continue by ferry or bus to the Amalfi Coast; the Salerno port is only a few blocks from the train station. The other option is to take the Circumvesuviana commuter train from the Naples train station to Sorrento and continue by bus to the Amalfi Coast. While there is limited ferry service from Sorrento to the Amalfi Coast, if you're traveling by train from Naples, it's a bit of a hike or a bus ride to reach the port in Sorrento from the train station, and ferry service is far more limited.

PLANNING TIPS

If you're arriving in, or departing from, Naples and plan to visit the Amalfi Coast, it can be a good idea to schedule your time in Naples for the end of your trip prior to departure, especially if you're headed to the United States—flights from Naples for US connections often depart extremely early in the morning. The airport is located near the center of Naples and easy to get to using public transportation.

If you're traveling through Naples and have limited time, head straight to the **Castel Nuovo** and enjoy a stroll from there to the **Galleria Umberto I, Piazza del Plebiscito,** and along the waterfront to the Santa Lucia neighborhood to see the **Castel dell'Ovo** and beautiful views along the waterfront of the city with Mount Vesuvius in the distance.

Piazza Dante down to the grand Piazza Trieste e Trento in the area called San Ferdinando. Not far from Via Toledo, **Spaccanapoli** also cuts through the centro storico and is just one of the important streets to explore in the ancient Greek-planned city center.

San Ferdinando

Where Via Toledo ends (or starts) to the south of the centro storico lies the San Ferdinando neighborhood, the setting for royal palaces, the grandiose **Galleria Umberto I,** and the **Piazza del Plebiscito.**

Waterfront

Along and near the waterfront there are a few neighborhoods to explore. The **Santa Lucia** neighborhood juts out where the Castel dell'Ovo sits on an islet surrounded by the **Borgo Marinari**, a charming harbor with the atmosphere of a small fishing village. Follow Via Partenope along the waterfront until it becomes Via Caracciolo and runs along the edge of the Villa Comunale gardens. Not far beyond the western edge of the gardens is the **Mergellina** harbor, one of the most scenic spots to enjoy views of the Gulf of Naples on the waterfront. North of the Villa Comunale is the **Chiaia** neighborhood, a stylish area for shopping, dining, or an evening aperitivo.

Vomero

High above Chiaia, the Vomero neighborhood offers bird's-eye views from the **Castel Sant'Elmo** and **Certosa di San Martino**. Several funicular trains connect the Vomero with Chiaia and the historic center.

Capodimonte

In the hills north of the city center, the Capodimonte neighborhood is noted especially for its fine **Museo di Capodimonte,** surrounded by a wooded park.

PLANNING YOUR TIME

With more than 2,700 years of history and culture to explore, Italy's third-largest city deserves at least 2-3 days for you to cover just the top sights. If you only have a couple of days, read our Itinerary Ideas for the top things to see and do in 2 days in Naples. Whether you're just visiting for a day or for longer, allow time to explore the centro storico to walk along **Spaccanapoli,** visit the churches and layers of history underground, and enjoy the best pizza in Italy. A longer stay means you'll also have time to explore the incredible museums—both the large ones and the smaller artistic gems—and time to take the funicular train up to **Vomero** to see the Castel Sant'Elmo and enjoy sweeping views across the city and Gulf of Naples.

In Naples there are plenty of transportation options right at your fingertips, which makes it a convenient base to explore the entire region. You can easily spend up to a week if you plan day trips to popular destinations nearby, such as Pompeii, Herculaneum, Sorrento, or the islands of Capri, Ischia, and Procida. Ferries depart regularly from Naples's port for the islands and Sorrento, or you can reach Sorrento on the Circumvesuviana commuter train, which includes stops at Pompeii and Herculaneum.

Sightseeing Passes

The **Campania Artecard** (www.campaniartecard.it) is an excellent sightseeing pass for Naples and sights throughout Campania. It covers many artistic and cultural sights in Naples, including museums, archaeological sites, churches, and more. The pass also includes access to nearly all public transportation systems. A 3-day **Naples Card** (€22 adults, €13 ages 18-25) covers only sights in the city, whereas a 3-day **Campania Card** (€32 adults, €25 ages 18-25) covers Naples and all of the region; the latter is the better bet if you plan to visit the archaeological cities of Pompeii and Herculaneum. For longer visits, a 7-day Campania Card (€34 adults) is also available. All of the cards provide free entry to the first two to five sights, depending on the card selected, and then discounts of up to 50 percent are given for admission to subsequent sights. If you plan to visit many sights in Naples or the surrounding area, the Campania Artecard quickly pays for itself.

Itinerary Ideas

In a city with such an extensive history, seeing all the sights in Naples would require a lifetime. Yet the highlights of the city can be enjoyed in a 48-hour tour that covers the essential sights, panoramic views from the best vantage points, and the gastronomic delights of Naples.

NAPLES ON DAY 1

Day 1 starts with a walking tour through the centro storico (historic center), a stop for pizza for lunch, and a visit to the remarkable Museo Archeologico Nazionale. This neighborhood is incredibly rich with historic sights and rewarding museums. So put on some comfortable walking shoes and set off to discover Naples!

1 Start the day with a walk down **Spaccanapoli** through the most characteristic area of Naples.

2 Stop in **Scaturchio** for a shot of strong Neapolitan espresso.

3 Take a left on Via Duomo to visit the **Duomo di Napoli** (Naples Cathedral) with its sumptuous chapel dedicated to the city's patron saint, San Gennaro.

4 Detour down **Via San Gregorio Armeno** to see artisans selling presepi (Nativity scenes).

5 Go inside the **Complesso Monumentale di San Lorenzo Maggiore** to see the soaring Gothic nave and explore the archaeological area below the church with Greek and Roman ruins.

6 Stop for a pizza break at **Sorbillo** along Via dei Tribunali.

7 After lunch, stop by the **Museo Cappella Sansevero** to see the *Cristo Velato* (Veiled Christ) statue by Giuseppe Sanmartino.

8 Go down Via Santa Maria di Costantinopoli to the world-class **Museo Archeologico Nazionale.**

9 Enjoy an aperitivo and people-watching in **Piazza Bellini,** where nightlife options abound.

NAPLES ON DAY 2

Day 2 begins high in Vomero and continues down to Piazza del Plebiscito, Palazzo Reale, and the waterfront castles of Naples.

1 Make your way to the **Castel Sant'Elmo** in the Vomero neighborhood for panoramic views.

2 Stop for lunch at **Borbonika Napulitan Restaurant** and enjoy a dish of pasta with traditional Naples genovese (meat) sauce.

3 Head to Piazza Ferdinando Fuga to take the **Funicolare Centrale** down to the Augusteo stop at the bottom on Via Toledo.

4 Cross Via Toledo and see the **Galleria Umberto I** and stop for a traditional sfogliatella pastry at La Sfogliatella Mary.

5 Across Piazza Trieste e Trento, visit the **Palazzo Reale,** the stunning royal palace of Naples.

6 Admire **Piazza del Plebiscito** and continue along the waterfront to the Borgo Marinari.

7 Enjoy a seaside stroll to see the **Castel dell'Ovo** up close and the charming Borgo Marinari nearby.

8 Have one last Neapolitan pizza at **Sorbillo Lievito Madre al Mare** by the sea with incredible views of the Gulf of Naples with Vesuvius and the island of Capri in the distance.

NAPLES LIKE A LOCAL

Naples is a city with strong ties to tradition and a somewhat nonchalant attitude toward things that might be termed touristy. However, walking down Spaccanapoli in the centro storico, stopping in little restaurants or even busy pizzerias, you can start to feel like a local, thanks to the natural exuberance and warmth of the Neapolitans. Often characterized as a living theater, Naples pulls you into the fabric of daily life.

1 Start the day with a traditional Neapolitan espresso at the historic **Gran Caffè Gambrinus.** Enjoy your coffee standing at the bar like the locals.

2 Walk down pedestrian-only **Via Chiaia,** where you'll find iconic shops like Camiceria Piccolo and Rubinacci that continue the sartorial tradition in Naples.

3 Stop for lunch at **Ristorante Amici Miei** to enjoy hearty Neapolitan pasta dishes.

4 Admire the Liberty-style (art nouveau) buildings along **Via dei Mille** and catch the funicular train from Parco Margherita up to the Vomero.

5 Visit the **Certosa e Museo di San Martino** to see its lovely art collection, peaceful cloister, and fabulous views overlooking Naples.

6 Enjoy the local atmosphere and shopping along pedestrian-only **Via Alessandro Scarlatti.**

7 For dinner, take a short taxi ride to **Pizzaria La Notizia** for what is often considered the very best of the best traditional Neapolitan pizza.

8 After dinner, taxi back to the waterfront. A wine shop by day and wine bar by night, **Enoteca Belledonne** is a lovely spot to sample fine wines as the evening winds down.

Itinerary Ideas

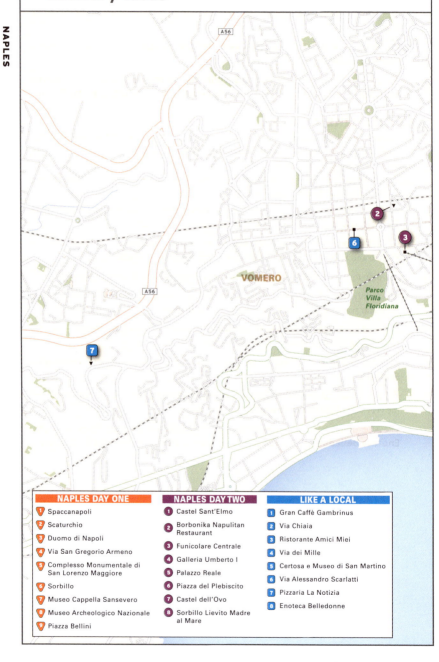

NAPLES DAY ONE	NAPLES DAY TWO	LIKE A LOCAL
1 Spaccanapoli	1 Castel Sant'Elmo	1 Gran Caffè Gambrinus
2 Scaturchio	2 Borbonika Napulitan Restaurant	2 Via Chiaia
3 Duomo di Napoli	3 Funicolare Centrale	3 Ristorante Amici Miei
4 Via San Gregorio Armeno	4 Galleria Umberto I	4 Via dei Mille
5 Complesso Monumentale di San Lorenzo Maggiore	5 Palazzo Reale	5 Certosa e Museo di San Martino
6 Sorbillo	6 Piazza del Plebiscito	6 Via Alessandro Scarlatti
7 Museo Cappella Sansevero	7 Castel dell'Ovo	7 Pizzaria La Notizia
8 Museo Archeologico Nazionale	8 Sorbillo Lievito Madre al Mare	8 Enoteca Belledonne
9 Piazza Bellini		

Sights

From the waterfront with romantic views across the gulf to the narrow alleys of the historic center and the view from on high in Vomero, Naples is a city to be explored. It's also a city that is best seen on foot to get a feel for all its little quirks and its soul. Most significant sights in Naples are clustered in the historic center and famous Spaccanapoli street, and down Via Toledo to the Piazza del Plebiscito. Plan also to spend some time in the Chiaia area with its chic shopping, take a funicular train up to Vomero to enjoy the views from Castel Sant'Elmo, and explore the fine collection at the Museo di Capodimonte.

CENTRO STORICO

The centro storico (historic center) of Naples is incredibly rich with sights, including beautiful Gothic and baroque churches, remarkable small museums, and one of the world's finest archaeological museums. Located over the heart of the ancient Greek and later Roman city, the centro storico is basically the city center, from Via Toledo east to the area around the Duomo di Napoli. The center is divided by the decumani, three parallel streets dating back to the Greek city, that run roughly east-west and are crossed by a series of streets. Here among this tight grid of narrow streets lie some of Naples's most iconic streets, like Spaccanapoli, one of the decumani, which cuts a straight line through the center of the city. This is an area for exploring on foot, as it's not very large and, quite literally, around every corner there's something incredible to discover.

TOP EXPERIENCE

★ Museo Archeologico Nazionale

Piazza Museo 19; tel. 848/800-288; www.mann-napoli.it; 9am-7:30pm Wed.-Mon.; €22

For history lovers, a visit to the Museo Archeologico Nazionale di Napoli (MANN), before or after exploring the ancient Roman towns of Pompeii and Herculaneum, is a must. A treasure trove of archaeological finds from the ancient world are on display at this museum, and many of the objects are here thanks to Bourbon kings of Naples, who were fascinated with the discovery and exploration of the ancient sites around Vesuvius. Over the course of the 18th century, Pompeii, Herculaneum, and other sites were excavated, and the finest pieces were gathered together in a collection housed in this museum's current location.

Start on the ground floor in the large galleries of the Farnese Collection of antiquities, which includes spectacular sculptures. Some of these statues are on a monumental scale, like the *Farnese Bull,* a Roman copy of an earlier Greek sculpture that stands over 12 ft (3.7 m) tall, or the *Farnese Hercules,* a massive statue dating from the 3rd century. Also part of the Farnese galleries is a collection of carved gems, where the Farnese Cup, one of the largest carved cameos in the world, is not to be missed. Spread over the ground floor and two upper floors, the collection of pieces from Campania's archaeological sites is also on display, including mosaics, frescoes, sculptures, the numismatics collection, and a unique room called the Gabinetto Segreto (Secret Cabinet) entirely dedicated to ancient art with an erotic theme. There are also artifacts from prehistoric and protohistoric times as well as galleries that tell the story of ancient Naples. On the lower level, you'll find a fine Egyptian collection as well.

From exquisitely detailed Roman mosaics to awe-inspiring marble sculptures, the Museo Archeologico Nazionale offers a fascinating exploration of the ancient world and is well worth a visit, even if your time is limited in Naples.

Naples Overview

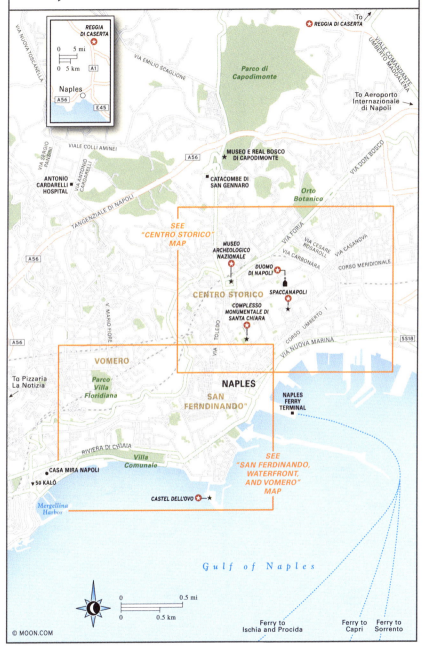

Centro Storico

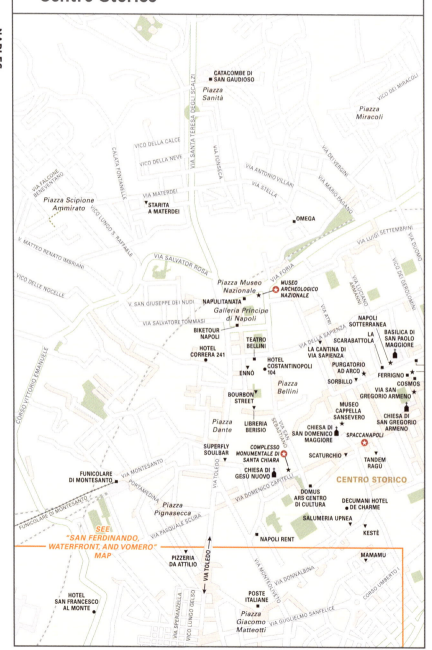

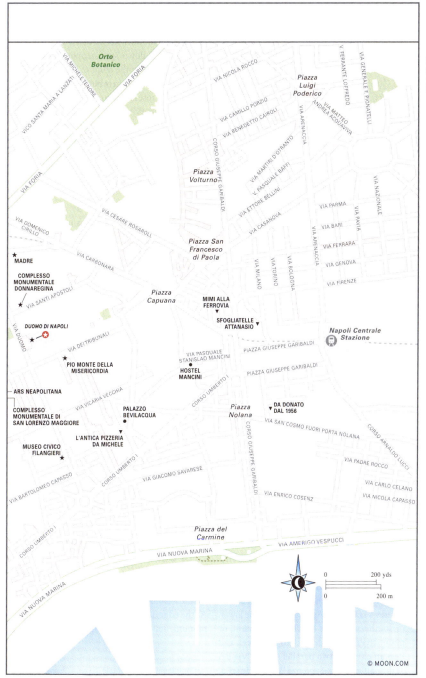

Piazza Dante

Just a short walk south from the Museo Archeologico Nazionale, this large semicircular piazza is named for the statue of the poet Dante Alighieri that stands in the center. Once the setting for a market in the 16th century, the piazza was renovated in 1757 by Neapolitan architect Luigi Vanvitelli for the Bourbon king Charles III. Vanvitelli's elegant colonnade design is the backdrop to a bustling piazza lined with shops and cafés. It marks the starting point for Via Toledo, which runs all the way to Piazza Trieste e Trento. In the northeast corner of the piazza, you'll find the Port'Alba, a large arch from the early 17th century that was an entrance gate to the city. Through the grand arch is an arcade lined with **bookstores** that leads to the nearby Piazza Bellini.

Piazza Bellini

Tucked away behind Piazza Dante, this small square is a lively nightlife spot and is worth a visit to see the ancient Greek walls that are visible below a part of the piazza. Take a look down at the defensive walls that once marked the edge of the Greek city of Neapolis in the 4th century BCE. The walls are located well below the modern street level, as the city has been built up in layers over the centuries, literally covering the ancient city.

★ Spaccanapoli

Via Benedetto Croce and Via San Biagio dei Librai, from Piazza Gesù Nuovo to Via Duomo

Running through the heart of Naples's historic center, Spaccanapoli is the popular name for a very straight and long street. Literally meaning "Split Naples," it takes its name from the way it cuts down the middle of the city. Starting in Piazza del Gesù Nuovo, the street now is labeled Via Benedetto Croce, which then becomes Via San Biagio dei Librai until it crosses Via Duomo. Spaccanapoli is the lower, or southernmost, of the three decumani, or main streets that date back to the Greek and Roman city. The two parallel streets, Via dei Tribunali and Via Sapienza/Via Anticaglia, form the upper two decumani, and all three are crossed by a grid of streets that form the backbone of the ancient city that is still visible today. A stroll down Spaccanapoli is a must, not only to take in the ethos of Naples that is so perfectly captured here but also to see many of the city's most important churches and historic monuments in a very short distance. The streets in the historic center are narrow and can be crowded, especially during the lead-up to the Christmas season with so many people heading toward Via San Gregorio Armeno to see the Christmas Nativity workshops.

Chiesa di Gesù Nuovo

Piazza del Gesù Nuovo 2; tel. 081/557-8111; www.gesunuovo.it; 8am-1pm and 4pm-7:30pm daily; free

The beautiful Piazza del Gesù Nuovo is one of the city's loveliest, with its ornate Guglia dell'Immacolata (Spire of the Immaculate, an 18th-century decorative obelisk), elegant palazzos, and the very striking facade of the Chiesa di Gesù Nuovo. Its dark-gray stone facade is almost completely covered with carved pyramid-shaped projections, an imposing design that reflects the building's origins as a private palazzo in the 15th century. The Jesuits later confiscated the building, completely gutted the interior, and transformed the space into an architectural and artistic treasure. Inside you'll find artworks by some of the most important Neapolitan artists of the 17th century, including Luca Giordano, Francesco Solimena, and Giovanni Lanfranco. The church is free to visit and worth the time to admire the resplendent interior and explore the highly decorated chapels.

★ Complesso Monumentale di Santa Chiara

Via Santa Chiara 49c; tel. 081/060-6976; www.monasterodisantachiara.it; 9:30am-5:30pm Mon.-Sat., 10am-2:30pm Sun.; €6

At the edge of Piazza del Gesù Nuovo sits the monumental religious complex of the Chiesa

---

1: Spaccanapoli **2:** exterior of the Duomo di Napoli **3:** Complesso Monumentale di Santa Chiara

di Santa Chiara. Built in the early 14th century, the basilica has a stark Gothic facade that stands in striking contrast to the Chiesa di Gesù Nuovo across the piazza. Near the entrance stands a tall bell tower, which also dates from the 14th century yet shows baroque decorations from a later restoration. The church itself was also restored during the baroque period, yet was unfortunately almost completely destroyed by World War II bombardments. After the war, the church was rebuilt in a style to recapture the majestic beauty of the original Gothic design. The chapels along the nave hold tombs of aristocratic Neapolitan families and Angevin sovereigns from the 14th-15th centuries. Behind the main altar is the intricately carved Gothic-style tomb of King Robert of Anjou, created by Florentine sculptors Giovanni and Pacio Bertini in the 14th century.

The monastery features three cloisters. The most remarkable is the Chiostro Maiolicato (Majolica Cloister), which was designed by Domenico Vaccaro in 1739-1742 and includes beautiful hand-painted majolica tiles on the 64 octagonal pillars and benches throughout the cloister. Look closely at the benches, which feature a series of scenes from daily life in the 18th century. Off the cloister, look for the room with the large Neapolitan presepe (Nativity) from the 1700s-1800s.

Beyond the cloister is the **Museo dell'Opera,** which houses a collection of religious artworks saved from the church and archaeological finds from excavations on the site. Part of the museum includes ruins of a Roman bath complex, dating from the 1st century CE, that were discovered during restorations after World War II.

Chiesa di San Domenico Maggiore

Piazza San Domenico Maggiore 8A; tel. 333/863-8997; www.museosandomenicomaggiore.it; 10am-6pm daily; from €5

Stroll a few minutes down Via Benedetto Croce from Santa Chiara to Piazza San Domenico Maggiore, which you can't miss because it's marked by another distinctive obelisk. Gaze up to see the exterior of the apse of the massive Chiesa di San Domenico Maggiore. This remarkable Gothic church was built 1283-1324, and together with its museum offers visitors a masterpiece of religious architecture and art in Naples. The soaring basilica is divided into three aisles and is as ornate as Santa Chiara is austere. Here, the Gothic church still retains its resplendent baroque decorations with gilded details and a coffered ceiling. The lavish chapels are the burial place for Aragonese kings and aristocratic families of Naples.

The massive complex, now called **Museo Doma,** can be visited on a guided tour to delve deeper into this rich history. Visits cover the basilica, the sacristy, Aragonese tombs, and highlights of the art collection, which includes 16th-century garments and a painted *Salvator Mundi* attributed to the school of Leonardo da Vinci. Standard visits last about 30 minutes, while the complete visit lasts 60 minutes and includes additional interesting stops like the room where San Tommaso d'Aquino (Saint Thomas Aquinas) lived during his stay at the monastery.

Museo Cappella Sansevero

Via Francesco De Sanctis 19/21; tel. 081/552-4936; www.museosansevero.it; 9am-7pm Wed.-Mon.; €10

For its intensity and artistic masterpieces, the small Cappella Sansevero is a jewel of Neapolitan baroque design. With pride of place in the center of the chapel is the remarkable *Cristo Velato* (Veiled Christ) statue by Giuseppe Sanmartino. This marble sculpture from 1753 depicts Christ after being taken down from the cross and covered with a sheet. It is so finely carved as to capture the pain and suffering of Christ through the incredible lightness of the sheet. While this fine statue is utterly captivating, the rest of the museum, featuring works by the most prominent 18th-century sculptors and artists, is no less worthy of attention.

Museo Civico Filangieri

Via Duomo 288; tel. 081/203-175; www.museofilangieri.org; 9:30am-7pm daily; €6.50

A massive entrance portal and rusticated 15th-century facade greet visitors to the Museo Civico Filangieri, a small museum set in the former home of Prince Gaetano Filangieri (1824-1892). The prince was an avid art collector and historian. In 1888, he transformed the historic palazzo into a home and museum filled with his collection of paintings, sculptures, weapons and armor, decorative arts, and an extensive library with 30,000 volumes. The upper room of the museum features carved wood paneling, an intricate majolica tile floor, and a skylight that fills the room with light. The gallery level of the room has wood cabinets displaying pieces from the museum's porcelain collection.

★ Duomo di Napoli

Via Duomo 147; tel. 081/449-087; www.chiesadinapoli.it; 8:30am-1:30pm and 4:30pm-7:30pm daily; cathedral entry free

In a city with no shortage of impressive religious sights, the Duomo (Cathedral of Naples) holds an important place not only as the largest and most important church in the city, but also for its strong connection to Neapolitan traditions and life. Behind the Gothic-revival facade designed by Neapolitan architect Errico Alvino at the end of the 1800s lies a church with layers of history dating back to the 13th century, when the Gothic cathedral was built. Over the centuries the cathedral was rebuilt, expanded, and decorated in a variety of different styles that blend together to tell the story of art in Naples from the 13th to the 19th centuries. The central nave soars to about 157 ft (48 m) and combines Gothic elements with later baroque decorations and a coffered and gilded 17th-century ceiling with painted panels. On the upper band of the nave are paintings by celebrated Neapolitan artist Luca Giordano depicting the Apostles and Doctors of the church, and on the lower band are round portraits of important patron saints of Naples.

To the left of the entrance is a large chapel that was once the Basilica of Santa Restituta, dating to the 4th century, offering an interesting look at early Christian architecture. Don't miss the **Battistero di San Giovanni in Fonte** (8:30am-12:30pm and 2:30pm-6:30pm Mon.-Fri., 8:30am-1pm Sun.), a Byzantine baptistery that is the oldest surviving in the Western world. As in much of the centro storico, the history below the Duomo dates to Greek and Roman times. Archaeological excavation has uncovered a Greek street made of tufa with traces of cartwheels carved into the stone, beautiful Roman mosaics, and architectural ruins. Unfortunately, the archaeological area below the Duomo is closed indefinitely for restoration.

The heart and soul of the Duomo is the gleaming **Reale Cappella del Tesoro di San Gennaro,** a sumptuous baroque chapel built in the early 17th century. Dedicated to the city's patron saint and protector San Gennaro (Saint Januarius), the chapel holds artifacts, reliquaries, and the much-treasured vial of the saint's blood that, the faithful say, miraculously liquefies three times a year (first Sun. in May, Sept. 19, and Dec. 16). Besides the chapel, take time to visit the **Museo del Tesoro di San Gennaro** (Via Duomo 149; tel. 081/294-980; www.tesorosangennaro.it; 9am-6:30pm daily with reduced hours for the Chapel of the Treasury; €12) to see the collection of exquisite religious silver objects, textiles, jewels, sculptures, and artwork.

Pio Monte della Misericordia

Via dei Tribunali 253; tel. 081/446-944; www.piomontedellamisericordia.it; 10am-6pm Mon.-Sat., 9am-2:30pm Sun.; €10

Just around the corner from the Duomo, the Pio Monte della Misericordia church is located across from a small piazza with an exquisite obelisk designed by Cosimo Fanzago in 1637. This church was founded in 1602 by seven Neapolitan noblemen to provide charitable works to help the city's poor, offer care for the sick, shelter pilgrims, and help inmates. The institution is still active doing charitable works and is located in the same 17th-century building where it was founded. With more than four centuries of history, Pio Monte della Misericordia has amassed a fine collection of artworks, with the most important and significant being Caravaggio's masterpiece *The Seven Works of Mercy*, created for the main altar in 1607. The cappella is a stunning place to admire this important work along with other paintings on display around the chapel. Take time to explore the rest of the church's collection, which includes both historical and contemporary donations by local and international artists such as Mimmo Jodice, Francesco Clemente, Mimmo Paladino, Anish Kapoor, and many more.

Napoli Sotterranea
(Underground Naples)

Piazza San Gaetano 68; tel. 081/296-944; www.napolisotterranea.org; tours 10am-6pm daily; €15

With two striking churches, Piazza San Gaetano is a natural spot to pause along Via dei Tribunali while exploring the centro storico (historic center). This historic piazza is in the exact location of the Greek agora and later Roman forum, the heart of ancient Neapolis. Descend deep below the busy streets of Naples and you can explore layers upon layers of history. The Napoli Sotterranea tour starts in the caves excavated in the 4th century BCE by the Greeks. The caves were later used for cisterns for the city's water supply. The visit includes the remains of a Roman theater and city, World War II air raid shelters, a War Museum, and more. The tour includes steps, but most of the area explored is spacious and well lit, except for one optional part where the space is narrower and darker, but everyone is given a candle to light the path. Tours last about 1 hour and are available in English every 2 hours daily.

Complesso Monumentale di San Lorenzo Maggiore

Piazza San Gaetano 316; tel. 081/211-0860; www.laneapolissotterrata.it; 9:30am-5:30pm daily; €9

To delve deeper into the fascinating tapestry of Naples's history, pay a visit to the Chiesa di San Lorenzo Maggiore, where you'll learn the city's story, from the ancient city to the creation of this important religious complex in Piazza San Gaetano. Beyond the baroque facade designed by Ferdinando Sanfelice in 1742, the interior of the church dates from the 13th century and has largely been restored to its original Gothic design.

Don't miss the **cloister,** which was located on the spot of the ancient Roman market, with its central stone well carved by Cosimo Fanzago. Travelers should also visit the **Museo dell'Opera** (museum) and the **Sisto V Hall,** the refectory with 17th-century frescoes covering the ceiling. Just off the cloister, a staircase leads down to the **archaeological excavations** below the church, where you can see the Greek and Roman footprint of the city; you'll see a well-preserved Roman street and the ruins of the ancient market shops, including mosaic paving from the 1st-2nd centuries BCE. It's a unique historical experience to walk down through the medieval layers of the church and to stand in what was the heart of Naples in antiquity.

Basilica di San Paolo Maggiore

Piazza San Gaetano 76; hours vary; free

A statue dedicated to San Gaetano stands near the grand double staircase entrance to the Basilica di San Paolo Maggiore. Before visiting, take a moment to look closely at the 17th-century baroque facade of the church and notice the two large Corinthian columns standing about 36 ft (11 m) tall. These are from the Roman Temple of Dioscuri that once stood on this spot. The church is surprisingly large and bright, which is excellent for admiring the many paintings and frescoes adorning the interior. Significantly damaged during World War II bombings, the church was later restored. Repairs can be seen in the transept and roof in this area, which completely collapsed.

The Nativity Tradition in Naples

Nativity scenes in Naples

Of the many artistic traditions of Naples, one of the most unique is the **presepe,** Italian for Nativity scene, or Christmas crib. Dating back to Saint Francis of Assisi in the 13th century, the Nativity is still an important part of Christmas celebrations throughout Italy. Starting in the mid-14th century, artists in Naples began creating both small and large-scale presepi for churches, private chapels for wealthy families, and eventually for displaying in homes during the Christmas season.

By the 1700s, the Neapolitan presepe was a work of art that extended far beyond the traditional manger scene. In addition to figures related to the birth of Jesus, the Nativity grew to include an entire landscape that was representative of Neapolitan life in the 1700s. These figures, called **pastori,** include a host of characters, from peasants to farmers, animals, and houses.

VIA SAN GREGORIO ARMENO
The heart of the presepe tradition is Via San Gregorio Armeno in the historic center, where artisans have been handmaking nativities for centuries. Strolling down the street, you'll find one workshop after the next with elaborate displays of figures and elements for creating presepi of all sizes. Traditional figurines are made with terra-cotta or papier-mâché; the finest are delicately painted and feature handmade clothing. Leading up to the Christmas season the street becomes very crowded, but throughout the year you can stop by workshops to see artisans at work.

SHOPS
Ferrigno (page 327) is an excellent shop to see traditional Neapolitan Nativity scenes created by brothers Giuseppe and Marco Ferrigno. Or just around the corner, stop by **Ars Neapolitana** (page 328) to see the remarkable figures crafted by hand by Neapolitan artist Guglielmo Muoio.

OTHER PLACES TO SEE PRESEPI
Some of the finest examples of 18th-century Neapolitan presepi can be seen at the **Certosa e Museo di San Martino** (page 319), which has a special section dedicated to nativities from the 1700s-1800s in Naples. Just off the Chiostro Maiolicato (Majolica Cloister) at the **Complesso Monumentale di Santa Chiara** (page 304) there's a special room with a large Neapolitan presepe from the 18th century. If you visit the **Reggia di Caserta** (page 322) outside Naples, you'll have the chance to see the Royal Nativity Scene, a massive presepe scene re-created based on a design from 1844.

Via San Gregorio Armeno

Via San Gregorio Armeno from Via dei Tribunali to Via San Biagio dei Librai

As the hub of Naples's presepe (Nativity) artisan workshops, this short street is one of the most entertaining in the historic center. Displays with Nativity scene figurines and decorations of all sizes spill out onto the street. Take time to look closely at the detailed pieces that are handmade from terra-cotta and require meticulous work. Often in the workshops along the street you can see artisans at work creating new pieces. It's a tradition that has been passed down for generations, and the craftsmanship is spectacular to witness firsthand. The street itself has a heritage of terra-cotta since ancient times, when shops produced votive figurines that were popular offerings to take to the temple dedicated to Ceres, which was located nearby in ancient Neapolis. The holiday season is a particularly busy time to visit the street because the Nativity tradition is still an integral part of Christmas celebrations in Italy, but the workshops are open year-round.

Chiesa di San Gregorio Armeno

Via San Gregorio Armeno 1; 9:30am-1pm daily; €4

Take a break from the Nativity scenes to visit the Chiesa di San Gregorio Armeno, located about midway down the street. Though it's hard to take in the dark stone baroque facade from the narrow street, go inside to admire the lavish baroque decorations, complete with gold paneling on the walls and ceiling. There are many fine paintings, including more than 50 by Neapolitan artist Luca Giordano. The church and adjacent convent were founded in the 8th century by a group of nuns who fled from persecution in Constantinople with the relics of San Gregorio, a bishop from Armenia. The convent has a peaceful cloister with a marble fountain flanked by two large statues from the early 18th century representing Christ and the Samaritan woman at the well.

Madre

Via Luigi Settembrini 79; tel. 081/197-37254; www.madrenapoli.it; 10am-7:30pm Mon. and Wed.-Sat., 10am-8pm Sun.; €8

Located in the 19th-century Palazzo Donnaregina, the Madre (Museo d'Arte Contemporanea Donnaregina) museum has a fine collection of contemporary art. The permanent collection, exhibitions, and educational spaces are spread across three floors and 77,500 sq ft (7,200 sq m). With a unique juxtaposition of historic and modern architectural styles, the collection includes works by the biggest names in Italian and international art from the past 50 years, including Mimmo Paladino, Richard Serra, Sol LeWitt, Francesco Clemente, Jeff Koons, Anish Kapoor, and many more.

Complesso Monumentale Donnaregina

Largo Donnaregina; tel. 081/557-1365; www.museodiocesanonapoli.com; 9:30am-4:30pm Mon. and Wed.-Sat., 9:30am-2pm Sun.; €7

Covering a large area north of the Duomo, this religious complex dates from the 8th century with the foundation of the earliest church, Santa Maria Donnaregina Vecchia (vecchia means old). The complex today also includes the Santa Maria Donnaregina Nuova (new) church and the Diocesan Museum of Naples, where a wonderful collection of religious art is on display. Visiting the complex, you can see both the Gothic architecture of the Vecchia church and the baroque majesty of the 17th-century Nuova church.

Purgatorio ad Arco

Via dei Tribunali 39; tel. 081/440-438; www.purgatorioadarco.it; 10am-2pm Mon.-Sat.; €7

Out of all of the churches in Naples, this little one dedicated to Santa Maria delle Anime del Purgatorio is truly one of the city's most unusual. The elegant 17th-century church that you step into on the main level reveals little of what you'll find in the lower church. There lies a burial area housing anonymous remains that are part of a special devotion to the ancient cult of the Purgatory Souls. In the underground church, you'll see tombs, skulls, and wooden boxes used for burial. Though a visit to the church is free, you'll need to buy a ticket and join a guided tour to see the museum and burial site.

SAN FERDINANDO

The area called San Ferdinando is the political and administrative center of Naples—just as it has been for centuries. Yet most travelers head to this part of Naples to stroll through the grand Piazza del Plebiscito, shop at the glass-domed Galleria Umberto I, visit the royal palace, and see the impressive Castel Nuovo and other top sights nearby. Here you can go from the depths of the city in **Napoli Sotterranea** (Naples Underground) on one of the city's two underground tours to the heights of Bourbon dynasty in Naples at the Palazzo Reale.

The **Quartieri Spagnoli** (Spanish Quarter) is a tight grid of narrow streets west of Via Toledo sitting at the base of the steep slope up to Vomero. This is where the Spanish Viceroy's soldiers lived in the 16th century, which explains how this intensely Neapolitan neighborhood got its name. This neighborhood's tiny streets, crisscrossed with laundry, make for an interesting stroll.

Castel Nuovo

Piazza Municipio; tel. 081/795-7722; www.comune. napoli.it/maschioangioino; 8:30am-6:30pm Mon.-Sat.; €6

Sitting grandly on the waterfront, the imposing Castel Nuovo, also called the Maschio Angioino, is a castle dating from the late 13th century. Built by the French King Charles I of Anjou, it was later expanded under the Aragonese control of the city. The stunning Triumphal Arch with marble bas-reliefs at the entrance dates from the Aragonese period. Entering through the massive bronze gates, look for the cannonball still embedded in one of the gates, a reminder of the battles this castle has seen over its long history. The view inside the courtyard is an impressive sight. Don't miss the **Cappella Palatina** from the 14th century, **Sala dell'Armeria** (armory), and the **Museo Civico** (Civic Museum), displaying artwork from the medieval period to the late 1800s.

Palazzo Reale

Piazza del Plebiscito 1; tel. 081/580-8255; www. palazzorealedinapoli.org; 9am-8pm Thurs.-Tues.; €11

Occupying appropriately fine waterfront real estate, the Palazzo Reale is the royal palace of Naples and was built starting at the beginning of the 17th century for Spanish royalty. Originally designed by noted architect Domenico Fontana, the palace has changed in many ways over the years, including the addition of the grand entrance staircase. Standing in the immense Scalone d'Onore (Staircase of Honor), it's hard to imagine an entryway more impressive with its multiple types of marble, soaring ceiling, and sober yet regal neoclassical design. Following the grand hallways, it's possible to visit the 17th-century Cappella Palatina (Palatine Chapel) and a series of grand royal apartment rooms, including the throne room, all beautifully decorated with historic furniture and artwork from the days of Bourbon rule in Naples. With its frescoes and outstanding sculptural work, the court theater is a sparkling gem, designed by architect Ferdinando Fuga to celebrate the marriage of Ferdinand IV to Maria Carolina of Austria in 1768. An audio guide, available in English, is available for a small additional fee and brings the history of the state apartments and richness of the decor and artwork on display to life. Included in the ticket price is entrance to the Museo Caruso, dedicated to the famous Neapolitan tenor Enrico Caruso.

Piazza del Plebiscito

The largest piazza in Naples, and one of the largest in Italy, Piazza del Plebiscito is where much of the city's history has played out over the centuries. Opening from Piazza Trieste e Trento, the large piazza is an impressive sight with the **Palazzo Reale** on the left, a striking colonnade with the **Basilica di San Francesco di Paola** on the right, and

San Ferdinando, Waterfront, and Vomero

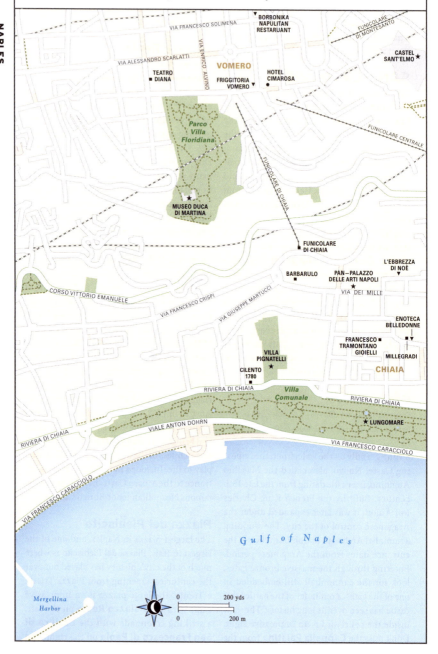

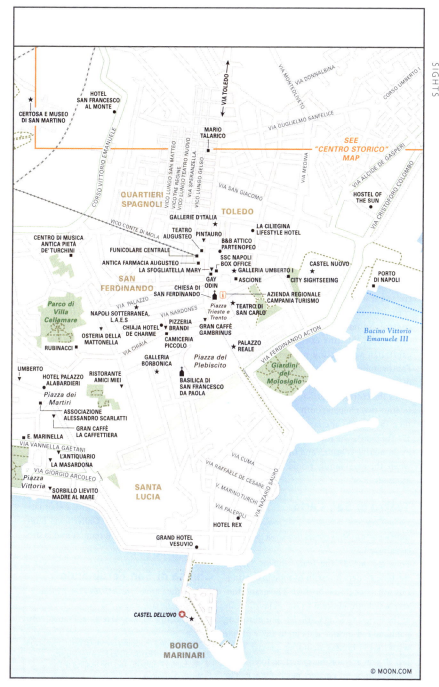

a glimpse of the sea in the distance. Two large equestrian statues stand in the piazza, one representing Bourbon king Carlo III and the other his son Ferdinando I. While firmly rooted in the city's royal past, the name Piazza del Plebiscito today refers to the referendum, or plebiscite, in 1860, when the Kingdom of the Two Sicilies was annexed to the Kingdom of Italy during the unification. While the Piazza del Plebiscito is occasionally the setting for concerts and events, the rest of the time the large, open piazza is a popular spot for kids to run and play, and for locals to enjoy a walk away from the traffic and hustle and bustle of the city.

Basilica di San Francesco da Paola

Piazza del Plebiscito; hours vary; free

Built 1817-1846, this impressive church was created at the wish of Ferdinando I as an ex-voto after reclaiming Naples from French control. Situated in the center of a curved colonnade, this fine example of neoclassical Italian architecture was inspired by the Pantheon in Rome. Walk up the small flight of marble steps past the six Ionic columns that mark the entrance portico. Enter the church to find two chapels, both with domes, and then the central and largest dome, rising to 174 ft (53 m). The round nave is surrounded by 34 marble columns and includes a gallery where the royal family would sit during religious services.

Teatro di San Carlo

Via San Carlo 98/F; tel. 081/797-2331; www.teatrosancarlo.it; performances throughout the year; guided tours €9

Founded in 1737, the Teatro di San Carlo is the oldest opera house in Europe in continuous use since it first opened. The grand theater was built adjacent to the Palazzo Reale at the behest of King Carlo III. The glittering gold and red theater seats up to 1,379 people with its 184 boxes, including a lavish royal box. It's an extraordinary setting to enjoy an opera, dance, or concert performance. The Teatro di San Carlo welcomes visitors outside of performance times with guided tours that are also available in English (daily; €9). English-language tours are limited, and reserving in advance is advised. Tours include a visit to MeMus (10am-5pm Mon.-Tues. and Thurs.-Fri., 10am-3pm Sun.), the museum and archive of the Teatro di San Carlo.

Galleria Umberto I

Via San Carlo 15; 24 hours daily

The distinctive soaring glass and metal ribbed dome of the Galleria Umberto I is an arresting sight amid the urban landscape of Naples. Built at the end of the 19th century, the Galleria was a key part of the city's revival and regeneration, called the Risanamento (Restoration), which saw massive changes in the historic center. Located across the street from the Teatro di San Carlo, the Galleria was envisioned as a public space that would bring together shops, cafés, and living with private apartments on the upper floor. The architectural style is reminiscent of the Galleria Vittorio Emanuele II in Milan. The glass dome rises to 187 ft (57 m) and is an impressive sight, especially when you stand below the central dome, where a large mosaic in the floor depicts the zodiac signs. The ground level has shops and simple restaurants and cafés.

The best way to experience the Galleria is to find a spot and simply look up to admire the incredible level of architectural detail and the richness of the decor, with its decorative arched windows, rows of columns, and ornate friezes and sculptures. The Galleria was built to impress in the late 19th century and is still a splendid sight today.

Chiesa di San Ferdinando

Piazza Trieste e Trento 5; tel. 347/769-7274; 7:30am-noon and 4:30pm-7pm daily; free

Overlooking Piazza Trieste e Trento, you

1: glass-domed shopping center Galleria Umberto I
2: Chiesa di San Ferdinando **3:** Castel Nuovo
4: Piazza del Plebiscito and the Basilica di San Francesco di Paola

Coral and Cameos

HISTORY

The art of coral and cameo carving is an ancient one in the Naples area. Since Greek and Roman times there has been a tradition of fine craftsmanship when it comes to creating elegant jewelry from locally sourced coral. In ancient Rome, finely detailed cameos were highly prized, and coral was valued because it was thought to protect the wearer from bad luck. From a renewed appreciation of coral carving in the Renaissance to royal patronage in the 1800s and the appeal of the artisanal tradition to travelers on the Grand Tour, coral harvesting has long been a part of the local economy, especially in **Torre del Greco,** a seaside town located on the Gulf of Naples between Naples and Pompeii.

ETHICAL CONCERNS

Due to significant harvesting and the slow growth of the *Corallium rubrum* (red coral) that grows in the Mediterranean, there are many environmental and ethical concerns around the production of coral jewelry. Yet because of the importance of the tradition to the local communities, families have passed down the art form for generations, and some producers and shops in the area, such as **Ascione** in Naples (page 328) and **Cellini Gallery** in Pompeii (page 361), claim a commitment to sustainable harvesting and ethically sourced coral. Meanwhile, shoppers should be aware that, though you'll see many stores selling cameos and coral jewelry, much of what's for sale isn't real *Corallium rubrum*, and real coral sometimes is imported from other parts of the world that may or may not have a commitment to sustainability.

---

might miss the facade of this church, seemingly absorbed into the surrounding buildings. The church was originally founded by the Jesuits in the early 17th century and dedicated to San Francesco Saverio (Saint Francis Xavier), with a design that has been attributed to Cosimo Fanzago (1591-1678), one of the top architects working in Naples during the baroque period. The interior is richly decorated and noted for the stunning baroque frescoes by Paolo de Matteis from the early 1700s. After the Jesuits were expelled from the Kingdom of Naples in 1767, the church was eventually dedicated to San Ferdinando III di Castiglia, a 13th-century Spanish king who was canonized, and the neighborhood now takes its name from this saint.

Napoli Sotterranea, L.A.E.S.
(Underground Naples)

Vico S. Anna di Palazzo 52; tel. 081/400-256; www.lanapolisotterranea.it; tours every 2 hours 10am-6:30pm Mon.-Fri., more frequently 10am-6pm Sat.-Sun., reservation required; €12

Far below the street level in Naples lies a hidden world that dates to the Greek settlement of the city from 470 BCE. While this tour doesn't feature as many Roman ruins as the Napoli Sotterranea tour in the centro storico, it is nevertheless a fascinating journey through the underground city and tells the story of Naples in an intriguing way. You'll see how the city has been built for centuries by excavating the stone from below, and you'll get an up-close look at the cisterns that gathered water for the buildings above. You'll also see the areas that were used for refuge during World War II bombings, including graffiti dating from the war period. Some passageways can be quite narrow, so this tour may not be suitable for everyone. However, alternative routes are available for people who might feel claustrophobic in tight tunnels. Excursions are available with an English-speaking guide (10am, noon, 2pm, and 4:30pm Mon.-Fri., 10am, 11am, noon, 2pm, 4:30pm, and 6pm Sat.-Sun.). The starting point is in Piazza Trieste e Trento outside the historic Bar Gambrinus. Advance reservation is required. The tour takes about an hour, and comfortable shoes are a good idea.

Gallerie d'Italia

Via Toledo 185; tel. 081/400-256; www.gallerieditalia. com; 10am-7pm Tues.-Fri., 10am-8pm Sat.-Sun.; €7

Along Via Toledo, not far from the Galleria Umberto I, it's hard to miss the imposing and ornate entrance to the beautiful Palazzo Zevallos Stigliano. Built in 1563 as a noble family residence, the palazzo has also served as headquarters for a bank, and in 2014 was transformed into an exquisite gallery space for the collection of the Intesa Sanpaolo bank. The outstanding permanent collection features artwork from the 16th-18th centuries, including important works by Caravaggio, Artemisia Gentileschi, Luca Giordano, and Francesco Solimena. Special exhibitions are hosted throughout the year and are included in the ticket price.

Galleria Borbonica

Vico del Grottone 4; tel. 081/764-5808; www. galleriaborbonica.com; tours Fri.-Sun.; €10-15

Built in the mid-19th century at the request of King Ferdinando II, this massive tunnel was created to connect the Palazzo Reale to the military barracks and the sea on the other side of Monte Erchie. Opened in 1855 after three years of work that was all done by hand with picks, hammers, and wedges, the tunnel has served many purposes over the years. During World War II, the tunnel and nearby cisterns were used for shelter by 5,000-10,000 Neapolitans during the extensive German and Allied bombings of the city. It's possible to visit the tunnel on different themed tours, from a standard tour offering a glimpse of the highlights to an adventure tour complete with helmet and flashlight, or a speleological tour for a unique experience deep underground in Naples. Tours are available throughout the day and last 1-1.5 hours. It's best to book your tour in advance via the website, especially for more specialized tours.

WATERFRONT

The waterfront of Naples, stretching from the Castel dell'Ovo to the harbor at Mergellina, is one of the loveliest spots in the city. From Piazza del Plebiscito south lies the Santa Lucia neighborhood, with elegant buildings overlooking the sea, and the islet with Castel dell'Ovo and the tiny harbor of Borgo Marinari. Heading west leads to the stylish Chiaia neighborhood, which stretches from the Villa Comunale gardens up to Vomero.

★ Castel dell'Ovo

Borgo Marinari; tel. 081/795-4592; www.comune. napoli.it/castellovo; check for hours; free

One of the most scenic and historic spots in Naples, the Castel dell'Ovo sits on an islet jutting out into the gulf south of Santa Lucia. The earliest Greek settlers landed on this spot and named the island Megaride. Over the centuries it has been a lavish Roman villa, a monastery in the 5th century, and what we see today as the Castel dell'Ovo. Legend says the name, meaning Egg Castle, comes from the story that the Roman poet Virgil buried an egg below where the castle stands today. The legend says as long as the egg remains unbroken, the castle will stand and Naples will be safe. The castle itself is a fascinating amalgam of styles, having been modified by many rulers of the city since it was first built by the Normans in the 12th century. The castle today largely dates from the Aragonese rulers of Naples in the 15th century. Climb to the top of the castle's terraces for a panoramic view of the Gulf of Naples.

At press time the Castel dell'Ovo was closed for renovation without a fixed date for reopening, but it's still pleasant to stroll out along the small causeway that leads to the castle, since it offers an extraordinary up-close view of the castle and the charming **Borgo Marinari,** a small harbor at its base. An old-world fishing village atmosphere, with boats bobbing in the harbor and seaside restaurants, makes this an especially romantic spot for dinner.

Villa Comunale

Via Francesco Caracciolo and Riviera di Chiaia from Piazza Vittoria to Piazza della Repubblica

Stretching along the waterfront in Chiaia from just west of the Borgo Marinari to Piazza della Repubblica, this large public garden along the lungomare (waterfront) offers green space and a place to stroll by the sea. The sprawling gardens were originally designed by Carlo Vanvitelli in 1778-1780 for the private use of the royal family of King Ferdinand IV. Following the unification of Italy, the gardens were opened to the public and renamed the Villa Comunale in 1869. The gardens are dotted with statues, sculptures, and an ornate art nouveau cast-iron and glass bandstand designed by Errico Alvino in 1887. In the center of the gardens you'll find the **Aquarium Napoli** (tel. 081/583-3442; www.aquariumnapoli.it; 10am-2pm and 3pm-7pm Tues.-Sun.; €8), founded in 1872 and the oldest aquarium in Europe.

Piazza dei Martiri

This elegant piazza is located at the end of **Via Chiaia,** not far from the lungomare (waterfront), and is right in the heart of the elegant shopping district of Chiaia. The triangular-shaped piazza dates to the westward expansion of the city in the 17th century and is lined by elegant palazzos. Find a spot outdoors at one of the cafés to enjoy a moment of people-watching and to admire the central column dedicated to all the Neapolitans who have died fighting for freedom in the long history of the city.

Villa Pignatelli

Riviera di Chiaia 200; tel. 081/761-2356; www.museicampania.cultura.gov.it; 9:30am-5pm Wed.-Mon.; €5

Set in a lovely garden, the Villa Pignatelli is a large home that was built in 1826 for Admiral Ferdinando Acton. Its neoclassical design features Ionic pilasters and references to Pompeian designs on its facade. Owned by Carl Mayer von Rothschild, of the German banking family, from Acton's death until after the unification of Italy, the villa now bears a name that refers to Diego Aragona Pignatelli Cortés, who purchased the property in the 19th century and whose heirs donated the villa and art collection to the Italian state. The historic rooms are richly decorated and offer the chance to explore the collection of furniture, porcelain, and decorative art in situ. An adjacent building houses the **Museo delle Carrozze** with a collection of antique

Castel dell'Ovo

Italian, French, and English carriages from the 1800s-1900s.

Mergellina
Mergellina Harbor

At the base of the hill leading up to Posillipo, this small harbor is a picturesque spot along the waterfront in Naples. Once a small fishing village, it was absorbed into the city as it expanded in the 17th century. As the beach area that once ran along the Villa Comunale was transformed into gardens and eventually paved for Via Francesco Caracciolo, the fishing boats once located along the beach were moved toward the Mergellina marina. Now more of a seaside tourist spot than a place for fishing boats, this area is lovely for a stroll along the harbor to enjoy the excellent view of the Naples waterfront with Mount Vesuvius in the distance. A great viewpoint is from the **Fontana del Sebeto,** a large fountain originally designed by Cosimo Fanzago in 1635. At the heart of the statue is an old man representing the Sebeto river, the ancient river that flowed through Naples.

The harbor is also a departure point for ferries to Ischia, Sicily's Aeolian Islands, and the Pontine islands of Ponza and Ventotene.

PAN-Palazzo delle Arti Napoli
Via dei Mille 60; tel. 081/795-8601; www.comune.napoli.it/pan; 9:30am-7:30pm daily; admission to the building free, exhibition prices vary

Set in the Palazzo Roccella, an elegant building dating to the 17th century, PAN, which stands for Palazzo delle Arti Napoli, has served as a large contemporary art exhibition space since 2005. PAN hosts traveling and specially organized exhibits throughout the year.

VOMERO

Rising steeply above the city center, the Vomero neighborhood is topped by Castel Sant'Elmo and the Certosa di San Martino. With its panoramic views and important historical sights, it's a lovely neighborhood to explore, and it's easy to reach via the three funicular trains that have connected Vomero with the lower areas of the city since the late 19th century.

Castel Sant'Elmo
Via Tito Angelini 22; tel. 081/558-7708; www.museicampania.cultura.gov.it; 8:30am-7:30pm daily; €5

Sitting atop the San Martino hill, the Castel Sant'Elmo is perfectly situated to take in views of the city of Naples and the entire Gulf of Naples. Naturally, with such a fine view, it has been the spot for an overlook for centuries. The original construction on this site goes back to the 1200s when the Normans built a fortified residence called Belforte. Expanded and modified many times, the unique hexagonal star-shaped design we see today dates from the 16th century under Spanish rule. The castle was a military prison 1860-1952 and then continued to be used for military purposes until 1976. After an extensive restoration, it was transformed into a space for the public to enjoy and visit. It's possible to explore many areas of the castle, which often hosts art exhibitions and events. The **Museo del Novecento** (9:30am-5pm Wed.-Mon.) in the castle is dedicated to 20th-century Neapolitan art. Don't miss the views overlooking the Certosa di San Martino and the Gulf of Naples from a variety of different lookout points on the castle walls.

Certosa e Museo di San Martino
Largo San Martino 5; tel. 081/229-4503; www.museicampania.cultura.gov.it; 8:30am-7pm Thurs.-Tues.; €6

Easily spotted atop Vomero hill next to the Castel Sant'Elmo, the Certosa di San Martino is a former Carthusian monastery, now a museum with a remarkable art collection. Visit to explore excellent examples of work by important Neapolitan painters from the 1800s, decorative arts, and historic presepi (nativities), and to admire the spectacular view over the Gulf of Naples. Although founded in the 14th century, the Certosa has a baroque design

Visiting the Catacombs of Naples

inside the Catacombe di San Gennaro

While in many places the traces of early Christianity have long since been covered with layers upon layers of history, in Naples the catacombs offer a chance to see some of the earliest records of its arrival in the city. The majority of the city's catacombs are located between the historic center and Capodimonte in the Rione Sanità neighborhood, and near the Museo di Capodimonte. Both the catacombs below are managed by the Catacombe di Napoli organization, and the entrance fee covers both sights. You pay at the first one you visit, and your ticket gives you free access to the other. Guided tours are available in English, and written information in English is also available at both catacombs.

CATACOMBE DI SAN GENNARO
Via Capodimonte 13; tel. 081/744-3714; www.catacombedinapoli.it; 10am-5pm Thurs.-Tues.; €11, includes admission to San Gaudioso
Located below the Basilica della Madre del Buon Consiglio, the Catacombe di San Gennaro is one of the oldest and most important catacombs to visit. The paleo-Christian burial area held a strong religious significance when San Gennaro was buried here in the 5th century. Divided into two levels and carved out of tufa rock, the catacombs offer the chance to see the different types of tombs, early chapels, and artwork from pagan designs, from 2nd-century works to Byzantine paintings from the 9th-10th centuries.

CATACOMBE DI SAN GAUDIOSO
Basilica Santa Maria della Sanità, Piazza Sanità 14; tel. 081/744-3714; www.catacombedinapoli.it; 10am-5pm Thurs.-Tues.; €11, includes admission to San Gennaro
Inside the Basilica Santa Maria della Sanità is the entrance to the fascinating Catacombe di San Gaudioso, dating from the 4th-5th centuries. The catacombs contain preserved frescoes and mosaics from the 5th-6th centuries, displaying early Christian symbols, including the lamb, fish, and grapevines. Abandoned during the late Middle Ages, the catacombs were rediscovered and used as a burial site again in the 16th century. To preserve and honor the location, builders constructed the basilica above in the early 17th century with a baroque design by Fra Nuvolo.

that dates to the mid-1600s and is the work of Cosimo Fanzago, the most noted architect working in Naples at the time. Take a stroll around the stunning large cloister surrounded by 60 marble arches and visit the church that is a museum in itself with beautiful paintings and sculptures from the 17th-18th centuries.

Museo Duca di Martina

Villa Floridiana, Via Cimarosa 77; tel. 081/578-8418; www.museicampania.cultura.gov.it; 9:30am-5pm Wed.-Mon.; €4

For decorative arts enthusiasts, a visit to the Museo Duca di Martina is a special experience while in Naples. This small house museum is located in the Villa Floridiana, a stunning neoclassical villa built on the slopes of Vomero for Lucia Migliaccio, the Duchess of Floridia, who was the second wife of King Ferdinand I. Surrounded by a lush park, the villa is at its most impressive on the south side, where a grand staircase leads down into the gardens with a view to the sea. Since 1931, the villa has been the home of the Museo Duca di Martina, which houses one of the finest collections of decorative arts in Italy. Created by Placido de Sangro, Duke of Martina, the massive collection of more than 6,000 objects dating from the 12th-19th centuries was donated to the city of Naples in 1911. The museum's collection is spread across three floors of the villa and includes Chinese porcelain and Eastern objects on the lowest level; ivories, corals, and majolica from the Middle Ages to the Renaissance and baroque periods on the ground floor; and an incredible collection of 18th-century porcelain on the upper floor.

CAPODIMONTE

Once a rural area in hills north of Naples, the Capodimonte area saw many changes during the 18th century, including the construction of the royal palace and development of expansive gardens and woods. Despite the treasures housed in the Museo di Capodimonte and the tranquility of the setting, the area was not particularly well connected to the city center until the early 1800s, when a long, straight road and bridge were built over the Sanità neighborhood. Today a visit to Capodimonte is a must for art lovers, but don't miss exploring the area's catacombs as well. Taking a taxi for the short ride from the historic center is the easiest way to reach the Capodimonte neighborhood. Taking a taxi for the short ride from the historic center is the easiest way to reach sights in the Capodimonte neighborhood.

Museo e Real Bosco di Capodimonte

Via Miano 2; tel. 081/749-9111; www.capodimonte. cultura.gov.it; 8:30am-7:30pm Thurs.-Tues.; €15

In the hills above Naples, the Museo e Real Bosco di Capodimonte was built in the 18th century by the Bourbon king Carlo III as a royal palace set amid a lush forest perfect for hunting. It was also intended from the beginning as the setting for the marvelous art collection belonging to Elisabetta Farnese, the mother of Carlo III. Today the Farnese Collection is the heart of the museum, which includes works by Titian, Botticelli, Raphael, and Caravaggio, to name only a selection of the highlights. One of the largest art museums in Italy, Capodimonte also houses an excellent collection of paintings and sculptures from the 13th-18th centuries. Decorative art enthusiasts will enjoy the elegant Royal Apartments and extensive porcelain collection, as well as the remarkable Salottino di Porcellana, an 18th-century rococo-style salon decorated with delicately painted porcelain. To complete the incredible walk through art history, the museum also includes a gallery dedicated to the 1800s and a contemporary art collection. Some of the levels and galleries of the museum can be closed or open only for selected hours. Check the museum's website for the latest schedule.

★ Reggia di Caserta

fountain of Aeolus at Reggia di Caserta

Piazza Carlo di Borbone; tel. 082/344-8084; https://reggiadicaserta.cultura.gov.it; 8:30am-7:30pm Wed.-Mon.; €15

Located about an hour from Naples in Caserta, the Reggia di Caserta royal palace and gardens have been called the Versailles of Italy. As a UNESCO World Heritage Site, the palace, with its colossal baroque architecture, lavish interiors, and tranquil gardens, make a splendid day trip from Naples. Of all the architectural treasures created by the Bourbon kings of Naples, this is the largest and most impressive, built in a secluded location chosen by King Charles VII in the 18th century.

THE PALACE

The first sight of the Reggia di Caserta is awe-inspiring. Created for the Bourbon king by Luigi Vanvitelli (1700-1773), the building has a rectangular plan divided into four sections, each with a large inner courtyard, and covers a surface area of about 506,000 sq ft (47,000 sq m). When multiplied by the building's five floors, that brings the space to a whopping 2.5 million sq ft (235,000 sq m).

Sports and Recreation

There are fun biking and kayaking tours for those looking for more active ways to explore the urban landscape or enjoy views of the city from the Gulf of Naples. Soccer is the main sport in Naples and one that Neapolitans are passionate about. For soccer enthusiasts, catching a game with the locals can be an exciting experience.

BIKING
Biketour Napoli

Galleria Principe di Napoli 27-28; tel. 379/136-2755; www.biketournapoli.com; tours daily; from €48 pp

Although Naples is known for its chaotic traffic, don't let that stop you from exploring the city on two wheels. This company offers small-group tours for 2-20 people. Bike

With its 1,200 rooms and 1,700 windows, the space is almost too large to conceptualize. Charles never lived in the palace he started; he left in 1759 to be crowned king of Spain. Building continued under Bourbon king Ferdinand IV and was finally finished in 1845 for King Ferdinand II of the Two Sicilies by Vanvitelli's son Carlo Vanvitelli. A century later, the end of World War II was marked here on May 7, 1945, with the signing of the unconditional surrender of German forces.

A visit to the Reggia offers the chance to step inside and see the opulence of the Bourbon court. Begin by climbing the imposing staircase guarded by two large marble lion statues and topped by an elliptical vault. See the splendid **Palatine Chapel** with its design inspired by Versailles, blending neoclassical, Renaissance, and baroque elements. The **Royal Apartments** span the 18th-19th centuries and include a series of richly decorated antechambers leading to the gilded **Throne Room,** the most resplendent of the palace's many rooms.

Also fascinating is the glimpse of more relaxed moments of royal life inside the **Murat Apartment,** set up for Gioacchino Murat, King of Naples, at the beginning of the 19th century. This part of the palace includes the apartments where Ferdinand IV and Queen Maria Carolina lived at the end of the 18th century, including the enchanting thematic **Rooms of the Seasons,** the **King's Apartment,** the **Queen's Apartment,** the **Palatine Library,** and the impressive **Royal Nativity Scene,** set up similar to the Nativity created at the palace in 1844.

THE ROYAL PARK

The grandeur of the Reggia di Caserta continues outside in the Royal Park, which was also designed by Luigi Vanvitelli and finished by his son Carlo. The massive park covers 297 acres (120 ha) and includes an English-style garden and a long alley called the Via d'Acqua that stretches more than 1.8 mi (3 km) and features a series of fountains inspired by classical mythology. At the very top of the alley is the impressive **Fountain of Diana and Actaeon** set at the base of a waterfall that was carefully constructed to appear natural. The view looking back toward the Reggia di Caserta from the end of the alley is a sight fit for royalty.

GETTING THERE

The Reggia di Caserta is located about 19 mi (30.6 km) north of Naples. Trains (www.trenitalia.com; every 20-30 minutes daily) run regularly from the Napoli Centrale train station, a journey of 40-50 minutes, depending on the type of train. The train station is located across Piazza Carlo III from the entrance to the Reggia di Caserta.

through the heart of Naples on a 3-hour Central Naples tour or explore more on the 4-hour Seaside Naples tour. Tours are family-friendly, but children must be accompanied by an adult. For safety, the tours take place in pedestrian areas and helmets are included. Bike tours are available in English, but advance booking is required.

KAYAKING
Kayak Napoli
Via Posillipo 68 and Via Posillipo 357; tel. 331/987-4271; www.kayaknapoli.com; tours from €25 pp

Located just west of Naples's historic center, the Posillipo coastline with its caves and beautiful seaside villas is the nicest area to kayak. Kayak Napoli offers both kayak and stand-up paddleboard rentals, as well as guided kayak tours along the coast. From Bagno Sirena (Via Posillipo 357), the Naples and its Villas tour offers a close-up look at some of the historic villas of the area. The Wild Posillipo tour highlights the natural landscape, archaeological ruins, and marine-protected area of Gaiola. Tours are offered with an English-speaking guide throughout the year, weather permitting. Bus 140 from the center of Naples runs along Via Posillipo and passes the starting points for both tours.

SOCCER
SSC Napoli
Piazza Giorgio Ascarelli; tel. 081/509-5344; www.sscnapoli.it; from €25 pp

If there's one thing that is deep in the heart of Neapolitans, it's their love for the local Napoli soccer club. Founded in 1926, the Napoli team has boasted many of the world's best soccer players, including the Argentinian player Diego Maradona 1984-1991. The Napoli team plays at the highest level (Serie A) of soccer in Italy and is regularly one of the top teams. The soccer season runs 38 games August-May.

The Stadio Diego Armando Maradona is the home stadium for Napoli, located west of the historic center of Naples.

To enjoy a game at **Stadio Diego Armando Maradona,** your best bet is to buy tickets in person in Naples. Advance ticket sales are hard to come by, given the regulations around sales. You'll find tickets for sale at various points around Naples, including the Box Office (Galleria Umberto I 17; tel. 081/551-9188; 10am-7pm Mon.-Fri.) or at the stadium in advance of a game. Bring your passport when purchasing tickets because your name will be printed on the ticket. You'll also need your passport as identification to get into the stadium, and the name must match the name on your ticket.

Entertainment and Events

The music and theater scene in Naples has a tremendous history, and for generations it has influenced scores of musicians from Italy and around the world. It's hard to find travelers who aren't familiar with the strains of popular Neapolitan songs like "O Sole Mio." Traditional Neapolitan music is very much alive; it's treasured by the locals and enjoyed by visitors. Naples also offers resplendent opera houses like Teatro di San Carlo and Teatro Bellini, and with so many locals dedicated to preserving music traditions, there are plenty of ways for visitors to experience Neapolitan music.

Tradition is also very much at the heart of the biggest religious events throughout the year. Whether it's a festival dedicated to the city's patron saint and protector San Gennaro or a celebration of the city's much-revered pizza, joining the locals in honoring their traditions is a moving experience in a city as full of passion as Naples.

PERFORMING ARTS
Centro Storico
Napulitanata
Piazza Museo Nazionale 10-11; tel. 348/998-3871; www.napulitanata.com

Set in the arcades of the Galleria Principe near the Museo Archeologico Nazionale, Napulitanata offers a live musical experience dedicated to traditional Neapolitan songs. The relaxed and small concert setting creates a friendly and intimate atmosphere where the heart of Neapolitan music is brought to life through song and dance.

Teatro Bellini
Via Conte di Ruvo 14; tel. 081/549-9688; www.teatrobellini.it

Located off of Via Toledo in the centro storico, Teatro Bellini is one of the city's important historic theaters. Inaugurated in 1878, the theater was restored in the 1980s, bringing back the original splendor of its six tiers of box seats, frescoed ceiling, and 19th-century details. A wide variety of theatrical, musical, and dance performances take place throughout the year.

Domus Ars Centro di Cultura
Via Santa Chiara 10C; tel. 081/342-5603; www.domusars.it

Right around the corner from Piazza del Gesù Nuovo, the Chiesa San Francesco delle Monache, originally founded in the 14th century, is the setting for classical concerts organized by the Domus Ars Centro di Cultura.

San Ferdinando
Teatro di San Carlo
Via San Carlo 98/F; tel. 081/797-2331; www.teatrosancarlo.it

The jewel of Naples's art scene and the oldest opera house in Europe in continuous use, the Teatro di San Carlo has been the setting for spectacular opera, dance, and musical performances since its doors opened in 1737. The richly decorated interior is beautiful enough to warrant a visit on its own, but if you can catch a show during your stay, you'll experience the celebrated history of this spectacular opera house in all its glory.

Teatro Augusteo
Piazzetta Duca D'Aosta 263; tel. 081/414-243; www.teatroaugusteo.it

Set in a lovely little piazza off of Via Toledo, this historic theater was built on the site of an earlier 18th-century theater designed by Luigi Vanvitelli. It opened at the same time as the adjacent Funicolare Centrale in 1929. The theater hosts musicals, plays, and concerts throughout the year.

Waterfront
Associazione Alessandro Scarlatti
Piazza dei Martiri 58; tel. 081/406-011; www.associazionescarlatti.it

Founded in 1918, the Associazione Alessandro Scarlatti is dedicated to chamber music, with a rich selection of classical and innovative performances. Concerts are held at various locations around Naples, including the historic Conservatorio di Musica San Pietro a Majella, the Teatro di Corte in the Palazzo Reale, and a variety of churches in the centro storico.

Centro di Musica Antica Pietà de' Turchini
Via Santa Caterina da Siena 38; tel. 081/402-395; www.turchini.it

Dedicated to preserving and highlighting the Neapolitan musical and theatrical heritage from the 16th-18th centuries, the Centro di Musica Antica Pietà de' Turchini presents concerts in the Chiesa Monumentale di Santa Catarina da Siena. The beautiful 16th-century baroque church couldn't be a more fitting setting for the classical concerts. Concerts are also held at various churches and the Gallerie d'Italia museum in the historic center.

Vomero
Teatro Diana
Via Luca Giordano 64; tel. 081/556-7527; www.teatrodiana.it

This theater in the heart of the Vomero was founded in 1933 and presents a variety of concerts and plays from noted Italian singers and actors. Performances are in Italian, and the theater also hosts classical concerts throughout the year.

Greater Naples
Complesso Palapartenope
Via Corrado Barbagallo 115; tel. 081/570-0008; https://new.palapartenope.it

One of the larger music and performance venues in Naples, the Teatro Palapartenope is located west of the historic center in the Fuorigrotta area. The venue has performance areas of various sizes and hosts concerts, musicals, dance, and family-friendly performances. This is often the setting for larger concerts by big-name Italian musicians.

FESTIVALS AND EVENTS

Wine & The City
Various locations; tel. 081/681-505; www.wineandthecity.it; events throughout the year

Launched in 2008 as a creative way to showcase wine in a variety of settings, Wine & The City is an annual festival where wine and gastronomic events take place in various locations across Naples. Events are set in museums, galleries, boutiques, restaurants, artist studios, and more, showcasing more than 100 wineries.

Napoli Pizza Village
Lungomare Caracciolo; tel. 081/404-089; www.pizzavillage.it; June

Every year at the beginning of June along the waterfront, the Napoli Pizza Village celebrates the city's most famous gastronomic contribution. More than 50 pizzerias are present, and there are competitions, events, and live music as well. This is the chance to sample some of the best pizza from Italy's top pizza makers on a festive and fun summer evening in Naples.

Festa del Carmine
Piazza del Carmine 2; tel. 081/201-196; www.santuariocarminemaggiore.it; July 15

One of the most historic religious celebrations in Naples is also one of the most explosive. The Festa del Carmine takes place July 15, the evening before the festival celebrating the Madonna del Carmine (Our Lady of Mount Carmel). After evening mass in the Santuario del Carmine Maggiore, fireworks are set off from all over the bell tower of the church to create the impression that the bell tower is on fire. Only the arrival of a celebrated portrait of the Madonna del Carmine stops the fire. At 246 ft (75 m), the bell tower is the tallest in Naples. The festival is popular with Neapolitans, who pack the Piazza del Carmine and surrounding area to watch the event and enjoy the music and stands selling sweets, toys, and food.

Festa di San Gennaro
Duomo di Napoli; Sat. before first Sun. in May, Sept. 19, Dec. 16

Every day of the year San Gennaro (Saint Januarius) is the beloved and revered patron saint of Naples, but there are a few very special days when all eyes are on the saint. This is when the reliquary vials holding the blood of the saint are said to miraculously liquefy during a special mass in the Duomo di Napoli. Tradition says that when the miracle doesn't occur it's a bad omen for the city of Naples, and has in fact coincided with natural disasters and unfortunate events over the centuries. For the festival, the Duomo and surrounding area are crowded with people eager to see the miracle, celebrate the saint with processions, and enjoy the festive atmosphere with stands selling candy, food, and toys.

Shopping

The artisanal tradition in Naples dates to ancient times when the Greek and later Roman craftspeople transformed coral into intricately carved treasures. However, it was in the 17th-18th centuries that Naples became known for its fine shopping and craftsmanship, thanks to the patronage of the Bourbon kings and the aristocracy of the time. Whether you're shopping for handmade Nativity figurines, being fitted for a custom shirt or suit, or slipping on a pair of gloves, in Naples you'll find talented artisans preserving family traditions and beautiful crafts.

Many shops in Naples, especially the artisan boutiques and smaller shops, respect the local custom of closing for lunch from 1pm or 1:30pm to about 4pm. If you want to shop during the mid-afternoon, head to Via Toledo, where some of the larger chain stores remain open. Many smaller shops will also close on Sunday for the afternoon or the entire day, and some take a break for a period in August surrounding the Ferragosto holiday on August 15.

SHOPPING DISTRICTS
Centro Storico
Via San Gregorio Armeno
Via San Gregorio Armeno from Via dei Tribunali to Via San Biagio dei Librai

If you love traditional crafts and Christmas nativities, a visit to Via San Gregorio Armeno is a must. This narrow street is lined with artisans' workshops full to the brim with handmade presepe (Nativity) figurines and decorations. No matter the size—from tiny figures to grand 18th-century-style scenes—you'll find holiday decorations to treasure for years to come.

San Ferdinando
Via Toledo
Via Toledo from Piazza Trieste e Trento to Piazza Dante

One of the busiest shopping streets in Naples, Via Toledo starts at Piazza Trieste e Trento by the Galleria Umberto I, the glass-domed 19th-century shopping center, and runs to Piazza Dante. The street is largely pedestrian-only and has shops on both sides. Here you'll find Italian and international stores as well as local brands and smaller shops.

Via Chiaia
Via Chiaia from Piazza Trieste e Trento to Via Gaetano Filangieri

Via Chiaia is lined with boutiques, the city's historic tailors, and other great shopping finds. The pedestrian-only street is also a pleasant stroll just for window shopping as it connects Piazza Trieste e Trento and Via Toledo with Piazza dei Martiri, another fine shopping area.

Waterfront
Via Dei Mille
Via dei Mille from Via Gaetano Filangieri to Via Vittoria Colonna

The spot for elegant shopping in Naples, this is where high-fashion designer boutiques vie for attention with ornately decorated palazzos, including some in the Liberty style (the Italian equivalent of the art nouveau style from the late 1800s-early 1900s).

Vomero
Via Alessandro Scarlatti
Via Alessandro Scarlatti from Piazza Vanvitelli to Via Luca Giordano

Vomero's stylish shopping district stretches from Piazza Vanvitelli down the tree-lined and pedestrian-only Via Alessandro Scarlatti to Via Luca Giordano. Be sure to meander down some of the cross streets for more little shops and cafés.

CENTRO STORICO
Leather Goods
Omega
Via Stella 12; tel. 081/299-041; www.omegasrl.com; 9am-6pm Mon.-Fri., by appointment Sat. Sept.-July

Since 1923, the Squillace family have produced the finest-quality leather gloves, and today the fifth generation is hard at work continuing the tradition. Each pair of gloves requires 25 steps to create, and the store is like a living museum where you can see gloves being made.

Ceramics
Cosmos
Via San Gregorio Armeno 5; tel. 081/193-51165; www.cosmosangregorioarmeno.com; 10:30am-6:30pm Mon.-Sat., 10:30am-2pm Sun.

In Naples, horn-shaped items called corni are considered good-luck charms and often take the shape of small, red hot peppers that look like the peperoncino used in many traditional Neapolitan recipes. Cosmos specializes in the production of handmade corni of all types, including customized requests.

Nativity
Ferrigno
Via San Gregorio Armeno 8; tel. 081/552-3148; www.arteferrigno.it; 10am-7pm Mon.-Fri., 10am-6pm Sat., 10am-2pm Sun.

Along Via San Gregorio Armeno, this very special store is where brothers Giuseppe and Marco Ferrigno continue a family tradition of handmade figures for presepi, or Nativity scenes. The figurines and Nativities are created using the same materials as when the workshop was founded in 1836, including terra-cotta details and silk fabrics, and all are created by hand in the on-site workshop.

La Scarabattola
Via dei Tribunali 50; tel. 081/291-735; www.lascarabattola.it; 10:30am-2pm and 4pm-7pm Mon.-Fri., 10am-2pm and 4:30pm-7:30pm Sat.

Created by three brothers, Salvatore, Emanuele, and Raffaele, this shop is a treasure of hand-carved and remarkably detailed figures for presepi as well as contemporary sculptures inspired by the Neapolitan masked figure Pulcinella and other Neapolitan traditions.

Ars Neapolitana
Via dei Tribunali 303; tel. 081/193-30967; www.arsneapolitana.it; 10am-7pm Mon.-Sat.

Combining family tradition and original talent, Guglielmo Muoio is a young, highly praised presepe artist. His wife, Laura Loinam, adds her tailoring and embroidery expertise to create inspired Nativity pieces in the 18th-century traditional Neapolitan style.

SAN FERDINANDO
Clothing
Camiceria Piccolo
Via Chiaia 41; tel. 081/411-824; www.camiceriapiccolo.com; 10am-1:30pm and 4pm-8pm Mon.-Sat.

One of the most important names in men's fashion in Naples, Camiceria Piccolo is especially noted for their fine custom-tailored shirts. Today the business is still family-run by the son and grandsons of the founder Sabatino Piccolo, and each shirt is handmade to measure with the highest-quality materials.

Rubinacci
Via Chiaia 149E; tel. 081/415-793; www.marianorubinacci.net; 10am-1:30pm and 4:30pm-8pm Mon.-Sat.

Distinguished for their bespoke clothing and tailoring since 1929, Rubinacci is an iconic store along Via Chiaia for men's fashion, custom tailoring, and accessories.

Accessories
Ascione
Angiporto Galleria Umberto I; tel. 081/421-111; www.ascione.it; 4pm-7:30pm Mon., 10:30am-2pm and 3:30pm-7:30pm Tues.-Sun.

Master craftspeople at Ascione have created high-quality coral jewelry for more than 150 years. Here you'll also find cameos, pearls, and fine gems. There is also an exquisite private museum that tells the story of the area's important coral-carving tradition through a display of remarkable coral pieces. Guided visits are available for a small fee and with advance reservation.

Chocolate
Gay Odin
Via Toledo 214; tel. 081/400-063; www.gay-odin.it; 9:30am-8pm Mon.-Sat., 10am-8pm Sun.

At the end of the 1800s, Isidoro Odin created a chocolate shop tucked away between tailors and coffee shops in the stylish Chiaia neighborhood, and set to work making delicious chocolate creations. Neapolitans were enchanted by the unique flavor combinations, and this success led to more shops around the city, with the Via Toledo shop opening in 1922. In the 1960s Isidoro Odin and his wife, Onorina Gay, passed the chocolate-making traditions to the Castaldi-Maglietta family, who still run the business's nine locations around Naples.

Specialty Items
Mario Talarico
Vico Due Porte a Toledo 4b; tel. 081/407-723; www.mariotalarico.it; 9am-8pm Mon.-Sat.

Umbrellas might not be at the top of your

holiday shopping list, but that's because you haven't been to Talarico yet. Founded in 1860, this small shop has been producing handmade umbrellas for five generations. Choose from a variety of styles and sizes to brighten up any rainy day with travel memories.

WATERFRONT
Clothing
E. Marinella

Via Riviera di Chiaia 287; tel. 081/335-9972; www.emarinella.eu; 6:30am-8pm Mon.-Sat.

If there's one shop to visit to experience Naples's sartorial tradition, it's E. Marinella, a tiny boutique known worldwide for its handmade ties. The family-run company was founded in 1914 and all of its ties are hand-sewn in a workshop just a few doors away using handprinted silk. Stepping inside is like being transported back in time with the original woodwork and handcrafted quality, yet the ties have a contemporary style that's fitting for one of the world's finest names in ties.

Cilento 1780

Via Riviera di Chiaia 203-204; tel. 081/552-7465; www.cilento1780.it; 9am-1:30pm and 4pm-8pm Mon.-Sat., 9am-1:30pm Sun.

Leaders of Neapolitan fashion since 1780, when the family business was founded, today Ugo Cilento is the eighth generation of the family to guide Cilento 1780. Here you'll find sartorial treasures, accessories, shoes, and shirts made to measure.

Accessories
Francesco Tramontano Gioielli

Via Vittorio Imbriani 44 bis; tel. 081/012-7855; www.tramontanogioielli.com; 10am-1:30pm and 4:30pm-8pm Mon.-Sat. Sept.-Aug. 15

Young goldsmith and designer Francesco Tramontano comes from a long family line of Neapolitan artisans. His jewelry pieces are inspired by Mediterranean elements and are handcrafted in gold, silver, and brass; each one is a unique piece of art.

Barbarulo

Piazza Amedeo 16/i-Passeggiata Colonna; tel. 081/403-512; www.gemellidapolso.it; 10am-1:30pm and 4pm-7:30pm Mon.-Fri., 10am-1pm and 4:30pm-7:30pm Sat. Sept.-July

To complement that bespoke suit or custom-made shirt, you need the perfect cuff links. Since 1894, the Barbarulo family have specialized in finely crafted handmade cuff links. Along with traditional pieces, you'll also find a line of women's jewelry and accessories for men.

Ceramics
Millegradi

Vico Belledonne 15; tel. 081/764-4959; www.millegradinapoli.com; 10:30am-1:30pm and 4:30pm-8pm Mon.-Sat., closed for the holiday around Aug. 15

From scenes of Vesuvius on tiles to boldly patterned vases and plenty of Mediterranean blues, this cheerful shop displays beautiful handmade ceramic objects inspired by the colors and traditions of Naples.

Bars and Nightlife

Naples is a vibrant city after dark with a lively and eclectic scene. Although it's a very large city, most of the nightlife spots are small clubs, literary cafés, or wine bars where you're more likely to rub elbows with locals than tourists. The city also has a rich musical heritage, and talented young musicians carry on the Neapolitan traditions. So whether your scene is more a glass of Campania wine, a formal concert, a good jazz club, or dancing until dawn, you'll find plenty of nightlife options, especially in the centro storico (historic center) area around Piazza Dante and Piazza Bellini. Many nightclubs in Naples will close for a short period in August around the Ferragosto holiday (August 15) for a summer break.

CENTRO STORICO
Bars
Ennò
Via Vincenzo Bellini 43; tel. 392/658-8623; 6pm-1am Sun.-Thurs., 6pm-2am Fri.-Sat.

Located in a great nightlife area not far from Piazza Dante and Piazza Bellini, this club offers a large selection of artisanal beers, wine, and cocktails alongside a dinner menu. The atmosphere is especially vibrant with live music on the weekends.

Libreria Berisio
Via Port'Alba 28-29; tel. 081/549-9090; berisio@libero.it; 10am-1:30am Mon.-Thurs., 10am-1:30pm and 5pm-2am Fri.-Sat., 5:30pm-1:30am Sun.

Along Via Port'Alba, lined with bookstores, Libreria Berisio opened its doors in 1956 and is now also a popular local wine and cocktail bar, especially late into the night. Check their schedule for live music events; this place often has a great jazz and blues vibe.

Clubs and Live Music
Kestè
Largo San Giovanni Maggiore Pignatelli 26/27; tel. 339/468-1248; info.keste@gmail.com; 6pm-1am Tues.-Sun.

Since 1997, Kestè has been a cornerstone in the music and nightlife scene in Naples. With a live music program throughout the year, as well as art, theater, stand-up comedy, and cultural events, it's a popular spot with locals, offering an artistic atmosphere on a little square in the historic center.

Bourbon Street
Via Vincenzo Bellini 52/53; tel. 338/825-3756; www.bourbonstreetjazzclub.com; 8pm-2am Tues.-Sun.

Around the corner from Piazza Dante, Bourbon Street is one of the city's classic nightclubs, completely dedicated to jazz. The setting is intimate, and live music is on the schedule regularly, along with jam sessions.

Superfly Soulbar
Via Cisterna dell'Olio 12; tel. 347/127-2178; gfiorito6704@yahoo.it; 7pm-1:30am Wed.-Thurs. and Sun.-Mon., 7pm-3am Fri.-Sat.

Superfly Soulbar is an iconic Naples nightlife spot with a good groove, just south of Piazza Dante in the centro storico. The cocktails are expertly mixed, and the setting is perfectly in tune with the jazz and soul music vibe.

Mamamu
Via Sedile di Porto 46; tel. 320/669-5222; mamamubar@gmail.com; 8pm-2am Thurs.-Sat.

Located near the university, this has been a popular local venue with a great vibe for live music performances since it first opened its doors in 1996. Check their schedule for upcoming live concerts and DJ sets.

WATERFRONT
Bars
Enoteca Belledonne
Vico Belledonne a Chiaia 18; tel. 081/403-162; www.enotecabelledonne.eu; 9:30am-1:30pm and 4:30pm-midnight Mon.-Thurs., 9:30am-1:30pm and 4:30pm-2am Fri.-Sat., 6:30pm-noon Sun.

At night, this well-stocked wine store transforms into a popular wine bar where you can sample a fine selection of wines accompanied by light meals and cheese and cured meat platters.

L'Antiquario
Via Vannella Gaetani 2; tel. 081/764-5390; https://lantiquarionapoli.superbexperience.com; 7:30pm-2:30am daily

L'Antiquario is everything a cocktail bar should be but with a special Neapolitan flair. Try the signature drinks inspired by the history of Naples.

Food

It's not an exaggeration to say that food is a way of life in Naples. While you're in its birthplace, it's a must to try true Neapolitan pizza. Tradition reigns here, whether you're grabbing a quick pizza fritta (fried pizza) on the street or enjoying a hearty dish of pasta with a ragù sauce that has bubbled away for hours. Neapolitans have strong opinions on the best ragù (although it might be their grandma's), the best pizza, and the best place to get a warm sfogliatella pastry. With so many options, there are few better pastimes in Naples than trying out different places to find your favorites.

Pizza is an art form in Naples and is taken quite seriously, especially at the historic pizzerie where often you'll find pizza, and sometimes only pizza, on the menu. However, at many pizzerie you can expect to find delicious fried appetizers, and some restaurants serve full menus in addition to making an excellent pizza. Expect lines at the most popular pizzerie because they don't take reservations. As pizza only takes 60-90 seconds to cook in a very hot wood-fired oven, the line usually moves quite quickly. Compared to most restaurant settings in Italy where lingering over a meal is the norm, Naples's pizzerie are often bustling places with simple decor and table settings, where it's all about the pizza.

Unlike in the coastal areas and on the islands, many restaurants in Naples close for a period in August. Some may close just for the Ferragosto holiday on August 15, while others will close for a 1-2-week holiday around Ferragosto or even for the entire month.

CENTRO STORICO
Regional Cuisine
La Cantina di Via Sapienza
Via Sapienza 40-41; tel. 081/459-078; www.cantinadiviasapienza.it; 12:30pm-3:30pm Mon.-Sat.; €5-8

A tiny little trattoria not far from the Museo Archeologico Nazionale, La Cantina di Via Sapienza gets its name from the setting in a former cantina, or wine cellar. Stop here for lunch to enjoy Neapolitan homecooked pasta dishes along with plenty of contorni (side dishes) of vegetables to choose from. You'll enjoy a delicious, affordable lunch in the centro storico.

Salumeria Upnea
Via San Giovanni Maggiore Pignatelli 34/35; tel. 081/193-64649; www.salumeriaupnea.com; 12:15pm-4pm and 7:15pm-11:45pm Thurs.-Tues.; €10-20

With an industrial-inspired decor and a great central location, this bistro has an engaging atmosphere and diverse menu where you'll find a series of tempting panini (sandwiches) and an extensive menu that includes vegan options, meat and cheese platters, perfectly prepared and seasoned freshly made potato chips, primi and secondi (first and second courses), and a good drink menu with lots of beer varieties.

Da Donato dal 1956
Via Silvio Spaventa 41; tel. 081/287-828; dadonato1956@gmail.com; 12:30pm-2:30pm and 7pm-10pm Tues.-Sun.; €8-15

Family-run for four generations, this trattoria and pizzeria is an excellent choice for a wide variety of homemade Neapolitan-style dishes like the traditional ragù or genovese pasta sauces that cook for 10-12 hours. The menu changes daily and the staff can guide your choice of a seafood or non-seafood menu, or you can order à la carte. Reservations are a good idea because it's a popular spot.

Mimì Alla Ferrovia
Via Alfonso D'Aragona 19/21; tel. 081/553-8525; www.mimiallaferrovia.it; noon-4pm and 7pm-midnight Mon.-Sat.; €10-22

A classic Naples address for beautiful dining, Mimì Alla Ferrovia is a favorite with locals and travelers alike. Start with the Passeggiata Napoletana, a series of classic Neapolitan appetizers, and try the delicately flavored ravioli with sea bass and lemon. The grilled fish is done superbly. Reservations are required for four or more people.

Tandem Ragù

Via Giovanni Paladino 51; tel. 081/190-02468; www.tandemnapoli.it; 11:30am-11:30pm daily; €10-16

In Naples, ragù is essential. This is a tomato sauce simmered for hours upon hours and enriched with various types of meat and quite possibly a touch of magic. Tandem Ragù has a simple menu dedicated to only a handful of ragù-based dishes available daily along with a selection of vegetarian options and second courses. As the restaurant is quite small, reservations are a good idea. You'll also find other locations in the historic center (Via Sedile di Porto 51 and Calata Trinità Maggiore 12) and one in Vomero (Via Bernini 74).

Pizzeria
Sorbillo

Via dei Tribunali 32; tel. 081/446-643; www.sorbillo.it; noon-3:30pm and 7pm-11:30pm Mon.-Sat.; €8-15

Coming from a big family of pizzaioli (pizza makers), Gino Sorbillo became an expert at a young age and has created one of the most notable pizzerias in Naples as well as locations in major Italian cities, Miami, New York City, and Tokyo. The original location on Via dei Tribunali is always packed, but there's also the **Lievito Madre al Mare** (Via Partenope 1) location near the waterfront.

L'Antica Pizzeria da Michele

Via Cesare Sersale 1; tel. 081/553-9204; www.damichele.net; 11am-11pm daily; €5-6

This is easily the most iconic pizzeria in Naples, thanks not only to its divine pizza but also to Elizabeth Gilbert's book *Eat, Pray, Love*. L'Antica Pizzeria da Michele is certainly worthy of all the praise, which is why you can expect to find a lengthy line here most days. Everything here is focused 100 percent on the pizza in its most traditional form. The menu only has two pizzas: the classic pizza Margherita and the marinara, topped with tomatoes, oregano, and garlic. Expect to wait a bit to enjoy this classic Naples experience, as reservations are not accepted.

★ Pizzeria Da Attilio

Via Pignasecca 17; tel. 081/552-0479; www.pizzeriadaattilio.com; noon-4pm and 7pm-midnight Mon.-Sat.; €5-10

Just off Via Toledo on the attractive and very typical Neapolitan street Via Pignasecca, this little restaurant is one of the top spots in Naples. Pizza maker Attilio Bachetti continues a long tradition of excellent pizza started by his grandfather (also named Attilio Bachetti) in 1938. From a young age Attilio has been making pizza, and the hard work has paid off as he is a true master of the craft.

Starita a Materdei

Via Materdei 27/28; tel. 081/557-3682; www.pizzeriastarita.it; noon-3:30pm and 7pm-midnight Tues.-Sun.; €6-11

A little off the beaten path compared to the pizzerie in the centro storico, this historic pizzeria is a favorite with locals and attracts a lot of pizza-hunting travelers as well. Don't be surprised if there's a line, but it's worth the wait. Along with a large selection of pizzas, this spot also makes one of the best gluten-free pizzas in Naples. Reservations are not accepted.

Bakeries and Cafés

★ Sfogliatelle Attanasio

Vico Ferrovia 1-4; tel. 081/285-675; www.sfogliatelleattanasio.it; 6:30am-7:30pm Tues.-Sun.; €2

Regularly voted the best spot for sfogliatelle in Naples, this tiny spot near the train station is easy to find thanks to the crowd and the heavenly scent wafting down the street. You'll want to sample both the sfogliatella riccia with its flaky crust and the traditional frolla variety made with short-crust pastry.

TOP EXPERIENCE

☆ True Neapolitan Pizza

traditional Neapolitan pizza Margherita at Sorbillo

In 2017, the art of the Neapolitan piazzaiuolo, or pizza maker, was added to UNESCO's list of Intangible Cultural Heritage of Humanity. It was a moment of great celebration in Naples, where the famous gastronomic delight is indelibly connected to the city's identity.

The most classic of Neapolitan pizzas is the **pizza Margherita,** which dates to 1889 when Raffaele Esposito made pizzas for King Umberto I and Queen Margherita di Savoia during their visit to Naples. The queen most enjoyed the pizza topped with tomatoes, mozzarella, extra virgin olive oil, and basil—to represent the green, white, and red of the Italian flag—and so Raffaele named the pizza in her honor. You'll find pizza Margherita on every pizzeria menu, along with the **marinara pizza** topped with tomatoes, oregano, garlic, and extra virgin olive oil (no cheese). These two pizzas are considered the most traditional, with some pizzerias only serving those two varieties. However, in most pizzerias you will find a large selection of toppings on the menu.

Pizza in Naples is usually considered individual sized and is served about the size of a large plate. Your pizza will arrive whole and not presliced, so grab your knife and fork and dig in. There are no rules; you can eat it with knife and fork or slice your pizza into quarters and pick up a quarter, fold it in half, and enjoy! Naples is also famous for its pizza fritta (fried pizza): This is pizza that's topped with a variety of different fillings, like ricotta and salami, and then folded in half and deep fried.

You don't have to go far in Naples to find an excellent pizzeria, and here are some suggestions to get you started.

- **L'Antica Pizzeria da Michele:** Try the classics here—Margherita and marinara are the only two options (page 332).
- **Sorbillo:** Among Sorbillo's multiple locations around the city are a restaurant in the centro storico and a seaside outpost with a view of the Castel dell'Ovo. Many of their branches specialize in pizza fritta (page 332).
- **Pizzaria La Notizia:** A bit off the beaten path, Pizzaria La Notizia serves the outstanding pizza created by Enzo Coccia (page 336).
- **50 Kalò:** This pizzeria is not far from the Mergellina harbor (page 336).
- **Starita a Materdei:** This classic pizzeria also serves gluten-free pizza (page 332).

Scaturchio

Piazza San Domenico Maggiore 19; tel. 081/551-6944; www.scaturchio.it; 7am-9pm daily; €2-4

This coffee shop and bakery is a classic stop along Spaccanapoli at Piazza San Domenico Maggiore. Join the locals at the bar inside, which is the traditional way to have coffee in Italy. Listen to the Neapolitan dialect flow as you sip a strong coffee and try something sweet like their delicious rum-soaked babà or other tempting pastries.

SAN FERDINANDO
Pizzeria
Pizzeria Brandi

Salita S. Anna di Palazzo 1/2; tel. 081/416-928; www.pizzeriabrandi.com; 12:30pm-3:30pm and 7:30pm-11:30pm Tues.-Sun.; €5-22

Every pizzeria in Naples has a good story, but no story is so intimately tied to the origins of Neapolitan pizza as Brandi's. Pizza maker Raffaele Esposito and his wife, Maria Giovanna Brandi, made pizza in 1889 for King Umberto I and Queen Margherita di Savoia, who were visiting Naples. Of the three types of pizza, the queen was most pleased by the pizza with mozzarella and tomato, which Esposito then named in her honor. This is how the pizza Margherita, the most classic of all Neapolitan pizzas, was born. In addition to excellent pizza, the restaurant has a full menu.

Bakeries and Cafés
Pintauro

Via Toledo 275; tel. 348/778-1645; www.pintauro.it; 9:30am-8pm daily; €3

In this small bakery along Via Toledo hangs a sign that honors Pasticceria Pintauro as the birthplace of the famous shell-shaped sfogliatella pastry in 1785. The origins of this pastry go back even earlier to a convent on the Amalfi Coast, but it was Pasquale Pintauro who perfected the sfogliatella with its flaky crust and citrus-infused ricotta filling that we know today. A stop here is a must on the tour of finding the best sfogliatella in Naples.

La Sfogliatella Mary

Via Toledo 66/Galleria Umberto I; tel. 081/402-218; 8am-8:30pm Wed.-Mon.; €2-4

Another classic stop for sfogliatelle in Naples, this small bakery is located in the Galleria Umberto I just off the entrance from Via Toledo. Yet you'll likely catch the sweet scent before you arrive. Although the specialty is certainly the sfogliatella, there are plenty of other traditional Neapolitan desserts, such as the rum-soaked babà cake, to try as well.

★ Gran Caffè Gambrinus

Via Chiaia 1/2; tel. 081/417-582; www.grancaffegambrinus.shop; 7am-midnight Sun.-Fri., 7am-1am Sat.; €2-10

Gambrinus is in a class of its own when it comes to coffee and pastries in Naples. Founded in 1860, the café has beautiful art nouveau rooms; it has been a literary salon and meeting place for generations of Neapolitans. Sitting right between Piazza Trieste e Trento and Piazza del Plebiscito, the café couldn't be better situated for taking a break or just stopping in to try their famous coffee or deserts.

WATERFRONT
Regional Cuisine
Ristorante Amici Miei

Via Monte di Dio 77/78; tel. 081/764-6063; www.ristoranteamicimiei.com; noon-3pm and 7:30pm-midnight Tues.-Sat., noon-3pm Sun. Sept.-June; €8-20

At this family-run restaurant, the focus is on preserving and sharing Neapolitan culinary traditions, especially recipes closely tied to the land. Try the pasta with mushrooms and truffles, or thick pappardelle noodles served with a tomato sauce enriched with lamb. Second courses include a wonderful selection of steak, grilled meats, and roasts, as well as beautifully prepared seasonal vegetables.

Umberto

Via Alabardieri 30; tel. 081/418-555; www.umberto.it; 12:30pm-3:30pm and 7:15-midnight Tues.-Sun. Sept.-July, 7:15-midnight Tues.-Sun. Aug.; €14-25

Founded in 1916, this restaurant has been

In Search of the Best Sfogliatella

sfogliatelle in Naples

Naples has many traditional desserts, but nothing quite tops the shell-shaped sfogliatella. This pastry has a citrus-infused ricotta filling and comes in two varieties: The classic **sfogliatella riccia** has a crispy and flaky crust that makes an unavoidable mess as you bite into it, and the **frolla** variety has a soft short-crust pastry shell. The pastry originated on the Amalfi Coast in Conca dei Marini but was modified at the end of the 1700s by Neapolitan pastry maker Pasquale Pintauro to the sweet treat enjoyed today. Now it is one of the desserts most commonly associated with Naples, and though it can also be enjoyed throughout the entire region, you've never tasted anything quite like the sfogliatella made right in Naples. Locals hotly debate where to find the best sfogliatella in the city, but the tastiest way to find the answer is to throw your diet out the window and try them all. Here's where to start your sfogliatella tasting tour in Naples.

- **Sfogliatelle Attanasio:** Often considered the top spot for sfogliatelle in the city, this tiny bakery is not far from the train station. Stop by to try them still warm from the oven (page 332).
- **Pintauro:** This small bakery on Via Toledo is the birthplace of the sfogliatella and a fine place to sample both the traditional sfogliatella riccia with its flaky crust as well as the frolla variety (page 334).
- **La Sfogliatella Mary:** Not far away, you'll find this popular bakery right off Via Toledo at the entrance of the Galleria Umberto I (page 334).

serving Neapolitan specialties for more than 100 years—and doing it exceedingly well. Here you can choose from a rich menu that changes seasonally to highlight locally sourced ingredients. Dishes include both seafood specialties like the paccheri di Gragnano "d' 'o treddeta" (large tube-shaped pasta served with tomatoes, baby octopus, black olives, and capers) or perfectly prepared baccalà (salted cod) and delicious non-seafood options like the incredible meatballs with ragù sauce. The pizza is also an excellent choice.

L'Ebbrezza di Noè

Vico Vetriera a Chiaia 8b/9; tel. 081/400-104; www.lebbrezzadinoe.com; 10am-1:30pm and 5pm-midnight Tues.-Fri., 10am-1:30pm and 7pm-midnight Sat., 11:30am-3pm Sun.; €14-22

This excellent wine store is also a cozy dining spot where sommelier and owner Luca shares his passion for all things wine and guides diners to the perfect wine-food pairings. It's a small space, so book ahead to ensure a spot to settle in and sample some lovely local Campania wines and fresh seasonal fare.

Osteria della Mattonella
Via Giovanni Nicotera 13; tel. 081/416-541; www.osteriadellamattonella.com; 12:45pm-3pm and 7:30pm-11pm Mon.-Tues. and Thurs.-Sat., 1pm-3:30pm Sun.; €22-28

A welcoming, rustic eatery where the walls are lined with bottles of wine, this osteria is a good choice in Chiaia. The menu includes hearty home-cooked fare like the genovese (meat and onion pasta sauce) and the rich yet heavenly pasta with potatoes and provola (smoked cheese) that keep the regular customers and locals coming back for more.

Pizzeria
La Masardona
Piazza Vittoria 5; tel. 081/245-2243; pizzeriamasardona@gmail.com; noon-4pm and 7pm-11:30pm Mon.-Sat., noon-4pm Sun.; €4-8

In Naples there's pizza, and then there's pizza fritta (fried pizza), which is a specialty in itself. Since 1945, La Masardona has specialized in authentic pizza fritta, which can be filled with different options like ricotta, provola, and salami or topped with arugula, tomatoes, and mozzarella. Above all, these pizzas are best enjoyed Neapolitan-style, by eating with your hands.

50 Kalò
Piazza Sannazzaro 201/b; tel. 081/192-04667; www.50kalo.it; noon-4:30pm and 6:30pm-12:30am daily; €5-10

Not far from the Mergellina harbor and waterfront, this is a spot that pizza enthusiasts from around the world flock to, to taste the creations of master pizza maker Ciro Salvo. Though it's relatively new (opened in 2014) compared to the iconic pizza establishments, 50 Kalò has quickly become a top choice for pizza in Naples.

Café
Gran Caffè La Caffettiera
Piazza dei Martiri 26; tel. 081/764-4243; www.grancaffelacaffettiera.com; 7:30am-11pm Mon.-Fri., 7:30am-midnight Sat., 8:30am-10pm Sun.; €4-8

This is a lovely spot in Chiaia to stop for coffee, tea, or drinks any time of the day, or late into the night. There's both indoor seating in a salon-style setting and outdoor seating on the elegant Piazza dei Martiri.

VOMERO
Regional Cuisine
Friggitoria Vomero
Via Domenico Cimarosa 44; tel. 081/578-3130; 10am-2:30pm and 6pm-9pm Mon.-Sat.; €2-5

This small friggitoria (fried food shop) is a great spot to try the classic pizza fritta, a type of local fried pizza filled with a variety of options like ricotta and salami. Also on the menu are a fried frittata of pasta and fried rice balls. You'll enjoy these tasty and inexpensive snacks while exploring Vomero.

Borbonika Napulitan Restaurant
Via Michele Kerbaker 112; tel. 081/1870-3243; www.borbonika.com; noon-3:30pm and 7pm-11:30pm Mon.-Sat., noon-3:30pm Sun.; €10-25

Just a couple of blocks from Piazza Vanvitelli in the Vomero, this welcoming restaurant has a menu dedicated to classic Neapolitan recipes. Try pasta with the traditional Naples genovese sauce made by slow-cooking onions and beef. Or try the delicious pasta with potatoes, smoked provola cheese, and porcini mushrooms. You'll also find seafood options for first and second courses, including an excellent fried baccalà served with a pumpkin cream and ricotta cheese.

GREATER NAPLES
Pizzeria
★ Pizzaria La Notizia
Via Michelangelo da Caravaggio 53; tel. 081/714-2155; www.pizzarialanotizia.com; 7:30pm-midnight Tues.-Thurs. and Sun., 7:30pm-1am Fri.-Sat.; €7-12

Born and raised in Naples and in the Neapolitan pizza tradition, Enzo Coccia opened his first pizzeria in 1994. With his dedicated attention to the highest-quality ingredients, as well as plenty of passion and hard work, Enzo has created not just one but two of the best pizza places in the city, both on the same street. The original pizzeria at Via Michelangelo da Caravaggio 53 is dedicated to tradition (think the best pizza Margherita of your life), while down the street at number 94 you'll find highly creative and delicious variations with other toppings.

Accommodations

With accommodations ranging from friendly hostels to family-run bed-and-breakfasts and historic palazzos transformed into modern hotels, Naples has a wide array of accommodations to suit every budget. If you want to be close to the top sights, look in the San Ferdinando, Quartieri Spagnoli (Spanish Quarter), and centro storico (historic center) areas. The historic center is an especially good option if you're traveling to the Amalfi Coast via public transportation because you'll be close to the Napoli Centrale train station. For sea views and a more tranquil atmosphere, look in Santa Lucia and Chiaia. For the most magnificent views over the city and Gulf of Naples, head for Vomero. Unlike the Amalfi Coast and Capri, Naples offers plenty of accommodations that are open year-round, and breakfast is usually included in the price of the room.

CENTRO STORICO
Under €100
Hostel Mancini

Via Pasquale Stanislao Mancini 33; tel. 081/200-800; www.hostelmancini.com; from €50 dorm, from €120 pp private room

Located near the Naples train station, this hostel offers comfortable and cost-effective accommodations in the historic center of the city. Owned by husband-and-wife team Alfredo and Margherita, the hostel welcomes guests to enjoy the large common room and use the fully equipped kitchen for cooking and dining. Mixed-gender dorms and women-only dorm rooms with private baths are available, in addition to private rooms with shared or en suite baths. This hostel is an excellent choice for a friendly and budget-conscious stay in Naples.

€100-200
★ Palazzo Bevilacqua

Via Pietro Colletta 35; tel. 081/015-2412; www.palazzobevilacquanapoli.com; €105 d

A B&B with a lovely family story, the Palazzo Bevilacqua is located in an elegant building built in 1911 by Pasquale Bevilacqua for his family to live close together. Today the B&B is run by Luigi and Margherita, the fifth generation to live in the palazzo. With a touch of creativity and modern style, they have created an enchanting little B&B with three stylish and comfortable rooms, each with an en suite bath. With some of the city's best pizzerie just steps away, as well as the top sights in the centro storico, it's a fine option for an authentic Neapolitan experience.

Hotel Correra 241

Via Correra 241; tel. 081/195-62842; www.correra.it; €140 d

In a city with a dynamic contemporary art scene, this small hotel offers a chance to stay close to the top museums and historic sites. Bright pops of color and modern design prevail here, contrasted with exposed stone walls and the hotel's remarkably well preserved Greek- and Roman-era aqueduct, which was used as a water cistern until the late 15th century. Double, triple, and two-level family rooms are available, all quite distinctive and contemporary.

€200-300

★ Decumani Hotel de Charme

Via S. Giovanni Maggiore Pignatelli 15d; tel. 081/551-8188; www.decumani.com; €220 d

In the historic center not far from Santa Chiara, this hotel is set in an 18th-century palazzo that was once the home of Cardinal Sisto Riario Sforza, a 19th-century bishop. Much of the historical charm has been preserved, including period furniture and the spectacular salon with its 18th-century mirrors and decorative stuccowork covering the walls and ceiling. The 39 rooms range from one single to many double and triple rooms, each one elegantly decorated and featuring large windows.

Over €300

Hotel Costantinopoli 104

Via Santa Maria di Costantinopoli 104; tel. 081/557-1035; www.costantinopoli104.it; €315 d

Conveniently located in the historic center not far from Piazza Dante and the Museo Archeologico Nazionale, this small hotel is set in a historic residence with a small garden and swimming pool. The 13 classic rooms are comfortably decorated with warm colors, and the six spacious junior suites are mostly on two levels, with the garden-facing suites offering private balconies.

SAN FERDINANDO

Under €100

Hostel of the Sun

Via Guglielmo Melisurgo 15; tel. 081/420-6393; www.hostelnapoli.com; €50 dorm, €100 private room

With a cheery atmosphere and a convenient location near the Castel Nuovo and ferry terminal, this hostel offers dorm-style shared rooms as well as private rooms for 2-4 people with private or shared baths. Wi-Fi access is fast and available throughout the hostel. The common spaces are welcoming and fun, and breakfast is included. The hostel can help organize excursions, or you can take advantage of the free walking tour of Naples offered by the hostel.

€100-200

Bed-and-Breakfast Attico Partenopeo

Via Santa Brigida 72; tel. 081/542-4248; www.atticopartenopeo.it; €150 d

This is a welcoming B&B with a fantastic central location right next to Galleria Umberto I. The entire B&B and its eight rooms are decorated with an elegant and artistic touch. Choose a superior room to enjoy a private terrace and views up to Vomero. The rooftop terrace overlooks the glass dome of the Galleria Umberto I and the Chiesa di Santa Brigida next door; hearing the antique bronze bells of the church, which chime on the hour, is a classic Neapolitan experience.

Chiaja Hotel de Charme

Via Chiaia 216; tel. 081/415-555; www.chiaiahotel.com; €180 d

Full of charm and antique decorative touches, this friendly small hotel is set in an 18th-century noble palazzo very near Piazza del Plebiscito. Rooms vary in size, and many are named after stories from the family and building's history. The Superior Rooms have a small balcony overlooking pedestrian-only Via Chiaia and its many shops and restaurants. The breakfast is excellent, with only fresh ingredients and locally made pastries.

€200-300

★ La Ciliegina Lifestyle Hotel

Via Paolo Emilio Imbriani 30; tel. 081/197-18800; www.cilieginahotel.it; €255 d

Well situated between Via Toledo and Castel Nuovo, this boutique hotel with 14 jewel-like rooms is an excellent choice for its refreshing Mediterranean style, location, and features. Every aspect of the hotel is beautifully detailed, from luxurious linens to the stylish custom-designed furniture in the rooms to the panoramic rooftop terrace complete with a jetted tub and sun beds. There's a friendly team dedicated to customer service, and each guest is sent a questionnaire before arrival so the concierge can prepare personalized suggestions and guidance.

WATERFRONT

€100-200

Casa Mira Napoli
Via Giordano Bruno 169; tel. 081/761-1035; www.casamiranapoli.it; €150 d

This small B&B lovingly run by Alessandra, her mother Gina, and family offers a welcoming stay with friendly service and lovely views overlooking the city and Gulf of Naples. Two of the three rooms include a terrace with panoramic views, while the third features a window that frames a view of Vesuvius, the Gulf of Naples, and the Castel dell'Ovo. This property is an easy 5-minute walk from Mergellina harbor and the Villa Comunale gardens nearby.

Hotel Rex
Via Palepoli 12; tel. 081/764-9389; www.hotel-rex.it; €170 d

Just moments from the waterfront and set in an art nouveau-style palazzo, this charming three-star hotel offers a very comfortable stay with excellent hospitality in one of the best areas of Santa Lucia. The 34 rooms are spacious and bright, and are decorated in a clean, modern style with unique artistic touches like the large paintings depicting Neapolitan scenes. Standard rooms include both doubles and triples, while the executive doubles with lateral sea views are worth the extra cost.

★ Hotel Palazzo Alabardieri
Via Alabardieri 38; tel. 081/415-278; www.palazzoalabardieri.it; €190 d

Only a few steps off of Piazza dei Martiri and surrounded by excellent shopping and dining options, this hotel captures the essence of Chiaia's style with its elegant and traditional decor. The classic and superior rooms are all comfortable, but for a splurge consider the junior suite with a view overlooking Piazza dei Martiri.

Over €300

Grand Hotel Vesuvio
Via Partenope 45; tel. 081/764-0044; www.vesuvio.it; €495

The peak of elegance and refinement in Naples, the Grand Hotel Vesuvio is situated in a prized location along the waterfront overlooking the Borgo Marinari, Castel dell'Ovo, and the Gulf of Naples. Opened in 1882, the hotel maintains a gracious air of old-world charm mixed with modern comforts, including a fitness club with an indoor pool, two restaurants with panoramic views, the Sky Lounge Solarium and Cocktail Bar on the 10th floor, and the top-quality service of a five-star hotel. The 160 rooms and suites are classically decorated and luxurious in every detail. This is a location where the sea view is well worth the splurge.

VOMERO

€100-200

Hotel Cimarosa
Via Domenico Cimarosa 29; tel. 081/556-7044; www.hotelcimarosa.it; €139 d

Enjoy a stay in the chic Vomero neighborhood at this boutique hotel situated along the pretty tree-lined streets near Piazza Vanvitelli and Castel Sant'Elmo. Three funicular stations are located nearby, making it easy to explore Naples while also enjoying the atmosphere of Vomero. The rooms offer a calming blend of minimal design with artistic touches, and some feature views over the city and Gulf of Naples all the way to Capri.

€200-300

Hotel San Francesco al Monte
Corso Vittorio Emanuele 328; tel. 081/423-9111; www.sanfrancescoalmonte.it; €260 d

One of the most scenic hotels in Naples, the Hotel San Francesco al Monte is set in a 16th-century monastery on the hillside below the Certosa di San Martino and Castel Sant'Elmo in the Vomero. The property was transformed into a luxury hotel while still preserving the important religious character of the site. The former monks' cells are now elegant accommodations decorated in soft colors, with breathtaking sea views that bring a sense of calm and reflection. Enjoy the same sweeping views of the Gulf of Naples from the floral roof garden with a swimming pool.

Information and Services

TOURIST INFORMATION
Azienda Regionale Campania Turismo
Piazza del Gesù 7; tel. 081/551-2701; www.agenziacampaniaturismo.it; 9am-7pm Mon.-Sat., 9am-2pm Sun.

The Naples tourist office has an info point in Piazza del Gesù that offers information on sights and tours and can help with any questions. Additional info points are at the Naples train station and the Molo Beverello at the port.

MEDICAL AND EMERGENCY SERVICES
For emergency services in Italy, dial 118 for an ambulance and urgent care. The **Antonio Cardarelli hospital** (Via Antonio Cardarelli 9; tel. 081/747-1111) is located northwest of the city center and has a pronto soccorso (emergency room) open 24 hours daily. Pharmacies are good resources if you have nonurgent medical issues or questions. Just look for the green cross or signs saying Farmacia. You'll find several right along Via Toledo in the historic center, including the **Antica Farmacia Augusteo** (Piazzetta Duca D'Aosta 263; tel. 081/416-105; 8am-8:30pm Mon.-Fri., 9:30am-2pm and 3:30pm-8pm Sat.) located just across the street from the Galleria Umberto I.

POSTAL SERVICES
For postal services in Naples, the main post office (Poste Italiane; Piazza Giacomo Matteotti 2; tel. 081/552-4410; www.poste.it; 8:20am-7:05pm Mon.-Fri., 8:20am-12:35pm Sat.) is located not far off Via Toledo on Piazza Giacomo Matteotti.

Getting There

As Italy's third-largest city, Naples is well connected to national and international transportation systems.

BY AIR
Aeroporto Internazionale di Napoli
NAP; Viale F. Ruffo di Calabria; tel. 081/789-6111; www.aeroportodinapoli.it

The Aeroporto Internazionale di Napoli, also referred to as Capodichino, is located about 3.7 mi (6 km) northeast of the city center. Though it's not a large airport, it handles more than 10 million passengers a year. Direct flights to Naples arrive from destinations across Italy as well as from 90-plus international cities. Direct flights from the United States are occasionally available during the peak travel season May-October. Most major European cities have direct flights to Naples. The airport has received many updates in recent years, including new dining and shopping options. Tourist information, car rentals, currency exchange, and public transportation options are available just outside the baggage claim in the arrivals hall.

BY TRAIN
Napoli Centrale Stazione
Piazza Giuseppe Garibaldi; www.napolicentrale.it

Located in the heart of Naples at Piazza Garibaldi, the Napoli Centrale Stazione is the city's main train station; nearly 400 trains pass through daily. **Trenitalia** (www.trenitalia.com) operates on the Italian railway lines and runs regional, intercity, and high-speed trains from destinations across Italy. Journey times and prices can vary greatly, depending on the season, time of day, number of transfers, and especially the speed of the train. The fastest and most convenient trains are the

Frecciarossa high-speed trains that travel from Rome to Naples in about 70 minutes. The journey from Rome on slower regional trains takes about 3 hours and can include a transfer. From Florence, the Frecciarossa is a great option; it's a direct journey of about 3 hours. From Venice, the Frecciarossa direct is about 5 hours, 20 minutes. There are cheaper options, but they take a lot longer and require transfers. From Milan, the Frecciarossa train takes a little over 5 hours.

The private company **Italotreno** (www.italotreno.it) offers high-speed trains from Milan, Venice, Florence, Rome, and many other smaller cities. The journey from Rome to Naples takes about 1 hour 15 minutes; from Florence, travel time is about 3 hours; from Venice, the trip is about 6 hours; from Milan, the journey is about 5 hours.

To reach Naples by train from the Amalfi Coast, you first have to take the bus or ferry to the closest train station at Salerno or Sorrento. From Sorrento, catch the **Circumvesuviana** train (www.eavsrl.it; departures about every 30 minutes daily; 1-hour journey; €4.20), which also connects Naples with Pompeii and Herculaneum, with the journey from Pompeii to Naples taking about 40 minutes (€3) and from Herculaneum about 20 minutes (€2.90). The Circumvesuviana train platforms are connected to the Napoli Centrale station via an underground walkway. From Salerno, Trenitalia trains depart every 15-30 minutes for the Napoli Centrale Stazione, taking from 35 minutes to 1 hour, depending on the type of train.

BY BUS

Flixbus (www.flixbus.it) offers bus service to Naples from destinations across Italy for affordable rates. Buses can be booked to or from the Napoli Centrale train station and at the Aeroporto Internazionale di Napoli. **Curreri Viaggi** (www.curreriviaggi.it) offers 8-10 daily bus connections from Sorrento and points along the Sorrento peninsula, as well as from Pompeii, to the Aeroporto Internazionale di Napoli for €10. The bus ride from Sorrento to the airport takes 1 hour 30 minutes. **SITA SUD** (www.sitasudtrasporti.it) has limited bus lines connecting Salerno and the Amalfi Coast to Naples, with a stop at Varco Immacolatella near the ferry terminal. **Pintour** (www.pintourbus.com) operates a shuttle bus service from Amalfi and towns east on the Amalfi Coast (Atrani, Minori, Maiori, Erchie, Cetara, and Vietri sul Mare) to the Aeroporto Internazionale di Napoli April-November for €20.

BY BOAT
Porto di Napoli

Port of Naples; tel. 081/228-3257; www.porto.napoli.it
As one of the largest ports in Italy, the Porto di Napoli (Port of Naples) handles cruise ships, cargo transport, and ferries from the Gulf of Naples and major ports around the country. Cruise ships usually dock near the **Stazione Marittima,** and the ferry terminal for arrivals from most destinations is nearby at the **Molo Beverello.** Both arrival areas are close to bus and metro options for public transportation at Piazza Municipio, or only a short walk from Castel Nuovo and Piazza Trieste e Trento. Some ferries from Ischia also arrive in the **Mergellina** port, to the west of Naples's main port.

BY CAR

Naples is well connected to the autostrade (highways) that crisscross Italy. If you're traveling to Naples from points north, take the **A1** (Autostrada del Sole) and follow signs indicating Napoli Centro/Porto Marittima/Stazione Centrale to reach the city center. If you're arriving from **Salerno** and points south, take the **A3** and look for signs for Napoli Centro/Porto Marittima/Stazione Centrale.

Driving in Naples can be quite the adventure and is not the recommended means of transportation for exploring the city. Parking in Naples is also challenging. If you're staying in the city center, it's a good idea to contact your hotel in advance for guidance on arriving by car, navigating to the exact location, and parking.

Getting Around

Naples has a busy city center and some of the wildest traffic in Italy. When you consider this, as well as the parking challenges and concentration of sights around the historic center and waterfront, navigating the city on foot and public transportation makes the most sense. When you're out walking, be cautious at all times, even when crossing at crosswalks. Keep an eye out for scooters that zip through traffic and along narrow streets. Although pedestrians do technically have the right of way, it's not something you'll want to test in Naples. Once you're in the city center, public transportation is a great way to get around the city. There are plenty of bus lines, a metro system with modern stations, funicular train lines running up to Vomero, and trains to the surrounding areas.

FROM THE AIRPORT

Alibus (ANM; tel. 800/639-525; www.anm.it; €5) offers a convenient bus line connecting the Aeroporto Internazionale di Napoli to three stops in the Naples city center: Piazza Garibaldi for the Napoli Centrale train station and other locations in the city center; Immacolatella/Porta di Massa; and Molo Angioino/Beverello, most convenient for reaching ferries and cruise ships. Tickets are €5 each way and can be purchased on board. The Alibus stop at the airport is about 300 ft (100 m) beyond the arrivals exit. Be sure to validate your ticket in the machine on board and keep it with you for the entire journey. Travel time from the airport to Piazza Garibaldi is about 15 minutes, and to the port about 35 minutes. Buses leave the airport every 20 minutes or so 6am-11pm daily.

You can also catch a taxi for the short ride from the airport into the center of Naples. The taxi stand is located right outside the arrivals exit at the airport. Fixed rates are available from the airport to the center of Naples, and taxis are required to display the tariff card in the taxi; fares are usually about €18 to the centro storico and Napoli Stazione Centrale, €21 to the port and the San Ferdinando areas, and €25 to Mergellina, Chiaia, and Vomero. It's essential to let the driver know you would like to have the fixed-rate fare before departing the airport; be sure to agree on the price in advance as well.

PUBLIC TRANSPORTATION
Metro and Railway

Naples has a convenient metro and railway system. **ANM** (Azienda Napoletana Mobilità; tel. 800/639-525; www.anm.it) operates line 1 and line 6 of the metro system. **Line 1** is particularly convenient for tourists, as it connects Piazza Garibaldi at the Napoli Centrale train station to the historic center, with stops at Municipio for the Piazza Municipio area, Toledo along the busy shopping street Via Toledo, Dante at Piazza Dante, Museo for the Museo Archeologico Nazionale, and Vanvitelli for the Vomero. **Line 6,** which was closed at press time for construction to extend the line, runs from Mergellina to the western suburbs of Naples. **Line 2** is a metro train line that's actually operated by **Trenitalia** (www.trenitalia.com; departures every 10 minutes; €1.70) and runs from Piazza Garibaldi as well, with stops at Cavour, Museo (to transfer to line 1), Montesanto, Amedeo, Mergellina, and points west to Pozzuoli.

To reach the archaeological sites of Pompeii and Herculaneum as well as points along the Sorrentine Peninsula to Sorrento, the Circumvesuviana train line operated by **EAV** (www.eavsrl.it; departures about every 30 minutes; 60-minute journey from Naples to Sorrento; €3 to Pompei, €2.90 to Herculaneum, €4.20 to Sorrento) departs from Piazza Garibaldi at the Napoli Centrale station.

Bus and Tram

ANM (Azienda Napoletana Mobilità; tel. 800/639-525; www.anm.it) operates a large bus transit network that covers the city center day and night. From the Napoli Centrale train station, Line **R2** runs from Piazza Garibaldi to Piazza Trieste e Trento to reach the Galleria Umberto I, Piazza del Plebiscito, and Via Toledo area. Bus line **151** connects Piazza Garibaldi with Piazza Vittoria in Chiaia, with stops for the port near Molo Beverello and Castel Nuovo. Line **V1** covers much of the Vomero area, including a convenient connection from near Piazza Vanvitelli and the Cimarosa and Morghen funicular train stations to reach the Castel Sant'Elmo and Certosa di San Martino. To reach the Museo di Capodimonte, catch bus **178** at the Piazza Museo outside the Museo Archeologico Nazionale and get off at the Tondo di Capodimonte piazza or the Museo di Capodimonte.

A single-ride ticket costs €1.20, or you can choose a 90-minute ticket for €1.70 that allows for transfers. Daily tickets for the ANM transit network (buses, funicular trains, trams, and metro lines 1 and 6) are €4.20, or weekly passes are available for €12.50. Buy your tickets at most tabacchi (tobacco shops), some newsstands, or at the ticket machines at some metro or train stations. Single-use or timed tickets must be validated at the machine when you board the bus or before boarding at the metro or train station. If you have a daily or weekly ticket, validate it the first time you use it and be sure to fill out the name and date information on the ticket. Be prepared to show ID if the ticket inspector asks. It is worth making sure you validate your tickets properly, or you may be fined.

Funicular

Naples has three funicular train lines, called funicolari, also operated by **ANM** (Azienda Napoletana Mobilità; tel. 800/639-525; www.anm.it) that connect the centro storico and Chiaia area with the Vomero. These train lines run on a grade up the mountainside, a convenient and unique way to get around in the city. The **Funicolare Centrale** line starts in the Augusteo station just off Via Toledo opposite the Galleria Umberto I and arrives at the Fuga station in Piazza Ferdinando Fuga in the Vomero. The **Funicolare di Chiaia** starts at the Amedeo station in Piazza Amedeo and ends at the Cimarosa station just south of Piazza Vanvitelli in the Vomero. The **Funicolare di Montesanto** starts in the Quartieri Spagnoli and runs to the Morghen station not far from the Castel Sant'Elmo in Vomero. The funicular trains are primarily used by locals to move between the higher and lower parts of the city. Each line makes several stops along the way, mostly connecting residential areas of Naples. It's not a problem to transport luggage on the trains.

Funicular trains run in both directions on all the lines, about every 10 minutes, 7am-10pm daily. Ticketing is the same as for buses, and a single ride costs €1.20. Daily and weekly ANM tickets also include rides on the funicular lines.

Taxi

Taxis in Naples offer either metered or fixed-rate tariffs for each ride. Fixed-rate fares are available to and from the main transportation hubs like the airport, train station, and port. If you opt for a fixed-rate tariff, you must tell the driver at the beginning of the journey. Metered fares start at €3.50 Monday-Saturday and €6.50 Sunday and holidays; the fare increases €0.05 every 157 ft (48 m) and every 8 seconds stopped. There are extra fees for bags, more than four passengers, airport pickups or drop-offs, and more. All taxis must display the tariff card (in Italian and English) regulated by the city of Naples. Though you can flag a taxi down, getting a taxi is much easier if you go to the nearest taxi stand, located throughout the city at transportation hubs and major landmarks and piazzas. Or call a taxi by phoning **Taxi Napoli** (tel. 081/8888; www.taxinapoli.it) or **Radio Taxi La Partenope** (tel. 081/0101; www.radiotaxi-lapartenope.it).

Ferry

The large **Porto di Napoli** (www.porto.napoli.it) offers frequent ferry connections that make it easy to get around the Gulf of Naples to Sorrento and the islands of Capri, Ischia, and Procida. Ferry service is available year-round from Naples, though reduced during the winter months. Ferry service direct from Naples to the Amalfi Coast is limited, but there are more options if you take a ferry to Sorrento or Capri and connect from those destinations to ferry services to the Amalfi Coast (usually May-Oct.).

Docking Areas

The Naples Port is divided into many different docking areas. Just across from the Castel Nuovo, the **Molo Beverello** is where the majority of the passenger ferries depart and arrive. Just to the left of the Molo Beverello (looking toward the sea), a very large pier juts out into the harbor with the **Stazione Marittima** (Piazzale Stazione Marittima; tel. 081/551-4448; www.terminalnapoli.it), where cruise ships usually dock. Continuing along the port to the left beyond Piazzale Immacolatella is the **Calata Porta di Massa**, where larger passenger and vehicle ferries depart for Ischia, Procida, and Capri. From Molo Beverello to the Calata Porta di Massa it's a 15-minute walk, or there is often a free shuttle bus that circulates between the two that you can take.

Boat Services

Many different companies run boat service from Naples's port, offering a variety of options, from high-speed jet boats to aliscafo (hydrofoil) and slower traghetti (ferries) that transport passengers and vehicles. Most ferry companies offer advance ticket purchase online, which is a good idea during the busy summer months. You can also purchase tickets from the ticket booths before boarding; just arrive with time to spare in case there are lines at the ticket booths.

- **NLG** (tel. 081/552-0763; www.nlg.it; from €16.50 per person) operates jet routes to Capri and Sorrento.

- **Gescab** (tel. 081/428-5259; www.gescab.it; from €26) has jet routes from Naples to Capri.

Funicular trains connect Chiaia and the historic center to the Vomero neighborhood.

- **SNAV** (tel. 081/428-5555; www.snav.it; from €25) operates lines to Ischia, Procida, and Capri.

- **Caremar** (tel. 081/189-66690; www.caremar.it; from €14 passengers, €42.20 vehicles) offers ferry service and can transport vehicles to Sorrento, Capri, Ischia, and Procida.

- **Medmar** (tel. 081/333-4411; www.medmargroup.it; from €14.10 passengers) also offers vehicle transport and ferry service from the **Calata Porta di Massa** in the Naples port to Ischia and Procida.

- **Alilauro** (tel. 081/497-2222; www.alilauro.it; from €15.20 per person) runs ferry departures from Molo Beverello to Sorrento, Capri, Procida, Ischia, and Amalfi and Positano on the Amalfi Coast.

CAR AND SCOOTER RENTAL

Navigating Naples's famously chaotic traffic and maze of streets in the historic center by car is not a recommended way to get around. Outside Naples, however, having a car gives you more freedom to move around.

Napoli Rent
Calata Trinità Maggiore 28; tel. 081/1925-9711; www.napolirent.it; scooters from €45 per day, cars from €50 per day

If you're willing to brave the streets or are looking to head out of Naples, Napoli Rent offers car and scooter rental options with different locations to pick up your rental in Naples, including the airport, Piazza Garibaldi at the Napoli Centrale train station, or near the Molo Beverello at the port.

BUS TOURS
City Sightseeing
Largo Castello Piazza Municipio; tel. 335/780-3812; www.city-sightseeing.it; from €25

For a worry-free way to get around Naples, City Sightseeing offers easy-to-spot, bright red, double-decker buses with open seating on the top. With the company's convenient hop-on hop-off policy, you can explore the city for an entire day, getting on and off as many times as you wish. Line A makes a loop through the historic center and includes stops at all the top sights, including the Museo Archeologico Nazionale and Museo di Capodimonte. Line B runs along the waterfront to Mergellina and along Posillipo to Capo Posillipo. Tickets are €25 per person for adults and €12 ages 5-15; under age 4 ride for free.

Pompeii, Herculaneum, and Vesuvius

Itinerary Ideas	349
Pompeii	351
Herculaneum	362
Vesuvius	368

Whether you're relaxing by the sea in Sorrento or strolling along the waterfront in Naples, the distinctive humpbacked slopes of Mount Vesuvius dominate the Gulf of Naples. Although its lush green appearance may make it seem innocuous, this volcano is considered one of the most dangerous in the world because of the densely populated areas surrounding its base. Among the urban sprawl are the ruins of the ancient cities of Pompeii and Herculaneum, two of the world's most important archaeological sites.

These two Roman towns were frozen in time by the explosive eruption of Mount Vesuvius in 79 CE. Though this massive eruption destroyed many luxurious Roman villas in the area as well, the sites of Pompeii and Herculaneum offer a rare look at life in ancient

Highlights

Look for ★ to find recommended sights, activities, dining, and lodging.

★ **Forum, Pompeii:** Stand in the middle of what was Pompeii's city center and imagine what everyday life was like for the people who lived here (page 355).

★ **Villa of the Mysteries, Pompeii:** A prime example of a Roman agricultural estate, its name comes from a series of stunning but mysterious frescoes (page 358).

★ **Amphitheater, Pompeii:** Visit this arena on the outskirts of the city for a glimpse into Roman sporting life (page 360).

★ **House of Neptune and Amphitrite, Herculaneum:** One of the loveliest houses in Herculaneum, this site is known for its intricate and colorful wall mosaics (page 365).

★ **House of the Deer, Herculaneum:** A series of statues, including some of deer being attacked by dogs, was uncovered in the garden of this sophisticated seaside villa (page 367).

★ **Hiking to the Crater, Vesuvius:** Hike to the summit of Vesuvius to take in panoramic views of the Naples area and the Sorrentine Peninsula (page 369).

Pompeii, Herculaneum, and Vesuvius

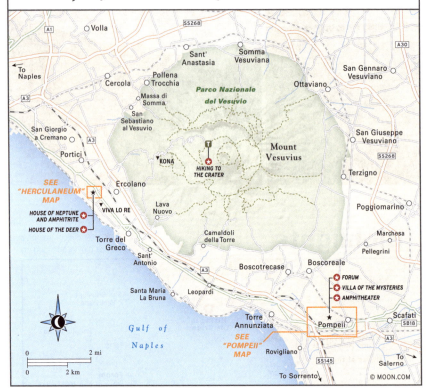

Roman times. Nowhere else can you literally stroll down the streets of a Roman city and see where wheels of countless carts left deep grooves in the stone, or admire brilliantly colored frescoes and minutely detailed mosaics preserved by volcanic ash. A full picture of daily life comes into focus as you discover everything from the advanced heating and plumbing systems of the ancient cities to street-food businesses, and see close-up how Romans of all social levels lived, worked, ate, and spent their free time.

A visit to Pompeii and Herculaneum, as well as the volcano that destroyed them so many centuries ago, is an eye-opening experience and an exceptional glimpse into the past.

PLANNING YOUR TIME

Mount Vesuvius and the ancient cities of Pompeii and Herculaneum are located southeast of Naples and north of the Sorrentine Peninsula, making them ideal day trip destinations from both areas. Though both archaeological sites can be visited in 1 day, it requires a good deal of walking on uneven surfaces and there's a lot of ground to cover, especially if you're getting around on public transportation. It's a good idea to break it up into 2 days of sightseeing if your travel schedule allows,

---

Previous: Pompeii street; mosaic in the Central Baths at Herculaneum; Vesuvius crater.

or elect to visit only one of the sites. Pompeii is the popular choice if time only permits one site, because its larger size offers a more complete look at an ancient Roman city. However, Herculaneum has many historical gems and is usually less crowded. A visit to either archaeological site can be combined with a visit to Mount Vesuvius. A guided tour is highly recommended for Pompeii and Herculaneum, and a group or private tour that includes transportation to the sites, or combines one or both of the cities with Vesuvius, can save you time and hassle.

Tours
Golden Tours
Via degli Aranci 25, Sorrento; tel. 081/878-1042; www. goldentours.it; Apr.-Oct.; group tours from €55 pp

For daily group excursions to Pompeii, Herculaneum, and Vesuvius from Sorrento, Golden Tours organizes a variety of half-day tours to individual locations as well as full-day combo tours. Group tours include pickup from your lodging and a guide as well as skip-the-line entrance tickets. Different tours are scheduled for different set days of the week, so check the schedule and book directly online in advance.

Sunland
Corso Reginna 82, Maiori; tel. 089/877-455; www. sunland.it; Apr.-Oct.; group tours from €90 pp

From the Amalfi Coast, the Sunland travel agency offers many tour options, including private and group excursions to Pompeii and Vesuvius, Pompeii and Herculaneum, or only to Pompeii on a half-day excursion. Tours include a guide and bus pickup in towns along the Amalfi Coast as well as skip-the-line entrance tickets. Tours of the archaeological sites take place on set days during the week and vary by tour, so it's worth checking the schedule ahead of time. Advance bookings are required and can be made online.

Private Tours
The easiest and most comfortable way to travel to Pompeii, Herculaneum, and Vesuvius from Naples, Sorrento, Salerno, and the Amalfi Coast is by private car. **Amalfi Turcoop** (Via A. Diaz 5, Agerola; tel. 089/873-1522; www.amalfiturcoop.it; private transfers from €110) offers transfers and both half-day and full-day excursions from all locations in the area. Transfers can also include a stop at Pompeii, Herculaneum, and Vesuvius for an additional fee.

Itinerary Ideas

DAY 1
Start your 2-day exploration with a visit to Pompeii followed by a visit to a local vineyard to sample local wines and even get a glimpse of how wine was made in ancient Roman times.

1 Arrive in **Pompeii** by car or by public transportation. Begin your visit at the Porta Marina entrance and follow the Walking Tour of Pompeii's Highlights (page 356).

2 Next, head to nearby **Bosco de' Medici Winery** for a tour of the vineyard and wine-tasting or a tour followed by lunch with wine-tasting in the relaxing garden.

Itinerary Ideas

DAY ONE
1. Pompeii
2. Bosco de' Medici Winery

DAY TWO
1. Herculaneum
2. Viva Lo Re
3. Mount Vesuvius crater
4. Kona

DAY 2

The second day focuses on the ancient city of Herculaneum and a visit to Mount Vesuvius. This is a good combination because Herculaneum is a more manageable size than Pompeii and is a bit nearer to the volcano.

1 Start your day by traveling to **Herculaneum** by car and spend 2-3 hours exploring the archaeological ruins.

2 Stop for lunch at **Viva Lo Re** near the archaeological site to enjoy dishes inspired by traditional recipes and seasonal ingredients.

3 Continue to **Mount Vesuvius** by car. From the parking area closest to the summit, continue on foot up to the Gran Cono (Big Cone) to hike around the edge of the volcanic **crater.** Enjoy panoramic views over the entire Gulf of Naples from the Sorrentine Peninsula to the islands of Capri and Ischia and over to Naples.

4 After your hike, pop into **Kona** for an early dinner.

Pompeii

With more than 3.5 million visitors annually, Pompeii is one of the most popular sights in all of Italy. Its massive appeal is due to the one-of-a-kind experience the archaeological ruins offer visitors to virtually step back in time. Before Mount Vesuvius erupted in 79 CE, freezing Pompeii in time, it was a large Roman city in Campania. The origins of the city date back to the 6th century BCE, when it was founded by the Oscans from central Italy. Over centuries, it passed from Etruscans to Greeks to Samnites, and eventually into Roman control. In the 1st century CE, Pompeii sat much closer to the coastline than it does today, and the city was prized for its location near the sea and the Sarno river, which made it an important trading city.

Pompeii is situated not far from the base of Mount Vesuvius, which the ancient Romans didn't know to be a dangerous volcano, as it had been dormant for more than 800 years. In 62 CE, a violent earthquake caused significant damage to Pompeii, but that was only a prelude to what was coming. The hustle and bustle of daily life came to a dramatic end for the people of Pompeii on a fateful day in 79 CE, when the explosive eruption of Mount Vesuvius covered the city with volcanic material, primarily pumice and ash, from the violent pyroclastic flows. Every part of life stopped in time and was preserved for centuries by the ash that covered the city. After the eruption, the city was abandoned and forgotten until it was accidentally rediscovered, first in 1599 and later in 1748 when official excavations began to uncover the city. Early archaeological treasures, including statues, mosaics, and frescoes, were uncovered and removed from the site, and many are now on display in the **Museo Archeologico Nazionale** in Naples.

There's a solemnity about Pompeii that lingers in the air. We can walk the same streets that the ancient Romans walked only because of the dramatic way in which the city and many of its residents were lost to time. Today, the massive amphitheater may be empty, but once thousands of Romans crowded its seats to watch spectacles like gladiator fights. Where the scent of bread once filled the air, the ovens are now empty. Walking through homes, you can see how families lived, worshipped, and conducted their daily business. Every detail of life, from how the city was run to everyday pleasures and entertainment, can be discovered while exploring Pompeii.

ORIENTATION

The massive archaeological site of Pompeii covers roughly 163 acres (66 ha), of which about 109 acres (44 ha) have been excavated, enclosed by about 2 mi (3 km) of city walls. Seven entrance gates to the city have been uncovered as well as the main streets that crisscrossed the city. **The Forum,** located in the southwest area of Pompeii, was the heart of the city. Two main streets, the **Via dell'Abbondanza** and **Via di Nola,** run southwest to northeast through the city and are crossed by the main street **Via Stabiana.** The **Via dell'Abbondanza** leads to the large amphitheater at the easternmost edge of Pompeii.

A Roman from 79 CE wouldn't be able to get around with the street names we use today because they are modern conventions, often based on important buildings and finds. Archaeologists have divided the site into nine areas (called regio), each subdivided into blocks with numbers for each building. The map and booklet you'll receive at the ticket booth is divided into these areas with the main sites numbered.

Entrance to the archaeological site is through the ancient entrance gate to Pompeii at **Porta Marina** in the southwesternmost point of Pompeii or at **Piazza Anfiteatro** on the easternmost side, mostly used for

Pompeii

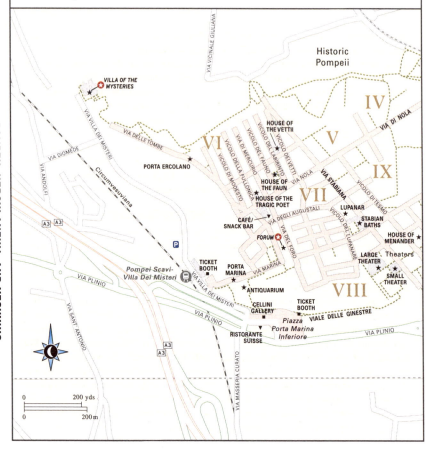

school groups. You can exit Pompeii from either gate or from the **Porta Ercolano** on the northwestern side of Pompeii (note that you cannot enter Pompeii via the Porta Ercolano). The most convenient entrance for most travelers is the main entrance at Porta Marina, which leads to Via Marina and the Forum. This entrance also makes it easy to start your visit at the Antiquarium museum to delve into the history of Pompeii before exploring the ruins. Another convenient entrance is southeast of Porta Marina at **Piazza Porta Marina Inferiore** (Piazza Esedra), where, after the ticket booth, you can follow the **Viale delle Ginestre** and enter the site on the southern side near the Teatro Grande.

VISITING POMPEII

Entrance to the **Parco Archeologico di Pompei** (tel. 081/857-5347; www.pompeiisites.org) includes access to the entire archaeological park, the Antiquarium, and all the sights. It is open 9am-7pm (last entrance 5:30pm) daily April-October, and 9am-5pm (last entrance 3:30pm) daily

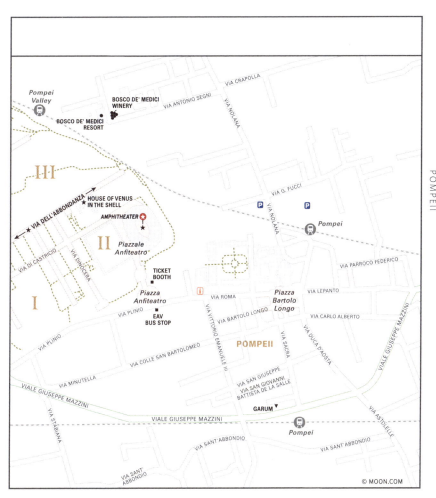

November-March. The site is closed January 1, May 1, and December 25.

Full-price admission to Pompeii is €18 per person. Tickets for kids under 18 are €3.50 and free under 6 years old, but be prepared to show identification for older kids. Tickets can be purchased online in advance via TicketOne (www.ticketone.it), and this will save you time in the ticket purchasing line. With your advance ticket, you can go directly to the entrance turnstiles with the printed or digital version of your ticket. Reduced-price tickets for children cannot be purchased in advance.

Pompeii is included in the **Campania Artecard** (www.campaniartecard.it), which offers free and discounted entrance to many sights in Naples as well as both Pompeii and Herculaneum. The Campania Artecard is available in a 3-day version (€32 adults, €25 ages 18-25) and a 7-day Campania Card (€34 adults) version. Entrance to Pompeii is free with the 3-day Artecard if it is one of the first two sights where you present the card; you'll receive a 50 percent discount if it's the third or subsequent sight visited. For the 7-day pass, Pompeii is free if it's one of the first five sights visited, or you'll receive a 50 percent discount if it is the sixth or subsequent sight visited.

Keep in mind that your ticket to Pompeii is valid for only one entrance. Once you enter, you won't be able to exit the park and reenter with the same ticket. However, there is a café for refreshments, and there are restrooms located throughout the excavation site.

Planning Your Time

With such a large footprint and so many archaeological treasures, Pompeii's ruins require at least 3-4 hours to see just the highlights, such as the Antiquarium, the Forum area, the baths, the city's theaters and amphitheater, homes in the city center, and the Villa dei Misteri outside the city walls. A longer visit will allow you to stop to see more homes and explore more areas of the city, but be prepared for a good deal of walking.

Given Pompeii's popularity, there's not necessarily a good time of day to avoid crowds. Early afternoon is often a good time to visit, but you will still have to navigate crowds and groups. Inclement weather can turn Pompeii muddy, so it's best to adjust your schedule if possible and avoid the site if it's raining hard.

Much of Pompeii requires walking on uneven stone roads, and there's limited shade on sunny days. Bring water, sunscreen, and a hat on hot days. Comfortable closed-toed walking shoes are the best option for the rough and dusty setting.

Audio Guides and Tours

An entrance ticket to Pompeii includes a map and a booklet with brief information on all the main sights within the archaeological site. Download the free official **MyPompeii** app from the Apple App Store or Google Play Store for access at your fingertips to maps, information about key sites to visit, and more. Audio guides and tours are available at an additional cost. **Audio guides** are available only at the **Porta Marina entrance** and cost €8 per person or €13 for two people. Be prepared to leave a personal ID of some kind in order to rent the audio guide.

Hiring a **private guide** or joining a **tour** is one of the best ways to get the most out of a visit to Pompeii. Authorized guides for the region of Campania can be hired near the Porta Marina and the Piazza Porta Marina Inferiore (Piazza Esedra) entrances. A 2- or 3-hour private tour with a guide will cost roughly €120. As Pompeii includes areas of active excavation as well as restoration to existing sights, it's not uncommon for some areas to be closed. Guides are up to date on the openings, and can save you a lot of time by showing you only the houses that are currently open. After seeing the highlights and learning about the history on a guided tour, you can always choose to stay in the archaeological site and continue exploring on your own.

SIGHTS

The sights included here are the top highlights of Pompeii, but this only scratches the surface of all that Pompeii offers with its multitude of houses, civic and religious buildings, and public baths to explore at the site.

Antiquarium

Via Marina near Porta Marina entrance

This small museum is a great place to start your visit by delving into the history of Pompeii before setting off to explore the ruins. Although the Antiquarium was first built in the late 19th century, it was heavily damaged by bombing during World War II and later by a strong earthquake in 1980. After extensive remodeling and updating, the Antiquarium reopened in 2021 and offers an excellent introduction to Pompeii as well as a fine collection of artifacts, artwork, and objects uncovered during excavations at Pompeii and other archaeological sites in the area. In addition to an in-depth history of Pompeii, you'll see detailed frescoes, mosaics, jewelry, household items, and a room dedicated to recent plaster casts made of victims of the eruptions. Pompeii is an active excavation site, and the Antiquarium also highlights and displays recent discoveries. Entrance to the museum is included in the ticket price for the Parco Archeologico di Pompei.

★ Forum

Via Villa dei Misteri at Via Marina/Via dell'Abbondanza

Located in the oldest part of the city, the Forum was the bustling city center and the heart of the political, religious, and commercial life of Pompeii. The large rectangular area is surrounded by temples dedicated to Jupiter, Apollo, Vespasian, and Venus. On the south side, what is called the Basilica today was home to the law and commerce courts. Along the western side, stop to peer into the Forum Granary, which was once a large fruit and vegetable market, where you'll now see row after row of tall shelves lined with archaeological finds, including amphorae (large vases used for storage), pots and pans for cooking, statues, and architectural details. The city's largest meat and fish market, called the Macellum, is located on the northeastern side of the Forum. Here you'll find replicas of plaster casts of the bodies of victims of Pompeii that were created by archaeologists during the excavation process. The terrifying final moments of life in Pompeii are captured in the different positions of the plaster cast bodies. Seeing them is a somber experience that can be unsettling to some visitors, especially young travelers. However, moments like this offer the chance to reflect on both the broad historical significance of Pompeii and the tragic loss of individual lives.

Standing in the middle of the Forum today, you can imagine Pompeiians of all types passing through here going about their business, shopping, or visiting a temple. Looking toward the Temple of Jupiter on the northern side of the Forum, you'll also find a perfectly framed view of Mount Vesuvius in the distance.

Stabian Baths

Via dell'Abbondanza 15

Located east of the Forum, the Stabian baths are the oldest public baths in Pompeii, dating back as early as the 3rd century BCE. The pristine state of the baths allows a rare glimpse into the splendid plumbing and heating systems that were used; the clever heating system is still quite intact. Public baths were a regular part of life in ancient Rome, and as was the custom, the Stabian baths are divided into separate areas for men and women. You can walk through the changing rooms to another series of rooms, each one with a different water temperature. While the men's rooms are larger and more lavishly decorated with paintings, both the men's and women's areas offer a look at the multistep bathing process as well as the heating system with double floors and terra-cotta pipes in the walls where hot air was circulated throughout the structure from a furnace. There are two other interesting public baths in Pompeii, including the **Forum Baths** just north of the Forum and the **Central Baths** north of the Stabian Baths along Via Stabiana.

Lupanar

Vicolo del Lupanare at Vicolo del Balcone Pensile

Among the variety of entertainments available in Pompeii, many brothels have been brought to light during archaeological excavations. The largest is located along Vicolo del Lupanare, and the name of both the structure and the street come from the Latin word *lupa*, meaning prostitute. Originally a two-level building, there are five rooms on the lower level, each one fitted with a built-in bed and that could be closed off with curtains. Along the main corridor are erotic-themed paintings that are thought to have encouraged clients or perhaps been used to communicate with clients who spoke different languages. Let's just say they set the scene.

A visit to the Lupanar is included in most guided visits to Pompeii, but it can be skipped if it's not to a visitor's taste. However, it is interesting to note that erotic themes weren't particularly taboo in Roman culture. A large amount of art with erotic themes has been uncovered in Pompeii over the centuries, and much of it can be seen at the Gabinetto Segreto (Secret Cabinet) room at the **Museo**

Walking Tour of Pompeii's Highlights

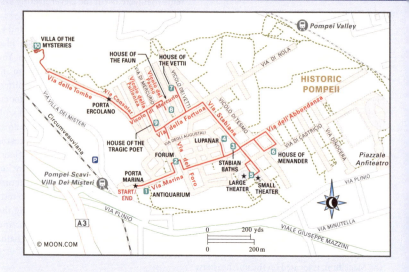

To see many of the highlights of Pompeii, pull on a comfortable pair of walking shoes and follow this itinerary of the top spots. To cover the sights included here, allow about 2 hours, and longer if you want to explore more of the buildings, temples, and sights you'll pass along the way.

1. Enter Pompeii through the Porta Marina gate, and soon after the entrance you'll find the **Antiquarium.** Start your visit by uncovering the history of the ancient city at this museum full of artifacts from Pompeii.

2. Continue along Via Marina until you reach the **Forum,** the heart of the ancient city. See

Archeologico Nazionale in Naples. It's also not uncommon in the streets and houses of Pompeii to find erotic symbolism, some of which are thought to have been a sort of porta fortuna (good luck symbol) for Romans.

Theaters

Near intersection of Via Stabiana and Via del Tempio d'Iside

South of the Stabian Baths, Via Stabiana leads to a beautiful part of Pompeii where the city's theaters are located. Here the **Large Theater** (Teatro Grande) is built into the hillside with steep seating and excellent acoustics. The theater was built around the 2nd century BCE and seated up to 5,000 people. Today it is still occasionally used as a particularly evocative setting for cultural and musical events. Next to the Large Theater, the Odeon or **Small Theater** (Teatro Piccolo) was originally a covered theater used for more intimate musical performances. Just south of the Large Theater, a large square—surrounded by 74 gray Doric columns—that was previously connected to the theater was transformed into a barracks for gladiators after the earthquake in 62 CE.

Via dell'Abbondanza

One of the main roads of Pompeii, the Via dell'Abbondanza runs from the Forum northeast all the way to the Porta Sarno on the

the temples, commercial buildings, and courts and enjoy a perfectly framed view of Mount Vesuvius.

3. From the Forum, follow Via dell'Abbondanza a few blocks east to see the **Stabian Baths,** the oldest public baths in Pompeii.

4. Walk north a couple of blocks on Vicolo del Lupanare to visit the **Lupanar,** one of the brothels of the ancient city.

5. Return down Vicolo del Lupanare, cross Via dell'Abbondanza, and continue to the two well-preserved **theaters** where plays, music, and events were held.

6. Go back the way you came, take a right on Via dell'Abbondanza, and continue along it as it heads northeast into a residential area of the city where you can walk through many fine Roman homes, like the **House of Menander.**

7. Turn back toward the center of Pompeii along Via dell'Abbondanza and take a right on Via Stabiana and a left on Via della Fortuna. Soon after, take a right on Vicolo dei Vetti and follow to the **House of the Vettii,** the most finely decorated house excavated at Pompeii.

8. Follow Vicolo di Mercurio in front of the House of the Vettii to see the **House of the Faun** to explore one of the largest houses in the ancient city.

9. Again returning to Vicolo di Mercurio, take a left on Via di Mercurio and follow a short distance to see the **House of the Tragic Poet,** which is famous for its entry mosaic depicting a large dog with the words *Cave Canem,* meaning "Beware of the Dog." Follow Vicolo del Foro to return to the Forum.

10. For a longer visit, return along Vicolo di Mercurio to Via Consolare and take a right. Keep walking as it passes through the ancient gate of Porta Ercolano and becomes Via delle Tombe, leading to the **Villa of the Mysteries.** This large country estate is fascinating to explore and is famous for its captivating frescoes.

You can exit the archaeological site near the Villa of the Mysteries or return along Via delle Tombe, Via Consolare, back through the Forum, and to Via Marina and the **Porta Marina gate.**

eastern side of the city. This area is one of the most intriguing and characteristic in Pompeii, with a mix of large and richly decorated private homes interspersed with shops, bakeries, and inns. Walking down the once busy street, where the wheels of countless carts left deep grooves in the stone paving, visitors can envision moments of daily life in ancient Pompeii. Archaeologists have discovered many of the original shop functions as well as incredible details that, in some cases, reveal the names of the original shopkeepers.

While walking down Via dell'Abbondanza, stop to see some well-preserved examples of thermopolia, which were somewhat like modern-day take-out or fast-food restaurants. You'll recognize them when you see their countertops with terra-cotta jars set into them, where ready-to-serve food was stored in the small restaurants, or dried goods were kept in the shops. Just beyond the crossroad of Vicolo dell'Efebo, stop to see the house and thermopolium (tavern) of Vetutius Placidus. Drinks and hot food were served at the front of the building, with the owner's house located at the rear. During excavation, about 6.6 lbs (3 kg) of coins were found in one of the terra-cotta pots set into the counter, a testament to the popularity of this particular tavern.

Pompeii's Houses

Pompeii has an embarrassment of riches when

it comes to residential architecture to explore, with more houses and villas than you could possibly visit in 1 day. One thing to keep in mind is that, unlike the larger buildings, many of Pompeii's houses may be closed at any given time for restoration work. It is hard to tell in advance if, or how long, a house will be closed. Yet, while some houses may have been closed for years, ongoing restoration and excavation means that houses are also continually reopening. The Pompeii website (www.pompeiisites.org) does include a list of buildings open to the public, but the surest way to avoid wasting time or disappointment is on a guided tour, as the local authorized guides are up to date on the latest openings and closures. Below are some fine houses that you'll want to see if they're open during your visit.

House of Menander
Vicolo del Menandro between Vicolo del Citarista and Vicolo di Pasquius Proculus
Follow Via dell'Abbondanza from the Forum into the southeastern part of the city, another particularly rich area with homes to explore. Take a detour south of Via dell'Abbondanza to reach the House of Menander, where you can explore one of Pompeii's most beautiful homes. Walking through the atrium you can see frescoes depicting scenes from Homer's *Iliad* and *Odyssey,* and the artistic theme continues in the frescoes around the large and elegant peristyle garden with a portrait of the Greek playwright Menander.

House of Venus in the Shell
Via dell'Abbondanza between Vicolo della Venere and Vicolo di Giulia Felice
Not far north of the Amphitheater, the House of Venus in the Shell is an appealing house with a garden atrium surrounded by rooms with detailed frescoes. The house is named after the impressive fresco of Venus reclining in a large shell.

House of the Tragic Poet
Via della Fullonica between Via delle Terme and Vicolo di Mercurio
Heading north from the Forum leads toward the northwestern section of the city where some of the largest homes were located. You won't have to go far to reach the House of the Tragic Poet. This somewhat small house has one of Pompeii's most famous mosaics right at the entrance. You'll go in through a side entrance where glass covers the mosaic of a large and rather intimidating black dog with the words *Cave Canem* (Beware of the Dog) below.

House of the Faun
Vicolo di Mercurio between Vicolo del Fauno and Vicolo del Labrinto
Continuing down Vicolo di Mercurio leads to the House of the Faun, among the largest houses in Pompeii. The name comes from a bronze statue of a faun in one of the atria. A replica stands in place of the original, which is now at the Museo Archeologico Nazionale along with the original of the remarkable mosaic scene depicting the Battle of Alexander, which has also been replaced by a replica.

House of the Vettii
Vicolo dei Vetti at Vicolo di Mercurio
Just beyond is the House of the Vettii, one of the richest and most finely decorated of all the houses excavated at Pompeii. The house belonged to rich merchants who spared no expense in filling it with paintings and friezes inspired by mythological themes. There's also a large garden with a central fountain that featured jets of water.

★ Villa of the Mysteries
Via Villa dei Misteri 2
As you work your way toward the periphery of Pompeii, you'll notice the houses tend to get larger as more space was available for gardens and private estates. The Villa dei Misteri (Villa of the Mysteries) is located outside the original city walls northwest of Pompeii;

1: remains of walls and columns of the House of the Faun **2:** one of the rooms in the Stabian Baths **3:** the Forum at Pompeii **4:** fresco in the Villa of the Mysteries

this large villa is a fine example of a wealthy Roman agricultural estate. Built around a large peristyle courtyard, the sprawling villa has many rooms you can explore on various levels. Because the villa received less damage during the eruption of Vesuvius than much of the rest of Pompeii suffered, you can get an excellent sense of the original spaces with many ceilings and frescoes remarkably well intact. Its name comes from one series of captivating yet cryptic frescoes that have puzzled art historians. This highly debated fresco frieze is beautifully detailed with a striking red background. It runs around three walls of a room and is one of the largest and finest examples of painting from antiquity. The frieze depicts scenes of women performing various rituals along with a host of mythological figures, and the prevailing thought is that they depict scenes from rites dedicated to Dionysus, who appears in the center of the frieze.

★ Amphitheater
Piazzale Anfiteatro

Set in the far southeastern part of the city, Pompeii's large Amphitheater offers a fascinating glimpse into an important element of Roman culture that is often of interest to modern-day travelers: gladiators. While smaller than more impressive amphitheaters like the Colosseum in Rome, Pompeii's oval Amphitheater is notable as the earliest known example of a large theater built primarily for gladiatorial combat. Built around 70 BCE, it seated up to 20,000 people, who crowded in to watch the popular fights between gladiators and animals. With so many people coming and going, the Amphitheater was built on the outskirts to lessen the noise and crowding impact on daily life in Pompeii. Though there's no roar of the crowd today, the Anfiteatro is an impressive place to stand right in the center, gaze around, and imagine the scene in all its glory.

VINEYARDS
Bosco de' Medici Winery
Via Antonio Segni 41, Pompei; tel. 081/856-4040; www.boscodemediciwinery.com; tour and wine-tasting from €45 pp

Located next to the archaeological site of Pompeii, Bosco de' Medici is a beautiful family-run vineyard that produces excellent wines. The tour takes you through the biodynamic vineyard where you'll also see an 18th-century farmhouse and the small necropolis of Porta Sarno from ancient Pompeii. You'll learn about the variety of local grapes used to

Large Theater of Pompeii

create their wines as well as unique varieties like the rare caprettone that only grows on the slopes of Mount Vesuvius. Then, visit the wine production rooms and cellar that blends modern technology with ancient techniques, such as the large terra-cotta amphoras where they produce white wine. Tours include a wine-tasting and an excellent lunch menu.

SHOPPING
Cellini Gallery
Piazza Porta Marina Inferiore 1, Pompei; tel. 081/862-4200; www.cellinigallery.com; 8:15am-5:30pm daily Apr.-Oct., 8:15am-4pm daily Nov.-Mar.

Near the main entrance to Pompeii, you'll find this shop specializing in beautiful cameos and coral. Founded in 1960, the shop upholds the antique tradition of coral and cameo carving, which dates to Greek and Roman times. You'll also find souvenirs of your visit to Pompeii.

FOOD
Inside the archaeological site of Pompeii, a **café,** located near the Forum, offers a variety of snacks, sandwiches, and light meals as well as drinks. The restaurants below are located outside the archaeological site.

Ristorante Suisse
Piazza Porta Marina Inferiore 10/13, Pompei; tel. 081/862-2536; www.suissepompei.it; 9am-11pm daily Apr.-Oct., 9am-5pm daily Nov.-Mar.; €15-30

This popular restaurant is located in the piazza between the Porta Marina entrance and the entrance nearby off Piazza Porta Marina Inferiore. With a full restaurant, self-service bar for a quick meal, and pizzeria, there are plenty of options to choose from for the whole family. Stop for a coffee and something sweet in the morning before starting your tour, or have a snack or meal after a visit to the ruins.

Garum
Viale Giuseppe Mazzini 63, Pompei; tel. 081/850-1178; www.ristorantegarumpompei.it; noon-4pm and 7pm-11:30pm Mon.-Tues. and Thurs.-Sat., noon-4pm Sun.; €8-16

Not far from the archaeological site, near the modern-day city of Pompei, this restaurant specializes in traditional dishes and Campania wines. Special attention is given to ingredients like the antique garum fish sauce used in ancient Rome, which is featured in a variety of dishes, including a lovely spaghetti with tomatoes, pine nuts, raisins, and local anchovies.

ACCOMMODATIONS
Bosco de' Medici Resort
Via Antonio Segni 43, Pompei; tel. 081/850-6463; www.pompeihotel.com; €200

For a peaceful stay very near Pompeii, this resort is surrounded by citrus gardens and the Bosco de' Medici vineyard. After a day exploring the archaeological ruins, cool off and relax by the large pool while enjoying the view of Mount Vesuvius in the distance. There are 18 modern and comfortable rooms available with four suites that include a hot tub. All rooms have a private patio and entrance from the gardens surrounding the resort. Free on-site parking is a great feature if you're exploring the area by car.

GETTING THERE
Located between Naples and Sorrento, the archaeological site of Pompeii is an easy day trip by train or car. If you're transferring between Naples and Sorrento or the Amalfi Coast, you can also stop to visit Pompeii along the way. With a private car transfer, your driver can wait while you visit the site. You can store your luggage while visiting Pompeii if you're traveling by train.

By Train
Pompeii is easily reached by train from Naples and Sorrento with the **Circumvesuviana** train operated by **EAV** (www.eavsrl.it; departures every 30 minutes daily). The journey is 40 minutes from Naples (€3) and 30 minutes from Sorrento (€2.60). Exit at the **Pompeii Scavi-Villa dei Misteri** stop, and across the street from the station you'll find the Porta Marina entrance to Pompeii. Keep in mind that the Circumvesuviana is a commuter

train for the area and can be quite crowded. However, it does provide an inexpensive way to reach Pompeii without the hassle of driving. If you are traveling with luggage, any bags larger than 30 by 30 by 15 cm are not allowed into Pompeii. You can leave luggage in the deposito bagagli (luggage storage) at the Pompei Scavi-Villa dei Misteri station for a fee (generally €8 per bag) or smaller bags can be left directly at the cloakroom lockers near the Porta Marina entrance to Pompeii for free.

By Bus

Multiple bus lines connect Pompeii with surrounding cities. From Naples and Sorrento, the journey is much faster and more convenient by train. From Salerno, **Busitalia Campania** (www.fsbusitaliacampania.it; €3.20) has two lines that connect the historic center of Salerno with Pompeii, stopping near Piazza Porta Marina Inferiore. Line 4 passes by the Salerno train station and takes about 1 hour 40 minutes to reach Pompeii. Line 50 also departs from Salerno's train station and takes about 1 hour 10 minutes to Pompeii.

To reach Pompeii from the Amalfi Coast, the easiest option is to first take the ferry or bus to Salerno and continue by bus, or first head to Sorrento and continue to Pompeii on the Circumvesuviana train.

By Car

Pompeii is located just off the **A3** autostrada (highway) connecting Naples and Salerno. The drive from **Naples** to Pompeii takes about 30 minutes, while from **Salerno** it is 35-40 minutes. To reach Pompeii from **Sorrento,** follow the **SS145** east along the Sorrentine Peninsula to where it meets the A3 autostrada, and shortly after joining the A3 you'll exit for Pompeii. Whether you're coming from Naples, Salerno, or Sorrento, exit at Pompei Scavi, and in moments you'll arrive at the Porta Marina entrance. There's a variety of paid **parking** areas around the archaeological site, including one conveniently located near the Porta Marina entrance operated by **Camping Zeus** (tel. 081/861-5320; www.campingzeus.it; from €3 per hour).

GETTING AROUND

Once you're at the Pompeii archaeological site, the only way to get around and explore the ruins is on foot. Expect to navigate hills, steps, and uneven stone walkways while visiting the site.

Herculaneum

The same devastating volcanic eruption that brought the ruin of Pompeii also destroyed the nearby city of Herculaneum. Much smaller than Pompeii, the town wasn't a commercial center like its larger neighbor but was instead a popular seaside resort town that was home to luxurious homes and villas. While Pompeii was covered with pumice and ash, Herculaneum's proximity to Vesuvius meant that it was buried below a very deep layer of mud combined with ash and volcanic materials. Though this was a horrendous end for the town's population, the volcanic mud preserved Herculaneum's buildings. That's why today we can still see wooden structures like ceiling beams, upper floors of buildings, furniture, and doors in more detail than what remains in Pompeii.

In the **Villa dei Papiri** (Villa of the Papyri), one of the most sumptuous private houses in Herculaneum, more than 1,800 papyrus scrolls were discovered—a truly rare and precious find. As the villa is unfortunately closed to the public, the scrolls are now housed in the Biblioteca Nazionale di Napoli (National Library of Naples), where they are still undergoing intense study. Its famous sculptures are located in the Museo Archeologico Nazionale in Naples. The architectural design of the lavish villa was the inspiration for the J. Paul Getty Villa museum in Los Angeles.

The ruins of Herculaneum, located in modern-day Ercolano, were discovered in 1709 before those of Pompeii. Yet the excavation of Herculaneum has always been a challenge compared to Pompeii because the 52 ft (16 m) of volcanic mud covering the town turned into solid rock. And unlike Pompeii, much of the ancient city of Herculaneum lies below the city of Ercolano. However, what has been uncovered so far of ancient Herculaneum has revealed true archaeological gems, and the site is certainly worth a visit.

ORIENTATION

The excavation site of Herculaneum is located well below the street level and is accessed via a long inclined walkway that offers a great view over the ruins before you even arrive. However, much of the ancient city remains covered; only about 11 acres (4.5 ha) of the estimated 49 acres (20 ha) has been excavated. Based on the areas that have been brought to light, it's possible to get an idea of the city's original layout. As was traditional in Roman cities, Herculaneum is laid out in a grid, divided by at least three decumani, or main streets. Two of these have been uncovered, the **Decumano Inferiore** and the **Decumano Massimo,** running roughly southwest-northeast and crossed perpendicularly by five roads, called Cardo III, Cardo IV, and Cardo V on today's maps of Ercolano. The remaining two of the five crossroads lie in an unexcavated area northwest of the archaeological site. Since the Decumano Massimo is a noticeably larger street, researchers think it may mark where the Forum or center of the city started.

Before the eruption of 79 CE, Herculaneum sat right at the edge of the sea. The volcanic material from the eruption moved the coastline much farther out to where we see it today. After you pass the ticket booth, look down to the right as you walk by the barrel-vaulted buildings below; these were originally boathouses opening to the beach. Herculaneum's most noted sight, the Villa of the Papyri, remains only partially excavated and is not open to the public. The ancient theater, which was the first site at Herculaneum discovered in the early 18th century, is completely underground north of the archaeological area below modern-day Ercolano, and it is only rarely open to the public.

the ancient Roman ruins at Herculaneum

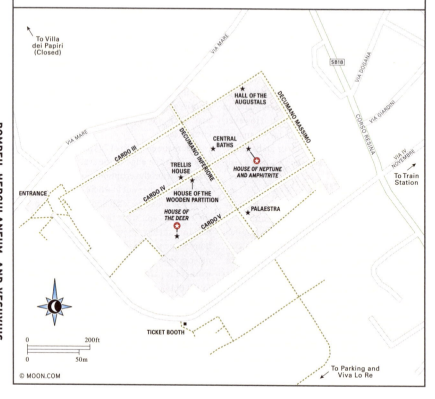

VISITING HERCULANEUM

The Herculaneum archaeological site is managed by the **Parco Archeologico di Ercolano** (Corso Resina, Ercolano; tel. 081/777-7008; www.ercolano.beniculturali.it) and is open 8:30am-7:30pm (last entrance 6pm) April-October, and 8:30am-5pm (last entrance 3:30pm) November-March. The site is open daily throughout the year and is only closed on January 1 and December 25.

Full-price admission to Herculaneum is €13 per person. Kids under 18 get free admission, but bring identification, especially for older kids.

If you purchase the **Campania Artecard** (www.campaniartecard.it), it includes many sights in Naples as well as free admission to both Herculaneum and Pompeii if the sites are the first two where you present the card; the card gives you a 50 percent discount if it's the third or subsequent site you visit. The Campania Artecard is available in a 3-day version (€32 adults, €25 ages 18-25) and a 7-day version called the Campania Card (€34 adults).

Planning Your Time

Herculaneum doesn't receive the massive number of visitors that Pompeii gets, but you should still expect to find groups here. The flow of visitors depends on the season and the number of cruise ships docked in nearby Naples and Sorrento, which means there's no one best time to plan a visit. However, if possible, try to explore the site during good weather. Herculaneum requires 2-3 hours for you to see the site well. You'll do plenty of walking on uneven surfaces, although the inclined walkway and bridge down to access the site help to minimize the number of steps.

Audio Guides and Tours

Similar to a visit to Pompeii, admission to Herculaneum includes a **map** and **detailed booklet** with information on the most important sights. An excellent **audio guide** (€10 per person) is available for rent and can be booked in advance online (www.ercolano. tours) or at the audio guide desk after entering. As the archaeological site is smaller than Pompeii, Herculaneum is fairly easy for visitors to navigate with the booklet and audio guide combo.

Also like Pompeii, the ruins of Herculaneum really come to life if you hire an **authorized tour guide.** Authorized guides for the region of Campania are available near the ticket booth for **private tours.**

SIGHTS

At Herculaneum, you'll find examples of many of the same types of buildings as at Pompeii, including public baths, shops, and eating establishments, and you'll enjoy the experience of walking down the streets of an ancient Roman town. Herculaneum has fine examples of houses, many with details that are even better preserved than at Pompeii. Each site has something different to offer, so history buffs in particular will enjoy exploring both. The sights mentioned here are a selection of the top highlights, but there are many more to explore during a visit to Herculaneum.

Hall of the Augustals

Cardo III Superiore near Decumano Massimo
This large building was the location of a cult called the Augustals that was dedicated to worshipping the Emperor Augustus. Becoming a part of the Augustals was an important step for freed slaves to move upward in Roman society. Meetings and religious celebrations took place in these rooms, which still retain traces of the original floors and wall decorations. There are frescoes depicting Hercules—according to legend the founder of Herculaneum—in battle with the Etruscan god Achelous, and entering Olympus surrounded by a host of gods.

Central Baths

Cardo III Superiore and Cardo IV Superiore
The Central Baths in Herculaneum are divided in two, with separate areas for men and women. Built in the second half of the 1st century BCE, the baths were fed by a large well. The Men's Baths area is accessed from Cardo III Superiore and includes a dressing room where you can still see the niches where garments and personal items were stored. Beyond is a domed frigidarium for cold bathing and a tepidarium for warm bathing that includes a black-and-white mosaic of Triton, a sea god, surrounded by dolphins and a host of sea creatures. Beyond that is a caldarium, the hot room of the baths.

The Women's Baths are entered from Cardo IV Superiore and follow a similar progression of rooms, from the barrel-vaulted changing room to the tepidarium, where shelves were located for personal items. This is followed by the caldarium, with a large vaulted ceiling, and two unusually fancy seats: one made of marble and the other a dark red stone. Behind the caldarium is the furnace used to heat the rooms and the water, in addition to the well for the baths that drew water from a depth of about 27 ft (8.25 m). Adjacent to the baths is a large courtyard, surrounded by porticos, that was used as a palaestra, or gymnasium.

★ House of Neptune and Amphitrite

Cardo IV Superiore
One of Herculaneum's loveliest houses, this building is noted for its remarkable wall mosaics, which are often considered the most beautiful uncovered in Herculaneum. Although not a particularly large house, its

highly detailed decor indicates its owner was wealthy. The most impressive mosaic depicts the god Neptune and his wife, Amphitrite, surrounded by decorative floral patterns and columns, and topped with a fan-shaped design, all in brilliantly preserved shades of deep red, blue, yellow, and green. Nearby, there's also a nymphaeum, or water garden, covered with floral and animal-themed mosaics and topped with marble theatrical masks. Admiring the brightly colored mosaics with all of the captivating intricacies of their designs, it's fascinating to imagine just how lavish the fully decorated room would have looked before the eruption of Vesuvius.

Trellis House
Cardo IV Inferiore

Easy to spot from the street with its wooden balcony supported by brick columns, this was originally a two-level boardinghouse with space for several families on the upper level; there's a separate entrance from the apartment on the lower level. Not only was the wooden balcony structure discovered remarkably intact, but archaeologists also found carbonized wooden remains of furniture.

House of the Wooden Partition
Cardo IV Inferiore

Just across the street from the Trellis House, this house is named after a very particular detail that was remarkably preserved. Beyond the atrium entry that's standard in most Roman homes, the family here added a wooden partition, an ancient version of a sliding door that could be closed for more privacy between the atrium and the tablinum, the room located between the atrium and the peristyle garden. The wooden partition survived and is the only known example of this type of design from Greek or Roman antiquity.

★ House of the Deer
Cardo V Inferiore

This elegant villa covers about 11,840 sq ft (1,100 sq m) and includes many rooms around a central garden. This is where archaeologists uncovered statues of deer being attacked by dogs, as well as statues of a Satyr and one of drunken Hercules, and round marble tables with ornately carved legs. Replicas of these statues and tables are located in the center of the garden. Surrounding the garden is a cryptoporticus, a covered passageway with windows, that has frescoes along the walls and a white mosaic floor. On the north side you'll find a large portal entrance to a sitting room with traces of highly detailed mosaics depicting cherubs riding sea animals and the head of the sea god Oceanus. With the villa's position near the walls of the city by the sea, there would have once been a fine sea view from the terrace located off the garden. Since the ancient city sits well below street level today, and the sea is no longer in sight, it takes some imagination to picture the enviable seaside setting villas like this one once boasted.

Palaestra
Cardo V Superiore at Decumano Inferiore

The entrance to this building, between two large columns, leads into what was once a very large complex used for sporting activities. In the center there was originally a grand open space with a cross-shaped pool in the center, surrounded on three sides by arcades with columns and a corridor on the north side. The gymnasium complex included a variety of rooms, including a vast hall that was likely used for religious or cult ceremonies. Only a small area of the central garden and pool has been uncovered, but one of the finds includes a bronze fountain sculpture of the Lernaean Hydra, a frightening mythical monster with many snake heads.

1: garden statue in the House of the Deer
2: mosaic of Neptune and Amphitrite **3:** the ruins of Herculaneum

FOOD
Viva Lo Re
Corso Resina 261, Ercolano; tel. 081/739-0207; www.vivalore.it; 12:30pm-3:30pm and 7pm-11pm Tues.-Sat., noon-4pm Sun.; €15-22

South of the archaeological park in Ercolano, this osteria and enoteca (wine bar) is a good spot to stop for a meal before or after visiting Herculaneum. Locally sourced ingredients are key, and they are used beautifully to create traditional dishes with a twist on the menu that changes seasonally. The excellent wine list offers more than 1,500 labels.

GETTING THERE
By Train
The **Circumvesuviana** train run by EAV (www.eavsrl.it; departures every 30 minutes daily; from Naples 20 minutes, €2.40; from Sorrento 40 minutes, €3.10) is the most comfortable public transportation option to reach Herculaneum. Exit at the **Ercolano Scavi** stop and head straight down Via Vittorio Veneto toward the sea and across the traffic circle to continue along Via IV Novembre for about 10 minutes. This will take you right to the entrance gate of the ruins. If you are traveling with luggage and can walk the distance (or take a taxi) from the station to the entrance, you can leave bags in the deposito bagagli (luggage storage) next to the ticket office for free.

By Car
Herculaneum is located off the **A3** autostrada (highway) that connects Naples and Salerno. It's about a 30-minute drive from **Naples** and at least 45 minutes from **Salerno.** Exit at either the Ercolano or Portici/Ercolano exit and follow the signs indicating Scavi di Ercolano for a short distance to the archaeological site. There are paid **parking** lots southeast of the site with rates usually starting at €3 per hour.

GETTING AROUND
Once you're at the Herculaneum archaeological site, the only way to navigate the ruins is on foot. The area is significantly smaller than Pompeii, so it's a good choice if extensive walking is an issue. However, you should still be prepared for uneven surfaces, and sturdy, comfortable shoes are recommended.

Vesuvius

In ancient Roman times, the massive volcano Mount Vesuvius, called Vesuvio in Italian, was known as Monte Somma. The fertile land surrounding the mountain southeast of Naples was valued by the Romans, who were largely unaware that the lush green slopes of Vesuvius concealed a deadly explosive volcano. Until the massive eruption in 79 CE, only a few Roman scholars suspected the true nature of Monte Somma. Pliny the Elder had been studying the mountain, and the geographer Strabo had written about stones on the mountain that looked as if they had been burned by fire. Yet the devastation of the eruption left no doubt of the fierce natural power below Vesuvius. Letters written by Pliny the Younger describe the events of that fateful day that killed his uncle Pliny the Elder as he tried to escape.

Though there hasn't been an eruption of the same level of devastation as in 79 CE, Vesuvius has erupted regularly over the centuries. It is classified as a stratovolcano, a type of volcano made up of many layers of hardened lava, pumice, ash, and other materials. This type of volcano is known for periodic and violent eruptions, similar to Mount St. Helens in the United States. Vesuvius is considered one of the most dangerous volcanoes in the world due to its unpredictable nature and the nearly 3 million people who live in the area surrounding the volcano. The last major eruption was in 1944 during World War II and was captured on film and video by the US Army Air Forces stationed near Naples at the time.

Today you can only occasionally catch a glimpse of wisps of steam coming out of the crater, but Vesuvius remains as much a threat as ever. It will come as no surprise that it's a heavily studied and constantly monitored volcano. Nevertheless, its gently curved slopes are an undeniable symbol of Naples. A climb to the top of the crater is a moving experience, both for the spectacular views and for the chance to be so close to such an incredible force of nature.

PARCO NAZIONALE DEL VESUVIO

Strada Provinciale Ercolano-Vesuvio; tel. 081/865-3911; www.parconazionaledelvesuvio.it; crater 9am-3pm daily Nov.-Feb., 9am-4pm daily Mar. and Oct., 9am-5pm daily Apr.-June and Sept., 9am-6pm daily July-Aug.; €12, tickets must be purchased in advance

The Parco Nazionale del Vesuvio (Mount Vesuvius National Park) was created in 1995 to protect the entire area surrounding the volcano, along with its natural landscape, animal and plant species, and unique geological elements. The vast park covers 20,959 acres (8,482 ha), from the base of the volcano to the upper part around the cone. The fertile soil of the volcano has created a rich forest of pine and holm oak trees, along with maples, alders, chestnuts, and oaks. The park is especially rich in Mediterranean vegetation, with up to 23 types of orchids and several varieties of broom. Following the meandering road up the slopes of Vesuvius to the top leads through the natural landscape from the forested base up to the rugged rocky area around the Gran Cono, the main cone of the volcano.

Even though the volcano is surrounded by a dense urban environment, the park is home to many different species of mammals, birds, and reptiles. Foxes, rabbits, and beech martens all call the slopes of the volcano home, along with more than 100 different bird species, including migratory, wintering, and breeding birds. It's a beautiful sight to catch a glimpse of a peregrine falcon gliding through the air along the slopes of the volcano.

Tickets for the climb to the Gran Cono can only be purchased in advance. Since phone service and signals are intermittent near the entrance, it's best to purchase your ticket before arriving at the 3,280-ft-elevation (1,000-m) parking area.

★ Hiking to the Crater

Distance: *2.5 mi round-trip*
Time: *1-1.5 hours round-trip*
Trailhead: *Piazzale di Quota 1,000 (parking area nearest the crater)*
Information and Services: *Basic visit information available at the ticket stand and often at the top along the Gran Cono crater*

By far the biggest draw at Vesuvius is the experience of hiking around the crater, or Gran Cono, the highest point of the volcano. To hike to the crater, start with a drive or bus ride to the parking lot located at about 3,280 ft (1,000 m) elevation. Parking can be booked in advance (www.parkingsuvio.it; from €3). Be sure to purchase a ticket (€12 per person) in advance and then enter the e-gate to access the pathway up to the crater. The steep and rocky pathway zigzags up to the edge of the crater. The path up is not shaded at all and rugged in parts, but there are plenty of spots to stop and rest. Along the way, look over to the peak on the other side of the volcano; it rises to 4,203 ft (1,281 m) and the lava flow from the 1944 eruption is visible in the valley below.

Once you're at the top, the pathway levels out and opens to great views down into the crater and panoramic views over the entire Naples area south to the Sorrentine Peninsula, and on a clear day to the islands of Capri, Ischia, and Procida in the Gulf of Naples. Along the crater you'll find an information and services booth where you can get more details on the volcano (available in English). Enjoy exploring the crater area and walking along the rocky pathway leading around a long section of the crater. The pathway has wooden fences along either side and is a good vantage point to look down into the steep slopes of the crater. The hike up takes 20-30 minutes, depending on the number of photo stops or breaks you take. Plan to spend at least that long visiting the crater before doubling back on the same pathway for the 20-30-minute walk down. Mornings are the best time to visit the crater, as the view over the Gulf of Naples tends to be clearer, and in the summer you can avoid the midday heat. To avoid having to rush, be sure to park in the lot area 1.5-2 hours before the park closes.

Keep in mind that the temperature at the summit can be quite cool, so it's a good idea to bring layers, even in the summer. Services are quite limited, so be sure to bring water and sunscreen. Comfortable footwear is strongly recommended for the climb, but hiking boots are certainly not required. Note that the summit of Mount Vesuvius can be closed due to adverse weather conditions. To find out in advance if the crater is open, call the Parco Nazionale del Vesuvio for information (tel. 081/865-3911).

FOOD
Kona
Contrada Osservatorio, Ercolano; tel. 081/777-3968; ristorantekona@gmail.com; 11:30am-6pm daily, dinner 7pm-11pm Fri.-Sun. May-Sept.; €8-15

Located along the road leading from the town of Ercolano up the slopes of Vesuvius, this restaurant is a convenient stop for a pizza or hearty lunch while you're driving to the crater. There's a large dining area with indoor and outdoor seating and great views. The service is friendly and welcoming, and you can't go wrong with either the pizza or menu with traditional first- and second-course options. Set menus feature plenty of seafood and other choices.

GETTING THERE
Vesuvius is located about 6 mi (9.7 km) from Naples, 5 mi (8 km) from Pompeii, and 4.3 mi (7 km) from Herculaneum. The volcano is a popular day trip often combined with a visit to Pompeii or Herculaneum. Given the expanse of the park, a car is by far the most convenient way to reach the Gran Cono and explore the area. If you aren't driving while visiting the area, see the tours suggested at the opening of this chapter for suggestions on small group and private tours that include transportation and can be combined with a visit to Pompeii or Herculaneum.

By Train
The **Circumvesuviana** train (www.eavsrl.it)

path on Mount Vesuvius

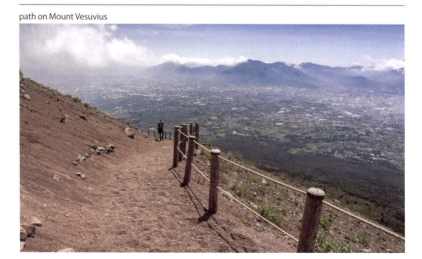

stops at both the Pompeii and Herculaneum archaeological sites, where you can then connect to buses to reach the nearest point of the summit of Vesuvius before continuing on foot.

By Bus

From Pompeii, the public bus company **EAV** (www.eavsrl.it; 1 hour; departures every 50 minutes Apr.-Sept.; €3.10) operates a bus line during high season connecting Pompeii with the Gran Cono of Vesuvius. Buses depart from the Piazza Anfiteatro with a stop at the Pompeii Scavi-Villa dei Misteri Circumvesuviana train station near the Porta Marina entrance. Tickets can be purchased on board. Buses run about 8am-4pm from Pompeii and return from Vesuvius to Pompeii about 9:30am-6pm. Buses can be very crowded at times and may be standing room only during peak periods. Be prepared for a bit of an adventure and plan to be patient with crowds and schedules if you choose this inexpensive way to reach Vesuvius from Pompeii.

There are also companies that specialize in bus transfers to Vesuvius. From Ercolano, **Vesuvio Express** (tel. 081/739-3666; www.vesuvioexpress.it; €30 including entrance to Vesuvius) operates a bus route departing from the Ercolano Circumvesuviana train station. The round-trip transfer includes free time to hike to the crater of Vesuvius. From Pompeii, **Tempio Travel** (tel. 081/536-9869; www.pompeivesuvio.info; from €49 including entrance to Vesuvius) offers round-trip transfers and tickets with departure from the Pompei Scavi-Villa dei Misteri Circumvesuviana station. From Naples, **Tramvia Napoli** (tel. 081/777-2347; www.tramvianapoli.it; from €12) offers daily transfers to Pompeii, Herculaneum, and Vesuvius or a combination of the sites.

By Car

From the **A3** autostrada connecting Naples and Salerno, exit at Ercolano and follow signs for Parco Nazionale del Vesuvio. The road begins to climb up Via Vesuvio. The setting, landscape, and views improve as you continue to drive up. The road winds its way to a small parking area at an elevation of about 3,280 ft (1,000 m). You must park in the paid lot there before continuing on foot to the ticket booth. Expect to pay around €5 to park.

Background

The Landscape.........372
Plants and Animals.....374
History 376
Government and
   Economy 384
People and Culture 385

The Landscape

Whether you're gazing out the airplane window at the distinctive humpbacked slopes of Vesuvius or admiring the rugged mountains of the Amalfi Coast from the ferry, the first sight of Campania is captivating. The coastline, mountains, and fertile fields have shaped the history of this region for centuries.

The landscape explains a lot about the rich history of this area: how culture can change within such short distances, why words are pronounced differently from one area to the next, and how culinary traditions have developed. Nature has been instrumental in the development

of Italy. The vineyards, olive groves, hilltop villages, and mountain ranges that define the region's geography have evolved over centuries while people have adapted to and transformed the natural setting. From the fertile land around Vesuvius to the islands in the Gulf of Naples, and the soaring mountain peaks along the Sorrentine Peninsula, it's a land that has fostered genius and civilization, and a landscape that is as memorable as the food, art, and people you'll meet.

GEOGRAPHY

Roughly the size of Colorado, the long, boot-shaped Italian peninsula was formed millions of years ago in the Cenozoic Era, when tectonic plates underneath Europe and Africa slowly collided and transformed the earth's surface. Over the past million years, alternating warm and glacial periods shaped the terrain and formed mountain ranges, valleys, lakes, and rivers along with geographic features as diverse as Alpine peaks, active volcanoes, hot springs, and desert-like settings.

The region of **Campania** is the third most populous of Italy and covers an area of 5,247 sq mi (13,590 sq km), with a coastline of about 217 mi (350 km) on the Mediterranean Sea. It is bordered by the regions of Lazio to the northwest where Rome is located, Molise directly to the north, Puglia to the northeast, and Basilicata to the east and south. Its coastline and two large gulfs are divided by the Sorrentine Peninsula, with the Gulf of Naples to the north and the Gulf of Salerno to the south. The Gulf of Naples is home to the islands of Capri, Ischia, and Procida.

Volcanic Activity

Perhaps the most defining geographic feature of Campania is **Mount Vesuvius,** the massive volcano that soars 4,203 ft (1,281 m) above the city of Naples and surrounding areas. The volcano is only a part of the Campania volcanic region, which formed some 34,000 years ago and stretches along the coastline west of Naples to the Campi Flegrei and to the islands of Ischia and Procida. This volcanic area comprises active, dormant, and extinct volcanoes. You'll observe hydrothermal activity, steaming craters at the Solfatara in the Campi Flegrei, fumaroles and thermal hot springs on Ischia, and fascinating bradyseism in Pozzuoli, where the level of the earth's surface has moved up and down significantly over the centuries.

This volcanic activity has long made the Campania area prized for its rich soil and productive farming. During Roman times the area was called *Campania felix,* meaning "fertile countryside" or "happy countryside." Agriculture is still an important part of the economy, both on a large scale in the plains around Vesuvius and on a smaller scale with the lemon production on the Amalfi Coast and small vineyards that produce high-quality wines throughout much of the region.

CLIMATE

The weather in Campania is a Mediterranean climate with warm summers and mild winters, which makes Campania an appealing travel destination for much of the year. Summers are hot and dry with abundant sunshine, while the spring and autumn shoulder seasons are excellent times to travel, to enjoy pleasant weather and avoid the heat. In early spring, March-April, the weather begins warming up, with occasional rain and temperatures ranging from lows of 43-46°F (6-8°C) to highs of 59-64°F (15-18°C). May-June temperatures are among the most pleasant, with lows of 54-61°F (12-16°C) and highs of 72-79°F (22-26°C). The hottest period is July-August, with temperatures ranging from an average low of 64°F (18°C) to an average high of 86°F (30°C). Warm weather continues in September, with only a slightly cooler average low of 59°F (15°C) and a high of 79°F (26°C).

Temperatures cool off in late autumn,

Previous: Atrani at night.

October-November, when rainy days are mixed with gorgeous sunny days. Expect average lows to range 45-52°F (7-11°C) and highs 63-72°F (17-22°C). Although winters are relatively mild in the Amalfi Coast area, temperatures drop to their lowest December-February, with average lows of 37-41°F (3-5°C) and average highs of 54-55°F (12-13°C). It's not uncommon for temperatures to drop enough for a dusting of snow occasionally on the top of Mount Vesuvius or along the mountains of the Sorrentine Peninsula. November-January is when the most rainfall occurs on the Amalfi Coast.

If you're planning a seaside holiday, the beach season begins around May and continues through October in most coastal areas. The sea temperatures are the warmest during July-August, with an average of about 78.8°F (26°C). The water can be a bit chilly in the spring and autumn months, yet on a sunny day that can be quite refreshing. June and September are also excellent times for swimming, as the water is on average about 75°F (24°C). Although there are some brave locals who swim year-round, the winter sea temperatures drop to an average of about 57-59°F (14-15°C) January-April.

ENVIRONMENTAL ISSUES

Italy's environmental concerns range from poor building practices in earthquake-prone areas to air and water pollution. Over the past decade, seasons have begun to stray from their clockwork patterns and people have started to recognize the greater variability. Summers aren't just hot, they can be excruciating, and local TV broadcasts advise viewers throughout July-August on how to avoid sunstroke and heat exhaustion.

A waste management crisis in the 1990s and 2000s also led to an epidemic of illegal toxic waste dumping in Italy, especially in a region northeast of Naples. Unfortunately, the practice is very profitable and difficult to stop. Harmful chemicals and other forms of pollution found in agricultural products from the region have raised concerns, from residents to international trade partners, that still persist to this day.

Plants and Animals

The diverse natural landscape of the Amalfi Coast area supports rich and varied wildlife and plant life.

TREES

The mountainous slopes of the Sorrentine Peninsula and the surrounding areas are home to thick forests with many different types of trees, including pine, oak, beech, and chestnut. The towns of Scala and Tramonti on the Amalfi Coast are known for their large chestnut forests. Occasionally, you'll also see palm trees and the iconic umbrella pines, introduced to the area in Roman times. The noci di Sorrento are a variety of walnut typically found on the Sorrento coastline, but they're cultivated in many areas of Campania.

Limone Costa d'Amalfi and Limone di Sorrento

Though citrus trees like mandarin and orange are also common in the area, the lemons of the Amalfi Coast and Sorrentine Peninsula are world famous. Two types of lemons are grown in the area, the limone Costa d'Amalfi and the limone di Sorrento, and these two varieties have garnered the IGP (Indicazione Geografica Protetta) status, which indicates a protected product unique to a geographic area. The limone Costa d'Amalfi is the Sfusato Amalfitano variety, which is noted for its tapered shape, very bright and medium-thick peel, and intense aroma. It is rich in essential oils and the pulp is juicy with a moderate acidic level, making it popular for use in creating the classic limoncello liqueur as well as in traditional cooking. These lemons are exclusively grown in terraced groves along the Amalfi Coast, with large groves in the Amalfi, Minori, and Maiori areas.

Along the Sorrento coastline you'll find the limone di Sorrento, a slightly smaller and more oval-shaped lemon compared to the Sfusato Amalfitano. The juice has a higher acidity level and is rich in vitamin C. The peels are also extremely fragrant and are used to create excellent limoncello and lemon sweets.

Olives

Olive trees are typical at lower elevations along the Sorrentine Peninsula and Amalfi Coast, where groves climb nearly vertically up and down terraces on the mountain slopes. Their silvery-green leaves are a common sight throughout the year. During autumn harvest you can spot the black and green nets placed below the trees to catch the olives.

PLANTS AND FLOWERS

The mild Mediterranean climate is ideal for plants and flowers, which grow in abundance in the Campania area. Wildflowers fill the mountainsides with color and their sweet scent starting in the spring. You'll see many varieties of orchids, as well as cyclamen, crocuses, freesias, lilies, poppies, valerian, lavender, honeysuckle, buttercups, geraniums, and even wild garlic. Bright bursts of bougainvillea in various shades of purple and pink dot the area along with delicate wisteria in the spring. Jasmine grows particularly well here and fills the early summer air with a divine scent. Along rugged slopes you'll see the characteristic wisps of green and yellow of the many broom plants. Herbs grow wild here, including rosemary, thyme, oregano, and sage.

Along the footpaths of the Amalfi Coast it's common to see wild cyclamen popping out of tiny crevices in stone walls or large caper plants growing in the most unexpected spots. Deep in the Valle delle Ferriere above Amalfi you may find the rare Woodwardia radicans, a giant fern dating back to prehistoric times.

Far easier to spot is the prickly pear, a type of cactus with edible fruit.

Grapevines and vineyards are common in the area, and they can be found in the most unlikely places. Along the Amalfi Coast, for instance, a vineyard may spread vertically along terraces with the vines trained to grow on trellises. Keen to maximize every inch of space available, growers often plant small vegetable gardens below the trellises.

MAMMALS

In the mountains of the Sorrentine Peninsula and inland in Campania, it's possible to find wild boars, foxes, and hares. However, you're more likely to encounter the mules and donkeys traditionally used as pack animals in the area. Outfitted with metal baskets to carry their loads—which in the summer may be tourists' suitcases—these beasts of burden clatter up and down the steps in long rows. Sheep and goats are also common; you'll hear the tinkling of their bells before you see them making their way along the mountainside. On Capri, wild goats occasionally pick their way carefully along the steep, rocky cliffs.

REPTILES

While out hiking, you're sure to happen across lizards and geckos sunning themselves or darting across your path. There are snakes in rural areas, most commonly long, dark, and nonvenomous, but keep an eye out for vipers, which have a triangular head, lighter color, and smaller size. They'll stay away from you and are only defensive when startled.

SEA LIFE

The Mediterranean is home to a variety of sea life. Occasionally, dolphins can be spotted jumping alongside boats, especially in the early morning. The Gulf of Salerno and Gulf of Naples are home to many different types of fish, from the tiny alici (anchovies) to large tunas in the deeper waters off the coast as well as squid, octopuses, and sea urchins. While swimming, you might run into a medusa (jellyfish), an unpleasant experience but not dangerous. Locals are keen to spot jellyfish and will likely alert you if they have been seen in the area. If you are stung, you can find creams or lotions that offer relief at any local farmacia (pharmacy).

BIRDS

The cry of seagulls is a familiar sound in the coastal regions, where you'll see colonies perched on rocks along the shore or high atop rugged cliffs on the islands. It's also not unusual to see falcons and other birds of prey gently gliding through the air. At night, you may hear the calls of owls, especially in the mountaintop villages of the Amalfi Coast.

Many types of migratory birds pass through the area in the spring and autumn, on the way to breeding grounds in northern Europe or winter nesting areas in Africa. Capri is a popular resting place; in 1904, Swedish doctor Axel Munthe bought the entire mountain above his Villa San Michele in Anacapri to protect and study the native and migratory birds that stopped to rest on the island. The Capri Bird Observatory at Villa San Michele still welcomes ornithologists who study and track migratory patterns on the island.

History

GREEKS, ETRUSCANS, AND ITALIC TRIBES
(8th-5th Centuries BCE)

Inhabited since Paleolithic times, Campania was home to many ancient Italic tribes and was colonized by the Greeks and Etruscans. **Greek** colonists founded some of the earliest settlements along the coast; the first Greek colony in the area was Pithecusa on the island of Ischia, founded by Greeks from Euboea around 775 BCE near the modern-day town of Lacco Ameno. From there, the Greeks moved to the mainland to found many cities, including Neapolis (modern-day Naples) around the 7th century BCE.

Farther south, Greek colonists from Sybaris founded Poseidonia (now called Paestum) around 600 BCE, and Elea (Velia) was founded by settlers from Phocaea in 541-535 BCE. Poseidonia became a thriving Greek city, building three Doric temples between 560 and 450 BCE that are still visible today, impressive as anything built in Athens and in much better shape.

Meanwhile, the **Etruscans,** the first major civilization to settle in modern-day Italy, began to spread throughout the center of the peninsula in the 9th century BCE and continued south to Campania, founding colonies in the inland areas like Capua around 600 BCE.

It wasn't long before Greeks and Etruscans battled over the coastal areas, along with the Osci, a local Italic tribe that had founded towns such as Pompeii along the coastline. The Etruscans lost two major battles to the Greeks in Cumae in 524 and 474 BCE. Much weakened, the Etruscans were unable to resist the Samnites, an Italic tribe of Oscan-speaking people, who expanded their territory from mountainous internal Italy toward the coast in the 5th century BCE. The Lucanians, another Oscan-speaking Italic tribe, moved into Campania from the south to conquer Poseidonia in 400 BCE, and the Samnites took Cumae in 421 BCE.

ROMANS
(4th Century BCE-4th Century CE)

The Romans began their expansion south in the 4th century BCE, meeting great resistance from local Italic tribes and especially from the Samnites. During the period from 343 BCE to 290 BCE, Rome fought three wars with the Samnites until the Romans finally took control of the area, including Neapolis. It took even longer, however, for the Romans to dominate the Samnites, who continued to rebel. By

273 BCE, Romans had arrived in Poseidonia, which they called Paestum.

Over the following centuries, Campania became fully Romanized. Roman ruins are still visible in Salerno, Sorrento, Capri, on the Amalfi Coast, and especially in Naples, where Roman ruins lie just below modern-day streets. Take a Napoli Sotterranea (Naples Underground) tour to literally walk along the streets of ancient Neapolis and see the ruins of markets, theaters, and more.

Lavish Villas

For the Romans, Capri had a particular appeal. Emperor Augustus (63 BCE-14 CE) was so enamored of the island that he started many large-scale building projects, finished by Tiberius, his successor, who ruled the Roman Empire from the island for the last 10 years of his life (27-37 CE). During this time, there were 12 imperial villas across the island. Today, only the ruins of a few remain. Villa Jovis, the largest, sits atop Monte Tiberio. The ruins of Villa Damecuta in Anacapri reveal a grand terrace where the emperor could take in fine views of the Gulf of Naples.

Wealthy Romans also built lavish villas along the Sorrentine Peninsula and Amalfi Coast. Brilliantly colored frescoes have been found below the Chiesa di Santa Maria Assunta in Positano, and you can walk through the ancient Villa Romana in Minori.

Roman Decline

The Roman cities of Pompeii and Herculaneum around the base of Mount Vesuvius thrived until the violent eruption of the volcano in 79 CE completely destroyed the cities. As the Roman Empire started to decline, much of the once-thriving agricultural plains in Campania were abandoned. **Constantine** (272-337 CE) moved the capital to Constantinople (modern-day Istanbul) in 312 CE, which led to the split of the Roman Empire. Though the eastern half survived for another 1,000 years in the guise of the **Byzantine Empire,** the west could not stop the Vandals, Franks, and Visigoths from pouring over the Alps in the north. The western Roman Empire officially came to an end in 476 CE, with some sources indicating that the last emperor, Romulus Augustulus, died at the Roman villa that once stood where the Castel dell'Ovo stands in Naples today.

Despite persecution, **Christianity** grew and eventually became an officially recognized religion. The first Christian temples that were built later formed the foundations (literally) on which the Duomo di Napoli and many other churches in the area were built.

MIDDLE AGES
(5th-13th Centuries CE)

After the fall of the Western Empire, Italy was subject to repeated foreign invasion from the **Lombards** followed by the **Franks** and **Charlemagne** (742-814), who was eventually crowned Holy Roman Emperor. The Lombards then moved south and vied for control of much of Campania. In the south, **Saracen** pirates landed in Sicily and Campania, and **Normans** built impressive fortifications. The **Byzantine Empire** continued to fight for control of the area after taking Naples in the 6th century.

Many battles for Naples, Salerno, and the Amalfi Coast areas were waged between the Byzantines and the **Goths,** invading from the north, until the Goths were finally driven out. Later, the Lombards arrived and took much of Campania, with the Byzantines only managing to keep hold of Naples, Sorrento, and the Amalfi Coast. Salerno fell to the Lombards in 646 and was absorbed into the Duchy of Benevento. Naples would continue on as an independent duchy under Byzantine influence until the 12th century.

Independent Republics

In the fray of the early Middle Ages many cities managed to form independent republics. Along with Venice, Genoa, and Pisa, Amalfi became one of the most powerful maritime republics of Italy. The peak of the **Duchy of Amalfi** stretches from the 10th to the 11th centuries, when the republic included much of the Amalfi Coast. As its trading ships crisscrossed the Mediterranean, traveling as far as Africa, Constantinople, and Jerusalem, this was the peak of wealth and culture on the Amalfi Coast. Many of the richly decorated churches and sprawling estates, like the Villa Rufolo in Ravello, date from this period. The Duchy of Amalfi was sacked by the Republic of Pisa in 1137, which was the beginning of the area's decline as powers shifted to the cities of Salerno and Naples. After a series of attacks, plagues, and misfortunes, the Amalfi Coast settled into a simple rural existence as the centuries passed.

Salerno grew in prominence during the late Middle Ages under the Lombards. After the Duchy of Benevento was moved to Salerno in 774, the city thrived as a center of culture and art, founding the Schola Medica Salernitana, among the earliest medical schools in the world. In 954, the relics of San Matteo (Saint Matthew) were brought to Salerno and the city's grand cathedral was built.

The relative stability of the area was turned on its head with the arrival of the Normans. From their first settlement near Naples, they would go on to conquer all of southern Italy over the next century. Amalfi fell to the Normans in 1073, and in 1076 they took Salerno, which became an important center for Normans in the area. Naples was the final territory in the area to fall to the Normans in 1139. Under the Normans, Naples was fortified with the construction of walls and the Castel dell'Ovo.

In 1194, power shifted in Naples and the south, from the Normans to the Swabians, the Hohenstaufen dynasty of kings from Germany. The period was not an easy transition for the population of Naples, who were highly resistant to their new leaders. Nevertheless, Naples began to grow under King Frederick II Hohenstaufen, who founded the University of Naples—the first state-run secular university in the West—in 1224. Yet after the king's death in 1250, the city revolted once again under Swabian rule.

ANJOU AND ARAGONESE RULE
(13th-15th Centuries)

The Swabian rule of Naples came to an end when Charles I of Anjou arrived in the city in 1266. The ruler of the French Angevin kingdom, which covered all of southern Italy and Sicily, Charles set about developing Naples as an intellectual and artistic European capital, efforts continued by his grandson, Robert of Anjou (1275-1343). Defending Naples was also key, and it was Charles I who built the Castel Nuovo along the waterfront in Naples; later Angevin rulers built the Castel Sant'Elmo in the hills above the city.

Religious Monuments

Grand building plans during this period weren't limited to castles. The Gothic Complesso Monumentale di Santa Chiara religious complex was built under Angevin rule; inside are a number of chapels and tombs, including that of King Robert of Anjou. Other Gothic masterpieces in Naples include the Duomo di Napoli cathedral, the Complesso Monumentale di San Lorenzo Maggiore, and the Chiesa di Santa Maria Donnaregina Vecchia with its marvelous frescoes inspired by Giotto.

Power Shifts and Cultural Growth

In the early 15th century, the Angevin dynasty's internal family squabbles led the Aragonese to attempt an attack. After a bloody battle, Alfonso of Aragon conquered Naples in 1442, arriving triumphant in early 1443. Aragonese rule only lasted a little over half a century, though, and was marked by near constant turmoil. The Aragonese rulers were widely disliked, but it was a vibrant period for the arts and learning, attracting notable Renaissance poets and painters to the city. In addition to enlarging the Castel dell'Ovo in Naples, the Aragonese expanded the Castello Aragonese on Ischia, connecting the castle to the island with a stone bridge.

Though the Aragonese controlled much of the Campania area, Salerno and its territory came under the rule of the Princes of Sanseverino, feudal lords who controlled the area starting in the 14th century. The wealthy lords were pulled into the battle between the Angevin and Aragonese rulers, taking sides back and forth between the two, depending on what was most beneficial for Salerno.

SPANISH RULE
(16th-17th Centuries)

By the end of the 15th century, both France and Spain were vying for the Kingdom of Naples. The French first took control in 1501 but power passed to the Spanish King Ferdinand III by 1504. This began about 200 years of Spanish rule, largely under the Hapsburg dynasty, with Naples governed by a series of viceroys. One of the most notable was Pedro Álvarez de Toledo, viceroy from 1532 to 1552. Known for urban planning initiatives like expanding the city walls, constructing Via Toledo, and building the tightly packed residential area to house the Spanish troops (still called the Quartieri Spagnoli or Spanish Quarter), he was also a harsh ruler.

Growth of Naples

Nevertheless, under Spanish rule Naples very quickly grew into one of the largest cities in Europe. Overcrowding and poverty became significant issues. However, the 17th century was one of the peak moments of art and architecture for Naples. Many fine churches and monasteries were built in the lavish Neapolitan baroque style, and Cosimo Fanzago (1591-1678) was one of the most notable architects of the day. The first truly Neapolitan school of painting began in the early 17th century, largely inspired by the work of Caravaggio (1571-1610), who spent a short time in the city and gifted it with masterpieces like *The Seven Works of Mercy* at the Pio Monte della Misericordia. Neapolitan artists, such as Battistello Caracciolo (1578-1635), Luca Giordano (1634-1705), and Francesco Solimena (1657-1747), to mention only a few, were hard at work decorating all of the new churches built during the period.

The Spanish rule was also punctuated by a series of revolts to oppressive taxes. A 1647 uprising led by young fisherman Tommaso Aniello (called Masaniello, 1620-1647) turned into a citywide uprising that lasted until the leader's assassination on July 16, 1647. Capitalizing on the disorder, the French attempted to take back Naples, but by 1648 order was restored under a new Spanish viceroy.

By the second half of the 17th century, the Kingdom of Naples was falling apart. In 1656, the plague hit Naples and Campania in full force, killing more than half of the population in Naples alone. A strong earthquake in 1688 caused significant destruction in the historic center of Naples, setting the city's recovery back even more. Outside Naples, Salerno finally passed from the last descendants of the Sanseverino family to the Kingdom of Naples.

THE BOURBONS
(18th Century)

After the tumultuous Spanish period, the 1700s brought great changes to Naples. During the War of the Spanish Succession (1701-1714), as the Austrian Habsburg and Bourbon families fought over the Spanish Empire, Naples was ceded to Austria in 1707. The Austrian viceroyalty rule lasted only until 1734 when the Bourbon king Charles VII (future Charles III, King of Spain) conquered Naples and set about transforming it into a European capital. Grand urban plans and a focus on public works marked the Bourbon era in Naples and the surrounding areas.

Under Charles VII, and later his son Ferdinand IV, the arts flourished along with new industries like silk production at the Real Borgo di San Leucio and the prized porcelain of the Real Fabbrica di Capodimonte (Capodimonte Royal Factory). During this period, the Teatro di San Carlo became one of the most celebrated opera houses in Europe. In the hills above the city center, the grand museum known as the Museo e Real Bosco di Capodimonte was developed as a palace, home to the royal art collection. The finest Bourbon addition to Naples is the grand Reggia di Caserta, built to rival Versailles.

Rediscovering Pompeii and Herculaneum

During Bourbon rule, Herculaneum was accidentally rediscovered in the construction of yet another royal residence. The first real exploration of the archaeological site began in 1738. In 1748 Pompeii was rediscovered after an intentional search for the ancient city. The treasures uncovered were highly valued by the kings of Naples and extremely influential to the neoclassical movement.

Naples garnered attention across Europe, and the first tourists began to arrive on the Grand Tour, a popular tour across Europe that was an integral part of an aristocratic and upper-class education in the 18th century. After visiting Florence, Venice, and Rome, many travelers continued to Naples to appreciate the fine music, art, and cultural experiences, as well as to marvel at the ancient temples in Paestum and walk among the ruins of Pompeii and Herculaneum. Many travelers would continue on to Sorrento during this period, drawn by the romantic views across the Gulf of Naples and artisan traditions like intarsia (inlaid woodwork). A few travelers also braved the boat ride or mountainous journey to visit villages on the Amalfi Coast, which were still extremely isolated. By the early 1800s, especially after the rediscovery of the Grotta Azzurra in 1826, Capri's allure as an international travel destination had begun.

PARTHENOPEAN REPUBLIC AND UNIFICATION
(19th Century)

At the end of the 18th century, the wave of revolutionary ideas of the French Revolution arrived in Naples. When Marie Antoinette—who was the sister of King Ferdinand IV's wife Maria Carolina—was beheaded in 1793, the revolution became personal to the Bourbon rulers of Naples. After battling with the French, the king and queen escaped to Palermo and left Naples to the French, who established the Parthenopean Republic in 1799. This was a short-lived moment of confusion, which ended after only 6 months when a counterrevolution led by the Bourbons ousted the republic and brutally executed republican sympathizers.

Despite the return of the Bourbon monarchy, the beginning of the 19th century in Naples was a period of turmoil. The French returned in 1805, this time more successfully. In 1806, Napoleon made his brother Joseph Bonaparte king of Naples, a role that was passed to Napoleon's brother-in-law Joachim Murat in 1808. The French were never fully embraced by the Neapolitans, and when the French lost power in 1815, the Neapolitans welcomed Ferdinand IV back to rule as Ferdinand King of the Two Sicilies.

Resurgence and Restoration

The Bourbon family continued to rule Naples for first half of the 19th century, a period of great unrest in Naples, when a nationalist movement, known as the **Risorgimento** (Resurgence), began to spread across Italy, aiming to unite the peninsula against foreign domination. **Giuseppe Garibaldi** (1807-1882) was one of the movement's great leaders, and southern Italy posed a major hurdle to unification. The **Kingdom of the Two Sicilies** was overseen by Bourbon monarchs who ruled from their capital in Naples. Garibaldi set off from Genoa with a ragtag team of volunteers who were able to capture Palermo and the rest of Sicily with little violence. Campania was tougher, but the Bourbons eventually surrendered Naples, and the Kingdom of the Two Sicilies was incorporated into the Kingdom of Italy.

The period of post-unification in Naples saw widespread poverty in the densely populated city center. A terrible cholera epidemic in 1884 led to a massive urban renewal plan, called the **Risanamento** (Restoration). Streets were widened and entire neighborhoods were demolished and rebuilt in an attempt to revitalize the city. Large-scale building projects like the Galleria Umberto I date from this period, as well as the city's first funicular train to the Vomero neighborhood of Naples.

WORLD WAR I
(1914-1919)

Newly united Italian citizens were challenged by the tumultuous onset of World War I, with leaders and the intelligentsia divided on which side to join, until the Allies offered to expand the country's territory into lands that were then under Austrian control. Predicting a short conflict, Italy did little to prepare, equip, or train its army and its leadership, leading to a major defeat at the 1917 **Battle of Caporetto.** The ensuing campaign against the Germans and Austro-Hungarians was long, bloody, and of little strategic import, with more than 650,000 Italians dead and more than a million wounded by 1919.

FASCISM
(1920-1945)

In the grim postwar period, droves of Italians emigrated to the United States, Argentina, and Australia, many embarking from Naples. Conditions for those who remained were poor, with little food and much discontentment with the unfulfilled promises of war. The Russian revolution caused a stir among workers worldwide, including in Italy, and frustration against the liberal government grew.

Amid the unrest, **Benito Mussolini** (1883-1945), a former Socialist Party newspaper editor, came to prominence, spreading fascism that relied heavily on widely circulated, successful propaganda. Mussolini announced a march on Rome in October 1922, and in response, King Emmanuel III promoted him to prime minister. It wasn't long before the fascists turned Italy into a virtual dictatorship. Large-scale public works projects kept workers employed, and propagandized cinema and radio glorified Mussolini's achievements. In Naples, the Palazzo delle Poste, which still serves as the main post office, was built 1928-1936 in the sleek rationalist style typical of fascist architecture. The Stazione Marittima in the port also dates from this period and was part of the fascist regime's plan to increase the productivity and importance of the port of Naples in Mediterranean trade.

WORLD WAR II
(1939-1945)

Under Mussolini, Italy invaded Ethiopia and sided with Francisco Franco in the Spanish Civil War, leading to an ill-fated alliance with Hitler in World War II. Once again unprepared, Italy's military and civilian casualties were greater than during World War I, suffering demoralizing defeats in North Africa and the Balkans.

By the time US and British troops landed in Sicily in July 1943, Mussolini and the Axis powers' decline was evident, but Germany wasn't ready to give up the fight, brutally struggling against Allied advances up the peninsula after the **Landing of Salerno** on September 9, 1943. After a 4-day popular uprising in Naples against German forces, the allied troops arrived on October 1 for the **Liberation of Naples.**

The Most-Bombed City in Italy

Naples suffered significant damage from allied bombing during World War II, with more than 200 air strikes 1940-1944, making it the most-bombed Italian city of the war. The approximate civilian toll ranges 20,000-25,000. During bombing raids, the city's residents fled to the underground areas of the city, which can now be visited on Napoli Sotterranea (Naples Underground) tours. To cap it all off, Mount Vesuvius erupted in 1944 (its last major eruption), destroying towns around the volcano as well as planes from the United States Army Air Forces (USAAF) 340th

Historical Timeline

8th century BCE	Greek settlers arrive on Ischia.
7th century BCE	Greek city of Neapolis (modern-day Naples) is founded.
474 BCE	First castle is built on the site of Castello Aragonese in Ischia.
560-450 BCE	Three large Greek temples are built in Paestum.
3rd century BCE	Romans arrive in Campania and establish settlements.
27-37 CE	Emperor Tiberius rules Roman Empire from his lavish Villa Jovis on Capri.
79 CE	Violent eruption of Mount Vesuvius destroys Roman cities of Pompeii and Herculaneum.
5th century	Campania area is ruled by Byzantines, Goths, and Lombards.
9th century	The Schola Medica Salernitana, the first medical school of its kind, is founded in Salerno.
954	Relics of San Matteo (Saint Matthew) arrive in Salerno and construction of the cathedral already underway is ramped up.
10th-11th centuries	The Republic of Amalfi reaches its peak.
1057	Bronze doors of the Duomo di Amalfi are cast in Constantinople.
1139	Naples becomes part of the Norman kingdom that already includes Amalfi and Salerno.
1208	Relics of Sant'Andrea (Saint Andrew) arrive in Amalfi.
1266	Angevin dynasty gains control of Naples.
1343	Massive tsunami hits Amalfi and destroys much of the town.
1442	Alfonso of Aragon conquers Naples and begins the Aragonese dynasty in Naples.
1504	Naples becomes a colony of Spain and two centuries of Spanish rule begin.
1558	Sorrento is sacked by Barbary pirates.
1647	Masaniello leads revolution in Naples against Spanish rule.
1734	Bourbon dynasty begins in the Kingdom of Naples.

Bombardment Group, based near Naples at the time.

The **Surrender of Caserta** was signed at Reggia di Caserta on April 29, 1945. This written agreement ended the Italian campaign of World War II and formalized the surrender of German forces in Italy.

POSTWAR AND CONTEMPORARY TIMES
(1946-Present)

A 1946 referendum was held to decide whether the Italian government would be a monarchy or a democracy. A majority of Italians voted for democracy (although Naples as a city voted

1737	Teatro di San Carlo opens in Naples.
1738	Herculaneum is rediscovered, and 10 years later Pompeii is found again.
1752	Construction begins on the massive Reggia di Caserta royal palace.
1799	Parthenopean Republic established after bloody revolution in Naples.
1815	Bourbons take back control of Naples.
1835	Construction begins on the Amalfi Coast Road.
1861	Italian city-states and regions unify into a single nation governed by a constitutional monarchy.
1883	Earthquake on Ischia causes severe destruction in town of Casamicciola Terme.
1886	A school dedicated to teaching the inlaid woodwork tradition opens in Sorrento.
1943	Operation Avalanche, also known as the Landing of Salerno, during World War II takes place on September 9.
1943	Naples is liberated from German occupation September 27-30.
1945	The Surrender of Caserta is signed at the Reggia di Caserta on April 29, ending the Italian campaign of World War II.
1946	Italians choose to become a democratic republic in national referendum.
1953	John Steinbeck writes influential essay on Positano for *Harper's Bazaar*.
1962	First Lady Jacqueline Kennedy spends a summer vacation on the Amalfi Coast and visits Capri.
1987	Napoli soccer team wins the scudetto (Coppa Campioni d'Italia) and the Coppa Italia with Diego Maradona on the team.
1988	Russian dancer Rudolf Nureyev buys the Li Galli islands off of Positano.
1997	The Amalfi Coast, Pompeii, Herculaneum, and the Reggia di Caserta are listed as UNESCO World Heritage Sites.
2010	The Auditorium Oscar Niemeyer is inaugurated in Ravello.
2022	Island of Procida is named the Italian Capital of Culture.
2023	After 36 years, the Napoli soccer team wins the scudetto again.

for the monarchy), leading to the adoption of a new constitution and the establishment of the **Italian Republic.** Italy's recovery from the war was slow, and Naples had a significant uphill battle to rebuild from the extensive damage. However, by the late 1950s and 1960s, Naples, along with much of Italy, began a period of growth. In many parts of Naples, especially the Posillipo area, indiscriminate unchecked building was a widespread problem. Postwar recovery was also hindered by the Camorra, the mafia of Naples and Campania. Industrialization was slower in Naples than in other areas as well, which led to high unemployment and mass emigration, this time mostly to the north of Italy and throughout Europe.

Largely untouched by the war, the Amalfi Coast and island of Capri quickly became popular tourist destinations in the 1950s and 1960s. Capri offered the epitome of the La Dolce Vita, attracting the jet-set crowd of movie stars, royalty, and other rich celebrities.

Starting in the 1990s, political leaders in Naples began a war on corruption and criminality as well as a focus on preserving and enhancing the historic treasures of Naples and Campania. The region has seen a remarkable transformation and is now one of Italy's top tourist destinations. The Naples public transportation network continues to be improved, along with large pedestrian-only areas in the historic center. Initiatives like the Grande Progetto Pompeii (Great Pompeii Project), dedicated to preservation, management, and new archaeological excavations, have invigorated the interest in the region's heritage and improved the visitor experience.

Government and Economy

GOVERNMENT

Campania is divided into five provinces: Avellino, Benevento, Caserta, Salerno, and Naples. The city of Naples serves as the capital for the entire region. Italian government can appear enigmatic to visitors, and it often is to Italians as well. While Rome is the seat of the Italian government, all regional legislation takes place in Naples. The president of Campania governs the region along with the Regional Council of Campania (Consiglio Regionale della Campania). Elected in 2015, Vincenzo De Luca is currently serving his second 5-year term as president of Campania after his reelection in 2020. A member of the Partito Democratico (Democratic Party), De Luca continues in Campania's generally more center-left political tradition.

ECONOMY

Italy's economy is the world's 10th largest, with a GDP of $2 trillion. Although the region of Campania ranks seventh in terms of the national GDP, the average per capita income is one of the lowest in Italy. Unemployment hovers around 18 percent, which is among the highest in Italy and double the national average. The economy is mainly fueled by the agricultural and food sector and mechanical industries, with the largest industrial areas around Naples. As one of the most visited destinations in Italy and home to significant UNESCO World Heritage Sites, tourism forms an important part of Campania's economy, especially in the Naples, Capri, and Amalfi Coast areas.

Industry

Campania's potential was noted even by its earliest settlers, referred to as *Campania felix,* or "happy countryside," by the ancient Romans. The fertile soil has long been a valuable resource, and agriculture is still an important industry, producing fruit, vegetables, nuts, and legumes. Many of the region's agricultural specialties are famous worldwide, and the food industry is extremely active, including canned tomatoes, pasta, and dairy. Carefully controlled and protected, buffalo mozzarella production is a thriving industry, with the cheese exported throughout the world. Campania is also noted for its wine, especially the internal provinces of Avellino and Benevento but also the Amalfi Coast, island of Ischia, and the areas surrounding Vesuvius.

Other industries include high-end automotive production, the busy shipyards in Castellamare di Stabia and Naples, and the aerospace industry. Naples is a major port for cargo transport and is one of the Mediterranean's busiest port cities.

Traditional crafts play a smaller yet integral part of the regional economy. Ceramics in Vietri sul Mare on the Amalfi Coast, the artisanal Nativity scenes in Naples, the coral carving tradition, and inlaid woodworking in Sorrento all play a vital role in the economy at a local level and keep the nation's "Made in Italy" movement going strong.

Tourism

Italy is the fifth most visited country in the world and attracted more than 74 million visitors in 2022. The Naples and Amalfi Coast areas in Campania are among the most popular destinations in Italy, with a notable increase in visitors every year. Cruise ships dock in the large ports of Naples and Salerno, while at Amalfi, Sorrento, and Capri, cruise ships drop anchor and tender travelers to shore. Despite the region being such a popular travel destination, overtourism is a concern, especially given the small size of many of the most popular towns and islands and the limitations of the existing infrastructure to handle the volume of visitors.

Some cities have been taking a deeper look at how to handle the mass influx of tourists. In 2011 the town of Amalfi opened a large parking area that was tunneled out of the mountain. In 2023 restrictions were placed on the Amalfi Coast to reduce the number of cars along the coastal road during peak season. Meanwhile, the island of Capri is revisiting ferry schedules and investigating other ways to help visitors get around the island more easily. Cultural initiatives like **Slow Tourism** are designed to address the impact of overtourism, encouraging travelers to slow down and get a deeper understanding of the places they visit.

People and Culture

DEMOGRAPHY

Campania is home to about 5.6 million people, making it the third-largest yet most densely populated region in Italy, which has more than 59 million inhabitants. Naples is Italy's third-largest city, with 3.1 million inhabitants. The average life expectancy is relatively high, 85 years for females and 80 for males, with a median age of 47.3 and plenty of people pushing 100.

IMMIGRATION

Until the late 20th century, Italy was often more associated with emigration than immigration. Today, foreign-born residents make up close to 9 percent of the total population, with the largest immigrant numbers coming from African countries (including Morocco), Romania, Albania, Poland, and China. Immigration from Syria and sub-Saharan Africa to Europe has become a crisis, leading to a wave of anti-immigrant sentiment and policy. Though Italians generally favor legal immigration, it's a hot political issue.

RELIGION

Roman Catholicism is the dominant religion in Italy, though the country is growing more secular. That doesn't stop almost every town from celebrating its patron saint with festivals each year.

Islam, Buddhism, and Orthodox Christianity are also growing in Italy. In Naples, the Jewish presence dates to the 1st century under Roman control of the city. The 15th-16th centuries brought much persecution, with all Jews being forced to leave in 1541. In the 19th century, the number of Jewish residents grew thanks to the thriving branch of the Rothschild family bank in Naples. Today there are only around 200 Jewish people in Naples.

LANGUAGE

Modern Italian derives from Latin. **Dante Alighieri** (1265-1321) was the first to codify and utilize the dialects spoken during the Renaissance, but there is a big difference in the accent you'll hear in the north and the one you'll hear in Rome and central Italy, or farther south around Naples and the Amalfi Coast. Dialects mixed with minority languages such as Sardo, spoken in Sardinia, and Friulano have led to colorful words and expressions that you won't learn in an Italian class.

Neapolitan

In Naples and much of southern Italy, your ear will pick up a highly expressive and unique dialect called Neapolitan. Though it's not officially a language and isn't taught in school, the dialect sounds distinctly different from Italian even though it shares a great deal of vocabulary. The pronunciation of Neapolitan is what largely sets it apart from Italian, although there are significant grammatical differences as well. The dialect can even be almost incomprehensible to Italian speakers. Yet one thing Neapolitans excel at is the use of highly demonstrative gestures, which is a seemingly integral part of communication in the area. Stay long enough and you'll likely find yourself gesturing to communicate as well. The Neapolitan dialect is indelibly linked with the cultural history of Naples, thanks to an especially rich musical, theatrical, and literary heritage that is still appreciated around the world today.

LITERATURE AND PHILOSOPHY

Naples and the surrounding areas have been important cultural centers since ancient Greek and Roman times. South of Paestum, the town Elea (Velia) was home to the Greek philosopher Parmenides, founder of Eleaticism, an important pre-Socratic school of philosophy that also counted philosopher and mathematician Zeno of Elea as a member. Naples was later a center of Epicureanism, a school of philosophy arguing that pleasure or happiness is the chief good in life. Writings by noted Epicurean philosopher Philodemus of Gadara have been uncovered among the charred papyrus scrolls at the Villa dei Papiri in Herculaneum.

Classic and Renaissance Literature

Roman writer and natural philosopher Pliny the Elder was among the many victims of the eruption of Mount Vesuvius in 79 CE that destroyed Pompeii and Herculaneum. His nephew, **Pliny the Younger,** wrote two letters to the historian Tacitus describing the eruption of Vesuvius and death of his uncle; the letters serve as remarkable pieces of historical evidence of the tragic events.

The Roman poet **Virgil** (70-19 BCE), author of the epic poem the *Aeneid,* is also associated with Naples, from the legend of the egg he placed below the Castel dell'Ovo to the mysterious allure of his supposed tomb west of Naples (in fact, it is not his tomb at all). Naples was a place of pilgrimage for other writers, including Dante Alighieri (1265-1321), Francesco Petrarca (1304-1374), and Giovanni Boccaccio (1313-1375), who lived there for years and used the city as the setting for *The Decameron* and later works.

Influential philosopher and theologian **San Tommaso d'Aquino** (Saint Thomas Aquinas) lived and worked in Naples at the Chiesa di San Domenico Maggiore in the 13th century. The city was also home to philosophers Giordano Bruno (1548-1600), Giambattista Vico (1668-1744), and Benedetto Croce (1866-1952), who adopted Naples as his hometown.

Contemporary Writers

The allure of Naples has continued to tempt many writers over the centuries. More recent examples include Neapolitan writer **Roberto Saviano,** who gained fame for his stories of the Camorra crime syndicate; and best-selling author **Elena Ferrante,** whose Neapolitan novels have captivated readers around the world.

VISUAL ARTS
Architecture
With its remarkable churches, royal palaces, and castles, Naples has an incredibly rich architectural heritage. It's a city that has, at many moments in its history, been a center of culture and arts in Europe. Below the street level today lie the ruins of the ancient Greek and Roman city, where you can walk down Roman streets and see ruins of markets as well as a theater where performances were once held. It is fascinating to explore on a Napoli Sotteranea (Naples Underground) tour. Above the ancient city, layer upon layer of history has created modern-day Naples, which is an intriguing blend of soaring Gothic churches and lavishly decorated baroque ones: all masterpieces of architecture, full of artistic treasures around every corner.

Greek and Roman Ruins
Beyond Naples, the greater region of Campania is home to many remarkable ancient architectural treasures. Just south of Salerno at Paestum you can see some of the best-preserved ancient **Greek temples** and explore the Greek and Roman ruins of the ancient city. The archaeological sites of Pompeii and Herculaneum offer the rare chance to walk through ancient Roman towns. The ruins of the Villa Romana in Minori and a Roman villa below the Chiesa di Santa Maria Assunta in Positano offer a glimpse into Roman seaside villas, and the ruins of Villa Jovis on Capri were once the lavish villa where Emperor Tiberius ruled the Roman Empire.

Fortified Cities
Centuries of turmoil gave the entire coastal region a great deal of defensive architecture, such as **watchtowers,** like Cetara's 14th-century Torre di Cetara. **Castles** are abundant in the area, from the Castello Aragonese in Ischia, founded in 474 BCE, to the 8th-century Castello di Arechi, high above Salerno. In Naples, three of the city's castles are easy to spot: Along the waterfront, the Castel dell'Ovo sits on a small islet where some of the earliest settlers of the city landed. The grand Castel Nuovo, dating from the 13th century, sits right on the waterfront, and its dark crenellated towers are an impressive site. High above the city, the Castel Sant'Elmo dates to the 1200s but has a unique hexagonal star-shaped design from the 16th century.

Gothic and Baroque Churches
The first of many extraordinary churches in Naples dates to the Angevin rule in the 13th century. The Complesso Monumentale di San Lorenzo Maggiore is a fine example of Gothic architecture. Many churches in Naples were remodeled during the baroque period, a time when creativity flourished and the city became one of the great centers of architecture in Italy. The work of Cosimo Fanzago (1591-1678) exemplifies the Neapolitan baroque style, including his work at the Certosa di San Martino, the Chiesa di San Ferdinando, and various sculptures in Naples.

Naples is full of baroque gems, and inside the Museo Cappella Sansevero, itself a jewel of baroque architectural design, you'll find the superb *Cristo Velato* (Veiled Christ) statue created by Giuseppe Sanmartino (1720-1793). From the end of the 1600s to the beginning of the 1700s, Neapolitan painter, sculptor, and architect Domenico Antonio Vaccaro (1678-1745) worked on many churches in Naples, including the splendid Chiostro Maiolicato (Majolica Cloister) in the Complesso Monumentale di Santa Chiara.

Many churches in the area were remodeled in the baroque style, including the Duomo di Amalfi and the Cattedrale di Salerno. Yet it's often the smaller churches that reveal architectural treasures, like the exquisite 18th-century hand-painted ceramic tile floor of the Chiesa Monumentale di San Michele in Anacapri, depicting the Garden of Eden, or the Chiesa del Soccorso atop a picturesque promontory in Forio on the island of Ischia, where you'll find votive offerings of sailing ships incorporated into the architecture.

Royal Palaces

As the capital of the Kingdom of Naples, the city is home to many splendid **royal palaces**. In the 17th century, Domenico Fontana (1543-1607) designed the grand Palazzo Reale on the waterfront in Naples, and later Ferdinando Fuga (1699-1782) added the lavish court theater inside. Next came a royal palace in Capodimonte, now the Museo e Real Bosco di Capodimonte, which was built in 1738 in the hills above Naples by the Bourbon king Charles VII as a royal palace for hunting. However, from the beginning it was also used to store the royal art collection, and today it is one of the finest art museums in Italy. Yet the jewel in the crown of royal palaces is the Reggia di Caserta, a masterpiece of 18th-century architecture designed by prominent architect Luigi Vanvitelli (1700-1773). It is one of the largest palaces in Europe, with 1,200 rooms and immense gardens.

The shift toward **neoclassicism** in Naples was greatly influenced by the rediscovery of the ruins of Herculaneum and Pompeii in the mid-18th century. Naples was at the forefront of this shift in styles, and classical influences, symmetry, and simplicity reigned in architecture and design. In Piazza del Plebiscito, the grand curved colonnade and the Basilica di San Francesco da Paola, inspired by the Pantheon in Rome, are the most striking examples of neoclassicism in the city. The Villa Pignatelli in Naples is a fine example of neoclassical residential architecture, including references to designs from Pompeii in its elegant facade.

Urban Renewal

The urban footprint of Naples was dramatically changed in the 19th century, during a period called the Risanamento (Restoration), a revival and regeneration of the city similar to large-scale urban renewal projects that took place in other cities across Europe. Streets were widened and old buildings were cleared and replaced with some of the impressive architectural sights of Naples today, such as the soaring glass dome of the Galleria Umberto I, built at the end of the 19th century.

A few interesting examples of **modern and contemporary architecture** can be found while exploring the Campania area, including the unusual Villa Malaparte on Capri, a striking red villa created by Italian writer Curzio Malaparte. In more contemporary times, the Auditorium Oscar Niemeyer in Ravello was opened in 2012 and is named after its Brazilian architect. The venue makes a bold and rare contemporary addition to the UNESCO World Heritage-protected Amalfi Coast. Not far down the coastline, the Stazione Marittima in Salerno, with its sleek roofline and smooth lines, was designed by Zaha Hadid and opened in 2016.

Painting

For a glimpse of incredible frescoes and pictorial decorations from the ancient world, a stroll through the ruins of Pompeii and Herculaneum is a one-of-a-kind experience. Many fine examples of frescoes uncovered at the archaeological sites are on display at Museo Archeologico Nazionale in Naples. You can go back even farther in time at the Museo Archeologico Nazionale in Paestum as you admire the Tomb of the Diver, a rare example of an ancient Greek burial tomb with painted figures.

The **Neapolitan School** of painting only began in the early 17th century. In 1606, Caravaggio (1571-1610) arrived in Naples, and though he only spent about 8 months in the city, his stay created a lasting impression on many artists of the day, including Battistello Caracciolo (1578-1635). In Naples, you'll find impressive works by Caravaggio, including *The Seven Works of Mercy* at the Pio Monte della Misericordia, *Martirio di Sant'Orsola* (*The Martyrdom of Saint Ursula*) at the Gallerie d'Italia (likely his final painting), and other works at the Museo di Capodimonte. In addition, you'll find many paintings in churches and museums in Naples by local artists who were inspired by Caravaggio's dramatic use of chiaroscuro, defined by its strong contrast between light and dark.

Also very active in the 17th century, the noted Italian painter Luca Giordano (1634-1705) was born in Naples and contributed his lively and particularly colorful style to many churches. Exploring the city's churches, you'll also find masterpieces by local artist Francesco Solimena (1657-1747), who was the most important painter in the 1700s in Naples. In addition to the churches in Naples, head to the Museo di Capodimonte to explore an extensive collection of paintings from the 13th-18th centuries.

By the 19th century, painting styles had become decidedly more naturalistic and romantic, and the **Posillipo School** of painters were drawn to the natural beauty of the Gulf of Naples. Domenico Morelli (1823-1901), a leading artist of the 19th century, was known for his fine historical and religious paintings. He was also an influential professor at the Accademia di Belle Arti di Napoli (Naples Academy of Fine Arts) and later its president. Morelli was the designer of the mosaics depicting the Triumph of Christ and the Twelve Apostles on the facade of the Duomo di Amalfi.

In the 1970s, the **Transavanguardia movement,** an Italian version of neo-expressionism, was developed by a group of artists in Naples, including Francesco Clemente and Mimmo Paladino. Visit the Madre (Museo d'Arte Contemporanea Donnaregina) museum in Naples to see fine examples of their work as well as pieces by other top Italian and international artists from the past 50 years.

Decorative Arts and Crafts

The creative talents of generations of artisans have always brought an artistic touch to Campanian daily life. A strong artisan tradition still thrives in the dramatic baroque-influenced **presepi** (nativities), still hand crafted in Naples, and the intricate **intarsia** (inlaid woodwork) in Sorrento. You can still walk down the Via San Gregorio Armeno in the historic center of Naples and see artisans at work creating Nativity figures. In Sorrento, the labor-intensive tradition of inlaid woodwork is passed down through generations; many examples of the craft are on display at the excellent Museobottega della Tarsialignea museum dedicated to intarsia.

Ceramic production is traditional in the entire area but is especially strong in the town of Vietri sul Mare on the Amalfi Coast. There you'll find streets lined with ceramic workshops as well as the Museo della Ceramica, a small museum dedicated to the history of ceramic production in Vietri sul Mare. Since ancient times, **coral** and **cameo** carving has been a tradition in the Gulf of Naples, especially in Torre del Greco, located between Naples and Pompeii.

Famous for producing European porcelain, Capodimonte flourished under Bourbon control of Naples. The Real Fabbrica di Capodimonte (Capodimonte Royal Factory) produced remarkable porcelain pieces 1743-1759, and many fine examples can be seen at the Museo di Capodimonte in Naples. After the Real Fabbrica di Capodimonte was transferred to Madrid, **porcelain production** continued to be a popular local craft throughout the 18th century. Some small factories still produce pieces in the Capodimonte style today.

MUSIC, THEATER, AND DANCE
Music

Nothing captures the spirit of Naples quite like traditional Neapolitan songs. The city's contributions to musical history began in the 16th century, when many important conservatories were founded. During the baroque period, Alessandro Scarlatti was the founder of the Neapolitan school of opera and was known for his operas and chamber cantatas. Known as the "conservatory of Europe," Naples was noted not only for its many important composers, such as Domenico Cimarosa, but also for attracting other famous composers like the young Mozart, who was smitten with the city, as well as Gioachino Rossini. Opened in 1737, the Teatro di San Carlo is the oldest continuously active opera house in the world.

Starting in the 1800s, traditional Neapolitan popular songs, called *canzone napoletana,* took center stage. Songs like **"O Sole Mio," "Torna a Surriento,"** and **"Funiculì Funiculà"** became internationally known and are just as popular today. Neapolitan tenor Enrico Caruso had great success in America and was an important ambassador of opera and Neapolitan song around the world. Later, the recordings of Renato Carosone had an international success with songs like "Tu Vuò fà l'Americano," which was later performed by Sophia Loren in the movie *It Started in Naples* with Clark Gable. In Naples, you can enjoy a live performance of iconic Neapolitan songs at Napulitanata (www.napulitanata.com).

Neapolitan music is popular throughout the region of Campania. On the Amalfi Coast, the town of Ravello is known as the City of Music, with a long tradition of opera and other musical performances. In 1880, German composer Richard Wagner visited Ravello, finding inspiration for the scenography for his opera *Parsifal* among the terraced gardens of the Villa Rufolo. A Wagnerian music festival started in the 1930s eventually transformed into the **Ravello Festival,** an annual summer music and performing arts festival.

Theater

There's one masked figure that you'll encounter often in Naples. This is **Pulcinella.** With a long nose and distinctive black mask, a baggy white costume, and often a pointy white hat, Pulcinella is a much loved and often mischievous character from the 17th-century commedia dell'arte theater tradition in Italy. The character of Pulcinella inspired many different iterations across Europe, most notably Mr. Punch, of Punch and Judy, in London in the 17th century.

Naples's theatrical heritage is equally rich. Eduardo Scarpetta (1853-1925) was one of the most notable theatrical actors and writers working in the Neapolitan dialect from the end of the 1800s to the beginning of the 1900s. He created an artistic dynasty that was continued by his son Eduardo de Filippo (1900-1984) and siblings, Peppino and Tatiana de Filippo. Eduardo de Filippo was active as an actor, playwright, screenwriter, and author, and is widely regarded for his artistic contributions.

Naples wouldn't be Naples without **Totò** (1898-1967), one of the country's most characteristic and entertaining actors, often considered the most popular Italian comedian of all time. Neapolitan through and through, Totò first gained success as a stage actor before appearing in many films from the 1940s-1960s, many of which are still regularly aired on TV. One of the classics is *Totò, Peppino e la Malafemmina,* featuring Totò and Peppino de Filippo and including the beautiful song "Malafemmena," written by Totò.

Dance

Popular throughout southern Italy, the Tarantella is a folk dance, and the **Tarantella Napoletana** is the traditional variation that is connected to Naples. Dating back to the 1700s, it's a lively and flirtatious dance typically performed by couples or groups of couples, and accompanied by tambourines and castanets. You can see performances of the dance in Sorrento at the Sorrento Musical Show at the Cinema Teatro Armida.

On Ischia in the small mountain town of Buonopane, the traditional dance **'Ndrezzata** is a fascinating folk dance that features 18 men dressed in traditional fishermen's costumes from the 17th century. The dance, accompanied by a song and rhythmic beating of wooden sticks and swords, is a tradition passed down from one generation to the next. You can see it during the festival of San Giovanni Battista on June 24 and on the Monday following Easter.

Essentials

Transportation

Transportation	391
Visas and Officialdom	396
Festivals and Events	398
Recreation	399
Food	400
Shopping	403
Accommodations	403
Health and Safety	405
Conduct and Customs	406
Practical Details	407
Traveler Advice	412

GETTING THERE
By Air
The **Aeroporto Internazionale di Napoli** (NAP; Viale F. Ruffo di Calabria; tel. 081/789-6111; www.aeroportodinapoli.it), also referred to as the Capodichino airport, is the Naples International Airport, located about 3.7 miles (6 km) northeast of Naples city center. Although it's not a large airport, it handles more than 10 million passengers a year and is the main airport for Naples and the region of Campania, including

travelers visiting the Amalfi Coast, Sorrentine Peninsula, and the islands of Capri, Ischia, and Procida.

From North America

Direct flights from the United States to Naples are very limited, but **United** (www.united.com) offers one or two daily direct flights from Newark to Naples during the peak travel season (late May-mid-Oct.). However, there are many daily nonstop flights from the United States to Italy, with most landing in Rome or Milan. There are many connecting flights daily from Rome and Milan to Naples. **ITA Airways** (www.ita-airways.com), **Delta** (www.delta.com), **American** (www.aa.com), **United** (www.united.com), and **Air Canada** (www.aircanada.com), along with their European partners, operate most of the flights from major North American cities to destinations in Italy, with connecting service to Naples.

From Europe and Britain

ITA Airways (www.ita-airways.com) operates most domestic flights within Italy to Naples. Direct flights to Naples are available from most major cities across Italy as well as from more than 110 European and international cities. There are many direct flights from London, Paris, Frankfurt, and Amsterdam via **Air France** (www.airfrance.com), **British Airways** (www.britishairways.com), and **Lufthansa** (www.lufthansa.com). Low-cost airlines like **EasyJet** (www.easyjet.com), **Vueling** (www.vueling.com), and **Ryanair** (www.ryanair.com) also fly to Naples from many major European cities.

From Australia and New Zealand

There are no direct flights from Australia or New Zealand to Naples or even to larger cities like Rome. **Quantas** (www.qantas.com), **Emirates** (www.emirates.com), and **Etihad** (www.etihad.com) operate daily departures to Italy from Sydney, Melbourne, and Perth. Most flights require a transfer in Dubai or Abu Dhabi, and total travel time is around 24 hours. Travelers from Auckland can transfer in Australia with these airlines or fly **Qatar** (www.qatarairways.com), **Korean Air** (www.koreanair.com), and **Emirates** on single-stop flights with transfers in Hamad, Seoul, or Dubai. You then have to catch a connecting flight to Naples. The low-cost airline **Flydubai** (www.flydubai.com), based in Dubai, offers direct flights from Dubai to Naples.

From South Africa

There are no direct flights from South Africa to Italy, but you can fly from Durban, Cape Town, or Johannesburg to Italy with **Ethiopian Airlines, Qatar, Emirates,** and **Turkish Airlines.** You can then take a connecting flight to Naples with those airlines' European partners.

By Train

Though Europe has a good train network, travel between countries can still be slow. There are daily overnight departures from Paris to Naples on the TGV high-speed train or the Trenitalia high-speed train; for the most comfortable experience, purchase a berth in one of the sleeping cabins. There are also many trains from northern European cities to Naples, often with a transfer in Milan or Rome. Single tickets can be purchased through www.trenitalia.it. A rail pass from **Eurail** (www.eurail.com) or **Rail Europe** (www.raileurope.com) can be worthwhile if you're traveling to many European countries.

Due to massive government investment in high-speed trains over the last 10 years, traveling to Naples or Salerno from major cities like Milan, Rome, Florence, and Venice is fast, easy, and convenient. Trains are comfortable, clean, have Wi-Fi, and food and drink is served on board. The state-owned **Trenitalia**

Previous: Amalfi Coast Road near Conca dei Marini.

(www.trenitalia.com) and private **Italo** (www.italotreno.it) both provide frequent daily departures to the Napoli Centrale station in Naples and to Salerno. The Trenitalia **Frecciarossa** (red arrow) service is slightly more expensive and frequent, making it popular with business travelers. Journey times vary significantly, depending on the type of train and number of stops or transfers, but the high-speed direct journey time to Naples is about 1 hour 15 minutes from Rome, about 3 hours from Florence, about 5 hours from Venice, and about 4 hours 30 minutes from Milan. Salerno's train station is also served by both Trenitalia and Italo trains, with the travel time 35-40 minutes longer than to Naples. Buy your tickets in advance online or at the train station.

Trenitalia also operates local and intercity trains throughout Italy. These are slower and make more stops, but tickets are fairly cheap, a very affordable way to reach Naples and Salerno from destinations across Italy.

By Bus

Buses are an inexpensive, if much slower, alternative to trains. **Flixbus** (www.flixbus.com) is the main company offering bus service to Naples and Salerno from many points throughout Italy, and more limited service to Sorrento. Buses seat around 40 passengers with one-way tickets starting as low as €4.99. Buses arrive and depart from near the Napoli Centrale train station and the airport in Naples, from Piazza della Concordia in Salerno, and from Corso Italia right outside the train station in Sorrento. All are equipped with free Wi-Fi, electrical outlets, restrooms, and baggage storage.

By Boat

Naples is one of the busiest ports in Italy, handling a large number of ferries, cruise ships, and commercial vessels daily. Many of the cruise ship companies offering Mediterranean cruises stop in Naples. Cruise ships usually dock at the Stazione Marittima. Naples is well connected by ferries from destinations across Italy, including Sicily and Sardinia, as well as destinations around the Mediterranean. Ferries from around the Gulf of Naples, such as Sorrento, Capri, Ischia, and Procida, arrive at either the Molo Beverello near the Stazione Marittima or the Calata Porta di Massa, where larger passenger and vehicle ferries from Ischia, Procida, and Capri arrive. Ferries from Ischia, the Aeolian Islands, and Ponza also arrive at the Mergellina port in Naples.

Farther south, Salerno continues to grow as a popular cruise ship destination. Ferry service also connects many ports around the Mediterranean to Salerno. Ferry service to the Amalfi Coast and Capri is also available seasonally April-October.

By Car

It's usually possible to cross the borders of countries that are members of the European Union without a document check, under the **Schengen Agreement.** But recent issues with immigration mean some governments have reinstated a bit more control. Entering Italy usually isn't a problem, but leaving Italy can be trickier as border officials check incoming vehicles.

Italy's autostrade **(highways)** are generally very good. Drivers collect tickets at booths as they enter the network and pay tolls in cash or credit, based on distance traveled, upon exiting. **Autostrade** (www.autostrade.it) manages highways and provides real-time traffic information in English. Signage should be familiar to international drivers; to review the rules of the Italian road, visit the **Italian Office of Tourism** (www.italia.it).

GETTING AROUND
By Train

Trenitalia (www.trenitalia.com) operates frequent train service between Naples and Salerno daily with travel times ranging 40 minutes to 1 hour 25 minutes, depending on the type of train. Salerno is the closest major train station to the Amalfi Coast. From the station you can catch buses to the Amalfi Coast or walk a short distance to the port nearby, where ferries depart for Amalfi Coast towns and to Capri seasonally April-October.

The **Circumvesuviana train** line operated by EAV (www.eavsrl.it) connects Naples with the archaeological sites of Pompeii and Herculaneum as well as Sorrento. The full journey from Naples to Sorrento takes about 60 minutes. This regional commuter train runs frequently throughout the day and is an inexpensive way to travel between Naples and Sorrento. To reach the Amalfi Coast from Sorrento, you can catch a bus right outside the Sorrento train station.

By Car and Scooter

Cars can be rented from **Avis** (www.avisautonoleggio.it), **Budget** (www.budget.com), **Europcar** (www.europcar.com), **Maggiore** (www.maggiore.com), **Hertz** (www.hertz.com), and other companies on arrival at the Aeroporto Internazionale di Napoli, from rental offices located near the train stations in Naples and Salerno, or with smaller local companies along the Amalfi Coast. **Skyscanner** (www.skyscanner.it) and **Kayak** (www.kayak.com) can help find the best rental prices.

Naples is famous for its chaotic traffic, and driving in the city is not for the timid. Given the extensive public transportation system, challenging parking, and the **limited traffic zone** (ZTL) in the historic center of Naples, getting around by car in Naples is not recommended. It's best to park at a supervised lot and continue to explore the city via public transportation.

The Amalfi Coast Road is known for its beautiful views and twists and turns. However, the road is not the easiest to negotiate, and parking is limited, so getting around the area by car can be more of a hassle than it's worth. Scooters are a popular choice because they're easier to maneuver along the winding road and are usually easier to park as well. With extremely narrow and busy roads, it's also not recommended to get around the islands of Capri, Ischia, and Procida by car. The small size of Capri and Procida make public transportation a good choice. Ischia is larger, and renting a scooter can be helpful for getting around the island. You'll find scooter rental agencies in many of the towns along the Amalfi Coast, as well as Sorrento, Capri, Ischia, and Procida.

Rules and Documentation

You'll need a **passport** and a **driver's license** if you plan to rent a scooter or car. (Specify automatic transmission for cars if you're unfamiliar with manual drive.) For US residents, an **international driver's permit** is not required but can help you avoid confusion if you're pulled over. It's available from **AAA** (www.aaa.com) for $20. The **minimum driving age** in Italy is 18. Police and Carabinieri frequently set up control posts along roads and randomly stop cars. The **blood alcohol limit** in Italy is 0.5, which is lower than in the United States and Britain (both 0.8) but is on par with most European nations.

Driving Tips

Whether you rent a car or a scooter, always get the maximum insurance. Anything can happen on Italian roads, especially the ones around Naples and the Amalfi Coast. Most cars have manual transmissions, so be sure to request or reserve an automatic if you're not comfortable tackling the mountains and tight curves of the Amalfi Coast with a stick shift.

In contrast to the relaxing atmosphere on much of the coast, drivers in the area are usually in a hurry. Passing is a very common practice, especially on the Amalfi Coast. If traffic seems to want to move faster than you're comfortable, find a straight section to slow down or pull over to let traffic pass. Naturally, if you're the one passing, pay extra careful attention to the curves, taking advantage of the mirrors placed on the side of the road in especially tight curves for guidance. Scooters, motorcycles, and cyclists can appear very suddenly around curves, so it's best for drivers who are unfamiliar with the road to go with the flow of traffic.

By Bus

On the **Amalfi Coast,** buses are operated by **SITA SUD** (www.sitasudtrasporti.it), with Amalfi as the central hub. The main lines run from Amalfi to Sorrento and from Amalfi to Salerno, with stops in all the towns along the way. Buses for Ravello and Scala depart from Amalfi. In Positano, an internal bus line operated by **Mobility Amalfi Coast** circles through the town's internal road and extends to the hamlets located in the mountains above.

For the **Sorrentine Peninsula,** buses are operated by both **SITA SUD** (www.sitasudtrasporti.it) and **EAV** (www.eavsrl.it). Within Sorrento, EAV runs four lines that circulate around the city, connecting main spots like Marina Piccola, Piazza Tasso, and the train station. To explore the Sorrentine Peninsula, **SITA SUD** buses run from the train station in Sorrento to Nerano, Marina del Cantone, and Sant'Agata sui Due Golfi.

On **Capri,** the island's small public buses are operated by **A.T.C.** (tel. 081/837-0420) and connect all the main points on Capri, including Marina Grande, Capri town, Anacapri, Marina Piccola, Punta Carena, and the Grotta Azzurra. **Ischia** and **Procida** are well connected via many bus lines that go to all the towns on the islands. All buses are operated by **EAV** (www.eavsrl.it) and offer an inexpensive option for exploring the island.

While you're in Naples, you can get around on public buses operated by **ANM** (www.anm.it). The large bus transit network covers the city center day and night. The **City Sightseeing** (www.city-sightseeing.it) hop-on, hop-off buses in Naples are often more convenient for reaching top sights in the historic center.

Tickets in all cities must be **validated** upon boarding the bus; this is done with a small machine located near the driver. Controllers do occasionally check passengers and will fine anyone without a ticket. Daily and multiday travel cards are available in most areas and can be more convenient and affordable than single tickets.

By Boat

Ferries are the most comfortable and scenic modes of transportation between destinations in the Gulf of Naples and Gulf of Salerno. **Travelmar** (www.travelmar.it) and **Alicost** (www.alicost.it) are the main ferry companies connecting Salerno, the Amalfi Coast, Capri, and Sorrento. On the Amalfi Coast, ferry service runs between Positano, Amalfi, Atrani, Minori, Maiori, Cetara, Vietri sul Mare, and Salerno. Amalfi and Positano serve as the main ferry terminals on the Amalfi Coast with the most departures daily. In Positano, **Positano Jet** (www.lucibello.it) also offers ferry service connecting Positano, Amalfi, and Capri. Ferry service is highly seasonal on the Amalfi Coast, running April-early November.

The Naples port (www.porto.napoli.it) is very large and offers frequent ferry connections to destinations around the Gulf of Naples, including Sorrento and the islands of Capri, Ischia, and Procida. Many different companies operate ferry service from Naples, ranging from high-speed jets to aliscafo (hydrofoil) and slower traghetti (ferries) that transport passengers and vehicles. **NLG** (www.nlg.it) operates jet routes to Capri, Sorrento, and the Amalfi Coast, while **Gescab** (www.gescab.it) has jet routes from Naples to Capri and Sorrento as well. **SNAV** (www.snav.it) operates lines to Ischia, Procida, and Capri. **Alilauro GRU.SO.N** (www.alilaurogruson.it) has routes connecting Sorrento and Capri. To transfer vehicles, you'll need to book through **Caremar** (www.caremar.it) for ferry service to Sorrento, Capri, Ischia, and Procida, or **Medmar** (www.medmargroup.it) for service to Ischia and Procida. Ferry departures are also available from the Mergellina port in Naples to Ischia with **Alilauro** (www.alilauro.it). Though ferry service is available year-round from Naples, the number of ferries daily is reduced during the winter months. Ferry service direct from Naples to the Amalfi Coast is very limited, but you can take a ferry to Sorrento and Capri and connect to ferry services to the Amalfi Coast; these are available seasonally (usually May-Oct.).

All ferries to Capri arrive in the island's Marina Grande port. Service is seasonal from Salerno, the Amalfi Coast, and the islands of Ischia and Procida, while it is available year-round from Sorrento and Naples. On Ischia, the island's main port is in Ischia town, with more limited ferry service to the towns of Casamicciola Terme and Forio. Procida is connected by frequent ferry service from Ischia and Naples, and all ferries arrive in the port of Marina Grande. Ferries to Ischia and Procida run throughout the year from Naples, while they operate seasonally during the summer from Capri, Sorrento, and the Amalfi Coast.

You can purchase tickets in advance online from most ferry companies, which is a good idea during the busy summer months. Tickets are also available to purchase before boarding from ticket booths in the ports.

By Taxi

In Naples, rather than hailing a cab from the street, you'll find them stationed at taxi stands near large squares, at the train station, and near the port, 24 hours daily. They are usually white, with signage that indicates whether cars are free or in service. You can also reserve taxis by phone; call the local companies **Taxi Napoli** (tel. 081/8888; www.taxinapoli.it) or **Radio Taxi La Partenope** (tel. 081/0101; www.radiotaxilapartenope.it). Taxis operate 24 hours, and vehicles for special-needs passengers are available.

Taxi fares in Naples are relatively high, especially on weekends and at night, calculated according to time and distance. It is not necessary to tip your driver. Fixed tariffs for popular journeys are set by the city of Naples and rates must be posted inside the taxi. However, it is essential to notify the driver before departure that you want the fixed-rate fare. The same goes for Capri, Ischia, and Procida, where you'll want to inquire about fares in advance in order to avoid a higher rate than expected upon arrival.

Taxis on the Amalfi Coast can be found in the center of most towns. It's important to note that taxis in this area function more like private transfers than a taxi, with costs much higher than a city taxi. Many cities have fixed tariffs determined by the city for journeys between towns on the Amalfi Coast, but some do not. If there are not fixed-rate fares, be sure to negotiate a rate with the driver in advance.

Visas and Officialdom

PASSPORTS AND VISAS
United States and Canada

Scheduled to launch in 2025, a pretravel electronic registration system (European Travel Information and Authorization System, or ETIAS) is planned for travelers from Schengen visa-waiver countries like the United States and Canada. Travelers will be required to apply for an ETIAS visa waiver before entering Italy. Check the official ETIAS website (https://travel-europe.europa.eu/etias_en) for the latest information. Apply well in advance to avoid any delays before your travel dates. The ETIAS visa waiver costs €7 and is valid for 3 years or until the end of the validity of your passport.

Also check that your passport is valid at least 3 months after your intended departure from the European Union.

EU/Schengen

Citizens from all 27 countries belonging to the European Union as well as citizens of the non-EU member states of the European Economic Area (EEA) and Switzerland can travel visa-free within the European Union. A passport or National Identity Card is all that is needed for entering Italy.

United Kingdom
After the United Kingdom's exit from the European Union, all UK citizens can enter Italy with a UK passport and an ETIAS (https://travel-europe.europa.eu/etias_en) visa waiver for visits of fewer than 90 days within any 180-day period. Check your passport in advance as it must be less than 10 years old and valid for at least 6 months beyond your travel dates.

Australia and New Zealand
Australian or New Zealand citizens who visit Italy for 90 days or less within any 180-day period in the Schengen Area (European Union) will also be required to apply for an ETIAS (https://travel-europe.europa.eu/etias_en) visa waiver. New Zealanders ages 18-30 can apply for a special working holiday visa at the Italian Embassy in Wellington.

South Africa
Visas are required to visit Italy from South Africa and can be obtained through **VFS** (www.vfsglobal.com). The application process begins on the website and requires stopping into one of the visa application centers located in Cape Town, Durban, Johannesburg, Port Elizabeth, and Pretoria. Getting a visa takes 2 weeks and there is a fee.

CONSULATES
The majority of foreign embassies in Italy are located in Rome. However, the **US Consulate General in Naples** (Piazza della Repubblica, Naples; tel. 081/583-8111; https://it.usembassy.gov/embassy-consulates/naples) offers passport and emergency services for US citizens. For emergencies, call the consulate at tel. 081/583-8111, which is a 24-hour hotline. For help with **lost or stolen passports,** you can apply in person for same-day emergency passports at the consulate in Naples. The consulate is closed during Italian and US holidays. For emergencies while abroad or to report lost or stolen passports, call the **US Department of State** (tel. 1-888/407-4747 from the United States, 1-202/501-4444 from other countries; 8am-8pm eastern time Mon.-Fri.).

CUSTOMS
Travelers entering Italy are expected to declare any cash over €10,000 and are prohibited from importing animal-based food products into the country. Duty-free imports for passengers from outside the European Union are limited to 1 liter of hard alcohol, 2 liters of wine, 200 cigarettes, 50 cigars, and 250 grams of smoking tobacco.

Bags are likely to be heavier upon leaving Italy than they were when you packed. US citizens are limited to return with $800 worth of goods deemed for personal use. Anything over that amount must be declared and will be taxed. Fresh fruit and vegetables, cheese, and animal-based products are not allowed into the United States. Further details regarding what can and cannot be imported into the country are available from the **US Department of State** (www.state.gov).

Canadian regulations are fairly lenient and allow cheese, herbs, condiments, dried fruits, baked goods, and candies; for a complete list, visit the **Canadian Border Services Agency** (www.cbsa-asfc.gc.ca). Australian regulations are particularly stringent, and customs officers go to great lengths to avoid contamination. All fruit, vegetables, and meat products are forbidden. Fake designer goods will also be confiscated and may lead to a fine. Consult the **Australian Department of Immigration and Border Protection** (www.homeaffairs.gov.au) for a complete list of items that need to be declared upon entry.

Festivals and Events

From moving religious processions to gastronomic events, festivals offer a unique chance for visitors to experience local life and traditions in Italy. There are many festivals throughout the year in this region. Here are a few highlights to mark on your calendar.

AMALFI COAST
Positano
Ferragosto

Aug. 15

While Ferragosto is a national holiday, it is also a religious festival celebrating the Assumption of the Virgin Mary in the main church of Positano. Watch the traditional processions and spectacular fireworks displays over the sea. **Maiori** hosts a similar celebration.

Festa del Pesce

Last Sat. in Sept.

Seafood enthusiasts will love the annual Fish Festival held in Positano on the Spiaggia di Fornillo.

Amalfi
Festival of Sant'Andrea

June 27 and Nov. 30

The biggest festivals of the year in Amalfi are dedicated to Sant'Andrea, the town's patron saint and protector. Don't miss seeing the incredible running of the statue of the saint up the steps of the Duomo di Amalfi at the end of the procession.

New Year's Eve

Dec. 31

Amalfi rings in the new year with a massive fireworks display over the harbor and music in Piazza Duomo that lasts well into the early hours of the morning.

Ravello
Ravello Festival

July-Sept.

Called the City of Music, Ravello hosts an important music and performing arts festival every year with concerts and other events.

Cetara
Notte delle Lampare

July

The town famous for anchovies hosts a food festival on the beach and re-creates the traditional fishing method of using light to attract fish after dark.

SORRENTO
Easter Holy Week

Good Friday

Easter is a major holiday in Italy, and in Sorrento you can see two impressive processions through town.

ISCHIA
Festa a Mare agli Scogli di Sant'Anna

July 26

A fun blend of tradition, folklore, and religious celebrations, this festival includes a boat procession and fireworks over the Castello Aragonese in Ischia.

NAPLES
Festa di San Gennaro

Sat. before the first Sun. in May, Sept. 19, and Dec. 16

The patron saint of Naples is celebrated three times a year with important religious festivals complete with processions and miracles.

Napoli Pizza Village

June

The traditional Neapolitan pizza is celebrated in this fun food festival that takes over the waterfront in Naples.

Recreation

HIKING
Outdoor enthusiasts will find plenty of hiking opportunities on the Amalfi Coast, Sorrentine Peninsula, and the islands of Capri and Ischia. Most walks are along stone steps and pathways, but you can certainly go deeper into the woods of the Monte Lattari, the mountains that run down the Sorrentine Peninsula. Hiking boots are not essential for most hikes in the area, unless you're doing serious hiking up into the mountains or are more comfortable with the support. For the walks and hikes included in this book, regular sneakers or athletic shoes with support will be fine. Most hikes include a significant change in elevation, so be prepared for a lot of steps and steep walking up or down. However, the fine views are a wonderful compensation for the effort.

BEACHES
The beaches are among the biggest draws to the Amalfi Coast and islands in the Gulf of Naples. Like the rugged and mountainous landscape, the beaches here are rocky and often tucked away in scenic spots along the coastline. Expect anything from small pebbles to larger rocks on the beaches instead of sand. A handful of beaches do have finer dark sand, but it's a good idea to pack water shoes or flip-flops to make walking on the beaches and wading into the sea more comfortable.

Going to the beach in Italy might be a different experience from what you're used to at home. Beaches are divided into two areas, one that is free and the other where you must pay to gain access. The free areas are called spiaggia libera, literally meaning free beach, where you can simply throw down a towel and enjoy swimming. However, if you see rows of sun beds and umbrellas neatly lined up, that is a stabilimente balneare, or a private beach club. To access those beach areas, you will need to pay to rent a sun bed and umbrella for the day. The rental also includes beach services that vary depending on the size of the stabilimente balneare, but usually you'll have access to changing rooms and showers. Most stabilimenti balneari will also offer snack bar and drink options, or even complete seaside restaurants. Given the rocky nature of the beaches, renting a sun bed and having beach services is certainly the most comfortable way to enjoy a relaxing day at the beach.

WATER SPORTS
Water sports are not as popular in the Amalfi Coast area as might be expected. Yet there are some great experiences to be had, and many are highlighted in individual chapters where water sports options are available. Kayaking is one of the best ways to experience the coastlines of the Amalfi Coast and Sorrentine Peninsula up close. Glide along the sea to discover little coves and beaches only accessible from the sea and to swim in secluded spots. To explore the undersea beauty of the region, there are scuba diving centers on the Amalfi Coast, Capri, and Ischia. Windsurfing is also possible along the Amalfi Coast with equipment rental and lessons available at beaches in Amalfi and Praiano.

Food

ITALIAN EATERIES
Restaurants

Sit-down eateries in Italy are usually known as **ristoranti, trattorias,** and **osterie.** Trattorias and osterie are often more rustic, older, and cheaper. More popular in Naples, an osteria has fewer items on the menu and rarely strays from tradition. While the style can change from seaside restaurants to city dining, a ristorante is often more expensive and elegant, with uniformed waiters, a wine cellar, and nicer table settings, with more likelihood to play with new flavors, ingredients, and variations on old recipes. Though continuous food service throughout the day is not the norm—usually all three types of eateries close between lunch and dinner—during the summer months on the Amalfi Coast and Capri, you can usually find a handful of restaurants in the main piazzas that are open from lunch through dinner.

Pizzerias and Street Food

With the strong Neapolitan pizza tradition, you don't have to go far to find an excellent pizzeria, especially in Naples. While pizza is on the menu in many restaurants, in Naples there are pizzerias dedicated just to making the classic wood-fired-oven pizza. In these iconic pizzerias, the menus will focus only on pizza and perhaps a few appetizer options. However, on the Amalfi Coast, islands, and remaining areas in Campania, most pizzerias also offer a variety of menu options.

The most popular street food in Naples also happens to be pizza. Both **pizza al taglio** (pizza by the slice) style and **pizza fritta** (fried pizza) are available in small food shops from midmorning onward. In Naples you can also find excellent friggitorie (fried food shops), which offer pizza fritta, fried pizza filled with a variety of options like ricotta and salami, as well as other typical fried snacks like frittata of pasta or fried rice balls. They make a tasty and inexpensive snack while sightseeing. In seaside areas, enjoy a cuoppo (cup) of fried seafood served in a paper cup with a slice of lemon to squeeze over the top.

Bakeries and Pasticcerie

Fornaio (bakeries) are often the first businesses open in the neighborhood, to supply locals with all types of bread, buns, and sweets, usually priced by weight. **Pasticceria** shops are entirely dedicated to sweets; they open early in the morning and remain busy until midafternoon. If combined with a coffee bar, they may be open all day and late into the night. The Neapolitan tradition of pastries is strong in the entire area, and there are unique varieties of cakes and sweets to be found from Naples to the Amalfi Coast and islands. In Naples, don't miss the classic sfogliatella, a shell-shaped pastry with flaky crust and citrus-infused ricotta filling. On the Amalfi Coast, try lemon-infused sweets like the delizia al limone, a cake with lemon filling and topped with a lemon cream. Procida is famous for its lingue di bue (ox tongues), a name that refers to the pastry's long oval shape. This puff-pastry dessert filled with lemon cream can only be found on the island. In Capri, you'll often find torta Caprese, a rich flourless almond and chocolate cake.

Coffee Bars

Coffee bars and cafés open nearly as early as bakeries; in the morning, locals come for an espresso or cappuccino and **cornetto** (croissant), a cheap and tasty breakfast. While at the coffee bar, remember that the counter service, where most locals eat and drink, is cheaper and faster. Sitting at a table to linger over your coffee and pastries will cost more than standing inside, but the experience may be worth it. If you're sitting at a **café** in Capri's Piazzetta or the Piazza Duomo in Amalfi, you can expect prices to be higher than what you'd pay at a small bar tucked away on a small street. In other words, you'll pay for the view and the atmosphere, and the tables outside are usually filled with tourists.

MENUS

Italian menus are divided into **antipasti** (starters), **primo** (first course), and **secondo** (second course), distinct and served in order. Antipasti are meant to whet the appetite; try local specialties like prosciutto and mozzarella di bufala (buffalo milk mozzarella) or alici (anchovies) fried or marinated, and share them with the table to try more options.

The primo, usually pasta or risotto, can be any of hundreds of traditional pasta shapes, served with vegetable, meat, or fish sauces. Pasta with seafood is featured at many restaurants, especially on the coast and islands. Risotto is often served with a simple yet beautiful lemon infusion, or with seafood and crustaceans.

While it's fine to order just one course, try to leave room for the secondo, which can include fish or meat. Typical **contorni** (sides), ordered separately, include grilled vegetables or roasted potatoes. It's worth checking out daily specials, often listed on a separate menu.

DRINKS

Italy is known for its natural spring water, which Italians drink more of per capita than any other people in the world. Water usually does not come free at Italian restaurants, and you'll be asked by your waiter whether you want **acqua** (water) **frizzante** (sparkling) or **naturale** (still), sometimes with a choice of brands (around €3 per liter). **Acqua del rubinetto** (tap water) in Italy is regularly tested by authorities and safe to drink, but will rarely be an option while dining.

Most restaurants have a decent **wine** list of local, regional, and international bottles. House wine is also generally very good. It can be ordered by the glass or in different-size carafes.

Most Italians end lunch with an **espresso** and usually conclude dinner with a **digestivo** (digestif). The latter is some kind of high-grade alcoholic spirit infused with a variety of fruits or herbs and reputed to help digestion. The most famous of these in the area is limoncello, a very strong lemon-infused liqueur. It is served ice-cold in small glasses and is sipped. Each area has its typical digestivo options to try, including other citrus fruits, wild fennel, or licorice liqueurs on the Amalfi Coast, and the rucola liqueur infused with arugula (rocket) made on Ischia. **Soft drinks** are widely available but are not often seen on Italian restaurant tables.

REGIONAL AND SEASONAL SPECIALTIES
Seafood

The Mediterranean coastal setting of the Amalfi Coast and surrounding areas means seafood is the top regional specialty. Yet that doesn't mean you won't find anything you'll like if you don't care for seafood or are vegetarian or vegan. The regional cuisine is divided into mare (sea) and terra (land), reflecting the sea and the mountainous setting as well as the strong agricultural tradition of Campania. The majority of dining spots, even ones specializing in seafood, will have primi and secondi options highlighting seasonal vegetables and meat as well.

If you do enjoy seafood, you are in for some excellent gastronomic experiences, as it is fresh and prepared in an unfussy way that highlights the natural flavors. You'll often find spaghetti or linguine with vongole (clams) or cozze (mussels). Pasta with freshly caught fish is another classic, as is grilled or baked fish for a second course. Cetara, a small fishing village on the Amalfi Coast, is noted for alici (anchovies), which are prepared in a variety of ways. Squid and octopus are also popular, and are served fried as an appetizer, prepared with pasta or potatoes, and grilled or stuffed for secondi. Even if you've not tried squid or even ricci (sea urchins), it's well worth stepping out of your comfort zone to try local seafood specialties.

Meat

Though Campania isn't particularly noted for its steak, like some other regions of Italy, you will still find nicely prepared beef on many menus. The local tradition, especially on the Amalfi Coast, leans more toward pork. The sausage is excellent, especially in autumn when it's served grilled with the seasonal broccoli. Rabbit is traditional on the islands of Ischia and Procida, especially on the slopes of Monte Epomeo on Ischia.

Vegetables and Legumes

Vegetables and legumes are important parts of the traditional Campania diet, especially when it comes to home cooking. Pasta with zucchini is a classic dish to try in Nerano, a seaside town near the tip of the Sorrentine Peninsula, and in many other towns on the Amalfi Coast. Pasta is also served with chickpeas, beans, and lentils. Some areas are known to combine mare and terra with dishes like a thick soup of cozze e fagioli (mussels and beans). Grilled locally grown vegetables are a popular antipasto, as is the famous parmigiana di melanzane (eggplant parmesan). Vegetables appear on menus very seasonally, from artichokes and asparagus in the spring to zucchini, eggplant, and peppers in the summer, and pumpkin and broccoli in the autumn. Other notable seasonal specialties include Amalfi Coast chestnuts, which are celebrated in the town of Scala with a food festival every October.

Pizza

Nothing compares to pizza in Naples, where it is truly a gastronomic art form. Be sure to try the classic pizza Margherita topped with tomatoes, mozzarella, basil, and olive oil. Or go even more traditional by enjoying the pizza marinara with tomatoes, oregano, garlic, extra virgin olive oil, and no cheese. Of course, you'll find plenty of options for toppings at most pizzerias. In Naples, you won't want to miss the pizza fritta (fried pizza). This is a pizza filled with a variety of different fillings, like ricotta and salami, which is then folded in half and fried. Forget the diet for the day—you're in Naples!

Lemons

No visit to the Amalfi Coast region is complete without trying the local lemons. It's an easy task since the famous lemons cultivated in the area are incorporated into many of the regional specialties. Squeeze lemons over your fresh fish or salad, enjoy traditional lemon desserts, and finish off your meal with a chilled glass of limoncello, a lemon-infused liqueur.

HOURS

Restaurants are typically open 12:30pm-2:30pm for lunch and 7:30pm-10:30pm for dinner; Italians tend to eat later, especially in the summer, waiting for the sun to go down and for cooler temperatures. Most eateries close one day a week, except during the peak of summer, and many take an extended break January-March in the coastal areas and islands. Reservations are a good idea to guarantee a seat, especially at popular eateries and during the busy summer season. Bakeries open before sunrise and close in the midafternoon, while coffee bars remain open all day long and pizzerias and gelaterie stay open late.

TIPPING

While tipping is generally not required in much of Italy, in the Amalfi Coast area it's traditional to leave a small tip. Rounding your bill up or leaving €3-5 behind after a good meal is one way to show appreciation. The other way to express gastronomic gratitude is with words. Italians are proud of their cuisine and compliments are always welcome. Note that it's not as common to add tips when paying by credit card at restaurants, so it's a good idea to have some cash on hand. Customers at coffee bars often leave a low-denomination coin on the counter. Tipping your tour guide, driver, or boat captain is also welcome when you've enjoyed your experience.

Shopping

Shopping is a fun local experience as the majority of family-owned shops are dedicated to one thing, like shoes, hats, books, clothing, or furniture, or materials like leather, ceramics, or paper. These shops are true treasures in Campania, where you can often see artisans at work painting ceramics on the Amalfi Coast, carving wood in Sorrento, or creating traditional presepe (Nativity) figures in Naples.

There are department and flagship stores in the center of Naples and Salerno, but they attract as many tourists as locals, who shop more at malls and outlets. If you're looking for luxury boutiques, you'll find them concentrated around Via Dei Mille in Naples and even more in the shopping haven that is Capri. From the Piazzetta down Via Vittorio Emanuele and along Via Camerelle, you'll find just about every name in high-end Italian and international fashion design.

SHOPPING ETIQUETTE

Italians entering a shop (or bar) nearly always greet shopkeepers with buongiorno or buonasera (good morning/good evening), and acknowledge them once more upon leaving with a grazie (thank you) or arrivederci (good-bye), whether or not they've bought something. It's certainly okay and even encouraged to browse in Italian shops, and shopkeepers are generally helpful, professional, and appreciate being asked how an object was made.

SHIPPING ITEMS HOME

If something larger than your suitcase catches your eye, stores, especially ones selling ceramics, can often arrange for shipment back to your home, usually for about 10 percent of the purchase price.

HOURS

Even more so than restaurants, family-owned stores and smaller businesses nearly always close in the early afternoon, as well as on Sunday and Monday morning. However, larger stores and those located in heavily trafficked areas have continuous hours. If you're shopping in Naples, Salerno, and on Ischia, plan on shops closing mid-afternoon for a break. However, if you're in Amalfi, Positano, Sorrento, or Capri, you'll find shops open daily and with continuous hours. If you're traveling off-season, many shops on the Amalfi Coast and Capri close for a period after Christmas through early spring, but the length of time varies from a couple of weeks to a month or longer. Just keep in mind that early January-March, many shops will be closed in those areas. This is not the case in larger cities like Salerno and Naples.

Accommodations

MAKING RESERVATIONS

The Amalfi Coast and Capri are among the most popular travel destinations in Italy, so accommodations fill up very quickly. Despite the large number of options on the Amalfi Coast, many hotels in the area can be fully booked well in advance. If you have your eye on a particular hotel for its features or views, it's wise to book ahead of time, especially if you're going to be traveling in July-August. Yet even during the shoulder seasons certain hotels can be booked up many months ahead of time. Lower-priced hotels in Positano, Amalfi, and Capri fill up especially fast. Keep in mind that many hotels and B&Bs might only have a handful of rooms and are relatively small compared to large chain hotels in other parts of the world.

Accommodations in Naples and Salerno are open throughout the year, but most hotels on the Amalfi Coast, Sorrentine Peninsula, and the islands of Capri, Ischia, and Procida close for a period in the winter. This may be the entire winter season November-March or for a shorter period January-March. Some smaller B&Bs will operate year-round, or you will find vacation apartment rentals available throughout the winter season in these areas.

HOTELS

Like in other parts of the world, Italian hotels are graded on a system of one to five stars based on amenities and services. The Amalfi Coast is a popular tourist destination, and the quality of accommodations on the coast and other areas covered in this book is very high. Breakfast is included, and all hotel rooms include en suite baths. It's possible to book online; most hotels have multilingual websites. A **passport** or ID card is required when checking in, and smaller hotels often have a "leave the key" policy in which keys must be left and retrieved whenever entering or leaving the lodging. Expect to be charged a city **hotel tax** of €1.50-5 per guest per day depending on the number of stars and the type of lodging; kids under age 10 are exempt. Some towns only collect the city hotel tax seasonally April-November, while others charge it year-round. The city tax is usually required to be paid in cash when you leave.

HOSTELS

Ostelli (hostels) in Italy aren't just for young travelers; they provide clean accommodations as well as a sense of community for good rates, and most include private or semiprivate rooms in addition to dormitories. Baths are often shared, but some private rooms may have en suite baths. Expect higher than usual hostel rates in locations like Positano.

BED-AND-BREAKFASTS AND APARTMENTS

Italy boasts thousands of bed-and-breakfasts, a great option to mingle with the owners for a truly local stay. Another option is to rent an **apartment** or **villa** through **Airbnb** (www.airbnb.com) or **VRBO** (www.vrbo.com), an especially good choice and usually affordable for those traveling in large groups; it allows you to prepare your own meals and enjoy the other amenities of fully equipped housing. A word to the wise if you're considering a short-term vacation rental on the Amalfi Coast: Be sure to check for the number of stairs to access the property. Though most hotels have easy access or elevators available, many private residences or villas may require climbing a significant number of steps to reach them. If the number of steps or access information is not indicated on the website where you're searching, it's a good idea to ask in advance before booking if there are steps and how many. It is far better than arriving at your vacation rental and finding a daunting flight of stairs to navigate daily.

LOCATION RECOMMENDATIONS

Choosing a holiday destination can be a challenging task with so many fine options on the Amalfi Coast. If you're planning a visit of only a few days, Amalfi is the most convenient choice for its easy ferry and bus connections to the entire area. If you're staying longer, Positano and Ravello are also fine choices. For an experience a bit more off the beaten path, consider Minori or Cetara, two smaller towns that also offer convenient ferry and public transportation options.

If you're booking a short-term rental on the Amalfi Coast, keep in mind that many towns are quite spread out and include frazioni, or hamlets, that can be quite a distance from the town center. In some towns, like Positano or Amalfi, you will find rentals available in frazioni that are located very high in the mountains above the center of town. In this case, you will need to use local buses to reach the town for beaches, shopping, and dining options. These more remote lodging options offer a quieter experience, but if you're not prepared, it can be a surprise and you may use up some valuable vacation time waiting for buses that can be very crowded in the summer months. Don't assume that a town name in an address guarantees a short-term rental will be conveniently located. Map the precise location before booking so you know exactly what you're getting.

Health and Safety

EMERGENCY NUMBERS

In case of a **medical emergency,** dial **118.** Operators are multilingual and will provide immediate assistance and ambulance service. The **US Consulate General in Naples** (tel. 081/583-8111) offers US citizens phone access any time for matters regarding illness or emergencies of any sort. **Carabinieri** (112), **police** (113), and the **fire department** (115) also operate around-the-clock.

POLICE

The law enforcement in Italy is divided into different agencies. The two main agencies are the polizia and the Carabinieri, who are responsible essentially for the same duties. The Carabinieri are a military corps that perform both military and civilian police duties, whereas the polizia is the more customary civilian police force. Either one can help in an emergency situation because they both handle law enforcement, investigations, and traffic incidents. The polizia tend to be more involved in patrolling the Autostrade (highways), yet both forces also perform periodic random traffic stops. If you are driving and see the polizia or Carabinieri on the side of the road flag you to stop, be prepared to show your documents and vehicle registration or rental information. The Carabinieri uniforms are black with a red stripe on the pants and their vehicles are dark blue, also with red stripe details. Polizia uniforms are gray and blue, and their vehicles light blue and white.

Although you're less likely to encounter them while sightseeing, the Guardia di Finanza are another military police force who are responsible for policing financial and drug crimes. They are usually outfitted in gray uniforms and the vehicles are also gray. On a city level, the vigili urbani, which are part of the polizia municipale (municipal police), are usually on hand in every town to help with traffic, parking violations, and local law enforcement.

MEDICAL SERVICES

Italian medical and emergency services are relatively modern and are highly rated by the World Health Organization. First aid can be performed by all public hospitals, and urgent treatment is entirely free of charge. A symbolic copayment is often required for non-life-threatening treatment but does not exceed €30. The emergency medical service number is **118.** If you can't wait, go directly to the pronto soccorso (emergency room) located in most hospitals.

Vaccines

For the most part, vaccines are not required for entering Italy, but a flu shot can prevent unnecessary time in bed if you're visiting in winter. Check the latest vaccine guidelines and restrictions for travel with your local health authority as well as Italian and European health departments.

PHARMACIES

A pharmacy is called a farmacia in Italian, and they are recognizable by their green neon signs. They are very common in cities and even smaller town centers. If a pharmacy is closed, you can often find a list of the closest open ones posted in the window. Pharmacists can be very helpful in Italy and provide advice and nonprescription medicine for treating minor ailments. You'll also find practical items such as toothbrushes, sunscreen, baby food, and dietary foods like gluten-free

CRIME

Italian cities are safe, and muggings and violent crime are rare. The Amalfi Coast area, along with Sorrentine Peninsula and the islands of Capri, Ischia, and Procida are very safe. Of course, you'll want to keep an eye on your personal items, but even petty crimes are rare.

Though Naples has a reputation regarding organized crime, violent crimes are usually restricted to the Camorra (local mafia) and generally do not affect tourists. Petty crime is the main issue, as in any large city in the world. Being street savvy is your best defense against thieves. Most petty criminals work in teams and can be quite young. Crowded train stations and public transportation are ideal places for thieves. Leave the eye-catching jewelry and expensive accessories at home and opt for a cross-body bag, carried in front, that closes well. It's best to keep wallets and other valuables in a front pocket or locked in a hotel safe. Distribute what you carry with you in different front pockets, or even better, use a money belt and leave out just the cash that you need to be easily accessible for the day. Keep smartphones and cameras out of sight as much as possible, and always keep a close eye on your bags.

If you're driving in Naples, it's best to park your car in an attended parking garage rather than on the street. Be sure to lock the vehicle and leave no valuables in the car.

Before traveling, make a photocopy of your passport and other vital documents and call your credit card company immediately if your wallet is stolen. If you are the victim of a pickpocket, have a bag snatched, or have issues with car theft, report it within 24 hours to the nearest police station. You'll need a copy of the denuncia (police report) in order to make an insurance claim.

Conduct and Customs

LOCAL HABITS

Many of the most noticeable Italian habits are related to food: strict mealtimes, almost always eaten sitting down—you'll hardly ever see Italians eating on the go. Breakfast is generally light to save room for lunch and dinner, served around 1pm and 8pm. When eating out, Italians usually divide the bill between friends, and each person buys his or her own drink. Drinking is generally considered part of a meal, rather than with the intention of intoxication.

Though most etiquette in Italy will feel fairly familiar to most travelers, one exception is cutting in line, which is a frequent occurrence. If you don't defend your place, you may be waiting all day, and don't expect an orderly line while waiting to get on the bus or other forms of transportation. Often there is an order to a queue based on order of arrival. If you're unsure, you can ask who is the last in a waiting group and then remember that your turn is after that person.

GREETINGS

Italians' interactions with friends and acquaintances often involve physical contact, and kisses on both cheeks are common (though a handshake is just as acceptable). Conversation in public spaces, from the café or square, is unhurried; the proliferation of the cell phone has only fueled Italians' passion to communicate, and in some cases has led to an overreliance that can be witnessed on public transportation and sidewalks of Italian cities.

ALCOHOL AND SMOKING

In Italy, alcohol can be consumed in public and purchased by anyone over 18. Attitudes toward alcohol are relaxed, and excessive drinking is rare. Smoking has been banned in bars, restaurants, and public spaces since 2005, and the number of smokers is falling, though you'll still see plenty of people smoking in outdoor spaces, including seating at outdoor cafés and restaurants.

DRUGS

Italy's geographical position between Europe and North Africa and its extensive coastline mean smuggling of drugs, including heroin, cocaine, hashish, and synthetic drugs, is a problem here. Hashish (derived from cannabis and mixed with tobacco) is the most common drug here, and most dealers aren't too pushy, while cocaine or amphetamines may be present at discos and nightclubs. Cannabis has been decriminalized for decades, but harder drugs are illegal. Though personal use of cannabis in public will not lead to arrest, it's not worth the risk of a fine or warning.

DRESS

Style is second nature to Italians. It can be easy to feel out of place when surrounded by their more formal attire and attention to detail when it comes to appearance. Clothing is generally elegant and fits well; to fit in style-wise, think about packing your Sunday best for the trip, or doing some shopping to pick up some of that easy Italian elegance.

That being said, style in the coastal areas of the Amalfi Coast and the islands is more relaxed than in many Italian cities. People are often dressed resort-chic, including a lot of linen for both men and women, flowing summer dresses to keep cool, and handmade sandals or leather loafers. And while the skimpy Speedo-style swimsuits for men and the proliferation of bikinis on the beach might give the idea of a relaxed beach vibe everywhere, Italians cover up when leaving the beach. It's not appropriate, or even allowed in many towns, to walk around in only swimwear, except on the beach. A beach cover-up and flip-flops are fine for getting from your accommodations to the beach, but you won't see Italians dining anywhere except a beachside restaurant in a beach cover-up.

At Places of Worship

It is assumed travelers will dress more conservatively when visiting churches in Italy. Though modest dress codes are not as strictly enforced in this region as in other parts of Italy, if you are revealing too much skin, you might be denied entry. Even if a sign isn't posted, it's polite to avoid going into churches while wearing short skirts or shorts, or bare midriffs or shoulders. For women, it can be handy to carry a scarf to cover your shoulders while visiting religious sites during the summer months.

Practical Details

WHAT TO PACK

Traveling to an area famous for its many steps can quickly make you regret packing those extra five pairs of shoes; it's best to err on the side of packing light, and to leave expensive watches and jewelry at home, especially if you'll be spending time in Naples. Finally, it's a good idea to email yourself a copy of your passport and any important credit card codes or customer service numbers as backup in case you lose your wallet or bag.

Luggage: Wheeled suitcases can be bumpy going on Italy's cobblestone streets, but it's often still worth it to avoid carrying heavy bags. Bring a backpack or handbag with zippers for daily excursions, and a money belt can be useful for cash and valuables.

Paperwork: You'll need your passport and a driver's license if you plan on renting your own transportation.

Clothing, shoes, and accessories: Bring comfortable shoes and clothes for long days of walking, and layers, especially in spring and fall, when mornings and evenings can be chilly. Bring at least one fancier outfit for nicer restaurants or clubs, and clothes that cover knees and shoulders to visit places of worship. You'll thank yourself for bringing flip-flops to the rocky beaches. If you have very sensitive feet, consider packing a pair of water shoes. You might not win style awards, but being comfortable on your beach holiday is more important. Pack some beach cover-ups for seaside dining and getting to and from the beach. Sunglasses and hats are useful for sunny summer days. For hiking and walking, a good pair of supportive athletic shoes will be fine, and you can save space by leaving your hiking boots at home.

Toiletries and medication: You can pick up most normal toiletries and common medications like aspirin at Italian pharmacies, but pack a high-SPF sunscreen, which can be quite costly in seaside locations. If you take medication, make sure to bring enough, and a copy of your prescription in case you need a refill. **Hand sanitizer** is now a must while traveling and is especially useful on the go. If you're concerned about crowded spaces, bring a **face mask** especially for public transportation. Tuck several **travel tissue** packs into your bag, as it's not uncommon to find restrooms without toilet paper.

Electronics: Voltage is 220 in Italy and plugs have two round prongs. Pack a US-to-European **travel adapter,** which are harder to find once you're in Italy; that said, many hotels supply them to guests free of charge. A portable battery charger can prevent phones and other devices from going dark while out and about during the day. Digital photographers will definitely want to bring extra memory cards too. If you're a film photographer, bring plenty of film because it's becoming increasingly difficult to find film for sale on the Amalfi Coast.

LAUNDRY AND LUGGAGE STORAGE

If you need to do laundry while traveling, keep in mind that laundromats are often small and offer washing services as well as dry-cleaning options. Self-service laundromats can be hard to find, but they are available as a budget-friendly option or if you're traveling light.

Luggage storage can make day trips and transfers easy if you're staying in multiple places on the Amalfi Coast or exploring Campania. In general, look for deposito bagagli (luggage storage) signs and be sure to check on timing because some locations only offer storage during the day.

Laundry
Rosy Laundry
Corso Italia 321; tel. 331/912-1122; 24 hours daily; from €6 per wash

This is a good option for travelers in Sorrento who need to do laundry on the go, with self-service machines.

Luggage Storage
Amalfi Porters
Piazza Flavio Gioia 1; tel. 339/276-8989; www.amalfiporters.it

As the main transportation hub on the Amalfi Coast, it can be convenient for day trips to leave your luggage stored at your lodging or at a deposito bagagli (luggage storage) in Amalfi. With stairs to many accommodations, especially vacation rentals and smaller bed-and-breakfasts, hiring porters to help with your luggage can help ease your arrival and departure. The local porter service in Amalfi can also advise on storing your luggage if needed.

Sorrento Luggage
tel. 338/431-7323; www.sorrentoluggage.com; 8am-8pm daily; from €7 per day

Sorrento Luggage offers a storage service as well as the possibility to have your bags picked up and dropped off from your lodging. Contact them to reserve in advance.

Stow Your Bags
Via Venezia 64; www.stowyourbags.com; 7am-11pm daily; from €2.49 per locker

In Naples, it's best to request to leave your luggage at your lodging, but if needed there are luggage storage options. Stow Your Bags is located near the Napoli Centrale train station and offers lockers in two sizes for luggage.

MONEY
Currency
The euro has been Italy's currency since 2000. Banknotes come in denominations of €5, €10, €20, €50, €200, and €500 (which is currently being phased out). Denominations are different colors and sizes to facilitate recognition. Coins come in €0.01, €0.02, €0.05, €0.10, €0.20, €0.50, €1, and €2 denominations; these also vary in color, shape, and size.

Currency Exchange
Fluctuation between the dollar and the euro can have a major impact on expenditures. One dollar is now worth roughly €0.90. To obtain euros, you can exchange at your local bank before departure, use **private exchange** agencies located in airports and near major monuments, or simply use **ATMs** in Italy. Banks generally offer better rates but charge a commission, while agencies charge a low commission but offer poor rates. Certainly the easiest and best option is to withdraw the cash you need from ATMs as you go.

ATMs and Banks
ATMs are easy to find and use throughout Italy, providing instructions in multiple languages and accepting foreign debit and credit cards. Before withdrawing cash in Italy, ask your bank or credit card company about fees. Italian banks also charge a small fee for cardholders of other banks using their ATMs.

The maximum daily withdrawal at most banks is €500, and banks are generally open weekdays 8:30am-1:30pm and 2:30pm-4:30pm. Be aware of your surroundings when withdrawing cash late at night or on deserted streets.

Debit and Credit Cards
Debit and credit cards are ubiquitous in Italy, and recent legislation meant to encourage cashless transactions has removed monetary limits. Yet it's still best not to assume you can use a card absolutely everywhere, and to contact your bank before leaving to let them know about your trip, so your card doesn't get frozen. Do plan on always having some cash on hand for transactions like bus tickets or small purchases, as not all small businesses are equipped to process cards. However, you can use credit cards at most museums, restaurants, and shops. It's useful to have a card with a chip-and-PIN system, the most common form of bank card in Italy. Credit cards often provide the most advantageous exchange rates, with a 1-3 percent commission fee per transaction.

Sales Tax
There's a value-added tax (IVA) of 22 percent on most goods, but visitors who reside outside the European Union are entitled to **tax refunds** (www.taxrefund.it) on all purchases over €154.94 on the same day within stores that participate in the tax-back program. Just look for the **Euro Tax Free** or **Tax Free Italy** logo, have your passport ready, and fill out the yellow refund form. You'll still have to pay tax at the time of purchase, but you are entitled to reimbursement at airports and refund offices. Forms must be stamped by customs officials before check-in and brought to the refund desk, where you can choose to receive cash or have funds wired to your credit card. Lines move slowly and it's usually faster to be refunded at private **currency exchange agencies** such as **Forexchange** (www.forexchange.it) in Naples. They facilitate the refund process for a small percentage of your refund. All claims must be made within 3 months of purchase.

COMMUNICATIONS
Telephones
To call Italy from outside the country, dial the **exit code** (011 in the United States and Canada), followed by **39** (Italy country code), and the number. All large Italian cities have a 2- or 3-digit **area code** (081 for the city of Naples and surrounding areas and 089 for the province of Salerno), and numbers are 6-11

digits long. Landline numbers nearly always start with a zero, which must be dialed when making calls in Italy or calling Italy from abroad. Cell phone numbers have a 3-digit prefix (347, 390, 340, etc.) that varies according to the mobile operator, and cell phone numbers are 10 digits long in total. Numbers that start with 800 in Italy are toll-free, 170 gets you an English-speaking operator, and 176 is **international directory assistance.**

Most smartphones, such as iPhones, Samsung Galaxy, and Google Pixel devices, will work in Italy, but roaming rates vary widely. Before leaving, check whether your service provider offers an international plan to avoid unexpected bills. You can also visit a mobile shop on arrival in Italy to purchase an Italian SIM card from operators like **Wind** (www.wind.it), **Tim** (www.tim.it), and **Vodafone** (www.vodafone.it). You need a passport or photo ID to purchase a SIM card, but this is a cheap option that usually allows the most generous use of minutes and data. Or, save on charges by connecting to Wi-Fi whenever possible—in hotels, bars, and many other places throughout the region.

Wi-Fi

Many towns in Italy have free Wi-Fi networks that make it simple to stay connected throughout a journey, as do train operators, airports, and hotels. You must register to access Wi-Fi, and there are often time and traffic limits.

Postal Services

Yellow **Poste Italiane** (www.poste.it) offices range from larger branches, usually open 8:30am-7pm Monday-Friday, to smaller branches, open about 8:30am-1:30pm Monday-Friday. A postcard to the United States costs €2.40 as long as it doesn't exceed 20 grams and remains within standard dimensions. The cost of sending letters and other goods varies according to weight; just know that it may take many weeks for your items to reach their destination. Some tabacchi (tobacco shops) also have standard francobolli (stamps) available for purchase. Mailboxes are red and may have slots for international and local mail, so take a close look before mailing.

OPENING HOURS

Opening hours can vary based on the season and location throughout the region of Campania. In larger cities like Naples and Salerno, you can expect to find many shops, especially smaller ones, closed in the afternoon around 1:30pm-4:30pm. In Salerno, shops often close Monday morning as well, especially during the winter, while in more popular tourist spots like Amalfi, Positano, Ravello, Sorrento, and Capri, shops will be open daily and offer continuous hours April-October. On Ischia and Procida, many shops close for the afternoon around 1:30pm-4:30pm even in the peak of summer.

Shop hours also vary significantly by season. In the top tourist spots, shops will likely be open daily with continuous hours during the summer months, with extended evening hours in July-August. Hours will be shorter in the winter months, and some shops may close entirely on the Amalfi Coast and islands for a period after Christmas or for the entire winter period.

Restaurants will often close one day a week, possibly Monday, Tuesday, or Wednesday. In the coastal areas and islands, restaurants will usually be open daily in August or for the entire summer period, but will close for much or all of the winter season.

Nothing is worse than arriving at a museum you are eager to visit and finding it closed. Most of the major museums in Naples, including the Museo Archeologico Nazionale, Madre museum, and many smaller museums are closed Tuesday. The Reggia di Caserta is also closed on Tuesday, while the Museo di Capodimonte and Certosa e Museo di San Martino are closed Wednesday. In Sorrento, the Museo Correale di Terranova is closed Monday, while the Museobottega della Tarsialignea is open daily. As for museums in Salerno, the Museo Archeologico Provinciale and Pinacoteca Provinciale are closed Monday. On the Amalfi Coast, the Museo della Carta in Amalfi is closed Monday November-January and is closed for the entire month of February, while the Museo della Ceramica is closed Monday throughout the year.

PUBLIC HOLIDAYS

Public holidays in Italy usually mean that banks and offices will be closed. It also means that grocery stores will be closed, or open for reduced hours. In addition to public holidays, each town has one or more days dedicated to celebrating its local patron saint. Though this usually doesn't impact the hours of banks or public offices, you may sometimes find that shops keep more limited hours. However, along the Amalfi Coast, on the islands and other peak tourist spots, you will find all restaurants and shops open during the summer months and for public holidays, like the Festa della Repubblica and Ferragosto.

- **January 1:** Capodanno (New Year's Day)
- **January 6:** Epifania (Epiphany)
- **Pasqua** (Easter Sunday)
- **Pasquetta** (Easter Monday)
- **April 25:** Festa della Liberazione (Liberation Day)
- **May 1:** Festa del Lavoro (International Workers' Day)
- **June 2:** Festa della Repubblica (Republic Day)
- **August 15:** Ferragosto (Assumption Day)
- **November 1:** Tutti i Santi (All Saints' Day)
- **December 8:** Immacolata (Immaculate Conception)
- **December 25:** Natale (Christmas)
- **December 26:** Santo Stefano (Saint Stephen's Day)

WEIGHTS AND MEASURES

Italy uses the **metric system.** A few helpful conversions:

- 5 centimeters = about 3 inches
- 1 kilogram = a little more than 2 pounds
- 5 kilometers = around 3 miles

Celsius is used to measure temperature; room temperature is about 20°C (68°F). When summers temperatures break the 35°C (95°F) barrier, head to the beach early in the day and spend the hottest midday hours indoors as many Italians do.

Italy is on **Central European Time,** 6 hours later than the US East Coast and 9 hours later than the West Coast. Military or 24-hour time is frequently used, as in 13:00 for 1pm and 20:15 for 8:15pm. Italians order dates by day, month, and year, which is important to remember when booking hotels and tours.

TOURIST INFORMATION
Tourist Offices

You'll find tourist offices in major destinations: on the Amalfi Coast and the islands, and in Sorrento and Naples, where city travel cards, maps, and event information can be obtained. Hours vary but most are open non-stop from 9:30am until around 6pm during the tourist season, with more limited hours during the winter months. Staff are multilingual and can help put you in touch with local guides, order tickets, or get directions. Tourist offices are located in the city center and are usually well indicated with signs.

Sightseeing Passes

The **Campania Artecard** (www.campaniartecard.it) is the main sightseeing pass for Naples and sights throughout Campania. It covers many art and cultural sights in Naples, including museums, archaeological sites, churches, and more. The pass also includes access to nearly all public transportation systems when traveling to sights included in the pass. Available passes include a 3-day Naples card (€22 adults, €13 ages 18-25) that covers only Naples and a 3- or 7-day Campania card (3-day: €32 adults, €25 ages 18-25; 7-day: €34, no youth card available) that covers Naples and the region. As the Campania card includes the archaeological cities of Pompeii and Herculaneum, it is often the better choice. The cards provide free entry to the first 2-5 sights, depending on the card selected, and reductions of up to 50 percent for subsequent sights visited. If you plan to visit many sights in Naples or the surrounding area, the Campania Artecard quickly pays for itself and saves you money on sightseeing and travel.

Maps

Maps are available at most tourist offices and at newsstands and bookstores in Naples. Keep in mind that the towns of the Amalfi Coast and the islands are all quite small and easy to navigate. Usually there are only one or two main streets or piazzas, and a maze of little passageways weaving through the town. Given the labyrinthine layout, street names can be tricky to follow on the Amalfi Coast. Google Maps is a useful app, especially for determining the right bus stop. Yet keep in mind that not even Google Maps can handle the Amalfi Coast with much accuracy. Give yourself extra time to get lost and plan on plenty of steps along the way.

Asking for directions is the best way to start a conversation with a stranger and learn something new. One of the most enjoyable experiences on the Amalfi Coast or the islands is putting away the map and simply meandering through town. You'll happen across moments of daily life and experience the joy of discovering quiet spots.

For hiking on the Amalfi Coast, Sorrentine Peninsula, and Capri, **Cart&guide** (www.carteguide.com) produces the most in-depth maps of the hiking and walking paths. These maps are available online and in bookstores in the area. The Amalfi Coast is divided into four separate maps that cover the entire coastline from Vietri sul Mare to Punta Campanella, and a there's a separate Capri map that details 14 walks on the island.

Traveler Advice

OPPORTUNITIES FOR STUDY AND EMPLOYMENT

With unemployment rates quite high in Italy, finding job opportunities in the area is challenging at best. An easier option is to consider studying abroad in order to experience a more extended time in Italy, learn about the history and culture of the area, and to learn and practice Italian. Language study programs are among the best options in the area, with the **Accademia Italiana Salerno** (www.accademia-italiana.it), the **Istituto Italia 150** in Naples (www.istitutoitaliaclaps.it), and the **Sant'Anna Institute** in Sorrento (www.santannainstitute.com) offering a variety of courses throughout the year.

ACCESS FOR TRAVELERS WITH DISABILITIES

For a country with predominantly historic buildings that were not designed to be wheelchair-accessible, Italy has been making great strides to improve accessibility in airports, train stations, hotels, and sights. However, not all historic churches and sights, or even restaurants, are wheelchair-accessible, so it's always a good idea to call in advance before visiting to confirm. Calling ahead is also a good idea because some sights offer wheelchair access, but it must be reserved.

The Amalfi Coast presents many barriers for travelers with disabilities or mobility issues simply due to the mountainous setting and many steps involved in navigating the towns along the coastline. Positano is one of the most challenging places to visit with a wheelchair because the town center is located near the beach and is only accessible on foot along a steep pathway that includes many steps. Of all the towns along the Amalfi Coast, Amalfi is one of the most wheelchair-friendly. The waterfront and historic center—including Piazza Duomo and the main street through town, lined with shops and restaurants—are relatively flat. Large cobblestones in the historic center make it a bit bumpy, but along the waterfront the sidewalks are smoother and there are ramps. The Marina Grande beach is accessible via a ramp on the western side of the beach nearest Piazza Flavio Gioia. The towns of Minori and Maiori are also relatively flat and wheelchair-friendly, with Maiori offering a long waterfront area and main street with smoother sidewalks and ramps.

The historic center of Naples has many pedestrian-only areas, but the cobblestone streets and chaotic atmosphere can present challenges for travelers with disabilities. Sorrento is somewhat easier to navigate in that it is not as chaotic, but those Italian cobblestones are ubiquitous. Yet cultural sightseeing in Naples and Sorrento is well ahead of the curve in Italy. It's safe to say that nearly all the museums are accessible and offer special services. The Museo Archeologico Nazionale in Naples (www.mann-napoli.it) is entirely wheelchair-accessible and offers an **International Sign Language Tour** via the website. **Tactile itineraries and workshops** are available for blind and partially sighted travelers, but must be reserved in advance.

Though the uneven terrain and large stone streets of the archaeological sites of Pompeii and Herculaneum present challenges, there are new initiatives to make them both more accessible. **Pompeii** has a special route called Pompei per tutti (Pompeii for All) that leads through a specially designed 2.2-mile (3.5-km) tour of the ruins, with ramps to make it more manageable. While it's a fantastic endeavor, you'll still want to keep in mind that you're entering an archaeological site; there are ramps or slopes of more than 8 percent at times, as well as stretches of ancient and uneven pavement and certain points that may present challenges for wheelchair users to move independently. **Herculaneum** is a much smaller site than Pompeii and offers wheelchair-accessible ramps and walkways to enter the ancient city. Movement within is, again, somewhat challenging given the uneven terrain and steps required to enter some of the houses. **Paestum** has some barrier-free paths through its archaeological park as well as wheelchair access to all areas of the museum.

Turismo Accessibile (www.turismoaccessibile.org) provides detailed information on accessibility in Naples, yet much of the information is only available in Italian. **Sage Traveling** (www.sagetraveling.com) is a travel company specializing in disabled travel. In the Naples area, the company offers a number of day tours that are wheelchair-friendly, including tours to Pompeii, Herculaneum, Sorrento, Capri, and the Amalfi Coast.

TRAVELING WITH CHILDREN

Italians go crazy for kids, and if you're traveling with a baby or toddler expect people to sneak peeks inside the stroller or ask about your child. Restaurants and hotels generally welcome young travelers, and some high-end accommodations offer babysitting services for parents who want to sightsee on their own. Not all restaurants offer booster seats or high chairs, but many will create mezza porzione (half-size portions) for small appetites. Tickets to museums and public transportation are usually discounted for children under 12, and are free for kids under 6.

Strollers

Keep in mind that steps, and often a lot of them, are hard to avoid on the Amalfi Coast, which can make getting around with a stroller

Fun for Families

While the Amalfi Coast is famous as a honeymoon and romantic destination, it's also a fun and memorable area to visit for families. From exploring the beautiful coastline on a clear-bottomed kayak to climbing castles and eating pizza in its birthplace, here are some of the best experiences for families.

AMALFI COAST

- Spend a day swimming and collecting sea glass and pebbles at the beautiful **Spiaggia di Fornillo** in Positano, where the clear water and calmer beach is a great option for families (page 53).

- Learn firsthand how paper was traditionally made and even try to make it yourself on a tour at Amalfi's **Museo della Carta.** Kids won't look at paper the same way again after seeing how much work used to go into its creation (page 86).

SORRENTO AND THE SORRENTINE PENINSULA

- Stroll through a historic lemon grove at **La Limonaia** to learn how lemons grow and enjoy tasty samples. The grove is located largely on one level and is easier to navigate with young kids than groves on the Amalfi Coast (page 182).

- **Rent a clear kayak** from Chasing Syrens at the Marina del Cantone beach in Nerano and set off on a family adventure exploring the coastline from the sea (page 193).

ISLANDS

- Thrill the kids with a ride up the chairlift to the top of Capri's **Monte Solaro** for incredible views overlooking the island (page 210).

- Enjoy a **boat tour** around the island of Capri for the best views of the famous grottoes and caves. Watch the excitement as the boat cruises right through the hole in the middle of the Faraglioni rocks (page 217).

- Explore the **Castello Aragonese** on Ischia: Complete with macabre crypts, abandoned prisons, and interesting ruins, there are a lot of real-life tales to uncover here (page 244).

NAPLES

- Climb to the top of **Castel Sant'Elmo** for a view dominating Naples and see who can point out first the other two castles of Naples, the Castel Nuovo and the Castel dell'Ovo, along the waterfront far below (page 319).

- Older kids will find a **Napoli Sotterranea** tour fascinating and spooky as it leads deep into the underground of the city to reveal intriguing layers of the past (page 308).

HERCULANEUM AND VESUVIUS

- Get a look at ancient Roman life at **Herculaneum,** which is much smaller and easier to explore for kids than Pompeii (page 362).

- For the adventurous young travelers, a climb to the top of **Mount Vesuvius** is a thrilling travel experience (page 369). Maybe you'll even see a glimpse of steam seeping from the crater!

challenging. You're going to want a lightweight and easy-to-fold stroller in order to navigate steps. For infants and young children, baby wraps, carriers, or a hip seat can be helpful to make handling the steps a little easier. Be sure to check the number of steps required to reach your accommodation. The vertical setting of Positano is particularly challenging for strollers and tiring for little legs. However, if Positano is your dream family destination, just look for accommodations close to the beach to make it easier to get around once you've arrived.

The archaeological sites like Pompeii, Herculaneum, and Paestum can also be challenging to navigate with a stroller. Herculaneum is a much smaller site to cover, yet offers all of the intriguing aspects of ancient Roman life to capture the interest of young visitors. A tour guide can also help bring the history to life for children in fun and engaging ways.

Beaches

Most of the beaches in this area have pebbles or are rocky, so a pair of beach shoes will keep little feet safe and can help make the beach experience more enjoyable for the whole family. (Adults will want water shoes or flip-flops for the beach as well.) Hiring a boat or booking a boat excursion is a family-friendly way to explore the coastline and islands, allowing you to stop and swim in beautiful coves and older kids to explore the rugged coastline and little grottoes.

Managing the Heat

During the hot days of summer, do like the Italians do and head to the beach in the morning. Then return to your lodging for a midafternoon break during the hottest part of the day to rest up for evening adventures. You'll find that most Italian children have later bedtimes, especially during the summer, and it's normal for families to be out to dinner late, even with young children. With some advance planning, it's hard for kids not to love Italy. Involving them as much as possible in the journey will help leave an impression they'll never forget.

WOMEN TRAVELING ALONE

Women travelers may find that Italians in general are less shy about staring than they may be accustomed to at home. This may make women feel uncomfortable, but for the most part, men in southern Italy are respectful. The stereotype of Italians and their wandering hands is uncommon here and would be looked upon as shameful by the locals. Advances are usually not aggressive and can simply be ignored. Enter a shop, bar, or other public space if unwanted attention is threatening; if harassment persists, call the **police** (113) from a crowded area. In Naples women should be more aware of their surroundings at all times and avoid unlit streets and train stations at night. Having a cell phone handy is a wise precaution, and periodically keeping in touch with family back home never hurts. Hotels will be happy to order a taxi or make reservations whenever necessary.

SENIOR TRAVELERS

Italy's high life expectancy (84) and median age (47) means visiting seniors may feel right at home, and there's a general respect for older people. You'll see that the steps of the Amalfi Coast don't stop local seniors from getting around. They just take the slow and steady approach and stop to chat along the way. Take a cue from them and enjoy sightseeing at a relaxed pace. If mobility and steps are problematic, be sure to check on the number of steps at your accommodations and confirm there is an elevator. Nearly all hotels have elevators, but smaller lodgings and bed-and-breakfasts may not.

Special Discounts

People over age 65 are entitled to discounts at museums, theaters, and sporting events as well as on public transportation and for many other services. **Trenitalia** offers over-60s up to a 50 percent discount, while **Italo** offers 40-60 percent off selected ticket classes. Find out the latest details on the Trenitalia (www.trenitalia.com) and Italo (www.italotreno.it) websites.

LGBTQ+ TRAVELERS

Though Italy was one of the last European countries to enable civil unions for same-sex couples, violence against LGBTQ+ people is rare (although cases of physical and verbal harassment in Naples do occasionally make headlines). In modern Italy, it's not uncommon to see same-sex couples holding hands. Capri has long been known for its open community and appeal for gay travelers. For LGBTQ+ nightlife, your best bet is Naples, though the scene is more modest than in other large cities in Italy like Rome or Milan. The **Mediterranean Pride of Naples** (www.napolipride.org) parade and festival take place in June or July in the streets of Naples.

TRAVELERS OF COLOR

Over the last few decades, Italy has become increasingly diverse, with growing communities of Eastern Europeans, Asians, South Americans, and Africans. Still, the country's population is 91 percent Italian, though that group itself comprises many different cultural, linguistic, and historical subgroups. In an area where travelers arrive from all corners of the world, most Italians are welcoming to travelers of color. However, it's a good idea to keep in mind that Italians are known for staring, which isn't something just reserved for travelers. Although this cultural quirk makes some people uncomfortable, blatant discrimination is rare. That said, growth in immigration from African countries has led to an increase in anti-immigration sentiment across the country, and an uptick in incidents of racial violence. If you think you've been refused service based on race, report the incident to local police or Carabinieri, who treat all acts of racism seriously.

Resources

Glossary

A
aeroporto: airport
albergo: hotel
alcolici: alcohol
alimentari: grocery store
aliscafo: hydrofoil (high-speed ferry)
ambasciata: embassy
analcolico: nonalcoholic
aperitivo: appetizer
aperto: open
arrivo: arrival
autista: driver
autobus: bus
autostrada: highway

B
bagaglio: suitcase
bagno: bathroom
banca: bank
bibita: soft drink
biglietteria: ticket office
biglietto: ticket
buono: good

C
calcio: soccer
caldo: hot
cambio: exchange
camera: room
cameriere: waiter
carta di credito: credit card
cartolina: postcard
cassa: cashier
cattedrale: cathedral
centro storico: historic center
chiesa: church
chiuso: closed
città: city
climatizzato: air-conditioned
coincidenza: connection (transport)
consolate: consulate
contante: cash
conto: bill

D E
destinazione: destination
discoteca: disco
dogana: customs
duomo: cathedral
edicola: newsstand
enoteca: wine bar
entrata: entrance
escursione: excursion

F G I
farmacia: pharmacy
fermata: bus/subway stop
ferrovia: railway
fontana: fountain
forno: bakery
francobollo: stamp
gratuito: free
grazie: thanks
isola: island

L
letto: bed
libreria: bookshop
limone: lemon
lontano: far

lungomare: waterfront

M N O
macchina: car
mare: sea
mercato: market
metropolitana: subway
moneta: coin
monumento: monument
mostra: exhibition
museo: museum
negozio: shop
orario: timetable
ospedale: hospital
ostello: hostel

P Q R
palazzo: building
panino: sandwich
parcheggio: parking lot
parco: park
partenza: departure
passeggiata: walk
pasticceria: pastry shop
pasto: meal
periferia: outskirts
piazza: square
polizia: police
ponte: bridge
prenotazione: reservation
prezzo: price
quartiere: neighborhood
ristorante: restaurant

S T
sconto: discount
soccorso: assistance
spiaggia: beach
spuntino: snack
stabilimento balneare: seaside beach club
stazione: station
strada: road
tabacchi: tobacco shop
teatro: theater
torre: tower
traghetto: ferry
trattoria: restaurant (casual)
treno: train

U V
uscita: exit
via: street
viale: avenue

Italian Phrasebook

Many Italians in the Amalfi Coast area have some knowledge of English, ranging from managing basic communication to being fully fluent. Of course, whatever vocabulary they lack is compensated for with gesticulation. It is, however, more rewarding to attempt to communicate in Italian, even a little bit, and your efforts will often be greeted with encouragement from locals.

Fortunately, Italian pronunciation is straightforward. There are 7 vowel sounds (one for *a*, *i*, and *u*, and two each for *e* and *o*) compared to 15 in English, and letters are nearly always pronounced the same way. Consonants are familiar, although the Italian alphabet has fewer letters (no *j*, *k*, *w*, *x*, or *y*). If you have any experience with French, Spanish, Portuguese, or Latin, you have an advantage, but even if you don't, learning a few phrases is simple and will prepare you for a linguistic dive into Italian culture. Inquiring how much something costs or asking for directions in Italian can be a little daunting, but it's also exciting and much more gratifying than relying on English.

PRONUNCIATION
Vowels
a like *a* in *father*
e short like *e* in *set*
é long like *a* in *way*
i like *ee* in *feet*
o short like *o* in *often*, or long like *o* in *rope*

u like *oo* in *foot*, or *w* in *well*

Consonants
b like *b* in *boy*, but softer
c before e or i like *ch* in *chin*
ch like *c* in *cat*
d like *d* in *dog*
f like *f* in *fish*
g before e or i like *g* in *gymnastics* or like *g* in *go*
gh like *g* in *go*
gl like *ll* in *million*
gn like *ni* in *onion*
gu like *gu* in *anguish*
h always silent
l like *l* in *lime*
m like *m* in *me*
n like *n* in *nice*
p like *p* in *pit*
qu like *qu* in *quick*
r rolled/trilled similar to *r* in Spanish or Scottish
s between vowels like *s* in *nose* or *s* in *sit*
sc before e or i like *sh* in *shut* or *sk* in *skip*
t like *t* in *tape*
v like *v* in *vase*
z either like *ts* in *spits* or *ds* in *pads*

Accents
Accents are used to indicate which vowel should be stressed and to differentiate between words with different meanings that are spelled the same.

ESSENTIAL PHRASES
Hi Ciao
Hello Salve
Good morning Buongiorno
Good evening Buonasera
Good night Buonanotte
Good-bye Arrivederci
Nice to meet you Piacere
Thank you Grazie
You're welcome Prego
Please Per favore
Do you speak English? Parla inglese?
I don't understand Non capisco
Have a nice day Buona giornata
Where are the restrooms? Dov'è il bagno?
Yes Si
No No

TRANSPORTATION
Where is ...? Dov'è ...?
How far is ...? Quanto è distante ...?
Is there a bus to ...? C'è un autobus per ...?
Does this bus go to ...? Quest'autobus va a ...?
Where do I get off? Dove devo scendere?
What time does the bus/train leave/arrive? A che ora parte/arriva l'autobus/treno?
Where is the nearest subway station? Dov'è la stazione metro più vicina?
Where can I buy a ticket? Dove posso comprare un biglietto?
A round-trip ticket/a single ticket to ... Un biglietto di andata e ritorno/andata per ...

FOOD
A table for two/three/four ... Un tavolo per due/tre/quattro ...
Do you have a menu in English? Avete un menu in inglese?
What is the dish of the day? Qual è il piatto del giorno?
We're ready to order. Siamo pronti per ordinare.
I'm a vegetarian. Sono vegetariano (male)/Sono vegetariana (female)
May I have ... Posso avere ...
The check, please. Il conto per favore.
beer birra
bread pane
breakfast colazione
cash contante
check conto
coffee caffè
dinner cena
glass bicchiere
hors d'oeuvre antipasto
ice ghiaccio

ice cream gelato
lunch pranzo
restaurant ristorante
sandwich(es) panino (panini)
snack spuntino
waiter cameriere
water acqua
wine vino

SHOPPING
money soldi
shop negozio
What time do the shops close? A che ora chiudono i negozi?
How much is it? Quanto costa?
I'm just looking. Sto guardando solamente.
What is the local specialty? Quali sono le specialità locali?

HEALTH
drugstore farmacia
pain dolore
fever febbre
headache mal di testa
stomachache mal di stomaco
toothache mal di denti
burn bruciatura
cramp crampo
nausea nausea
vomiting vomitare
medicine medicina
antibiotic antibiotico
pill/tablet pillola/pasticca
aspirin aspirina
mask maschera
thermometer termometro
I need to see a doctor. Ho bisogno di un medico.
I need to go to the hospital. Devo andare in ospedale.
I have a pain here . . . Ho un dolore qui . . .
Can I have a facemask? Posso avere una maschera?
She/he has been stung/bitten. È stata punta/morsa.
I am diabetic/pregnant. Sono diabetico/incinta.
I am allergic to penicillin/cortisone. Sono allergico alla penicillina/cortisone.
My blood group is . . . positive/negative. Il mio gruppo sanguigno è . . . positivo/negativo.

NUMBERS
0 zero
1 uno
2 due
3 tre
4 quattro
5 cinque
6 sei
7 sette
8 otto
9 nove
10 dieci
11 undici
12 dodici
13 tredici
14 quattordici
15 quindici
16 sedici
17 diciassette
18 diciotto
19 diciannove
20 venti
21 ventuno
30 trenta
40 quaranta
50 cinquanta
60 sessanta
70 settanta
80 ottanta
90 novanta
100 cento
101 centouno
200 duecento
500 cinquecento
1,000 mille
10,000 diecimila
100,000 centomila
1,000,000 un milione

TIME

What time is it? Che ora è?
It's one/three o'clock. E l'una/sono le tre.
midday mezzogiorno
midnight mezzanotte
morning mattino
afternoon pomeriggio
evening sera
night notte
yesterday ieri
today oggi
tomorrow domani

DAYS AND MONTHS

week settimana
month mese
Monday Lunedì
Tuesday Martedì
Wednesday Mercoledì
Thursday Giovedì
Friday Venerdì
Saturday Sabato
Sunday Domenica
January Gennaio
February Febbraio
March Marzo
April Aprile
May Maggio
June Giugno
July Luglio
August Agosto
September Settembre
October Ottobre
November Novembre
December Dicembre

VERBS

to have avere
to be essere
to go andare
to come venire
to want volere
to eat mangiare
to drink bere
to buy comprare
to need necessitare
to read leggere
to write scrivere
to stop fermare
to get off scendere
to arrive arrivare
to return ritornare
to stay restare
to leave partire
to look at guardare
to look for cercare
to give dare
to take prendere

Suggested Reading

HISTORY AND CULTURE

Banks Amendola, Barbara. *The Mystery of the Duchess of Malfi*. In-depth research and fine storytelling bring to life the enigmatic Giovanna d'Aragona, the Duchess of Amalfi, and detail the historical context of her life, her secret marriage, and her death, which has since been shrouded in mystery.

Beard, Mary. *The Fires of Vesuvius: Pompeii Lost and Found*. This is an excellent look at life in Pompeii, written in a compelling narrative style that brings the history of the ancient city to life.

Camuto, Robert V. *South of Somewhere: Wine, Food, and the Soul of Italy*. A memoir centered on Vico Equense near Sorrento that captures the essence of a place through flavors and family.

D'Acierno, Pellegrino, and Stanislao G. Pugliese, eds. *Delirious Naples: A Cultural History of the City of the Sun*. A fascinating selection of essays on an interdisciplinary range of topics by Neapolitan and American scholars, artists, and writers.

Hazzard, Shirley. *The Ancient Shore: Dispatches from Naples*. Celebrated Australian writer Shirley Hazzard first visited Naples in the 1950s, beginning a lifelong love affair with the city. This volume brings together her many writings on Naples.

Kelly, Chantal. *The Amalfi Coast Up Close & Personal*. In a beautiful homage to the Amalfi Coast, author and photographer Chantal Kelly shares a personal look at the history, culture, and charms of the area through her stories and many photos. This is a follow-up to her entertaining travel narrative *Gelato Sisterhood on the Amalfi Shore*.

La Capria, Raffaele. *Capri and No Longer Capri*. This intriguing portrait of Capri by an Italian novelist and screenwriter blends the island's history with personal tales and beautiful descriptions of Capri.

Lancaster, Jordan. *In the Shadows of Vesuvius: A Cultural History of Naples*. Lancaster delves into the history of Naples with a special focus on ancient Naples to the Medieval, Spanish, and Bourbon eras of the city.

Lewis, Norman. *Naples '44: A World War II Diary of Occupied Italy*. This is a classic look at Naples during World War II by noted British writer Norman Lewis, famous for his travel writing, who was stationed in Naples in 1944 as an intelligence officer.

Lima, Chiara. *Mamma Agata: Traditional Italian Recipes of a Family That Cooks with Love and Passion in a Simple and Genuine Way*. Both a cookbook and the story of a family dedicated to traditional cooking on the Amalfi Coast, this book will enchant you with its photos and help you re-create the delicious recipes in your own home.

Munthe, Axel. *The Story of San Michele*. The memoir of Swedish-born doctor Axel Munthe was a best seller when it was published in 1929 and offers a captivating glimpse into his life and his beloved Villa San Michele on Capri.

Robb, Peter. *Street Fight in Naples*. An intriguing look at nearly 3,000 years of history in Naples.

Saviano, Roberto. *Gomorrah*. Saviano provides a frightening and unforgettable insider's account of the inner workings of the Camorra, the organized crime network in the Naples area.

Seward, Desmond. *Naples: A Traveller's Reader*. An interesting selection of excerpts from letters, memoirs, books, and more telling the story of travelers visiting the city of Naples.

FICTION

Adler, Elizabeth. *The House in Amalfi* and *Sailing to Capri*. International best-selling author Elizabeth Adler has brought a charming combination of romance, intrigue, and love of travel to her two novels set on the Amalfi Coast and Capri. This is fun and light travel reading for a beach holiday.

Ferrante, Elena. *Neapolitan Novels: My Brilliant Friend, The Story of a New Name, Those Who Leave and Those Who Stay, The Story of the Lost Child*. This four-part novel follows a captivating friendship between two young girls and throughout their lives, set in the Naples area—with parts of the first book, *My Brilliant Friend,* taking place on Ischia. Her latest novel, *The Lying Life of Adults,* is also set in Naples.

Hazzard, Shirley. *The Bay of Noon*. This novel, set in Naples after World War II, was written by Australian writer and Naples enthusiast Shirley Hazzard. It's not generally considered one of her best works, but it depicts Naples beautifully.

Kwan, Kevin. *Sex and Vanity*. A lively retelling of E. M. Forster's classic *A Room with a View* but set between Capri and New York City.

de Lamartine, Alphonse. *Graziella*. Published in 1852 and based on the firsthand experiences of French writer Alphonse de Lamartine in Procida, the novel is the story of an ill-fated relationship between a young French man and poor young woman named Graziella, the granddaughter of a fisherman.

Mazzoni, Jan. *Dreamland and Other Stories*. A collection of 15 short stories based in the Amalfi Coast in the 1980s.

Moran, Jan. *The Chocolatier*. A mystery and romance as sweet as its title unfolds in this novel set on the Amalfi Coast in the 1950s.

Morante, Elsa. *Arturo's Island*. Set on the island of Procida, this celebrated novel written by Italian author Elsa Morante in 1957 follows Arturo and his family life on the island.

Probst, Jennifer. *The Secret Love Letters of Olivia Moretti*. Three sisters are brought together after their mother's death as they unravel a mystery from her past in Positano.

Serle, Rebecca. *One Italian Summer*. An inspirational story about the powerful love between mothers and daughters set in Positano.

Sontag, Susan. *The Volcano Lover*. A compelling historical novel about Sir William Hamilton, British Ambassador to the Kingdom of Naples 1764-1800, his wife, Emma Hamilton, and her scandalous affair with Lord Nelson.

Storey, Nicki. *A Boatful of Lemons*. Written by a longtime Positano expat, this fun and uniquely personal story was inspired by one unforgettable summer the author spent on the Amalfi Coast.

HIKING GUIDES AND MAPS

Cart&guide Maps. For the most in-depth maps of the hiking and walking paths of the Amalfi Coast and Capri, get your hands on the series of maps by Cart&guide (www.carteguide.com). The Amalfi Coast is divided into four separate maps, stretching from Vietri sul Mare to Punta Campanella. A Capri map with 14 walks is also available.

Cavaliere, Gabriele. *Ravello*. Full of color photos, maps, and information about Ravello, this book includes six walks in Ravello and the surrounding area, including Minori, Atrani, and Scala, as well as the Valle delle Ferriere.

Cavaliere, Gabriele. *Strolling Through Amalfi*. Divided into seven walks themed around art, history, and tradition, this book is packed with detailed trail maps, information, and photos.

Price, Gillian. *Walking on the Amalfi Coast: Ischia, Capri, Sorrento, Positano and Amalfi*. This is a helpful Cicerone guide by experienced Italian hiker Gillian Price.

Tippett, Julian. *Sorrento, Amalfi and Capri: 7 Car Tours, 72 Walk Segments*. Tippett's pocket-size book includes drives on the Sorrentine Peninsula as well as detailed walking and hiking directions on the Amalfi Coast and Capri. Walks in Ischia, Capri, Sorrento, and the Amalfi Coast are also included.

Suggested Films

Beat the Devil (1953), John Huston. An entertaining and, at times, comic parody of a film noir, this movie was filmed in Ravello and various spots on the Amalfi Coast, and stars Humphrey Bogart, Jennifer Jones, and Gina Lollobrigida. Bogart's character teams up with a band of crooks to buy a uranium-rich piece of land in Africa. While they are waiting in Italy to depart for Africa, a series of encounters sets off a chain of unexpected events.

L'Oro di Napoli (1954), Vittorio De Sica. Meaning "The Gold of Naples," this film is a tribute to the city by Italian director and actor Vittorio De Sica. Composed of six episodes, the film features some of the most iconic names in Italian film, including Totò, Eduardo De Filippo, and Sophia Loren.

It Started in Naples (1960), Melville Shavelson. This fun love story features the great duo of Clark Gable and Sophia Loren. Despite the title, the movie was filmed mostly on Capri and shows off the island as it was in the 1960s.

Avanti! (1972), Billy Wilder. Set on Ischia, this comedy features Jack Lemmon, who arrives on the island after his father is killed in a car accident only to discover that nothing is quite as it seemed. The movie was filmed on Ischia, in Sorrento, and various other locations on the Amalfi Coast and Capri.

Il Postino (1994), Massimo Troisi, Michael Radford. This now iconic film featuring Massimo Troisi was nominated for five Academy Awards in 1995, winning the Academy Award for Best Music for an Original Dramatic Score. Filmed on Procida, it's a story of an unlikely friendship between the poet Pablo Neruda and his postman.

Only You (1994), Norman Jewison. This romantic comedy with Robert Downey Jr. and Marisa Tomei follows a grand tour from Venice to Rome and Positano. The poolside scenes in Positano were filmed at the Le Sirenuse hotel.

The Talented Mr. Ripley (1999), Anthony Minghella. A movie adaptation of Patricia Highsmith's 1955 novel, this thriller has the powerhouse cast of Matt Damon, Jude Law, and Gwyneth Paltrow. For the film, Procida was used for the novel's fictional seaside town of Mongibello, with scenes also shot in Positano.

Under the Tuscan Sun (2003), Audrey Wells. This much-loved film, based on the book of the same name by Frances Mayes, has a Positano interlude featuring Italian actor Raoul Bova.

A Good Woman (2004), Mike Barker. Based on *Lady Windermere's Fan* by Oscar Wilde, this captivating film, set in the 1930s, features Helen Hunt and Scarlett Johansson. It was filmed on the Amalfi Coast, with especially beautiful scenes in Atrani.

And While We Were Here (2012), Kat Coiro. Ischia is the backdrop to this drama starring Kate Bosworth and Jamie Blackley, showing the transformational power of unexpected love.

Love Is All You Need (2012), Susanne Bier. This romantic comedy with Pierce Brosnan tells the story of Brosnan's character falling in love alongside the character played by Danish actor Trine Dyrholm. Sorrento shines as the setting, and you'll easily fall in love with the place as well as the characters.

Si Accettano Miracoli (2015), Alessandro Siani. Neapolitan actor and director Alessandro Siani shot this film on the Amalfi Coast, with much of the filming taking place in the peaceful town of Scala near Ravello.

Tenet (2020), Christopher Nolan. This science fiction, action, and thriller film all in one has scenes filmed on the beautiful Terrace of Infinity at Ravello's Villa Cimbrone and in Amalfi.

The Equalizer 3 (2023), Antoine Fuqua. Former government assassin Robert McCall, played by Denzel Washington, finds his peaceful life in southern Italy transformed into a war against the local mafia. It was filmed primarily in Atrani, Ravello, and along the Amalfi Coast.

Internet and Digital Resources

TRAVEL AND TOURIST TIPS

www.incampania.com
The official tourist website for Campania is a great place to start looking for inspiration, with information on the landmarks, museums, culture, gastronomy, and natural landscape of the region.

www.visitamalfi.info
Find travel information, excursions, and ideas to enhance your time in Amalfi by visiting the official website from the Amalfi tourist board.

www.scabec.it
Scabec (Società Campania Beni Culturali) is a society dedicated to preserving and sharing Campania's cultural heritage through organizing and promoting events, concerts, and exhibitions throughout the region.

TRANSPORTATION

www.skyscanner.com, www.kayak.com, www.momondo.com
These flight aggregators help find the cheapest fares. Momondo often pulls in the lowest fares, but they can all offer great savings and simplify planning as well as offering hotel and car-rental services.

www.rome2rio.com
Door-to-door transportation details with distances, departures times, and prices for planes, trains, buses, and ferries.

www.seatguru.com
Learn your legroom options and read unbiased advice on where to sit on a flight. The database includes all major airlines, along with diagrams, photos, and descriptions of Airbus and Boeing interiors.

www.italotreno.it, www.trenitalia.com
These are the sites of Italy's high-speed rail operators. Tickets can be printed at home or saved on mobile devices. If your trip is still months away, sign up for the Italo newsletter and receive monthly travel offers.

www.aeroportodinapoli.it
The Aeroporto Internazionale di Napoli website offers travel information in English for arrivals, departures, traveling to and from the airport, and amenities available while you're in transit.

www.autostrade.it
Drivers can calculate mileage (in kilometers) and toll costs for planned routes. Rest areas are listed, as are the cheapest gas stations. It's

also useful for traffic alerts and brushing up on the rules of the Italian road in English.

ACCOMMODATIONS
www.airbnb.com, www.booking.com, www.slh.com
Search for bed-and-breakfasts, apartments, or boutique hotels. Sites include realistic visuals, plus advice and reviews from people who have traveled before you.

www.tripadvisor.com
Get feedback and user ratings on sights, services, and hotels. Comments are detailed and often highlight inconveniences like a bad view or small bath.

www.xe.com
Calculate what a buck is worth and know exactly how much you're spending. The site's sister app is ideal for the financially conscious and allows travelers to track expenditures on the go.

APPS
Alitalia
Italy's main airline has an app with flight status, boarding information, and baggage claim info.

Trenitalia, Italo
Italy's two train companies offer English-language apps with timetables, the latest train status information, and the ability to purchase tickets via the apps.

Unicocampania
On this useful app, check schedules, plan your journey, and buy tickets for a variety of different transportation systems in Campania, including SITA SUD bus tickets for the Amalfi Coast, Sorrento, and Naples bus tickets on EAV as well as Circumvesuviana train tickets.

Moovit
This excellent app covers transportation for the entire area, including trains, metro, buses, funicular trains, and ferries. Offline maps of Naples's train and Metro lines are available to download.

Travelmar
Find schedules and purchase tickets in advance for ferries along the Amalfi Coast to Salerno, Vietri sul Mare, Cetara, Minori, Maiori, Amalfi, and Positano.

Google Translate
This helpful dictionary and translation app helps travelers decipher and pronounce Italian.

The Weather Channel
Here you'll find the latest reliable weather information and forecasts for the Amalfi Coast area.

Index

A

Abbazia di San Michele Arcangelo: 283
accessibility: 412–413
accommodations: 403–405; see also specific place
Aeroporto Internazionale di Napoli: 23, 391–392
A. Gargiulo & Jannuzzi: 179, 185
air travel: 22, 340, 391–392
alcohol: 406–407
Amalfi: 80–101; accommodations 97–98; arts 43; beaches 42, 86–88; festivals and events 90–91, 398; food and dining 94–97; information and services 98–99; itinerary 24; map 82–83; nightlife 97; recommended activities 21; shopping 91–94; sights 81–86; sports and recreation 88–90; travel and transportation 99–101
Amalfi Coast: 35–165; Amalfi 80–101; Atrani 101–105; best of 24–26; Cetara 136–142; Conca dei Marini 76–80; festivals and events 398; Furore 72–76; highlights 36; hiking 112–113; itinerary 44–47; Maiori 130–135; map 36, 38–39, 40–41; Minori 126–130; planning tips 18, 43–44; Positano 48–65; Praiano 66–72; Ravello 105–119; Salerno 149–165; Scala 119–123; Tramonti 124–125; travel and transportation 37–43; Vietri sul Mare 142–149
Amalfi Lemon Experience: 34, 89–90
Amphitheater (Pompeii): 347, 360
Anacapri: accommodations: 229; festivals and events 220; food and dining 226–227; nightlife 228; shopping 223; sights 207–211; sports and recreation 215–216
anchovies: 36, 140
animals: 375–376
Antiche Terme Belliazzi: 256
Antiquarium: 354–355
apartments; see accommodations
architecture: 387–388
Arco Naturale: 204–206, 219
Arco Naturale to Belvedere di Tragara Walk: 197, 214–215
Arienzo: 53, 54
Arsenale: 85
Ars Neapolitana: 309
art(s): best towns for 43; cameos 316; ceramics 27, 144, 145–146, 327, 329; general discussion 387–390; intarsia 27, 176–178, 179; Naples 324–325; Positano 58; Praiano 69; Ravello 113; Salerno 154–156; Sorrento 27, 176–178, 179, 184; see also museums

Ascione: 316
Associazione Alessandro Scarlatti: 325
ATMs: 409
Atrani: 101–105; map 82–83
audio guides: 354, 365
Auditorium Oscar Niemeyer: 113

B

Bagni della Regina Giovanna: 192
Baia di Sorgeto: 249, 259, 276–277
baked goods: 34, 335, 400
banks: 409
Barano d'Ischia: 274–281
bars; see nightlife
Basilica di San Francesco da Paola: 314
Basilica di San Paolo Maggiore: 308
Basilica di Sant'Antonino: 178
Basilica di Santa Trofimena: 126
Basilica di Sant'Eustachio: 121
Battistero di San Giovanni in Fonte: 307
beaches: Amalfi 86–88; Atrani 102; best 31, 54; best towns for 42; Blue Flag 30, 52–53; Capri 211–214; Casamicciola Terme 256; Cetara 138; children, traveling with 415; Conca dei Marini 77; Forio 271; general discussion 399; Ischia Town 247–249; Lacco Ameno 263–264; Maiori 54, 132; Minori 127; Positano 52–55; Praiano 68; Procida 248–249, 285; Serrara Fontana, Sant'Angelo, and Barano d'Ischia 276–277; Sorrentine Peninsula 193; Sorrento 180; tips for 30–31; Vietri sul Mare 144–145
bed-and-breakfasts; see accommodations
Belvedere della Migliera Walk: 215–216
biking: 322–323
BIPOC travelers: 416
birds: 376
Blue Flag beaches: 30, 52–53
boat rentals: 133, 272
boat tours and trips: 57–58, 77–79, 89, 209, 217–219, 249, 277–279
boat travel: 393, 395–396
bus tours: 345
bus travel: 23, 393, 395
Byzantine New Year: 91

C

cable cars; see funicular
cameos: 316
Campania Artecard: 295, 353–354, 364, 411–412
Campania Card: 295

Campanile dell'Annunziata: 127
Cantine Giuseppe Apicella: 75, 124
Cantine Marisa Cuomo: 74
Capo di Conca: 77
Capodimonte: 321
Capri (island): 196-233; accommodations 228-229; beaches 211-214; best views 208-209; festivals and events 220; food and dining 224-227; grottos 197, 218-219; highlights 197; information and services 230; itinerary 25-26, 28-29, 200-201; map 197, 198-199, 201; nightlife 227-228; planning tips 19, 200; recommended activities 21; shopping 221-223; sights 201-211; sports and recreation 214-220; travel and transportation 230-233
Capri Rooftop: 209
Capri Town: accommodations 228; festivals and events 220; food and dining 224-226; map 203; nightlife 227-228; shopping 221-223; sights 202-207; sports and recreation 214-215
Carnival: 133
Cartaromana: 248-249
car travel and rentals: 23, 393, 394
Casa e Bottega: 61
Casa Mariantonia: 229
Casamicciola Terme: 255-261
Casa Rossa: 210-211
Castel dell'Ovo: 291, 317
Castello Aragonese: 235, 244-247
Castello di Arechi: 154
Castel Nuovo: 311
Castel Sant'Elmo: 319
castles: Ischia 235, 244-247; Naples 291, 309, 311, 317, 319, 322-323; Salerno 154
Catacombe di San Gaudioso: 320
Catacombe di San Gennaro: 320
catacombs: 320
Cattedrale di Salerno: 150
Cattedrale di Sorrento: 167, 173-176, 179
Cattedrale Santa Maria dell'Assunta: 247
Cavallo Morto: 132
Cellini Gallery: 316, 361
Central Baths (Herculaneum): 365
Centro Caprense Ignazio Cerio: 202
Centro di Musica Antica Pietà de' Turchini: 325
Centro Storico (Naples): 293-294, 300-311, 327-328, 330-334; map 302-303
Centro Storico (Salerno): 36, 150, 152
Centro Storico (Sorrento): 167, 176
ceramics: 27, 144, 145-146, 327, 329
Certosa di San Giacomo: 204
Certosa e Museo di San Martino: 309, 319-321
Cetara: 21, 36, 42, 45, 136-142, 398
Chiesa dell'Annunziata: 121
Chiesa del Soccorso: 235, 269
Chiesa di Buon Consiglio: 255-256

Chiesa di Gesù Nuovo: 304
Chiesa di San Domenico Maggiore: 306
Chiesa di San Ferdinando: 314-316
Chiesa di San Francesco: 108-110
Chiesa di San Francesco and Cloister: 178
Chiesa di San Francesco d'Assisi: 138, 269
Chiesa di San Gaetano: 269-271
Chiesa di San Gennaro: 66
Chiesa di San Giovanni Battista: 142-144
Chiesa di San Giovanni del Toro: 108
Chiesa di San Gregorio Armeno: 310
Chiesa di San Luca Evangelista: 66-68
Chiesa di San Michele: 279
Chiesa di San Pancrazio: 77
Chiesa di San Pietro Apostolo: 136-138
Chiesa di San Salvatore de Birecto: 102
Chiesa di Sant'Agostino: 108
Chiesa di Santa Maria a Gradillo: 108
Chiesa di Santa Maria Assunta: 48-50
Chiesa di Santa Maria Visitapoveri: 269
Chiesa di Sant'Antonio: 85
Chiesa di Santa Restituta: 261
Chiesa di Santo Stefano: 201-202
Chiesa Monumentale di San Michele: 210
children: traveling with: 413-415; see also families
churches and cathedrals: Amalfi 36, 81-85; Atrani 102; Capri 202, 210; Casamicciola Terme 255-256; Cetara 136-138; clothing 407; Conca dei Marini 77; Forio 235, 269-271; Ischia Town 247; Lacco Ameno 261; Minori 126; Naples 291, 304-306, 307-308, 310-311, 314-316; Positano 48-50; Praiano 66-68; Ravello 107, 108; Salerno 150-152; Scala 121; Sorrento 167, 173-176, 178; Vietri sul Mare 142-144
50 Kalò: 333
climate: 373-374, 415
clothing: 27, 59, 407; see also fashion
coffee bars: 400-401
Collegiata di Santa Maria a Mare: 131-132
Collegiata di Santa Maria Maddalena: 101-102
color, travelers of: 416
communications: 409-410
Complesso Monumentale di San Lorenzo Maggiore: 308
Complesso Monumentale di San Pietro a Corte: 153
Complesso Monumentale di Santa Chiara: 291, 304-306, 309
Complesso Monumentale Donnaregina: 310
Complesso Palapartenope: 325
Conca dei Marini: 21, 42, 76-80
conduct: 406-407
consulates: 397
cooking classes: 58, 112, 182, 218-219
coral carving: 316
Crater (Vesuvius): 347, 369-370

crime: 406
currency exchange: 409
customs, cultural: 406-407
customs regulations: 397

DE

Da Gelsomina: 226
Dalla Carta alla Cartolina: 85
dance: 390
Da Vincenzo: 60
Decumani Hotel de Charme: 338
demographics: 385
disabilities, travelers with: 412-413
discounts, senior: 415-416
diving: 69, 250
Domus Ars Centro di Cultura: 325
dress; *see* clothing; fashion
drugs: 407
Duoglio: 54, 88
Duomo di Amalfi: 36, 81-85
Duomo di Napoli: 291, 307
Duomo di Ravello: 107
Duomo di San Lorenzo: 121
Easter: 90, 184, 398
Eco Capri: 222
economy: 384-385
emergency numbers: 405
employment, opportunities for: 412
entertainment and events: general discussion 324-326; Praiano 69-70; Ravello 112-114; Salerno 154-156; Scala 122; Sorrento 184; *see also* festivals and events
environmental issues: 374
ETIAS (European Travel Information and Authorization System) visa waiver: 22

F

families: best beaches for 54, 249; spas 259; *see also* children
Faraglioni: 204, 212, 219
fashion: 27, 59; *see also* clothing
Ferragosto: 58, 398
Ferrigno: 309
ferry travel: 23
Festa a Mare agli Scogli di Sant'Anna: 250, 398
Festa del Carmine: 326
Festa Della Castagna (Chestnut Festival): 122
Festa del Pesce: 398
Festa di San Costanzo: 220
Festa di San Gennaro: 326, 398
Festa di San Giovan Giuseppe della Croce: 250
Festa di San Michele Arcangelo: 286
Festa di Sant'Antonio: 220
Festa di Santa Restituta: 264
Festa di San Vito: 272

Festa San Michele Arcangelo: 279
Festival of La Maddalena: 102
Festival of San Giovanni Battista: 145
Festival of San Lorenzo: 122
Festival of San Matteo: 156
Festival of San Pantaleone: 113-114
Festival of San Pietro: 138-139
Festival of Santa Maria a Mare: 133
Festival of Sant'Andrea: 91, 398
Festival of Sant'Antonino: 184
Festival of Sant'Antonio: 90
Festival of Santa Trofimena: 129
Festival of Santi Anna e Gioacchino: 184
festivals and events: Amalfi 90-91; Atrani 102; Capri 220; Cetara 138-139; Forio 272; general discussion 398; Ischia Town 250; Lacco Ameno 264; Maiori 133; Minori 127-129; Naples 326; Positano 58; Praiano 69-70; Procida 286; Ravello 113-114; Salerno 156; Scala 122; Serrara Fontana, Sant'Angelo, and Barano d'Ischia 279; Sorrento 184; Vietri sul Mare 145; *see also* entertainment and events
Fiordo di Furore: 72
fishing: 57
Fonte delle Ninfe Nitrodi: 259, 275-276
food and dining: Amalfi 94-97; anchovies 36, 140; best towns for 42; Capri 209, 224-227; cooking classes 58, 112, 182, 218-219; general discussion 34, 400-402; lemons and lemon products 34, 89-90, 374-375, 402; lingue di bue (ox tongues) 34; Minori 129; Naples 34, 291, 331-337; olives 375; pizza 34, 291, 326, 333, 398, 402; Positano 58, 60-61; Praiano 70; recommended places 21; Salerno 157-158; sfogliatelle 34, 335; Sorrento 173, 182, 186-188
Forio: 268-274; map 262
Forum (Pompeii): 347, 355
funicular: 232, 343
Furore: 21, 72-76

G

Galleria Borbonica: 317
Galleria Umberto I: 314
Gallerie d'Italia: 317
geography: 373
Giardini di Augusto: 197, 203-204, 208-209
Giardini La Mortella: 235, 268-269
Giardini Poseidon Terme: 259, 271
Giardini Ravino: 271
Giardino della Minerva: 154
glossary: 417-418
government: 384
Gran Caffè Gambrinus: 334
Greek temples: 36, 162-164
greetings: 406
Grotta Azzurra: 207-208, 218, 219

Grotta Bianca: 219
Grotta dello Smeraldo (Emerald Grotto): 76-77
Grotta Meravigliosa: 219
Grotta Verde: 219
grottos: 197, 218-219
Gusta Minori (A Taste of Minori): 129

H

Hall of the Augustals: 365
health and safety: 405-406
Herculaneum: 346-350, 362-368; highlights 347; itinerary 349-350; map 348, 350, 364; planning tips 20, 348-349, 364-365; recommended activities 21; rediscovery 380
hiking: Amalfi 88-89; Amalfi Coast 36; best towns for 43; Capri 215-217; general discussion 112-113, 399; Ischia 235; Minori 127; Positano 21, 55-57; Ravello 110-111; recommended places 21; Scala 121-122; Serrara Fontana, Sant'Angelo, and Barano d'Ischia 277; Sorrentine Peninsula 193-194; Sorrento 182; Vesuvius 347, 369-370
history: 376-384; recommended places 21
holidays: 411
hostels; see accommodations
Hotel Canasta: 228
Hotel La Minervetta: 189-190
Hotel La Tosca: 228
Hotel Luna: 229
Hotel Palazzo Alabardieri: 339
hotels; see accommodations
hours of operation: 402, 403, 410-411
House of Menander: 358
House of Neptune and Amphitrite: 347, 365-367
House of the Deer: 347, 367
House of the Faun: 358
House of the Tragic Poet: 358
House of the Vettii: 358
House of the Wooden Partition: 367
House of Venus in the Shell: 358

IK

I Faraglioni: 204, 219
Il Geranio: 209, 224-226
immigration: 385
industry: 384-385
information and services; see specific place
intarsia: 27, 176-178, 179
Ischia (island): 234-281; Casamicciola Terme 255-261; festivals and events 398; Forio 268-274; highlights 235; Ischia Town 244-255; itinerary 29, 240-241; Lacco Ameno 261-268; map 235, 236-237, 242-243; planning tips 19, 239; Procida 281-289; recommended activities 21; Serrara Fontana, Sant'Angelo, and Barano d'Ischia 274-281; thermal spas 235, 256, 258-259
Ischia Film Festival: 250
Ischia Town: 244-255; map 245
itineraries: Amalfi Coast 44-47; by available time 22; best of Amalfi Coast 24-26; Capri 200-201; Ischia and Procida 240-241; Naples 296-299; outdoor recreation and seaside relaxation 32-33; Pompeii, Herculaneum, and Pompeii 349-350; Sorrentine Peninsula 170-171; Sorrento and island hopping 28-29
kayaking: 57, 69, 89, 193-194, 285, 323-324

L

La Casa di Graziella: 283
Lacco Ameno: 261-268; map 262
La Ciliegina Lifestyle Hotel: 338
La Colonna Sunset Bar: 173
La Crestarella: 144-145
La Gavitella: 68
La Limonaia: 173, 180, 182
La Marinella: 86
landscape: 372-374
language: general discussion 386; glossary 417-418; Italian phrasebook 418-421
L'Antica Pizzeria da Michele: 333
L'Antica Trattoria: 173
La Piazzetta: 201-202
Large Theater (Pompeii): 356
La Sfogliatella Mary: 335
laundry: 408-409
Laurito: 53-55
lemons and lemon products: 34, 89-90, 374-375, 402
Le Sirene: 86-88
Le Vigne di Raito: 75, 144
LGBTQ+ travelers: 416
Li Galli Islands: 51-52
lingue di bue (ox tongues): 34
literature: 386
Luci d'Artista: 156
luggage storage: 408-409
Luminaria di San Domenico: 69-70
Lungomare di Salerno: 154
Lupanare: 355-356

M

Madre (Museo d'Arte Contemporanea Donnaregina): 310
Maiori: 130-135
Maiori Beach: 54, 132
Maison Tofani: 189
Maliblu Sunset: 209
maps: 412
Marina Corricella: 235, 281-282

Marina del Cantone: 167, 192–193
Marina di Atrani: 54, 102
Marina di Cetara: 54, 138
Marina di Conca (Conca dei Marini): 77
Marina di Erchie: 132–133
Marina di Praia: 54, 68
Marina di Vietri: 144
Marina Grande (Amalfi): 86
Marina Grande (Capri): 211, 217, 224
Marina Grande (Sorrento): 167, 180
Marina Piccola: 197, 209, 212–214, 217–218
MAR Positano (Museo Archeologico Romano Santa Maria Assunta): 50
Massine, Léonide: 58
medical services: 405
Mergellina: 319
metro and railway: 342
Minori: 42, 126–130
money: 402, 409
Monte Epomeo: 235, 277
Monte Gambera: 52
Montepertuso: 52
Monte Solaro: 197, 209, 210, 215–217
Museo Angelo Rizzoli: 263
Museo Archeologico di Pithecusae: 261–263
Museo Archeologico Nazionale: 164, 291, 300
Museo Archeologico Provinciale: 153
Museo Archeologico Romano Santa Maria Assunta (MAR Positano): 50
Museobottega della Tarsialignea: 167, 176–178, 179
Museo Cappella Sansevero: 306
Museo Civico del Torrione: 269
Museo Civico Filangieri: 306
Museo Correale di Terranova: 179–180
Museo del Corallo: 108
Museo della Carta: 86
Museo della Ceramica: 144
Museo dell'Opera: 306
Museo dell'Opera del Duomo: 107
Museo del Tesoro di San Gennaro: 307
Museo Diocesano: 152–153
Museo Doma: 306
Museo Duca di Martina: 321
Museo e Real Bosco di Capodimonte: 321
Museo Etnografico del Mare: 247
museums: Amalfi 86; Forio 269; Ischia Town 247; Lacco Ameno 261–263; Naples 291, 300, 306–307, 309, 310, 319–321; Paestum 36, 164; Positano 50; Procida 283; Ravello 107, 108; Salerno 152–153; Sorrento 167, 176–178, 179–180; Vietri sul Mare 144
music: 69, 184, 324, 325, 389–390

NO

Naples 290–345; accommodations 337–339; catacombs 320; entertainment and events 324–326; festivals and events 398; food and dining 331–337; highlights 291; information and services 340; itinerary 26, 296–299; language 386; map 291, 292, 293, 298–299, 301, 312–313; nativities 27, 309, 327–328; nightlife 329–330; pizza 34, 291, 326, 333, 398, 402; planning tips 20, 295; recommended activities 21; shopping 326–329; sights 300–322; souvenirs 27; sports and recreation 322–324; travel and transportation 340–345; World War II 381–382
Naples Card: 295
Napoli Centrale Stazione: 340–341
Napoli Pizza Village: 326, 398
Napoli Sotterranea, L.A.E.S. (Underground Naples): 308, 316–317
Napulitanata: 324
nativities: 27, 309, 327–328
'Ndrezzata: 279
Neapolitan: 386
Negombo: 259, 263
Nerano: 21, 192–193
New Year, Byzantine: 91
New Year's Eve: 398
nightlife: Amalfi 97; Capri 227–228; Naples 329–330; Positano 61–62; Salerno 158–159; Sorrento 188–189
Nocelle: 43, 52
Nonna Flora Sorrento Family Kitchen: 173, 182
Notte delle Lampare: 139, 398
olives: 375
opening hours: 402, 403, 410–411

P

packing tips: 23, 407–408
Paestum: 21, 36, 162–165; map 38–39, 163
Palaestra: 367
Palazzo Bevilacqua: 337
Palazzo D'Avalos: 283
Palazzo Mezzacapo: 132
Palazzo Reale: 311
PAN—Palazzo delle Arti Napoli: 319
Parco Archeologico di Ercolano: 364
Parco Archeologico di Paestum: 162–164
Parco Archeologico di Pompei: 352–353
Parco Castiglione Resort & Spa: 256, 259
Parco Nazionale del Vesuvio: 369
passports and visas: 22, 396–397
Pasticceria Pansa: 95–97
Pathway of the Gods: 21, 36, 55–57, 112
Pathway of the Lemons: 113, 127
pharmacies: 405–406
philosophy: 386
Piazza Bellini: 304
Piazza Dante: 304

Piazza dei Martiri: 318
Piazza del Plebiscito: 311–314
Piazza Fontana Moresca: 108
Piazza Marina: 255
Piazza Municipio: 119
Piazza San Rocco: 275
Piazza Tasso: 172–173
Piazza Umberto I: 101
Pinacoteca Provinciale di Salerno: 153
Pintauro: 335
Pio Monte della Misericordia: 307–308
pizza: 34, 291, 326, 333, 398, 400, 402
Pizzeria La Notizia: 333, 336–337
Pizzeria Da Attilio: 332
planning tips: Amalfi Coast 43–44; Capri 200; Herculaneum 364–365; Ischia and Procida 239; itinerary 24–26; laundry and luggage storage 408–409; Naples 295; packing tips 23, 407–408; passports and visas 22, 396–397; Pompeii, Herculaneum, and Pompeii 20, 348–349, 354; Sorrentine Peninsula 169–170; when to go 20; where to go 18–20
plants: 374–375
police: 405
Pompeii: 346–350, 351–362; highlights 347; itinerary 26, 349–350; map 348, 350, 352–353; planning tips 20, 348–349, 354; recommended activities 21; rediscovery 380
Pontone: 121
Porto di Cetara: 138
Porto di Napoli: 341
Positano: 48–65; accommodations 62–63; beaches 42, 52–55; fashion 59; festivals and events 58, 398; food and dining 60–61; information and services 63; itinerary 24–25, 45; map 50–51; nightlife 61–62; recommended activities 21; shopping 58–60; sights 48–52; souvenirs 27; sports and recreation 55–58; travel and transportation 63–65
Positano Premia la Danza Léonide Massine: 58
postal services: 410
Praiano: 66–72
Praiano NaturArte: 66–68
Procida: 281–289; beaches 248–249; itinerary 29, 241; map 235, 237, 242–243, 282; planning tips 19, 239
Punta Carena: 214, 219
Purgatorio ad Arco: 310–311

R

Ravello: 105–119; accommodations 117–118; entertainment and events 112–114; festivals and events 398; food and dining 116–117; hiking 43; information and services 118; itinerary 25, 44; map 106; recommended activities 21; shopping 114–116; sights 107–110; sports and recreation 110–112; travel and transportation 118–119
Ravello Festival: 113–114, 398
Reale Cappella del Tesoro di San Gennaro: 307
recreation: 399; *see also specific place*
Regatta of the Ancient Maritime Republics: 92
Reggia di Caserta: 291, 309, 322–323
Regina Isabella: 259, 263
Regional Ristorante Don Alfonso: 1890 194–195
relaxation: itinerary 32–33; recommended places 21
religion: 385
reservations: 403–404
Riserva Naturale Statale Isola di Vivara: 285–286
Ristorante Marina Grande: 95
rock climbing: 57
Rolex Capri Sailing Week: 220

S

safety: 405–406
Salerno: 149–165; accommodations 159; arts 43; Centro Storico 36, 150, 152; entertainment and events 154–156; food and dining 157–158; information and services 159–160; map 151; nightlife 158–159; Paestum day trip 162–165; shopping 156–157; sights 150–154; sports and recreation 154; travel and transportation 160–162
sales tax: 409
Salicerchie: 132
San Ferdinando: 311–317, 328–329, 334; map 312–313
Santa Croce (Amalfi): 54, 88
Sant'Angelo: 235, 274–281
Scala: 43, 119–123
scooter travel and rentals: 394
seafood: 34, 36
seasons: 20, 31
Sedile Dominova: 176
senior travelers: 415–416
Serrara Fontana: 274–281
Serrara Fontana Belvedere: 275
Settembrata Anacaprese: 220
Settimana Santa: 286
sfogliatelle: 34, 335
Sfogliatelle Attanasio: 332, 335
shopping: general discussion 403; *see also specific place*
sightseeing passes: 295, 353–354, 364, 411–412
Small Theater (Pompeii): 356
smoking: 406–407
soccer: 324
Sorbillo: 333
Sorrentine Peninsula: 166–171, 192–195; map 168–169
Sorrento: 172–192; accommodations 189–190;

beaches 180; entertainment and events 184; festivals and events 398; food and dining 173, 186–188; highlights 167; information and services 190; itinerary 25, 28–29; map 171, 174–175; nightlife 188–189; planning tips 18–19; recommended activities 21; shopping 185–186; sights 172–180; souvenirs 27; sports and recreation 180–182; travel and transportation 190–192
Sorrento Musical Show: 184
souvenirs: 27
Spaccanapoli: 291, 304
spas and baths: Casamicciola Terme 256; Forio 271; Herculaneum 365; Ischia 235, 258–259; Lacco Ameno 263; Pompeii 355; Serrara Fontana, Sant'Angelo, and Barano d'Ischia 275–276
Spiaggia degli Inglesi: 247
Spiaggia dei Maronti: 249, 276
Spiaggia dei Pescatori: 247–248
Spiaggia della Chiaia: 249, 285
Spiaggia della Chiaiolella: 285
Spiaggia della Marina: 256
Spiaggia del Lannio: 138
Spiaggia delle Fumarole: 277
Spiaggia del Porto: 86
Spiaggia del Pozzo Vecchio: 249, 285
Spiaggia di Castiglione: 102
Spiaggia di Chiaia: 271
Spiaggia di Citara: 248, 271
Spiaggia di Fornillo: 51, 53, 54
Spiaggia di San Francesco: 249, 271
Spiaggia di San Montano: 249, 263–264
Spiaggia di San Pietro: 247
Spiaggia di Sant'Angelo: 248, 276
Spiaggia Grande (Minori): 54, 127
Spiaggia Grande (Positano): 53, 54
Spiaggia San Francesco: 180
Spiaggia Torre Saracena: 212
sports and recreation: 399; see also specific place
SSC Napoli: 324
Stabian Baths: 355
Stadio Diego Armando Maradona: 324
Starita a Materdei: 333
Stinga Tarsia: 179
study, opportunities for: 412

T

taxes: 409
taxis: general discussion 396; see also specific place
Teatro Augusteo: 325
Teatro Bellini: 324–325
Teatro Diana: 325
Teatro di San Carlo: 314, 325
Teatro Giuseppe Verdi: 154–156

telephones: 409–410
Tenuta San Francesco: 75
Tenuta San Francesco Vineyard: 124
Terme di Cavascura: 275–276
Terra Murata: 235, 282–283
That's Panaro: 173
theater(s): 356, 390
thermal spas; see spas and baths
tipping: 402
Torre dello Ziro Watchtower: 113, 121–122
Torre di Cetara: 136–142
Torre di Sant'Angelo: 275
Torre Trasita: 51
tourism: 385
tourist information: 411–412
tours: Amalfi 89–90; Capri 214–215, 217–220; Herculaneum 365; Ischia Town 249; Naples 345; Pompeii 354, 356–357; Salerno 152
train travel: 22–23, 392–394
tram: 343
Tramonti: 21, 75, 124–125
travel and transportation: 22–23, 391–396; see also specific place
trees: 374–375
Trellis House: 367

V

vaccines: 405
Valle delle Ferriere: 21, 88–89, 113
Vesuvius: 20, 346–350, 368–371; map 348, 350
Via dell'Abbondanza: 356–357
Via Krupp: 203–204
Via Positanesi d'America: 50–51
Via San Gregorio Armeno: 309, 310
Vietri sul Mare: 27, 43, 75, 142–149
Villa Cimbrone: 36, 110
Villa Comunale: 153–154, 178, 318
Villa delle Palme: 62
Villa di Damecuta: 211
Villa Fiorentino: 184
Villa Jovis: 197, 206–207, 209
Villa Lysis: 206–207
Villa Malaparte: 215, 219
Villa of the Mysteries: 347, 358–359
Villa Pignatelli: 318–319
Villa Romana: 126–127
Villa Rufolo: 107–108
Villa San Michele: 197, 209–210
vineyards: Amalfi Coast 75; Forio 272; Furore 74; Pompeii 360–361; Tramonti 124; Vietri sul Mare 144; see also wine
visas: 22, 396–397
volcanic activity: 373; see also Vesuvius
Vomero: 319–321, 336; map 312–313
Vrasa Wine Tasting: 182

WZ

walking tours: Capri 214-215; Pompeii 356-357; Salerno 152
waterfront (Naples): 317-319, 329, 330, 334-336; map 312-313
water sports: general discussion 399; Naples 323-324; Positano 57; Praiano 69; Procida 285; Serrara Fontana, Sant'Angelo, and Barano d'Ischia 277-279; Sorrentine Peninsula 193-194; Sorrento 180-182
weights and measures: 411
Wi-Fi: 410
wildlife: 375-376
windsurfing: 69
wine: 34, 58, 182, 326; *see also* vineyards
Wine & The City: 326
women traveling alone: 415
ziplining: 74

List of Maps

Front Map
Amalfi Coast: 2–3

Welcome to the Amalfi Coast
chapter divisions map: 19

Amalfi Coast
Amalfi Coast and Paestum: 38–39
Amalfi Coast: 40–41
Itinerary Ideas: 46–47
Positano: 50–51
Amalfi and Atrani: 82–83
Ravello and Scala: 106
Salerno: 151
Paestum: 163

Sorrento and the Sorrentine Peninsula
Sorrento and the Sorrentine Peninsula: 168–169
Itinerary Idea: 171
Sorrento: 174–175

Capri
Capri: 198–199
Itinerary Idea: 201
Capri Town: 203

Ischia and Procida
Ischia and Procida: 236–237
Itinerary Ideas: 242–243
Ischia Town: 245
Lacco Ameno and Forio: 262
Procida: 282

Naples
Greater Naples: 292–293
Itinerary Ideas: 298–299
Naples Overview: 301
Centro Storico: 302–303
San Ferdinando, Waterfront, and Vomero: 312–313

Pompeii, Herculaneum, and Vesuvius
Pompeii, Herculaneum, and Vesuvius: 348
Itinerary Ideas: 350
Pompeii: 352–353
Walking Tour of Pompeii's Highlights: 356
Herculaneum: 364

Photo Credits

All interior photos © Laura Thayer except: title page photo: Vogelsp | Dreamstime.com; page 5 (top) Lorenzobovi | Dreamstime.com; (top middle) © Sirio Carnevalino | Dreamstime.com; page 6 © Josef Skacel | Dreamstime.com; page 10 © (top) Massimobuonaiuto | Dreamstime.com; (bottom) Flaviu Boerescu | Dreamstime.com; page 12 © Lev Levin | Dreamstime.com; page 14 © (top) Anamaria Mejia | Dreamstime.com; (bottom) Giovanni Gagliardi| Dreamstime.com; page 16 © Ramon Ivan Moreno Prieto | Dreamstime.com; page 17 © (top) Pfeifferv | Dreamstime.com; (bottom) Ig0rzh | Dreamstime.com; page 21 © Mezzatorre Hotel & Thermal Spa; page 24 © Ig0rzh | Dreamstime.com; page 25 (middle) © Jef Wodniack | Dreamstime.com; (bottom) © Nicola Pulham | Dreamstime.com; page 26 © (top) Erdalakan | Dreamstime.com; page 27 © Laudibi | Dreamstime.com; page 29 (bottom) © Cezary Wojtkowski | Dreamstime.com; page 30 © Daniel Schreurs | Dreamstime.com; page 32 © Laudibi | Dreamstime.com; page 33 © (bottom) Massimobuonaiuto | Dreamstime.com; page 34 © Nelly Kovalchuk | Dreamstime.com; page 36 © (top left) Giovanni Cardinali | Dreamstime.com; (top right) Rinofelino | Dreamstime.com; page 56 © (bottom) Massimobuonaiuto | Dreamstime.com; page 67 © (top left) Gastonebaldo | Dreamstime.com; page 73 © (top) Antonel | Dreamstime.com; (bottom) Cherylramalho | Dreamstime.com; page 84 © (top left) Daniel M. Cisilino | Dreamstime.com; page 92 © Salvatore Conte | Dreamstime.com; page 115 © (top) Fondazione Ravello; (bottom) Iciar Cano Fondevila | Dreamstime.com; page 155 © (top) Lucamato | Dreamstime.com; page 156 © Stefano Valeri | Dreamstime.com; page 162 © Fotografiche | Dreamstime.com; page 166 © Neirfy | Dreamstime.com; page 197 © (top left) Gary Along | Unsplash; page 205 © (bottom) Roman Plesky | Dreamstime.com; page 206 © Roman Plesky | Dreamstime.com; page 208 © Witold Ryka | Dreamstime.com; page 213 © (bottom) Mikolaj64 | Dreamstime.com; page 216 © (bottom) DiegoFiore | Dreamstime.com; page 218 © Casadphoto | Dreamstime.com; page 246 © (bottom) Ig0rzh | Dreamstime.com; page 258 © Morozova Oxana/Shutterstock.com; page 265 © (top) Eugenesergeev | Dreamstime.com; page 270 © (top right) Mariyasiyanko | Dreamstime.com; (bottom left) Mezzatorre Hotel & Thermal Spa; (bottom right) Maddalena Di Gregorio | Dreamstime.com; page 272 © Lucamato | Dreamstime.com; page 278 © (top left) Massimo Buonaiuto | Dreamstime.com; page 290 © Minnystock | Dreamstime.com; page 291 © (top left) Konstantin Malkov | Dreamstime.com; (top right) Greta6 | Dreamstime.com; page 294 © Bruno Coelho | Dreamstime.com; page 305 © (top left) Giuseppe Anello | Dreamstime.com; (top right) Alvaro German Vilela | Dreamstime.com; (bottom) Dudlajzov | Dreamstime.com; page 315 © (top) Christophefaugere | Dreamstime.com; (bottom) Laraslk | Dreamstime.com; page 320 © Enrico Della Pietra | Dreamstime.com; page 335 © Stefano Carnevali | Dreamstime.com; page 346 © Scaliger | Dreamstime.com; page 347 © (top left) Porojnicu | Dreamstime.com; (top right) Vaclav Volrab | Dreamstime.com; page 359 © (top) Pablo Boris Debat | Dreamstime.com; (left middle) Maxim Sergeenkov | Dreamstime.com; (right middle) Alexandre Fagundes De Fagundes | Dreamstime.com; (bottom) Floriano Rescigno | Dreamstime.com; page 360 © Yi Liao | Dreamstime.com; page 363 © David Moreno | Dreamstime.com; page 366 © (top left) Merlin1812 | Dreamstime.com; (top right) Bographics | Dreamstime.com; (bottom) Nicolas De Corte | Dreamstime.com; page 370 © Rcgcristi | Dreamstime.com; page 372 © Aleh Varanishcha | Dreamstime.com; page 391 © Oleksandr Ryzhkov|Dreamstime.com.

Acknowledgments

A place as beautiful as the Amalfi Coast is a dream for inspiration, especially when it's what first sparked and continues to sustain my creativity. While it may seem unusual to thank a place, I wouldn't be the person or the writer that I am without the Amalfi Coast. There are hardly words to capture the immensity of my gratitude and love for this place.

The warmth of the locals in Campania makes a project like this a celebratory occasion. My continued thanks to everyone I encountered who helped me with details, history, and stories while creating and updating this book. A big thank-you for the readers who have enjoyed and shared the first two editions. I hope this new one continues to inspire beautiful journeys on the Amalfi Coast!

This book never would have happened without the inspiration of my mother, Sandra Thayer, who brought me on a serendipitous mother-daughter trip to the Amalfi Coast in 2007. Thank you for always being my biggest cheerleader and for supporting my journey every step of the way. And thank you to my father, Richard Thayer, for sharing the same enthusiasm and pride with each new edition.

Writing is essentially a solitary journey, but one made so much better by dear friends around the world—what every expat needs. If you sent words of encouragement or music playlists, sat with a more than slightly frazzled version of myself for an aperitivo, or simply made me laugh, you know who you are, and your support means the world to me.

Many thanks to the entire team at Moon Travel Guides for bringing this book to life. Each editor has added a special touch, but grazie mille to Devon Lee, Grace Fujimoto, Courtney Packard, and the entire editing and design team for making the third edition the best yet.

Finally, a special thank-you to my husband, Lello Brandi, for sharing this beautiful place in the world and our life together.

MAP SYMBOLS

═══	Expressway	○	City/Town	🛈	Information Center	♣	Park
───	Primary Road	◉	State Capital	🅿	Parking Area	⛳	Golf Course
───	Secondary Road	⊛	National Capital	⛪	Church	✦	Unique Feature
───	Unpaved Road	✪	Highlight	🍇	Winery/Vineyard	≈	Waterfall
----	Trail	★	Point of Interest	🚹	Trailhead	▲	Camping
····	Ferry	●	Accommodation	🚉	Train Station	▲	Mountain
----	Railroad	▼	Restaurant/Bar	✈	Airport	⛷	Ski Area
	Pedestrian Walkway	■	Other Location	✈	Airfield	~	Glacier
⋮⋮⋮	Stairs						

CONVERSION TABLES

°C = (°F - 32) / 1.8
°F = (°C x 1.8) + 32
1 inch = 2.54 centimeters (cm)
1 foot = 0.304 meters (m)
1 yard = 0.914 meters
1 mile = 1.6093 kilometers (km)
1 km = 0.6214 miles
1 fathom = 1.8288 m
1 chain = 20.1168 m
1 furlong = 201.168 m
1 acre = 0.4047 hectares
1 sq km = 100 hectares
1 sq mile = 2.59 square km
1 ounce = 28.35 grams
1 pound = 0.4536 kilograms
1 short ton = 0.90718 metric ton
1 short ton = 2,000 pounds
1 long ton = 1.016 metric tons
1 long ton = 2,240 pounds
1 metric ton = 1,000 kilograms
1 quart = 0.94635 liters
1 US gallon = 3.7854 liters
1 Imperial gallon = 4.5459 liters
1 nautical mile = 1.852 km

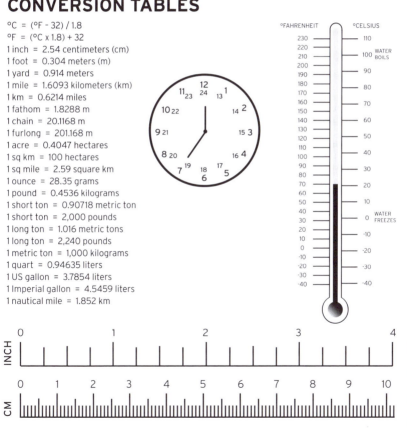

MOON AMALFI COAST
Avalon Travel
Hachette Book Group
555 12th Street, Suite 1850
Oakland, CA 94607, USA
www.moon.com

Editor: Devon Lee
Managing Editor: Courtney Packard
Copy Editor: Christopher Church
Graphics and Production Coordinator: Rue Flaherty
Cover Design: Toni Tajima
Interior Design: Avalon Travel
Map Editor: Kat Bennett
Cartographers: Abby Whelan, Mark Stroud (Moon Street Cartography), Erin Greb, John Culp, Kat Bennett
Proofreader: Brett Keener
Indexer: Rachel Lyon

ISBN-13: 9798886470482

Printing History
1st Edition — 2019
3rd Edition — September 2024
5 4 3 2 1

Text © 2024 by Laura Thayer.
Maps © 2024 by Avalon Travel.
Some photos and illustrations are used by permission and are the property of the original copyright owners.

Hachette Book Group supports the right to free expression and the value of copyright. The purpose of copyright is to encourage writers and artists to produce the creative works that enrich our culture. The scanning, uploading, and distribution of this book without permission is a theft of the author's intellectual property. If you would like permission to use material from the book (other than for review purposes), please contact permissions@hbgusa.com. Thank you for your support of the author's rights.

Front cover photo: Positano © Pietro Canali / Sime / eStock Photo
Back cover photo: Cetara harbor, Amalfi coast © Cezary Wojtkowski | Dreamstime.com

Printed in China by RR Donnelley APS

Avalon Travel is a division of Hachette Book Group, Inc. Moon and the Moon logo are trademarks of Hachette Book Group, Inc. All other marks and logos depicted are the property of the original owners.

All recommendations, including those for sights, activities, hotels, restaurants, and shops, are based on each author's individual judgment. We do not accept payment for inclusion in our travel guides, and our authors don't accept free goods or services in exchange for positive coverage.

Although every effort was made to ensure that the information was correct at the time of going to press, the author and publisher do not assume and hereby disclaim any liability to any party for any loss or damage caused by errors, omissions, or any potential travel disruption due to labor or financial difficulty, whether such errors or omissions result from negligence, accident, or any other cause.

The publisher is not responsible for websites (or their content) that are not owned by the publisher.